DICKENS STUDIES ANNUAL
Essays on Victorian Fiction

DICKENS STUDIES ANNUAL

Essays on Victorian Fiction

EDITORS

Stanley Friedman
Edward Guiliano
Michael Timko

DICKENS
STUDIES
ANNUAL

Essays on Victorian Fiction

VOLUME
29

Edited by
Stanley Friedman, Edward Guiliano, and Michael Timko

AMS PRESS
NEW YORK

DICKENS STUDIES ANNUAL
ISSN 0084–9812

COPYRIGHT © 2000 by AMS Press, Inc. *Dickens Studies Annual: Essays on Victorian Fiction* is published in cooperation with Queens College and the Graduate Center, CUNY.

International Standard Book Number
Series: 0–404–18520–7
Vol. 29:0–404–18549–5

Dickens Studies Annual: Essays on Victorian Fiction welcomes essay- and monograph-length contributions on Dickens and other Victorian novelists and on the history of aesthetics of Victorian fiction. All manuscripts should be double-spaced and should follow the documentation format described in the most recent *MLA Style Manual*. The author's name should appear only on a cover-page, not elsewhere in the essay. An editorial decision can usually be reached more quickly if two copies of the article are submitted, since outside readers are asked to evaluate each submission. If a manuscript is accepted for publication, the author will be asked to provide a 100– to 200–word abstract and also a disk containing the final version of the essay. The preferred editions for citations from Dickens's works are the Clarendon and the Norton Critical when available, otherwise the Oxford Illustrated or the Penguin.

Please send submissions to The Editors, *Dickens Studies Annual*, Ph.D. Program in English, The Graduate Center, CUNY, 365 Fifth Avenue, New York, NY 10016–4309. Please send inquiries concerning subscriptions and/or the availability of earlier volumes to AMS Press, Inc., 56 East 13th Street, New York, NY 10003–4686.

Manufactured in the United States of America

Contents

List of Illustrations   vii
Preface   ix
Notes on Contributors   xi

MALCOLM ANDREWS
Dickens, Washington Irving, and English National Identity   1

SEAN C. GRASS
Pickwick, the Past, and the Prison   17

DAVID PARKER
Oliver Twist and the Fugitive Family   41

CATHERINE ROBSON
Down Ditches, on Doorsteps, in Rivers: *Oliver Twist*'s
      Journey to Respectability   61

GOLDIE MORGENTALER
The Long and the Short of Oliver and Alice: The Changing
      Size of the Victorian Child   83

COLETTE COLLIGAN
Raising the House Tops: Sexual Surveillance in Charles
      Dickens's *Dombey and Son* (1846–48)   99

ANNETTE R. FEDERICO
Dickens and Disgust   145

JAMES HILL
Authority and the *Bildungsroman:* The Double Narrative of
      Bleak House   163

v

DAVID A. WARD
Distorted Religion: Dickens, Dissent, and *Bleak House*   195

DANIEL P. SCOGGIN
Speculative Plagues and the Ghosts of *Little Dorrit*   233

KAREN C. GINDELE
Desire and Deconstruction: Reclaiming Centers   269

KEITH HALE
Doing the Police in Different Voices: The Search for Identity
        in Dust Heaps and Waste Lands   303

CAROL-ANN FARKAS
Beauty is as Beauty Does: Action and Appearance in Brontë
        and Eliot   323

LISA STERNLIEB
"Three Leahs to Get One Rachel": Redundant Women in *Tess
        of the d'Urbervilles*   351

CYNTHIA NORTHCUTT MALONE
Near Confinement: Pregnant Women in the Nineteenth-
        Century British Novel   367

HARLAND S. NELSON
Recent Dickens Studies: 1998   387

DAVID GARLOCK
Recent Studies in Thomas Hardy's Fiction 1987–99   465

Index   489

Illustrations

Two Cruikshank illustrations, *Rose Maylie and Oliver*   58
William Hogarth's *The Foundlings,* Subscription Document
   for Coram's Foundling Hospital   78
Four figures illustrating preformation and emboitement   95–96
Twenty-one Hablot K. Browne illustrations for *Dombey
   and Son*   124–44
Hablot K. Browne's *Mr. Pecksniff on his Mission*   381

Preface

John Forster, in his biography of Dickens, tells of an elderly charwoman's great surprise on learning that *Dombey and Son* had been written by just one author: "Lawk ma'am! I thought that three or four men must have put together *Dombey!*" This volume of *Dickens Studies Annual,* however, was "put together" not by just one person, nor even by three or four. We therefore take pleasure in acknowledging the contributions of the many members of our support system.

First, we thank all who sent their essays for our consideration. Second, we express our deep gratitude to the numerous outside readers who generously devoted their time and expertise to evaluating these submissions. Our reviewers, located in different parts of the world, enable us to remain open to widely disparate critical and scholarly perspectives.

We thank Professor Harland S. Nelson for his survey of Dickens studies published in 1998, and we thank Professor David Garlock for his examination of studies of Hardy's fiction that were published from 1987 through 1999.

In addition, we express our appreciation to the following administrators for encouragement and essential practical assistance: President Frances Degen Horowitz, Provost William P. Kelly, Ph.D. Program in English Executive Officer Joan Richardson, and Linda Sherwin, Assistant Program Officer, Ph.D. Program in English, all of The Graduate Center, CUNY; President Allen Lee Sessoms, Provost David H. Speidel, Dean Raymond F. Erickson, and Department of English Chair Nancy R. Comley, all of Queens college, CUNY; and President Matthew Schure of New York Institute of Technology.

We are also grateful to Professor John O. Jordan, Director of The Dickens Project at the University of California, Santa Cruz, and to Jon Michael Varese, the web programmer for The Dickens Project, for placing on the Project's website the tables of contents for volumes 1–27 of *DSA* and the tables of contents as well as abstracts for later volumes. (These materials are included in the Project's Dickens Electronic Archive.) The Dickens Project can be reached at http: //humwww.ucsc.edu/dickens/index.html

We greatly appreciate the interest and steady support of Gabriel Hornstein, President of AMS Press, and the resourcefulness and genial cooperation of

Jack Hopper, our editor at AMS Press. Finally, during the preparation of this volume we have benefited very much from the help given first by our editorial assistant Jody R. Rosen and then by her successor, Andrea Knutson.

—The Editors

Notes On Contributors

MALCOLM ANDREWS is professor of Victorian and Visual Studies at the University of Kent at Canterbury (UK). He is the author of *Dickens on England and the English* (1979), *Dickens and the Grown-up Child* (1994), and *Landscape and Victorian Art* (1999). He is currently editor of *The Dickensian*.

COLETTE COLLIGAN is a doctoral candidate at Queen's University, Canada. Her research interests include Victorian literature and the history of sexuality. She is currently working on a study of Victorian pornography.

CAROL-ANN FARKAS is currently completing her doctoral thesis for the University of Alberta. Her project is a study of late nineteenth-century novels about women doctors in England and America.

ANNETTE R. FEDERICO teaches Victorian literature and Women's Studies at James Madison University. Her book, *Idol of Suburbia: Marie Corelli and Late-Victorian Literary Culture,* has recently been published by the University Press of Virginia.

DAVID GARLOCK is an adjunct assistant professor in the Department of Modern Languages and Comparative Literature at Baruch College, the City University of New York. Previous publications include a recent essay on Hardy and Darwin in *DSA* (vol. 27).

KAREN C. GINDELE is assistant professor of English at Indiana University, South Bend. Her fields are Victorian fiction and critical theory. She has published an article on laughter and desire in works by Thackeray, Oliphant, and Meredith entitled "When Women Laugh Wildly and (Gentle)men Roar: Victorian Embodiments of Laughter," in *Look Who's Laughing: Gender and Comedy,* edited by Gail Finney. Two essays forthcoming concern George Eliot's formulation of a theory of ideology (*Texas Studies in Literature and Language*) and the conjunction of wonder and thought in Wilkie Collins's *The Woman in White* (*Literature and Psychology*). Ms. Gindele is writing a book which theorizes relationships among thought, feeling, ideology, and dialogue in nineteenth-century English fiction.

SEAN C. GRASS is a lecturer in English at the Pennsylvania State University, University Park. He has published articles on Christina Rossetti in *Nineteenth-Century Literature* and on Dickens in the *Journal of English and Germanic Philology* and received the Edwin Erle Sparks Fellowship at Penn State in 1996. He is now completing a book titled *The Self in the Cell: Narrating the Victorian Prisoner* which investigates authority, psychology, and self-narration in novels of the Victorian prison.

KEITH HALE is an assistant professor of English at the University of Guam. His most recent book is *Friends and Apostles: The Correspondence of Rupert Brooke and James Strachey, 1905–1914.*

JAMES L. HILL is a professor in the Department of English, Michigan State University. He has published on Shakespeare, and writers of the Romantic and Victorian periods, and is currently working on a book concerned with the question of authority in Victorian fiction.

CYNTHIA NORTHCUTT MALONE is associate professor of English at the College of St. Benedict and St. John's University in Minnesota. She writes about visual and textual representations of pregnancy. She also practices and teaches papermaking, letterpress, and bookbinding.

GOLDIE MORGENTALER is assistant professor of English at the University of Lethbridge in Alberta, Canada. She is the author of *Dickens and Heredity: When Like Begets Like.* She has also published articles on Dickens in *SEL* and *Dickens Quarterly.*

HARLAND S. NELSON, professor emeritus of English at Luther College in Decorah, Iowa, taught there 1962–94 (with time out for Fulbright professorships at Bergen Innsbruck). He has published articles on Conrad, E. M. Forster, Stephen Crane, Steinbeck, and Updike, as well as on Dickens (most recently "Dickens, Religion, and Nubile Girls" in *Dickens Quarterly,* March 1997). His *Charles Dickens* (1981) is still in print. The working title of his current project is "War News in *All the Year Round*, Summer 1859."

DAVID PARKER retired last year after twenty-one years as Curator of the Dickens House Museum in London. Before that he taught for the University of Sheffield, the University of Malaya, and the Open University. He is author of numerous papers on Dickens and other literary subjects, and edited the Everyman Paperback Edition of *Nicholas Nickleby.* Now he is concentrating on writing and lecturing, and is at work on a book, *The Doughty Street Novels,* to be published by AMS Press.

CATHERINE ROBSON is an assistant professor of English at the University of California, Davis. Her first book, *Men in Wonderland: The Lost Girlhood of the Victorian Gentleman,* is forthcoming from Princeton University Press. Her current work focuses on the figure of the inadequately buried body in the literary and cultural imagination of nineteenth-century Britain.

DANIEL P. SCOGGIN is the headmaster of Tempe Preparatory Academy in Tempe, Arizona. He is a recent graduate of the doctoral program in English literature of the Claremont Graduate University. Forthcoming publications include "A Speculative Resurrection: Death, Money, and the Vampire Economy of *Our Mutual Friend*" in *Victorian Literature and Culture,* "Surveying the Vampire in Nineteenth-Century English Literature" in the MLA volume *Approaches to Teaching Gothic Fiction,* and "Reflections on Reception: Heidegger, Technology, and Television" in *Negations.*

LISA STERNLIEB is assistant professor of English at Wake Forest University. Her essays have appeared in *ELH* and *Nineteenth-Century Literature.* She is currently writing a book about redundant women in Victorian literature and culture.

DAVID A. WARD is lecturer in Professional Communication at the University of Wisconsin-Madison. He has previously published essays on Joseph Conrad and Jane Austen.

Dickens, Washington Irving, and English National Identity

Malcolm Andrews

It has long been recognized that Dickens drew on Washingon Irving's
Sketch-Book *and* Bracebridge Hall *for scenes and characters in* Pickwick Papers, *especially for the Christmas sequence. This essay explores
Dickens's debt to Irving in more depth and suggests that the influence
is both more widespread in early Dickens and more radical than might
hitherto have been recognized. Irving's England, as it is portrayed
in his two texts, is predominantly a traditional, conservative nation,
functioning within a residually feudal political and economic dispensation. Irving, the tourist from the New World, has come to see old-world
Europe still flourishing in romantic and eccentric ways, and to fabricate
it imaginatively where he could not see it in actuality. The young Dickens's sense of English national identity is a mix of often unsteadily
focussed radicalism and affectionate traditionalism (the latter typified
in the quasi-feudal structure of the Dingley Dell community, where
Wardle is modelled on Squire Bracebridge). This ideological mix is
matched in Irving's mix of republican loyalty with a comic-sentimental
attachment to the world of Bracebridge Hall. The two writers thus seem
to have a great deal in common: in combination, their writings strongly
colored the nation's sense of its own identity in the early nineteenth
century.*

I want to begin by registering the warmth of the relationship between Dickens
and Washington Irving. It began long before they met each other in person,

Dickens Studies Annual, Volume 29, Copyright © 2000 by AMS Press, Inc. All
rights reserved.

and took the form of a strong literary kinship that each was happy to acknowledge. Dickens grew up on Irving's *The Sketch-Book of Geoffrey Crayon, Gent.,* which was published in 1819–1820, when Dickens was 7 or 8 years old. Irving's *Bracebridge Hall* appeared in 1822 and was an expansion of the descriptions of an old English manor-house and its inhabitants that he had introduced in the *Sketch-Book. Tales of a Traveller* (1824) and *The Alhambra* (1832), like the two books on England, were anecdotal and whimsical travel books, which Dickens seems to have read over and over again.

Irving became an ardent admirer of the early works of Dickens, and shortly after *The Old Curiosity Shop* had finished its run, in March 1841, he wrote to Dickens to express his "heartfelt delight" not only with the *Shop* but with his writings generally. Dickens was quite obviously thrilled to receive this unsolicited praise from someone whose opinions he so much valued. This much is evident from his effusive letter to Irving on 21 April 1841:

> There is no living writer, and there are very few among the dead, whose approbation I should feel so proud to earn. And with everything you have written, upon my shelves, and in my thoughts, and in my heart of hearts, I may honestly and truly say so. . . . I wish I could find in your welcome letter, some hint of an intention to visit England. I can't. . . . I should love to go with you—as I have gone, God knows how often—into Little Britain, and Eastcheap, and Green Arbour Court, and Westminster Abbey. I should like to travel with you, outside the last of the coaches, down to Bracebridge Hall. It would make my heart glad to compare notes with you about that shabby gentleman in the oilcloth hat and red-nose who sat in the nine-cornered back parlor at the Mason's Arms—and about Robert Preston—and the tallow chandler's widow whose sitting room is second nature to me—and about all those delightful places and people that I used to walk about and dream of in the daytime when a very small and not over-particularly-taken-care-of boy.[1]

The recollection of details from the *Sketch-Book* that comes tumbling out of this letter strikes me as authentic testimony to the fact that Dickens had long ago furnished the curiosity shop of his own imagination with hundreds of odd bits and pieces from Irving's book; and that in quiet moments he loved to go back in there and pick over the strange miscellaneous material. That this imaginative sympathy was reciprocated by the older writer is clear from Irving's reply the following month to Dickens's letter:

> My dear Sir,
> I cannot tell you how happy the receipt of your letter has made me, for it has convinced me that I was not mistaken in you; that you are just what your writings made me imagine you, and that it only wanted a word to bring us together in heart and soul. Do not suppose me, however, a man prompt at these spontaneous overtures of friendship. You are the only man I have ever made such an advance to. In general I seek no acquaintances and keep up no correspondences out of my family connexion; but towards you there was a strong

impulse, which for some time I resisted, but which at length overpowered me; and I now am glad it did so.

You flatter my languid and declining pride of authorship by quoting many of my sketchings of London life, written long since, and too slight as I supposed, to make any lasting impression; but what are my slight and isolated sketches to your ample and complete pictures which lay all the recesses of London life before us? . . . I have a peculiar relish for your pictures of low English life, and especially those about the metropolis, and connected with public fairs &c., from my having studied them much during my residence in England. I had a perfect passion for exploring London, and visiting every place celebrated in story or song . . . I wanted to write about all these scenes . . . but some how or other my pen seemed spell bound; . . . I felt too much like a stranger in the land . . . All this makes me the more sensible to the fullness as well as the fidelity of your picturings[2]

Irving goes on to rhapsodise about Pickwick and the Wellers, Bob Sawyer and Ben Allen, Dick Swiveller and Mantalini. I have quoted fully from the early part of the letter because, together with Dickens's letter, it outlines the common area of interest between Dickens and Irving: London life and topography. This is one of the two areas which I want to examine in more detail later. The other one is Bracebridge Hall and its relationship to Dickens's picturings of traditional English life in the early books. Irving conveys a sense that what he started, in his sketchings of English life, was only a start, and that he was now happy to leave the rest of the job to the native writer, young Dickens. It is seen almost in terms of a collaboration, or a continuity of projects. Irving's combined focus on London and the old-fashioned country estate, foreshadowing Dickens's concentration in *Pickwick Papers* on London life and old-fashioned Dingley Dell, makes me think that these two writers were, in effect, collaborating in an imaginative effort to construct an idea of English national identity in the period following the end of the Napoleonic Wars—a period when that identity has become peculiarly complicated. That will be the principal focus of my essay.

Just before embarking on the main task, let me add one more instance of the admiration Dickens felt towards Irving's work. Forster remarked that Irving's opening letter to Dickens "very strongly revived" Dickens's idea of going to America. In February 1842 Dickens arrived in New York. On the 18th of that month he was guest of honor at a banquet at the City Hotel. Washington Irving took the Chair, and gave the toast of the evening, to "Charles Dickens—Literary Guest of the Nation." Dickens's speech of reply acknowledged at great length his affection for and admiration of Irving. "It is," he said, "the crowning circumstance to me of the night that he is here in this capacity." He went on:

Why, gentlemen, I don't go upstairs to bed two nights out of seven, as I have a credible witness very near at hand to testify [he here gave a comic side look at his wife and laughed: Catherine blushed, hid her face in her handkerchiefs, and laughed too: everyone was laughing] . . . I don't go to bed two nights out of seven without taking Washington Irving under my arm upstairs to bed with me . . . Washington Irving! Why, when I visited Shakespeare's birthplace not long ago, and went beneath the roof where he first saw light, whose name but *his* was the first that was pointed out with pride upon the wall?—Washington Irving!—Diedrich Knickerbocker, Geoffrey Crayon! Why, where can we go that they have not been before us? In the English farmhouse, in the crowded city, along the beautiful lanes, across the pleasant fields of England, and amidst her blessed, happy homes, his name above every name rises up with hallowed recollections of his virtues and talents, and like his memory will continue to be hallowed in those bright and innocent sanctuaries, until the last tick of the clock of Time!

If we go into the country are there no Bracebridge Halls in existence? If we visit the crowded city, has Little Britain never had a chronicler? Is there no Boar's Head in Eastcheap? Why, gentlemen, when Mr. Crayon left England he left sitting in the small back parlour of a certain public house near that same Boar's Head, a man of infinite wisdom, with a red nose and an oilskin hat, who was sitting there when I came away. Yes, gentlemen, it was the same man—not a man that was very *like* him, but the self-same man—his nose in an immortal redness, and his hat in an undying glaze. Why, Mr. Crayon was also on terms of intimacy, in a certain village near that same Bracebridge Hall, with a certain radical fellow, who used to go about very much out at elbow, with his hat full of old newspapers. Gentlemen, I knew the man. He's there to this very hour, with the newspapers in his hat, very much to the dissatisfaction of Mr.Tibbets the elder. And he has not changed a hair; and when I came away he charged me to give his best respects to Washington Irving![3]

Even allowing for flattery, there is something very special about Dickens's sense of the importance to him of Irving's writings. I have selected from the letters and this speech just those mentions of Irving's writings about England, and that is, as I have indicated, the area I am going to be concentrating on. I don't think it is an exaggeration to suggest that Dickens's England in the early years of his life and writing career is very much Irving's England. The fields, farmhouses, city streets, and public houses were to Dickens, from his early years, saturated with associations from Irving's writings—partly, indeed, constituted in their identity by Irving's portraits of them. The London of the *Sketches by Boz*, the England of *Pickwick Papers* and of parts of *Oliver Twist, Nicholas Nickleby* and *The Old Curiosity Shop* would have been different without Irving's *Sketch Book* and *Bracebridge Hall*. As has often been suggested, the Christmas at Dingley Dell owes a great deal to Irving's evocations of Christmas at Bracebridge Hall. Dickens is said to have invented Christmas. What that usually means is that Dickens revived the old Christmas for early Victorian England; in the countryside for *Pickwick Papers* and in the metropolis for *A Christmas Carol*. It will be an heretical notion to some, but Washington Irving has a very strong claim to have invented the English

Christmas, via Dickens. However, it is my purpose to suggest that Irving contributed considerably more than just Christmas character to early nineteenth-century England.

A nation's identity is invented by its writers and politicians. It involves a lot of conscious myth-making in the interests of promoting certain characteristics that are culturally or politically useful at any given time. In Britain in the last five years our politicians have consciously manipulated versions of British national identity to suit their political agenda. Thus Prime Minister John Major sighed for the old-fashioned world of cricket on the village green and warm beer. Tony Blair's New Labour regime opted briefly for "Cool Britannia"—an attempted revival of a vigorous, youth-led, creative popular culture to take us into millennial Britain.

We can fit Washington Irving into this kind of myth-making of England. Tourism is never undertaken with a wholly disinterested curiosity about the country visited. We have our preconceptions and prejudices about what we are going to see, and we have a habit of comparing what is new with what is familiar. So it was with Irving in his travels to England over the years 1815 to the mid 1820s. As an American in the young republic, undergoing "one of the greatest political experiments in the history of the world," [4] he was, like most of his countrymen, highly sensitive to the bigoted and patronising criticisms of his country made by visiting Europeans. He lamented that "It has been the peculiar lot of our country to be visited by the worst kind of English travellers" (*SB* 53). The newness of America as a political organisation, the sense that the "national character is yet in a state of fermentation" (ibid.), makes Irving defensive as a traveller to England, but it also makes him particularly curious about all those things in England which are *not* American. Thus Americans need not look beyond their own country for stupendous and varied natural scenery; but "Europe held forth the charms of storied and poetical association"(*SB* 2). "My native country was full of youthful promise: Europe was rich in the accumulated treasures of age" (ibid.). "I longed to ... escape ... from the commonplace realities of the present, and lose myself among the shadowy grandeurs of the past" (*SB* 2–3). For Irving to be travelling in ancient, storied Europe in the period just after the end of the Napoleonic Wars, it was inevitable that he should echo some of the same sentiments as the most famous verse travelogue of that period, Byron's *Childe Harold's Pilgrimage*. That passion to meditate among the ruins of history he shares with Byron's hero.

So the *context*, cultural and political, in which Irving sets out as a tourist determines his agenda. Since the *Sketch Book* was primarily aimed at an American readership, it is the *otherness* of Europe that he is going to stress: *those* features are the ones that will be new and curious for his New World audience. This sense of the otherness of the English experience is reflected in the topics indicated in the various titles to the sketches: "Rural Life in England," "A Royal Poet," "The Country Church," "A Sunday in London," "The Boar's Head Tavern, Eastcheap," "Rural Funerals," 'The Inn Kitchen," "Westminster Abbey," "The Stage Coach," "London Antiquities," "Little Britain," "John Bull," "The Pride of the Village."

I intend now to concentrate on Irving's sketches of London, and to explore their relationship to Boz's London. The first point to make is that Irving's London, as Dickens's letters and speeches show, became part of Dickens's mental map of London. Here again is part of that first letter Dickens wrote to Irving:

> It would make my heart glad to compare notes with you about that shabby gentleman in the oilcloth hat and red-nose who sat in the nine-cornered back parlor at the Mason's Arms—and about Robert Preston—and the tallow chandler's widow whose sitting room is second nature to me—and about all those delightful places and people that I used to walk about and dream of in the daytime when a very small and not over-particularly-taken-care-of boy.

This is an interesting piece of biography. Is he here referring to the blacking warehouse period when he speaks of himself as a very small and not over-particularly-taken-care-of boy? It's clearly not the Chatham period: if, as he says, he used to walk around those places, he must be referring to the London period of his boyhood, 1822 onwards. He mentions London places and people that were specifically portrayed by Irving in the *Sketch Book* and that wasn't published in England until 1820/21. The likelihood is that, since *The Sketch Book* made such a strong impression on English readers in the early 1820s, the boy Dickens knew of it soon after its publication and meshed his growing knowledge of London's highways and byways with Irving's romantic portraits of the odd and antique corners of the great city. Dickens's London anyway was a composite of his readings and his actual knowledge of its streets, so much so that romantic and literary associations were inseparably a part of his geography of the city. But if Dickens's London was as much a literary site as a real city, so too was it for Irving. London for him, as he arrived in the city for the first time, was already a literary anthology. "Storied" England and "storied" London suggest the degree to which the imaginary and real are scarcely divisible.

Dickens famously wrote in his Preface to *Bleak House*, "I have purposely dwelt on the romantic side of familiar things." This is exactly what Irving does again and again in his sketches, as real places and people mingle in his mind with their literary prototypes, and as the combination triggers romantic reveries in the tourist's imagination. This mingling of the real and the illusory is what he loved about Shakespeare: "Ten thousand honours and blessings on the bard who has thus gilded the dull realities of life with innocent illusions'' (*SB* 304). I will take one example of this characteristic dissolving of the mundane world with the world of fantasy.

In the sketch "The Art of Book-Making," Irving describes one summer's day when he wanders into the British Museum and soon finds himself in one of the Reading Rooms. "About the room were placed long tables, with stands for reading and writing, at which sat many pale, studious personages, poring intently over dusty volumes, rummaging among mouldy manuscripts, and taking copious notes of their contents"(*SB* 79). The room was filled with huge book-cases and dark portraits of ancient authors. Silence reigned, except for the scribbling of pens and the occasional deep sigh from a reader (little has changed in the British Library's move to St. Pancras, except that the scribbling of pens has given way to the pitter-patter of fingers on key-boards). Induced by the soporific atmosphere of the place, the visitor falls into a doze, in the course of which he dreams that the room and the readers are transformed. The readers have become ragged beggars who, when they seize on any one of the books, find that it turns into a garment of foreign or antique fashion. They clothe themselves bit by bit with these magically transformed books and thereby become the animated spirit of whatever books they appropriate. One very puny reader, "had bolstered himself out bravely with the spoils from several obscure tracts of philosophy, so that he had a very imposing front"'(*SB* 83). Bit by bit the whole scene becomes a "literary masquerade" (*SB* 84). This is abruptly stopped by a change in the portraits of the ancient authors all round the room. The authors come alive, climb out of their pictures in a fury at all the literary pilfering of their works going on below, and chase the culprits out of the room, in such a comical fashion that the author bursts out laughing. That wakes him from his reverie and he opens his eyes to find all the readers staring at him in astonishment and the librarian demanding to know whether he had a Reading Room ticket. End of sketch.

I commend this piece to post-structuralists, as a sprightly allegory of the constitution of a text: all texts, so it is said, derive from and refer to, not any objective reality but other texts. Old works undergo, in Irving's words, "a kind of metempsychosis, and spring up under new forms" (*SB* 81). So "book-making" is really not original authorship but a kind of literary recycling. This is very much the practice of the young Dickens, as so many of his early reviewers were quick to point out. *Pickwick*, for instance, was judged to be compounded of "two pounds of Smollett, three ounces of Sterne, a handful of Hook, a dash of grammatical Pierce Egan. . . . "[5] Dickens's father-in-law, George Hogarth, reviewing *Sketches by Boz*, wrote that " 'Christmas Dinner' was a charming paper, which might have been written by Washington Irving in one of his happiest hours."[6] Dickens's mental map of London, as I have suggested, was partly composed of his beloved *Sketch-Book* readings. But, more importantly perhaps, his early *writings* were heavily dependent on Irving's. The title of his first book, *Sketches by Boz*, no doubt carried an implied debt to Irving's *Sketch Book*. Take the "Book-Making" piece I have just described. This was surely a principal source for one of Dickens's best Boz sketches, "Meditations in Monmouth Street." Dickens visits a street in the Giles Rookery where second-hand clothes are on display for sale. He falls into a reverie there and imagines the various clothes coming alive as people, with distinct identities and life stories. The imagined characters, dressed in their Monmouth Street cast-offs, accumulate as a motley crowd and the narrative rises to a crescendo as they all start dancing. The fantasy is abruptly dispelled by an officious local, and the embarrassed Boz flees the scene. The parallels between this and Irving's sketch are very close. It's hard not to think that Dickens was trying his hand here at something which he had so enjoyed in Irving's book. Irving had even explicitly mentioned Monmouth Street's clothing trade in his Reading Room reverie, when he compared the ragged, threadbare scholars with the throng so often seen "plying about the great repository of cast-off clothes, Monmouth-street" (*SB* 82). The irony, of course, is that Irving's sketch was all about literary pilfering. Dickens pilfers from this very sketch; and then, several years later, rounds on the Americans over the issue of copyright!

I want to look at one other London piece from Irving's *Sketch Book* before moving on to Bracebridge Hall. In fact it is a kind of hinge piece to enable us to turn easily to the later book. This is "Little Britain."

Little Britain is the small area in the City of London where Smithfield market and St. Bartholomew's Hospital are located. The sketch itself is purportedly a paper given to Irving by "an odd-looking old gentleman in a small brown wig and a snuff-coloured coat" who lives in one of the oldest of Little Britain's buildings. In his old wainscoted, panelled chamber and array of high-backed, claw-footed chairs, this gentle, retiring old man in his venerable little lodging seems to me to be an original for Dickens's Master Humphrey. It is interesting, incidentally, that in July 1839, when Dickens was beginning to think about his new project, *Master Humphrey's Clock*, he wrote to Forster of his idea for "a series of papers descriptive of places and people I see, introducing local tales, traditions, and legends, something after the plan of Washington Irving's *Alhambra*."

Little Britain is described as "the strong-hold of true John Bullism" (*SB* 269). It has an air of faded grandeur and remains a place where some of the ancient English traditions persist: St. Bartholomew's Fair is one such festival. The inhabitants are highly superstitious, good-natured, and somewhat insular. In short, Little Britain is a microcosm of Great Britain, where one can study the changing culture of the nation:

> Thus wrapped up in its own concerns, its own habits, and its own opinions, Little Britain has long flourished as a sound heart to this great fungous metropolis. I have pleased myself with considering it as a chosen spot, where the principles of sturdy John Bullism were garnered up, like seed corn, to renew the national character, when it had run to waste and degeneracy. (*SB* 277)

The change that now threatens Little Britain comes in the form of an *arriviste* butcher's family. The butcher has suddenly come into money, and therefore come out of trade. His daughters aspire to high fashion. The family set up a one-horse carriage, put a bit of gold lace round the errand boy's hat, scorn playing any of the old-fashioned games, such as Pope-Joan or blindman's-buff (precisely the games that are played at Dingley Dell), reject the old English country dance, Sir Roger de Coverley (the high point of the Fezziwigs' Christmas party) in favor of the modish quadrilles. Worse still, "they took to reading novels, talking bad French, and playing on the piano" (*SB* 279). The national character is seriously threatened. The Little Britain community is highly indignant; but little by little the innovations start to spread, and others follow the example of the *nouveaux riches*. The narrator testifies with horror, "I even saw, in the course of a few Sundays, no less than five French bonnets, precisely like those of the Miss Lambs, parading about Little Britain" (*SB* 281). The dreadful prospect has to be faced: "I apprehend that it will terminate in the total downfall of genuine John Bullism" (*SB* 283).

This sketch represents a paradigm of the social changes happening in nineteenth-century England. Dickens from first to last was fascinated by it. His early sketch "The Tuggses at Ramsgate" is a comic variation on the fortunes of Irving's butcher's family. And in his last complete novel, *Our Mutual Friend*, the Boffins—especially Mrs Boffin—are affectionately mocked as they go in for high fashion. Irving the American tourist has clearly come to England in search of the old national character, the John Bullism he describes in "Little Britain." He enlarges a little on this character in another sketch, "John Bull."

John Bull is "a plain, downright, matter-of-fact fellow [with] little of romance in his nature, but a vast deal of strong natural feeling . . . continually volunteering his services to settle his neighbours' affairs" (*SB* 341). He is a kind, indulgent master on his country estate. His family mansion is solid, weather-beaten and picturesque, "full of obscure passages, intricate mazes, and dusky chambers. Additions have been made to the original edifice from time to time, and great alterations have taken place; towers and battlements have been erected during wars and tumults; wings built in time of peace; and outhouses, lodges, and offices, run up according to the whim or convenience of different generations, until it has become one of the most spacious, rambling tenements imaginable" (*SB* 344). It bears a close resemblance to the old-fashioned, rambling and irregular Bleak House, just as Mr. Jarndyce is a

kind of latter-day, retiring version of John Bull. John Bull's house is like a
historical document, or, to change the analogy, like the sedimentary layers
of Englishness that have grown up over a long period to form the present
national character.

In these respects it resembles Bracebridge Hall, just as Squire Bracebridge
resembles John Bull. Squire Bracebridge's mind, like his house, is a picturesque accumulation of styles: "Though the main ground-work of his opinions
is correct, yet he has a thousand little notions, picked up from old books,
which stand out whimsically on the surface of his mind"[7] (*BH* 436). Young
Frank Bracebridge, son of the Squire, describes his father as "a bigoted
devotee of the old school, [who] prides himself upon keeping up something
of old English hospitality" (*SB* 214). He patterns his values on "honest"
Henry Peacham's *The Compleat Gentleman* (1622), rather than (like Sir John
Chester) on the polished sophistications of Lord Chesterfield's *Letters*. In his
country fastness Squire Bracebridge promotes the old English sports and past-
times, cherishes only the old-fashioned English writers. All this, of course,
is meat and drink to the American visitor brought down from London to
spend some days at Bracebridge. "To a man from a young country, all old
things are in a manner new; and he may surely be excused in being a little
curious about antiques, whose native land, unfortunately, cannot boast of a
single ruin"(*BH* 363).

Washington Irving's *Bracebridge Hall* is subtitled *A Medley*. He describes
his authorial intentions as the making of occasional sketches, not the writing
of a novel with an intricate plot. The reader is invited to ramble with the
author, stopping now and then to admire the prospect, or listen to a bird sing,
recounting any particularly curious information about the history of the house
or any of its occupants, passing on stories that are told to him in the course
of his stay. This loose structure and relaxed descriptive mode, the plotless
narrative, the array of colorful, eccentric characters, the appetite for curious
tales that can be incorporated into the larger story frame—what else is this
but the form Dickens exploits in *The Pickwick Papers*? The formal similarities
between the two books extend to other parallels. Just as Bracebridge Hall is
a model for Dingley Dell, as both a pastoral refuge and a repository of old-
fashioned English values that have been lost in the great metropolis, so Mr.
Wardle is a version of Squire Bracebridge, a patriarchal figure to his family
and servants, ferociously protective, exuberantly hospitable, and deeply preju-
diced in favor of the old-fashioned ways of doing things. Christmas at Dingley
Dell, modelled, as often observed, on the Christmas Sketches by Irving in his
Sketch-Book, is Christmas in the old style. Squire Bracebridge was called by
his son "a devotee of the old school." In *Pickwick Papers* , in a passage
deleted in later editions, Christmas was personified as "quite a country gentleman of the old school."[8] Bracebridge and Wardle epitomize the old-fashioned

English Christmas spirit, and are, in spite of their eccentricity, forces for moral good.

In *Bracebridge Hall*, Irving creates a mythic England of the past, stuck in a kind of feudal time-warp. He is clearly influenced by Walter Scott's historical recreations, and Bracebridge Hall bears a strong resemblance to such ancient households as Waverley Honour or Tully Veolan in Scott's first historical novel, *Waverley*, published just six years before the *Sketch Book*. But, like Scott in *Waverley*, Irving is always aware of the forces of change operating on this antique social order. Just as in "Little Britain" Irving had chronicled the arrival in that old-fashioned culture of disruptive modern values, so he sees Bracebridge as prey to the intrusions of the new world, of an industrialized, urbanized and politically more egalitarian order. Old England is changing, as Irving foresees:

> The old Hall will be modernised into a fashionable country-seat, or, peradventure, a manufactory. The park will be cut up into petty farms and kitchen-gardens. A daily coach will run through the village; it will become, like all other commonplace villages, thronged with coachmen, post-boys, tipplers, and politicians: and Christmas, May-day, and all the other hearty merry-makings of the "good old times," will be forgotten. *(BH* 728)

Now what is an American, from the young New-World republic doing celebrating this quasi-feudal, aristocratic social order from the Old World? In the last part of this essay I want to reflect on the political perspective taken by Irving and to compare it with Dickens's representations of the social order in *Pickwick*. It seems to me that in both the American and the English writer there is considerable ambivalence about their political attitudes.

In a letter to Irving of 28 Sept 1841, Dickens broached the subject of a subscription to help the bereaved family of Theodore Hook. That family included four illegitimate daughters, a circumstance that had dissuaded some of the more puritanical of his acquaintances from offering any help. "I hardly know what your politics are," Dickens wrote to Irving; "remembering the Squire in Bracebridge Hall and the radical.—But I am sure this is not your creed" (Letters: 28/9/41). It is not surprising that Dickens was unsure what Irving's politics were. The Squire is an entrenched Tory of the old school: that much is obvious. The "radical" to whom Dickens refers appears in the chapter "A Village Politician." In *Bracebridge Hall*. He is thin, bilious, ill-shaven and somewhat aggressive. The pockets of his shabby clothes are stuffed with newspapers and pamphlets. His recent arrival in the village has caused consternation. He "has grievously puzzled the brains of many of the oldest villagers, who had never thought about politics, or scarce anything else, during their whole lives"*(BH* 581). It is indeed he who suggests that it would be better if the Hall park were cut up into small farms and kitchen-gardens as a means of giving the poorer members of the community some share in land. This is the shape of the new egalitarian age, and where does the ideological backing for this come from? From France of course—like the fashionable bonnets sported by the butcher's daughters, to the distress of the old community of Little Britain. The radical's greatest adversary in the village pub is Jack Tibbets, a sturdy old yeoman in the John Bull mould, extremely slow-witted and unswervingly loyal to King and Country. "Whatever does not square with Jack's simple and obvious creed, he sets down for 'French politics'; for, notwithstanding the peace, he cannot be persuaded that the French are not still laying plots to ruin the nation, and to get hold of the Bank of England" (*BH* 582).

Irving has offered a stereotyped portrait of the disaffected radical of the period, who was nearly always represented as emaciated, fiery, and embittered. So it might be inferred that by caricaturing the figure in this way Irving sides with the older Tory interest. But he also caricatures Jack Tibbets, the radical's adversary. He caricatures Squire Bracebridge, and laughs affectionately at the Squire's foibles and prejudices. In other words, Irving maintains a detachment that is appropriate to his position as a worldly, much-travelled outsider in this insular community. In the chapter "English Country Gentlemen," he reflects on his own political identity and his feelings for the English dispensation:

> Though born and brought up in a republic, and more and more confirmed in republican principles by every year's observation and experience, yet I am not insensible to the excellence that may exist in other forms of government, nor to the fact that they may be more suitable to the situation and circumstances of the countries in which they exist: I have endeavoured rather to look at them as they are, and to observe how they are calculated to affect the end which they propose. Considering, therefore, the mixed form, I have looked with admiration at the manner in which the wealth and influence and intelligence were spread over its whole surface; not, as in some monarchies, drained from the country and collected in towns and cities. I have considered the great rural establishments of the nobility, and the lesser establishments of the gentry, as so many reservoirs of wealth and intelligence distributed about the kingdom, apart from the towns, to irrigate, freshen, and fertilise the surrounding country.

As to the matter of class-divided society, Irving has this to say:

> There is no rank that makes [a man] independent of the opinions and affections of his fellow men; there is no rank nor distinction that severs him from his fellow-subjects; and if, by any gradual neglect or assumption on the one side, and discontent and a jealousy on the other, the orders of society should really separate, let those who stand on the eminence beware that the chasm is not mining at their feet. The orders of society, in all well constituted governments, are mutually bound together, and important to each other.   (*BH* 548–49)

This analysis of Britain just after the Napoleonic Wars idealizes the situation. The idea that the politically and economically powerful members of society distribute "wealth and intelligence," "irrigate" and "freshen" the country as a whole, doesn't really conform with the historical condition of England in this period, an England that is beginning to agitate for political reform, and is a decade away from carrying through the Reform Bill. But the more general observations Irving makes about the dangers of social division are well taken. And here we turn back to Dickens.

I have mentioned that Dickens's London was an amalgam of all the literary Londons stored in his imagination as well as the physical city of the nineteenth century, itself in continual change. In the same way, Dickens's England, in the early years of his career, was partly a literary invention. Literary associations were indelibly attached to and enriched specific places that he knew (Gad's Hill and the Falstaff episode, for instance, which was so precious an association for him). Irving's England is grafted onto Dickens's England, particularly when it comes to describing the idealized community of Dingley Dell. Dingley Dell is a more demure version of Bracebridge Hall, and does not quite so obviously stand as a miniature representation of old England. But the presiding patriarch, Mr. Wardle, has much in common with Squire Bracebridge. He presides over a traditional, organic, hierarchical community: the male head of family, beneath him the dependent relatives, beneath them the domestic staff. Everyone knows his or her place, and the stability of the small society depends on that kind of structure. Christmas is a time when a greater egalitarianism is encouraged, and the whole family gathers in the great kitchen to mingle with the servants on Christmas Eve:

> "Our invariable custom," [said] Mr Wardle. "Everybody sits down with us on Christmas eve, as you see them now—servants and all." *(PP 28)*

The ceremonial tradition that Wardle emphasises—the ritualistic temporary relaxing of the social hierarchy—accentuates the anciently established hierarchical relations that obtain throughout the rest of the year. All newly cemented relationships within that community subscribe to its social rules. In *Bracebridge Hall*, the narrator arrives to discover that a wedding is shortly to take place, and towards the end of the book the wedding takes place, as a kind of climax to the visit. The Christmas visit of the Pickwickians to Dingley Dell is also an occasion for the celebration of a marriage: Wardle's daughter, Bella, is to be married. This is done in the heartiest manner possible, blessed by Wardle and Pickwick himself, and celebrated in traditional style, just as at Bracebridge:

> The carpet was up, the candles burnt bright, the fire blazed and crackled on the hearth, and merry voices and light-hearted laughter rang through the room.

If any of the old English yeomen had turned into fairies when they died, it was
just the place in which they would have held their revels.   (Ibid.)

Dingley Dell's community is a kind of model of how a small, mixed society
might function. Consider the alternative to which Pickwick has to return.
Instead of a romantic country wedding, he is going to face a trial for breach
of promise of marriage. Instead of the decorous hierarchical relations that
govern and give stability to Dingley Dell, the dignified old Pickwick on his
very first outing into the world has a punch-up with cabman and is duped
several times over by a clever scoundrel from the world of low theater. There
seem to be two Englands in *Pickwick Papers*, each the inverse of the other.
One is an old-fashioned, semi-feudal, patriarchal organization of mutual de-
pendencies among all orders of society, surviving in the country (the Bracebridge Hall type); the other, an egalitarian, individualist, acquisitive culture
that belongs particularly in the city, where community is so much harder to
sustain. The two Englands are brought into partnership, symbolically as it
were, when the sharp Londoner Sam Weller is united with the old-school
gentleman, Mr. Pickwick. Thus what continue as confrontational worlds in
the larger structure of the novel, become partially reconciled in that blessed
partnership.

Washington Irving was an inspirational figure for the young Dickens. That
the *Sketch Book* and *Bracebridge Hall* inspired features in Dickens's early
writings has long been acknowledged; though I believe, and hope to have
shown, that the extent of that literary debt has been underestimated. But there
is a larger sense in which Irving was important for Dickens. Irving brought
to life a mythic England of the past at a time when England was undergoing
radical change: he imagined a stable, old-world culture based on a residual
patriarchal feudalism, at the same time as he saw (vividly, from the fresh
experience of a New-World republican) social and political and cultural
change overtaking that older order. This is exactly what Dickens inherited as
he began his career: how to make sense of a changing England, and where
to establish one's political loyalties. Both Irving and Dickens have a strong
sentimental attachment to the patriarchal, feudal model—the idea of the organic family unit as a microcosm of the ideal political order. But, both also
have strong republican, meritocratic leanings that threaten to disturb settled
hierarchical ordering of society. The ideological ambivalence which joins
these two great writers together is far from being a flaw: it is what gives
vitality, color, and dramatic energy to their portraits of early nineteenth-
century England.

NOTES

1. To Washington Irving, 21 April 1841: The Pilgrim Edition *The Letters of Charles Dickens*, vol. 2 ed. M. House & G.Storey (Oxford,1969), 267–68.
2. Irving to Dickens, 26 May 1841: *ibid.*,269n.
3. *The Speeches of Charles Dickens*, ed. K. J. Fielding (Harvester Wheatsheaf, 1988), 29–30.
4. *Sketch Book,*p.53. All quotations from the *Sketch Book* are taken from *Washington Irving's Sketch Book* (London: George Bell, 1906): hereafter abbreviated in the text to *SB*. All subsequent page references to this work will appear in parenthesis after the citation and refer to this edition.
5. *The Athenaeum*, 3 December 1836, 841.
6. *Morning Chronicle*, 11 February 1836.
7. Washington Irving, *Bracebridge Hall: The Works of Washington Irving: The Adventures of Captain Bonneville; Bracebridge Hall*, New York & London: The Co-operative Publication Society, n. d.), 436. This edition is hereafter abbreviated to *BH*: all subsequent page references to this work will appear in parenthesis after the citation and refer to this edition.
8. Robert Patten ed., *The Pickwick Papers* (Penguin Books, 1972), 944: note 1 to ch. 28.
9. To Washington Irving, 21 April 1841: The Pilgrim Edition, *The Letters of Charles Dickens*, vol.2 ed. M. House & G. Storey (1969), pp. 267–68.
10. Irving to Dickens, 26 May 1841: ibid., p.269n.
11. *The Speeches of Charles Dickens*, ed. K. J. Fielding (Harvester Wheatsheaf, 1988), 29–30.
12. *Sketch Book,*p.53. All quotations from the *Sketch Book* are taken from *Washington Irving's Sketch Book* (London: George Bell & Sons, 1906): hereafter abbreviated in the text to *SB*. All subsequent page references to this work will appear in parenthesis after the citation and refer to this edition.
13. *The Athenaeum*, 3 December 1836, 841.
14. *Morning Chronicle*, 11 February 1836.
15. Washington Irving, *Bracebridge Hall: The Works of Washington Irving: The Adventures of Captain Bonneville; Bracebridge Hall*, New York & London: The Co-operative Publication Society, Inc, n. d.), 436. This edition is hereafter abbreviated to *BH*: all subsequent page references to this work will appear in parenthesis after the citation and refer to this edition.
16. Robert Patten ed., *The Pickwick Papers* (Penguin Books, 1972), 944: Note 1 to chapter 28.

WORKS CITED

Dickens, Charles. *The Letters of Charles Dickens,* 1840–41. Ed. Madeline House and Grahem Storey. Oxford: Clarendon Press, 1969. Vol.2 of The Pilgrim Edition. 11 vols. to date. 1965– .

————. *The Speeches of Charles Dickens*. Ed. K. J. Fielding. Hemel Hempstead, Hertfordshire, 1988.

————. *The Pickwick Papers*. Ed. Robert Patten. Harmondsworth: Penguin Books, 1972.

Irving, Washington. *Washington Irving's Sketch Book*. London: George Bell & Sons, 1906.

————. *The Works of Washington Irving: The Adventures of Captain Bonneville; Bracebridge Hall*. New York & London: The Co-operative Publication Society, n. d.

Pickwick, the Past, and the Prison

Sean C. Grass

Critics have typically regarded the Fleet prison chapters of Charles Dickens's Pickwick Papers as merely a plot device, a site of resolution for the novel's difficulties, and an episode in which the prison has only historical relevance as part of Dickens's early social reformism. I argue, however, that Pickwick*'s Fleet is rather a site of significant psychological transformation, in which the misshaping of the mind is legible in the marks left upon the body. Thus focusing upon the Fleet's psychological consequences, I reconceive* Pickwick *as a novel that, despite its carefree present, constantly investigates the past, and particularly the psychological past of the prisoner.* Pickwick*'s prisoners all bear the marks of their confinement, and the novel encourages readers to interpret those marks as part of the psychological legacy of the cell. More, by suggesting* Pickwick*'s concern with memory, transformation, and psychological wounding, I illustrate too the significance of the novel to Dickens's greater career, which includes countless narrative returns to the prison.* Pickwick Papers *does not prefigure later Dickens works in its delightful characters and social reformism only; rather, it also foreshadows Dickens's incessant return to the prison as a site for investigating the darkest horrors of the psychological self.*

No sensible critic would suggest that *Pickwick Papers* (1837) is primarily an exploration of the Victorian debtors' prison. The novel is Charles Dickens's greatest comic masterpiece, wholly set in an exuberant present tense filled with picturesque pre-Victorian characters who engage in a series of remarkable and often farcical adventures. The most egregious acts carry no serious

Dickens Studies Annual, Volume 29, Copyright © 2000 by AMS Press, Inc. All rights reserved.

17

consequences: characters drift in and out of the novel without disturbing the serenity and good-humor of its action. Indeed, as many critics have noted, a great deal of *Pickwick Papers*'s comedy arises from this wandering menagerie of characters, whose different social classes and various dialects and figures of speech create a lively linguistic playfulness.[1] Within a discussion of these comic aspects, the Fleet chapters serve only as a site of resolution, where the main characters of the novel—Pickwick, Sam, Mrs. Bardell, Alfred Jingle, Job Trotter, and even Mr. Perker and old Anthony Weller—are reunited, the conflict between Pickwick and Mrs. Bardell is worked out, and Pickwick's education regarding the wide world the Pickwickians have sent him to explore is finally completed.[2] Aside from acknowledging these functions of the Fleet in the novel's plot, critics have more or less dismissed the prison from scholarly discussions. Philip Collins's landmark *Dickens and Crime*, concerned primarily with imprisonment as a punishment for criminals rather than for the financially irresponsible, understandably ignores *Pickwick Papers* and its portrayal of imprisonment for debt.[3] Angus Easson has paid considerably more attention to the Fleet, demonstrating the ways in which Dickens's account may be mined to determine its accuracy in portraying imprisonment for debt in the late 1820s and thus entered as early evidence of Dickens's explicitly reformist social aims.[4] The suggestion that the Fleet chapters comprise an overt indictment of contemporary imprisonment for debt is by no means incorrect. Dickens was unquestionably concerned with the physical conditions and cruelties inflicted by prisons of all kinds, and throughout the 1830s and 1840s he visited jails in both England and the United States in order to discover the miseries they concealed within their walls. A great deal of Dickens's aim in his account of the Fleet is to educate Pickwick—and by association the reader—regarding the particular injustices inflicted upon debtors. The novel abounds in rhetorical claims to authenticity, to its status as an edited chronicle of sorts, and its authority and credibility as a documentary text help to legitimate the education that Dickens proposes to give his readers and protagonist.

As three decades of fictional returns to the prison suggest, however, in texts from *Pickwick Papers* to the condemned-cell ending he had planned for *The Mystery of Edwin Drood* (1870), Dickens never viewed the prison as a place of merely physical, factual significance. Rather, Dickens's novels about the prison present the cell as a place of hidden narratives, psychological upset, and terrible transformations of those confined. Scholarly discussions of the prison these days almost inevitably return in some measure to Foucault, and to analyses of surveillant strategies, disciplinary regimens, and psychological transformations—discussions that have produced thoughtful investigations by, for instance, D. A. Miller and Audrey Jaffe into surveillance, ideology, and omniscience in the Victorian novel.[5] Dickens unquestionably recognized the prison's physically and psychologically transformative power, as his portraits of prisoners from Alfred Jingle to Alexandre Manette illustrate, and imprisonment in Dickens's novels always carries an element of psychological destruction as its most significant consequence. Yet Dickens's imaginative engagement with the prison and its psychological effects depends little upon surveillant or disciplinary strategies like those Foucault describes. Dickens of course knew the contemporary reformative penitentiaries from repeated visits and returns in the 1830s and 1840s, and his analysis of Philadelphia's Eastern Penitentiary in *American Notes* (1842) accorded him, in Philip Collins's estimation, "a respectable place in penological history."[6] But the Fleet was no reformative criminal penitentiary; it operated according to no surveillant or disciplinary strategies for transforming the mind. Moreover, as anyone acquainted with Dickens's personal history is aware, his most significant intellectual apprehension of the prison—especially the debtors' prison—emerged much earlier than the 1830s, during his father's imprisonment in the Marshalsea. Terribly wounded by his deeply-felt shame over his father's incarceration and determined to overcome and erase his own trials at Warren's Blacking during this same period, Dickens concealed for decades what he had seen and known of the prison and its miseries. But even in 1837, at the time he wrote *Pickwick Papers*, Dickens continued to struggle privately with the meanings of his boyhood shame, continually feeling the prison's indelible imprint upon his character and his mind. For Dickens, as novels like *Little Dorrit* (1857) and *A Tale of Two Cities* (1859) make clear, the simple physical fact of confinement created a hidden psychological text much more significant, and his long fictional engagement with the prison largely reflects a continuous effort to bring to narrative light the private, psychological horrors of the cell.

Pickwick Papers is an early indication of this desire, and as a result it is as well a novel infinitely more complex in its presentation of the prison than criticism has allowed. On one hand, there is no question that Dickens is explicitly concerned with the physical realities of the contemporary Fleet and with educating Pickwick and his readers regarding the miseries of the prison. The saturation of squalid detail in Dickens's depictions of the Fleet suggest as much, as do the narrative claims to authority in which the novel abounds both in the Fleet chapters and elsewhere. Yet having been made acutely aware in his own history of the prison's psychologically transformative power, Dickens paints in *Pickwick Papers* a portrait of the Fleet that far transcends in importance its contemporary or factual relevance. Each physical mark left upon the bodies of Dickens's Fleet prisoners—each indication of emaciation, sorrow, and despair—attests to a greater psychological meaning of imprisonment that rests beneath the story's surface. The novel contains two interpolated tales that treat the prison experience, both of which investigate the significance of this concealed psychological story; moreover, Pickwick's education includes not only an initiation into the Fleet's physical hardships but also an insistence that the hidden psychological story created by confinement must be read and interpreted to arrive at a full comprehension of the meaning of the prison. In part, the novel thus marks a return to Dickens's boyhood, to what he had seen and suffered during his father's time in the Marshalsea. The first of many narrative returns to the prison, however, *Pickwick Papers* marks also the earliest stirrings of Dickens's impulse to narrate the cell, an impulse that Dickens continually indulged and refined through more than three decades of authorship. By insisting upon the Fleet as a place of both physical and psychological concern, Dickens creates in *Pickwick Papers* a novel that achieves its comic aims even as it foreshadows Dickens's darker and later work in narrating the story of the Victorian prisoner.

II

Dickens's apprehension of the prison as a place charged with devastating psychological consequences stems in the main from his personal experience with the Marshalsea, and from his lifelong reconsideration of the meaning of that experience as a shaping influence upon his character. Young Charles even in early boyhood exhibited a fascination with prisons and prisoners, a tendency that his experiences with the Marshalsea rather tended to strengthen.[7] His career as a novelist could almost be said to begin in the Fleet with Samuel Pickwick, and to have ended in preparation for John Jasper's time in the condemned cell, though Dickens died himself before he could complete the execution he planned for this enigmatic character. Yet even this intended finale for John Jasper returned to Dickens's earliest sketch of the prison, undertaken in 1835 and called "A Visit to Newgate," which imaginatively portrays the thoughts of a man condemned to hang. "Fagin's Last Night Alive" in *Oliver Twist* (1838), too, returns to this early consideration of Newgate's condemned cell. These accounts differ from the Fleet chapters, of course, because those condemned to die are presumably guilty of crimes, and the psychological portraits that Dickens undertakes are primarily attempts—like William Godwin's *Caleb Williams* (1794) and Edward Bulwer-Lytton's *Paul Clifford* (1830) and *Eugene Aram* (1832)—to wrestle narratively with the psychological dimensions of guilt. The debtors imprisoned in Dickens's Fleet hardly share in such terrible guilt as Fagin's, and none confront the same horrors of solitude and conscience. Yet this very fact makes the Fleet chapters all the more crucial for an understanding of how Dickens understood the effects of confinement, for the psychological upset we witness is exclusively that caused by squalor, sorrow, and the long misery of the cell.

Portraying Pickwick's confinement in the Fleet thus required, despite the episode's relative levity compared with the episode of Fagin, a deeper consideration of confinement itself than is contained in these other works. Perhaps no author was better qualified than Dickens to contemplate and to narrate both the physical and psychological experience of the prison.

His knowledge of contemporary prisons, both debtors' and criminal, was prodigious, garnered in part through his experiences as a free-lance and then full-time journalist for a number of London papers. Edgar Johnson suggests that during the young man's seven years as a reporter focusing upon Parliamentary matters, Dickens watched lengthy and heated debates over the 1832 Reform Bill, discussions of labor law reforms like Sadler's Ten Hours Bill and attempts to limit the working hours of adults, and the passage of the new Poor Law of 1834, which Dickens so mercilessly attacks in *Oliver Twist*.[8] Johnson omits, however, the penological debates which Dickens may also have witnessed during these years. Scholars working to recover Dickens's writing from these early years have met with limited success, for his contributions to newspapers were unsigned, but debates he may have observed as a Parliamentary reporter include those over an 1828 riot and consequent disciplinary adjustments at Millbank Penitentiary, for instance, and the creation of the Prison Inspectorate—which ushered in a move toward a more unified English prison system predicated upon separate confinement—in 1835.[9] In addition to his journalistic experience with the prisons, Dickens conducted several visits to prisons in and around London during the 1830s and concentrated upon prisons during his visit to America in early 1842.[10] While preparing materials for various *Sketches by Boz* in 1835 and 1836, Dickens visited both Newgate and George L. Chesterton's silent-system prison at Coldbath Fields, and he returned to both prisons several more times, at least once with John Forster and other friends in tow.[11] Forster recalls a Dickens fond of discussing "the improvement during the last few years of the London prisons," and remembers another tour of nearly all these prisons during the period 1838–1839.[12] Dickens struck up a friendship with Chesterton as a result of his visits to Coldbath Fields, and he befriended penal experimenter Alexander Maconochie when the latter returned from his office as governor of the Norfolk Island penal colony in Australia. Dickens began his career as a novelist amid a time of remarkable change in penal practices and reformative discipline, and his remarkable breadth of prison knowledge coupled with his keen eye for observational detail molded him into an author who, when he wrote of the prison, could render scenes that achieved his earliest hopes as a shaper of fiction: the "higher recognition of these as bits of actual life."[13]

Familiar as Dickens became with criminal prisons during his early career as a novelist, however, his experience with a prison of another kind pushed him beyond this physical realism and into the hidden psychological world of the Victorian prisoner. Biographers from Forster and Johnson to Peter Ackroyd and Michael Allen have emphasized the psychic consequences of Dickens's childhood experiences at the Marshalsea, ensuring that his boyish traumas at both the debtors' prison and at Warren's Blacking remain a familiar part of Dickens lore.[14] We know, for instance, that John Dickens was imprisoned in the Marshalsea because of "the Deed" on February 20, 1824, only two weeks after Charles's twelfth birthday, and that the elder Dickens was released from the prison when his mother died three months later, on May 28, leaving him a small estate sufficient to settle his debts.[15] As was typically the case in both the Marshalsea and the Fleet debtors' prisons—both of which eventually received lengthy treatment in Dickens's fiction—John Dickens took his wife and the smaller Dickens children into the prison with him, where they lived together in the tiny room he contracted for with the warden. The two elder children, Fanny and Charles, lived away from the prison. Fanny had earned an award to study at the Royal Academy of Music and therefore had every reason to live away from her family, but Charles was simply sent to work so that he could pay his own way rather than drain the meagre family income. He was let a dingy room near his place of employ across London from the Marshalsea and endured miserable evenings isolated from his family. Each morning he walked to work, where he earned his tiny income labelling bottles, a job he had received through the "charity" of a cousin. Forced into shabby company while at work and isolation away from it, the boy spent his free time ferreting about the streets of London in search of cheap bread and pleasant sights that could take his mind away from his dismal situation. Years later he recalled to Forster: "I know that I have lounged about the streets, insufficiently and unsatisfactorily fed. I know that, but for the mercy of God, I might easily have been, for any care that was taken of me, a little robber or vagabond."[16] This terrible period lasted only a couple months before John Dickens noticed the boy's misery and found him a room nearer the prison, after which time Charles regularly took supper with his family and spent Sunday with them all—Fanny included—at his father's tiny room. During these visits Charles was "endlessly curious about all the prisoners and their histories, and untiringly observant of their characters and behavior."[17] He even, according to Forster's recollections, said that he "made out [his] own little character and story for every man" he watched while in the prison, each of their "different peculiarities of dress, of face, of gait, of manner . . . written indelibly upon [his] memory."[18] Understandably he was most observant of his father, who initially despaired at his situation and developed the nervous play of the fingers about the mouth that Dickens later attributed to William Dorrit.[19] From Dickens's earliest acquaintance with the Marshalsea, then, he associated the prison with the fashioning of a narrative past and narrative identity from the visible marks of confinement.

Yet what Dickens suffered—not what he observed—makes his writing on the prison so powerful and distinguishes his accounts from those of lesser authors, for Dickens realized through the slow round of years the internal, psychic, lasting consequences of his early trials. Though John Dickens had been imprisoned for only about three months, Charles was left to labor at bottle-labelling for more than a year, and the boy's deep shame at having been so reduced—having been denied companionship, education, and a more genteel upbringing—became in later life a distinguishing characteristic of his sense of self.[20] He had not himself been a Fleet prisoner, but he had been imprisoned by circumstance, exposed to the squalor and misery of the debtors' prison, left isolated, as he thought, from the wider world. As he reached manhood and earned literary success, Dickens came to recognize the period as a central formative influence upon his behavior and identity. For most of his life, Dickens says he hid this brief period from the view of the world, his wife included; he never broached the subject with his parents. By his own account, not until he spilled forth the whole story to John Forster did he fully disburden his long-aching mind:

> From that hour until this at which I write, no word of that part of my childhood which I have now gladly brought to a close, has passed my lips to any human being. I have no idea how long it lasted; whether for a year, or much more, or less. From that hour, until this, my father and mother have been stricken dumb upon it. I have never heard the least allusion to it, however far off and remote, from either of them. I have never, until I now impart it to this paper, in any burst of confidence with any one, my own wife not excepted, raised the curtain I then dropped, thank God.[21]

How accurate this account of his silence may be is uncertain, for Kate at any rate may have known his story. Regardless of the truth of his claim, however, Dickens never dropped fully the curtain that he claimed separated his boyhood trials from his adult life. Early after his liberation from Warren's, Dickens felt the difference between himself and his schoolfellows that his days of misery had created, and after revealing his past to Forster he continually found "at extreme points in his life, the explanation of himself in those early trials."[22] In other words, Dickens came to recognize that physically suppressing his childhood experiences could not expunge them, and that any coherent self-narrative he could give must deal with the psychological ramifications of his brief foray into the prison. *David Copperfield* (1850) and the Micawbers testify to this truth. Like the prisoners whose histories he both learned and invented while visiting his father at the Marshalsea, Dickens had come to own a miserable narrative of the cell. Though not subjected to prison discipline or technically imprisoned himself, he had been indelibly marked by his boyhood experience of the prison. More importantly, he recognized the presence of an essential psychological account concealed beneath the outward fact of his confinement.

Natalie McKnight suggests that Dickens's muteness on his days at Warren's and the Marshalsea explains his determination to voice "experiences with poverty, alienation, and marginalization" through the downtrodden characters he creates, but in making this attribution she misses a fundamental part of the point.[23] Dickens did attest to this deeply felt and shameful period of his life, whether to Forster only, as the author claimed, or whether to Kate, and in so doing he recovered crucial reasons and strategies for narrating the prison. First, he came to understand that imprisonment, regardless of any explicit disciplinary aims, produces psychological transformations that can hardly be measured through the body alone. In Dickens's narratives of imprisonment the marks left upon the physical body always indicate a concealed psychological story that must be read, inferred, and interpreted to understand fully the prison story. He relies upon the sense and logic created by his own experience of imprisonment and misery, which he later discovered had left visible and quantifiable marks behind in his behavior and character, and uses this understanding to depict prisoners whose habits, ticks, and idiosyncrasies always bear the hidden psychological meaning of their imprisonment. Second, Dickens understood that any narrative of the self in the cell must investigate the prison in its psychologically transformative dimension, an imperative that grew stronger during the 1840s as criminal prisons, at least, increasingly became great reformative penitentiaries explicitly designed to effect psychological transformations upon the confined. Dickens wrote of such prisons in 1842 in *American Notes*, and he returned to the images of that travel book for much of his presentation of the irrevocably altered Alexandre Manette in *A Tale of Two Cities*. Even in *Pickwick Papers*, however, Dickens was astute enough to recognize that the narrative of imprisonment could not be merely an account of physical conditions, of social injustices, and of "bits of actual life" but must rather fuse these details with an imaginative invasion of the inscrutable human mind, tormented and altered by the cell. Taking up, for several chapters at least, the subject of imprisonment for debt in the Fleet, *Pickwick Papers* achieves the earliest such fusion. On one hand, relying upon the images that Dickens had himself witnessed at the Marshalsea and perhaps other London prisons as well, it establishes itself as a documentary text concerned with facts, details, and the physical prison and intended to educate Pickwick and the reader regarding the debtors' prison. On the other, it intimates all the while that an essential and more terrible psychological story of imprisonment lurks beneath the novel's pleasant and matter-of-fact world, and that we must peer beyond the plain facts if we are to penetrate the deeper truths and mysteries of the self in the cell.

III

Pickwick Papers establishes, both in its early passages and in its Fleet chapters, an authoritative narrative stance that suggests the documentary nature of the physical facts and details that comprise the bulk of the novel. Steven Marcus has thoughtfully called attention to the "cluster of negations, othernesses and circumstances" that mark the various prefaces Dickens wrote for the novel, and the book's origins in both the drawings of the unfortunate Robert Seymour and Dickens's fertile imagination partially confuse the question of the project's imaginative ownership.[24] Prefaces aside, however, the novel from its first page announces itself as authorized and indisputable, ostensibly a "true" account of the

> Transactions of the Pickwick Club, which the editor of these papers feels the highest pleasure in laying before his readers, as a proof of the careful attention, indefatigable assiduity, and nice discrimination, with which his search among the multifarious documents confided to him has been conducted.[25]

At the outset Dickens through his narrator negates his own role as a shaper of fiction and the fictional status of the novel itself. What will be presented in the following pages, we are told, is a true narrative that has been sifted by a persistent and insightful editor in order to assemble its narrative meaning. The avowal of narrative authority persists until, by the end of chapter one, the narrator claims that the facts of the account, while not an "official statement," have been "carefully collated from letters and other MS. authorities, so unquestionably genuine, as to justify their narration in connected form" (7). The comment implies that only authenticity justifies coherent narrative, and that the text is primarily an editorial undertaking designed to provide with its necessary meaning the otherwise chaotic accounts that form the basis of the novel. Later chapters of the novel are attributed to "the notebook of Mr. Snodgrass" (53), and the seeming intrusion of the interpolated tales is validated by their having been "recorded in the Transactions of the club" (41). After the first several chapters, Dickens drops the pretense of the novel as an editorial chore—stops insisting so loudly, that is, upon the novel as truth—and admittedly the narrative ploy has been little more than convention anyway, designed like many eighteenth- and early-nineteenth-century novels to present an appearance of authenticity and thus authority to speak. Convention or not, however, the novel's claims to authority and truth tend to ground even its most farcical events, to say nothing of its more sober and realistic prison scenes, in the world of credible and thus true human experience.

In the Fleet chapters Dickens underscores this authenticity—perhaps to ensure that the reader will not miss the truth of his social critique—by saturating his descriptions with details and intrusions that affirm the truth of his portrayal. Upon Pickwick's initial entry into the Fleet, he views through the open doors of its cells "four or five great hulking fellows, just visible through a cloud of tobacco-smoke . . . engaged in noisy and riotous conversation over half-emptied pots of beer, or playing at all-fours with a very greasy pack of cards. . . . [or] some solitary tenant . . . poring, by the light of a feeble tallow candle, over a bundle of soiled and tattered papers, yellow with dust and dropping to pieces from age" (632). When Pickwick is "chummed" to his new room, he immediately notices the "still remnants of loaves, and pieces of cheese, and damp towels, and scraps of meat, and articles of wearing apparel, and mutilated crockery, and bellows without nozzles, and toasting-forks without prongs" (650). Such vivid descriptions leave us little room to doubt their accuracy. Dickens also takes an opportunity to render the fetid interior of the Insolvency Court, a significant yet obscure feature of imprisonment for debt in pre-Victorian years, by gratuitously introducing old Anthony Weller's friend George, who otherwise plays little role in the novel.[26] These minor touches only anticipate, however, the lengthy narrative intrusion that announces the indisputability of the novel's portrait of the Fleet. Eschewing the playful tone that usually characterizes his storytelling, the narrator begins his account of the Fleet's "poor side" by invoking the reader's contemporary knowledge of the prison:

> Most of our readers will remember, that, until within a very few years past, there was a kind of iron cage in the wall of the Fleet Prison, within which was posted a man of some hungry looks . . . Although this custom has been abolished, and the cage is now boarded up, the miserable and destitute condition of these unhappy persons remains the same. We no longer suffer them to appeal at the prison gates to the charity and compassion of the passers by; but we still leave unblotted in the leaves of our statute book, for the reverence and admiration of the succeeding ages, the just and wholesome law which declares that the sturdy felon shall be fed and clothed, and that the penniless debtor shall be left to die of starvation and nakedness. *This is no fiction* [emphasis mine].
>
> (654)

Dickens the reformer has made his plea, at once denouncing the injustice of the poor laws, invoking the principle of less eligibility for felons (that is, the belief that the lot of even the poorest free citizen ought to be better than that of criminals housed and fed by the state), and hinting at the increasing separation and privacy of the prison from the society beyond its walls. And he has done so within an intrusive passage offered as a gauge of the veracity of the novel's account. Though part of a novel, the passage concludes with its paradoxical "This is no fiction," placing a premium upon the truth of its contemporary portrait of life within the Fleet and emphasizing that disclosure of that truth through narrative is the chief purpose of these several chapters.

The profession of truth-telling is not limited to Dickens's narrator, either, as the cobbler—Sam Weller's Fleet roommate—illustrates in his "story," itself a curious fusion of fact and fiction. The cobbler relates to Sam that he has been imprisoned in the Fleet as a victim of inheritance, having acted as trustee for a will later contested by one of the deceased's nephews. The disgruntled nephew has entered a caveat—what Sam calls the "brother-in-law o' the have-his-carcase" (680)—against the cobbler, and as a result the poor trustee has been taken to the Fleet, where he must remain until the case, in true *Bleak House* (1853) fashion, works itself out in Chancery. At the conclusion of this lengthy account of his unmerited sufferings, the cobbler proclaims, "And this is God's truth, without one word of suppression or exaggeration, as fifty people, both in this place and out of it, very well know" (681), and we are certain that we have just witnessed another of the text's claims to truth and authority. But a letter from Dickens to George Beadnell in July 1837 indicates that, in this case, the story really is true and reflects the sufferings that a Mr. Clarke related to Beadnell earlier that year. Mr. Clarke's story, Dickens tells Beadnell, has been "put into a Cobbler's mouth who tells it in the next number," though Dickens asks that Beadnell not inform Mr. Clarke that the author has even heard the remarkable tale.[27] The letter goes on to express Dickens's desire to be free of any inundation of actual accounts of imprisonment in composing his novel, and to insist that the inclusion of Clarke's tale has been "the only reality in the whole business of and concerning the Fleet."

The statement is of course troublesome, for in it Dickens separates the idea of narrative truth from the idea of reality, suggesting that a true portrayal of the potential abuses and likely events within the prison need not be based upon the actual experiences of a particular individual. The truth that Dickens seeks is qualitative rather than quantitative, divorced from facts to a degree that will permit the true power of the prison narrative to emerge. Explaining to Beadnell later in the same letter his desire to avoid real accounts , Dickens says: "Fictitious narratives place the enormities of the system in a much stronger point of view, and they enable one to escape the personalities and endless absurdities into which there is a certainty of rushing if you take any man's account of his own grievances." Placing Clarke's story in the mouth of the cobbler, Dickens assumes the editorial role that his narrator claims as well, and the result is a novel that both authorially and narratively seeks to imbue with greater meaning and truth the factual threads of the prison account. Of course, it is also likely that in the end Dickens's decision to include this real story indicates that the idea of the hopelessly entangled will—which reemerges in Jarndyce v. Jarndyce fifteen years later—was simply too absurd and telling to ignore.

More importantly, Dickens's admonition against using the personal experience of any single individual to create a narrative of the prison illustrates that the aim of *Pickwick Papers* is to educate Pickwick and the reader regarding the prison as a whole rather than to unearth any particular story of confinement. The cobbler's story contains much of caveats, councils, lawyers, and Chancery but virtually nothing of his time in the Fleet, and even such as it is the story falls, apparently unheard, upon the ears of a dozing Sam. Other prisoners similarly seem to lack their essential stories. We receive no explanation of the "young woman, with a child in her arms, who seem[s] scarcely able to crawl" (PP 636), for observing her physical state is all the novel allows. The worn and hollow Alfred Jingle, whom we have frequently met earlier in the novel, relates the entire prison experience that has brought him so low with the words, "Live on a pair of boots—whole fortnight. Silk umbrella—ivory handle—week—fact—honour—ask Job—knows it" (658). The novel permits us to see the physical marks left by long confinement, but the psychological effects and hidden meanings of those marks remain—like Jingle's atemporal present-tense speech—veiled by an incompleteness that requires the reader to rely wholly upon observable evidence. The whole of the novel's explicit concern seems to be the factual, physical disclosure of the prison's miseries to the innocent Pickwick, as the substance of his education.

Having established the veracity of his novel's account, Dickens moves Pickwick through the corridors and cells of the Fleet, showing him the world of cruelty and altered meanings that exists within the prison. It is an educative journey that we share. Just after his arrest but prior to his imprisonment, Pickwick demonstrates his ignorance of the horrors of confinement by reveling in the misfortunes of a "mere boy of nineteen or twenty" (618) confined at Namby's who exhibits what Pickwick considers a scornful brazenness in the face of adversity. At first, the boy receives visitors who he believes will "make it all right" (62) for him, but moments later he expresses his anguish over the impossibility of his visitors' removing his present difficulties. Uncharacteristically cold, Pickwick finds himself "[v]ery much satisfied with this sudden bringing down of the youth's valour" (620). First admitted to the Fleet, Pickwick notes as well the "vagabondish" air of the more swaggering of those confined, and he concludes shortly after that "imprisonment for debt is scarcely any punishment at all" (623). Hardly the compassionate and sensitive man here that we have seen throughout the novel's first forty chapters, Pickwick exhibits an unconscionable satisfaction at the misfortunes of this mere "boy," and his reaction is perhaps very much our own at seeing this devil-may-care self-assurance on the part of those confined, the apparent lack of punishment supplied by the debtors' prison. Dickens knew better, however, and Pickwick's education will teach him just how wrong he is about what he sees. Like Pickwick, we too will learn that this underworld—or at least other-world—represented by the debtors' prison is neither so kind nor so simple as it seems.

In part Pickwick's education as a Fleet prisoner is linguistic, as we see from the moment of his arrest, when Officer Namby turns up at the George and Vulture and enters Pickwick's room just in time to hear a request to Sam for "[s]having water" (616). "Shave you directly, Mr. Pickwick" (616), Namby interjects, the implicit meaning of his words intelligible to Sam but not to Pickwick. During his ensuing trip to the Fleet, Pickwick encounters other familiar phrases that have come detached from their typical meanings. "Sitting for your portrait" means undergoing scrutiny by the warders so that they may tell prisoners from visitors (626); the "paper" that has been Smangle's ruin is "bills" rather than a job as a stationer (642); "chummage" is a cell assignment (647); and a "bail" is one who will accept money to commit perjury before the court—only a "legal fiction," we are told (623). To Sam the bird-cage in the lobby of the Fleet becomes a woeful reminder of the prison itself, "Veels within veels, a prison in a prison. Ain't it, Sir," a "philosophical remark" (626) that escapes Pickwick, for the latter has not yet come to understand the way meaning changes within the walls of the prison—the way that the physical world always indicates a darker world of hidden and terrible truths. Nothing is what it seems to Pickwick's eyes and ears, as he discovers most disturbingly when, coming upon a row of "stone vaults beneath the ground," he mistakes them for little coal-cellers for the "convenient" use of the prisoners (631). Mr. Roker quickly corrects him:

> "Yes, I shouldn't wonder if they was convenient," replied the gentleman, "seeing that a few people live in there pretty snug. That's the Fair, that is."
> "My friend," said Mr. Pickwick, "you don't really mean to say that human beings live down in those wretched dungeons?"
> "Don't I?" replied Mr. Roker, with indignant astonishment; "why shouldn't I?"
> "Live!—live down there!" exclaimed Mr. Pickwick.
> "Live down there! yes, and die down there, too, wery often!" replied Mr. Roker; "and what of that?"   (631)

Here the Fleet yields up its darkest horror—terrible dungeons that house both life and death—to the unsuspecting Pickwick, and the disclosure is surely meant to shock the ignorant reader as well. As both Pickwick and the reader have learned, the debtors prison confines, maims, and even kills its prisoners in a private world beyond the scrutiny of those outside the walls.

These realizations, these horrors to which poor gentle Pickwick is exposed, constitute his prison education and ours as well. Only after witnessing the world within the prison's walls can Pickwick fathom the full horror of confinement: that the prison is capable of inflicting a slow, hidden, inexorable destruction upon those it confines. This realization emerges fully in the figure of the Chancery prisoner, who has "been slowly murdered by the law for six months'' (*PP* 686). When Pickwick occupies the Chancery prisoner's bedside during the man's final hours and realizes that he "had grown so like death in life, that they knew not when he died" (688), the former's education in the horrors of the prison is complete, and the end of the next chapter finds a disconsolate Pickwick proclaiming that he has "seen enough" (707) and locking himself away from the rest of the world of the Fleet. He takes Sam's early advice upon his arrest—"Don't witness nothin', Sir . . . Shut your eyes up tight, Sir" (617)—only after it is too late to blot from his memory the evils he has witnessed during this voluntary imprisonment. The measure of his education comes in weighing his gift of money to the wasted Jingle, and his determination not to let Mrs. Bardell suffer the continued evils of imprisonment, against his earlier satisfaction at the fate of the brazen young-ster, and his assessment of debtors' prison as hardly a place of punishment at all. The Fleet chapters of *Pickwick Papers* insist everywhere that the 1820s debtors' prison is a place of punishment out of all proportion to the social offense of being poor, and that the physical hardships imposed by poverty and imprisonment are such, as Perker reminds Pickwick, "to which no man should ever be consigned, if I had my will, but the infliction of which, on any female, is frightful and barbarous" (726). The Fleet chapters work throughout toward an illustration and iteration of this charge, and the explicit concern of the novel's address of the debtors' prison has been, as one would expect from the pen of a young reform-minded author, to disclose the very real physical horrors of confinement in the contemporary Fleet prison.

Even more importantly, the novel does not permit us, either in the Fleet chapters or elsewhere, to remain wholly situated in and concerned with the contemporary physical world of its action. The Bardell v. Pickwick lawsuit may, as Anny Sadrin suggests, disappear during the chapters between the court decision and Pickwick's arrest, but the effects of the lawsuit do finally interrupt the novel's celebration of the "passing moment."[28] The remarkable fat boy, Joe, who at first seems to require constant stimulation in order to stay awake, proves sentient indeed when he witnesses an event that will make the spinster aunt's "flesh creep" (*PP* 119), or when food is involved. And even Mr. Blotton's apparent solution to the mystery of "BIL STUMPS HIS MARK" (157), which would deny any significant meaning to the past world of the novel, is decried by the other Pickwickians, who turn the giant stone into an antiquarian riddle. As Stan Rubin suggests in discussing the novel's political content, *Pickwick Papers* is not devoid of history, and looking more closely at Dickens's exploration of the prison, we may see ways in which the past, particularly the past of prison experience, comprises one of the novel's primary preoccupations.[29] Like Pickwick's giant stone, the prisoner bodies of the Fleet bear marks inscribed by their imprisonment—marks that must be read and interpreted to reach a history of imprisonment that carries profound and private meanings for the individual self. In 1837 Dickens may still have been only dimly aware of the Marshalsea's effect upon his own psychological identity, but he remained too astute an observer of life to ignore those effects entirely. In the interpolated tales that litter the novel, in the indelibly marked prisoner bodies that inhabit the Fleet, and in the continuous acknowledgment of a concealed psychological narrative that rests beneath the scars of confinement, *Pickwick Papers* affirms the significance of the narrative past in the meaning of the present, especially in the story of the Victorian self in the cell.

IV

The fundamental lesson that Pickwick must learn during the novel's Fleet chapters is that understanding the story of the self in the cell entails reading the essential psychological past in the physical marks of confinement displayed in the present. Confined within the Fleet, the other convicts display in every haunted glance and wasted form the legible marks of their imprisonment. Some prisoners show signs of the Fleet's physical hardships, like the woman of "emaciation and misery" (636) and the Chancery prisoner with his "tall, gaunt, cadaverous" assortment of "sunken cheeks" and "bloodless" lips and "bones [worn] sharp and thin" by "the iron teeth of confinement and privation" (652). We must also recall the gauntness and pallor of Alfred Jingle and Job Trotter when Pickwick reencounters them in the Fleet, walking evidence of the violence done to two men who, only a handful of chapters earlier, had been hale enough to dupe Pickwick and Sam at Miss Tomkin's boarding-school. Other physical details indicate a deeper and more terrible narrative of confinement. The "strong-built countryman" absently strikes his riding boot with "a worn-out hunting whip" while he mutters commands to his imagined mount (657). A grandfather—curiously foreshadowing *The Old Curiosity Shop* (1840)—ignores the "thousand childish devices" with which his granddaughter plies him, his face having "settled into an expression of the deepest and most hopeless despair" (657). And of course the Chancery prisoner's fatal incarceration mercifully ends an existence made so grotesque by the prison that it resembled death even in life. Even the indomitable and lovable Pickwick, we are directed by Anthony Weller to fear, will be the worse for wear as a result of his confinement. "'He goes in rayther raw, Sammy,' said Mr. Weller metaphorically, 'and he'll come out done so ex-ceedin' brown, that his most familiar friends won't know him. Roast pigeon's nothin' to it, Sammy'" (668). In the Fleet the outward signs of incarceration abound while the disclosure of the hidden prison narrative is held in abeyance. The Fleet chapters insist upon a physically and psychologically transformative prison past that they choose then not to reveal.

If Dickens's account of the Fleet denies access to this hidden psychological story, though, we may find that story laid bare in the interpolated tales that incorporate the experience of the prisoner. The novel's nine "official"—that is, formally titled—interpolations all allow the past to intrude fantastically and often grotesquely upon the novel's present, and "The Old Man's Tale about the Queer Client" and "The Story of the Convict's Return" explicitly dwell upon the past of the Victorian prisoner. The former relates the story of George Heyling, who, like Dickens's father, falls upon financial woes and is taken to the Marshalsea, though in Heyling's case for debts he owes to his "wife's own father—the man who had cast him into prison, and who, when his daughter and her child sued at his feet for mercy, had spurned them from his door" (317). Heyling's son is blighted in childhood by the privations of confinement, and "though the form of childhood was there" (312), the boy sinks into despondency and physical decay, eventually dying while his father stands powerless to assist him. Heyling's wife soon follows suit, and he himself contracts a fever and is haunted by visions of death visited upon his father-in-law. Recovering from his illness, Heyling finds nothing within his breast but hatred, vengeance, and bloodlust for the man who has allowed his own daughter and grandson to waste away in the debtors' prison. In part, this tale offers a prison more obviously insidious than the Fleet into which Pickwick descends, and it is worth noting that this darker account unfolds in the prison that blighted Dickens's own boyhood. More importantly, this interpolation indicates Dickens's awareness of the body as a legible reminder of past sufferings both physical and psychological. The "hunger and thirst, and cold and want" shatter the boy's body, but he also declines because "[h]is recollections . . . were all of one kind—all connected with the poverty and misery of his parents" (312). The prison has become a place of external restraint but profoundly internal significance, and George Heyling is given a narrative being that contains the most fascinating psychological exploration of the novel. We witness his violent dreams, we comprehend his desire for revenge, and we witness and comprehend these things through the lens of his indelible past experience of the prison. His actions in allowing his brother-in-law to drown and in suing his father-in-law for debt acquire a meaning beyond cruelty only when they are measured against the anguish and fury of his confinement.

"The Story of the Convict's Return" is a different sort of tale, but like the first it suggests the importance of the past in narratively accounting for the prisoner's present. Indeed, the convict of this tale is able to return from transportation and resume a normal life—is able, in essence, to stop being a convict—only by shedding his self-narrative of imprisonment and transportation. Changed in physical appearance by age and his life of hardship in Australia, "No one," save the clergyman relating the story, "knew in that

man's life-time who he was, or whence he came'' (93). Eradicating the mark
of the convict means abandoning and concealing the story of imprisonment
as well, and entering the world again as an individual with no past and no
identity except in physical being—means undergoing, in fact, rebirth into a
world of present and future only. To have a past associated with the prison
is to continue to be a convict, to exist always as the product of the prison.
Like the story of the ''Queer Client,'' this tale hints at the ways in which the
dark narrative of the prison past threatens the pleasantness of the present.
Even unofficial interpolations like the ''Wellerisms'' attributable to Sam's
cockney wit—the parable, for instance, of the ''patent-never-leavin-off sas-
sage steam 'ingine'' (464)—function to make present meaning dependent
upon the the experiences and proper interpretation of the past. As the recipient
of these bits of wisdom, and as the reader and auditor of the official interpolations, Pickwick encounters over and again this logic enforcing the intercon-
nectedness of past and present and requiring that he read present signs for
hints of their past or hidden significance. Pickwick's whole reason for landing
in the Fleet approximates this interpretive process, as the court excavates
''Chops and Tomata sauce'' for its latent meanings; likewise, the marks that
Pickwick views in the wasted countenances of the Chancery prisoner, Jingle,
and Trotter bear witness in the present to the dreadful psychological transformations wrought in the convict past.

The novel's portrayal of the Fleet is more complex even than this, however,
for it insists in a pre-Foucauldian fashion upon the levelling nature of this
alteration, the presence and even production of sameness among those confined within the prison walls. The prison replicates the ''great hulking fellows'' who smoke and play cards in one room, for ''in a fourth, and a fifth,
and a sixth, and a seventh, the noise, and the beer, and the tobacco-smoke,
and the cards, all came over again in greater force than before'' (632). Other
of Pickwick's observations upon entering the prison further emphasize this
sameness, even beneath a veneer of difference and individualization. He
observes in the galleries of the prison:

> many classes of people . . . from the labouring man in his fustian jacket, to the
> broken down spendthrift in his shawl dressing-gown, most appropriately out at
> elbows; but there was the same air about them all—a kind of listless, jail-bird,
> careless swagger; a vagabondish who's-afraid sort of bearing, which is wholly
> indescribable in words . . .   (632–3)

Dickens has of course just described it in words, and he suggests that even
within the world of a debtors' prison—devoid of disciplinary schemes that
attempt to normalize and reform its inmates—the prison becomes its own
world with its own particular sort of inhabitants, what Dickens calls in *Little
Dorrit* the Marshalsea's ''race apart.''[30] Moreover, he has shown us in too

many other places the insidious and piteous transformations that the Fleet has inflicted upon its individual prisoners, all of whom eventually arrive at the same end in misery, frailty, and despair. These two narrative avenues imply in Dickens the possibility that in the end the experience of imprisonment produces—rather than simply houses or discovers—the sameness of its prisoners.

Despite these constant intimations that the essential prison story lies in the psychological account of the confined, *Pickwick Papers* stubbornly denies us more than oblique and momentary access to the hidden narrative that could complete the story of the self in the cell. The marks the prisoners bear miss their psychological roots, and indeed almost the whole novel remains closed off from the psychological processes of imprisonment, an idea best illustrated by the experience of Pickwick himself. Each time the novel approaches psychological disclosure, it recoils and omits. Early in Pickwick's imprisonment he feels "the depression of spirit and sinking of heart, naturally consequent upon the reflection that he was cooped and caged up" (636), but we see neither his gloomy thoughts nor his private reflections or fears, even though the novel has insisted all along that we are to be educated about a Fleet prison the effects of which we do not understand. After the lengthy narrative intrusion on the matter of debtors' prisons, we are told that Pickwick is "[t]urning these things in his mind" (654), but the reflections have decidedly been in tone and address an intrusion rather than psychological reflections of Pickwick's, and his mind remains unavailable to the text. After his friends visit the prison, Pickwick "ruminates" on Mr. Winkle's strange behavior, but we are privy to none of his suspicions or expectations, nor is he willing to consider what Winkle's secretive discussions with Sam presage. As Pickwick says, "I have no right to make any further enquiry into the private affairs of a friend, however intimate a one. . . . There—we have had quite enough of the subject" (684). Nor can we be surprised when Pickwick's attempt to comprehend the prison becomes a sudden withdrawal within the walls of his cell for three weary months. Repeatedly shrinking in this manner from the invasion of psychological privacy, from the reading of hidden thoughts, and from the disclosure of the missing narrative that everywhere underlies the prison experience, the novel becomes at best a partial account of the prison, a narrative that produces only the most basic and most superficial sort of truth about the cell. Sam's attempt to stare Mr. Smangle out of countenance becomes a metaphor for the book's narration of the prison, for, like Smangle, the prison and its prisoners are examined "steadily . . . with every demonstration of lively satisfaction, but with no more regard to . . . personal sentiments on the subject, than . . . had he been inspecting a wooden statue, or a straw-embowelled Guy Faux" (645). As such, it explicitly remains, even at its conclusion, much the contemporary portrayal of the Fleet that Angus Easson has suggested: a story of imprisonment that fully records the physical body only, and that can be defeated in its telling by Pickwick's disappearance within his private cell.

V

In the end, it may seem curious to premise an essay upon psychological meanings of imprisonment that *Pickwick Papers* fails to reveal, and to insist upon the significance of precisely what the novel does not contain. On one hand, it is tempting to suggest that Pickwick, and perhaps his novice author, lacks the imaginative capacity to apprehend the psychological experience of incarceration. Early in his imprisonment, Pickwick sees himself as "without prospect of liberation" (636) though he has entered voluntarily, and it is Sam rather than Pickwick who sees the symbolic significance of the Fleet's bird-cage, the "prison within a prison." Pickwick cannot even recognize the irony or analogy of Sam's arrest and his refusal to pay his creditor on "principle," nor the irony of his own observation that the lazy fly that crawls over his pantaloons is incomprehensible in its desire to stay within the Fleet "when he [has] the choice of so many airy situations" (639). Garrett Stewart sees Pickwick's educative journey as one toward not only awareness but also the expansion and liberation of his imagination, so that it may handle the "imaginative intensity" of what he sees in the prison.[31] Stewart may well be correct, for Pickwick is imaginatively ill-equipped to investigate the concealed narrative of imprisonment that the novel insists is everywhere present in the bodies, the habits, and the language of those confined within the Fleet. Indeed, even Pickwick's confinement must be voluntary, subject to end at any time, almost as if the protagonist and the author need the certainty of swift release from the necessity of delving too deeply into the psychological truths of the cell. But Dickens was not incapable of psychological portraiture, even this early in his career, as particularly his writings of the prison illustrate. In "A Visit to Newgate" and *Oliver Twist*, Dickens proved himself effectively and powerfully able to portray the condemned's psychological confrontation with death and guilt, instances that make all the more curious his refusal to do the same in *Pickwick Papers* for a kind of imprisonment that he knew much more intimately.

But in this very refusal—this insistence upon the privacy of both the prison cell and the individual mind—we discover the early dimensions of a narrative engagement with the prison that permeates Dickens's entire career. *American Notes* of course returns to pivotal images of the prison, as do *Barnaby Rudge*, *David Copperfield*, *Little Dorrit*, and *A Tale of Two Cities*. Indeed, finding a Dickens novel that does not contain some convicts, criminals, and cells is rather a difficult task. Particularly in his later fiction, however, and in those novels that treat the prison with a great degree of physical and imaginative detail, Dickens pressed increasingly upon the question of psychological privacy and the quandary of how to narrate the hidden mysteries of the mind. *Bleak House*, splitting its narrative duties between the voice of omniscience and the voice of Esther Summerson's private self, grapples with this question of how the hidden mind may enter the world of narrative. Invoking the Marshalsea Prison, *Little Dorrit* attacks the same question, offering Society as a great imprisoning power that drives each individual mind to constant self-policing, self-censoring, and concealment—a perspective that makes each individual mind both prison and prisoner, and that offers each character as almost inviolably private, available to narrative only in first-person confessions of past guilt and hidden anguish. *A Tale of Two Cities* reinscribes this question, and recovers images of *American Notes* as well, offering the sudden disclosure of Alexandre Manette's long-hidden prison narrative as the center of the novel's plot. In other words, Dickens's years of grappling with the imaginative and narrative possibilities of the prison returned constantly to claims for the privacy of the cell and the psychological story it contains, even as he constantly suggested that the psychological transformations wrought by confinement were the centers of his accounts. *Pickwick Papers*'s missing psychological story is thus neither accident nor failure: it is rather a precursor to the same concerns with privacy, narrative, and the prison that shaped many of Dickens's greatest novels and that make him the most gifted and intriguing author of the Victorian prisoner.

NOTES

1. For fuller discussions of this linguistic aspect of Dickens's comedy, see Garrett Stewart, *Dickens and the Trials of Imagination* (Cambridge: Harvard UP, 1974); Robert L. Patten, "'I Thought of Mr. Pickwick and Wrote the First Number': Dickens and the Evolution of Character," *Dickens Quarterly* 3.1 (1986): 18–25; and Steven Marcus, "Language into Structure: Pickwick Revisited," *Daedalus* 101.1 (1972): 188–203.

2. Many critics consider Pickwick's journey from innocence to knowledge the fundamental theme of the novel. See for instance Stewart; Elliot Engel, "The Maturing of a Comic Artist: Dickens' Leap from *Sketches by Boz* to *Pickwick Papers*," *Victorians Institute Journal* 9 (1980): 39–47; and Anny Sadrin, "Fragmentation in *The Pickwick Papers*," *Dickens Studies Annual* 22 (1993): 21–34.

3. Philip Collins, *Dickens and Crime* (3rd ed. New York: St. Martin's, 1994). Collins makes very little of *Pickwick Papers* and the Fleet, mentioning only a handful of times a particular episode or character from the novel. While his silence is

understandable in part, it is nonetheless worth noting that he dwells much longer upon William Dorrit's confinement in the Marshalsea—and upon *Little Dorrit* as a whole—than upon *Pickwick Papers*, almost as if the latter novel merits little attention not because it portrays the debtors' prison but rather because that portrayal is uninteresting or unworthy of analysis in light of Dickens's other fictions of imprisonment.

4. Angus Easson, "Imprisonment for Debt in *Pickwick Papers*," *Dickensian* 64 (1968): 105–12. In *Dickens, from Pickwick to Dombey* (New York: Basic Books, 1965), Steven Marcus argues that the novel is completely situated in the present-tense, in certain regards reformulating Easson's suggestion that *Pickwick Papers* is primarily preoccupied with its contemporaneous world. That contemporaneous world is the world of 1827–1828, in which almost the whole of the novel's action is set. For a thorough discussion of the novel's temporal setting, see Robert L. Patten, "Serialized Retrospection in *The Pickwick Papers*," *Literature in the Marketplace: Nineteenth-Century British Publishing and Reading Practices* (eds. John O. Jordan and Robert L. Patten. Cambridge: Cambridge UP, 1995), especially p. 125.

5. I refer here to D. A. Miller, *The Novel and the Police* (Berkeley: U of California P, 1988); and Audrey Jaffe, *Vanishing Points: Dickens, Narrative, and the Subject of Omniscience* (Berkeley: U of California P, 1991). Jeremy Tambling has also conducted recent post-Foucauldian work on the Victorian novel in *Dickens, Violence and the Modern State: Dreams of the Scaffold* (New York: St. Martin's, 1995), but his work is more concerned with social ideologies than with questions of narrative voice.

6. Collins, p. 134.

7. For a complete account of Dickens's childhood fascination with prisons and prisoners, see Edgar Johnson's biography *Charles Dickens: His Tragedy and Triumph* (2 vols. New York: Simon and Schuster, 1952), especially v. 1: 17–18.

8. Johnson, v. 1, p. 88. For more thorough accounts of Dickens's career as a journalist, see Johnson, pp. 47–105; and Kathryn Chittick, *Dickens and the 1830s* (Cambridge: Cambridge UP, 1990), ch. 1.

9. The editors of Dickens's *Collected Papers* (2 vols. Eds. Arthur Waugh, Hugh Walpole, Walter Dexter, and Thomas Hatton. Bloomsbury: Nonesuch Press, 1937) provide only one example of his reporting, aside from opinion pieces and literature reviews written later in his career. The example is his now-famous account of Lord Grey's reception at Edinburgh, "probably the first newspaper report by Dickens that was ever printed," which appeared in the *Morning Chronicle* on September 17 and 18, 1834. v. 1: 3.

10. For a complete discussion of Dickens's engagement with the American prisons during his tour of the United States, see Sean C. Grass, "Narrating the Cell: Dickens on the American Prisons," forthcoming in *Journal of English and Germanic Philology* 99.1 (2000): Ms. 30 pp.

11. This according to a letter from Dickens to W. Harrison Ainsworth on June 21, 1837 (*The Letters of Charles Dickens* [7 vols. Eds. Madeline House, Graham Storey, Kathleen Tillotson, et. al. Oxford: Clarendon P, 1974], v. 1: 275. I am indebted as well, of course, to Collins's thorough account of Dickens's various

visits to and familiarities with London prisons. One can also see in Dickens's letters from the mid-1830s other passing references to appointments made and letters of introduction composed for his plans to visit the London prisons. See for instance in Letters, v. 1, his letters to: John Macrone, 10/27/35, p. 83; Macrone, 10/29/35, p. 84; Catherine Hogarth, 11/5/35, p. 88; George Cruikshank, 12/8/35, p. 102; and Macrone, 12/9/35, p. 103.

12. John Forster, *The Life of Charles Dickens* (2 vols. London: Chapman and Hall; New York: Oxford UP, n. d.), v. 1: 166; 106.

13. Forster, v. 1: 70. According to Forster, this narrative realism was Dickens's proudest achievement in his early fiction.

14. See especially Forster, v. 1: 19–33; Johnson, v. 1: 27–46; Peter Ackroyd, *Dickens* (New York: Harper Collins, 1990), pp. 56–105; Michael Allen, *Charles Dickens' Childhood* (Basingstoke; Hampshire: Macmillan, 1988). Of all these texts, Allen's is perhaps the most thorough and well-researched, and of course it is as well the most focused upon Dickens's childhood before, during, and after the Marshalsea.

15. For a detailed discussion of the dates associated with John Dickens's imprisonment, see Allen, pp. 79–95.

16. Dickens, quoted in Forster, v. 1: 25.

17. Johnson, v. 1: 42.

18. Dickens, quoted in Allen, 91.

19. Johnson, v. 1: 35.

20. Allen argues persuasively, in distinction to earlier Dickens biographers, that Dickens's period at Warren's lasted from just before his twelfth birthday until March or April of 1825. See pp. 101–03.

21. Dickens, quoted in Forster, v. 1: 10.

22. See Johnson, v. 1: 48, for an account of Dickens's return to school. Forster, v. 1: 34.

23. Natalie McKnight, *Idiots, Madmen, and Other Prisoners in Dickens* (New York: St. Martin's, 1993), p. 10.

24. Marcus, "Language into Structure," 184.

25. Charles Dickens, *Pickwick Papers* (Oxford: Clarendon P, 1986), 1. Future references to the novel are to this edition and appear parenthetically in the text.

26. Throughout the eighteeenth century, Parliament passed a number of successive though erratically-timed Insolvency Acts aimed at alleviating debtors' prisons from the burden of confining those with no hope of paying. By an act of 1813, however, the Insolvency Court became a permanent feature of debtor law, allowing all prisoners of three months or more standing to apply to court for their discharge. Aside from his desire to achieve a realistic portrayal of the life of the imprisoned debtor, Dickens seems to have no reason for introducing George or his suit into the account of the Fleet. Indeed, in *Little Dorrit* Dickens includes no mention at all of the Insolvency Court, though William Dorrit is in prison for a quarter-century. For a fuller account of the Insolvency Court and the various acts that preceded it, see Roger Lee Brown, *A History of the Fleet Prison, London: The Anatomy of the Fleet* (Lewiston: Edwin Mellen, 1996), especially pp. 144–148; and Paul Elliott Brown, *Making People Pay* (London: Routledge and Kegan Paul, 1973) 310–15.

27. Dickens, Letters, v. 1: 289.
28. Sadrin, 24.
29. Stan S. Rubin, "Spectator and Spectacle: Narrative Evasion and Narrative Voice in *Pickwick Papers*," *Journal of Narrative Technique* 6 (1976), p. 195.
30. Charles Dickens, *Little Dorrit* (Oxford: Clarendon Press, 1979), 87.
31. Stewart, 35.

Oliver Twist and the Fugitive Family

David Parker

There is a systematic dissonance between developments in Dickens's life when he was writing Oliver Twist, *and what we find in the novel. He was starting a family. Very few characters in the novel get married, have a child or children, and bring them up with the help of a spouse in the usual way. Dickens was experimenting in* Oliver Twist, *an essay in Grand Guignol, but he was also restimulating feelings from his past. Private memories can be detected in it, which underpin Dickens's public indignation at the new Poor Law.* Oliver Twist *abandons the normal and the normative for the marginal and the transgressive. The novel is pervaded by irony against the family, and parody of it. Consanguinity is marginalized. The arbiters of decency and solvers of problems are old bachelors. In* Oliver Twist, *Dickens met a need to write something different from* Pickwick Papers *and* Nicholas Nickleby, *by revisiting emotions inimical to family life. Recognizing this helps explain Dickens's rejection of Cruikshank's original final illustration for* Oliver Twist, *too cozy for Dickens's somber vision.*

One of the pleasures of reading Dickens is to be found in the difference between successive novels.[1] Each is a new venture, a new fictional strategy. But Dickens's second novel, *Oliver Twist*, is not merely different from the others. There is something shrill and unappeased about it. I believe this to be explicable, and worth explaining for the glimpse it yields of the roots of Dickens's art.

It has been suggested that Dickens thought of the story of *Oliver Twist*, or something like it, in 1833 or even earlier (Tillotson xv–xvii). In a letter to

---

Dickens Studies Annual, Volume 29, Copyright © 2000 by AMS Press, Inc. All rights reserved.

Kolle of that year, Dickens speaks of a plan to write "a series of papers (the materials for which I have been noting down for some time past) called *The Parish*" (*Letters* 1: 33–34). This is echoed, not only by "Our Parish," title of the first group of *Sketches by Boz*, but also by *The Parish Boy's Progress*, subtitle of *Oliver Twist* in *Bentley's Miscellany*. Also in 1833 Dickens finally broke with Maria Beadnell after what was, for him, a painful first love affair. Like any twenty-one-year-old at such a time, he must have been reconsidering his hopes of marriage and, consequently, the prospect of fatherhood.

Whenever he first thought of the story, we know he began writing the novel at the end of 1836 or the beginning of 1837, at just the time he first became a father. The first number was published in February 1837. Charley, his and Catherine's first child, had been born a month earlier. There is no evidence of Dickens having actually written anything very much in advance of publication. He finished the novel the year he became a father for the second time. His daughter Mamie was born in March 1838. The volume edition of the novel was published in November.

I draw attention to these biographical data, because there is an odd and uncharacteristic lack of correspondence between the events of Dickens's life at this time, and what is to be found in the novel. Or, to be more precise, there is a systematic dissonance between them. Very few characters in *Oliver Twist* get married, have a child or children, and bring them up with the help of a spouse in the usual way. From what we are told, at any rate, it seems very few ever have. The novel is full of parentless children, single parents, childless couples, bachelors, widows, and widowers—not to mention characters for whom it is next to impossible to imagine any kind of family or family life. More often than not, transgression or misfortune have damaged or destroyed the families of which the narrative tells. Characters whose family background we know to be more or less normal are rare.

Needless to say, Oliver's own family history is the least normal in the book. He is illegitimate, the son of a man forced into an unsuitable marriage by an unsympathetic family, and of a woman the man loved, but could not marry because of this. Oliver is dispossessed, thanks to a conspiracy between his father's lawful wife and her son, his half-brother. The lawful wife, dead before the action begins, and the half-brother, still malevolently alive, hated each other, but were united in their hatred of Oliver. The family of Oliver's mother had foundered beneath the weight of her shame (ch. 51).

Disruption of family life and its reestablishment are, to be sure, traditional themes of narrative literature, as are illegitimacy and mysterious origins. Think only of *Tom Jones*. But rarely has the pudding been as over-egged as it is in *Oliver Twist*. Until the very end of the novel, such families as readers encounter are all deficient or unsatisfactory. From the beginning, the text accustoms readers to a vision of family dysfunction.

None of the families comprising more than one generation, encountered near the beginning of the novel, is exemplary. For instance, we are told that Noah Claypole "could trace his genealogy all the way back to his parents, who lived hard by; his mother being a washerwoman, and his father a drunken soldier, discharged with a wooden leg, and a diurnal pension of twopence-halfpenny and an unstateable fraction" (ch. 5). A pauper family introduced in chapter five comprises three generations, but the mother has just died of starvation and fever, the children are ragged and terrified, the father half mad, the grandmother completely so, and unnatural: "Lord, Lord! Well it is strange that I who gave birth to her, and was a woman then, should be alive and merry now, and she lying there: so cold and stiff! Lord, Lord!—to think of it; it's as good as a play—as good as a play!"

Other families are of one generation only, or depleted. Dickens does obliquely promise readers a family of more than one generation for Mr. Sowerberry, who complains of the difficulty of making a living from coffins for paupers, "especially when one has a family to provide for" (ch. 4). But the promise is not kept. The Sowerberry establishment is evidently childless. Mr. Brownlow's housekeeper is declared to be a "motherly old lady" (ch. 12), and she does indeed have a family, but her "kind good husband" has been dead twenty-six years, and though her "aimiable and handsome daughter" is married to "an aimiable and handsome man," her son in the West Indies writes "dutiful letters home" only four times a year (ch. 14). Gentle irony leaves readers uncertain quite how to receive Mrs. Bedwin's stories of her family. Only one thing is certain: misfortune has touched it, perhaps even transgression.

One of the strangest families in the novel is one readers are invited to see as exemplary. Mrs. Maylie, typically, has long been a widow. She and Rose Maylie, we are at first encouraged to think, are aunt and niece (ch. 29). The Reverend Harry Maylie, Mrs. Maylie's son, is in love with Rose, but both Mrs. Maylie and Rose caution him against marriage, because of a stain on Rose's name—her supposed illegitimacy, we later learn. Harry fell in love with Rose as a boy, he declares, when they were being raised together. At the time, he says, he was "ignorant of my own mind." But he claims to have been considering his feelings for "years and years": "I have considered ever since I have been capable of serious reflection" (ch. 34).

The implications are startling. Harry is about twenty-five, we are told, Rose seventeen. Assume he had been nineteen when he first came to love her—if anything, a little on the late side for the onset of "serious reflection." Rose would have been eleven. Assume, more realistically, he had been sixteen. She would have been eight. Nor have we even begun to think about their having been raised as brother and sister, or about Harry's first having declared his love when he still supposed them cousins. The hint of paedophilia and of other transgressions, however, though detectable by the analytic reader, almost certainly went unnoticed by Dickens. It impairs the exemplary status of the Maylie family and can best be explained by the supposition that Dickens simply neglected to do the arithmetic. But dismiss the hint of transgression, and we are still left with a fantasy which stopped him doing sums he might have done had he been imagining more constructively.

Rose and Harry learn the facts eventually, as does the reader. Rose is neither Mrs. Maylie's niece, nor illegitimate. They are unrelated. Supposing Rose illegitimate, Mrs. Maylie had pretended kinship only to protect her. So Harry and Rose can marry without anxiety, and do. At the end of the novel the narrative alludes to "joyous little faces that clustered round her knee" (ch. 53). At last a family is created which seems both normal and exemplary—a family, moreover, in which Oliver is included, since it is discovered that Rose is his aunt. The blood family for Oliver, however, the exemplary and normal family, have been arrived at by a route thick with transgression and abnormality.

And there are so many dysfunctional families in the novel. There is the disastrous marriage of Mr. Bumble and Mrs. Corney, for instance, a "jining of hearts and housekeeping," Mr. Bumble vainly gloats (ch. 27). There are the Sowerberrys, too. Mrs. Sowerberry, we are told, is given to hysterical laughter which greatly frightens Mr. Sowerberry, "a very common and much approved matrimonial course of treatment, which is often very effective," the narrator advises (ch. 5). The less conventional relationships of Sikes and Nancy, Noah and Charlotte, lead to murder in the one case, fraud in the other. One thing they do not lead to is children, let alone marriage.

We ask questions akin to "How Many Children Had Lady Macbeth?" when we wonder about the families of Fagin, the Artful Dodger, Bill Sikes and their like, but it is not irrelevant to note that Dickens's imagination invites little inquiry in this direction. Fagin articulates a doctrine irreconcilable with family life: "Some conjurers say that number three is the magic number, and some say number seven. It's neither, my friend, neither. It's number one" (ch. 43). Even Bill Sikes finds it difficult to envisage a family for him. "There never was another man with such a face as yours," he says, "unless it was your father, and I suppose *he* is singeing his grizzled red beard by this time, unless you came straight from the old 'un without any father at all betwixt you; which I shouldn't wonder at, a bit" (ch. 44). In accused prisoners and their friends, Noah Claypole can see "several women who would have done very well" for the Dodger's mother or sister, "and more than one man who might be supposed to bear a strong resemblance to his father" (ch. 43), but that is as near as we get to a family for him.

There is, then, a striking lack of correspondence between the events of Dickens's life when he was writing *Oliver Twist*, and the content of the book, a lack of correspondence unusual at this stage in his career. Chronologically, *Oliver Twist* stands between *Pickwick Papers* and *Nicholas Nickleby*. *Pickwick Papers*, I have suggested elsewhere, is a novel concerned with mobility, in more than one sense: geographical mobility, which leads through error to wisdom, and social mobility, the getting of status, unattainable, in Mr. Pickwick's case at any rate, without wisdom ("Mr. Pickwick and the Horses"). It projects Dickens's own experience, as a newspaperman of modest origins, turning novelist and rising through the class system. The relationship of money and love, I have also suggested elsewhere, is the principal theme of *Nicholas Nickleby* (*Nicholas Nickleby* xxv–xxxvi). Again, it projects Dickens's own experience. By the end of the 1830s, Dickens was famous, acquiring wealth, and raising a family, but worrying about its future. No such direct relationship between the novel's theme and the novelist's experience is to be found in *Oliver Twist*.

To construct an intelligible chronology, we have to speak of *Oliver* standing between *Pickwick* and *Nickleby*, but to do so is of course to oversimplify. At this stage in his career, Dickens was starting a new novel before completing the old. During the twenty-one months that elapsed between the appearance of the first instalment of *Oliver Twist* in *Bentley's Miscellany*, and the publication of the three-volume edition of the novel, no more than five months passed—November 1837 to April 1838–when Dickens need not have been working on either *Pickwick* or *Nickleby* (or indeed on "The Mudfog Papers," another current project). He doubtless thought it expedient to convey a different kind of vision in *Oliver Twist*, turning to the dark side of his imagination, in order to differentiate the tasks he was performing, and to offer readers something other than more of the same. Perhaps in this book, for artistic and commercial reasons alone, he needed to deny what he was affirming in his behaviour: marriage, parenthood, responsibility. Those, after all, are affirmed elsewhere, in other books. Whatever the reason, *Oliver Twist* dwells relentlessly on the failure of the family, on misfortunes and transgressions that ruin it. Dickens was always fascinated by the dysfunctional family, but in no other novel is the normal family so marginalized as in *Oliver Twist*.

It would be possible to leave this as a purely formal observation. We could agree that *Oliver Twist* is simply a different kind of novel. It was only Dickens's second. Unsurprisingly, he was experimenting. This was his essay in Grand Guignol. He wanted to make his readers' flesh creep. But I do not believe *Oliver Twist* is simply the result of a teleological choice by Dickens, though doubtless such a choice was made, and should not be neglected. As always with Dickens, strong feelings were restimulated in the course of composition, and you can only restimulate what has gone before.

Echoes of three emotional crises in Dickens's life can be detected, I believe, in *Oliver Twist*—emotional crises which, whatever their role in shaping Dickens's later life, were certainly episodes he revisited in search of material for fiction. Memories of his father's imprisonment in the Marshalsea Gaol, and of his own year in Warren's Blacking Warehouse, I suggest, have something to do with the special character of *Oliver Twist*. So do the relationships Dickens had with Maria Beadnell on the one hand, and with his wife Catherine on the other. So does the death of Mary Hogarth, Catherine's younger sister, three months after he had launched *Oliver Twist*. Feelings to do with these crises underpin Dickens's public indignation at the policy encouraged by the new Poor Law, of deliberately destroying family ties. In *Oliver Twist*, which has such a different tone and texture from *Pickwick* and *Nickleby*, Dickens, I suggest, much more systematically and intensely than in either of the other books, was taking a holiday from the normal and the normative, taking a holiday from what he sought in life for himself, to immerse himself in the marginal and the transgressive, to wallow in emotions which perhaps he could leave behind or call up at choice, but which here he saturated himself in. Throughout his career, his imagination required periodic immersion in these emotions. Arguably, all good novelists need something similar. But at this stage in his life, the pressures of the normal and the normative seem to have prompted an unusually thorough and protracted immersion.

Warren's and the Marshalsea had separated him from his family, damaged his sense of the family as something to be relied upon. The episodes had humiliated him, but had also given him the experience of intense emotion, and conferred street wisdom upon him. One way he had of dealing with that period was to enact in play an even worse condition. John Forster reports a tale told by Dr. Henry Danson, one of Dickens's classmates at Wellington House Academy, who spoke of Dickens, within months of leaving Warren's, "heading us in Drummond-street in pretending to be poor boys, and asking the passers-by for charity—especially old ladies" (Forster bk. 1, ch. 3). *Oliver Twist*, I suggest, is such play writ large. Parallels have often been drawn between Oliver's solitary condition and the isolation suffered by Dickens when he was at Warren's, between the moral catastrophe which threatens Oliver, and Dickens's sense that, "but for the mercy of God, I might easily have been, for any care that was taken of me, a little robber or a little vagabond" (Forster, bk. 1, ch. 2). Less has been made of the fact that Oliver's predicament is immeasurably worse than Dickens's had been. If we are to see the novel as a cathartic exercise for Dickens, we have to acknowledge that, to achieve catharsis, he evidently needed imaginatively to go way beyond Warren's, deeper into the abyss, for every shudder it was worth. Nor should we neglect the figure, above all others, of the Artful Dodger, who inhabits the abyss very comfortably, coping by means of roguish insouciance and anarchic wit, personal qualities Dickens did not manage to cultivate at Warren's, but which he did later, perhaps not least because of Warren's.

Speculation to the contrary and Dickens's own hindsight notwithstanding, I think it is now generally accepted that Dickens loved his wife Catherine, at least until the early 1850s, and certainly when he was writing *Oliver Twist*, but there are different fashions and degrees of loving. It is impossible not to see in the letters he wrote to Catherine during their engagement, the resolution of a man still nursing wounds of a less happy courtship, and determined this time to be in control, to temper passion with authority, to shape his new consort to his will. "With regard to your note my love," he could write,

> I will only say, that it displays all that aimiable and excellent feeling which I know you possess, and for which I believe from my heart, you are unrivalled;—if you would only determine to *shew* the same affection and kindness to me, when you feel disposed to be ill-tempered, I declare unaffectedly; I should have no one solitary fault to find with you. (*Letters* 1: 104)

This is not the unhappy victim who wrote to Maria Beadnell, "Our meetings of late have been little more than so many displays of heartless indifference on the one hand, while on the other they have never failed to prove a fertile source of wretchedness and misery" (*Letters* 1: 16–17). But it is the voice of someone constructing a family of his own at a price. With the experience of one unhappy courtship behind him, and of one successful thanks to emotional discipline and repression, it must have been tempting for Dickens to forget the frustration he had suffered in the one relationship, the rigorous control he exercised over the other, and to escape into a fantasy of overwhelming illicit love, self-immolation on the altar of passion, and its unforeseen fruit, illegitimate offspring. As he became a father, as responsibilities accrued, the notion of erotic self-abandon, regardless of consequences, must have seemed something worth at least imagining very thoroughly.

It is difficult not to believe that the death of Mary Hogarth released in Dickens a torrent of fantasies about what might have been, not excluding fantasies about relationships forbidden within families (see Parker, "Dickens and the Death of Mary Hogarth"). Evidence suggests the feelings he and Mary had for each other, while she lived, were not at all unconventional. Extravagant things he said about her after her death suggest an intensification of feeling, not merely permitted but caused by it. Only death made safe passion for a sister-in-law, with whom congress was prohibited both by the law of the land and by the Book of Common Prayer. Some features of the relationship of Rose and Harry Maylie may be traced to this. The similarities between Rose and Mary Hogarth have often been noted; not so often those between Harry and Dickens. Twenty-five and seventeen were precisely the ages of Dickens and Mary when she died. Harry "was of the middle height; his countenance was frank and handsome; and his demeanour easy and prepossessing" (ch. 34). This echoes many descriptions of Dickens as a young man. His height is repeatedly described as average. Forster speaks of his face's "candour and openness of expression." "The head was altogether well-formed and symmetrical,'' he says, ''and the air and carriage of it were extremely spirited'' (bk. 2, ch. 1). Harry is engaged in ''high and noble pursuits,'' which a liason with Rose could damage (ch. 35). There is a problem in her family background. There are suggestions of prohibited degrees of relationship. The point need not be labored.

To appreciate what we find there, however, it is important not to misunderstand how aspects of the relationship of Dickens and Mary Hogarth transfer into the novel. There is no evidence that Dickens used his relationship with Mary as a model for the relationship of Harry and Rose. On the contrary, the latter has all the marks of a fantasy compensating for disappointment in life—deviating, that is to say, from what might have been a model: fantasy as a substitute for creative imagination, something usually marked by stronger roots in experience and more attention to detail. Unresolved personal passion in a novelist is as likely to produce rootless fantasy as imaginative creation rooted in fact. Dickens's unhappiness over the death of Mary Hogarth, I suggest, led him to fantasize an enduring attraction between Harry and Rose, unmindful of the fact that, when you do your sums, you realize she would have been about eight when it started. He put something of himself into Harry, and a lot of Mary into Rose, because of fantasies he had after her death, not of experiences and desires before it.

The failure of imagination shows in the melodrama:

> ''If your inclinations chime with your sense of duty—'' Harry began.
> ''They do not,'' replied Rose, colouring deeply.
> ''Then you return my love?'' said Harry. ''Say but that, dear Rose; say but that, and soften the bitterness of this hard disappointment!
> ''If I could have done so, without doing heavy wrong to him I loved,'' rejoined Rose, ''I could have—''
> ''Have received this declaration very differently?'' said Harry. ''Do not conceal that from me, at least, Rose.''
> ''I could,'' said Rose. ''Stay!'' she added, disengaging her hand, ''why should we prolong this painful interview? Most painful to me, and yet productive of lasting happiness, notwithstanding; for it *will* be happiness to know that I once held the high place in your regard which I now occupy, and every triumph you achieve in life will animate me with new fortitude and firmness. Farewell, Harry! As we have met today, we meet no more; but in other relations than those in which this conversation would have placed us, we may be long and happily entwined; and may every blessing that the prayers of a true and earnest heart can call down from the source of all truth and sincerity, cheer and prosper you!''   (ch. 35)

The combination of strong feeling with logic-chopping and elaborate rhetoric is weirdly potent, but it is evidently an end in itself, replacing any need for the reader to think about character, motivation, or relationships.

Strange families and unconvincing relationships are two of the manifestations of Dickens's holiday from the normal and the normative in *Oliver Twist*.

Much more pervasive is narrative irony against the family. The novel begins with an ironic commendation of the foundling condition, brutally emphasised: "The old story . . . : no wedding-ring, I see," says the workhouse doctor. The newborn Oliver fails to breathe immediately. "Now, if, during this brief period, Oliver had been surrounded by careful grandmothers, anxious aunts, experienced nurses, and doctors of profound wisdom," the reader is told, "he would most inevitably and indubitably have been killed in no time" (ch. 1). Left to nature and without a family, Oliver learns the trick himself—unlike little Charley Dickens, we can be quite sure, at about the time his father was writing these words. Another early irony is to be detected in Oliver's triumph as a professional mute in Mr. Sowerberry's employment. He leads funeral processions, "in a hat-band reaching down to his knees, to the indescribable admiration and emotion of all the mothers of the town" (ch. 5). They are deeply moved by what they know to be simulation of grief. The child simulating, moreover, has neither mother nor father to grieve for.

Irony is often developed into parody, to evoke family in the novel. There are multiple parodies of family life and feeling, most of them repugnant, just one of them disturbingly seductive. The cruel, rapacious, and evidently solitary Mrs. Mann, mistress of the baby farm, provides one of the first. She tells Mr. Bumble she gives the children "Daffy" when they are unwell: that is to say, a supposedly medicinal dose, laced with gin, guaranteed at least to keep fretful infants quiet. Sampling the gin, Mr. Bumble declares himself impressed: "You feel as a mother, Mrs Mann," he observes (ch. 2).

The workhouse board enacts a parody of family solicitude. More than once, members deliberate over Oliver's future. On one occasion the parody is made explicit:

> in great families, when an advantageous place cannot be obtained, either in possession, reversion, remainder, or expectancy, for the young man who is growing up, it is a very general custom to send him to sea. The board, in imitation of so wise and salutary an example, took counsel together on the expediency of shipping off Oliver Twist, in some small trading vessel bound to a good unhealthy port. This suggested itself as the very best thing that could possibly be done with him: the probability being that the skipper would flog him to death, in a playful mood, some day after dinner, or would knock his brains out with an iron bar; both pastimes being, as is pretty generally known, very favourite and common recreations among gentlemen of that class. (ch. 4)

But the chief parody of family life in *Oliver Twist*—the disturbingly seductive one—is provided by Fagin and his gang. It is important not to be mistaken about this. The structure of *Oliver Twist*, and repeated indications in the narrative, make it clear that Fagin is evil, that he gladly conspires to ruin Oliver, that he cares as little for all his associates. Unlike Lionel Bart's musical *Oliver*, the novel eschews the suggestion that genuine warmth and belonging are to be found among a community of loveable working-class rogues. On the contrary, it shows such a supposition to be dangerous. But Dickens's imagination was at work on Fagin. He is dangerous precisely because we can see him to be clever and subtle. We see he knows about relationships, and takes pains with them. Oliver's meeting with the Artful Dodger, and his introduction to Fagin, are the nearest he has ever known, at that stage of the story, to admission into a family. Whatever it threatens, it offers something better than the loneliness he had experienced at the workhouse (ch. 4).

The gang communicates much of the time through underworld cant: "Hullo, my covey! What's the row?''; "Now, then!'' .... "Plummy and slam!'' (ch. 8). This may be a warning to the reader, but there is also warmth in its informality, not at all to be found at the workhouse, even in discourse between Oliver and Little Dick. The cant might almost be the private language of a close family, especially since Oliver is warmly welcomed by Fagin, and unstintingly given food and drink.

And Fagin calls him "my dear.'' (ch. 8). No one has ever called him that before, for all that others do afterwards. Fagin's feigned affection, moreover, is a sign of a real intimacy he contrives between himself and the boy, however perfidious on his part. Forget about their cruelty for the moment. Mrs. Mann, Mr. Bumble, the workhouse Board, are unrelentingly distant, patronising and admonitory in what they say to Oliver, and of him. They submit him to arbitrary, capricious, always unsympathetic definition, exemplified by the refrain of the gentleman in the white waistcoat: "That boy will be hung'' (ch. 2). Nor is this hectoring confined to characters condemned by the narrative. Initially at any rate, even Mr. Grimwig, one of a team of eccentric old bachelors who finally solve all the problems, is scarcely less dismissive of Oliver. He knows of only two categories of boy: "mealy boys, and beef-faced boys'' (ch. 14), and assigns Oliver to the former. That is enough for Mr. Grimwig, to start with at any rate. Whatever his motives, Fagin seeks to know and to understand Oliver. Regardless of what he says of him, what he says to Oliver has about it, by contrast to what others say, a refreshing normality and directness, undiminished by the underlying hypocrisy. He never speaks down to him. Enraged by Oliver's observing him gloating over his booty, Fagin goes so far as to threaten him with a carving knife, but remembers himself in time. He plays "with the knife a little, . . . as if to induce the belief that he had caught it up, in mere sport.'' He knows the importance of encouragement and praise. "You're a brave boy,'' he tells Oliver (ch. 9).

Whatever the signs are for us to question Fagin's "benevolence,'' his behavior towards the Dodger, for instance, and Charley Bates, demonstrates warmth hitherto unknown to Oliver. "Good boys, good boys,'' he calls them.

Whatever the sinister undertones, the gang provide Oliver with his first experience of teasing and playfulness:

> "You'd like to be able to make pocket-handkerchiefs as easy as Charley Bates, wouldn't you, my dear?" said the Jew.
> "Very much indeed, if you'll teach me sir," replied Oliver.
> Master Bates saw something so exquisitely ludicrous in this reply, that he burst into another laugh; which laugh meeting the coffee he was drinking, and carrying it down the wrong channel, very nearly terminated in his premature suffocation.   (ch. 9)

Nobody laughs much in *Oliver Twist*, except members of the gang, and Charley Bates especially who, when Oliver is snatched back, has to ask, "Hold me, somebody, while I laugh it out" (ch. 16). We are told Mr. Losberne cracked jokes, and that people laughed at them (ch. 34), but no sample is vouchsafed us.

Like the workhouse Board, Fagin parodies a father in the way he offers judgment and advice on conduct. We see what is wrong, when he says of the Dodger and Charley, "Make 'em your models, my dear" (ch. 9), but we feel he is more engaged in his advice than the Board member who tells Oliver, "I hope you say your prayers every night, . . . and pray for the people who feed you, and take care of you—like a Christian" (ch. 2). Fagin no more eschews violence than Mrs. Mann or Mr. Bumble, but the irony conspires with him rather than against him:

> Whenever the Dodger or Charley Bates came home at night, empty-handed, he would expatiate with great vehemence on the misery of idle and lazy habits; and would enforce upon them the necessity of an active life, by sending them supperless to bed. On one occasion, indeed, he went so far as to knock them both down a flight of stairs; but this was carrying his virtuous precepts to an unusual extent.   (ch. 10)

Nor are his pupils unappreciative. "Why don't you put yourself under Fagin, Oliver?" asks Charley Bates:

> "And make your fortun' out of hand?" added the Dodger, with a grin.
> "And so be able to retire on your property, and do the gen-teel: as I mean to, in the very next leap-year but four that ever comes, and the forty-second Tuesday in Trinity-week," said Charley Bates.   (ch. 18)

Oliver's first experience of female warmth is provided by the gang. On first meeting them, he is charmed by Bet and Nancy: "Being remarkably free and agreeable in their manners," the narrative dryly tells us, "Oliver thought them very nice girls indeed. As there is no doubt they were" (ch. 9).

Nor is it long before a parody of consanguinity is enacted. It is agreed that Nancy should go to the police court to find out what has happened to Oliver after his arrest:

> "Oh, my brother! My poor, dear, sweet, innocent little brother!'' exclaimed Nancy, bursting into tears, and wringing the little basket and the street-door key in an agony of distress. "What has become of him. Where have they taken him to! Oh, do have pity, and tell me what's been done with the dear boy, gentlemen; do, gentlemen, if you please gentlemen!''

Far from being diminished by it, the reader's awareness of parody is sharpened by this being only a rehearsal, for the benefit of Fagin and Bill Sikes. It offers Sikes an opportunity for commentary. He declares Nancy "a honour to her sex'' (ch. 13). One ironic effect of Nancy's play-acting is to remind us that no such concern has been shown for Oliver before, feigned or unfeigned. A similar parody of consanguinity is enacted when Oliver is snatched back into the gang, from Mr. Brownlow's care, by Sikes and Nancy:

> "What the devil's this?'' said a man, bursting out of a beer-shop, with a white dog at his heels; "young Oliver! Come home to your poor mother, you young dog! Come home directly.''   (ch. 15)

The parody is complicated, of course, by the fact that Nancy really does mother Oliver. She won't have him attacked by Sikes's dog: "the child shan't be torn down by the dog, unless you kill me first'' (ch. 16). Nor is Fagin right in his dismissal of Nancy's maternal feelings. "The worst of these women is, that a very little thing serves to call up some long-forgotten feeling,'' he reflects; "and the best of them is, that it never lasts'' (ch. 19). Nancy confounds Fagin by risking her life to protect Oliver, and forfeiting it.

There is even a kind of parody tug-of-love for possession of Oliver's heart. Contemplating the planned burglary in Chertsey, Fagin says, "Once let him feel that he is one of us; once fill his mind with the idea that he has been a thief, and he's ours. Ours for his life'' (ch. 19).

The everyday texture of family life is conjured as much by parody, in the novel, as by unironic narrative. Consanguinity proper is repeatedly marginalised as something established and signalled by nature alone, regardless of nurture, something declaring itself in untaught behaviour, detected in mysterious recognition. Oliver's courage and spirit—he famously asks for more, fights Noah Claypole, runs away—cannot be explained by circumstances. "But nature or inheritance,'' we are told, "had implanted a good sturdy spirit in Oliver's breast'' (ch. 2). He is fiercely loyal to the mother he has never known, ready to defend and indeed fight for her honor (ch. 6). He is honest without the least training in honesty (ch. 15). Having loved his aunt, Mr.

Brownlow recognizes Oliver. "There is something in that boy's face," he muses. "He looked like. . . . No, . . . it must be imagination" (ch. 11). Oliver is instinctively drawn to his mother's portrait in Mr. Brownlow's house (ch. 12). As the tears of his mother's sister, Rose, drop on his sleeping face, "The boy stirred, and smiled in his sleep, as though these marks of pity and compassion had awakened some pleasant dream of love and affection he had never known." And Rose instinctively sees what he lacks: "he may never have known a mother's love, or the comfort of a home" (ch. 30). Monks instinctively knows and hates Oliver. He had "seen him accidentally with two of our boys on the day we first lost him," Nancy tells Rose, "and had known him directly to be the same child that he was watching for, though I couldn't make out why" (ch. 40). "If you buried him fifty feet deep, and took me across his grave," Monks snarls, "I fancy I should know, if there wasn't a mark above it, that he lay buried there" (ch. 34).

Monks apart, a creature entirely of melodrama, the criminal characters in the novel are famously more vital than the honest ones. And they are the ones who stand free of families. As, curiously, do the arbiters of decency in the novel. The center of normality it proposes is the prosperous old bachelor, preferrably eccentric. Old bachelors, though given to aimiable error, are ultimately the fount of wisdom, decency and the good things in life. Old bachelors solve the problems. Mr. Brownlow, of course, is central in the rescue of Oliver. Mr. Brownlow, Mr. Grimwig, and Mr. Losberne, between them, constitute a kind of Pickwick club composed entirely of Samuel Pickwicks—advanced in years, prosperous, benevolent, wilful, scarcely touched by the perplexities of sexuality. In chapter forty-one, it is the old bachelors who successfully plot the resolution of the story, and at the end of the novel, the community in the village where the Maylies, Mr. Brownlow and Oliver settle, seems half made up of contented old bachelors, one of whom has adopted Oliver.

I submit that Dickens met a need to write something different from *Pickwick Papers* and *Nicholas Nickleby*, by revisiting powerful emotions he had experienced, inimical to the family life he was privately constructing. *Oliver Twist* is an experiment in anarchy at the expense of family order. Within the world of this novel, family is too unreliable an institution to withstand the tide of anarchy. The old bachelors can withstand it because they are strong solitary bulwarks, unencumbered by family. The criminals, equally unencumbered, are the tide itself. What are the great set pieces of the novel—the murder of Nancy by Bill Sikes, the pursuit and death of Bill Sikes, Fagin's responses at his trial, and his last night in the condemned cell—if they are not enactments of anarchy, licentious celebrations of the break-down of order? Turn from the normal and the normative: anarchy is what offers itself first. You can see this, moreover, not only in the Grand Guignol set pieces. It is to be found at its best in the committal proceedings for the Artful Dodger.

"Now then! Wot is this here business? I shall thank the madg'strates to dispose of this here little affair, and not to keep me while they read the paper, for I've got an appointment with a genelman in the City, and as I'm a man of my word and wery punctual in business matters, he'll go away if I ain't there to my time, and then pr'aps there won't be an action for damage against them as kep me away. Oh no, certainly not!"

At this point, the Dodger, with a show of being very particular with a view to proceedings to be had thereafter, desired the jailer to communicate "the names of them two files as was on the bench." Which so tickled the spectators, that they laughed almost as heartily as Master Bates could have done if he had heard the request.

"Silence there!" cried the jailer.

" What is this?" inquired one of the magistrates.

"A pick-pocketing case, your worship."

"Has the boy ever been here before?"

"He ought to have been, a many times," replied the jailer. "He has been pretty well everywhere else. *I* know him well, your worship."

"Oh! you know me, do you?" cried the Artful, making a note of the statement. "Wery good. That's a case of deformation of character, anyway."

Here there was another laugh, and another cry of silence.

"Now then, where are the witnesses?" said the clerk.

"Ah! that's right," added the Dodger. "Where are they? I should like to see 'em."

This wish was immediately gratified. . . .

"Have you anything to ask this witness, boy?" said the magistrate.

"I wouldn't abase myself by descending to hold no conversation with him," replied the Dodger.

"Have you anything to say at all?"

"Do you hear his worship ask if you've anything to say?" inquired the jailer, nudging the silent Dodger with his elbow.

"I beg your pardon," said the Dodger, looking up with an air of abstraction. "Did you redress yourself to me, my man?"

"I never see such an out-and-out young wagabond, your worship," observed the officer with a grin. "Do you mean to say anything, you young shaver?"

"No," replied the Dodger, "not here, for this ain't the shop for justice; besides which, my attorney is a-break-fasting this morning with the Wice President of the House of Commons; but I shall have something to say elsewhere, and so will he, and so will a wery numerous and 'spectable circle of acquaintance as'll make them beaks wish they'd never been born, or that they'd got their footmen to hang 'em up to their own hat-pegs 'afore they let 'em come out this morning to try it on upon me. I'll—"

"There! He's fully committed!" interposed the clerk. "Take him away."

(ch. 43)

This is the trick, writ large, played in the Dodger's characterization of Fagin as "a 'spectable old genelman," an intoxicating parody of order.

Formally, of course, Dickens endorses order, the normal and the normative, endorses the family where they are nourished. But it is clear his imagination yearned for the dark side. It is especially clear, I submit, in one detail of the production of the novel which has puzzled many, but which may be explained with the help of the observations I am making.

Oliver Twist ends with a description of the memorial tablet to Oliver's mother in the church over which Harry Maylie presides. The narrator expresses the belief that her shade "sometimes hovers round that solemn nook. I believe it none the less because that nook is in a Church, and she was weak and erring." Dickens chose to leave readers with an image of transgression rather than of the normal and normative.

Cruikshank's original final plate for the novel (fig. 1), shows Oliver with Rose and Harry Maylie, and old Mrs. Maylie, gathered contentedly round the domestic fireside. Dickens loathed this.[2] Because of production schedules, he was unable altogether to stop it appearing, but he managed to have it suppressed before many copies were printed, and to have another substituted. He wrote to Cruikshank, regretting "its being what it is," and demanding another design (*Letters* 1: 450–451). The words tellingly foreshadow the denunciation of the Circumlocution Office, responsible for the public condition being "what it was" (*Little Dorrit*, ch. 20). Less restrained and less subtle, Forster called the etching "a vile and disgusting interpolation on the sense and bearing of the tale," and spoke of its being "long known as a Rowland Macassar frontispiece to a sixpenny book of forfeits" (*Letters* 1: 451 n. 1).

It is not hard to understand why Dickens and Forster disliked the plate, but it is hard to understand why they disliked it so much. Various explanations are proffered, none very satisfactory. One has it that the domestic milieu depicted in it is too suburban for the country parsonage—the "rustic dwelling"—in which Rose and Harry finally make their home. But why so much anger at something merely inappropriate? Another has it that the peacock feathers arranged round the top of the mirror exemplify a fashion far too lower-middle-class. But that too would be merely inappropriate. Michael Slater suggests that Dickens was angry at the inclusion of Harry Maylie in the illustration, that Dickens wanted his projection of Mary Hogarth to stand free of adult male attachments (94). That is persuasive only if you see Harry Maylie as an interloper introduced by necessities of plot, rather than as a projection of Dickens himself.

The key to the indignation, I am tempted to think, is to be found in Forster's curious charge, that the image had been "long known as a Rowland Macassar frontispiece to a sixpenny book of forfeits." I am unfamiliar with the precise advertisement, if there was one, to which Forster was alluding, but an unchanging principle of advertising provides sufficient answer. Associating use of a product with happy normal life is not a discovery of the twentieth-century copywriter. Detach the image from the story, and it is possible to read it as a fine head of hair and whiskers yielding domestic bliss: Mum, Dad and the nipper, with Gran in the corner. Readers of the novel, of course, know that is not what is depicted, but ending the novel with this image seems almost to suggest that appropriate closure is achieved by as near a simulacrum as possible of Mum, Dad, the nipper and Gran around the fireside. Forster was not raging incoherently, but saying something precise, when he called the etching "a vile and disgusting interpolation on the sense and bearing of the story."

Confirmation of the grounds of Dickens's and Forster's objection is to be found in the replacement plate they procured from a reluctant Cruikshank. At first, it seems, Cruikshank tried adapting the original, but Dickens rejected that. Then he supplied an earlier version of the etching (fig. 2) showing Rose and Oliver sadly contemplating the memorial tablet, but with Rose wearing a light-colored dress. We can only suppose that, prompted by Dickens, he eventually etched the dress more heavily, to produce the version you see, with Rose soberly clad, perhaps indeed in mourning for a sister whose loss she only now knows of.

The final visual image with which readers were to be left had evidently to dwell upon transgression. It had to reinforce the narrator's final words. Nothing was to detract from the thought that the shade of Oliver's mother might hover around the nook where she is commemorated by her loved ones, "none the less because that nook is in a Church, and she was weak and erring."

This bleak final note crystallizes what I have in mind when I say there is something shrill and unappeased about *Oliver Twist*. There is also, it has to be admitted, something immensely powerful. For all its revisiting of unquiet emotions, *Oliver Twist* has embedded itself in popular consciousness, and not only in the English-speaking world. How Dickens contrived a novel which is both discordant and enduring is a mystery I have not attempted to probe. Perhaps it addresses something shrill and unappeased within all of us.

Figure 1. George Cruikshank's original final plate for *Oliver Twist*

Figure 2. Cruikshank's replacement plate of Oliver and Rose Maylie

NOTES

1. This paper is a version of a lecture delivered at the University of California Dickens Project, Dickens Universe, Santa Cruz, 1998.
2. Patten disputes this, and suggests Dickens was following Forster (84–86), but I take the view that Dickens's coldness is proportionate to Forster's heat.

WORKS CITED

Dickens, Charles. *The Pilgrim Edition of the Letters of Charles Dickens*, vol. 1, 1820–1839. Ed. Madeline House and Graham Storey. Oxford: Clarendon, 1965.

Forster, John. *The Life of Charles Dickens*. Ed. J. W. T. Ley. London: Cecil Palmer, 1928.

Parker, David. "Dickens and the Death of Mary Hogarth." *Dickens Quarterly* 13 (1996): 67–75.

———. "Mr. Pickwick and the Horses." *The Dickensian* 83 (1989): 81–98.

——— (ed). *Nicholas Nickleby* by Charles Dickens. London: Everyman, 1994.

Patten, Robert L. *George Cruikshank's Life, Times, and Art*, vol. 2, 1835–1878. Cambridge: Lutterworth, 1996.

Slater, Michael. *Dickens and Women*. London: Dent, 1983.

Tillotson, Kathleen (ed.). *Oliver Twist* by Charles Dickens. Oxford: Clarendon, 1966.

Down Ditches, on Doorsteps, in Rivers:
Oliver Twist's Journey to Respectability

Catherine Robson

To resolve the moral ambiguities created by the hero's birth to an unmarried woman in the workhouse, Oliver Twist, *I argue, makes canny use of three archetypal locations: the ditch, the doorstep, and the river. In the first place, the novel exploits the long-lived cultural icon of the illegitimate baby, abandoned at the side of the road. Saved from early death by official intervention,* Oliver Twist *nevertheless plays the role of the murdered baby in the ditch at a later stage in the text, and indeed, thanks to serial publication, remains in this invidious position for a disproportionately lengthy time. When he manages to move himself to the doorstep of a well-to-do house, however, he takes up residence in a far more acceptable story: Oliver dies the death of the least-wanted baby, in order that he may begin the life of a very different kind of baby, the fortunate foundling. From this point onwards Oliver is placed on a clear route to a happy conclusion, but just as importantly, the novel begins to work towards the regeneration of his mother's reputation. When Monks consigns Agnes's jewels to the turbid waters of the river, the last remaining traces of any possible kinship between Oliver's mother and the prostitute are removed from the book, and she is finally able to rejoin the family, and allowed to "hover round the solemn nook" of an old country church.*

Something rather strange happens almost exactly half-way through *Oliver Twist* (1837–39). Sikes, Crackit, and Oliver are on the run from the bungled

---

Dickens Studies Annual, Volume 29, Copyright © 2000 by AMS Press, Inc. All rights reserved.

burglary at Chertsey: Oliver has been hit by a pistol-ball, pulled out of the window of the house by Sikes, and wrapped in a shawl. Then, as we learn in chapter 22's final paragraph, "came the loud ringing of a bell, mingled with the noise of fire-arms, and the shouts of men, and the sensation of being carried over uneven ground at a rapid pace. And then, the noises grew confused in the distance; and a cold deadly feeling crept over the boy's heart; and he saw or heard no more" (215). At this point in the original publication scheme, not only did the chapter come to an end, but so did the monthly part and the first book of the novel. When readers of *Bentley's Miscellany* picked up their new copies one month later in February 1838, they were returned not to the unconscious Oliver, but to a description of a "bitter[ly] cold" night:

> The snow lay on the ground, frozen into a hard thick crust, so that only the heaps that had drifted into by-ways and corners were affected by the sharp wind that howled abroad . . . Bleak, dark, and piercing cold, it was a night for the well-housed and fed to draw round the fire and thank God they were at home; and for the homeless, starving wretch to lay him down and die. Many hunger-worn outcasts close their eyes in our bare streets, at such times, who let their crimes have been what they may, can hardly open them in a more bitter world.[1]   (215)

Although this depiction of the poor wretch collapsed outside in the cold may have reminded readers of the hero's plight, they would have soon discovered, as indeed the chapter heading had already declared, that they were to spend the next few pages basking inside in the warmth of Mr. Bumble and Mrs. Corney's hearthside courtship. And even though the next chapter drags Mrs. Corney from her comfortable chair to attend the deathbed confession of Old Sally, those original readers remain, as do we contemporary readers, at a considerable distance from little Oliver. The final chapter of February's installment may then move to his more recent circle of intimates, Fagin's gang, but only in its closing moments do we (and most particularly an unusually anguished Fagin) hear the returned Toby Crackit deliver his long-deferred account of the failed housebreaking, and Oliver's fate:

> "Bill had him on his back, and scudded like the wind. We stopped to take him between us; his head hung down, and he was cold. They were close upon our heels; every man for himself, and each from the gallows! We parted company, and left the youngster lying in a ditch. Alive or dead, that's all I know about him."   (234)

The following month the narrative immediately picked up the thread of Fagin's crazed reaction which had concluded the previous chapter: thus we follow his "wild and disordered" progress through Snow Hill, Saffron Hill, and Field Lane until he reaches the insalubrious interior of the Three Cripples

(234). Here we learn from his conversation with the landlord that he is in search of an individual by the name of Monks, but before he can find this mysterious new character, he encounters an apparently drink-befuddled Nancy, and attempts to goad her with an emotive summary of Crackit's news:

> "And the boy, too," said the Jew, straining to catch a glimpse of her face.
> "Poor leetle child! Left in a ditch, Nance; only think!"   (239)

Nancy's response is violent: "The child . . . is better where he is, than among us; and if no harm comes to Bill from it, I hope he lies dead in the ditch, and that his young bones may rot there" (239–40). All this talk of Oliver's desperate state, however, takes us no closer to his actual location. On the contrary, in the next chapter, we are back with Mr. Bumble, waiting for Mrs. Corney's return from the "wicious paupers" so that he can press his marital suit, and it is only at the close of this installment, after the beadle has indulged in a little extra-curricular discipline of Noah and Charlotte at the undertaker's, that the narrator promises to "set on foot a few inquiries after young Oliver Twist, and ascertain whether he be still lying in the ditch where Toby Crackit left him" (253).

For the novel's original readers, then, it is only in April 1838, three months after his last true appearance in the narrative, that Oliver Twist returns to center-stage. But perhaps to their—and our—surprise, he is *not yet* lying in the ditch that has been mentioned so many times in the preceding chapters: instead we hear Sikes's muttered imprecation "Wolves tear your cursed throats!" and quickly realize that the narrative has rolled back to a moment which has long since been left behind in the overall scheme of things. After a few fevered exchanges between Sikes and Crackit, Oliver is indeed "la[id] in a dry ditch," covered by "the cape in which he had been hurriedly muf-fled" (254, 255) and then abandoned by the two robbers, whose escape is not greatly hampered by the timorous attempts of Giles, Brittles, and the tinker to apprehend them. Only now does the period of Oliver's experience in the ditch truly commence: as the hours pass, and night turns to day, he lies "stretched, helpless and unconscious, on his bed of clay" until, awakened by his own "low cry of pain," he manages to stagger towards the nearest building, which of course is the "very house" Sikes and Crackit had been attempting to rob (258–59). He summons his last remaining strength to "knock faintly at the door" and promptly collapses on the doorstep (259).

The peculiar ordering of these chapters within Dickens's novel, and particu-larly the extended absence of the titular hero, have already attracted critical comment.[2] It is fair to say, however, that the author himself had foregrounded a discussion of these kinds of structural issues even before he had written the sections of the text I have recounted at such length. Explicit reference had been made at the beginning of chapter 17 to the narrative conventions allowed within, and even expected of, the genre:

> As sudden shiftings of the scene, and rapid changes of time and place, are not only sanctioned in books by long usage, but are by many considered as being, by such critics, chiefly estimated with relation to the dilemmas in which he leaves his characters at the end of every chapter: this brief introduction to the present one may perhaps be deemed unnecessary.   (169)

Even in the light of this authorial proclamation, chapters 22 through 28 contain features which demand further attention. Most marked, perhaps, is the definite kink in the temporal progression of the narrative which allows us to see Toby Crackit on his return to central London three days after the botched robbery, and then, some twenty pages later, to witness his behavior back in the Chertsey fields at the moment when Oliver was abandoned. Critics who have noticed this kink have usually explained it away as a sign of the novelist's youthful inexperience, or, alternatively, as a sign of his youthful ingenuity.[3] It is not my concern here to allot censure or praise: instead I am interested in analyzing the result of this unusual presentation of events. If we focus on the time-loop's effect on our perception of Oliver's plight, we notice that what we later learn is only a five- or six-hour period in the ditch[4] has already been experienced as a lengthy, drawn-out episode—as long as three months for those original readers of the serialization, and still a considerable stretch for those of us with the complete text. It is my argument that this phantasmal extension of the hero's time in the ditch serves an extremely important role in the overall design of the novel: it allows Oliver to die the death of one kind of baby, in order that he may begin the life of quite a different kind of baby. From this point in the book onwards, Oliver is placed on a clear route to a fortunate conclusion, but the combined events of this section of the story do not benefit the boy alone. Just as importantly, Oliver's mother is rescued from an ambiguous, and potentially dangerous, position on a scale of female morality, the nadir of which is represented in this novel by the prostitute Nancy's existence "at the bottom of the weed-choked well" (37). After the remedial actions set in train in chapters 22 to 28, Agnes is able to move up to a much loftier level—if not to the sphere of the angels and Rose Maylie, then at least to where she may "hover round the solemn nook" of an old country church (480).

To make this argument, I shall be relying in the first place on a dramatic work which has frequently been cited as an important literary influence both on this specific novel and Dickens's entire oeuvre—Shakespeare's *Macbeth*. Critics have carefully documented the numerous echoes from *Othello*, *King Lear*, and *The Merchant of Venice* which sound through the pages of *Oliver Twist*, but the looming presence of the Scottish tragedy has long attracted special note in the novel's reception history.[5] As Philip Collins has argued, when the great actor William Macready gasped out "Two Macbeths!" in laudatory appreciation of Dickens's superlative *Sikes and Nancy* reading, he may well have been commenting more on the parallel stresses of performing these two pieces, than on overt similarities between the two murderers (*Dickens and Crime*, 158). Nevertheless, even if Bill makes a poor thane, few would deny that the narrative is thick with allusions which mount up with inevitable urgency around and after Nancy's bludgeoning. But here I wish to direct our attention to significantly different places in both play and novel. My text comes from the witches' famous cauldron chant, and perhaps constitutes its most disturbing phrase: "Finger of birth-strangled babe/Ditch-delivered by a drab" (IV i 30–31). [6] Unsanctified by Christian baptism, in common with the "Liver of blaspheming Jew," the "Nose of Turk, and Tartar's lips" (IV i 26, 29), the dead baby's finger is just one more of the revolting ingredients in the weird sisters'—and *Macbeth*'s —horrific stew.[7] Within *Oliver Twist*, I argue, these particular lines carry a far-reaching resonance.

Twists upon the bare linguistic elements of Shakespeare's lines appear in a variety of locations and guises in Dickens's narrative—the word "ditch," as my opening summary indirectly demonstrated, recurs throughout the novel's central chapters, and I shall consider the appearance of the other key words "strangled" and "drab" in due course. First of all, and perhaps most importantly, I want to establish how it is made possible that an approximately twelve-year-old boy can take on the status of a baby at this stage of the novel.[8] As I have already described, as soon as Oliver drifts out of consciousness, we are transported not only to the general location of his birth, the workhouse, but eventually to the actual room in which he was born (the lying-in room, which conveniently doubles as the laying-out room). Then, by virtue of Old Sally's need to confess her heinous crime of robbing a young woman on her deathbed, we are taken back to the precise moment of Oliver's birth:

> "Now listen to me," said the dying woman aloud, as if making a great effort to revive one latent spark of energy. "In this very room—in this very bed—I once nursed a pretty young creetur', that was brought into the house with her feet cut and bruised with walking, and all soiled with dust and blood. She gave birth to a boy, and died." (227)

Thus the memory of Oliver as a newborn baby, saved at that time from death in the fields or the streets by the intervention of official "care," is superimposed upon our image of the current incarnation of Oliver, who is lying comatose on his bed of clay.

If the newborn babe and the ditch are thus securely present in this section of the novel, then perhaps the witches of Shakespeare's imagination are not as far away as we might desire either: chapter 24 presents us not with one hideous old woman, but three. As Old Sally draws her last troubled breaths, Martha and Anny, variously described as "hags" or "old crones," wait out the time before they will commence their "dreadful duties" upon the corpse by adopting the witches' archetypal position:

> ... the two old women rose from the bed, and crouching over the fire, held out their withered hands to catch the heat. The flame threw a ghastly light on their shrivelled faces, and made their ugliness appear terrible ...   (225)

Just as one day in *Great Expectations* Pip will see Jaggers's housekeeper's face "as if it were all disturbed by fiery air," and be unable to banish from his mind "the faces [he] had seen rise out of the Witches' caldron" "a night or two before" at "*Macbeth* at the theatre" (235), so does the memory of Shakespeare's "secret, black, and midnight hags" haunt the presentation of these "withered old female paupers" of the workhouse (222).

To return to the newborn babe: as we remember from the very first chapter, far from being strangled at birth, Oliver has cause to thank the casual neglect of his unpropitious birthplace for the fact that he managed "to take upon himself the office of respiration" at all: had he "been surrounded by careful grandmothers, anxious aunts, experienced nurses, and doctors of profound wisdom," we are informed, "he would most inevitably and indubitably have been killed in no time" (45). But if Oliver escapes suffocation at birth, threats to his power to breathe are levied with startling frequency throughout his childhood, as J. Hillis Miller, Robert Patten, and John O. Jordan have pointed out. While his continued breathing is endangered by the possibility of being "overlooked in turning up a bedstead" at the baby farm (49) or menaced by Fagin's and Sikes' ominous designs upon his "windpipe" (142, 159), references to strangulation in the form of death by hanging are easily the most marked. "That boy will be hung ... I know that boy will be hung" (58) intones the gentleman in the white waistcoat, initiating a constant stream of comments which are so many turns of the hangman's noose, and heralding repeated gesticulations with handkerchiefs and neckerchiefs and cravats. True hanging—both accidental, and state-ordered—has of course a crucial presence within this novel, but the rope does not actually touch Oliver's neck. Nevertheless, the hero, just as much as the lowlife villain, is so completely encircled by the threat of strangulation that we are forced to wonder in what ways the baby who was *not* killed at birth might be connected to crime.

As I shall shortly be examining at greater length, the infant Oliver's offense is that he appears to prove someone's unwed love a whore. Consequently it is significant that in the section of the novel under scrutiny, we should be privy to the prostitute's reaction to the news of Oliver's apparent fate—remember Nancy's impassioned response: "I hope he lies dead in the ditch, and that his young bones may rot there'' (239–40). In the bitter exchanges which immediately follow, Shakespeare's coarse noun appears for the first time in the novel, spat out in exasperation from Fagin's lips: "Listen to me, you drab'' (240). As we shall see, the word will be spoken on two further significant occasions, once in oblique reference to Oliver's mother and once again about Nancy.

All of the key phrases of Shakespeare's lines, and more importantly, some of the concepts invoked by them, are thus scattered around the novel, cropping up with particular density during the period of Oliver's phantasmal ditch-lying. My aim in pointing this out, however, has been strategic rather than terminal: I do not wish merely to prove that the literary influence of *Macbeth* upon *Oliver Twist* extends beyond Dickens's borrowings from the realm of guilt and gore to enhance Nancy's murder. Instead I am much more interested in the idea that these lines from the play constitute a particularly memorable and historically long-lived evocation of a distressing social problem. Or to put it another way: the disposed body of the unwanted baby, whether prostitute's or not, is frequently imagined, in a range of discourses, and at different historical moments, through this icon. This is not to imply, I should stress, that what we are dealing with here is solely a literary or representational construction: no doubt, in an age before organized garbage collection, the abandoned dead baby, already reduced to the category of waste, would often be consigned to the place where all the rest of the rubbish went—which is to say, the ditch, or its urban cousin, the gutter, or, most disturbingly, their more specialized variant, the privy. Certainly the unwanted dead (or nearly dead) baby could also end up in any number of other locations—hidden in the servant's box, as was the case in the inquest for which Dickens was himself a juryman ("Some Recollections of Mortality"), or discarded on a bleak hillside, or thrown on a roof—but whether or not it comes about because of actual fact, or the power of a particular representation, or a combination of these two factors, the idea of the dead baby in the ditch forms one of the most pervasive images of abandonment and infanticide in Britain up and into the nineteenth century.

A notable example of this occurs in the history of London's Foundling Hospital, which opened in 1741. Indeed, the very etiology of Thomas Coram's desire to found such an institution is ascribed by a contemporary commentator to the spectacle of the baby in the ditch. As Richard Brocklesby recounts, back in the 1720s, Coram's routine of walking from his home in Rotherhithe to the City on dark winter mornings, and returning late at night "afforded him frequent Occasions of seeing young Children exposed, sometimes alive, sometimes dead and dying" (12, 13), at the side of the roads, and convinced him that he must do something about this pressing problem. When Hogarth was later asked to design an illustrative "head piece" for a document soliciting subscriptions for the hospital, he featured the emotive image not once but

twice [see fig. 1]. While Coram forms the focal point of the engraving, standing between a weeping mother who has just been stopped from killing her
baby, and a kindly beadle who now wraps the infant in the folds of his cloak,
two other babies in the picture have not been so fortunate: one, in the extreme
right background, is suspiciously swaddled and being dumped by a woman
behind a gate, and the other, in the right foreground, lies naked and abandoned
in a hollow besides a stream.[9] (The entire left-hand side of the picture, it
should be noted, is given over to depictions of docile and obedient children
in uniform, who are carrying tools emblematic of the various useful trades
they are learning at the Foundling Hospital.) This engraving was certainly
not the only visual image connected to the institution which associated the
baby in the ditch with the hospital's mission: Coram's Art Gallery, which
rapidly grew in size thanks to the influence of patrons like Hogarth, soon
contained a rich selection of works carrying a similar message: paintings
inspired by the Bible stories of Hagar and Ishmael, the baby Moses and the
Massacre of the Innocents simultaneously underscored the scriptural prece-
dents of the necessity of child-rescue and reinforced the cultural centrality of
this particular image of the abandoned babe.

In addition to subscription documents and high-art canvases, numerous
other cultural forms kept the image in general currency. Scandal sheets like
the mid-seventeenth century pamphlet *Natures Cruell Step-Dames* include
any number of terse accounts of women who throw their bastard children
into ditches (Dolan 162), while the popular ballad provides a wealth of examples: given that seduced and forsaken maidens feature so frequently in this
genre, it is not surprising to find metrical descriptions of numerous carelessly
or callously disposed-of infants. Variants of "The Cruel Mother," which
originated in the seventeenth century, often focus first on the woman in labor
in the fields ("She leaned her back against the stile/There she had two pretty
babes born") before proceeding to the swift dispatch of the infants, and the
mother's subsequent remorse. "The Babes in the Wood," on the other hand,
which came to be just as familiar from nursery-tales and pantomime as from
song versions, are the victims of a cruel uncle; the story, first registered for
publication as a street ballad in 1595, was based on an actual incident in
Norfolk. Here the uncle simply leaves the infants to die of exposure, as an
early-Victorian re-telling explains:

> No burial these two pretty babes
> Of any man received
> Till Robin Redbreast painfully
> Did cover them with leaves.

The high-tragical image of the baby in the ditch, then, was so well-estab-
lished by the mid-nineteenth century that Dickens himself could exploit its

hyperbolic potential for comic effect. When Mr. Bounderby, the self-aggrandizing fantasist of *Hard Times,* wishes to construct for himself the worst possible beginning in life (all the better, of course, to show off the astounding achievements of his self-made manhood), he consigns both his child and infant selves to what should now be a very familiar location:

> "I hadn't a shoe to my foot. As to a stocking, I didn't know such a thing by name. I passed the day in a ditch, and the night in a pigsty. That's the way I spent my tenth birthday. Not that a ditch was new to me, for I was born in a ditch."
> ... Mrs. Gradgrind hoped it was a dry ditch?
> "No! As wet as a sop. A foot of water in it," said Mr. Bounderby.   (59)

This is not a man to leave a rich theme alone: when he next refers to his imaginary sufferings, he adds dramatic tension by creating a stark contrast between the miserably repellent but entirely innocent being that was the infant Bounderby, and the wicked woman of the piece, his mother:

> "Very well," said Bounderby. "I was born in a ditch, and my mother ran away from me. Do I excuse her for it? No. Have I ever excused her for it? Not I. What do I call her for it? I call her probably the very worst woman that ever lived in the world, except my drunken grandmother."   (74)

Like Bounderby, I now turn from cultural representations of the dead or neglected baby to the child's mother herself. In so doing, I should make it clear that I wish to separate our knowledge of Oliver's *actual* mother, Agnes, from the phantasmal image of the mother which is raised by the text when Oliver is left for dead in the fields: just as Oliver is not really a new-born babe at this stage of the novel, neither is the woman who died in chapter 1 in any way identical to the murdering drab of Shakespeare's imagination. I shall examine the peculiarities of Agnes's situation at a later stage, but first wish to focus on the images of motherhood which accompanied the picture of the abandoned infant in popular consciousness in this period of British history.

When abandonment crosses the line and appears to resemble infanticide, the crucial question of the character, and motives, of the woman under suspicion becomes highly charged. This issue has always been seen as central to any kind of examination of infanticide, be it juridical, medical, journalistic, artistic or otherwise. The recent waves of historical and literary analyses of the prevalence of this crime, and its representation in the eighteenth and nineteenth centuries, have been no less attentive to the ways in which maternal responsibility has been understood and depicted. Christine Krueger's article, "Literary Defenses and Medical Prosecutions: Representing Infanticide in

Nineteenth-Century Britain,'' like many of its predecessors, invokes what has come to stand as the unholy trinity of infanticide texts—William Wordsworth's poem "The Thorn," which appeared in *Lyrical Ballads* in 1798, and two historical novels, Sir Walter Scott's *Heart of Mid-lothian* and George Eliot's *Adam Bede*, which were published in 1818 and 1859 respectively.

For Krueger, these works and many other lesser-known literary representations of this crime deliberately locate baby-killing in a pastoral setting in order, as she says "to render mothers as rural innocents inhabiting a sacrosanct natural space," and thus, by extension, "to naturalize infanticide" and place "women who killed their infants . . . outside the state's jurisdiction." Certainly women accused of infanticide in the nineteenth century seem often to have been objects of sympathy rather than condemnation: juries were consistently unwilling to find women guilty of the crime, often in the face of powerful evidence, and preferred instead to convict on the much lesser charge of "concealment of pregnancy" which levied only short custodial sentences. It can be argued then, that the literary tradition of the pastoral wronged maid, as pitiful herself as the child she desperately murders, carried considerable sway in the shaping of public opinion towards this particular problem: as Krueger asserts, those campaigners who were in favor of more hard-headed adjudication could not rely on professional and scientific reasoning to make their case, but were forced to come up with "sensational and sentimental narratives" of their own making to counter the dominant narrative. Thus figures like Thomas Wakley, elected in 1839 by West Middlesex as the nation's first medical doctor to carry the office of coroner, and his successor Dr. Edwin Lankester, sought to replace the vision of the distraught and isolated country girl with a picture of widespread urban vice, in which careless city slatterns regularly disposed of their innocent babes in any convenient nook or cranny of the immoral metropolis.

I cite Krueger's analysis of these competing representations of the midnineteenth century to give some sense of the discursive field in which *Oliver Twist*'s visions of the abandoned child must be located. The Shakespearean archetype which, I have been arguing, determines our perspective of Oliver's plight in the central portion of the novel, refuses to sit neatly with either the Romantic pastoral tradition or the newly-forming picture of urban vice. By virtue of *Macbeth*'s earlier provenance—both with respect to its early seventeenth-century date of composition, and its putatively eleventh-century Scottish setting—the crime of infanticide is, on the one hand, definitely not allied to a vision of urban corruption. On the other, while clearly set in the countryside, the crime is nevertheless wholly unredeemed by the Romantic evocations of natural scenery which will provide an explanatory and exculpatory context for the desperate mothers of later literary periods.

Even more important, of course, is the fact that this mother is by no means a frantic country maiden robbed of her innocence and driven to an unimaginably horrible and personally devastating deed—all that we know about her is that she is a "drab," a prostitute who seems to have dealt with the arrival of an unwanted infant encumbrance in a business-like manner. As such, she occupies a significantly different position in a moral universe than either those wronged maids of literary and popular imagination, or the city's loose-living (but not professional) sluts of the counter-narratives. Moreover, she is considerably removed from the juridical realm as well: documentary evidence from nineteenth-century infanticide trials reveals that the perpetrators of the crime (at least those brought before the courts) appeared very rarely to have been prostitutes—rather the overwhelming majority of the accused were employed in domestic service. If Oliver lies in that ditch under the sign of the Shakespearean "birth-strangled babe," then, the imaginary woman who has brought him to this pass is the most unpalatable, because the most callous, incarnation of the murdering mother that it is possible to invoke, and an incarnation that has little, if any, presence in records, be they literary, historical or otherwise.

Indeed, it was often claimed in the eighteenth and nineteenth centuries that the very concept of the prostitute's murdered child was untenable, either for moral or physiological reasons. For Mandeville in 1714, the infanticidal mother is driven to the deed by an acute sense of her sin, whereas "common whores, whom all the world knows to be such, hardly ever destroy their children, nay even those who assist in robberies or murders seldom are guilty of this crime; not because they are less cruel or more virtuous, but because they have lost their modesty to a greater degree, and the fear of shame makes hardly any impression upon them" (108–09). More common, perhaps, was the popular conception that prostitutes simply didn't get pregnant, a belief held either because of the spurious, but long-lived, medical reasoning that promiscuous sexual intercourse with numerous men "produced in the female an imperfect elaboration of secretion necessary for impregnation," or, more plausibly, because of sterility caused by venereal disease (Walkowitz 19). To be the prostitute's murdered child, then, in the face of these resolute denials of the possibility of such a category, is to occupy the very lowest and most despised position of all—is to be the victim of the most unmaternal and least redeemable female figure imaginable.

While Oliver exists in our readerly consciousnesses as an inert, ditch-lying figure, then, he is placed at the center of the very worst-case scenario of infanticide. Fortunately for Oliver, for his mother's reputation, and for the ultimate resolution of the narrative, Dickens grants his protagonist the ability to translate himself to the center of the best-case scenario of infant abandonment. With painful, staggering movements, Oliver drags himself towards the detached house on the horizon, "tottered across the lawn; climbed the steps; knocked faintly at the door; and, his whole strength failing him, sunk down against one of the pillars of the little portico'' (258). With these actions, the boy places himself in the very location that the distressed mother unable to keep her child would herself choose for her offspring. For a short period, Oliver must make a superhuman assumption of two roles—both of himself as needy babe, and of his caring yet desperate mother[10]—before he can revert to the single state of wordless infant: by the time Brittles answers that faint knock and opens the door, the assembled group of household servants behold ''no more formidable object than poor little Oliver Twist, speechless and exhausted, who raised his heavy eyes, and mutely solicited their compassion'' (261). Oliver is now in the position of the baby who is meant to be found; indeed, who is deliberately placed on the doorstep of a self-evidently well-to-do house which offers the best possible prospects for a candidate for adoption. (Neither Oliver nor the reader knows as yet that this particular house just happens to be an excellent advertisement for adoption, being both the home of a lady who has already proved herself more than willing and able to take on the role of adoptive mother, and of a blood-relation of Oliver's who has already modeled the role of the adopted child to perfection.) Simply by moving himself from the desolate ditch to the doorstep of a substantial dwelling, Oliver has exchanged a lamentable archetypal position for a location no less archetypal, but entirely superior in its cultural connotations.

If ditches and dead babies proliferate in a wide variety of texts of the seventeenth, eighteenth, and nineteenth centuries, then so do doorsteps and fortunate foundlings, with the houses of the nobility and the squirearchy particularly prone, both in literature and actual fact, to find bundles of joy laid at their portals.[11] In 1810 it was the turn of the Earl of Darlington to discover ''a fine beautiful male infant left at his door. The dress of the child was elegant, and in the basket was a letter strongly recommending the care of the infant to his lordship's daughters'' (Hopkirk 89). (In this particular case, the mother's ploy was unsuccessful: the chronicle proceeds to report that ''it was, however, deemed prudent to send the little foundling to the parish, lest an encouragement might be given to similar unwelcome presents.'') Despite this local failure, perhaps only one other position could be deemed more propitious than the doorstep for the infant's future well-being: as readers of *Tom Jones* will remember, the placement of the baby hero within the sheets of Squire Allworthy's bed results in his subsequent embrace within the family. In *Oliver Twist* circumstances make it impossible for Oliver to get himself any closer to eventual security than the doorstep, but Dickens makes quite sure that his hero, as at so many other points in this novel, is soon carried upstairs and tucked into the safest spot of all.

Transformed from the drab's strangled baby to a child on the brink of happy adoption, Oliver is manifestly in a far better position at the close of chapter 28 than at its midpoint—or indeed, at any previous juncture in his past history. Given, though, that I have claimed that the amelioration of his mother Agnes's reputation is also a necessary element of the novel's ultimate resolution, how does Dickens achieve this end? While one could certainly make the case that the direct metamorphosis of Oliver which I have been describing is bound to play an indirect role in repairing his mother's image, I maintain that the novel takes an additional, and a more overt, move to achieve the desired goal of separating Agnes from the imputation of prostitution. To make this argument, I need first to review the impressions of Agnes that we receive in the first half of the book.

Certainly we never really think Agnes a whore, common or otherwise: although we hear her speak only one sentence, and see her only in the act of imprinting "her cold white lips passionately on [her baby's] forehead" (46) before she dies, these moments are sufficient to establish her gentility from the start. And yet her presence within the workhouse, and more importantly, the emergence of a baby from a body whose left hand wears no wedding-ring, make it abundantly clear that the young woman's refined sensibility is at odds with her current position: we are, as the surgeon states and Robert Tracy has discussed, evidently witnesses to a version of "the old story," the story of a woman's fall, of sex outside the sacrament of marriage. Just how deeply-dyed this inherently sinful story might be, though, is not immediately clear, although we may surmise, both from our knowledge of the mother and of her preternaturally innocent son, that it will turn out to be as pale and faint as Agnes herself is in chapter 1. The ambiguous nature of Agnes's narrative, however, leaves the door wide open for those who feel inclined to disseminate their own colorful versions. Noah Claypole is the most insinuating and offensive tale-teller in the early portion of the novel:

> " . . . *Your* mother, too! She was a nice 'un, she was. Oh, Lor! . . . Yer know, Work'us, it can't be helped now; and of course yer couldn't help it then; and I'm very sorry for it; and I'm sure we all are, and pity yer very much. But yer must know, Work'us, yer mother was a regular right-down bad 'un."
> "What did you say?" inquired Oliver, looking up very quickly.
> "A regular right-down bad 'un, Work'us," replied Noah coolly. "And it's a great deal better, Work'us, that she died when she did, or else she'd have been hard labouring in Bridewell, or transported, or hung; which is more likely than either, isn't it?" (87–88)

This series of insults to his dead mother's reputation is the occasion for Oliver's violent attack on Noah and his subsequent flight, but neither the strength of his blows nor his departure from the scene of calumny can play any concrete role in walling up the slanderous tide. On the contrary, the immediate result of Oliver's removal to London is his immersion in a world teeming with characters destined for the criminal fates Noah hypothesized.

Even worse, Oliver is not only consorting with those already, or soon to be, familiar with hard labor, transportation or hanging, but is actually brought into direct relation with real prostitutes, those creatures whose professional connection to sexual sin stands in some uneasy relation to his mother's unexplained fall.

It is not hard to fathom Dickens's ostensible motive for dropping his protagonist into this moral and criminal cess-pit—after all, the more vile and corrupting the company and the environment, the more impressive and touching is Oliver's utter imperviousness to taint—but this narrative strategy carries a certain risk. Even though we feel convinced of Oliver's own personal innocence, the rapidity of his descent into such a society, followed by the sheer difficulty he faces trying to climb out of it, has a worrying tendency to suggest that he may bear some external—and possibly mother-related—connection, if not to this milieu exactly, then to its aura of sin. Despite the best efforts of Mr. Brownlow to secure Oliver within an upstanding, well-to-do home—a home which in its possession of a portrait of a female version of Oliver seems to offer the best chance yet of providing Agnes with a fuller narrative—despite these advantages, Oliver is unable to extricate himself from a morally dangerous world until, as I have been arguing, he reaches rock-bottom and exchanges the ditch for the doorstep in Chertsey. After this point, as critics and readers have always noticed, Oliver's position in the narrative undergoes a radical change. Safely tucked into the boring bosom of middle-class respectability, Oliver is insulated from danger and drama; now separated from the boy by a study window, or by a Brownlow-chaperoned visit in the condemned cell, vice can only look, but not touch.

Oliver's rebirth as a different kind of baby necessarily implies, as I have already claimed, a profoundly different kind of mother, but Dickens is not content to trust the regeneration of Agnes's reputation to this effect alone. An important plot-development occurs when Oliver is lying in the ditch: Monks makes his very first appearance in the novel. The late and unheralded introduction of this character, I argue, supplements Oliver's remedial actions by providing the novel with a new representative of middle-class wrongdoing: thus is the pallid, and we highly suspect, "more sinned against than sinning" figure of Agnes replaced by an incarnation of dynamic and purposeful malevolence. Monks, I maintain, not only displays a flamboyant wickedness which makes Agnes's crime pale into insignificance, but quite literally disposes of the traces of prostitute-identity which linger around the unexplained corners of her story.

Monks performs this exorcism by moving the action of the novel to a location which bears a much more famous relation to nineteenth-century English prostitution than the ditch. In the novels of Dickens and other writers, in paintings and poems, just as much as in the newspaper reports of the day, the river, and more specifically the River Thames, is always the place of the prostitute's suicide, or at the least, her suicidal thoughts. As the Uncommercial Traveller hears on the way to visit "Wapping Workhouse," female sexual sinners are "always a headerin' down" to the river to drown both in his fiction and in his journalism. Dickens repeatedly presents us with images of the desperate harlot either on the brink of, or immersed within, the swirling waters which represent her muddied moral turbulence and will secure her release from a hated world. In *Oliver Twist,* too, the prostitute announces her conviction that the river will witness her final moments. Standing on the steps of London Bridge, the meeting place she herself has appointed, Nancy rejects Mr. Brownlow's optimistic visions of a new life in a foreign country, and insists that Rose Maylie contemplate the only end she can imagine for herself:

> "Look before you, lady. Look at that dark water. How many times do you read of such as I who spring into the tide, and leave no living thing to care for or bewail them. It may be years hence, or it may be only months, but I shall come to that at last." (415)

Although Nancy does not in fact "come to that at last," meeting instead a far more brutal death of blows in a squalid room, I would argue that the novel still contains a scene of the prostitute's drowning. Eight chapters before Nancy's impassioned declaration on the bridge, Monks arranges a rendezvous at night with Mr. and Mrs. Bumble in a disused manufactory suspended over a dark stream—if not the Thames, then a river as vile and ominous as Dickens's descriptive powers can make it. After Monks has seized what he believes to be the last remaining tokens of Oliver's mother's identity, he opens a trap-door, and invites his visitors to look down: "[t]he turbid water, swollen by the heavy rain, was rushing rapidly on below; and all other sounds were lost in the noise of its splashing and eddying against the green and slimy piles" (342). Into this swirl of foul waters, Monks casts the little gold locket and the plain gold wedding-ring:

> [he] drew the little packet from his breast, where he had hurriedly thrust it; and tying it to a leaden weight, . . . dropped it into the stream. It fell straight, and true as a die; clove the water with a scarcely audible splash; and was gone.
> (342)

The woman that Monks thus drowns in this symbolic act is certainly not the Agnes we glimpsed in the first chapter, nor the mother of the boy whose adventures we have followed up to this point: instead she is a lurid creation of Monks's own hysterical imagination. So much is clear to us from the prelude to this scene, in which Monks plies Mr. Bumble with gin and water, and then pumps him for information. Just as old Sally's deathbed confession

took us back to the place and time of Oliver's birth, so now does Monks lead
the beadle step by step towards the same event:

> "Carry your memory back—let me see—twelve years, last winter."
> "It's a long time," said Mr. Bumble. "Very good. I've done it."
> "The scene, the workhouse."
> "Good!"
> "And the time, night."
> "Yes."
> "And the place, the crazy hole, wherever it was, in which miserable drabs
> brought forth the life and health so often denied to themselves—gave birth to
> puling children for the parish to rear; and hid their shame, rot 'em, in the
> grave!"   (331)

The unhinged intemperance of Monks's last utterance is so marked that the
beadle, unsurprisingly, has difficulty interpreting his meaning: " 'The lying-
in room, I suppose?' said Mr. Bumble, not quite following the stranger's
excited description" (332). Monks then moves on to question Bumble about
the whereabouts of "the hag that nursed [Oliver's] mother," but we should
perhaps pause to consider that speech more closely. Not only does it feature
the second of the novel's three instances of the word "drab"—this time, in
connection with Agnes, not Nancy—but still more disturbing is Monks's
creation of the bizarrely anatomical expression "crazy hole" to indicate the
lying-in room. One might argue that the turbulent opening below the trap-
door appears later to literalize Monks's fearful vision of that gaping space,
but even at this point in the narrative we sense that his words reveal some
kind of fevered and woman-loathing slippage between bodies and
places—that they display a confused and maniacal disgust centered on the
physical site of birth itself. What is the effect of this outright revelation
of the diseased misogyny of Monks's mind? When Noah Claypole makes
insinuating remarks about Oliver's mother, the casual nastiness of his intent
allows the innuendoes to linger, but Monks's insane persecution of this woman's reputation is quite another matter: the man who numbers Agnes amongst
the "miserable drabs" is in the grip of delusions with which no-one would
care to identify. Dropping her last effects into the river, Monks does indeed
do away with Agnes-the-drab for once and for all, but not in the way that
he imagines.

The deaths of Oliver as prostitute's child and Agnes as prostitute clear the
way for Oliver's rebirth and the resolution of his mother's story: now the
sisterhood of Agnes and Rose can be revealed, and Agnes's sin, if not as
entirely unfounded in fact as Rose's "stain," can be accommodated within
the respectable family and the church. For the real prostitute in this book,
however, matters do not reach such a happy conclusion. Of all the novels'

characters, Nancy travels the longest personal journey from vice to morality, and indeed goes the furthest, at the greatest risk, to promote the cause of goodness in the face of evil—as Monks mutters in the final showdown, "I began well; and, but for babbling drabs, I would have finished as I began!"(459). Yet despite Nancy's valiant deeds and moral regeneration, she is not saved, for *Oliver Twist*'s resolution is predicated on the removal of all signs of the prostitute. The unparalleled brutality of Nancy's murder is a clear indication of the absolute necessity of this: whereas the faint specter of Agnes's prostitute-identity can be exorcised through symbolic acts, the drab's flesh-and-blood existence is expunged, quite literally, on the level of flesh and blood.

Fig. 1. William Hogarth's *The Foundlings*, subscription document for Coram's Foundling Hospital

NOTES

1. Paroissien notes that "Dickens wrote this installment during January 1838 when unusually cold temperatures added to the misery of the homeless" (178).
2. See for example, Burton M. Wheeler, "The Text and Plan of *Oliver Twist.*"
3. See for example, Lance Schachterle, "*Oliver Twist* and Its Serial Predecessors."
4. According to internal evidence, the band of robbers hear the church-bell strike two when they are still about a quarter of a mile from the house (211). Oliver is then left in the ditch about thirty to forty minutes later, and drags himself out of it at around daybreak, which would probably fall between half-past seven and half-past eight in this wintry season (257).
5. Shifra Hochberg provides a useful summary of criticism on Dickens's debt to Shakespeare in his essay "The Influence of *King Lear* on *Bleak House.*" For a specific study of *Oliver Twist*'s Shakespearean borrowings, see for example, Laurence Senelick, "Traces of *Othello* in *Oliver Twist.*"
6. I have been unable to ascertain whether Dickens would have heard these lines in performances of the play in this era. He would, however, have been familiar with the passage from his private reading of *Macbeth.*
7. This is not to deny that it fits into a complex—and much studied—pattern of references to newborn (and other) babes throughout the play. See for example, Paul A. Jorgensen, *Our Naked Frailties: Sensational Art and Meaning in Macbeth.*
8. Inconsistencies within the novel make it impossible to define Oliver's exact age at many stages in the narrative.
9. Krueger reads this engraving rather differently, identifying the baby by the stream as the infant who has just escaped the maternal dagger. Whichever version one prefers, my general point still stands: the baby is depicted as having been abandoned in a ditch.
10. Molly Farren Cass's toddler, the soon-to-be Eppie, effectively makes the same move in *Silas Marner.*
11. The placement of an infant on a given individual's doorstep was frequently interpreted as an indication of paternity. Parish registers sometimes used the expression "laid at the door of Mr. X" indiscriminately, leaving it unclear whether a literal or metaphorical sense should be understood (Hopkirk 89).

WORKS CITED

Brocklesby, Richard. *Private Virtue and publick spirit display'd in a Succinct Essay on the Character of Capt. Thomas Coram.* London, 1751.

Collins, Philip, ed. *Dickens: The Critical Heritage.* New York: Barnes and Noble, 1971.

————. *Dickens and Crime*. London: Macmillan, 1962.

Dickens, Charles. *Great Expectations*. Ed. Angus Calder. Harmondsworth: Penguin, 1985.

————. *Hard Times*. Ed. David Craig. Harmondsworth: Penguin, 1969.

————. *Oliver Twist*. Ed. Peter Fairclough. Harmondsworth: Penguin, 1985.

————. "Some Recollections of Mortality." *All the Year Round* 16 May, 1863.

————. "Wapping Workhouse." *All the Year Round* 3 February, 1860.

Dolan, Frances. E. *Dangerous Familiars: Representations of Domestic Crime in England, 1550–1700*. Ithaca: Cornell UP, 1994.

Eliot, George. *Silas Marner*. Ed. Q. D. Leavis. Harmondsworth, Penguin, 1967.

Fielding, Henry. *Tom Jones*. Ed. R. P. C. Mutter. Harmondsworth, Penguin, 1982.

Hochberg, Shifra. "The Influence of *King Lear* on *Bleak House*." *The Dickensian* 87 (1991): 45–49.

Hopkirk, Mary. *Nobody Wanted Sam: The Story of the Unwelcomed Child, 1530–1948*. London: John Murray, 1949.

Jordan, John O. "The Purloined Handkerchief." *Dickens Studies Annual* 18 (1989): 1–17.

Jorgensen, Paul A. *Our Naked Frailties: Sensational Art and Meaning in Macbeth*. Berkeley: U of California P, 1971.

Krueger, Christine. "Literary Defenses and Medical Prosecutions: Representing Infanticide in Nineteenth-Century Britain." *Victorian Studies* 40 (Winter 1997): 271–94.

Mandeville, Bernard. *The Fable of the Bees*. Ed. Phillip Horton. Harmondsworth: Penguin, 1970.

Miller, J. Hillis. *Charles Dickens: The World of His Novels*. Bloomington, Indiana: Indiana UP, 1969.

Paroissien, David. *Oliver Twist: An Annotated Bibliography*. New York: Garland, 1986.

Patten, Robert. "Capitalism and Compassion in *Oliver Twist*." *Studies in the Novel* 1 (1969): 207–21.

Schachterle, Lance. "*Oliver Twist* and Its Serial Predecessors." *Dickens Studies Annual* 3 (1980): 1–13.

Senelick, Laurence. "Traces of *Othello* in *Oliver Twist*." *The Dickensian* 70 (1974): 97–102.

Shakespeare, William. *Macbeth*. Ed. G. K. Hunter. Harmondsworth: Penguin, 1967.

Tracy, Robert. " 'The Old Story' and Inside Stories: Modish Fiction and Fictional Modes in *Oliver Twist*." *Dickens Studies Annual* 17 (1988): 1–34.

Walkowitz, Judith. *Prostitution and Victorian Society*. Cambridge: Cambridge UP, 1980.

Wheeler, Burton M. "The Text and Plan of *Oliver Twist*." *Dickens Studies Annual* 12 (1983): 41–46.

The Long and the Short of Oliver and Alice: The Changing Size of the Victorian Child

Goldie Morgentaler

This essay seeks to relate the changing sizes of Lewis Carroll's Alice in Alice in Wonderland *and the small stature of Oliver in Charles Dickens's* Oliver Twist *to biological theories of development and growth, especially as these pertain to chidren. The essay explores how the Victorians understood size and how that understanding was reflected in their fictional presentation of children. For instance, was the small stature of the child perceived as a sign of its weakness and vulnerability, thereby defining childhood as a state distinct from and alternative to adulthood, or were children regarded as adults in miniature, as essentially mature in everything except size? By relating the two historically significant theories of growth—preformation and epigenesis—to* Alice in Wonderland *and* Oiver Twist, *the essay explores the literary ramifications of size and suggests that while these two child-centered novels appear to reflect diametrically opposite theories of growth, they are in fact not as contradictory as they may at first appear.*

It is a truism that children are always growing, and are therefore always in the process of changing size. Not surprisingly, this fact is reflected in children's literature which has become the repository for stories about dwarfs and giants, and which has made a classic out of the first two voyages of *Gulliver's Travels*—a satire which Swift intended for adults—because Gulliver's first

Dickens Studies Annual, Volume 29, Copyright © 2000 by AMS Press, Inc. All rights reserved.

journey is to the kingdom of the tiny Lilliputians, and his second to the land of the giant Brobdingnagians. A related truism states that size is relative, that we are really dependent on others for our sense of our own height—which is, after all, one of the ironies illustrated by *Gulliver's Travels*, since Gulliver himself never changes size; he is a giant or a midget only in relation to the height of those around him.

What I want to explore here is how *Oliver Twist* and *Alice's Adventures in Wonderland*—the two novels that did the most to revolutionize the presentation of childhood in English literature—reflected the Victorian understanding of size and its relationship to human development.[1] How, for instance, did the Victorians regard the small stature of children? Was lack of height considered an integral part of childhood, a token, not merely of the weakness and vulnerability of children, but of a time of life distinct from and alternative to adulthood? Or did the Victorians regard children as simply adults in miniature, as essentially mature in everything except their size, as Philippe Ariès has suggested was the case with earlier eras?[2] In other words: what is the cultural and literary significance of size in the nineteenth century, and how does it relate to childhood? Since the subject is vast, I will limit myself to one particular approach. I intend to answer this question in biological terms—that is, by relating size to theories of heredity and growth that were current both before and during the nineteenth century.

The immensity of the infinitesimal first became evident in the mid-seventeenth century when Antony von Leeuwenhoek perfected the microscope and so made possible Blake's poetic injunction "to see a world in a grain of sand," although in Leeuwenhoek's case it was a drop of water. What Leeuwenhoek saw when he put his drop of water under the lens of his microscope was an entire world of what he called "animulculi," which had hitherto been invisible. Ironically, the brave new world that Leeuwenhoek discovered under his microscope seemed to corroborate many of the assumptions of what we would today call popular belief, since the microscope confirmed the fact that the invisible existed, that there were beings so tiny that the unaided eye could not see them, that—to take an example from theology—it was theoretically possible for multitudes of angels to balance on the head of a pin.

Among the other up-to-then invisible things which Leeuwenhoek noted under his microscope was the existence of spermatozoa in semen. This finding seemed to corroborate preformation, one of the two battling theories of how living things grow that have dominated scientific thinking in Europe for the last three centuries—the other being epigenesis.[3] In fact, preformation—the idea that the individual has been preformed before conception and therefore is identical with his or her eventual adult self in everything except size—was the dominant theory of development until the dawn of the nineteenth century, when it gave way before a mass of new evidence from embryology that living things grow through accretion and differentiation, that they do not simply change size. This understanding of growth as a process of development caused by cells dividing and multiplying is called epigenesis and it is the accepted model of today. In fact, it is so widely accepted and is so obviously the right way to understand growth that it seems odd that anyone should ever have thought differently.

The problem with epigenesis, from the historical point of view, is that in order to accept and substantiate it, one must know, first, that cells exist, and secondly, that they divide. Until the 1830s, when two German biologists, Matthias Schleiden and Theodore Schwann, promulgated cell theory on the basis of Robert Brown's 1831 discovery of the cell nucleus, naturalists had no understanding of the significance of cells, and so were left with the problem of trying to account for the growth of living things without having a mechanism to explain it. It was this lack of available information that gave rise to the theory of preformation in the middle of the seventeenth century.

Preformation is the belief that all future generations of human beings had been created fully formed but in miniscule by God at the dawn of time, that they were encapsulated within each other like Russian dolls, and that sex—far from creating new individuals—merely supplied the trigger which permitted the preformed being to grow.

Where the capsule was located, whether in the ovaries of women or in the sperm of men, was a matter of great debate, with implications for the gender politics of the time. For instance, the ovists insisted that God had located the first capsule within the ovaries of Eve, thereby singling out women as the repositories of the germ in subsequent generations and making literal the biblical claim that Eve was the mother of humankind. But this belief seemed to "detract much from the dignity of the Male sex," in the words of William Cowper, as well as contradicting widely accepted Aristotelian assumptions about the secondary role of women in procreation.[4] With the discovery of the existence of sperm, it became possible to argue that the capsule was in fact located within the semen of men. As Leeuwenhoek said, "the foetus proceeds only from the male semen and the female serves merely to feed and develop it."[5] (See figures 1–4 for representations of seventeenth-through early twentieth-century concepts of preformation and epigenesis.)

Thus preformation had various ramifications for the way in which people understood generation and growth, not least the fact that it seemed to validate the biblical account of the Creation. But preformation also represented a static approach to life, because predetermined organisms are immune to change, all stages of development being identical, except for their size. Thus the young are understood to be little more than miniaturized versions of their future full-grown selves.

In contrast to this, epigenesis posited that organisms grow through accretion, that the germ cell is structureless and that the embryo develops as an original creation through the action of the environment on the protoplasm. As we know now, it is the blueprint for development, as encoded in DNA, that is passed on from parent to child, not the structure itself. Epigenesis defines sex as the originating act of conception and it defines generation as a dual-seed phenomenon, requiring the equal contribution of female and male. It describes growth by incremental stages, as addition and differentiation, not mere unfolding.[6] The fully-formed adult grows out of the child but is not identical with the child. Childhood in this model becomes a state unto itself, separate and distinct from adulthood.

The Victorians lived in the era that saw the transition between these two modes of thought: they inherited the remains of the theory of preformation, which by the nineteenth century had been largely discredited, but they could not yet fully document the fact that living matter grows through the division and multiplication of cells.[7]

While preformation had been discarded as a viable scientific theory by the nineteenth century, it was nevertheless an idea of great imaginative potential, with philosophical and literary implications which lingered throughout the century. In what follows I am going to argue that *Oliver Twist* and *Alice's Adventures in Wonderland* can be viewed as representing these two theories of growth—preformation and epigenesis—especially in the manner in which they present their respective child protagonists.

The young Dickens was a hereditary determinist, as is clearly demonstrated by *Oliver Twist* and *The Old Curiosity Shop*. Furthermore, he was attracted to a generational theory that closely resembled preformation. This theory recurs in several of his novels, and can be found even in such relatively late works as *A Tale of Two Cities*, where the hero Charles Darnay is doubled and duplicated by the anti-hero Sydney Carton just as the cruel excesses of the mob during the French Revolution are portrayed as a reiteration in identical terms of what had pertained during the reign of the aristocracy. I do not wish to suggest that Dickens deliberately propounded preformationism or even that he was necessarily aware of its existence as a biological theory. But in his approach to character development and in his imaginative grasp of the workings of history, Dickens was attracted to a view that favored the notion of endless repetition through the generations. We can see this in his frequent descriptions of children as "the living copies," or "the express likenesses" of their parents, and in such passages as the following from *The Old Curiosity Shop*:

"If you have seen the picture-gallery of any one old family, you will remember how the same face and figure . . . come upon you in different generations; and how you trace the same sweet girl through a long line of portraits—never growing old or changing . . . "   (OCS 637)[8]

This model of the generations repetitively succeeding one another with little or no variation is at the heart of preformationist theory.

And preformationism can certainly be found in *Oliver Twist*, especially in Dickens's presentation of Oliver. Oliver resembles both of his parents perfectly; as the text says, he is their "living copy" (OT 132).[9] And at the end of chapter 12, there is this description of Oliver's resemblance to his dead mother: "The eyes, the head, the mouth; every feature was the same. The expression was, for an instant, so precisely alike, that the minutest line seemed copied with an accuracy that was perfectly unearthly" (OT 132).

Perfect physical resemblance of this kind suggests preformation, but Oliver resembles his parents in more than looks. He embodies their social class in his very veins, another hallmark of preformationist theory. Oliver begins as illegitimate, illiterate, and impoverished, a mere "item of mortality" (OT 45), a member of the vast Victorian underclass of the disenfranchised and marginalized. He is brought up in the workhouse and at the age of nine he is put out to work. He runs away to London, where he falls in among thieves, prostitutes, and murderers. Despite all this, Oliver remains the quintessential little gentleman, a model of honesty and integrity whose character is untouched by his environment and unblemished by the slightest hint of moral stain.[10]

Oliver Twist is a fairy tale in which the magical element is located within the domain of heredity. It is his biological inheritance which protects Oliver from the corrupting effects of his surroundings. He requires neither education nor experience to instruct him; he is incorruptible from birth. Not even exposure to Fagin and his gang of boy thieves can shake Oliver's imperviousness to temptation.

Oliver exists in virtual isolation from his environment, because he is by right—that is, by biological right, by the right of his bloodline—a member of the middle class. What Oliver inherits from his parents is their moral essence as defined by their social class. Virtue in *Oliver Twist* is a middle-class characteristic, bound up with such traits as respectability, honesty, hard work, personal honor, good manners, and an excellent command of the English language.

The predetermined quality of Oliver's personality means that he is a static character. He does not change, and this lack of change is evident in other aspects of the novel, not least in the mystifying ending which neglects to stipulate a future for Oliver. Alone among the major child figures of Dickens's fiction, the Little Nells, Paul Dombeys, David Copperfields and Pips, Oliver neither dies in childhood nor matures. He remains as much a boy at the end of the novel as he was when the action started.

The novel's last chapter, which describes the future careers of all the other characters—even such marginal characters as Brittles, Mrs. Maylie's "boy," who over the years grows quite grey—this last chapter has absolutely nothing to say about Oliver's adulthood. Oliver remains forever Mr. Brownlow's adopted son, and Rose Maylie's "dead sister's child" (OT 479). He is the one immutable point among characters who change and age. His nature, as it develops, reveals only "the thriving seeds" (OT 479) of all that Mr. Brownlow wishes him to become. Oliver, in other words, is always in the seed stage. He never truly sprouts. He may begin life as an item of mortality, but he never makes any progress along the road to death. His is a case of arrested development—arrested because Dickens has philosophical reasons for wanting to keep Oliver boyish and small.

Oliver, after all, is an idea, not a boy. In his preface to the third edition, Dickens wrote: "I wished to show in little Oliver, the principle of Good surviving through every adverse circumstance, and triumphing at last."[11] Note the word "little." Oliver's lack of stature is requisite to the idea of virtue and innocence triumphing against overwhelming odds. Oliver represents the weak, the vulnerable, and the small victimized by the strong, the powerful and the tall—and winning in the end.

As weakness personified, Oliver must be small and must remain small. He is described as "a pale, thin child, somewhat diminutive in stature, and decidedly small in circumference" (OT 49). In other words, Oliver lacks dimension in all dimensions. The lack of stature works fictionally in several ways. Oliver's small size becomes a commodity that others can exploit. It makes him ideal for climbing up narrow chimneys and squeezing through small unlocked lattice windows, thus bringing the boy to the unwanted attention of chimney sweepers and burglars. His small size and sad pinched face also make him ideal to serve the purposes of the undertaker Mr. Sowerberry, who exploits the pathetic aspect of Oliver's size by having him walk mournfully and mutely in front of funeral processions for young children.

But Oliver's lack of stature is also given a certain emotional resonance, as in the following exchange with Mr. Bumble when Oliver is being taken to be apprenticed to Mr. Sowerberry. Oliver breaks into tears, saying

"I am a very little boy, sir; and it is so—so—"
"So what?" inquired Mr. Bumble in amazement.
"So lonely, sir. So very lonely!" cried the child. "Everybody hates me."

(OT 73)

The statement is a plea for compassion at the same time as it is an assertion of the self and of the needs of the self. It tells us what it is like to be Oliver

Twist, alone, unloved and small in a big world. It is one of the few times in the novel that we are given a glimpse into Oliver's inner life, so it is significant that Oliver's misery and his loneliness are linked to his being small. Even Mr. Bumble is moved, if only for the few seconds it takes to clear his throat. The incident illustrates the doubleness of being small—on the one hand it renders the child insignificant, contemptible, easily put-upon and dismissed. On the other hand it calls forth the pity due to naked newborn babes. Dickens famously returns to this equation of being small and alone in an immense universe in the opening paragraphs of *Great Expectations*, where Pip becomes aware of his own small self and his own large loneliness at virtually the same moment.

The strategy of using size to illustrate the undercurrents of plot occurs frequently in nineteenth-century literature. When Jane Austen wants to call attention to the vulnerability of Fanny Price at Mansfield Park, she makes her "small of her age," especially in comparison to her large and self-assured cousins who are "tall of their age."[12] Fanny even finds the rooms at Mansfield Park too large for her to move in. Ironically, Henry Crawford, the male heart-breaker in this novel, is also described as "under-sized." "Nobody can call such an under-sized man handsome," declares the jealous Mr. Rushworth. "He is not five foot nine." (MP 86).

Charlotte Brontë too emphasizes the size of her eponymous heroine in *Jane Eyre*, where Jane's being small and Jane's being plain are made to appear synonymous, as well as indicative of her inferior position, first in the Reed household, and then as a governess at Thornfield Hall. Jane's final triumph in marrying Mr. Rochester is thus all the more amazing, not least because Mr. Rochester's taste in women runs to the large. He likes big women, whom he calls "strappers." But he marries little Jane.

These examples suggest that considerations of size are seldom value-free, that we attribute aesthetic, erotic, and moral qualities to size. This value-system is encoded into our language, where, as a general rule, bigger is better. The very concept of greatness, of being large and expansive, carries all kinds of positive connotations. We speak metaphorically of "giants" in the fields of sports or science, and we mean this as the highest—note the word—praise. The word "largesse" is related to the positive qualities associated with being "large," as are "magnanimous" and "magnificent," which are formed from the Latin word for big, "magnus."

There are many other examples of how large size is positively encoded into our language, but they are small beer compared to the numerous expressions that define smallness negatively. To be big-hearted is good, small-minded is bad. To be petty—from the French word for small—is to be niggardly. To be small-time is to be irrelevant, to be base and low is to be beneath contempt. Small talk is trivial, small-potatoes are unimportant. To fall short is to be inadequate; to be short-sighted is to lack vision.

In fact there are very few expressions or terms which define small size positively, and those that do exist center almost exclusively around the young and around women. "Littleness" is, after all, a much-prized attribute of the Dickensian heroine—witness Little Nell and Little Dorrit and Ruth Pinch in *Martin Chuzzlewit*, who is called "little" seven times in two paragraphs, and this is not counting the times she is called "small."[13] Nor was Dickens the only writer to compound womanliness with lack of stature. Being small was a desirable trait in Victorian heroines generally. Littleness in women went along with daintiness and femininity, with being vulnerable and in need of protection from men.

George Eliot makes this clear in *Adam Bede*, when she has Adam say to the beautiful milk-maid Hetty Sorrel: "Such big arms as mine were made for little arms like yours to lean on."[14] The upper-class Arthur Donnithorne is also given to this kind of language when expressing his attraction to Hetty: "You little frightened bird, little tearful rose! silly pet!" (AB 136), he says to her. "Trot along quickly with your little feet" (AB 137). Clearly, Dickens was not the only Victorian writer to cloyingly confuse small stature with sexual allure. (Just as clearly, George Eliot resented the sex appeal associated with small women. Her narrator can never resist commenting deflatingly on Hetty's attractiveness: "How pretty the little puss looks in that odd dress" (AB 151).)

This equation of feminine small stature with erotic appeal risks turning adult women into children, and—depending on your point of view—either eroticizes the child, or unsexes the woman. But it is also indicative of a tendency among the Victorians to define men and women as opposite sexes, whose attributes are complementary rather than shared—and being small was definitely considered a female trait.[15]

All of which makes Lewis Carroll's *Alice's Adventures in Wonderland* the more remarkable, because it seems to call into question Victorian assumptions about size, especially as it relates to girls and women. At one point, Alice grows so large that she literally outgrows the house that should contain her, thereby, on the one hand, subverting Victorian notions that a woman's place is in the home, and on the other depicting female domestic power as potentially monstrous, the obverse side of the angel in the house. What is more, the over-sized Alice is aggressive and mean with no compunction whatsoever about kicking the poor lizard Dick out of the chimney.

And Carroll permits Alice to undergo some very unladylike changes of shape. Not only does Alice experience extreme variations in size, but her body becomes distorted as well. At one point she shrinks so quickly that her chin hits against her feet, effectively eliminating all torso in-between; another time she expands like a telescope, and soon after that, her neck grows so long that it "curves into a graceful zigzag,"[16] and gets entangled among tree branches, so that every now and then Alice must stop and untwist it. Yet none of these distortions calls into question Alice's essential femininity, although they do suggest the infinite plasticity of the human form, especially when encased in a girl's body.

In the accordion expansion and retraction of its heroine, *Alice's Adventures in Wonderland* is markedly different from the later *Through the Looking-Glass*, where it is the creatures of the looking-glass world—for instance, the Red Queen, or the Gnat in the railway car—who change size, not Alice. Because *Alice's Adventures in Wonderland* is the story of a little girl whose body—to quote Alice— cannot "keep the same size for ten minutes together!" (AAW 50), the book may be read as a fable of growth grown wild, of epigenesis out of control. Unlike *Oliver Twist*, a novel which describes its two societies—the perfidious criminal and workhouse worlds, and the virtuous domain of the good-hearted middle class—as antithetical, distinct, and immutable categories, and which, furthermore, pits good against evil without any complicating shades in between, *Alice's Adventures in Wonderland* describes a fantasy world of great fluidity, where no distinctions exist between the animate and the inanimate, between the human, the animal, or the vegetable; where there is no good and no evil, because there is no cause and effect, so that morality itself is in a state of flux. It is a land of infinite metamorphosis, where nothing can be predicted because nothing stays the same, a wonderworld where the only stable element is instability. Alice's constant changes of size seem to hint at a Darwinian universe in which boundaries are not fixed and any one species may transmute into any other, just as the duchess's baby turns into a pig.[17]

In this world epigenesis is the operative method of growth, since Alice grows or shrinks in response to her surroundings, specifically in response to what she eats or drinks—that is, she demonstrates on her own body the effects of environment on protoplasm. In this respect Alice is a direct contrast to Oliver Twist. Nothing in Oliver's environment causes him to change, because he has been preformed, whereas Alice is endlessly responsive to her surroundings and constantly attempting to adjust to her new circumstances. At first the changes in height appear to be beyond her control, and she is never the right size for her needs, but with the help of the caterpillar—another symbol of metamorphosis—she eventually learns to control her size, and hence her surroundings, although even then her control is not perfect, since she grows again during the trial scene.

Alice also differs from Oliver in having no parents that we know of, so that she remains unburdened by both heredity and history. She is nobody's "living copy." She cannot be preformed, because her parents are as completely irrelevant to who she is as they are to her adventures in Wonderland. This means that Alice is presented to us as sui generis, as essentially her own person and her own creation, a being whose essence has been shaped entirely by her surroundings—witness all the cultural baggage she has absorbed, from maxims, to didactic poems, to the Latin form for addressing a mouse—and whose response to those surroundings is infinitely adaptable.

Unlike *Oliver Twist*, where the language for the most part means what it says—I am ignoring here Dickens's frequent nudging references to Charlie Bates as "Master Bates"—the many puns in *Alice's Adventures in Wonderland* hint at the fluidity of language, at the way in which the same word or words may change from meaning one thing to meaning another. For example, one of the most telling dual allusions in *Alice's Adventures in Wonderland* is the confusion between physical size and chronological maturity that is inherent in the term "grown up" (being tall) and "grown up" (being mature). When Alice is in her giant state and bursting out of the house, she says to herself that when she grows up she will write a book about herself, and then suddenly realizes that she is "grown up" after all. When she chastises herself for crying, saying "you ought to be ashamed of yourself, a great girl like you," the narrator cannot resist calling attention to the pun, remarking parenthetically that "she might well say this" (AAW 27).

Being grown-up literally and being grown up chronologically are two different things—and yet they are the same thing, because the term "grown-up" equates adulthood with size. This puts Alice in a strange position, because how can she be grown up and still cling to her status as a child? Alice, after all, is very firm in her insistence that she is a "little girl" and not a serpent, or any other strange creature. But her abrupt changes in size seem to undermine the definition of childhood as a state of littleness, at the same time as they blur the demarcation line between childhood and adulthood as two distinct times of life.

Furthermore, Alice's changing size effectively splits her in two, allowing her to feel opposing emotions connected to her changing size. When she is little, she feels that it is impossible for her to give herself advice because there just isn't enough of her there, but when she grows very tall, she partitions her body, and speaks to her own feet as if they no longer belonged to her: "Good-bye feet. Who will put on your shoes and stockings for you now, dears" (AAW 26). The huge Alice, bursting out of the house, is unkind and bossy. The tiny Alice, who trembles before the oxymoronic "enormous puppy" (AAW 46) is meek and frightened. Being both tall and small means that Alice can become a particle of her own particles, an excretion of her own excretions, as when she nearly drowns in the ocean of her own tears. It means that she can be everywhere at once and can experience all the dualities of life equally—the large and the small, the aggressive and the meek.

On the face of it, then, Alice and Oliver could not be more different. But appearances can be deceiving. Despite the malleability of its heroine, despite the Darwinian allusions to dodos, primordial seas and adaptation, despite the fluidity and pliability of the fantasyland which Carroll paints—it, nevertheless, remains a fantasy land.

I have suggested that *Alice's Adventures in Wonderland* is a fable of epigenesis, of the living being responding to her surroundings, a response that is embodied in the cycles of growth and shrinkage which she experiences. And this is so. But while Wonderland is full of the imagery of change, of constant growth and retraction, of states merging into other states, of races run in every direction without beginning or end, the fact remains that Carroll's Wonderland world is not so different from Dickens's underworld land as it might appear; that what lies at the heart of *Wonderland* in much the same way as it lies at the heart of *Oliver Twist* is the romance of stasis, the longing for time stopped, for childhood made eternal. The difference is that Dickens seems to have wished such an outcome for his surrogate self as embodied in Oliver, whereas Carroll longed to bestow eternity on a beloved child.

So let me suggest another way to understand Alice's changes of size. By distorting her shape, by pushing her height to extremes, by defining her body as pliable matter, conformable to any shape whatsoever, Carroll translates Alice into the realm of limitless transformation, where death has no meaning. If, in the real world, the growing child is also proleptically the dying child, since life carries within itself the seeds of death, then, by permitting Alice to grow huge, and then allowing her to shrink, by distorting her body beyond what is humanly possible, Carroll pushes Alice beyond mortality.

There is no death in Wonderland, just a frightened flirtation with the idea of death, as embodied, for instance, in jokes about growing so small as to go out like a candle or falling so far as if off the top of a house. Just as the Queen of Hearts' constant threats to behead everybody in sight never result in any actual executions, so Alice's shape-changing has no real consequences for her health—nor, more importantly, for her maturity.

In *Alice's Adventures in Wonderland* the child may grow tall without ever growing old, which means that changes of size are without implication for development, just as the distortions of Alice's body are without implication for her mortality. No matter how grown up she may appear, Alice never really grows up, but remains—like Oliver—eternally a child.

Wonderland ends with Alice's sister dreaming the dream that Alice has just dreamt, and then imagining Alice retelling the story of Wonderland to future generations of bright and eager-eyed children. It is a Dickensian ending of preformationist cycles projected into the future, where "the same sweet girl" traced through a long line of portraits is identical with Alice, who listens, like Alice, to the grown Alice's retellings of her adventures in Wonderland.

In *Looking Glass* Alice claims that she never asks advice about growing, because "one can't help growing older," (TLG 186), but the thrust of *Wonderland* is that one can grow and yet stay perpetually young. It is an irony of history that the Victorians, who were so committed to the concept of progress and change, who lived, moreover, in the era when epigenesis was gaining ascendency as the dominant theory of growth, should have produced so many literary classics—*Peter Pan* is another example—in which stasis rather than growth is the operative and idealized element. It seems to bespeak a longing to slow down the rush of time, to hearken back to the past while plunging headlong down the rabbit-hole of the future.

The nineteenth century may justly be called the century of the child, since for the first time in literary history children become a central focus of novelistic concern, just as they begin to play a larger role in social awareness generally. Dickens was the writer who helped bring this about, when in *Oliver Twist*, for the first time, he placed a child at the center of a novel intended for adults. But I would suggest that the figure of the child in nineteenth-century literature tends to be regressive, that it is always tainted with the stasis inherent in Dickens's preformationist bias, because the fictional child embodies a tension that tends to negate the future when childhood is outgrown. Since children cannot mature and still be called children, childhood must always be celebrated within the context either of time past or time stopped. The many dying children in Victorian fiction are part of this wish to eternalize childhood, since the only thing that can truly destroy childhood is to outgrow it. The figure of the child in nineteenth-century literature is thus emblematic of a wish to arrest time, to keep the springtime of life eternally green—and eternally unchanging.

So I conclude with a paradox: While Oliver and Alice never change, because they do not mature; nevertheless, the answer to the question with which I began this essay—whether the Victorians regarded childhood as a distinct state unto itself—is, resoundingly, yes. As I suggested during my discussion of the two developmental theories, it was the growing acceptance of epigenesis that made it possible for the Victorians to regard childhood as a distinct stage of life and not merely as a miniature form of adulthood. The irony is that in focusing on childhood in this way, writers like Dickens and Carroll present the child as static, as incapable of change. The reason for this lies, perhaps, in the fact that epigenesis represents the reality of life, of growth as it actually occurs; while preformation—bankrupt scientific theory though it was by the nineteenth century—represents the reality of fiction. It is the nature of fiction to compartmentalize experience and to play tricks with time. In fiction, it is possible for Oliver and Alice never to grow up.

Fig. 1. Gautier d'Agoty's 1750 attempt to imagine the preformed foetus visible in a glass of water into which semen has been dischaged.

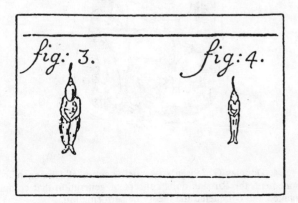

Fig. 2. François de Plantade's drawings for Leeuwenhoek in 1699. They attempt to depict the homunculi who become visible in sperm when it is placed under a microscope.

Fig. 3. Nicholas Hartsoeker's 1694 rendition of a homunculus curled inside a sperm head.

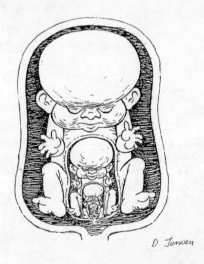

Fig. 4. Douglas G. Jensen's twentieth-century illustraion of emboitement, the Russian-dolls concept of generation that complemented and completed the theory of performation.

(Figures 1–3 are taken from Clara Pinto-Correia's *The Ovary of Eve: Egg and Sperm and Preformation*, University of Chicago Press, 1997, pp. 101, 212, 231.)

NOTES

1. An important study dealing with size in literature is M. M. Bakhtin, *Rabelais and His World*, tr. H. Iswolsky (Cambridge: MIT P, 1968). For feminist criticism dealing with size, see, among others, Helena Michie, *The Flesh Made Word: Female Figures and Women's Bodies* (New York: Oxford UP, 1987) and Patricia Ingram, *Dickens, Women and Language* (Toronto: U of Toronto P, 1992), 18–20.

2. Philip Ariès, *Centuries of Childhood: A Social History of Family Life*, tr. Robert Baldick (New York: Vintage, 1962).

3. For a detailed account of the history and ramifications of preformation see Clara Pinto-Correia, *The Ovary of Eve: Egg and Sperm and Preformation* (Chicago: U of Chicago P, 1997).

4. The quote is from William Cowper's *The Anatomy of Human Bodies* (London, 1737) and can be found in Thomas Laqueur's *Making Sex: Body and Gender from the Greeks to Freud* (Cambridge: Harvard UP, 1990). Aristotle believed that the male supplied the blueprint for reproduction, while the female provided the matter, which the male then fashioned. Or to quote him directly: "The male provides the form and the principle of the movement, the female provides the body, in other words, the material." From *Generation of Animals*. trans. A. L. Peck. Loeb Classical Library. (Cambridge: Harvard UP, 1965) 109.

5. Quoted in Clara Pinto-Correia, *The Ovary of Eve: Egg and Sperm and Preformation* (Chicago: U of Chicago P, 1997) 70.

6. I am borrowing here from Stephen J. Gould, whose phrase is "embryology is addition and differentiation, not mere unfolding." See Gould, *The Flamingo's Smile: Reflections in Natural History* (New York: Norton, 1985) 143.

7. Victorian misconceptions about how growth works found their most damaging expression in the belief that masturbation stunts growth because it represents a loss of vital energy. See for instance Edward Carpenter's dictum: "To prolong the period of continence [purity] in a boy's life is to prolong the period of growth . . . To introduce sensual and sexual habits . . . at any early age, is to arrest growth, both physical and mental." Quoted in James R. Kincaid's *Child-Loving: The Erotic Child and Victorian Culture* (New York: Routledge, 1992), 106. In her article on "The Nervous Diseases of Infancy and Childhood" in *Woods's Household Practice of Medicine, Hygiene and Surgery* (1881) Mary Putnam-Jacobi wrote that bodily growth "involves an expenditure of nerve force—in other words, a drain upon the store accumulated in the masses of cells and networks of fibres of the central nervous system." Quoted in Kincaid, 109.

8. References to Dickens's novels are to the 1985 Penguin editions and occur in the text.

9. To be perfectly accurate, the phrase "living copy" is used only to describe Oliver's resemblance to the portrait of his mother in chapter 12. But, as the text makes clear, Oliver is a perfect duplicate of his father as well. In fact, Monks first realizes that Oliver is his half-brother through "his resemblance to his father" (OT 439).

10. The notion that class was inborn was common among the Victorians. In volume 2 of *London Labour and the London Poor* (New York: Dover, 1968), Henry Mayhew cites the case of a young child stolen from his parents to become a chimney sweep, who, when rescued reverted immediately to his middle-class origins. "From various circumstances, it is thought impossible he should be the child of the woman who sold him, his manners being very civilized . . . His dialect is good and that of the south of England." The little boy at the time of rescue was about four years old. See p. 348.

11. Dickens, "Preface," *Oliver Twist* (Penguin) 33.

12. Jane Austen, *Mansfield Park*, (London: Penguin, 1996) 12.

13. The counting was done by Juliet McMaster in *Dickens the Designer* (Totowa, N.J.: Barnes and Noble Books, 1987) 65.

14. George Eliot, *Adam Bede* (London: Penguin, 1985) 222. Further references are to this edition and occur in the text.

15. See Thomas Laqueur, *Making Sex: Body and Gender from the Greeks to Freud.* Laqueur argues that it is in the nineteenth century that the sexes first come to be thought of as "opposite," both anatomically and emotionally.

16. Lewis Carroll, *Alice's Adventures in Wonderland and Through the Looking-Glass* (New York: Signet, 1960) 55. All future references are to this edition and occur in the text.

17. For a Darwinian reading of certain aspects of Alice, especially the pool of tears and the Dodo, see William Empson, "Alice in Wonderland: The Child as Swain," in *Aspects of Alice: Lewis Carroll's Dreamchild as Seen Through the Critics' Looking-Glasses* (New York: Vanguard, 1971) 344–73.

Raising the House Tops: Sexual Surveillance in Charles Dickens's *Dombey and Son* (1846–48)

Colette Colligan

Drawing on Laura Mulvey's theory of the gaze, Michel Foucault's notion of the panopticon, and recent criticism on nineteenth–century detective fiction, this essay examines surveillance in Charles Dickens's Dombey and Son. *Surveillance in this novel is concerned with detecting sexual guilt. At first, the novel's panopticon is directed at Florence and Edith to imply their sexual fallenness; however halfway through the novel, it shifts onto Dombey. What becomes clear is that the sexual guilt that the novel anxiously seeks to uncover by raising the house tops off lies less within the female characters than it does within the male—Dombey in particular. In other words, it is anxiety about the male characters that ultimately drives the novel's surveillance. The questions this essay addresses, then, are as follows: why does the novel displace its true surveillance of Dombey onto the female characters; why does the surveillance shift halfway through the novel; and, most saliently, what are Dombey's sexual secrets?*

> Oh for a good spirit who would take the house-tops off, with a more potent and benignant hand than the lame demon in the tale, and show a Christian people what dark shapes issue from amidst their homes. . . .
> Charles Dickens, *Dombey and Son* (620)

Nearly every character in Charles Dickens's *Dombey and Son* (1846–48) is

---

Dickens Studies Annual, Volume 29, Copyright © 2000 by AMS Press, Inc. All rights reserved.

under constant visual surveillance. It seems almost as if the novel were based on the panopticon, Jeremy Bentham's ideal mechanism of prison observation and control—an unseen, though all–seeing mode of surveillance devised to be "permanent in its effects, even if . . . discontinuous in its action" (Foucault, *Discipline* 204).[1] Good Mrs. Brown threatens that "potent eyes and ears . . . cognizant of all" are scrutinizing Florence (75). Later, "blank walls" look down upon Florence "as if they ha[ve] a gorgon-like mind to stare her youth and beauty into stone" (311). Young Paul Dombey surveys Master Blitherstone from "head to foot, . . . watching all the workings of his countenance" (101) and "gaz[es] fixedly [at] Mrs. Pipchin" (104). Most importantly, James Carker penetrates everybody's "[innermost]-secret thoughts" (564) with his "catlike and vigilant gaze" (567). Hablot K. Browne's illustrations to the novel, which not only make literal the images in the text, but frequently supplement them,[2] also give the effect of the panopticon. In his illustrations, portraits and busts of male politicians fix a curious, and often an opprobrious, gaze initially on the female figures and later on Mr. Dombey (figs. 1–3). Browne also shows Rob the Grinder, secretly employed by Carker, watching Florence through the skylight (fig. 4) and later staring fixedly at Captain Cuttle (fig. 5). Other illustrations show Major Bagstock intently spying on Miss Tox with his double-barrelled opera-glass (fig. 6), and Good Mrs. Brown, crouching low among the crowd of onlookers, directing a furtive, side-long glance at the newly-wed Dombeys (fig. 7). Finally, the figure at the bottom center of the monthly wrapper who looks through the telescope surely allegorizes the watchful surveillance which extends throughout the novel (fig. 8).[3]

The scrutinizing gaze in *Dombey and Son* not infrequently takes the form of an innocent and even playful curiosity. Paul openly observes Mr. Dombey, Master Blitherstone, and Mrs. Pipchin, for instance, because of his childlike fascination with the different and unusual. Rob the Grinder's gaze—at least at first—also shares some of Paul's natural inquisitiveness. In Browne's illustrations, his expression initially reflects a guileless curiosity (figs. 4–5) and only becomes wily and suspicious after he is quite corrupted by Carker (fig. 9). More frequently, however, the novel's watchful surveillance is less curious than disapproving. Specifically, it is concerned with uncovering secrets and establishing blame. This suspicious and denunciatory gaze is initially directed at the female characters, especially Florence and Edith: the staring portraits, the classical busts, and the watchful Carker all represent a male gaze preoccupied with uncovering their sexual guilt.

Not only do the specific details in the text identify the gaze directed at the female characters as male, but the gaze has been labeled male in theoretical terms as well: Laura Mulvey's essay "Visual Pleasure and Narrative Cinema," which describes women's objectification by the patriarchal male gaze, has now become a theoretical keynote. Using psychoanalysis as her conceptual framework, Mulvey suggests that the male gaze originates from men's castration anxiety, which is evoked implicitly by women's lack of a penis (Mulvey 21). More recently, critics such as bell hooks in *Black Looks* and E. Ann Kaplan in *Looking for the Other*, have problematized the use of psychoanalysis in gaze theory, objecting to its occlusion of race, class, nationality, and sexuality as determinants of the gaze. When considering the disciplinary gaze in *Dombey and Son*, therefore, I find Mulvey's theory of the male gaze useful, but I prefer socio-historical explanations of the gaze over psychoanalytic models. In *Myths of Sexuality*, Linda Nead suggests that although Victorian domestic ideology gave women considerable responsibility, in that their "moral purity maintained the home as a spiritual haven for [their] husband[s] and children," men could not quite trust them to carry out this role (48): "[f]ears of illegitimate inheritance and the breakdown of the bourgeois family" (48) persuaded them to regulate carefully women's sexuality (80). Anne McClintock's *Imperial Leather* and Robert Young's *Colonial Desire*, furthermore, locate male anxiety about female sexual malfeasance within a broad-ranging concern about social transgressions of all kinds; in Victorian England, "a triangulated, switchboard analogy . . . emerged between, racial, class, and gender deviance which was " bound in a regime of surveillance" (McClintock 56)—perhaps to counter the sense of "fragmentation and dispersion brought about by the rapid change and transformation of both metropolitan and colonial societies" (Young 4). In *Dombey and Son*, then, the scrutinizing gaze of the portraits, busts, and individual male characters, which identifies Florence and Edith with monstrous or sexually illicit women (such as the Medusan Mrs. MacStinger, the Cleopatran Mrs. Skewton, the corrupt Mrs. Brown, and the fallen Alice), reflects and creates a specific historical anxiety about transgressive female sexuality.

Halfway through the text, however, the novel's surveillance shifts. The investigating gaze is transferred from Florence and Edith onto Mr. Dombey. After the climactic chapter 47, when Edith elopes with Carker, Dombey strikes Florence, and Florence runs into the streets, Dombey becomes uncomfortably aware of scrutiny, feeling that "the world is looking at him . . . [even] in the stares of the pictures" (682). This gaze is different from that which scrutinizes Florence and Edith, in that it is both male and female, but, like the gaze directed at the female characters, it is preoccupied with exposing sexual guilt and delineating normative sexuality. Prying eyes—represented in staring portraits of both sexes, the eyes of his daughter, and the metonymic representations of the eyes of the world—attempt to uncover Dombey's sexual deviance: there are a number of veiled references to his sexual impotence as well as his homosexual proclivities (the homosexual act was criminalized in Britain during the nineteenth century [Pool 190]). Because Dombey is the novel's central character—as suggested by Dickens in his original plan (Forster 360) and by Dombey's prominent position on the wrapper design (fig. 8)—I think that uneasiness about his sexuality is at the heart of the novel. However, this anxiety about him seems to be initially deflected onto the female characters, where it is manifested as concern about illicit female sexuality and where it partly impels the surveillance of both Florence and Edith. When we recall how sensitive Dombey is to public scrutiny, always endeavoring "to hide the world within him from the world without" (682), we sense that the secrets that the novel hopes to uncover by raising the "house-tops off" do not entirely dwell within the female characters, but most saliently within Dombey himself (620).

I

The novel's scrutinizing gaze is first directed at Florence. Although *Dombey and Son* overtly sympathizes with and celebrates this "most devoted and most patient and most dutiful and beautiful of daughters" (589) who is "thrown away" by a father preoccupied with patriarchal lineage (28), the novel also keeps her under close surveillance.[4] Browne's illustration of Florence petting her dog Diogenes (fig. 1) clearly reflects this ambivalent attitude toward her. On the one hand, a male bust scrutinizes her censoriously from the corner of its eye. On the other hand, a caged bird to the right of the drawing, which appears throughout the novel as a symbol for women's humiliation and subjugation, suggests that Florence is imprisoned within an unloving home.[5] Elsewhere, the novel again engenders pity for Florence while simultaneously awakening doubt and suspicion about her. The narrator fosters our sympathy for her, for instance, by informing us that Dombey leaves his daughter alone in his "neglected" (311) and "deserted" (312) London home while he and Major Bagstock sojourn at Leamington. The emphasis placed on the dusty, mildewed, and rat-infested condition of the house especially heightens our sympathy (312). However, the fact that "blank" (311), "cold" (312), and "monotonous walls [look] down upon her with a stare, as if they ha[ve] a Gorgon-like intent to stare her youth and beauty into stone" (315) mitigates this initial response. Are these staring walls, which are alluded to three times, meant simply to create a greater effect of neglect, thus increasing our pity, or do they hint at Florence's potential infamy? We also wonder why "a glowering visage, with its thin lips parted wickedly, survey[s] all comers from above the archway of the door" instead of "two dragon sentries keeping ward . . . , [which] in magic legend are usually found on duty over wronged innocence imprisoned" (311). On the part of both narrator and illustrator, there are quiet, but insistent suggestions that Florence requires close scrutiny.

Acts of looking and surveillance are not only carried out by the narrator, but also by individual characters in the novel, most notably James Carker. Before shifting his gaze onto Edith, he watches Florence intently. He "picks his way softly past the [Dombey] house, glancing up at the windows, and trying to make out the pensive face behind the curtain looking at the children opposite" (311). When he comes across Florence in the company of Sir Barnet and Lady Skettles, moreover, he "look[s] particularly at Florence; and . . . he bow[s] to her before saluting Sir Barnet and his lady" (343). We later learn that he visits Florence on three separate occasions while she is visiting with the Skettleses (383). At the same time, Carker also manages to spy indirectly on Florence, instructing Rob the Grinder to take especial note whenever she visits Sol Gills: "There is a very young lady who may perhaps come to see him. I want particularly to know all about her" (304). Carker's interest in Florence is both self-serving and perverse. On the one hand, it is pecuniary. Should Carker marry Florence, he would inherit the firm of Dombey and Son. This is insinuated by the narrator who, after Paul Dombey's untimely death, remarks that "there is something gone from Mr. Carker's path—some obstacle removed—which clears his way before him" (326). On the other hand, Carker's interest in Florence is very nearly voyeuristic. In theoretical terms, voyeurism is a type of violent scopophilia (pleasure in looking); the voyeur, who watches unobserved, fixes a controlling gaze onto the objectified female other (Mulvey 16–17). According to Mulvey, it "has associations with sadism" because the pleasure in looking "lies in ascertaining guilt, asserting control and subjugating the guilty person" (21–22).[6] Unlike the voyeur, Carker does not endeavor to conceal his surveillance; but like that of the voyeur, his gaze is concomitant with his desire to subjugate and condemn. He initially gains power over Florence through his knowledge of her friendship with Walter. With this information, he assumes "a confidence between himself and [Florence]—a right on his part to be mysterious and stealthy, . . . a kind of mildly restrained power and authority over her—that ma[kes] her wonder, and cause[s] her great uneasiness" (384–85). As the narrator informs us, he obtains "a secret sense of power in her shrinking from him" (502). Later, Carker attempts to cast aspersion on Florence by deliberately misconstruing the nature of her friendship with Walter, suggesting that it is somehow illicit. He tells Edith that "Miss Florence . . . necessarily wanted some guide and compass in her younger days, and, naturally, for want of them, has been indiscreet, and has in some degree forgotten her station. There was some folly about one Walter, a common lad . . . " (504). Edith recognizes that Carker distorts his information, but cannot easily refute him because he is dealing with half-truths (504). Florence is indeed alone and unprotected "with no one to advise her" except her maid Susan Nipper, and with no one to protect her except her dog Diogenes (385, 678).[7] It is

Florence's very vulnerability—the fact that she enters puberty without any solid guidance—that engenders sympathy for her, but also creates uneasiness about her sexuality. Even though we are not encouraged to align ourselves emotionally with Carker, who exposes Florence's potential infamy with his sadistic gaze, both text and illustration nonetheless induce us to feel a little anxious about her sexual vulnerability.

Following Freud, Mulvey also argues that scopophilia has an erotic basis, being "one of the component instincts of sexuality" (16). The erotic undertones of Carker's (near) voyeuristic scopophilia are evident in his attempt to take advantage of Florence's vulnerability with his mesmeric power. In his chapter on "The Sexuality of Power" in *Dickens and Mesmerism*, Fred Kaplan argues that Carker gains control over Rob the Grinder by means of mesmerism (198). Using the vocabulary of mesmerism, Dickens describes Rob's capitulation to Carker (Kaplan 183): "the boy . . . could not help staring wildly at the gentleman with so many white teeth" (296); "he was fascinated with Mr. Carker and never took his round eyes off him for an instant" (297); "Rob . . . [is] fixed by Mr. Carker's eye, and fruitlessly endeavour[s] to unfix himself" (565). According to Lisa Surridge, Carker also attempts to control Florence (and later Edith) with his mesmeric gaze (87). The fact that Florence's "eyes [are] *drawn* towards him every now and then, by an *attraction* of dislike and distrust that *she [can]not resist*" indeed suggests that Carker uses his mesmeric force on her (Dickens 494; my emphasis). Browne also depicts Carker as possessing the power of the mesmerist. A careful examination of the illustration in which Carker is on horseback looking down at Florence will reveal that his eyes are strangely dilated and that Florence seems irresistibly drawn to them (fig. 10). In Dickens's time, as Kaplan points out, this mesmeric gaze was perceived as implicitly sexual. "The power to usurp the other's will," he writes, "was seen as inseparable from sexuality" (190). Indeed, *The Lancet* often printed stories about the seduction of young women by licentious male mesmerists, in one instance writing about "a young French lady . . . [who] was placed under the care of a Mesmeriser . . . [and] by some species of 'dislocation,'—or other 'anomalous transposition of the sense' . . . was thrown into a profound sleep, [whereupon] the quack stole her honour" (qtd. in Kaplan 189). It is clear, then, that Carker's mesmeric gaze gives evidence of Florence's sexual vulnerability and, as a result, demonstrates the need to watch her closely. Indeed, who is to say that he will not seduce Florence as he did Alice Marwood?

So far, I have suggested that Florence is subject to an opprobrious male gaze, having shown that Carker as well as the busts of male politicians look upon her suspiciously, and I have also suggested that this gaze is linked to uneasiness concerning Florence's sexuality. This apprehension about Florence, I now want to argue, pertains specifically to her potential sexual fall.[8]

The "penetrating" gaze that Carker fixes on Florence certainly hints at her sexual vulnerability, but chapter six especially introduces the possibility of her fall. In this chapter, Florence is separated from her nurse and finds herself lost in the city; Mrs. Brown, who "seem[s] to have followed [her]," lures her to her decrepit house, where she compels Florence to remove her clothes and don filthy rags (73). Florence's flight into London's streets in and of itself signals her imperiled virtue (409); as Alexander Welsh insists, "No one acquainted with Victorian euphemisms can mistake what it means for a homeless girl to be in the streets" (90).[9] In her provocative essay "Good Mrs. Brown's Connections," Joss Lutz Marsh further argues that Florence's virtue is symbolically threatened when she is abducted and robbed by Mrs. Brown. Besides revealing the striking similarities between this scene and John Cleland's pornographic work *Memoirs of a Woman of Pleasure* (410–12), where the artful Mrs. Brown beguiles the innocent young Fanny into prostitution, Marsh draws attention to the sexual suggestiveness of the incident itself. Mrs. Brown (masculinized by the fact that she smokes a pipe and carries large, pointy scissors) becomes unaccountably excited when she sees Florence's "luxuriant" curls escape accidentally from her bonnet and tumble down her shoulders:

> Mrs. Brown whipped out a large pair of scissors . . . ruffling her curls with a furious pleasure, [but] after hovering about her with the scissors for some moments . . . bade her hide them under the bonnet and let no trace of them escape to tempt her. Having accomplished this victory over herself, Mrs. Brown . . . smoked a very short black pipe. . . . (74–5)

The sexually redolent language of the passage—"whipped," "furious pleasure," "hovering," "tempt"—powerfully suggest the "sexual substratum" of this scene (Marsh 410). The attempted "rape of the lock," in other words, is described as a sexual assault, signaling Florence's threatened virtue; she even appropriates the rhetoric of the fallen women when she admits that she is "lost" (77). Finally, Florence's long, disheveled curls also imply her fallenness. Marsh mentions that "loosened, 'wild' hair comes to signify what it does in a host of Pre-Raphaelite paintings: sexual abandonment" (410), and, similarly, Elisabeth Gitter in "The Power of Women's Hair in the Victorian Imagination" links loose hair to wanton sexuality:

> [T]he more abundant the hair, the more potent the sexual invitation implied by its display, for folk, literary, and psychoanalytic traditions agree that a luxuriance of hair is an index of vigorous sexuality, even of wantonness. Anthropological literature too, makes little distinction between the sacrifice of genitals, or sexual surrender, and the sacrifice of the hair. (938)

Florence's luxuriant hair also connects her with Mrs. Brown's fallen daughter Alice Marwood, for it reminds her of her daughter who "was proud of her hair'' (75).[10] It will also later link her to the (nearly) adulterous Edith, whose "dark hair [is] shaken down" (420) "in beautiful abandonment" (426). In connecting Florence with other sexually notorious women in the text, the novel suggests her potential fallenness, but it also implicitly reveals how all these women are potentially the victims of men's (or male-identified women's) callous seduction.

The doubt raised about Florence's innocence in chapter six reverberates throughout the text, but especially in chapter 47, the "storm-centre of the novel," which includes Edith's elopement with Carker, Dombey's violence toward Florence, and Florence's desperate flight into the streets (Butt and Tillotson 103). Text and illustration collaborate here to suggest that Florence is "in league" with Edith, in that she is contaminated by her step-mother's (assumed) sexual guilt (637).[11] When Edith encounters Florence on the staircase, she recoils and shrieks: "Don't come near me! . . . Keep away! Let me go by! . . . Don't speak to me! Don't look at me . . . don't touch me" (632). The accompanying illustration (fig. 11), however, suggests that in spite of Edith's efforts to distance herself—and her guilt—from Florence, Florence is nonetheless tainted. Surridge examines this illustration closely, noting how Browne emphasizes their similarities:

> Edith's shawl, flying out beside and behind her, emphasizes her hurry. Florence's garments also trail behind her, echoing this detail. Edith's hair, as befits a soon-to-be fallen woman, is loose; Florence's is tied back but a loose tendril associates her with Edith's fallen state.   (82–83)

Both Florence and Edith also stretch out their arms, a gesture that still further affiliates them and thus immediately raises questions about Florence's innocence.

After Dombey strikes Florence across the breast, she is again found in the streets. She loses herself "in the wide wilderness of London" (638), seeing "long shadows coming back upon the pavement; and [hearing] voices that [are] strange to her asking where she [is going], and what the matter [is]" (638). The suggestion that various nefarious types are swooping down upon her at this point was such that Dickens decided against concluding number 15 with her flight, as he originally intended, and instead shows her finding refuge with the kind-hearted Captain Cuttle (Butt and Tillotson 107).[12] Keeping in mind the myriad allusions to her potential infamy, it becomes very clear why the seemingly blameless hearth angel and Dombey's "unknown Good Genius" is kept under close surveillance (Dickens, qtd. in Forster 360). Though we never entirely align ourselves with the narrator's disapproving gaze or Carker's nearly voyeuristic gaze, the novel encourages us to feel uneasy about Florence's sexual vulnerability, dreading that she may fall under the influence of Carker or the pimps and bawds in the streets.

II

Edith—like Florence—is identified with illicit sexuality in that she virtually prostitutes herself by marrying the wealthy Dombey whom she "scorn[s]" (374). Dickens and Browne draw attention to her sexual guilt in a number of ways, such as identifying her with Potiphar's wife, the Egyptian queen who attempts to seduce Joseph in Genesis 39 (455; Nunokawa 153) and connecting her to Lesbia, the adulterous woman loved by the Roman poet Catullus (fig. 11; Surridge 83). Most notably, however, they link her to the fallen woman. After Edith becomes engaged to Dombey, for example, we frequently see her sitting beside an open window, watching "the faded likeness of her sex [namely, prostitutes] . . . wander[ing] past outside" (415–18). Victorian literature and painting typically suggest a woman's uncontained or transgressive sexuality by depicting her by a window, a liminal site in constant negotiation between inside and outside, private and public, licit and illicit. We have only to recall Elizabeth Gaskell's novel *Ruth* (1853), where the fallen heroine presses her "hot forehead against the cold glass" straining against "the impulse . . . to snatch up a shawl . . . and sally forth" (5), or J. R. Spencer Stanhope's painting *Thoughts of the Past* (1859), where a prostitute stands by a window (Nead, plate 24; fig. 12). The novel also adopts the rhetoric of fallenness to describe Edith. She is not only depicted as "fallen" (383), "debased and lost" (409), and ashamed (408), but she is also viewed as both "corrupting" and "perverting" (418). Edith later perceives Florence "with strange dread and wild avoidance" because she fears she will somehow contaminate her (622). Dickens further implies Edith's sexual guilt by conflating her with Alice Marwood. When Edith and Alice encounter one another by chance, for example, the narrator suggests that Edith "may have . . . [seen] upon [Alice's] face some traces which she knew were lingering in her soul, if not yet written on that index" (550). In the illustration to chapter 40, Browne also identifies Edith with Alice by means of striking visual parallels (fig. 13). They look remarkably alike, both being dark and handsome. Alice's loose, unkempt hair, which signals her fallenness, is assailed by the wind; Edith's scarf is similarly blown. Dark, miasmic clouds also settle over each woman. It is precisely because of Edith's perceived sexual guilt, then, that she—like Florence—is subject to the scrutinizing gaze.

While the narrative (at least initially) shields Dombey from public scrutiny, allowing him to sit undisturbed "in the dark distance" (25) or to escape into his room where he can give relief to his feelings privately (204, 222–23), it denies Edith any such privacy.[13] The narrator fully depicts her passionate inner struggle in the woods (370) and shows her "wrest[ling] with her unquiet spirit" the night before her wedding (420). Also, the text will not let Edith conceal her guilt, but instead has her broadcast it vociferously:

[Dombey] sees me at the auction and he thinks it well to buy me. Let him! When he came to view me—perhaps to bid—he required to see the roll of my accomplishments. I gave it to him . . . I am too old now, and have fallen too low, by degrees, to take a new course, and to stop yours, and to help myself . . . I have nothing else to sustain me when I despise myself.   (382)

As Amanda Anderson writes, "Edith is continually subject to an enforced spectatorship of her fully public self" (86).[14] We are even invited to read Edith's body as a testament of her guilt; her repeated acts of self-mutilation, such as punching her breast (420), lacerating her wrist (542), and wounding her hand (578–79), bespeak her shame and self-loathing as well as her anger (Surridge 88–94). In effect, this narrative disclosure of Edith's most private feelings invites even further scrutiny.

The book's panoptic villain—Carker—soon takes up the novel's investigation of Edith's sexual guilt. Struck by Edith's beauty and intrigue, he transfers his gaze from Florence onto her. Dickens clearly reveals this shift in attention by describing how Carker no longer looks up at Florence's window, but instead observes Edith's. As Carker himself says, "time was . . . when it was well to watch [Florence's] rising little star, and know in what quarter there were clouds, to shadow [her] if needful. But a planet has arisen, and [she is] lost in its light" (617). Like Florence, Edith becomes subject to Carker's near voyeurism, which could also be described as his eroto-sadistic gaze. The erotic dimension of his gaze is implied in his keen attention to Edith's physical characteristics: "he admire[s] the graces of her face and form, and . . . they dwel[l] within his sensual remembrance" (577).[15] It is evident elsewhere in the novel that he views Edith as erotic spectacle, especially in that he displays a painting of a woman resembling her in his house and usually sits opposite it for optimum viewing purposes (455, 567; fig. 14). Other examples of Carker's erotic gaze suggest how his look is closely linked to sadism: "Mr. Carker, with his white teeth glistening approaches Edith, more as if he wanted to bite her, than taste the sweets that linger on her lips" (427) and with "glistening mouth . . . [he] thought, again, how beautiful she was" (598). According to Fred Kaplan, Carker's gleaming teeth take "the place of the usual 'visual ray' as the vehicle of the transmission of his mesmeric power" (198); this is evidenced by Rob the Grinder, who cannot help "staring wildly at the gentleman with so many white teeth" (296), and by the page Withers, who stands "amazed at the beauty of his teeth" (506). Carker's devouring look, therefore, intimates both the erotic and controlling aspect of his gaze, which in turn brings to mind Foucault's notion of the "sensualization of power" (Foucault, *The History of Sexuality* 44). Whenever we talk about Carker's cruelly vigilant surveillance of Edith, then, we must always keep in mind the erotic substratum of his gaze; as Foucault writes, "pleasure [can come] of exercising a power that questions, monitors, watches, spies, searches out, palpates, brings to light'' (45).

The sadistic element of Carker's gaze becomes apparent in his first few encounters with Edith. Soon after he meets her, for instance, he admits that ''he was not prepared for anything so beautiful and unusual together,'' referring specifically to a landscape drawing sketched by Edith, but certainly alluding to her as well (379). The fact that he finds her physically alluring is again made clear; however, we should not overlook the fact that he also adds that Edith is ''unusual.'' In so doing, he intimates that he finds something different, perhaps even ''askew'' about her, and thus reveals his (near) voyeurism, as Mulvey defines it. In fact, when Carker first catches sight of Edith in the woods while ''some passion or struggle [is] raging'' within her and then watches her surreptitiously from behind a tree (369–70), noticing how ''she h[olds] a corner of her under lip within her mouth, her bosom heave[s], her nostril quiver[s], her head tremble[s]'' (370), he becomes the paradigmatic voyeur who looks on unobserved.[16] Although it is the narrator who describes her passion, it is surely told from Carker's point of view, for he has just detected her and discovered her self-loathing and guilt. Later, Edith herself alludes to Carker's hypercritical observation of her. She informs her mother, for instance, that Carker ''knows [them] thoroughly, and reads [them] right'' and that before him she ''has even less self-respect or confidence than before [her] own inward-self: being so much degraded by his knowledge of [her]'' (382). Even in Carker's first few encounters with Edith, then, he fixes his scrutinizing gaze onto her, attempting to detect her sexual secrets and, with this knowledge, to subjugate and humiliate her.

The predatory imagery which surrounds Carker also suggests the sadistic nature of his gaze. Although he is identified with wolves, sharks, and snakes, he is most notably compared to a cat: ''in [Carker's] false mouth, stretched but not laughing; in [his] spotless cravat and very whiskers; even in [his] silent passing of his soft hand over his white linen and smooth face; there was something desperately cat-like'' (234). True to his feline nature, Carker relentlessly preys upon mice and birds. When Dombey, Bagstock, and the Skewtons are driving to Warwick Castle, for example, Carker ''canter[s] behind the carriage . . . and watche[s] it, during all the ride, as if he were a cat, indeed, and its four occupants mice'' (375). Even more significantly, ''the corner of his eye [is] ever on the formal head of Mr. Dombey . . . and the *feather* in the bonnet'' (375; my emphasis). This feather certainly stands in metonymically for Edith, for she is later strongly identified with Carker's ''chafing and imprisoned'' bird, ''a gaudy parrot in a burnished cage upon the table [who] tears at the wires with her beak . . . shaking her house and screeching'' (455); she also wears ''delicate white down'' on her robe (599), and has a ''pinion of some rare and beautiful bird at her wrist'' (600; Surridge

86). Later, Carker experiences sadistic pleasure in watching the bird-like Edith quiver under his gaze, musing on "how the white down [flutters] . . . how the bird's feathers [are] strewn upon the ground" (605).[17]

Carker's "lynx-eyed vigilance" (605) is such that Edith herself wonders "what was there in her he had not observed, and did not know?" (505). She nonetheless struggles fiercely against his violent scopophilia, and a battle for visual dominance consequently ensues between them. Carker, having detected that she not only despises her husband, but also feels guilt-stricken for having married him in the first place, uses this knowledge to degrade and subjugate her with his condemning gaze. His "eyes and his smile" are always fastened on her, watching "how she battle[s] with herself" (577). Edith endeavors to resist him, initially by avoiding eye contact (502–03) and later by "bending her dark gaze full upon him" (599). At first, Carker "[does] not shrink beneath her gaze" (600); "Edith watche[s] him attentively . . . but he watche[s] her too" (602). Edith's look, however, becomes incandescent and eventually overpowers him: "the towering fury and intense abhorrence *sparkling* in her eyes . . . made him stop as if a *fire* had stopped him" (723; my emphases). With what hooks identifies as "the oppositional gaze," Edith then takes possession of the scrutinizing look, surveying "him with a haughty contempt and disgust, that he shr[inks] under" (724). The illustration which depicts Edith threatening Carker with a "castrating gesture" reveals that he cannot meet her gaze; he can only look at her from the corner of his eye (fig. 15; Cohen 99). With Edith, as Homi Bhabha would argue, "the look of surveillance returns as the displacing gaze of the disciplined, where the observer becomes the observed" (89).[18] We are also invited to identify the "two red eyes" of the train which eventually crush Carker (741–42) with Edith's "kindling eyes" (600), thus recognizing that Edith symbolically murders him with her gaze and fulfills her earlier threat to kill him (723).

On the one hand, Edith's eventual usurpation of the male gaze suggests that she is both dangerous and unnatural, warranting careful observation. As E. Ann Kaplan writes in "Is the Gaze Male?", "the woman [who] takes on the 'masculine' role of the bearer of the gaze . . . nearly always loses her traditionally feminine characteristics in so doing—not those of attractiveness, but rather of kindness, humaneness, motherliness. She is now often cold, driving, ambitious, manipulating, just like the men whose position she has usurped" (29). Edith is certainly characterized in this way, being "so obdurate, so unapproachable, so unrelenting, one would have thought that nothing could soften such a woman's nature" (598). Both text and illustration, in fact, compare Edith to a number of dangerous women. In "Mr. Carker in his hour of triumph" (fig. 15), as Surridge notes, "Edith is framed by images of female aggression (with an Amazon statue to her right and a painting of Judith and Holofernes to her left)" (93). Edith's murderous gaze, moreover, also identifies her with Medusa, the menacing mythological figure who kills men with her stony glance. Dickens, intimating Edith's frenetic anger against Dombey, describes how she holds up her head "as if she were the beautiful Medusa, looking on him, face to face, to strike him dead" (623, cf. 628). Also, the emblematic details in Browne's illustrations associate Edith with Medusa. In "Mr. Dombey and the World" (fig. 3), for example, there seem to be two miniature depictions of Medusa's head upon the fireplace, which arguably symbolize Edith in that her recent elopement with Carker has exposed her infamy. In another illustration, Browne compares Edith to the comically terrible Mrs. MacStinger, who is clearly identified with Medusa in "The Midshipman is boarded by the enemy" (fig. 16). Both the head of Medusa as well as a painting bearing that name flank her. Steig convincingly draws attention to the visual linkage of these two women:

> Although the adjective in its title "Another wedding," is intended to refer to the recent marriages of Florence and Susan [Nipper], the depiction of the wedding of Jack Bunsby and Mrs. MacStinger recalls Dombey's wedding. It is one of the only three horizontal plates in the novel, and it clearly parallels the first one . . . in showing a wedding procession with the bride and groom at its head walking arm and arm, observed by casual onlookers in the background.
>
> (108; fig. 17)

Edith's conflation with Medusa as well as the Medusan MacStinger points to the underlying "woman-as-predator theme," the implicit fear that women will overpower men and perhaps dominate them sexually (Steig 109).

On the other hand, that Edith returns the gaze also suggests that it is not only she who should be scrutinized, but someone else. Furthermore, if we take into account Richard Currie's argument that Florence's nurse Susan Nipper, who flashes her sharp black eyes at Dombey and subsequently "nips" him for neglecting his daughter (Dickens 589), is Florence's literary double, we realize that Florence (albeit indirectly) also returns the gaze (Currie 114). This resistance to the patriarchal gaze induces us to ask whether only the female characters ought to be observed and, upon even further reflection, whether the sexual guilt rests entirely within them. After all, Florence and Edith seem to be victims of the gaze more than anything else.

III

After chapter 47, the scrutinizing gaze shifts from the female characters onto Mr. Dombey, a transference that suggests that he—like Florence and Edith—excites censure and unease. Soon after Edith elopes with Carker and Florence runs into the streets, Dombey begins to suspect that "the world . . . watch[es] him eagerly wherever he goes" (682). When Cousin Feenix and

Major Bagstock visit him, for example, "he feels that the world is looking at him out of their eyes. That it is in the stares of the pictures. That Mr. Pitt, upon the bookcase, represents it. That there are eyes in its own map, hanging on the wall" (682). Browne's illustration of this passage certainly suggests that everybody's gaze is fixed on Dombey (fig. 3). Cousin Feenix and Bagstock focus on him, the eyes in the carpet look up at him, the bust of Mr. Pitt looks down at him, the vase beside Mr. Pitt stares at him accusingly, the strangely personified map watches him with its two enormous eyes, the portrait of the man glances at him curiously, and finally the portrait of his first wife peeps out from behind its covering. Steig also draws attention to the "staring miniature of little Paul" (103), the watchful heads and naked woman depicted on the fireplace (103), and the peering eyes in the peacock feathers (104). Meanwhile, Dombey glances down as if he is attempting to retreat from the panoptic gaze by "hid[ing] the world within him from the world without" (682). In a later illustration of Florence returning to her fallen father, Browne again suggests that the gaze focuses on Dombey (795; fig. 18). The watchful eyes of the first Mrs. Dombey are emphasized by the fact that a divider conceals the lower half of her face. Also, the grimacing male bust on the bookshelf implies the world's gaze in that a map of the world lies just behind it. Furthermore, the narrative itself no longer shields Dombey from scrutiny; as Audrey Jaffe notes, the "narrator might seem to resemble the intrusive public world that haunts Dombey after the scandal of Edith's departure and the bankruptcy of the firm" (71). We are finally invited behind the closed doors where he privately releases his feelings; we learn that he suffers "in agony, in sorrow, in remorse, [and] in despair" (795). He fears "that all [the] intricacy in his brain w[ill] drive him mad; and that his thoughts [have] already lost coherence" (797), he weeps alone "upon the bare boards, in the dead of night," and he even contemplates suicide (798).

Dombey's cruelty toward Florence, his bankruptcy, and his subsequent shame are obvious explanations for this shift in focus onto him. Yet, from the very beginning of the novel, there are intimations that he is concealing something. This is suggested by his inordinate need for privacy. He "turn[s] the key, pac[ing] up and down [his] room in solitary wretchedness (20); he sits in "the dark distance . . . as if he were a lone prisoner in a cell" (25); he feels that Florence "watche[s] and distrust[s] him. As if she held the clue to something *secret* in his breast, of the nature of which he was hardly informed himself. As if she had an innate knowledge of one jarring and discordant string within him, and her very breath could sound it" (31; my emphasis); and he opens his first wife's letter, the contents of which are never revealed, behind a locked door (49). Dombey also resents that Mr. Toodle wears a black mourning band in memory of little Paul, feeling that it is an egregious invasion of privacy: "To think that he dared to enter . . . into the trial and disappointment of a proud man's *secret* heart, . . . having crept into the place wherein he would have lorded [his feeling], alone'' (275; my emphasis). With these repeated allusions to a secret, we cannot help but wonder what Dombey is hiding from the ''world without'' (682).[19]

The scrutinizing gaze does not shift until chapter 47 because up until this point the novel is still concerned about shielding Dombey from public scrutiny. As Anthea Trodd writes, ''an Asmodean desire to raise the roofs and examine the secret crimes which may be festering beyond the reach of public opinion conflicts with the emphasis on the need to keep the home as a sacred space, inviolable by the external world and under no external surveillance'' (4). When Dombey strikes Florence across the breast, however, he disbands his claims for privacy, for he publicizes his secret by imprinting it on her body; a ''darkening mark [appears] upon her bosom'' (655). Dombey's anger toward Florence, and therefore his reason for striking her, seems to stem largely from his secret feelings of unmanly impotence. From his patriarchal perspective, she is ''merely a piece of base coin that couldn't be invested—a bad Boy—nothing more'' (Dickens 3). That he engenders something of so little (perceived) value implicitly signals his debilitated manhood (Zwinger 429). Dombey also traces his exclusion from the female sphere (which hints at his inability to penetrate it) back to Florence. When reflecting upon how his first wife died in Florence's embrace, for instance, ''he [cannot] forget that he had had no part in it . . . he stood on the bank above them, looking down a mere spectator—not a sharer with them—quite shut out'' (31). Florence's close ties with his second wife also enervate Dombey because she influences Edith when he cannot:

> Who was it who could win his wife as she had won his boy! Who was it who had shown him that new victory, as he sat in the dark corner! Who was it whose least word did what his utmost means could not! . . . Who could it be, but the same child at whom he had often glanced uneasily in her motherless infancy . . . [and now] hate[d] . . . in his heart.   (539)

Dombey ruminates in this way when frustrated with Edith for not submitting to him sexually (see below). When Dombey strikes Florence, then, he broadcasts his private misgiving that he can neither dominate a woman nor satisfy one sexually. In so doing, he attracts the attention of the novel's panopticon as well as the reader's curiosity. It is at this point especially that ''the question of policing [moves] out of the streets, as it were, into the closet'' (Miller viii–ix).

Throughout *Dombey and Son*, there are a number of discreet allusions to Dombey's neutered sexuality. Nina Auerbach draws attention to the phallic rhetoric used to describe him, suggesting that he is a figure of ''emphatic masculinity'' or ''inveterate phallicism'' (99). He is ''*stiff* and stark [like the] fire-irons'' (54; my emphasis), "his walk is . . . *erect*, [and] his bearing [is] as *stiff* as ever (236; my emphases). It seems to me, however, that Dombey is merely donning a phallic veneer or performing a manly masquerade in an attempt to communicate a normative sexuality—which is one of vigorous heterosexuality. His hardness is really frigidity, and there is certainly nothing coital or fecund about his icy remoteness. Indeed, "when he look[s] out . . . at the trees in the little garden, their brown and yellow leaves c[ome] fluttering down, as if he blighted them'' (54). After ten years of marriage and in an age when one had virtually no recourse to effective birth control (Pool 187), moreover, he has begotten only two children. His formal demeanor around the first Mrs. Dombey indicates that there has been little intimacy between them; even though she has just given birth, he still formally addresses her as Mrs. Dombey (1). There is even the suggestion that his first wife was dissatisfied with him. In Dickens's manuscript version of the novel, Dombey discovers a private letter in his wife's writing-desk, and after carefully perusing it, he subsequently destroys it:

> He read it slowly and attentively, and with a nice particularity to every syllable. Otherwise than as his great deliberation seemed unnatural, and perhaps the result of an effort equally great, he allowed no emotion to escape him. When he had read it through, he folded and refolded it slowly several times, and tore it carefully into fragments.   (49)[20]

Though the contents of the letter are never disclosed, Dombey's peculiar response to it suggests that it is a letter from another lover or something of the kind, which, if the case, would imply his own sexual bankruptcy.[21] We have only to recall Browne's illustration "Joe B is sly Sir; devilish sly" to infer Dombey's sexual deficiency (fig. 19): a painting of Toby and the Widow Wadman (a reference to the man with the groin wound in Laurence Sterne's novel *Tristam Shandy*) is placed directly above his head.

During the time when little Paul physically wanes and then eventually dies—which again intimates Dombey's impotence insofar as he cannot produce a hardy boy—Dombey becomes acquainted with Major Bagstock, a man whose sexuality is as voracious and undiscriminating as his appetite. Dickens conveys Bagstock's ithyphallic permanency by means of barely veiled sexual language. The Major walks "with his cheeks *swelling* over his tight *stock*, his legs majestically wide apart, and his *great head wagging* from side to side'' (280). Also, his apoplectic fits of laughter remind us of an ejaculating penis: "his whole form, but especially his face and head, *dilated* beyond all former experience; and presented to [his servant's] view, nothing but a *heaving mass of indigo* . . . and when that was a little better *burst* into such *ejaculations* . . . ''(130; my emphases). In the illustrations, moreover, Bagstock's walking-stick always figures prominently and significantly points out rather than down (figs. 3, 20). Bagstock's vigorous sexuality has been noted by a number of critics (cf. Marsh 413), but, most notably, Steven Marcus writes:

> Dickens uses a variety of means to communicate to the reader the intense, disturbed, and corrupted sexuality of the Major; from his very name, which conceals a sexual pun, to the descriptions of him swilling hot spiced drinks and then swelling apoplectically and turning red and blue, to his frequent reference to the old "Bagstock breed," there is no doubt what Dickens had in mind.
>
> (110)

In Bagstock, it seems, Dombey finds a "perpetual cock-stand" who bolsters his own flagging sexuality (Marcus 234). It is the Major in fact who first introduces Dombey to his second wife, Edith. Without his encouragement and prompting, we may wonder whether Dombey would ever have remarried.

Significantly, Dombey's sexuality seems to wane after he marries Edith and visits with Bagstock less frequently. The Dombeys return from their honeymoon in Paris, for instance, claiming that the city was "cold" and "dull" (480). If they have even consummated their marriage, it is clear that they have not derived any pleasure from being sexually intimate. When Dombey later insists on sexual acquiescence from Edith, moreover, she altogether refuses (cf. Jackson 123). Dombey, resolving "to show her that he [is] supreme," enters his wife's room late in the evening insisting that "there is no time like the present . . . [he is] used to choos[ing his] own times; not to have them chosen for [him]" (540). Edith responds by folding her arms across her breast and looking away, signalling her sexual unavailability (540). "It seems you do not understand," she says, "that each of us shall take a separate course . . . I feel no tenderness towards you" (544–45). A later comment made by Carker also clearly indicates that Edith refuses Dombey sexually. When Edith also resists his sexual advances, Carker says, "Do you think to frighten me with these tricks of virtue . . . Do you mistake me for your husband?" (723). It becomes clear, then, that Dombey cannot control a woman sexually.[22] Browne's illustration "Mr. Dombey and the World" visually recapitulates Dombey's sexual deficiency (fig. 3). As Steig writes, "the withered and drooping flowers are suggestions of sexual impotence, while the Major's way of gesturing with his stick seems aggressively phallic in contrast to Dombey's present languidness" (103). The peacock feathers "hanging down instead of erectly" also intimate Dombey's impotent marriages, recalling the bird-like Edith and also Dombey's first wife insofar as one feather just lightly touches her portrait (104).

While the novel pointedly suggests that Dombey is sexually impotent, it also implies that he is profoundly male-identified. He is intently preoccupied with patriarchal lineage, masculinizes Mrs. Toodle by changing her name to Richards (18; Auerbach 99), feels excluded from the female sphere, separates the sexes by dividing the house into two spheres (253; Surridge 81), and attacks Florence's femininity by striking her breast; all of these actions reveal a man deeply troubled by the female principle and entirely absorbed by his patriarchal vision. Indeed, Dombey seems most comfortable when walking arm in arm with Bagstock or dining with him and Carker:

> Mr. Dombey, who had been so long shut up within himself . . . began to think this [his friendship with the Major] an improvement on his solitary life; and in place of excusing himself for another day, as her thought of doing when alone, walked out with the Major arm in arm. (280)

In her seminal work *Between Men*, Eve Kosofsky Sedgwick hypothesizes a contiguous relationship between the homosocial and the homosexual: "To draw the 'homosocial' back into the orbit of 'desire,' of the potentially erotic, then, is to hypothesize the potential unbrokenness of a continuum between homosocial and homosexual" (1). Drawing on Sedgwick's argument, we can see how Dombey's close friendships with Carker and Bagstock may incline toward the homoerotic.

There are a number of pointed innuendoes to Carker's and Bagstock's deviant sexuality, which in turn suggests Dombey's insofar as he associates with them both. Carker, with his "sleek look," "soft hand," and "smooth face," is the epitome of the "effeminate sodomite" (Elfenbein 208). He even admits to Bagstock that he plays a little backgammon, an activity that may seem harmless enough, until we realise that backgammon is a Victorian euphemism for sodomy (367; Pearsall 411). According to Fred Kaplan, moreover, there are "latent sexual implications" in Rob the Grinder's mesmerically induced submission to Carker (197). Bagstock also displays not-so-covert homosexual proclivities. He intimates, for example, that he was called "Flower" in his military days: "A man never heard of Bagstock . . . in those days; he heard of the Flower—the Flower of Ours. The Flower may have faded . . . but it is a tough plant yet, and constant as the evergreen" (356). In 1833, W. Bankes, a Member of Parliament, "was discovered and accused of 'standing behind the screen of a place for making water against Westminster Abbey walls, in company with a soldier named Flower, and of having been surprised with his breeches and braces unbuttoned at ten at night, his companion's dress being in similar disorder'" (Pearsall 450; cf. Elfenbein 210). Surely, there is little doubt what Dickens had in mind, especially considering that there are many other veiled references to the Major's homosexual inclinations. When Bagstock recounts his boyhood experiences at a public school, for instance, insisting that "none but the tough fellows could live through it . . . we put each other to the torture there" (128), he may likely be referring to the homoerotic initiation games played by the students (Pearsall 452–54;

Sedgwick 176). Furthermore, when Susan Nipper, referring to the Major, insists that she "would have natural-coloured friends, or none," she may not only be disparaging his unusual apoplectic hue, but also his "unnatural" predilections (250). Finally, when the Major "thrust[s] his cane among the Native's ribs, and continue[s] to stir him at close intervals . . . " (362), "using him as a counter-irritant against the gout, and all other physical vexations, mental as well as bodily" (362–63), we suspect that the Major demands sexual services from his servant. Is it not significant that Dickens insisted that Browne depict "the Native evidently afraid of the Major and his thick cane" in "Major Bagstock is delighted to have that opportunity" (Dickens qtd. in Horsman 838; fig. 21)?

Dombey is clearly the principal character in Dickens's novel about pride. Dickens's initial plan for the novel, which presents Dombey as the main protagonist, Dombey's position of prominence on the monthly wrapper, which depicts him as an enthroned patriarch (fig. 8), and Dombey's enormous influence on the lives of Mrs. Toodle, Rob the Grinder, Miss Tox, Florence, and Edith all suggest the primacy of his character. If his struggles are central to the novel, does it not follow that uneasiness about his deviant sexuality, rather than that of Florence or Edith, is really at the heart of *Dombey and Son*? That the narrator titillates us all throughout with allusions to Dombey's secrets certainly intimates that the desire to investigate him drives the novel's surveillance. But, if he is the real target of all this anxious spying, why does the novel deny its own surveillance for the first 47 chapters through a series of complex displacements? Anxiety about Dombey's sexuality seems to be initially deflected onto Florence and Edith, manifesting itself as concern about illicit female sexuality. The narrative clearly expresses anxiety about deviant femininity, but this seems somehow secondary to its uneasiness about Dombey. I think that there are at least two ways to account for the novel's denial of its true surveillance. First of all, as mentioned before, concern about an individual's privacy initially shields Dombey from the novel's gaze. "Dickens would have liked to see the narrator and panoptic observer as a 'good spirit,'" Trodd writes, "he was also aware that to intrude on secrets concealed beneath the roof of a private house is to incur suspicion of being a spy" (5). Women were not privileged with such claims to privacy, however, because of the proliferating concern throughout the nineteenth century about female fallenness, adultery, and deviance (Nead 48–52).[23] *Dombey and Son*, therefore, relieves the pressure of its surveillance by focusing on the more observable female characters. It is only when Dombey strikes Florence and inadvertently publicizes his sexual guilt that the gaze finally intrudes upon his privacy.

A Foucauldian reading also illuminates our understanding of the novel's complex displacements. In *The History of Sexuality*, Michel Foucault argues that the discourse on sex, until Freud, concealed and evaded its true concerns:

> The learned discourse on sex that was pronounced in the nineteenth century
> was imbued with . . . systematic blindness: a refusal to see and to understand;
> but further—and this is the crucial point—a refusal concerning the very thing
> that was brought to light and whose formulation was urgently solicited . . . E-
> vading this truth, barring access to it, masking it: these were the many local
> tactics which, as if by superimposition and through a last-minute detour, gave
> a paradoxical form to a fundamental petition to know.   (55)

The insistent observation of the female characters, then, can be viewed as an
elaborate evasion that masks and conceals "the unbearable, too hazardous
truth" about Dombey's sexual perversions (Foucault 53). In the Victorian
period, male-male sex particularly was "the locus of scandals considered so
heinous as to be designated unspeakable" (Cohen 75). In Dickens's novel,
Dombey's secrets are only finally divulged—and indirectly at that—when
Dombey himself symbolically imprints them on Florence's bosom. In *Byron
and the Victorians*, Stephen Elfenbein argues that Byron's poetics of intro-
spection and secrecy were a way to describe his homosexuality; perhaps,
Dickens's novel similarly employs the evasions of secrecy to imply Dombey's
sexual alterity. As William Cohen writes in *Sex Scandal: The Private Parts
of Victorian Fiction*, "silence about sexuality composes a strategic form, not
an absence, of representation" (2).

In *Dombey and Son*, almost everyone is subject to the scrutinizing
gaze—the minor figures, such as Miss Tox, Sol Gills, and Captain Cuttle, as
well as the principal characters, including Florence and Edith and later Dombey. Invoking "the good spirit" to take "the house-tops off," the narrator
discloses the sexual perversions which lurk behind seemly facades (620).
Florence and Edith, on the one hand, are predominately identified with the
fallen woman, who was perceived as a threat to England's moral purity.
Dombey, on the other hand, is described as sexually impotent and peculiarly
male-identified. The fact that the female characters are relentlessly scrutinized
suggests an underlying misogynous subtext; however, the novel also exposes
Dombey's debilitated and deviant sexuality, thus qualifying, though not entirely canceling, our earlier impression. Since the novel so clearly centers on
Dombey, his secrets, and his inner struggle, it seems likely that uneasiness
about his sexuality is the novel's overarching concern. In other words, the
real sexual perversions of the novel lie within Dombey, as well as Carker
and Bagstock. It is anxiety about male sexuality, therefore, which actually
drives the surveillance of transgressive female sexuality. With the raising of
the house tops, a truth so unexpected and hazardous emerges that the novel
first feels the need to conceal and deny it, almost as if it would have really
preferred to keep Dombey in the closet.

NOTES

I am indebted to Lisa Surridge and Mary Carpenter for their advice and direction during various stages of this paper.

1. The panopticon was largely imaginary; in Britain, for instance, it was never actually incorporated into prison architecture.
2. Dickens's first biographer, John Forster, indicates that the author worked closely with his illustrator: "even beyond what is ordinary between author and illustrator, [Dickens's] requirements were exacting" (364). When writing his serialized novel *Dombey and Son*, Dickens would often, although not always, send lengthy letters to Browne, specifying which scenes he wanted illustrated and which details he wished emphasized. Occasionally, Browne had a copy of the text from which he could work, but often he could only rely on Dickens's notes (Forster 364–69).
3. This informal, but all-pervasive regime of surveillance evinces what D. A. Miller in *The Novel and the Police* calls "the radical entanglement between the nature of the novel and the practice of the police" (2); according to Miller, the nineteenth-century novel, "systematically participates in a general economy of policing power" which is ultimately conservative in its enterprise (2).
4. Florence has, surprisingly, received a considerable amount of negative attention from Dickens scholars. Sylvère Monod accuses Florence of "sentimental blackmail" because Dombey apparently surrenders to her loving affection at the end of the novel (qtd. in Zwinger 432), and Julian Moynahan, in even stronger language, suggests that Florence is "in at the kill" (125) hoping "to get Dombey's head down on the pillow where she can drown him in a dissolving love" (126). This denunciatory attitude on the part of the critics, as Lynda Zwinger points out, problematically duplicates Dombey's attitude toward his daughter (434). These critics, in other words, repeat the novel's misogyny; they respond to the novel's subtle inferences that Florence is (potentially) guilty of transgressive sexual behavior and, therefore, must be carefully watched.
5. This metonymic connection between Florence and the bird is substantiated by the fact that she is later likened to a "bird in a cage" hunted by the catlike Carker (304) and that her step-mother, Edith, affectionately calls her a bird (484, 585).
6. Although Mulvey (as well as Kaplan and hooks) analyses the cinematic gaze, her observations also illuminate our understanding of the operations of the gaze in literature. In that her essay examines a general condition of Western patriarchy—patriarchy's tendency to subject women to a controlling look—her theory pertains to a number of artistic mediums.
7. Throughout the novel, Diogenes frequently comes to Florence's rescue. When Carker begins to show an interest in her, for instance, Diogenes "regardless of all soothing, barks and growls, and makes at him . . . , as if he would spring down and tear him limb from limb" (310). In the illustration where Carker introduces himself to Florence, moreover, an angry dog symbolically representing Diogenes appears to be chasing him (fig. 10). Later, Diogenes faithfully follows Florence when she flees from her father and runs into the streets (638).

8. From 1846 to 1858, Dickens established and managed Urania Cottage, a shelter for fallen women and prostitutes, with Miss Angela Burdett Coutts (Anderson 66–77). Many of his novels also demonstrate a concern for fallen women. In *David Copperfield*, for instance, he sympathizes with Martha and Little Emily, who fall victim to heartless seducers. In *Bleak House*, he never completely denounces Lady Dedlock, though she married for wealth and rank without informing her husband of her fallenness. Even in *Dombey and Son*, he suggests that the fall is socially and economically determined (Anderson 68). At the same time, however, it is evident that Dickens feels a certain uneasiness about female sexual transgression, for Martha becomes associated with the polluted Thames, Lady Dedlock becomes subject to Tulkinghorn's and Bucket's investigating gaze, and Florence also becomes subject to the scrutinizing male gaze.

9. The novel represents Florence's flight into the streets and subsequent encounter with the shady Mrs. Brown as doubly transgressive, not only linking her impːitly to street prostitutes, but also suggesting her class infraction. In her encounter with Mrs. Brown, where she is forced to don tattered clothes, Florence momentarily falls from her class station; in her "altered state," she is even mistaken for a street person (76). Florence's (symbolic) sexual transgression, therefore, becomes especially threatening because she disrupts the intersecting social boundaries of sex and class. Significantly, it is in this "altered state" that she meets Walter, the lower-class clerk in her father's firm whom she eventually marries. This circumstance may suggest the novel's anxiety about Florence's alliance with Walter, an anxiety which is only resolved with the fulfillment of the Dick Wittingdon plot where Walter eventually earns wealth and station through his imperial ventures.

10. Alice Mar/wood's sexual transgression is revealed in her very name.

11. As Butt and Tillotson point out, Dickens still intended for Edith to fall when he wrote this chapter. It was not until after he had written it and received Lord Jeffrey's letter, stating that he "positively refuse[d] to believe that Edith [was] Carker's mistress," that Dickens contemplated the "inverted Maid's Tragedy" (Dickens, qtd. in Forster 373; Butt and Tillotson 106).

12. Butt and Tillotson explain Dickens's change of mind in more detail: "All was ready for Number XV (chapters xlvi-xlviii), but in the original plan 'The Thunderbolt' would have fallen last, making the number conclude with Florence's stricken flight, but not its destination and consolation. The serial reader would then have remained in horrified suspense through December 1847. But as the chapter was written first, Dickens had time to change his mind; 'to leave a pleasanter impression on the reader' (had he perhaps the Christmas season on his mind?) he pushed this chapter back into the middle place, and added the chapter (xlvii) which shows Florence safely under Captain Cuttle's protection" (107).

13. Amanda Anderson correctly draws attention to Dombey's "solipsistic unreadability," suggesting that "the narrative actively shields Dombey even as it shows him to be rigidly unfeeling" (87). Dombey, however, becomes increasingly readable after chapter 47, when the gaze shifts from the female characters onto him, and he is exposed to public scrutiny.

14. As with Alice Mar/wood, Edith's sexual guilt is implied in her (maiden) name: Skewton.
15. Carker does not eroticize Florence to the same extent that he does Edith. With respect to her physical features, he merely says that she has "a very good face" (304).
16. In this scene, one could argue, Carker acts as surrogate for the voyeuristic reader. As he hides behind the tree watching Edith unobserved, so we, reading privately in our "hermetically sealed world," penetrate Edith's secrets with every word we read on the page (Mulvey 17). Of course, we can resist aligning ourselves with the sadistic element of the gaze, but we cannot entirely deny the fact that we, by the very act of reading, become like Peeping Toms.
17. This sentence was later deleted in the first proof.
18. In *The Location of Culture*, Bhabha suggests that there is always the threat that the colonial mimic will return the disciplinary gaze of the colonizer. His concept of the returned gaze—albeit articulated as a moment of colonial menace—can also explain the mechanics of the gendered gaze. hooks, in fact, uses a similar argument to describe the resistant gaze of the black female spectator.
19. Dickens was forced to cut this scene at the first proof stage because the number was overwritten by a few pages. Forster admits that this cut, among others, was "not without much disadvantage" as it showed "something of the struggle with itself that such pride must always go through" (364–65; cf. Butt and Tillotson 97).
20. That Dombey's first wife is named Fanny, a popular Victorian euphemism for female genitalia (Pearsall 412), may also imply the illicit nature of the letter.
21. The narrator also refers to horse-back riding to suggest Dombey's sexual inadequacy: while Carker is a "good horseman" (576; cf. 343 and fig. 10), Dombey rides "with very long stirrups, and a very loose rein, and very rarely look[s] down to see where his [horse goes]" (576).
22. In Mary Elizabeth Braddon's novel *Lady Audley's Secret* (1861–62), for instance, Robert Audley feels reluctant about investigating Lucy Audley's infamous past, not because he respects her privacy, but because he wants to shield her husband (his uncle) and the family name from public scandal.

WORKS CITED

Anderson, Amanda. *Tainted Souls and Painted Faces. The Rhetoric of Fallenness in Victorian Culture*. Ithaca: Cornell UP, 1993.

Auerbach, Nina. "Dickens and Dombey: A Daughter After All." *Dickens Studies Annual* 5 (1976): 95–114.

Bhabha, Homi K. *The Location of Culture*. London: Routledge, 1994.

Braddon, Mary Elizabeth. *Lady Audley's Secret*. Ed. David Skilton. Oxford: Oxford UP, 1987.

Cohen, Jane R. *Charles Dickens and his Original Illustrators*. Columbus: Ohio State UP, 1980.

Cohen, William A. *Sex Scandals: The Private Parts of Victorian Fiction*. Durham and London: Duke UP, 1996.

Dickens, Charles. *Bleak House*. Ed. Norman Page. Middlesex: Penguin, 1986.

———. *David Copperfield*. Ed. Trevor Blount. London: Penguin, 1985.

———. *Dombey and Son*. Ed. Alan Horsman. Oxford: Clarendon, 1974.

Elfendein, Stephen. *Byron and the Victorians*. Cambridge: Cambridge UP, 1995.

Forster, John. *The Life of Charles Dickens*. London: Chapman and Hall, 1878.

Foucault, Michel. *The History of Sexuality*. Trans. Robert Hurley. Vol. 1. New York: Vintage, 1980.

———. *Discipline and Punish: The Birth of the Prison*. Trans. Alan Sheridan. New York: Vintage, 1979.

Gaskell, Elizabeth. *Ruth*. Ed. Alan Shelston. Oxford: Oxford UP, 1985.

Gitter, Elisabeth G. "The Power of Women's Hair in the Victorian Imagination." *PMLA* 99 (1989): 936–54.

hooks, bell. *Black Looks: Race and Representation*. Toronto: Between the Lines, 1992.

Jackson, Arlene M. "Reward, Punishment, and the Conclusion of *Dombey and Son*." *Dickens Studies Annual* (1978): 103–127.

Jaffe, Audrey. *Vanishing Points. Dickens, Narrative, and the Subject of Omniscience*. Berkeley: U of California P, 1991.

Kaplan, E. Ann. *Women and Film: Both Sides of the Camera*. New York: Methuen, 1983.

———. *Looking for the Other: Feminism and the Imperial Gaze*. London: Routledge, 1997.

Kaplan, Fred. *Dickens and Mesmerism*. Princeton: Princeton UP, 1975.

Marcus, Steven. *The Other Victorians. A Study of Pornography in Mid-Nineteenth-Century England*. New York: Basic Books, 1966.

Marsh, Joss Lutz. "Good Mrs. Brown's Connections: Sexuality and Story-Telling in *Dealings with the Firm of Dombey and Son*." *ELH* 58 (1991): 405–26.

McClintock, Anne. *Imperial Leather: Race, Gender and Sexuality in the Colonial Contest*. London: Routledge, 1995.

Miller, D.A. *The Novel and the Police*. Berkeley: U of California P, 1988.

Mulvey, Laura. *Visual and Other Pleasures.* London: Macmillan, 1989.

Nead, Lynda. *Myths of Sexuality. Representations of Women in Victorian Britain.* Oxford: Basil Blackwell, 1988.

Nunokawa, Jeff. *Macropolitics of Nineteenth-Century Literature: Nationalisn, Exoticism, Imperalism.* Ed. Jonathan Arac and Harriet Ritvo. Philadelphia: U of Pennsylvania P, 1991.

Pearsall, Ronald. *The Worm in the Bud. The World of Victorian Sexuality.* London: Pimlico, 1993.

Pool, Daniel. *What Jane Austen Ate and Charles Dickens Knew.* New York: Touchstone, 1993.

Sedgwick, Eve Kosofsky. *Between Men: English Literature and Male Homosocial Desire.* New York: Columbia UP, 1985.

Stanhope, J. R. Spencer. *Thoughts of the Past.* Tate Gallery, London. Plate 24.

Steig, Michael. *Dickens and Phiz.* Bloomington: Indiana UP, 1978.

Surridge, Lisa. "Domestic Violence, Female Self-Mutilation, and the Healing of the Male in *Dombey and Son.*" *Victorians Institute Journal* 25 (1997): 3–23.

Trodd, Anthea. *Domestic Crime in the Victorian Novel.* London: Macmillan, 1989.

Welsh, Alexander. *From Copyright to Copperfield. The Identity of Dickens.* Cambridge: Harvard UP, 1987.

Zwinger, Lynda. "The Fear of the Father: Dombey and Daughter." *Nineteenth-Century Fiction* 39 (1985): 420–40.

Fig. 1. Poor Paul's Friend

Fig. 2. Mr. Toots becomes particular—Diogenes also

Fig. 3. Mr. Dombey and the World

Fig. 4. Solemn reference is made to Mr. Bunsby

Fig. 5. A Visitor of Distinction

Fig. 6. The eyes of Mrs. Chick are opened to Lucretia Tox

Fig 7. Coming home from Church

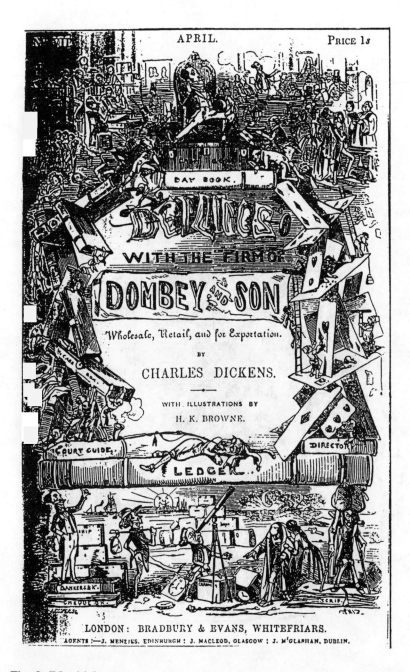

Fig. 8. [No title]

Fig. 9. Miss Tox pays a visit to the Toodle Family

Fig. 10. Mr. Carker introduces himself to Florence and the Skettles family

Fig. 11. Florence and Edith on the staircase

Fig. 12. J. R. Spencer Stanhope, *Thoughts of the Past*, Tate Gallery, London

Fig. 13. A Chance Meeting

Fig. 14. Mr. Dombey and his "confidential agent"

Fig. 15. Mr. Carker in his hour of triumph

Fig. 16. The Midshipman is boarded by the enemy

Fig. 17. Another Wedding

Fig. 18. ''Let him remember it in that room, years to come!''

Fig. 19. Joe B is sly, Sir; devilish sly.

Fig. 20. [No title]

Fig. 21. Major Bagstock is delighted to have the opportunity

Dickens and Disgust

Annette R. Federico

Despite his moral intentions, low comedy, or social satire, Dickens apparently possessed a genius for generating images that many of his contemporaries found disgusting. His unrestrained descriptions of slime and blood, rottenness and smells, bodily excretions and fleshy explosions frequently offended Victorian sensibilities. Dickens's novels invite a vivid appraisal of the nature of disgust for the Victorian imagination. This is a potentially important subject, according to William Ian Miller's The Anatomy of Disgust *(1997), because disgust implicates a culture's moral sensibility, its politics, and its social institutions. Charles Darwin was the first to theorize formally about disgust in* The Expression of the Emotions in Man and Animals *(1871). His acceptance of all emotions as subjects for analysis is similar to Dickens's virtual celebration of even the most loathsome aspects of physical life. Drawing on the work of anthropologist Mary Douglas, this essay argues that in his graphic evocations of human viscosity, slime, and scum, Dickens is an agent for change, an advocate of disproportion and anomalousness in a culture that cherishes order and symmetry.*

Another peculiarity of Dickens is his taste for nastiness. We do not mean that he tells dirty stories, or makes dirty jokes. Far from it. He is too much a man of the day to give in to anything of the kind. Yet he has a marvellous liking for whatever is physically offensive. He gloats over mould, damp, rottenness, and smells. . . . In the same way, he loves to dwell on the peculiarities in his characters. Thus, in *Bleak House* we have a disgusting lawyer with black gloves always picking the pimples on his face. The same story supplies one of the most unpardonably nauseous descriptions

Dickens Studies Annual, Volume 29, Copyright © 2000 by AMS Press, Inc. All rights reserved.

which ever disfigured a work of fiction. The details of the
spontaneous combustion of the miser Krook are positively
loathsome. Anything more sickening or revolting we
never read.

—James Augustine Stothert, 1854

James Stothert's 1854 article in *The Rambler* is more or less representative
of many Victorian readers' reactions to *Bleak House*, and indeed to Dickens's
somewhat grotesque artistic sensibility altogether. Although many more readers certainly admired Dickens for presenting eccentricities without "resorting
to what is profane, coarse, or indecent," to cite another critic of 1854 (Collins
295), others felt that he simply exhibited ugliness for its own sake. "His
choice of odious characters offer too frequently a disgusting picture of life,"
wrote a reviewer in *Blackwood's* in 1848. "[T]he vice of [some characters]
is disgusting" (Collins 231). Another reviewer for *Bentley's Miscellany* complained that unnatural characters "painted with a sickening minuteness" are
"simply revolting" (Collins 288). Even Walter Bagehot, in an influential
assessment of Dickens's novels published in 1858, admitted that Dickens's
range is so varied that the reader passes from "extreme admiration" to
"something like disgust" in a matter of moments (Collins 391).

Dickens's novels certainly invite a vivid appraisal of the nature of disgust
for the Victorian imagination. This is, potentially, an important subject, since,
according to William Ian Miller in *The Anatomy of Disgust*, disgust implicates
a culture's moral sensibility, its politics, and social institutions (x). While
conscientiously delineating these separate cultural domains, Miller insistently
argues that disgust is almost always about the corruptible body, and, inevitably, about human life, the "necessary consequence of our consciousness
itself—fat, greasy, teeming, rank, festering, viscous life" (21). *The Rambler*
reviewer of *Bleak House* objects to Dickens's taste for "mould, damp, rottenness, and smells," but as Miller emphasizes, such sensory perceptions are
crucial to disgust. "Disgust uses images of sensation or suggests the sensory
merely by describing the disgusting thing so as to capture what makes it
disgusting. We. . . talk of how our senses are offended, of stenches that make
us retch, of tactile sensations of slime, ooze" (9). Thus the emotion of disgust
is vitally important "in structuring our world and our stance towards the
world" (Miller 18), and the powerful "image-generating capacities" of disgust play an important role in organizing and internalizing collective moral
and social attitudes (18). Of course Dickens was a genius at generating images, including images of bodies which some of his contemporaries found
disgusting, despite his moral intentions, social satire, or low comedy. And
indeed, slime, ooze, and viscosity seem to be the primary sources of disgust
for Victorian readers of Dickens's novels. Particularly offensive are graphic
descriptions of the body's excretions, excrescences, and explosions.

Given the apparent materiality of the body for Dickens's readers, it is interesting to remark how some modern critics have suggested that the body in Dickens is repressed in his narratives.[1] Elana Gomel, for example, sees the body in Dickens as synecdochic: Carker's teeth, Jaggers's finger, and Silas Wegg's leg gain symbolic power by absorbing "the aggressive and erotic potential of the whole body, which it 'carves' into isolated parts" (49). Incorporating a discussion of Freud's theory of the castration complex, Gomel reads Bradley Headstone in *Our Mutual Friend* and Carker in *Dombey and Son* as "feminized" by "synecdochic dismemberment": "the male body is 'cancelled' by the force of excessive desire, and what is left—the head—hints at the ultimate feminization of castration" (52–53). Other critics, such as Timothy Clark and Nicholas Royle, offer interpretations of the body inspired by deconstruction and postmodern philosophy. Clark reads Dickens through Maurice Blanchot's view of the image, concluding that Dickens is ultimately anti-idealistic, his novels nightmares of "non-signifying materiality" (36). And in Royle's clever essay on *Our Mutual Friend*, bodies are figures, texts, always mysterious, encrypted, disintegrating, copreous (39–53). Similarly, Dennis W. Allen has suggested that the bodies in *Bleak House* are virtually non-present, that "the corporeal scarcely exists," and "the body . . . becomes a sign whose materiality vanishes into its signifying form" (92–94).

These interpretations are compelling. Yet surely the body in fiction existed for Victorian readers, and it apparently evoked pungent emotions. Victorian critics who found Dickens nauseating were responding not to gaps and fetishes, figures and signifiers, but to some image that was viscerally present to their imaginations. Krook's body certainly "vanishes," and Dickens is not subtle about its "signifying" the corruption of Chancery. But Krook's body also occupies a corporeal form in the text that may be read quite literally. Reduced to a "thick yellow liquid . . . which is offensive to the touch and sight and more offensive to the smell," Krook becomes a "stagnant, sickening oil, with some natural repulsion" (it makes poor Mr. Guppy shudder), a "smouldering, suffocating vapour . . . a dark greasy coating on the walls and ceiling." Krook "drips and creeps away down the bricks" and "lies in a little thick nauseous pool" (*Bleak House* 402–03). Indeed, Hablot K. Browne's illustration of Krook's death in chapter 32 of *Bleak House* does not stress its symbolic reference to Chancery as much as Guppy's and Jobling's expressions of horror and disgust in their awful confrontation with the stuff that was Krook.

Far from treating the body as an abstraction, Dickens frequently offers sensual representations of the physical. The description of Krook's demise may reasonably be called "sickening or revolting," but note that for *The Rambler* reviewer, Krook's death is only slightly more disgusting than those scenes in which the lawyer Mr. Vholes appears, picking at his pimples.

Vholes, with his "cold-blooded, gasping, fish-like manner" (541), is explicitly associated with cannibals and vampires (483, 720), and is indeed often seen "feeling the pimples on his face as if they were ornaments" (720). Or, more chromatically: "Mr. Vholes . . . secretly picked at one of the red pimples on his yellow face with his black glove" (541).

Other characters from Dickens's novels might also elicit disgust in sensitive readers. In *Dombey and Son*, Major Bagstock, who suffers from "apoplectic symptoms," frequently excretes, and is sometimes on the verge of exploding altogether (348). Major Bagstock (whose name is a sexual pun [page 152]), is often about to erupt—he "swelled and swelled, exceedingly" (347)—and usually in conjunction with moods of lust or gluttony. "The Major being by this time in a state of repletion, with essence of savoury pie oozing out at the corners of his eyes, and devilled grill and kidneys tightening his cravat" looks like a "leering . . . choking . . . over-fed Mephistopheles" (350). He is in this state virtually throughout the novel: "The Major . . . swelled, and swelled, and rolled his purple face about and winked his lobster eye, until he fell into a fit of wheezing" (445). Major Bagstock recalls the dreadful Captain Murderer from Dickens's "Nurse's Stories" (1860) who blows up after eating his murdered wife's body in a poisoned pie: "he began to swell, and to turn blue, and to be all over spots and to scream. And he went on swelling and turning bluer, and being more all over spots and screaming, until he reached from floor to ceiling and from wall to wall; and then at one o'clock in the morning, he blew up with a loud explosion" (*Uncommercial Traveller* 162).

Other characters are less explosive, but still seepy and rather disgusting. The unctuous Uriah Heep, from *David Copperfield*, is a fellow whose "clammy hand" evokes physical repulsion in young David, as does his reptilian body: "He had a way of writhing . . . which was very ugly," and he exhibits "snaky twistings of his throat and body" (292). Uriah Heep is consistently portrayed as sweaty, slippery, and slimy, and he has a powerful hold on David's imagination. He thinks of Heep as a "convulsive fish" and a "red-headed animal . . . [who] seemed to swell and grow before my eyes" (441). In a well-known scene, David watches Uriah asleep on his back "with his legs extending to I don't know where, gurglings taking place in his throat, stoppages in his nose, and his mouth open like a post-office. He was so much worse than in my distempered fancy that afterwards I was attracted to him in very repulsion" (443–44).

Perhaps *Our Mutual Friend* is the novel most readers have found too visceral for comfort, dealing as it does with heaps of refuse, as well as with drowned, dismembered, and swollen corpses. This novel introduces another character on the verge of violent discharges, the passionate lower-class schoolmaster Bradley Headstone, who had "enough of what was animal, and of what was fiery (though smouldering) still visible in him'' (267). Bradley Headstone explodes, in a way, but unlike the other characters I have mentioned, he does not ooze; he bleeds. In the homicidal love scene in chapter 15 of book 2, he brings ''his clenched hand down upon [a stone wall] with a force that laid the knuckles raw and bleeding'' and then stands before Lizzie Hexam, the woman he desires, holding out ''his smeared hand as if it held some weapon'' (457). Later he lifts his bleeding hand to his mouth and then wipes it on his sleeve (457). More significantly, Bradley Headstone bleeds spontaneously from an orifice. When ''a great spirt of blood burst from his nose,'' he cannot explain his body's betrayal: '''I can't keep it back. It has happened twice—three times—four times—I don't know how many times—since last night. I taste it, smell it, see it, it chokes me, and then it breaks out like this''' (704).

Krook, Vholes, Bagstock, Heep, and Headstone belong to different social classes, different generations, and different novels, but they have at least one thing in common: their physical viscosity. Their moral vices range from greed to vanity, ambition to violent obsession, but the crucial sign of their odiousness is their leaky bodies, and this is especially clear if we compare these characters to the staginess of some other villains in Dickens. Carker, for example, in *Dombey and Son*, with his feline attitude and sinister smile, or the foreigner Rigaud in *Little Dorrit*, may reasonably be reduced to a single gesture or body part as an emblem of their wickedness, but their actual bodies do not elicit disgust.

Just as Dickens's frequent dramatizations of what Harry Stone has called ''the night side'' of his imagination—taboos such as cannibalism and incest—lead us to ask about the hidden or secret dimensions of his art, these other half-comic, gross-out ''images of sense'' raise the question of how and why moralistic and entertaining novels may also incorporate scenes Victorian readers found nauseating. This is different from the fat boy's wish to make our flesh creep in *Pickwick*, to conjure emotions such as fear and terror, what Stone and other readers of Dickens might call the ''darker Dickens'' or the ''tragic Dickens.'' Elana Gomel asserts that it is ''the rhetoric of the fragmented body which is responsible for the 'uncanny' quality ascribed to Dickens by so many critics'' (49). Yet the feeling of disgust is distinct from the uncanny, for disgust is an emotion immediately connected to physical repulsion, and to ''the social and cultural contexts in which it makes sense to have those feelings'' (Miller 8). There are many Dickens characters who are physically strange or fantastic, but they were not, to Victorian readers, necessarily disgusting. In fact, the uncanny or aberrant body is often the opposite of fleshiness or fluidity: arid, skeletal, not at all porous, these bodies shrivel up or stiffen, become skin and bone, desiccated, mechanical. Like E. T. A. Hoffmann's weird characters, to which Freud alludes in his essay on

"The Uncanny" (1919), they are artificial, disturbingly non-human. Consider Grandfather Smallweed, with his black skull-cap and "spindle legs," like "a mere clothes bag" or "a bundle of clothes with a voice in it" (*Bleak House* 259, 268). When Mrs. Skewton, in *Dombey and Son*, prepares for bed she becomes a puppet or skeleton: "the form collapsed, the hair dropped off, the arched dark eyebrows changed to scanty tufts of grey; the pale lips shrunk, the skin became cadaverous and loose; an old, worn, yellow, nodding woman, with red eyes alone remained" (472). She is like the grotesque old Lady Tippins in *Our Mutual Friend*: "Whereabout in the bonnet and drapery announced by her name, any fragment of the real woman may be concealed, is perhaps known to her maid; but you could easily buy all you see of her in Bond Street; or you might scalp her, and peel her, and scrape her, and make two lady Tippins out of her, and yet not penetrate to the genuine article" (164). Similarly, young Pip associates Miss Havisham with "some ghastly waxwork" or a "skeleton in the ashes of a rich dress," her "figure . . . shrunk to skin and bone" (*Great Expectations* 87). And then there are the morally and physically hard, dry characters: the "metallic" Miss Murdstone in *David Copperfield*, the "gaunt and bony" Sally Brass in *The Old Curiosity Shop* (320), even the murderess Hortense in *Bleak House*, with her "feline mouth, and general uncomfortable tightness of face," her "eager" jaws and prominent skull, suggesting "something indefinably keen and wan about her anatomy" (143). There are probably even more examples of brittle or ossified characters, or those whose bodies have shrunken grotesquely into their costumery, cosmetics, and jewels—especially, it seems, female characters. These figures are bizarre and disconcerting, but they do not, for most readers, cross the line into loathsomeness. In describing Krook's demise, though, (to take the most offensive example) Dickens *does* step over a socially meaningful line about decency and what is allowed to be represented in middle-class, mid-Victorian fiction.[2] Even if spontaneous human combustion can be proven by medical testimony, wrote one Victorian reviewer, to describe it in a novel "would be false and repugnant in point of Art" (Collins 277).

Yet in Victorian society, it is precisely in the realm of the aesthetic, rather than in science or medicine, that the human condition can be most meaningfully and broadly addressed, where images of the body's deterioration, decay, or, worse perhaps, sudden disposal force readers to contemplate their corporeal existence. In this sense, the explosive potential of Krook and other bodies in Dickens offer another direction in the ongoing discussion of the cultural work of Dickens's representations, one which incorporates the emergence of anthropology as a scientific discipline in the nineteenth century. The Victorians were the first generation to theorize about disgust.[3] In his chapter on "Disdain—Contempt—Disgust—Guilt—Pride, Etc.," in *The Expression of the Emotions in Man and Animals* (1871), Darwin theorized that "the sensation of disgust primarily arises in connection with the act of eating or tasting"

(257).[4] But Darwin points out that customs and social context affect the nature and degree of one's disgust. Thus he explains that his own disgust for a naked Tierra del Fuego native who touched his preserved meat was matched by the native's disgust for the softness of the cold meat he touched (256–57). Dickens, too, would have understood the relative nature of disgust. Although known for his habits of cleanliness, on at least one American tour he found himself in conditions less than hygienic, according to Peter Ackroyd, "in frowsy and dirty shared sleeping quarters where all the men spat and where no one washed, except, of course, Dickens and his party" (Ackroyd 361). But Dickens reported in a letter home, "'I make no complaints, and shew no disgust'" (qtd. in Ackroyd 361). For Dickens and for Darwin, custom and cultural variance are complexly involved in constructing human emotion.[5]

For middle-class Victorian culture, in particular, the construction of disgust is related to constructions of difference. Ellen Handy, in a fascinating article on representations of excrement in *Our Mutual Friend* and the photography of Thomas Annan (1829–1887), has suggested that it is "the antithetical categories of wet and dry" that are evoked when Victorian writers or photographers seek to figure the reality of slums, sewers, and dustheaps, to represent the world which had been suppressed or sentimentalized in most Victorian cultural discourses. The same opposition of wet and dry may be applied to representations of the body, as in the examples I have given from Dickens of excess and ossification.[6] In perhaps the most acute modern analysis of the disgusting nature of wetness, Jean-Paul Sartre describes stickiness or slime in the light of existentialist philosophy: "What mode of being is symbolized by the slimy? I see first that it is the homogeneity and the imitation of liquidity" (*Being and Nothingness* 607). Sartre states that sliminess carries a dense interpretation in which the containment of the self is compelled to fuse with the world. "The slimy is at the moment that which is manifesting the world. . . . [The slimy] *symbolizes being*" (606–07, my emphasis). Indeed, the chief point of Sartre's *Nausea* (1938) is the narrator's insight that his inescapable corporeality—"flabby, languid, obscene, digesting, oily, callous, 'like a bruise or a secretion, an oozing'"—is the key to his very existence (Kern 243).

These evocations of wet and dry, of internal and external, of being and nothingness, are central to the moral meaning of disgust and connected to the representations of the specific bodies in Dickens with which I opened this essay. As I have suggested, disgust is very closely tied to a society's moral structures, and may be said to have a ritualistic function. Specifically, disgust is akin to ritual associations about the body, which is used to symbolize purity or impurity, pollution or perfection, contagion or containment within a given social hierarchy. Pollution beliefs and purity rituals have symbolic functions in a society; they reinforce claims to status, they define thresholds and boundaries. Dickens's disgusting bodies may therefore work as complex symbols which challenge bound systems of knowledge and the relationship between the individual and collective identity. Specifically, Dickens's evocations of exploding, erupting, and disintegrating bodies may have encoded fantasies and obsessions which caused some uneasiness among Victorian readers—uneasiness which becomes disgust, if disgust is a moral and social sentiment, not only an instinctive response. In any case, this must be true in reading a novel, in encountering complex symbolic and linguistic systems. Readers' reactions of disgust may suggest that Dickens's occasionally peculiar way of representing the body violated current ideological models of difference. Fluid rather than self-contained, fantastic figures such as Krook, Bagstock, Heep and others, approach the margins of representability by themselves representing marginality: their bodies leak, bleed, drip, and drool. No other representation of the body could force open the tidy categories of private and public, masculine and feminine, cleanliness and dirt, even human and animal, as do these viscous bodies. Anthropologist Mary Douglas writes in *Purity and Danger*:

> All margins are dangerous. . . . Any structure of ideas is vulnerable at its margins. We should expect the orifices of the body to symbolise its specially vulnerable points. Matter issuing from them is marginal stuff of the most obvious kind. Spittle, blood, milk, urine, faeces or tears by simply issuing forth have traversed the boundary of the body. (121)

Douglas goes on to say that "it is a mistake to treat bodily margins in isolation from all other margins" (121). The body in fiction, then, may work as a powerful metaphor for social boundaries and cultural margins. Disgust indicates an approach to the dangerous borders of Victorian social and moral sensibilities, and the image of the body is implicated in "the ordering of a social hierarchy" (Douglas 125).

This idea from a twentieth-century anthropologist who has studied rituals of pollution and purity in primitive societies intersects with Darwin's implicit awareness of the varied contexts for human expression. In *The Expression of the Emotions in Man and Animals*, Darwin writes: "A smear of soup upon a man's beard looks disgusting, though there is of course nothing disgusting in the soup itself" (257). Anticipating Sartre and Douglas, Darwin chooses to single out a *smear*, suggesting that there is something about the slimy, not-solid, marginal quality of smears which contributes to the feeling of disgust. Dickens's smeared bodies—Mr. Guppy says the "stuff" on the window ledge "smears, like black fat" (398), and recall Bradley Headstone holding out "his smeared hand" to Lizzie (457)—are transgressive representations, but, as I want to suggest, emphatically positive, culturally necessary and progressive. They do challenge social hierarchies, but not in ways we would expect.

Still, there are three possible approaches to Dickens's disgusting bodies worth briefly considering: feminist, biographical, and philosophical.

First, a reading informed by feminist theories of the body could interpret Dickens's excessive bodies as items in the Victorian catalogue of misogynist representations, focusing on the gender of these disgusting characters. Perhaps Victorian men, including Dickens, were squeamish about the boggy composition of the female body, and these disgusting males are symbolic approaches to the "bloody, uncontrollable flow, the dark otherness of woman" (Shuttleworth 59). This is quite possible. Sally Shuttleworth has discussed the Victorian medical establishment's "obsession with female secretions," figuring woman's body as an "internal drain" (47, 64). In this reading, Dickens's men are actually feminized figures: "When man is rendered grotesque, his body is usually feminized: it is penetrated, changes shape, swells, bleeds" (Creed 87). Thus Krook and Headstone are representations of the male fear, described by Freud, of being absorbed into fluidity, of being castrated. And yet I have to reject this interpretation when I look at Dickens's characters, who are not really "feminized" by their subordination, but are sexually rapacious, often physically large, and psychologically aggressive.[7]

A second, biographical approach makes us question whether Dickens imagined this condensation of the body into liquid matter as self-representation. Spontaneous combustion is certainly part of his imaginative repertoire. Harry Stone cites an article in the *Terrific Register*, a gory weekly periodical Dickens read when he was twelve, describing the death by spontaneous combustion of the Countess Cornelia de Bandi Cesante, the case Dickens uses in the defensive preface and in chapter 33 of *Bleak House* (Stone 573). Metaphors of explosion and implosion are fairly frequent in his novels; as early as 1843, in *A Christmas Carol*, Scrooge is "apprehensive that he might be at that very moment an interesting case of spontaneous combustion" (68). Dickens himself declared that he would "explode and perish" if he could not take long and vigorous walks. Although it is feasible to see these creepy characters in a biographical light, especially when we consider things like the *Terrific Register* and Dickens's high-pressure writing schedule, these explanations still do not address the question of how to interpret Victorian reactions of disgust to these fictional bodies. Psychobiography in this case does not really contribute to an analysis of the cultural work of Dickens's novels, and the emotions these novels evoked in a very wide cross-section of Victorian readers.

A more promising approach might be to see these exploding or viscous bodies as ontological problems for Victorian readers, since Dickens's novels often do present philosophical questions about the nature of existence. Nineteenth-century philosophers and scientists, including Darwin, who began to argue for a materialist analysis of human arrangements, contributed substantially to an "understanding of the corporeal determinants of human existence" (Kern 56). Is it one's own experienced body, however decayed, rather than the mind, which constitutes human life? To take one striking example from *Our Mutual Friend*, Rogue Riderhood, hovering between life and death, is described as "a dank carcase," "the outer husk and shell of Riderhood" (503). He is nothing, nobody, a carcase without "the spark of life within him [that] is curiously separable from himself now" (503). The narrator asks, "If you are not gone for good, Mr. Riderhood, it would be something to know where you are hiding at present. This flabby lump of mortality . . . yields no sign of you" (504). Is a "flabby lump of mortality" a human being? The same can be asked of the "little thick nauseous pool" that was Krook. Reading Dickens within the context of the mind-body problem as pursued by Victorian philosophers could be illuminating. In *Anatomy and Destiny*, Stephen Kern explains how Victorian thinkers such as Darwin and Marx repeatedly argued that an understanding of human existence must begin with our physical nature. The mind serves the body, and existence means material existence, the physical stuff from which humans developed and continue to evolve. Certainly Krook's death, and the threatening liquidity of other characters, may be "as much part of a metaphysical as a social viewpoint," as Timothy Clark argues, showing the horror of a "world without interiority" (27). Yet to me even this reading does not take into account the exuberance of Dickens's characterizations. What should we make of the comic detail (suggesting the triumph of "the social viewpoint") that the residents of Cook's Court demand that a six-foot coffin be constructed for Krook "though there is so little to put in it" (413)? Although disgusting, these fluid or perishable bodies are not objects of existential terror, and they are often terrifically funny.

I agree that ontology is linked to the disgusting in Dickens, but not in the way some contemporary critics have read Dickens's so-called dark novels, as visions of alienation, entropy, negativity.[8] The emotions these characters evoke in readers—of disgust, nausea, repulsion—are instead fruitful and affirming, or as Miller puts it, "human and humanizing" (11). And they are connected with Dickens's overall truth-telling mission and his acute criticism of Victorian system-making.

Victorian London was not a clean and sanitary city, and conditions in the metropolis were appalling. *Bleak House* is perhaps Dickens's most committed attack on aristocratic indifference and legal paralysis when it comes to improving the lives of the poor. He believed that all his novels had a humanitarian enterprise in exposing to the comfortable classes the squalor, disease, and filth which the poorer members of London's social body daily endured. But Dickens's humanitarianism embraces more than indignant outrage at social injustice or practical pleas for sanitary reform. His exploding, dripping, and often hilarious characters carry a symbolic load which Victorian society may have found disturbing or disgusting, but which was entirely necessary to serve its larger cultural needs. The anomalousness in representing leaking bodily fluids in a culture which values self-containment and purity, bodily discipline, Christian duty, and the virtue of stoical endurance supplies the necessary contradiction to exaggerated notions of purity, of virginity, of the body as an impermeable and perfect container, as well as to the Victorian habit of classification, especially in anthropological and medical discourses—the need for hard lines and clear taxonomies.

A writer for the *Athenaeum* complained, in 1853, that Dickens is often "beguiled into a cruel consideration of physical defects,—from the unnatural workings of the mind, the step to the painful agonies of the body is a short one" (Collins 277). The writer explicitly links moral disgust to descriptions of the unhealthy or contaminated body: "snub minds and pimpled tempers, principles that squint, and motives that walk on club feet" (Collins 277). Of course there *is* moral commentary in Dickens's disgusting bodies, and this is precisely the point: the disgusting lies in close and necessary proximity with moral feeling, moral *sense*. Outside of Guppy's and Tony Jobling's encounter with the exploded Krook, the most charitable and sympathetic characters in *Bleak House*, for example, are those who experience disgust, those whose *senses* are offended. When Esther and Ada visit the brickmakers' hovels with Mrs. Pardiggle, the philanthropist talks about "the untidy habits of the people" but Esther blatantly deplores "this damp offensive room" (98). Mr. Snagsby, "who has lived in London all his life, can scarce believe his senses" when he makes his Dante-esque descent into Tom-All-Alone's: he "sickens in body and mind, and feels as if he were going, every moment deeper down, into the infernal gulf" (277); the dirty room he finds himself in is "offensive to every sense" (279). Lady Dedlock "shrinks" when she approaches the disease-ridden burying ground, "putting out her two hands, and passionately telling [Jo] to keep away from her, for he is loathsome to her" (202), just as Allan Woodcourt "shrinks" from Jo with "horror," and must make "a strong effort to overcome his repugnance" in approaching him (556–58). Even Jo is compared to "a growth of fungus or any unwholesome excrescence produced there in neglect and impurity" (556–57).

Despite criticism of his vulgarity and coarseness, his fascination with sordid, filthy urban scenes, with crime and low-life, Dickens's huge readership invites us to think that his treatment of these physical and moral margins must have been a condition of his popularity, a necessary part of his appeal across his society's lines of class, gender, and religious belief. A journalist in 1865 complained that Dickens was constantly ferreting out "bright things in dirty places," always searching "among the sweepings, the odds and ends, and puddles of society'' for some ''undiscovered loveliness'' (Collins 458–59). The reviewer (of *Our Mutual Friend*) is being sarcastic, but he nevertheless inadvertently acknowledges the cultural potential of Dickens's dirt-accepting philosophy in a dirt-rejecting society (Douglas 164). Dickens's disgusting images point to a radical acceptance of the welter of modern existence. ''Purity is the enemy of change,'' writes Mary Douglas. ''[T]he facts of existence are a chaotic jumble. If we select from the body's image a few aspects which do not offend, we must prepare to suffer for the distortion'' (162–63).

Dickens should be understood, then, as an agent for change, a celebrator of disproportion and anomalousness in a culture that cherishes order and symmetry. In a way, his fictional figures counterbalance the analytical and taxonomic achievements of Victorian anthropologists, offering readers ''studies from nature'' colored by Dickensian exuberance, wit, and humanity. When he describes Major Bagstock as ''blue-faced and staring—more over-ripe . . . than ever . . . with his cheeks swelling over his tight stock'' (359), or the gluttonous dwarf Quilp, in *The Old Curiosity Shop*, horrifying women by devouring gigantic prawns, chewing water-cresses and tobacco, and swallowing boiling tea (86), or when he gives us vividly Mr. Vholes's mucousy pimples, or Mr. Chadband, ''a large yellow man, with a fat smile, and a general appearance of having a good deal of train oil in his system'' (235), who is described as ''dabbing his fat head for some time—and it smokes to such an extent that he seems to light his pocket-handkerchief at it, which smokes too, after every dab'' (321), or even presents Mr. Micawber, who, after successfully exploding ''that de-testable—serpent—HEEP!'' himself is in danger of erupting, ''steaming'' in his chair, ''with an endless procession of lumps following one another in hot haste up his throat, whence they seemed to shoot into his forehead'' (781), Dickens is not trying to gross out the reader with physical details of ingestion, eruction, sweat, and drool. I do not believe he is asserting a class hegemony, either, where social outcasts are physically repulsive. And he is not necessarily making a moral statement about personal hygiene. Nor, in my view, is he offering the reader some kind of coded archetype of male repulsiveness, a symbolical treatment of male ejaculation and semen, the substance William Ian Miller calls ''the most powerfully contaminating emission'' known to provoke disgust, which ''has the capacity to feminize and humiliate that which it touches'' (19). Elana Gomel sees the fragmentation of the male body in Dickens as the ''pressure of (illicit) desire that figuratively 'explodes' the confines of a stable corporeal identity'' (52). But some characters' explosions are more than figurative, they are literal, fleshy eruptions. For as Dickens keeps insisting in his prefaces and in letters, his project as a novelist is to tell the truth about his world, and here he does it through the symbolic medium of the physical body. For a strict pattern of purity and hygiene cannot be imposed upon a culture without some cracks and fissures. In this, again, Dickens has affinities with Darwin, who wholly believed in the moral as well as the scientific value of his study of human emotion, which he began as early as 1838: "[E]xpression in itself, or the language of the emotions, as it has sometimes been called, is certainly of importance for the welfare of mankind," he wrote, and no emotion, however unpleasant, should be exempt from scrutiny (Darwin 366). The same goes for our material existence, however nauseating. As Mary Douglas puts it, "That which is negated is not thereby removed" (163).

John Ruskin, who by all accounts had little liking for the physical details of human life, implicitly understood Dickens's ambivalent attraction of repulsion for Victorian readers. Although he called Dickens a "thorough cockney" and deplored his "diseased extravagance" (Collins 100), Ruskin seems to have appreciated that Dickens's own brand of "scholasticism," or "the Divinity of Decomposition" (358), spoke directly to a modern urban audience. In Ruskin's analysis, the "trained Londoner can enjoy no other excitement than that to which he has been accustomed . . . and the ultimate power of fiction to entertain him is by varying to his fancy the modes, and defining for his dulness the horrors, of Death" (359–60). In "Fiction, Fair and Foul," Ruskin gives a neat table counting the nine deaths in *Bleak House* (360), including, of course, the spontaneous combustion of Krook.

But if we look at Ruskin's language, there is the distinct impression, if tongue-in-cheek, that the "Divinity of Decomposition" has mitigating and cheering influences, and that Dickens's novels work in ways similar to religious or cultural rituals, and approach a legitimate system of belief:

> [A] philosophy develops itself, partly satiric, partly consolatory, concerned only with the regenerative vigour of manure, and the necessary obscurities of fimetic Providence; showing how everybody's fault is somebody else's, how infection has no law, digestion no will, and profitable dirt no dishonour. (358)

This "partly consolatory" philosophy in effect breaks down the strict binarisms of sacred and profane, clean and dirty, body and spirit, destruction and creation, even of male and female, since disgust is an entirely democratic emotion and can be evoked by any body with the messy or mucous qualifications. That Ruskin could refer, even ironically, to "the regenerative vigour of manure" suggests to me that despite his distaste, he smiled at the comprehensiveness of Dickens's willingness to embrace the whole of his world. And as Ruskin wrote approvingly in *Unto This Last*, Dickens's view of his world "was finally the right one, grossly and sharply told" (Collins 314).

In *Being and Nothingness*, Sartre writes:

> [W]e come to life in a universe where feelings and acts are all charged with something material, have a substantial stuff, are *really* soft, dull, slimy, low,

elevated, etc., and in which material substances have originally a psychic meaning which renders them repugnant, horrifying, alluring, etc.   (605)

Sartre insists that the *feeling* which comes from this materiality must not
be viewed only as a symbol, an image, but should be understood as *knowledge*. He concludes: "From the first appearance of the slimy, this sliminess
is already a response to a demand, already a *bestowal of self*" (606). Is it
possible to read Dickens's slimy characters in this affirmative way, to see
Bagstock's outbursts, Heep's handshakes, or Headstone's nosebleeds as representations of psychic knowledge, a response to a demand for life, as self-be-
stowal?
    In asking whether Victorian readers can find affirmation in Dickens's dis-
gusting bodies, it seems appropriate to return to *Bleak House* and the notorious description of Krook. Tony Jobling has looked into Krook's room, and
describes what he has seen to Mr. Guppy: "'And the burning smell is
there—and the soot is there, and the oil is there—and he is *not* there!'"
(402). But the omniscient narrator descriptively builds up to a thundering
avowal of the opposite:

> Here is a small burnt patch of flooring; here is the tinder from a little bundle
> of burnt paper, but not so light as usual, seeming to be steeped in something;
> and here is—is it the cinder of a small charred and broken log of wood sprinkled
> with white ashes, or is it coal? O Horror, he IS here!   (403)

Fearsome and horrible, yes. But in the authoritative pronouncement "He
IS here!" Dickens emphatically asserts being over not being, messy life over
pristine boundaries, identity over annihilation, thus weirdly and ambiguously
sounding the affirmative in Krook's greasy, gaseous, and gooey remains.

NOTES

1. The notable exception is James Kincaid's chapter on the "erotic fun" of reading
   The Pickwick Papers in *Annoying the Victorians* (New York: Routledge, 1995),
   21–34. As in my own readings of Dickens, Kincaid wants to bring us "back to
   the body, to restore it to us and us to it," rather than talking around it (23).
2. Dickens does not, obviously, work in the late-Victorian Gothic mode, where
   characters actually *are* slime. Kelly Hurley deals with the abjectness of such
   creatures in *The Gothic Body: Sexuality, Materialism, and Degeneration at the
   Fin de Siècle* (Cambridge: Cambridge UP, 1996).
3. Victorian anthropologists were not only the first to formally theorize about emotion; they were the first to use photography to scrutinize and exhibit "alien"

human bodies. Darwin was partly inspired by the French neurologist Guillaume-Benjamin Duchenne, who, with the help of photographer Adrien Tournachon (Nadar's brother) "undertook the analysis of facial expressions by applying an electrical current to specific muscles" (Ewing 109). Darwin uses photographs of frozen facial expressions throughout *The Expression of the Emotions in Man and Animals*. As an anthropologist, Darwin sought similarities in human physiognomies and believed certain emotions were instinctive or reflexive. He studied examples of human expression from places such as aboriginal Australia, New Zealand, Borneo, Malacca, China, India, and Africa, always taking into account differences in stimuli and degrees of emotional response.

4. William Ian Miller explains that Darwin is correct in associating disgust with "taste, oral incorporation, and rejection of food," since the etymology of the word means "unpleasant to the taste" (1). Darwin also claims, "As the sense of smell is so intimately connected with that of taste, it is not surprising that an excessively bad odour should excite retching or vomiting in some persons, quite as readily as the thought of revolting food does" (259). Stephen Kern's discussion of Victorian theories of smell is also relevant to disgust (recall *The Rambler* reviewer's dislike for Dickens's emphasis on "rottenness and smells"): "Society's willingness to recognize the role of smells in human affairs is a good index of its willingness to recognize that human beings are corporeal beings, closely linked to the animal world. The hairiness of man and his smells are constant reminders of his animal ancestry" (Kern 45). Kern points to the increase in research after 1850 on "the role of body odors and the sense of smell in human affairs" (45).

5. Like Victorian anthropologists, Dickens the novelist was interested in and accepting of the sometimes estranging physical diversity of human subjects—one could even argue that his observant imagination is a literary analogue to the scientist's microscope and camera. But if the brisk trade in anthropologic photographs and actual exhibits of the disgusting "other" (Ewing 239)—Zulu natives, bearded ladies, Siamese twins, etc.—is cruel and exploitative, Dickens, in my view, sustains a radically moral perspective on deformity, seldom presenting the body to Victorian readers solely within the context of cultural or racial alienation or "freakishness." Even the most conventionally "freakish" bodies in Dickens, from the Victorian standpoint—Quilp, Smallweed, Miss Mowcher, Jenny Wren—are not dehumanized, without personality and individual character. One could argue, too, that they are not slimy enough to qualify as disgusting, along the lines of Sartre and Miller.

6. In his discussion of the fleshy bodies in *The Pickwick Papers*, James Kincaid likewise argues that "the cultural binary—fat and bone," makes "fat the superior term," then (like a good deconstructionist) he "dissolve[s] the distinction, making the hard and soft, skeleton and flesh, bone and fat melt together in a formless vision of desire without limits or bounds" (24).

7. I have chosen not to emphasize gender in my approach to disgusting bodies in Dickens, though several feminist critics have proposed interesting theories on the female nature of physical viscosity. Elizabeth Grosz, a well-known theorist on the body, asks:

Can it be that in the West, in our time, the female body has been
constructed not only as a lack or absence but with more complexity, as a leaking, uncontrollable, seeping liquid; as a formless flow;
as viscosity, entrapping, secreting; as lacking not so much the
phallus but self-containment—not a cracked or porous vessel, like
a leaking ship, but a formlessness that engulfs all form, a disorder
that threatens all order?   (203)

"My hypothesis," concludes Grosz, "is that women's corporality is inscribed as
a mode of seepage" (203). She goes on to ask why the male body has been
"generally unrepresented," asserting that Western culture excludes "men's body
fluids from their self representation" (201). I will only suggest that the male
body has certainly not been unrepresented in Dickens, and most particularly with
attention to its fluids and its seepage.

  8. Probably the earliest and most influential examples are Edgar Johnson's *Charles
Dickens: His Tragedy and Triumph* (1952) and J. Hillis Miller's *Charles Dickens:
The World of His Novels* (1958).

WORKS CITED

Ackroyd, Peter. *Dickens*. New York: HarperCollins, 1990.

Allen, Dennis W. *Sexuality in Victorian Fiction*. Norman: Oklahoma UP, 1993.

Clark, Timothy. "Dickens through Blanchot: The Nightmare Fascination of a World
Without Interiority." *Dickens Refigured: Bodies, Desires and Other Histories*. Ed.
John Schad. Manchester: Manchester UP, 1996. 22–38.

Collins, Philip, ed. *Dickens: The Critical Heritage*. New York: Barnes and Noble,
1971.

Creed, Barbara. "Lesbian Bodies: Tribades, tomboys and tarts." *Sexy Bodies: The
Strange Carnalities of Feminism*. Eds. Elizabeth Grosz and Elspeth Probyn. London: Routledge, 1995. 86–103.

Darwin, Charles. *The Expression of the Emotions in Man and Animals*. New York:
Philosophical Library, 1955.

Dickens, Charles. *Bleak House*. New York: Norton, 1977.

———. *The Old Curiosity Shop*. Harmondsworth: Penguin, 1984.

———. *David Copperfield*. Harmondsworth: Penguin, 1978.

———. *Dombey and Son*. Harmondsworth: Penguin, 1970.

———. *The Uncommercial Traveller*. London: Mandarin, 1991.

———. *Great Expectations*. Harmondsworth: Penguin, 1965.

———. *Our Mutual Friend*. Harmondsworth: Penguin, 1971.

———. *A Christmas Carol*. Harmondsworth: Penguin, 1984.

Douglas, Mary. *Purity and Danger: An Analysis of Concepts of Pollution and Taboo*. London: Routledge and Kegan Paul, 1966.

Ewing, William A. *The Body: Photographs of the Human Form*. San Francisco: Chronicle, 1994.

Freud, Sigmund. "The Uncanny." *On Creativity and the Unconscious*. Ed. Benjamin Nelson. New York: Harper, 1958.

Gomel, Elana. "The Body of Parts: Dickens and the Poetics of Synecdoche." *The Journal of Narrative Technique*. 26.1 (1996): 48–74.

Grosz, Elizabeth. *Volatile Bodies: Toward a Corporeal Feminism*. Bloomington: Indiana UP, 1994.

Handy, Ellen. "Dust Piles and Damp Pavements: Excrement, Repression, and the Victorian City in Photography and Literature." *Victorian Literature and the Victorian Visual Imagination*. Eds. Carol T. Christ and John O. Jordan. Berkeley: U of California P, 1995. 111–33.

Hurley, Kelly. *The Gothic Body: Sexuality, Materialism, and Degeneration at the Fin de Siècle*. Cambridge: Cambridge UP, 1996.

Kern, Stephen. *Anatomy and Destiny: A Cultural History of the Human Body*. Indianapolis: Bobbs-Merrill, 1975.

Kincaid, James R. *Annoying the Victorians*. New York: Routledge, 1995.

Miller, William Ian. *The Anatomy of Disgust*. Cambridge: Harvard UP, 1997.

Page, Norman. *A Dickens Companion*. New York: Schocken Books, 1984.

Royle, Nicholas. "Our Mutual Friend." *Dickens Refigured: Bodies, Desires and Other Histories*. Ed. John Schad. Manchester: Manchester UP, 1996. 39–54.

Ruskin, John. *The Literary Criticism of John Ruskin*. Ed. Harold Bloom. Gloucester: Peter Smith, 1969.

Sartre, Jean-Paul. *Being and Nothingness*. Trans. Hazel E. Barnes. New York: Philosophical Library, 1956.

Stone, Harry. *The Night Side of Dickens: Cannibalism, Passion, Necessity*. Columbus: The Ohio State UP, 1994.

Shuttleworth, Sally. "Female Circulation: Medical Discourse and Popular Advertising in the Mid-Victorian Era." *Body/Politics: Women and the Discourses of Science*. Eds. Mary Jacobus, Evelyn Fox Keller, and Sally Shuttleworth. London: Routledge, 1990. 47–68.

Authority and the *Bildungsroman*: The Double Narrative of *Bleak House*

James Hill

Bleak House *is divided into two narratives of approximately equal length: "Esther's Narrative" and an omniscient present tense narrative. I argue that Esther Summerson's autobiographical narrative is an effort of self-fashioning. In responding to the narrative pattern for Esther's life proposed by her aunt, Miss Barbary, in which Esther is predetermined by the sin of her mother to a life of "submission, self-denial, diligent work," Esther attempts to construct the story of her life as a narrative of industry, contentedness and kind-heartedness, with the winning of love for herself as its goal. The second part of the essay treats the relationship between Esther's narrative and the omniscient narrative as an effect of historical conditioning. I argue that this present-tense narrative is a presentation of the modern, as a point that sees the past as deracination and decay and the future as intrinsically uncertain. Its version of the quest, driven by anxiety as a primary condition of the modern, is the detective story, exemplified by Inspector Bucket, and a range of amateur detectives.*

As a major category within English nineteenth-century realist narrative, the *Bildungsroman* raises the issue of authority in its own acute and specific terms. If one takes *Tom Jones* as perhaps the last example of the teleological narrative of providential, and therefore representative, realism, the *Bildungsroman*, by contrast, moves toward a realism of newly recognized and secularized individualism.[1] Asking its readers to attend to the formative processes

Dickens Studies Annual, Volume 29, Copyright © 2000 by AMS Press, Inc. All rights reserved.

that shape its characters into adulthood, it seeks to illuminate the biographies of a Dorothea Brooke rather than a St. Theresa, a David Copperfield rather than a Charles Dickens. In so doing, it enlarges the field of significant life from the public record of memorable achievement to the otherwise unremarked oblivion of the ordinary. Both in fictional and non-fictional biography, the eighteenth century maintained the Christian and the classical commitment to the exemplary life; neither Moll Flanders nor Dr. Johnson come before us as instances of the ordinary. But the *Bildungsroman* insists on the importance of private, as opposed to public life, suggesting a widening perspective on what constitutes history, and on what texts should notice both for the benefit of the present and the future.

In *The Way of the World*, Franco Moretti links its emergence in the late eighteenth century with the emergence of modernity, for which it provides the first powerful fictional narrative model.[2] If, as Moretti asserts, the discovery of modernity marks an historical juncture that manifests itself in a radical reconceptualization of self and society, the *Bildungsroman*, as the narrative of such reconceptualizing, cannot authorize itself by the unexamined invocation of older narrative forms. Since this reconceptualization involves a decisive interiorization of the self as well as the erosion or collapse of older status societies, and with those a new, if uncertain, social mobility (Moretti 4), older forms are no longer appropriate for its innovative procedures. When it uses older forms, it must use them either as antitexts (as *Prometheus Unbound* uses *Paradise Lost*), or as antetexts, which it must absorb and transform for its own purposes (as *Childe Harold* internalizes the quest romance, or as *Vanity Fair* secularizes *Pilgrim's Progress*).[3]

Moretti isolates as important characteristics of the *Bildungsroman* its elevation of youth to a position of significance in the wake of the French Revolution, its relegation of past history to the dustheap, and its inevitable recognition that youth, as an ideologeme (in both its conceptual and narrative senses),[4] is inherently limited because it is a cultural and biological process that inevitably comes to an end (Moretti 4–6).

The privileging of youth as the anodyne for the bankrupt wisdom of elders, the possibility of youth as the force to create a new world on the ruins of the old, the shifting of the significance of historical process from past to future—all of these as positive premises for the *Bildungsroman* would seem to place the authority for shaping the course of history on each successive emerging generation. For the first time, the new generation is seen not as inheriting the past, which it preserves, and which it also may modify to some degree, as in Burke, but as creating the future out of its own originating enterprise and energy.[5] Each generation, then, becomes the author of its own history, and history, in turn, becomes its construction. If the authority of that construction no longer derives from a grounding in past history, however; if authority is no longer conceived as received but initiated, a crucial question is who is granted that initiating authority, and for what reasons. Why should one narrative voice rather than another be attended to? The novel, particularly the *Bildungsroman*, raising the question of why it, as a text, should be attended to, does so in terms of origins. The question is implied when the narration comes from an omniscient narrator—implied in the very notion of narrational omniscience, which knows more than any human being can know.[6] Such omniscience is typically a given in older narrative, a consistent feature from the Homeric poems through Milton, and still present in Fielding. In the nineteenth century it begins to involve more urgently the narrator's authoritative relationship to the reader, in its presumption that the novel, as an instrument that may produce both pleasure and instruction, serves an ideological program as well, and that it competes with other ideologies for a readership much larger and more diverse than that of the eighteenth century. Harriet Martineau's withering dismissal of Dickens's treatment of the problems of industrialization in *Hard Times*, on the one hand, and Ruskin's praise of the novel as more effective than any number of government blue books, on the other,[7] testify both to the danger and effectiveness of narrative authority. When Dickens, writing to Wilkie Collins, asserted that "all art is but a little imitation" of "the ways of Providence,"[8] his primary purpose was to alert Collins to the superior effectiveness of showing, rather than telling, as a principal of narrative conduct. "The ways of Providence," however, while it indicates a narrative strategy that recuperates meaning retrospectively, as in a providential reading of history, also suggests that for Dickens the author/narrator imitates *in parvo* the authority of the Divine in history. The popular novelist, in this construction, is thus a demiurge, a secondary deity who is also a skilled workman for the people. If this view of narration seems incommensurate with the improvisatory exuberance of the youthful "Boz," it is firmly in place by the time of the careful planning of *Dombey and Son*.

II

The implicit issue of narrative authority becomes explicit when narration is conducted in first person, where it may be posed as a problem by the narrator. "I have great difficulty in writing my portion of these pages, for I know I am not clever" (17). After two chapters of powerful omniscient narration in the present tense, Esther Summerson couches her entry into *Bleak House* in terms of diffidence and responsibility. Her sense that she has been set a task specifically for her, and that she well may be unequal to it, that she has been designated an author, and that she may lack authority, establishes aspects of her personality that will continue consistently throughout the course of the novel, both in her conception of herself, and in her relations with other characters.

Esther's difficulty has been seen in terms of gender.[9] As a female author, she has been given responsibility for a portion of a larger text. The other portion, that of the omniscient narrator, is free to move as it will, from Chancery to Chesney Wold, into the slums of London, to France. While Dickens never identifies the gender of the narrator, its freedom of movement, like that of the detective, the reporter, the *flâneur*, or the male novelist, is male. Moreover, its use of present tense, echoing the authority of another male text, Carlyle's *The French Revolution*, gives it the authenticity of dramatic narrative. Beyond that, its recording eye knows the proper perspective in which to place its observations:

> It is but a glimpse of the fashionable world we want this miry afternoon . . . It is not a large world. Relative even to this world of ours, which has its limits too (as your Highness shall find when you have made the tour of it and are come to the brink of the void beyond), it is a very little speck.   (11)

Against that authority, which presumes to address—even to admonish—royalty, Esther must keep within her proper, domestic sphere, and attempt to produce significant narrative on the basis of a necessarily limited range of experience. Entering as if on cue, Esther begins her narrative in the present tense of the first two chapters. By the third paragraph, however, she shifts into narrative past tense, aligning her narrative with older, traditional modes of storytelling. The implied premise of this shift may well be that beginning at the beginning of what she knows best, her own life, in retrospect, offers the prospect of tracing a chronological sequence that will unfold, of its own, into meaning. At the same time, narrative past tense has the potential to gather to itself any of the narrative genres for which it has been used, and thus to reinscribe Esther's narrative within a genre, or even multiple genres, where an ideology of meaning is already present. Should this happen, the responsibility for meaningful narration shifts from author to the genre itself, in effect "solving" Esther's difficulty by displacing her as author. Audrey Jaffe's contention that Esther's self-creation is, paradoxically, a central function of her self-effacement, creating a self through the reflection of others (134), can be extended to the possibility that Esther's narrative, ostensibly a testament of individuality, can rescue itself from the frightening possibilities of absolute uniqueness by lapsing into the generic. Even here, there is a question as to the legitimacy, literal and metaphoric, of her own place within that "little speck." Esther's problem, involving the limitation of experience, the requirement that narrative be significant, and the legitimacy of any female claim for narrative authority, intruding into the larger world of male discourse, but intruding as if by command, may be taken as paradigmatic for the situation of the woman as author.

Moreover, while Esther's opening statement shows that she is aware that she is contributing her portion of a larger text, she is never privy to that text, even though several characters in her text appear in the omniscient narrator's text. The omniscient narrator, however, is aware of Esther, as the opening of chapter VII makes clear: "While Esther sleeps, and while Esther wakes, it is still wet weather down at the place in Lincolnshire"(76). That the omniscient narrator is aware of Esther, while she is not aware of him, appears to establish a dominant/subordinate relationship between the two narratives, a binary pattern also repeated in the series of relationships between Esther and other male figures in her own narrative: John Jarndyce, Inspector Bucket, and Allan Woodcourt. As controlling figures in Esther's life, they are also controlling figures in the shape of her narrative as well. We should keep in mind, however, that they appear in Esther's narrative because she writes it; we see them as she represents them. The voice that is not subject to Esther's narrative control is the voice of the omniscient narrator, a point to which I shall return.

But Esther's problem with narrative authority is paradigmatic not merely for women authors, but also for the novel itself, and is reflected in the opening of Dickens's first sustained first-person narrative. "Whether I shall turn out to be the hero of my own life, or whether that station will be held by anyone else, these pages must show." Long before the end of *David Copperfield*, David has found his vocation and established his credentials as an author. Thus, when he turns to write his autobiography, he does so after authoring other narratives; unlike Esther, he writes as a professional. But still, David poses the question of authority as urgent, and his tone, like Esther's, is self-effacing and diffident. Through a strategy of reticence that is also a sleight of hand, he transfers authority from narrator to narrative, a gesture that places responsibility on the reader as interpreter of his text.

III

The chronology of *Bleak House* shows us that Esther begins her assigned portion of the narrative seven years after the events that make up its plot. But if seven years leads us to infer that those events needed time to put them into proper perspective, and that Esther has composed them into the finished product of long meditation, the aposiopesis of her last sentence contradicts such inference. Her narrative does not close, but is suspended on the question of Esther's beauty, just as her opening had questioned her intelligence. Again, the question is put in terms of Esther's ability to evaluate herself, and is consistent with her behavior throughout the novel, but, like her opening statement, the issue is larger than one of self-image.[10,11]

Esther, like her mother, Lady Dedlock, is the center of a world that revolves around her. Her mother's beauty is achieved, rather than given: "She has a fine face—originally of a character that would be rather called very pretty than handsome, but improved into classicality by the acquired expression of her fashionable state"(13). Lady Dedlock has learned how to transform prettiness into classical beauty, and her self-improvement comes from her ability to read the fashionable world successfully enough to "acquire" its "expression." And the authority she wields in her world is built upon a lie, a commanding fiction that both conceals the facts of her past and is the center of gravity for the fashionable world orbiting around her.

Esther also functions in the context of her narration as a figure of authority, the center of a household that revolves around her, her keys as the manifest sign of her ability to order the smaller world of Bleak House. She has as much difficulty believing in the validity of that authority as she has with her qualifications as narrator, seeing her authority as a benign fiction created by communal conspiracy. And both Esther and Lady Dedlock, recognizing the fictive character of the power they appear to have in their respective worlds, are nevertheless trapped in an apparently suspended time, while the rest of the world goes on at its customary pace. In worlds where identity appears to be an almost immutable given, Esther and Lady Dedlock are freefloating and extraordinary, creating the necessary tension between character and environment that makes them narratable. Both Esther and Lady Deadlock identify themselves as "others" occupying acquired places in established systems whose members hold positions by some right of identity. They differ, however, because Lady Deadlock is aware of her own past, and thus of the falseness of her self-constructed position, while Esther, denied knowledge of her origins, is only aware of her "otherness," and the ambiguity attached to it.

Esther's situation provides the basis for what Fredric Jameson calls "magical" narrative (Political Unconscious 103–50)—and what Dickens, in his preface to the novel, called "the romantic side of familiar things"(4). The first, radical definition of her otherness comes on her birthday, when she asks to hear something about her mother. Her "godmother" (who will be demystified later as her aunt "in fact, though not in law"[21]), dismisses her questions with the formula of ritual:

> "Submission, self-denial, diligent work, are the preparations for a life begun with such a shadow on it. You are different from other children, Esther, because you were not born, like them, in common sinfulness and wrath. You are set apart." (19)

We recognize the extreme Protestant ethos of her aunt's pronouncement, placing her with characters like Joseph in Wuthering Heights in a specific historical setting, and we recognize also in Esther's reaction how traumatized she is by her aunt's statement:

> ... how often I repeated to the doll the story of my birthday, and confided to
> her that I would try, as hard as ever I could, to repair the fault I had been born
> with (of which I confusedly felt guilty and yet innocent), and would strive as
> I grew up to be industrious, contented, and kind-hearted, and to do some good
> to some one, and win some love to myself if I could.   (20)

Such a reaction opens itself to the psychological analysis of personality, the interiorization of the self that Moretti identifies as symptomatic of the modern. It provides the basis for understanding Esther's consistent behavioral pattern in the novel as neurotic defense formation, and perhaps helping to explain, and thus alleviate, both her submissiveness and her "angel in the house" tendencies that compromise her for many contemporary readers.

But her godmother's program for Esther, juxtaposed to Esther's program for herself, suggests two narrative possibilities for Esther's autobiography. As a child set apart, she may pray that the sins of her mother not be visited upon her, "according to what is written"(19; her godmother has paraphrased Numbers 14:18), but the tone of her godmother leaves little possibility that happiness will be her lot. Under this rubric, "the greatest kindness" would be to forget that she has a mother, but given the intensity with which Esther reacts in this scene, and the evocation of the generational inheritance of sin, forgetfulness is not an option. The narrative proposed by Esther's godmother, sanctioned by the Old Testament, is one of divine wrath.

Esther's program, on the other hand, proposes an alternate narrative. It replicates the triadic discipline of her godmother's program, submission, self-denial, and diligent work, but transforms them into industry, contentment, and kindheartedness, rewriting the harsh obligation entailed by wrath as the milder controlling reins of charity, in what appears to be a shifting of terms from Old to New Testament. Much in Esther's narrative would seem to reinforce that reading. We are introduced to example after example of false charity (Mrs. Jellyby, Mrs. Pardiggle, Mr. Skimpole, whose charity is that of the false recipient of the well-intended gifts of others, Reverend Chadband), as well as real charity (John Jarndyce, Mr. George, Esther, Allan Woodcourt, Ada, Gridley), with the High Court of Chancery hovering behind all these individual examples as the symbol of a public world from which charity has disappeared. And of course, such a case is strengthened by Dickens's intense involvement with charitable activity, his contempt for public and political institutions such as Chancery, and his version of Christianity.

But Esther's program also allows us to read her narrative as secular romance, in which the reward prepared for by a life of industry, contentment, and kindheartedness will be to "win some love" to herself. It is here that

Moretti measures the failure of the Dickensian version of the *Bildungsroman* against its Continental versions (185–89). Romance degenerates into fairy tale, and Dickens situates his central characters in a world that substitutes the inhabitants of fairyland for the characters one would expect in a realistic rendition of an emerging bourgeoisie during a century that underwent enormous change in its cultural, political, and economic configurations. Thus we meet Tulkinghorn, atavistically dressed in black, with ''Allegory'' as his sign, Detective Bucket, ready to draw ''Truth'' from the well, Miss Flite, whose name prepares us for her gnomically named birds, Mr. Krook, convinced of the ominous magical powers of written language, and dying of spontaneous combustion. That most of these characters, as well as others in the novel, are modelled from life, rather than being created wholly out of the Dickensian imagination, and that Dickens took pains to defend and document spontaneous combustion against charges of complete implausibility, is not in itself enough to refute Moretti's point. Nor does Dickens's attention to such contemporary issues as poverty, corruption or ineptitude in public institutions, or the appalling conditions of public health, quite serve to throw the balance of the narrative firmly into the camp of realism. For Moretti, the radical polarization of moral values in the Dickensian novel, so strong that it allows us to identify virtually every character with a tag of good or evil, prevents not only a realistic presentation of the psychological complexity of human behavior, but also projects a novelistic universe animated by polarized moral forces. What Moretti appears to overlook is that not all narratives that present their worlds in terms of polarized moral forces are fairy tales. The great allegorical narratives of the Middle Ages and the Renaissance, the tragedies of Shakespeare, *Paradise Lost*, and the mythopoeic narratives of Blake and Shelley create such polarities as well. It is of course true that these narratives, unlike *Jane Eyre*, *David Copperfield*, *Great Expectations*, and *The Mill on the Floss*, do not project these polarities through the eyes of childhood. The intervening voice may well be Wordsworth's, but that voice may be prompted less by the fairytale than by Matthew 18:3, ''Unless ye become as little children, ye shall not enter the kingdom of Paradise.'' However that may be, we may argue that moral polarization does not prevent Dickens from developing complex psychological characterizations.

IV

One aspect of the realistic novel is its tendency to suggest that the direction in which a given plot moves is controlled, at least to some degree, by unforeseen contingencies. The plot unfolding into the future is merely one possibility among a number of plots that might equally well have happened, with equal probability, if circumstances had been only slightly different. Some plots indeed hinge upon unexpected, but crucial contingencies that have no special vibrations, but appear to arise out of the very stuff of ordinary life.

It is not that such occurrences are not features of previous narratives, but rather that in those narratives they are unexpected only from the limited perspective of the characters involved, not from the larger perspective of the purposive teleology driving the plot. As such plots reach resolution, the perspective of the characters is usually realigned with the larger perspective, sometimes through explicit divine intervention, as in Athena's intervention in the final battle in the *Odyssey*, sometimes through an elevation of perception, as in Hamlet's "There is a special providence in the fall of a sparrow" (V,ii, 219–20).

At least one measure of the secular swerve of the novel is its effort to move away from a teleological account of accident, an account that had worked to construct fictive narrative according to a master narrative of providential history. Of the two plots initially proposed for Esther, it is clear that what I have called the narrative of wrath, the grounds of which her aunt has articulated, is a version of providential history. I wish here to lay out these grounds, because they are established by an older authority on the basis of scripture, because they define an irrevocable original identity for Esther, and because they remain in the background as a counter-possibility to the narrative that Esther herself writes. If Moretti is correct in his assertion that the novel, and in particular the *Bildungsroman*, is by its nature antithetic to tragedy, and to epic as well (54), the grounds for Aunt Barbary's narrative are antinovelistic in the extreme. They establish Esther as *sui generis* in her origins; she is not born as all others are, in common sin, but she is set apart. Her exceptionality, because it is a fact of her birth, rather than something she has achieved, is indelible; while it leaves no outward mark, it is as intrinsic to her as Oedipus's crippled foot. Aunt Barbary appropriately calls it her "shadow," the dark silhouette she will always cast, do what she will.

Esther's response to the knowledge of her sinful birth also underlines the potential tragedy of this narrative. She identifies it as "the fault I had been born with (of which I confusedly felt guilty and yet innocent)" (20). Such ambiguity is crucial to the identity of the tragic protagonist; Oedipus, we remember, is simultaneously the savior of Thebes and, as regicide, parricide, and incestuous king, its polluter as well, exceptional almost to the point of godhead and beyond the pale of polis in his violation of its deepest taboos.

Aunt Barbary's narrative is also antinovelistic in its iteration of the inheritance of sin by the children of succeeding generations. At least two premises, that sin, as the crucially determining fact of identity, is inherited, rather than a consequence of will, and that historical continuity is a form of repetition determined by God (it is God who speaks in Numbers 14:18), direct this account of Esther's future away from the possibility of realistic narrative. Exceptionality and divinely determined history point instead to a vision of preordained tragedy, in which the individual has been locked into the role of scapegoat, from which there is no escape.

Aunt Barbary has arranged Esther's life according to the demands of her narrative. Unlike other children, she has never been allowed to celebrate her birthday, and, as a daily ritual, she reads to her aunt from the Bible at nine o'clock every evening. In her brief summary of her early life, Esther cites only one example of her reading, John 8:7, during which her aunt has a fatal stroke. The text in question concerns the woman taken in adultery, Christ's writing in the dust with his finger, and his admonition, "He that is without sin, let him cast the first stone at her." Aunt Barbary responds with another biblical citation, Mark 13: 35–37, "Watch ye therefore! lest coming suddenly he find you sleeping. And what I say unto you, I say unto all, Watch!" These words, referring to the second coming of Christ, are her last, and mark the prophesied end of providential history.

Against this providential narrative, Esther writes her autobiography as secular romance. "I was brought up, from my earliest remembrance—like some of the princesses in fairy stories, only I was not charming—by my godmother" (17). I have referred earlier to Esther's sense that she is obliged to write her narrative, her "portion" of the novel, but at the same time she has not been instructed as to *what* that narrative is to be. "It seems so curious to me to be obliged to write all this about myself! As if this narrative were the narrative of *my* life! But my little body will soon fall into the background now" (27). Esther does in fact write subnarratives with other characters as principal subjects: the stories of Caddy Jellyby and of Ada and Richard. But her prediction that she will "fall into the background" is contradicted by her narrative, which is a refiguring of her aunt's model of generational history into another narrative paradigm.

Janet Larson has argued persuasively that Esther's narrative is a subtly managed conflict between biblical texts. Esther's narrative, like the other "multivocal" narratives of the later Dickens, shows us that the Bible, far from being a source of stability, or an authoritative text, "becomes a paradoxical book: it is at once a source of stability, with its familiar conventions of order, and a locus of hermeneutical instability reflecting the times of Victorian religious anxiety in which Dickens wrote" (101). Larson's detailed argument centers for the most part on Job and the Book of Esther, as well as on a strong tension between Old Testament Law and New Testament Gospel, and demonstrates how Esther both reads and misreads biblical texts for her own conflicted need. This reading reinforces earlier treatments of the novel that follow from Hillis Miller's insight that *Bleak House* "is a document about the interpretation of documents"(11), or to put it in my terms, that it makes the authority of texts and the interpretation of textual authority a crucial issue.

Esther's narrative is, as I have said, concerned at its opening with the difficulty of producing a text at all. If her document is to have authority by taking a narrative shape that will lead the reader to some kind of significance, it cannot be of the sort she produces so easily to please children, the fairy tale. Instead, it must either be a narrative that reproduces the accurately observed contents of the world ("I had always rather a noticing way—not a quick way, O no!—a silent way of noticing what passed before me, and thinking I should like to understand it better") (17), what we may call realistic narrative. Or it must be a symbolic narrative (of which the fairy tale is a demotic form) that arranges its materials along a syntagmatic axis pointing toward a higher, metaphysical truth.

With what seems almost an automatic gesture, she begins in the fairy tale vein, as if she is locating herself within her own narrative repertoire, but even as she begins, she feels somehow compelled to disenchant the genre. Unlike the princesses, she is "not charming," her godmother is not a fairy god-mother, and her doll, to whom she confides all her secrets, is not magical, but stares "at nothing." The properties for the fairy tale are in place, and will stay in place throughout her narrative (" 'Full of curiosity, no doubt, little woman, to know why I have brought you here?' 'Well, guardian,' said I, 'without thinking myself a Fatima, or you a Blue Beard, I am a little curious about it' ") (749), but they remain for the most part inert.

"A Progress," the title of Esther's first chapter, points in the direction of a royal progress, which the narrative enacts as the journey of Esther from Windsor, one of the seats of royalty, to Reading, and finally to London and the Court of Chancery, where Esther, Richard, and Ada are placed under the care of John Jarndyce by the Lord High Chancellor, the highest legal officer in England. In this version of a progress, elements of the fairy tale abound: the mysterious but unthreatening appearance and behavior of Mr. Kenge, the remarkable gentlemen in the carriage who tempts Esther with sweetmeats to stop her crying, and who refers to her aunt's housekeeper, Mrs. Rachel, by saying "Con-found Mrs. Rachel!. . . Let her fly away in a high wind on a broomstick!"(25), the six peaceful years at Greenleaf under the benign supervision of the twin Miss Donnys, where Esther almost transforms her former life with her godmother into a dream rather than a reality, the magical apparition of London, Esther's meeting with Ada and Richard, "half laughing at our being like the children in the wood"(34). Narrative movement also seems to be following a law in which Esther herself does nothing to forward things, but rather in which her life seems to be magically arranging itself for her according to a benign, if not divine, plan, which Mr. Kenge, as if casting about for the precise word, calls "Providence"(23).

At the same time, Esther's "noticing way" picks out particular details with memorial exactitude that anchors them within a more realistic context. Her account of her education at Greenleaf also introduces de-romanticized, realistic material as she re-defines her exceptionality. She makes it clear that her exceptionality, which is her illegitimacy within the framework of British law, continues to separate her from other children at Greenleaf, where, like Jane Eyre, another orphan, she begins to teach as a part of her training to become a governess. While such a position will provide her with a modest means of living, its social ambiguity (neither servant nor equal) will continue to represent her exceptionality, not as a fairytale princess, nor as the protagonist of an Old Testament tragedy, but as a marginalized woman on the fringes of a highly stratified social hierarchy.

To Dickens's Victorian readers, "A Progress" would also evoke Bunyan, and suggest that Esther's *Bildungsroman* would be a narrative of moral testing, and that it could shift into allegory. In this context, Esther's "noticing way" and her efforts "to understand . . . better" would serve as her weapons to defend her against moral pitfalls, not only those external to her, but also against her propensities to vanity and pride: "I have mentioned that, unless my vanity should deceive me (as I know it may, for I may be very vain without suspecting it—though indeed I don't)" (18). Certainly Esther subjects herself to moral self-examination, and if her humility seems occasionally specious, and her inability to be entirely honest with herself strikes us as repressive and neurotic, she is nevertheless following a program of moral self examination that is in no way unusual in the context of nineteenth-century Protestantism.

Bunyan's progress, however, is concerned with the difficulty of living a moral life in this world in preparation for the next world, a preparation suggested both by Esther's reading of 'He that is without sin among you, let him first cast a stone at her," and by Aunt Barbary's response "Watch ye therefore! lest coming he find you sleeping." Her response points toward the second coming of Christ, and with it the end of secular time. If Esther's narrative, from her aunt's death to her arrival in London, moves decisively away from the predestined narrative her aunt had set in motion, that narrative nevertheless returns at the conclusion of her first chapter. Precisely at the moment that Esther, Ada, and Richard have been "half laughing at our being like the children in the wood," Miss Flite appears. Both her appearance ("a curious little old woman in a squeezed bonnet and carrying a reticule, came curtseying and smiling up to us with an air of great ceremony") (34), and her first words to them ("Oh! . . . The wards in Jarndyce! Ve-ry happy, I am sure, to have the honour! It is a good omen for youth, and hope, and beauty, when they find themselves in this place, and don't know what's to come of it") retain the fairy tale mood. As she continues, however, the narrative moves from the fairy tale to Apocalypse: "I expect a judgment. Shortly. On the Day of Judgment. I have discovered that the sixth seal mentioned in the Revelations is the Great Seal. It has been open a long time! Pray accept my blessing."

Dickens's choice of the sixth seal is precise; the supernatural phenomena that follow its opening (darkening of the sun, earthquake, the fall of the stars, the emblematic fig tree, the *dies irae*) exactly recapitulate Christ's prophecy to the disciples in Mark 13, which is the chapter from which Aunt Barbary quotes as she has her fatal stroke.

V

My purpose here is not to give a sustained analysis of Esther's narrative. What I have sketched out so far suggests that a dominant motive for her narration comes from her need to discover a mode of narrative powerful enough to displace or dispel the preordained narrative model of her aunt, itself based on Biblical texts that formed the paradigmatic narrative of Christian history. If the death of Aunt Barbary implies that such a model no longer carries an absolute authority, and that there may be other versions of chronology that construct their own kinds of historical meaning, the shifting modes of Esther's narrative indicate that newer modes of chronology have not completely supplanted that authority, and that it continues to inhabit them in some shadowed way.

Thus the large pattern of Esther's narrative recapitulates the tragicomic Christian reading of the Old and New Testaments, tragedy appearing both in the subordinate plot ending with the death of Richard Carstone, and in the major plot with the death of Lady Dedlock, and comedy in the creation of a new Bleak House and in Esther's marriage to Allan Woodcourt.

VI

If a significant question for the *Bildungsroman* as fictional biography or autobiography is why we should attend to one voice rather than another—why Esther Summerson's life story has the authority to command our attention—that question has at least a partial answer in Esther's effort to cast the events of her life within a narrative paradigm that cancels the providential narrative of her aunt. It is of course obvious that Mrs. Barbary's narrative formula for Esther is one that few would wish to be forced to live, but the confrontation of narrative modes has mimetic implications that go considerably beyond that. Esther's aunt proposes a narrative in which Esther's individual personality is of virtually no importance. What is significant for Aunt Barbary is Esther's identity as defined by her illegitimate birth. Thus, the mimesis of Aunt Barbary's narrative is providential, resting on the interpretation of crucial biblical texts, and subsuming individuality in the symbolic and representative. One is reminded here of Elizabeth Rigby's remarks on *Jane Eyre*, a particularly grim example of the derivation of the ideology of hierarchical rank from the Bible, the Old Testament in particular.[12] Within this framework, identity is a function of origin, rather than development. The modernist thrust of the *Bildungsroman* is to replace this concept of a given identity with the ideology of individual character formation and development; against the biblical formula of the sins of the father being visited upon the son, it sets some version of Wordsworth's "The child is father of the man," the premise that generates Wordsworth's own *Bildungsroman, The Prelude*.

What matters most in Aunt Barbary's script is that Esther's illegitimacy sets her apart forever; what matters most in Esther's narrative is that her individual qualities become her legitimate identity, as John Jarndyce explains to Allan Woodcourt's mother, who dwells upon her son's royal Welsh lineage: " 'Come you, and see my child from hour to hour; set what you see against her pedigree, which is this and this'—for I scorned to mince it— 'and tell me what is the true legitimacy, when you shall have quite made up your mind on that subject' " (753).

To the extent that the closure of Esther's narrative fulfils her narrative program for herself on the basis of principles that she herself defines and substitutes for those of her aunt, her narrative both supersedes her aunt's, and cancels at least the relentless cycles that form her aunt's version of Providence. This is not to say that Esther's narrative escapes completely from the pattern of providential history by constructing a linear history that arrives at meaning on some quite different set of terms. Esther's narrative, in spite of its realistic elements, shifts the mode of tragic predestination into the mode of romance, in which the terms of deliverance depend upon exceptionality. Esther's qualities as an individual determine the closure of her story as her narrative asserts a modernist ideology that constructs identity on grounds other than those of origin. What characterized the hero of older romance narrative, exceptionality, is reregistered in modernist psychological terms as individuality, a historical construction of immense importance for a bourgeoisie that inhabited a world simultaneously defined by rank and class.

Yet Esther's apparently hard won individuality, worked out through her own narratizing activity, and pointed in the direction of what Jameson calls the salvational character of romance *(Political Unconscious* 105), finally accommodates or transposes itself to something quite different. Although it is her individuality, rather than her origin, that John Jarndyce stresses, that is itself subsumed within a specific historical context, as Esther becomes wife and helpmeet of Allan Woodcourt, and mother of his children. The opposition between freedom—the freedom to be oneself no matter what difficulties such freedom must carry with it—and comfort, the sense of relinquishing freedom for the security of dependence within a dominant structure that must be taken as benign if comfort is its promise, is resolved firmly in the direction of comfort.

Esther now sees herself not as Esther Summerson, but as the "Doctor's wife," and it is this new title that makes life meaningful for her. If Allan, descended from Welsh royalty, is not a Prince, but more secularly a physician, he is a healer, doing his good not by means of magic, but on the basis of scientific knowledge. This transmutation of magic (white or black) runs through the nineteenth-century re-writing of romance: Dr. Frankenstein, Count Fosco in *The Woman in White*, Lydgate, Ezra Jennings in *The Moonstone*, Dr. Jeykll. Moreover, Allan is the doctor as hero, in his efforts during the shipwreck, in his comforting of the dying Jo, where he functions both as physician and priest, and in his ministrations to Richard Carstone. And it is somehow from Allan's power, or the power of his speech, that the novel holds out as its last possibility the restoration of Esther's beauty.[13]

This reregistering of the heroic brings it within the compass of bourgeois realism and domesticates it. Esther's individuality is subsumed by Allan's exceptionality, which makes him an object of veneration, but his exceptionality is completely plausible within its secular context, and manifests itself within an exemplary work ethic. If the tendency of secular romance is to move toward a world re-envisioned as Utopian, or, as Frye puts it, "the quest-romance is the search of the libido or desiring self for a fulfilment that will deliver it from the anxiety of reality but will still contain that reality"(193), the conclusion of Esther's narrative is inarguably Utopian. The recreation of Bleak House as a vine covered cottage in Yorkshire and the provision there for all who are most dear to her, even while we know that the conditions under which Allan works are anything but Edenic, would seem to satisfy Frye's criterion for a world that remains itself, but is without anxiety. Death exists in this world ("I know that from the beds of those who were past recovery, thanks have often, often gone up, in the last hour, for his patient ministration. Is not this to be rich?") (796), but it is death far removed from the horror of Nemo's opium overdose, of Krook's combustion, the pathos of Jo and Gridley, the tragedies of Richard and of Lady Dedlock.

VII

Esther's narrative, concerned with the effort to discover or construct an authentic self, has parallels with *Jane Eyre, David Copperfield*, and *Great Expectations*. All are linear fictional autobiographies, and all, as internalized quests, rewrite romance in psychological terms. The shift from the heroic, external quest to the internal quest has far-reaching implications, and forms a a subject too large in scope to more than touch on here. Like all such shifts, such as the Christianization of classical genres, or the seventeenth-century shift from the tragedy of action to the tragedy of passion, it is both a response to, and a representation of, changing cultural pressures that force the adaptation of pre-existing forms to new uses. In the case of the quest, at least one possibility is that the external heroic no longer has an important cultural function in relation to modernity. Byron's "I want a hero," in the opening of *Don Juan*, marks an early instance of the withering away of the heroic in the wake of the Napoleonic wars and the Congress of Vienna, while the century's growing concentration on private life as a primary locus of ideological investment results in the novel's elaboration of "mute, inglorious Milton[s]" from Scott to Hardy's obscure Jude.

Notwithstanding the external adversities and adversaries that Dickens and Brontë provide in abundance in their narratives, the adversity and the adversary within are finally of greater significance for the process of self-discovery. Following Nietzsche and Freud, it is possible to see at least some of the "external" adversaries —Steerforth, Uriah Heep, Orlick, Drummle, and in *Jane Eyre*, Bertha, and perhaps even Rochester and St. John Rivers—as projections and objectifications of aspects of the self that cannot be consciously acknowledged. In Esther's case, the projection haunting her from childhood is the unknown mother, the beautiful and sinning Lady Dedlock, who is her mirror image, and whose sin her aunt has asserted Esther might well repeat. Another implication of the shift is that the struggle to achieve something like normal (Moretti would say "common") adulthood, given the conditions to which these characters are subject, becomes the modern equivalent of heroism. Of course, it is very much open to question that these characters *do* achieve normal adulthoods, if normalcy has any meaning beyond the statistical.

Unlike these narratives, which, like *Pride and Prejudice*, rework traditional genres, the omniscient narrative of *Bleak House* has, to the best of my knowledge, no fictional precedent. Linear narrative, essential to the *Bildungsroman*, is suspended in the omniscient narrative. Instead, Dickens adapts Carlyle's present tense from *The French Revolution*, without the benefit of the historical materials from which Carlyle shapes his narrative. While the physical settings of Dickens's narrative are historically real, the characters are Dickens's own. Carlyle's characters have documented individual histories that may or may not accord with Carlyle's presentation of them, but Carlyle's problem is in dramatizing them, not in creating them. For Dickens, the problem is to create characters that serve his thematic purpose; a purpose that appears to require extending the range of the novel beyond Esther's limited perspective.

I propose the following as a provisional way of suggesting the relationship between the two narratives. If the construction of an authentic self forms the principal subject of Esther's narrative, then the omniscient narrative serves to provide the broad historical context that establishes the environment providing the affective conditions, as well as the need, for such a quest. Its context is broader in the sense that these conditions bear not merely upon Esther, but on anyone and everyone at this juncture in time. These conditions are those of modernity, and a provisional definition of modernity, implicit in the present tense as trope, is that it is a moment in time that feels the past as deracination and decay (Tom All Alone's, Chancery, Chesney Wold), and the future, in the language of what Dickens calls ''the fashionable intelligence,'' as ''uncertain''(11).

In essence, Dickens has perceived in Carlyle's dramatized history precisely what Carlyle intended. For Carlyle (and Eric Hobsbawm), the French Revolution and the Industrial Revolution plunge Europe into the modern. Thus, to treat them in the past tense is to isolate them in the past, a refusal to recognize that they continue to act as forces in the present. Sir Leicester is the primary locus of the fear that the modern reveals itself as political change amounting to revolution, the overthrow of aristocratic hierarchy, but the omniscient narrator treats these fears ironically and comically. The Industrial Revolution and capitalism, represented by Rouncewell the iron master and the railroads under construction, as well as the change in function of Chancery, which I come to shortly, constitute the dominant force of change in the omniscient narrative.

A primary effect of the French Revolution was the levelling of the ranks of the ancien regime, so that the king himself became Citoyen Capet. It is in such levelling terms that Hazlitt describes the muse of the young Wordsworth, freshly returned from revolutionary France. And it is this levelling effect that pervades Dickens's omniscient narrative. Announced in the opening paragraphs, where fog and mud reduce everyone to a common identity in a world simultaneously suggestive of primordial geological development and imminent geological extinction (''the death of the sun'') it proceeds to the High Court of Chancery, the epitome of fog, mud, and, paradoxically, levelling. As a court, its original purpose was the securing or restoring of disputed property, so crucial to the British ideology of rank, and the basis of the socioeconomic power structure. Instead, it has become an instrument that in effect transforms property into money through its interminable court cases, and thus contributes to the ''cash nexus'' that for Carlyle (and Bulwer-Lytton) constitutes the value system for modern England. Money as the sign of the modern had already made its appearance in *Dombey and Son*, in little Paul's unanswerable question to Dombey, Sr., ''Papa, what is money?'' and would be the obsessive focus of the last novels. Here, its irrational, cancerous quality is reflected in Richard Carstone's fatal fascination with the Jarndyce suit (an element of the plot confined mostly to Esther's narrative, where it is treated

virtually as a mental disease), and in Grandmother Smallweed's senile lita-
nies, "Twenty thousand pounds, twenty twenty-pound notes in a money-box,
twenty guineas, twenty million twenty percent, twenty—'' (267).

Anxiety, uncertainty, and apprehension are the emotional markers of this
vision of modernity, and its other trope is the rhetorical question, directed
both toward the radically uncertain and obdurately mysterious future, and to
the inner life of characters such as Lady Dedlock and Tulkinghorn, masked
by their almost impenetrable facades. By making Lady Dedlock and Tulkinghorn the protagonist and antagonist of the omniscient narrative, Dickens
maximises anxiety and the modern need to read beneath the text. As a self-
created *arriviste* who has elevated manner into a protective art form, Lady
Dedlock acts a part with the skill of a great actress. She has, indeed, fulfilled
a dream of the bourgeoisie, which is to pass as an aristocrat. That Dickens
attaches her anxiety about discovery to a past that includes a love affair and
an illegitimate child may point to Victorian uneasiness with the manifestation
of female sexuality, and that Dickens makes her marriage to Sir Leicester
childless may underscore the fact that as Lady Dedlock she plays a mere stage
role, but that uneasiness may mask a deeper insecurity about the legitimacy of
the bourgeoisie as an emergent class.[14] Tulkinghorn, drinking ancient port,
dressed always in the costume of an earlier era, and holding the legal history
of the aristocracy under lock and key, whatever his motivation, effectively
purges her from her usurped place. Why this confrontation demands the death
of both is a question to which I shall return.

VII

While Esther's narrative makes use of the unexpected, it nevertheless manages to absorb the unexpected into pattern that has purposeful direction. The
omniscient narrative, on the other hand, takes the contingent and the fortuitous as the sources of its movement. The chance recognition by Lady Dedlock
of Captain Hawdon's handwriting on a Chancery document is enough to start
Tulkinghorn on his implacable quest to debase her, and the inability of the
omniscient narrator to do more than suggest Tulkinghorn's motivation in
pursuing Lady Dedlock, leaves us only with the uncertainty of hypotheses.
Tulkinghorn is a misogynist, Tulkinghorn wishes to remove the taint of Lady
Dedlock's sin from the aristocratic Dedlock family, or Tulkinghorn wishes
to bring Sir Leicester Dedlock to the level of ordinary mortals.

In such a world, in which appearances are registered with photographic
and sometimes hallucinatory clarity, interpretation becomes a compelling
activity. No matter how sharply the world appears, and its details are noted,
they may or may not be a guide to an underlying reality. The need to interpret

becomes essential in the context of the modern, because what seems fortuitous may be a function of cause and effect, while what seems part of a chain of cause and effect may merely be fortuitous. Lady Dedlock recognizes Captain Hawdon's personal handwriting somehow inhabiting standard Chancery script, Hawdon rents a room above Krook's rag and bottle shop, which happens to contain, among its endless piles of documents, the last will in the case of Jarndyce and Jarndyce, and Rachel, Aunt Barbara's housekeeper, somehow meets and marries Reverend Chadband. In *Hard Times*, Stephan Blackpool will describe this condition as "aw a muddle." In *Bleak House*, the process of proliferation and dissolution, represented both by the accumulation of documents and their turning to dust, and by the discovery of an endless web of connections between things, people, and events that seem too far separated in time or space to be connected, appears to be growing beyond the possibility of comprehension, or of being brought into the ordered perspective of diachronic narration.[15]

In this context, the motif of the search or quest assumes for the first time its peculiarly modern form, the detective narrative. As in Esther's narrative, these quests are for identity: Guppy begins his quest for Esther's identity after seeing her resemblance to Lady Dedlock's portrait in Chesney Wold, Mrs. Snagsby begins her quest for the identity of Jo as Snagsby's illegitimate child, Tulkinghorn his quest for Lady Dedlock's identity, and Inspector Bucket his quest for Tulkinghorn's killer and for the disguised Lady Dedlock. And here the quest also assumes its modern form as anxiety. In an essay on detective fiction, Moretti has asserted that the anxiety it arouses is conditioned by the fear that the criminal achieves success in the commission of a crime by his or her ability to appear as "one of us." Anxiety is allayed only when the detective has read beneath this disguise and identified the criminal as the alien in our midst; this, incidentally, becomes a stock in trade producer of anxiety in the shape changing or shape borrowing alien in science fiction. This is to say that one danger of homogeneity is that it may conceal the heterogeneous (*Signs* 134–35).[16]

The danger of the criminal or the alien is both in the subversion of law, and in the assertion of an individuality that threatens the status quo, but the assertion of individuality becomes dangerous only when it masks itself and does its work as part of the indistinguishable crowd. This applies also to the revolutionary, who sees the law as a superannuated system that either no longer works effectively, or preserves a society based upon inequities that are ideologically construed as inherent rights. Thus, for Sir Leicester, Mr. Rouncewell, the ironmaster, although he appears as a respectable and well-spoken member of the middle class, is analogous to Wat Tyler, leader of the peasant revolt, although England, as opposed to France, has had no true peasant class for centuries. And thus Madame Hortense, a French woman, disguises herself as Lady Dedlock, not only to murder Tulkinghorn, but also to level the house of the Dedlocks, striking both at the law and the aristocratic system it supports.[17]

Her exposure and capture are brought by the modern techniques of surveillance and entrapment, both engineered by Inspector Bucket, who functions as the primary reader of the most complex of modern texts, the city. What is ironic about Bucket is that, while he is successful in his imaginative construction of Hortense's plot, and in his divination of Lady Dedlock's flight narrative, he reaches his conclusions too late to stop the murder of Tulkinghorn, or to circumvent Lady Dedlock's death from exposure. These, then, become private histories that are fated to write themselves out, or to fulfil their destinies, and Bucket, as the discoverer of these histories, becomes their narrator. His narrative is the first of what is to become a classic scene in later detective fiction, the drawing room or library scene in which the detective, in the presence of the criminal, narrates the crime, the process of detection, and identifies the criminal.

In his discussions of *The Moonstone* and *Bleak House*, D. A. Miller makes the important point that the detection of a crime is essentially a process of simplification (33–34). In an initially overdetermined field where everything and everyone are charged with potential significance, the detective, by a process of deduction backed by previous experience, eventually reduces everything not pertaining to the crime to its usual and customary valence, so that the crime narrative is foregrounded in full clarity. It is of equal ideological moment that the act of detection recreates the common world as innocent (the world of "us"), and isolates the criminal as the radically self-directed alien who preys upon our innocence.

In *Bleak House*, however, the comforting neatness of the detective story is withheld. While Inspector Bucket is able to reconstruct the murder of Tulkinghorn on an inspiration that is almost divinely prompted—"By the living Lord it flashed on me ... that she had done it!" (649)—he never makes it clear how Madame Hortense has been able to arrive at a possible motivation for Lady Dedlock to murder Tulkinghorn, and thus, in murdering him herself, to make Lady Dedlock a plausible suspect. Bucket is limited to the "how" and the "why" (Hortense's hatred of Lady Dedlock), but essential details, which would be brought to light in a work such as *The Moonstone*, remain unexplained.

A preliminary way of accounting for this, which may seem at first as begging the question, is to fall back on genre. As Moretti remarks in his essay on detective fiction, the detective *novel* is a contradiction in terms because detective fiction is anti-novelistic (*Signs* 137). The process of detection is retrograde, moving backward from the crime to discover its origins in the past, while the temporal movement of the novel is forward, as in Esther's narrative, which moves from past to present, and an implied future. Moreover, the detective novel assumes a stable society that has been violated by a criminal act that is fundamentally antisocial, while the realistic novel, whether it endorses or attacks a status quo, sees it as a moment in history that is dynamic, rather than stable, where contradictory forces are struggling against each other, as in Mr. Rouncewell's bourgeois determination to remove Rosa, Lady Dedlock's maid, from the aristocratic influence of Chesney Wold, and to educate her to a new, presumably better, set of values.

More than that, the detective novel is anti-novelistic because it sees individuality as a threat; the fully developed and individuated being becomes autonomous, acting on self-generated principles that strike both at the heart of the victim and society; individuality and criminality are homologous. In fact, this construction of individuality is not only anti-novelistic, it is also anti-tragic. In tragedy, individuality is represented ambiguously as simultaneously innocent and guilty, and thus beyond simplification as good or evil. As an instance, Lear sees himself as the innocent victim of his scheming daughters, yet it is his initial and individual assertion of self that creates the model of autonomous will acting out its desires that activates the desires of Goneril and Regan, freeing them from their familial and communal identities as daughters, and releasing their individualities: Regan: "Hang him [Gloucester] instantly." Goneril: "Pluck out his eyes" (III,vii, 4–5). What distinguishes *King Lear*, with all its murders, from detective fiction is precisely this ambiguity, propelling the forward movement of tragedy.

In *Bleak House*, the novelistic impulse toward realism both contains the detective narrative and refutes its reductive procedures. Moretti asserts that "the *fabula* narrated by the detective in his reconstruction of facts brings us back to the beginning; that is, it abolishes narration"(*Signs* 148). But Bucket's narration does not end the novel by bringing it to the certainty of closure, where everything falls, once and for all, into place. That would, in effect, be the exclusively *literary* solution of the narrative, and a contradiction of the realistic premise driving the text, a premise embodied in the rhetorical question regarding the web of forces that somehow connects the most disparate phenomena. Any force exerted at any one point of the web will affect the whole in unpredictable ways—again, the fortuitous or contingent aspect of the web that keeps it from being reduced to a single linear narrative of cause and effect. This is the realist mode of Carlyle's *French Revolution*, which rejects linear narrative on the grounds that it falsifies the complex forces that are the dynamics of history. Thus, Bucket's activity generates, rather than closes narrativity. The effect of his revelations not only exposes Hortense, but just as importantly, unexpectedly triggers Sir Leicester's stroke, just as Madame Hortense's communication to Mrs. Rouncewell, leading to Mrs. Rouncewell's meeting with Lady Dedlock, along with Guppy's meeting with

Lady Dedlock, as well as the Smallweeds' demand for hush money, precipitates Lady Dedlock's flight.

And again, the realistic premise of the narrative refutes the detective novel's insistence on the changelessness of character, most obviously in what we can call Sir Leicester's growth, and what amounts to Lady Dedlock's anagnorisis. Inspector Bucket operates within the decorum of non-developmental assumptions about character in his consistent typing of characters as a way of understanding *and* controlling them, which is also a way of controlling his narratives. Esther is a "pattern," Sir Leicester is always addressed by his full title, which circumscribes and defines his character, Mr. Snagsby is not asked, but told who he is. But characters nevertheless have a way of escaping from Bucket's typing. His reading of Gridley will not allow Gridley to die, because it is untrue to type, but he dies, nevertheless. And Bucket's initial reading of Lady Dedlock results in a fatal mistake beyond his power to correct. There is a "messiness" about reality that eludes the orderliness of policing, as in the scene in the police station where the officers, quietly writing their reports, are accompanied by the descant of "some beating and calling out at distant doors underground"(675). If the world obeyed the laws of Bucket's typology, there would either be no need for further policing, or typical predictability would allow preventive intervention before damage is done.

This messiness may be interpreted in various ways; certainly in *Bleak House*, it may be interpreted as the monadal resistence of a given character to be typed by a meaning system other than the character's own; by insistently following its own laws, a character acts out its own destiny. Whether or not this is a character's freedom to be itself, or a manifestation of a character's limitation to be only itself, the consequence for Bucket is that he is limited to following the trajectory of a character who has already passed him. It is only when the character has arrived at his or her peculiar destination that Bucket can complete the narrative a posteriori. Even then, there is resistance; Madame Hortense resists Bucket's co-opting of her narrative with contempt and abuse.

VIII

The first and second chapters of *Bleak House*, both of which come from the omniscient narrator, center respectively on Chancery and Lady Dedlock; the resolution of the Chancery suit and of Lady Dedlock's narrative, however, both pass over to Esther's narrative, while the omniscient narrator's final chapter returns to the widowed and stricken Sir Leicester at Chesney Wold, waiting for death. This shift constitutes a *problem*, since Esther's narrative, engaged in the working out of her identity within the context of the liberal bourgeoisie (Mr. Jarndyce and Allan Woodcourt), seems at least on the surface far removed from Chancery, ostensibly concerned with the older, hierarchical rights of property, and from Lady Dedlock's self-constructed role as aristocrat. The omniscient narrative also represents most graphically what Mr. Kenge calls the "Grasp" of Chancery, its tentacles that reach throughout the country, that slowly crush Tom All Alone's, and that fill Mr. Krook's shop with endless documents.

The problem, then, is why Dickens moves the conclusion of the Chancery suit and the death of Lady Dedlock into what is essentially domestic romance. The obvious reasons for this are, of course, that Lady Dedlock is Esther's mother, and that Richard Carstone is intimately involved in Esther's life, making it appropriate for Esther to be present at their deaths. On the other hand, Chancery is a national institution, an important part of the public sphere, and Lady Dedlock, as the wife of Sir Leicester, and center of the fashionable world, is herself a public figure, as her picture in Weevle's collection of fashionable beauties testifies. Moreover, she is the wife of a member of the traditional ruling class, which underwrites her privileged social position.

What I would suggest is that the death of Lady Dedlock and Richard validate the conclusion of Esther's narrative, which has to do with the comforting domestication of desire. Lady Dedlock's history of desire is a reversal of Esther's. In order to achieve status, Lady Dedlock leaves a younger man whom she loves for an older man. Esther, capable of suppressing her desire for a younger man, and of marrying John Jarndyce out of gratitude, rather than because of a desire for status, is rewarded with an utopian Bleak House and Allan Woodcourt. Had Esther married Jarndyce, there would be at least the appearance that she has, as her aunt foretold, repeated her mother's actions. Even here, however, only the appearance of repetition would hold, because the motivations, self-aggrandizement and gratitude, are entirely different.

Richard, whose aspirations to status at first trace the customary professions open to a gentleman (medicine, the military, the law), falls back instead on the unravelling of the Chancery suit as the basis for achieving status, and is destroyed by the conflicted identity of the court itself. If Chancery were performing its original function, the adjudication of contested property rights in favor of the legitimate heir, Richard would inherit, and would gain the status that is rightfully his on the grounds of property, a vindication of the older hierarchical system of rank. But Chancery no longer functions in that way. It has instead become a game of chance, in which the "legatees" become gamblers for stakes, and in which the house wins by a long process of obfuscation where, as I said earlier, property, eaten up in cost, is transformed into money. The real function of Chancery, from this perspective, is not to proliferate itself as a modern bureaucracy (as in the Office of Circumlocution in

Little Dorrit), but to transform a traditional legal system into a system of speculation, masking its modern function as a recirculator of cash behind the forms of traditional law.

Chance, with its attendant anxieties, functions in this modern context as it does on the stock market, as an arbitrary leveller, and playing the game of Chancery is equivalent to playing the market. In Dickens's vision, however, it is even more efficient than the market because no one wins against the house. By the time that Richard has come—by chance—into possession of the winning ticket, the last will, there is nothing left to win, and the will that should give him legitimate status as a property owner has become merely one more meaningless document among all the others produced by the suit, which takes Richard's inheritance *and* his life.

Lady Dedlock's death, like Richard's, seems altogether too extreme or melodramatic as punishment for what the novel asserts are misplaced objects of desire. Having conquered the aristocratic world by a programmatic self-fashioning that has transformed her into a status symbol and an object of desire—Bob Stables has called her "the best groomed woman in the stud" (13), and Weevle hangs her picture prominently in his gallery of fashionable beauties—she has arrived at a point where status becomes stasis. I said earlier that Lady Dedlock, like Esther, is freefloating and extraordinary, creating a basis for narration. But Lady Dedlock, in order to keep her position, must *prevent* narration, because for her the only possible narration is one of exposure, the revelation that she has no legitimate claim to her position. In this, she is like the criminal, who must create a facade as "one of us" to prevent narration and exposure.

But Lady Dedlock is not, strictly speaking, a criminal; her affair with Captain Hawdon occurred before her marriage to Sir Leicester, and she has not, therefore, committed adultery, the only ground on which Sir Leicester could divorce her in English law. Thus, when Tulkinghorn proceeds against her, gathering evidence and slowly building the narrative which he finally presents at Chesney Wold, he is using the mechanisms of legal detection for a personal vendetta, rather than for bringing a criminal to justice. Tulkinghorn's vendetta against Lady Dedlock abuses the legal system by turning it into a personal instrument, but more than this, he conducts what is a private trial of Lady Dedlock and passes sentence on her. Moretti has noted that the interrogative, which is the proper mode of trial proceedings, is a peculiarly prominent feature of English fiction, and that fictional dialogue often takes the form of interrogative examination (209). We may extend his observation to drama, where we see, for instance, in Shakespeare, the structure of the trial appearing across the full range of dramatic genres, and from the earliest to the latest plays. Beyond England, the trial narrative is of central importance in Sophocles, where, if we follow René Girard, the creation of public law

serves to diffuse the energy of the vendetta across the public sphere, freeing
the individual from the guilt of scapegoating, and bringing to a halt the
inevitable generational cycle of the vendetta (52–3). It is exactly this characteristic of public law that Tulkinghorn violates, as if his atavistic black identifies him not merely with the eighteenth century, but with a time before the
law—before, that is, the Roman allegory in his chambers, below whose pointing finger his body is found.

It is after Tulkinghorn's death that Lady Dedlock's narrative is folded into
Esther's narrative, where it takes an extreme form of tragic recognition and
reversal. At this late point in the novel, Aunt Barbary's providential narrative
of wrath reappears, but Lady Dedlock, rather than Esther, takes the role of
scapegoat. Aunt Barbary's projected narrative is fulfilled, but in terms quite
other than she proposed. The initial text to which she reacts, concerning the
woman taken in adultery, is misapplied if the reference is to Lady Dedlock,
while Aunt Barbary's response, concerning the second coming of Christ and
the Last Judgment, reappears not as Apocalypse, but as Tulkinghorn's confrontation of Lady Dedlock with his knowledge of her past. Since the acts of
Providence cannot be understood except in retrospect, Aunt Barbary's narrative is an act of presumption. It is Esther, not Aunt Barbary, who finishes the
tragic narrative, and it should be clear that the tragedy is specific to the
individual will of Lady Dedlock and determined by her choice and action
alone.

The certainty of exposure precipitates Lady Dedlock's flight and death;
the question is *what* her exposure signifies. During Bucket's narration of
Lady Dedlock's past, the symptoms of Sir Leicester's stroke begin, suggesting
that his physical system (and the social system to which he belongs) cannot
tolerate her history of illicit love. But as Bucket says, and as Sir Leicester
must know, other aristocratic houses have such skeletons in their closets, and
Sir Leicester immediately forgives her and orders the search for her return.
Esther's narrative has made it clear long before Lady Dedlock's flight that
Esther is Lady Dedlock's child. Dickens has chosen not to make that revelation the prime point of suspense in her narrative, nor do I think that here the
major issue is that Lady Dedlock is a fallen woman.

What I would suggest is that Lady Dedlock's exposure is keyed to her
success, and what it proves is that her identity as an aristocrat is fraudulent.
The fact that she can have a child by Captain Hawdon, but not by Sir Leicester, implies that she has risen beyond her "natural" level, while Esther's
children with Allan Woodcourt imply a match between her personal identity
and her social status.

If Lady Dedlock's fraudulent success can be seen as somehow a threat to
the aristocracy, the nature of that threat or scandal remains to be defined.
One obvious line would be that Lady Dedlock, penetrating a closed world of

ancient precedent, threatens that world in the same way that the criminal, passing as ordinary, as "one of us," threatens the more general social stability. But what if we assume, as the omniscient narrator assumes, on the grounds of realism, that society is not stable, but that it is a field in which, as in Carlyle's *French Revolution*, a complex of forces is at work, so that Sir Leicester can respond to Mr. Rouncewell as a revolutionary, and so that disease may spread from Jo, at the bottom of society, to the top? What stands to be exposed here is not that Lady Dedlock, from her sister's point of view, is a more than common sinner, but that Lady Dedlock's successful appropriation of the characteristics of the aristocracy has led to her adoption of the "freezing mood"(13), which has become the quintessential characteristic of the aristocracy itself. It is not, after all, Lady Dedlock who is sterile, but Sir Leicester. Sir Leicester, called "old man gray" by Madame Hortense, is a relic, like Volumnia and all the ladies with "skeleton throats," dancing in a mimicry of youth under chandeliers that have lost their lustres, while Chesney Wold sinks into a "dull repose"(767). It is this that the last chapter of the omniscient narrator shows us, an aristocracy that has lost its function. The early history of Lady Dedlock exposes the sterility of the aristocracy, shatters its illusions of power and continuity, and reveals it as a superannuated system, that, like the external hero, capable of extraordinary feats as proof that he is *arista* (the best), no longer has significance for the modern context. Sir Leicester finally appears as a frail knight, escorted by Mr. George, his faithful squire; their habitual journey is to the Dedlock mausoleum, where he is soon to lie with his ancestors.

IX

The omniscient narrator links Chancery and the aristocracy as institutions of ancient precedent, representatives of an hierarchical system threatened, with good reason, by the levelling tendency of the modern. Yet if my analysis is correct, there is a radical difference between them. In Chancery the traditional machinery of the law has been put to unprecedented modern usage as an efficient instrument of levelling, as it transforms the ideological foundation of precedent and identity, property, into currency. Richard's renunciation of the traditional roles open to a gentleman for the equivalent of speculation on the market is analogous to the feverish speculation that followed the development of the railroad, and the revelation that Jarndyce and Jarndyce has been eaten up in costs mirrors the bust cycles that were a characteristic feature of the market.

The temptation of Chancery lies in the image it projects of tradition, the lure of rising to the status of the aristocracy, itself moribund. Against this,

Esther's narrative projects a bourgeois romance of identity formation and individuality, a vindication of selfhood simultaneously resistent to the aristocratic insistence on origins as definitive of the self (Sir Leicester's "family is as old as the hills, and infinitely more respectable"[12]), and to the levelling of people into statistics of modern economics. Although their means are different, Lady Dedlock and Richard fall to the temptation of upward mobility; their punishment is not that they are forced to acknowledge their place in the bourgeoisie, but that they are reduced to poverty and death.

The authority of the omniscient narrator is in the recreation of the conditions of modernity, where not even the acuteness of an Inspector Bucket can do more than trace out the individual narratives of Madame Hortense and Lady Dedlock, after the fact. Once these narratives are set in motion, Bucket's almost magical ability to appear virtually anywhere at will cannot stop the process, it can only record it. Linear narrative seems finally an inadequate means of describing the modern; inadequate because of its essentially arbitrary isolation of single narrative strands in the web of interacting forces. The model of diagnosis, operating most frequently post mortem (Nemo, Jo, Krook, Tulkinghorn, Gridley, Richard, Lady Dedlock), allows us to posit something like a scientific equivalent of Providence as the authoritative guide to truth. Providential readings of history are also retrospective, as in Henry V's "O God, thy arm was here!" (IV, viii, 108) after the battle of Agincourt, or Horatio's promised narration of "carnal, bloody, and unnatural acts,/Of accidental judgments, casual slaughters, Of deaths put on by cunning and forced cause,/And, in this upshot, purposes mistook/Fall'n on th' inventors' heads," in the final scene of *Hamlet*.

The problem with the scientific or diagnostic method of arriving at truth is the obvious one that the truth arrived at has little or no meaning in qualitative, or human, terms. If the link between Jo and Esther, for instance, is smallpox, smallpox does not infect its victims as a punishment for character flaws or sins. Jo, told constantly to "move on," may be a metonymy for the spread of disease, and disease, as a leveller, may be a metonymy for the modern condition, in its indifference to the status of its victims and to decorum, but disease, with perhaps the exception of Sir Leicester's gout, cannot, without the violence of metaphor, be brought within a teleological perspective.

But Dickens's omniscient narrative's presentation of modernity as a web or relationships too complex to be reduced, except arbitrarily, to linearity, is like the scientist's recognition that in selecting a specific phenomenon for study, he or she is making an arbitrary selection from the infinitely complex system that constitutes external reality. At the same time that the selective eye of the omniscient narrator is arbitrary, however, it is not reductive. It reads what it sees as individuality, or, if not fully differentiated individuality, as type, rather than stereotype. We may immediately recognize Chadband,

Guppy, and Grandfather Smallweed as types, but their languages—what Riffaterre calls idiolects—are specific and idiosyncratic.[18] The omniscient narrator gives us an anthropology, as opposed to a sociology, of the modern. In this anthropology, the city, an essentially human, but also alien creation, takes the place of nature as the external artifact against which the individual is forced to define himself or herself, and to create microcommunities resistant to the entropic drift towards anonymity, automatism, or statistics.

NOTES

1. The fullest discussion of *Tom Jones* as providential fiction is Leopold Damrosch Jr.'s in *God's Plot and Man's Stories: Studies in Fictional Imagination from Milton to Fielding* (Chicago: U of Chicago, 1985).
2. *The Way of the World: The Bildungsroman in European Culture* (London: Verso, 1987) 4-5. Throughout this essay I am indebted to Moretti's work on the *Bildungsroman*. Although there are points where I disagree with Moretti, particularly in his reading of the English *Bildungsroman*, he has given us the most lucid, imaginative, and provocative study of the form to date.
3. It may seem questionable here to invoke as first examples poetic, rather than prose narratives. But the ease with which Mary Shelley transmutes Prometheus into *Frankenstein*, which shares characteristics of the *Bildungsroman*, and the absorption of the Byronic hero by the novel (*Wuthering Heights, Jane Eyre, Moby Dick*), suggests their affinities with prose represntations of the new modernity.
4. "Ideologeme" is a critical term coined by Fredric Jameson; I quote his definition: "The ideologeme is an amphibious formation, whose essential structural characteristic may be described as its possibility to manifest itself as a pseudoidea—a conceptual or belief system, an abstract value, an opinion or prejudice—or as a protonarrative, a kind of ultimate class fantasy about the 'collective characters' which are the classes in opposition." *The Political Unconscious* (Ithaca: Cornell UP,1981), 87.
5. Even in Austen, an essential feature of the plot is the incompetence of the older generation, parents in particular, which places the responsibility for shaping their lives on the young. For her purposes, Austen shifts the blocking action by the older generation from the arbitrary imposition of a law or edict (the Duke in *Measure for Measure*, Duke Frederick in *As You Like It*, Leontes in *The Winter's Tale*) to incompetence. Since incompetence is inherent, rather than arbitrary, and thus susceptible to chastening, but not to change, plot resolution moves more definitively toward a future in which incompetence is not so much absorbed, but rather replaced by younger figures—Darcy, Mr. Knightley, Captain Wentworth.
6. See Audrey Jaffe, *Vanishing Points: Dickens, Narrative, and the Subject of Omniscience* (Berkeley, U of California P, 1991).
7. Both Martineau and Ruskin are quoted in *Hard Times*, eds. George Ford and Sylvère Monod (New York, London: W. W. Norton, 1966) 302-05, 331-32.

8. *The Letters of Charles Dickens*, ed. K. J. Fielding (London, Nonesuch Press, 1938), III:125.

9. For an analysis of the relationship between gendered narration and the issue of authority, see LuAnn McCracken Fletcher, "A Recipe for Perversion: The Feminine Narrative Challenge in *Bleak House* " (*Dickens Studies Annual*, 25, 1996) 67- 69. Fletcher argues that Esther's narrative acts as an implicit exposure of "the conventions we use when we read omniscient narratives. . ." (83). She also provides a useful survey of gender criticism of Esther's narrative from the first reviews to the present.

10. If Esther is neither clever nor beautiful, on what grounds do we pay attention to her? Traditionally, the reason for telling a woman's story was that she was one or the other, or both. Maggie Tulliver, for instance, is a bright child and becomes a beautiful woman; Becky Sharp lives up to her name, Amelia Sedley is beautiful, as is Tess Durbeyfield. What makes these woman narratable is their exceptionality—within the conventions of the nineteenth-century novel, with a beautiful and/ or intelligent woman there is seldom a dull moment.

11. Esther's story, like Ann Elliot's in *Persuasion* or Fanny Price's in *Mansfield Park*, is an obvious version of the Cinderella Story. That basic pattern, a movement from non-recognition to recognition and vindication, may well have served as powerful a purpose for nineteenth-century women readers as the self-made man rising from undistinguished beginnings to success had for Victorian male readers. Dickens, whose own life follows the pattern, exploits it in *David Copperfield* and explodes it in *Hard Times* and *Great Expectations*. These may be fairytales or fantasies of wish fulfillment, but their cultural power derives from the fact that they are ideological constructions, and is not conditioned by whether or not they are "realistic."

12. "It pleased God to make her an orphan, friendless and penniless—yet she thanks nobody, and least of all Him, for the food and raiment, the friends, companions, and instructors of her helpless youth. . ." Quoted in *Jane Eyre*, ed. Richard J Dunn (New York, London: Norton, 1977) 451.

13. The restoration of Esther's beauty, which has been talismanic in Mr. Guppy's construction of his own romance, where Esther is the object of his "heroic" desire, stimulated by his recognition of her resemblence to the portrait of Lady Dedlock at Chesney Wold, then shattered by her disfigurement, is an extreme form of Lady Dedlock's transformation from prettiness to classicality. With Lady Dedlock, however, this re-formation of the self is a conscious construct, while for Esther it is a process of which she is not conscious.

14. This anxiety is treated tragically in Mr. Dorrit's assumption of the role of English Milord in his European tour, and comically in Noddy Boffin's setting up of a fashionable establishment in *Our Mutual Friend*. That in both cases, wealth comes from an apparently gratuitous inheritance raises interesting questions for exploration.

15. ". . .the formal crisis of the novel today has its roots in the historical situation, which seems too complex for presentation in a narrative model." Fredric Jameson, *Marxism and Form*, (Princeton, Princeton UP, 1971) 350. Dickens's omniscient narrative appears to anticipate this crisis.

16. A prime example of this in early Dickens is Sikes's participation in the firefighting scene, presumably as another helpful citizen, during his flight after the murder of Nancy.

17. Mademoiselle Hortense's murder falls under common law, against which Dickens advances no brief in the novel, as he does against equity (Chancery).

18. Michael Riffaterre, *Fictional Truth* (Baltimore, Johns Hopkins UP, 1990) 28 *et passim.*

WORKS CITED

Austen, Jane. *Pride and Prejudice.* Ed. Donald J. Gray. New York: Norton, 1966.

Byron, George Gordon, Lord. *Byron.* Ed. Jerome J. McGann. Oxford: Oxford UP, 1986.Brontë, Charlotte. *Jane Eyre.* Ed. Beth Newman. Boston: St. Martin's, 1996.

Carlyle, Thomas. *Works.* Ed. H. D. Traill, 30 vols. London: Chapman and Hall, 1896–99.

Damrosch, Leopold. *God's Plot and Man's Stories: Studies in the Fictional Imagination from Milton to Fielding.* Chicago: Chicago UP, 1985.

Dickens, Charles. *Bleak House.* Eds. George Ford and Silvère Monod. New York: Norton, 1977.

———. *David Copperfield.* New York: Signet, 1962.

———. *Dombey and Son.* Ed. Peter Fairclough. London: Penguin, 1970.

———. *Great Expectations.* Ed. Janice Carlisle. New York: St. Martin's, 1996.

Fletcher, LuAnn McCracken. "A Recipe for Perversion: The Feminine Narrative Challenge in *Bleak House.*" *Dickens Studies Annual* 25 (1996): 67–89.

Frye, Northrop. *Anatomy of Criticism.* Princeton: Princeton UP, 1957.

Girard, René. *Violence and the Sacred.* trans. Patrick Gregory. Baltimore: Johns Hopkins UP, 1977.

Hobsbawm, E. J. *The Age of Revolution 1789–1848.* New York: Signet, 1962.

Jaffe, Audrey. *Vanishing Points: Dickens, Narrative, and the Subject of Omniscience.* Berkeley: California UP, 1991.

Jameson, Fredric. *The Political Unconscious: Narrative as a Socially Symbolic Act.* Ithaca: Cornell UP, 1981.

———. *Marxism and Form.* Princeton: Princeton UP, 1971.

Larson, Janet. *Dickens and the Broken Scripture*. Athens: Georgia UP, 1985.

Miller, D. A. *The Novel and the Police*. Berkeley: U of California P, 1988

Miller, J. Hillis. Introduction. *Bleak House*, by Charles   Dickens. Harmondsworth: Penguin, 1971.

Moretti, Franco. *Signs Taken for Wonders: Essays in the Sociology of Literary Forms*. London: Verso, 1988.

———. *The Way of the World: The Bildungsroman in European Culture*. London: Verso, 1987.

Shakespeare, William. *The Riverside Shakespeare*. Gen. ed. G. Blakemore Evans et al. Boston: Houghton Mifflin, 1997.

Distorted Religion: Dickens, Dissent, and *Bleak House*

David A. Ward

Nothing fired Dicken's imagination, Humphry House once suggested, like "the muddle he hated," and no work better demonstrates the muddled ways of Victorian England than Bleak House. *Critics have long recognized the special status of this novel among Dickens's works: it is the most comprehensive in its representation of British culture, the most complex in its analysis, and the most conflicted in its evaluation of the workings of power. What has not gained sufficient attention, however, is the religious dimension of the text, specifically, the extraordinary extent to which contemporary religious controversies inform* Bleak House *and its socio-political outlook. The role of religion in the novel goes far beyond the author's well-known antipathy to spiritual gloominess and hypocrisy. Dickens's supposed distaste for theological debate notwithstanding, he is at pains throughout the work to demonstrate the manifest inferiority of a particular segment of the country's Christian population, namely, religious Dissenters, and to represent the serious threat they posed to the moral and spiritual health of the nation. The novel imposes the practice of seeing Dissent as aberrant and corrupt, a deviation from a normaive Anglican—and more fully English—identity. Dickens's anti-Dissenting discourse in* Bleak House *is central to his criticism of mid-Victorian culture.*

> There have been at work among us three great social agencies: the London City Mission, the novels of Mr. Dickens, the cholera.
>
> —Anonymous nineteenth-century Dissenter

By 1852, the year in which *Bleak House* began publication in monthly parts,

Dickens Studies Annual, Volume 29, Copyright © 2000 by AMS Press, Inc. All rights reserved.

it was evident to Charles Dickens's readers that the light-hearted comicality of early works like *The Pickwick Papers* (1836–37) and the autobiographical musings of *David Copperfield* (1849–50) had given way to a dark strain of cultural criticism. England, Dickens felt, was in "a muddle." Although millions had flocked, the previous year, to the Great Exhibition, where the nation's material achievements were on elaborate display (popular attractions included the Nasmyth steam hammer, the Ross telescope, and a powerful hydraulic press), the novelist was in no mood to celebrate, as his memorable opening evocation of London mire and fog makes abundantly clear. Readers fresh from the imposing iron and glass Crystal Palace in Hyde Park, symbol of a new era of national well-being and optimism, stepped into a much different world at the outset of *Bleak House*: dreary city streets darkened by a "soft black drizzle" of smoke and soot, with inhabitants plodding about "in a general infection of ill temper" (17). Here were no rhetorical flourishes over growing British prosperity, no paeans to the wonders of human ingenuity (both in ready supply elsewhere at mid-century[1]), but rather bewilderment and anger over a culture in which things had gone terribly awry. With a famously abrupt identification of his setting—"London. Michaelmas Term lately over and the Lord Chancellor sitting in Lincoln's Inn Hall. Implacable November weather" (17)—Dickens sets in motion his most complex and today most critically acclaimed narrative, a somber vision of institutional disorder and the profound consequences of that disorder for Victorian society as a whole.

Parliament, he felt, had proven itself a "great dust heap of imbeciles and dandies" (Letter to Harriet Martineau, 3 July 1850, 6: 122), a contemptible "failure and nuisance" (Letter to Bulwer Lytton, 28 January 1857, 8: 270) incapable of grappling with the nation's considerable social ills. For generations, he remarked scornfully, lawmakers had "directed their entire attention to [the] graceful art" of folding their arms ("Why?" 98). Although Britain was becoming more democratic—Dickens himself had witnessed debates preceding passage of the Reform Bill of 1832 as a young Parliamentary reporter—extension of the franchise had hardly produced dramatic improvements: elections were by and large exercises in corruption and demagoguery, systems of patronage and family influence remained entrenched (Sir Leicester Dedlock of *Bleak House* can trace his "threads of relationship" throughout the ruling class [400]), and cumbersome bureaucracies had made inefficiency the norm in government, as would be demonstrated in the massive mismanagement of the Crimean War of 1853–56 and, fictionally, in the bunglings of the "Circumlocution Office" in *Little Dorrit* (1855–57). The public functionary, the novelist declared in an 1851 essay, "delights in Red Tape"; the purpose of his existence is "to tie up public questions great and small, in an abundance of this official article—to make the neatest possible parcels of them, ticket them, and carefully put them away on a top shelf out of human reach'' (''Red Tape'' 243).

But nothing fired Dickens's imagination, Humphry House suggests, like ''the muddle he hated'' (203), and from the start of *Bleak House*, which presents the hopeless inefficiency and corruption of the legal establishment, things are quite muddled, indeed. It wasn't the first time, of course, that Dickens had turned his attention to the disturbing realities of nineteenth-century England; an awareness of the country's social ills is in evidence in many of his texts. Even the sunny *Pickwick Papers*, renowned for its genial humor and its celebration of the communal pleasures of ''merry old England''—coach rides, country inns, and holiday feasts—had its moments of cultural critique when the title character is victimized by the unscrupulous lawyers Dodson and Fogg and is jailed in London's Fleet Prison, where he sees firsthand the distress of its ill-fed, poorly clothed inmates.

But *Bleak House*, Dickens's ninth novel, is different from his earlier texts in a number of ways: it is more comprehensive in its representation of British culture, more studied and complex in its analysis (as evidenced formally in its intricate network of parallel characters, scenes, and images), and, at the same time, more conflicted in its evaluation of the workings of power—despite his well-known frustrations with the nation's institutional abuses, there were certain elements of the mid-Victorian status quo that this author was quite eager to preserve. No other work better demonstrates the truth of George Ford's remark that Dickens was ''not so much the friend of the common man as the friend of the common Englishman'' (''The Governor Eyre Case'' 228); his indignation over incompetence and needless suffering was profound, but groups and practices that he perceived as *un*-English, even (perhaps especially) those present within Britain itself, warranted no sympathy and were, in some instances, worthy of careful surveillance and control by established authority. Hence, his reticence on the plight of the Irish during the Famine years and his surprisingly stern pronouncements on law and order. By mid-century, he had in fact become deeply ambivalent about the political and social structures he examined; if he was keenly aware of the serious shortcomings of Parliament and English courts, schools, and prisons, he also recognized their crucial role in defining cultural boundaries in a time of transition—the making of the modern English state—and in maintaining certain desirable hierarchies of status and privilege. *Bleak House* evidences this divided mind, as do his public statements at this time. Speaking to politicians and businessmen in 1855 on the subject of government reform, he was careful to temper his criticism: ''I wish to avoid placing in opposition here the two words Aristocracy and People. I am one of those who can believe in the virtues and uses of both, and I would elevate or depress neither, at the cost of a single just right belonging to either'' (Speech to Administrative Reform Association

203). In an earlier speech at the Mechanics' Institution of Liverpool he had declared, "Difference of wealth, of rank, of intellect, we know there must be, and we respect them" (Speech to Soiree 56).

Thus, it would be a mistake to cast Dickens solely as a rebel and outsider—as a writer who identified completely with the dispossessed and deprived of Victorian England whose interests were ignored by a corrupt and complacent ruling class. Thomas A. Jackson's early Marxist study, *Charles Dickens: The Progress of a Radical* [1937], exemplifies this sort of overemphasis on the author's antagonism to the British state. There is much in his life and work that runs counter to this view, and for those acquainted only with Dickens's egalitarian impulses, the contrasts that a thorough examination of his speeches and writings creates can be quite jarring. If he detested the inequity and hardship created by an inefficient government, he was repulsed as well by any threats to stability and public safety, even those arising out of a sincere desire for political change. During the Chartist uprisings of the late 1830s and 40s, Peter Ackroyd reminds us, Dickens was never more than "a concerned spectator" (326); and although he condemned despotic regimes abroad, he responded to the revolutions on the Continent not with sympathy but with the fevered and monitory mob scenes of *A Tale of Two Cities* (1859). Even George Bernard Shaw, who attributed his own leftist politics to his readings in Dickens, acknowledged that the novelist never showed an interest in joining "one of the dozens of political reform societies that were about him" (qtd. in Murray 26). Faced with the prospect of real social levelling, he sided squarely with the forces of hierarchy and control. "Democratic in principle, elitist in practice" is biographer Fred Kaplan's summation of his paradoxical politics (308).

Where established authority failed in its task, as was often the case, his own writings, he believed, might prove a bulwark for an endangered national identity, an imagined England helping to sustain the traditions and domestic virtues of the real one. Through fiction grounded in abundant social detail he might preserve the sense of community that modern urban life and its attendant evils, such as rampant materialism and crime, threatened to erode; as he openly acknowledged, he aspired to place his own conceptions and values "among the Household thoughts" of the English people ("A Preliminary Word" 107). Dickens was, of course, uniquely positioned for such a constitutive role in mid-Victorian culture. By this point in his career, Philip Collins notes, he had himself achieved "an institutional status in English life" (*Critical Commentary* 12). More than any other author of his day, he was understood as a "national" figure, "a master of the knowledge of English life" widely read across varying social strata (Andrews xv; Ford, *Dickens and His Readers* 22), who, as Peter Ackroyd describes it, "impressed his fiction upon his readers with almost mesmeric intensity" (856). Read aloud in homes, widely reviewed, frequently dramatized on stage, and even translated into domestic commodities (e.g., Pickwick hats and chinaware), his works became part and parcel of the country's self-image—at a time when the lineaments of "Englishness" were a matter of much concern and debate (Morse 45). If his phenomenal success with *Pickwick* had earned him an unprecedented audience among Victorian authors—its characters were present "in every reading Englishman's mind," claimed one contemporary (Richard Holt Hutton, qtd. in Engel 246)—Dickens cultivated that relationship, using his journalism and frequent public appearances to maintain a strikingly personal bond with his readers. He would have readily accepted Thackeray's estimation that the profession of novelist was "as serious as the Parson's own" (282); indeed, one might argue—and some have (e.g., W. E. H. Lecky in *Religious Tendencies of the Age*)—that during this period writers superseded the clergy as the primary shapers of thought and opinion in England.

Spiritual issues were certainly not left behind in this decisive shift, however, even if their presence in fiction is at times only "discreetly suggested and implied," as Kathleen Tillotson has observed concerning the domestic novels of the 1840s (qtd. in Coolidge 59). But for a culture steeped in religious controversy—in which the churchman's language and concepts "permeate[d] other forms of intellectual and cultural discourse" to a remarkable degree (Gilmour 71)—discreet suggestion and implication was often quite enough to register one's point. Subtle textual details concerning clerical dress and demeanor, the rituals of worship, and the handling of Scripture (by a character or narrator) could carry enormous significance; personal displays of guilt, forgiveness, submission, and self-assertion resonated in narratives in complex ways, given the thorough interpenetration of the religious, the social, and the political during this period. (Thus, the ease with which the questing heroine of *Jane Eyre* [1847] could be dismissed by early reviewers as not only unfeminine but "anti-Christian" [qtd. in "Charlotte Brontë" 50].) For a culture *not* steeped in religious controversy, such as our own, the full import of mid-Victorian texts, including those by Dickens, is easily lost; "We no longer breathe the same air," Robert Lee Wolff has remarked, regarding our present inacquaintance with the intense and complicated world of nineteenth-century faith and doubt (4), where a single phrase might conjure up an entire climate of opinion. A discussion of the distinctive features of *Bleak House* in Dickens's body of works—its comprehensiveness, complexity, and ambivalence—will lead, in this essay, to an analysis of this overlooked religious dimension of the text, which has a decisive bearing upon all of these matters, and is, as I will argue, far more thorough-going and detailed than critics generally acknowledge.

While few today would accept Arthur Quiller-Couch's stunning assertion that in approaching Dickens one must first "jettison religion" (65),[2] many

seem to have embraced the notion that religion figures into his social criticism
in only the most general and uncomplicated of ways, i.e., that what concerns
the novelist is simply the gloominess, hypocrisy, and ignorance that Christianity can give rise to rather than the creeds or practices of any particular
Christian groups or sects active in England. He "left religious convictions
alone," Douglas Woodruff flatly declares (542), a fact that, if true, would set
Dickens apart from the main currents of his day, since the "fights of rival
churches," to use the words of one contemporary observer (G. J. Harney,
qtd. in Machin 249), had become perhaps the most prominent aspect of British
public life. Controversy in religion, Robert Lee Wolff reminds us, was "omnipresent" during this era—it was "fought out in the press, in the pulpit of every
village church in England, and in the drawing rooms of every household" (6).
Still, critics persist in seeing Dickens's treatment of mid-Victorian religion
as largely disconnected from these pressing conflicts. The perceived anti-
clericalism of *Bleak House* becomes a sort of blanket condemnation, a non-
specific indictment of anyone insufficiently attuned to the social obligations
of the Gospel. Thus, Dennis Walder contends that in this novel Dickens
"largely resists the temptation to lay the blame on any specific party, sect,
or church, preferring the implication that nobody can escape responsibility" (153).

But at least Walder, whose *Dickens and Religion* appeared in 1981, can
be credited with addressing the issue at some length. More recent scholarship,
preoccupied with what James Shapiro (in *Shakespeare and the Jews*) calls
the "modern trinity of race, class, and gender" (3), has tended to overlook
it entirely. The purpose of this essay is to reveal the seriousness of this
omission, specifically, to show the extraordinary extent to which religious
issues inform *Bleak House* and its socio-political outlook. For in this text
Dickens is very much concerned with an identifiable social group; his supposed distaste for theological dogmatism and controversy notwithstanding,
he is at pains throughout the novel to demonstrate the manifest inferiority of
religious Dissenters (i.e., Protestant non-Anglicans), a growing presence in
Britain at this time, and to represent the serious threat that they posed to the
moral and spiritual health of the nation. Indeed, Dickens's anti-Dissenting
discourse in *Bleak House* is central to his criticism of mid-Victorian culture.

Dickens had never before attempted to analyze his own culture so exhaus-
tively. The story's multifarious settings and numerous characters (some one
hundred) make up a wide cross-section of English life, and its depiction of
diverse institutional practices and domestic relationships—we meet many
families here—clearly comes closer than his previous works do to articulating
a national identity. Just as the roving eye of the narrator in the novel's acclaimed opening passage moves over a panorama of England, spreading outward from London streets to Essex marshes, Kentish heights, and ships at

sea, the novel as a whole moves over an expansive realm, seeking to replicate in its shifting scenes and narrative discontinuities the sprawling world of nineteenth-century Britain. Critical commentary on *Bleak House* has been quick to note the enormous scope of Dickens's undertaking. It is the author's "first major assault on the England of his day" (Daleski 21), a groundbreaking effort at a "comprehensive picture of a complex modern society" (Page 3), a "vehicle of more concentrated sociological argument" than his earlier fictions (House 205). "In no other of his novels," J. Hillis Miller notes, "is the canvas broader, the sweep more inclusive" ("Interpretation" 179).

It is especially significant, then, given the novelist's efforts to picture the culture "at large" with emblematic characters and places, and to delineate its numerous social ills, that religious Dissenters and their practices have such a prominent role in the text. In Dickens's fecund imagining of mid-Victorian England, they are a pervasive presence, exercising an unhealthy influence (directly and indirectly) upon all levels of society. Like the epidemics of infectious diseases that threatened the physical health of the British population at this time (cholera alone killed 72,000 in England and Wales in 1848–49 [Wood 121]), Dissent was, in his view, a blight spreading throughout the nation in alarming and insidious ways. In fact, in an 1859 essay entitled "Hysteria and Devotion," he makes this analogy with disease explicit, describing excessive religious fervor, then on display in the famous Ulster Awakening, as a highly contagious (and decidedly abnormal) condition; it is a kind of "madness," which "may be caught literally like smallpox" (34). It is smallpox, of course, that the streetsweeper Jo in *Bleak House* unwittingly transmits to Esther Summerson, an occurrence that illustrated the need for slum clearance and health reforms; this novel is just as concerned, however, with the infectious power of deviant religious belief.

Whatever metaphor one employs, it is clear that as Dickens pondered the "Condition of England," Dissent loomed large in his imagination. If we accept J. Hillis Miller's assertion that in writing *Bleak House* "Dickens wants to tell how things got as they are, to indict someone for the crime" (181), then it is apparent that he regards Dissenters as guilty of grave offenses. Time and again, they appear at crucial points in the development of the narrative—always with injurious results for those around them—and their ways of thinking and acting are implicated in many of the social problems the work explores. Through this thorough exposure, the text seeks to give a determinate, readily recognizable shape to a cultural group Dickens perceived as a menace, to define its personality and character for an audience largely unfamiliar with its ways, and mark it as alien to the best interests of the English state and family. The novel imposes the practice of seeing Dissent as aberrant and corrupt.

Although by mid-century Dissent comprised no less than thirty separate Nonconformist traditions (Parsons, "From Dissenters to Free Churchmen"

71)—including Congregationalists, Baptists, Presbyterians, Quakers, and Methodists—and numerous scholars have attested to its diversity (e.g., Routley; Chadwick; Thompson), in *Bleak House* and elsewhere in Dickens's texts, it is homogeneous and singular, a uniform and predictable ground for Victorian readers. Through the discourse of his narratives one could see that these religious outsiders were invariably coarse and vulgar and that they were rightfully relegated to the fringes of society. "Observe the contrast," he directs readers of his early pamphlet *Sunday Under Three Heads* (1836), as he describes the strange goings-on at a Dissenting chapel. The worshipers here are "as different in dress, as they are opposed in manner" to those attending Anglican services (122). "There is something in the sonorous quavering of the harsh voices, in the lank and hollow faces of the men, and the sour solemnity of the women, which bespeaks this a stronghold of intolerant zeal and enthusiasm" (122). The preacher is a "coarse, hard-faced man of forbidding aspect, clad in rusty black," whose violent ravings on the tortures of hell produce "great excitement . . . among his hearers" and cause one young girl to fall senseless on the floor (122). Not much imagination is needed to see the difference between these odd and gloomy creatures and the "neat and clean, cheerful and contented" people who choose to spend their Sunday mornings elsewhere (120).

The sources of Dickens's divisive rhetoric lay within the crude stereotypes of Dissenting Christians circulated in eighteenth- and early nineteenth-century works, such as the fiction of Henry Fielding and Oliver Goldsmith, the *Spectator* papers of Joseph Addison and Richard Steele, and the essays of Leigh Hunt, William Hazlitt, and Sydney Smith, the last of whom once referred to Methodists as "nasty and numerous vermin" (qtd. in Cunningham 225); these texts, as well as various minor stage productions in which Dissenters were mercilessly lampooned, Dickens was quite familiar with (Cunningham 223). He did have some firsthand acquaintance with Dissenters, having, as a boy, occasionally visited a neighborhood chapel with his parents, although they were members of the Church of England. And his elder sister Fanny and her husband Henry Burnett converted to Congregationalism in the early 1840s. But these and other "direct" experiences seem not to have shaped his image of Dissenters as much as his early reading had, which, according to Fred Kaplan, formed "his lifelong models of human nature" (26). Thus, despite Dickens's legendary skills at observation and his persistent claims for the exacting verisimilitude of his texts (his prefaces and letters typically insist upon the truth of his representations [Ford, *Dickens and His Readers* 124]), his fiction's vigorous enacting of preconceived notions of religious identity, belies this pose of objectivity. It is his rigid adherence to biased and factitious conceptions of personal difference that Peter Ackroyd may have had in mind when he referred to Dickens's "blindness to reality in the act of composition" (258).

But whatever their origins, there can be little doubt that the distinctions his novels enforce (religious and otherwise) in a sense *became* reality as readers employed them to interpret and organize their experience in the ferment of mid-Victorian culture. The generative power of his works, therefore, went far beyond the quaint Pickwick clubs and holiday festivities that sprang up in conscious imitation of his fictional worlds and that linger to this day. His texts gave powerful impetus to spiritual discriminations and deeply ingrained them in the Victorian self-image; if it is true, as Fintan O'Toole has recently remarked that "nations exist in the mind" (56)—and that they are to a large extent created by poets and novelists, as Aldous Huxley once observed (Andrews xv)—then it is not extreme to assert that Dickens's novels, perhaps more than those of any other author, helped produce Victorian England. Just as his rich and complex vision of London "came to be added" to the actuality of the city itself (Ackroyd 260), his dark vision of Dissenters was ultimately inseparable from British assessments of their own character as a people. Those outside the Establishment formed an essential category, a group whose manifest "Otherness" helped define a contrasting normative English identity.

Not all English Dissenters, of course, were doctrinal conservatives and raving zealots. Indeed, Dickens himself experienced a much different form of Dissent when he attended Unitarian worship services for a time in the 1840s. But if historically Victorian Dissent was heterogeneous in belief and practice, it was anything but that in Dickens's fiction. His rigid model of Nonconformity became the vehicle for all the religious tendencies he wished to see banished from the national life: narrow adherence to the letter of Scripture, including the doctrines of original sin, eternal punishment, and the imminent Second Coming of Christ; gloomy Sabbatarianism and a dour stifling of fancy and the imagination; ranting, long-winded pulpit oratory and enthusiastic, undignified revivalism; a divisive and contentious spirit and the arrogant presumption of spiritual superiority; and a blinkered absorption in misguided missionary and philanthropic activities. Added to this was his conviction that Dissenters were often supreme hypocrites, capable, for example, of decrying fleshly pleasures while indulging to excess their own bodily appetites for food and drink. Mr. Stiggins of *The Pickwick Papers* is a preacher—and member of the United Grand Junction Ebenezer Temperance association—who imbibes freely of pineapple rum.

The attempt to mark and classify Dissent, to posit it as a fixed, immutable entity, arises, no doubt, out of the novelist's own fear that the traditional boundaries defining the difference of Dissenters in British life were becoming less clear—that their strange and joyless habits of mind and rigid values, once immured in obscure conventicles, were now being assimilated into the national culture. He disdained the growing alliances between Dissenters and the Low-Church Evangelicals (who espoused many of the same beliefs as Dissenters)—alliances that were strengthened considerably in the wake of the shocking "Papal Aggression" of 1850 (Chadwick 303). Cooperative efforts between Anglicans and non-Anglicans, such as those formed at Exeter Hall—"the great moral stock exchange of the Evangelical world" (Pope 1)—could never yield positive results for the country; "It might be laid down as a very good rule of social and political guidance," Dickens flatly declared in 1848, "that whatever Exeter Hall champions, is the thing by no means to be done" ("The Niger Expedition" 43). He was determined to prevent the Anglican Establishment—and the culture as a whole—from becoming more and more like Dissent, and *Bleak House* is a product of that determination.

This was the era, it is important to remember, in which the legal strictures that had previously blocked Dissenters' full participation in Victorian society were being gradually removed in a religious-political transformation that one church historian has described as a "fundamental change amounting to a minor revolution" (Parsons, "Reform, Revival, and Realignment" 17). And as the landmark Religious Census of 1851 demonstrated, by midcentury Sunday attendance at Anglican and Nonconformist services was nearly equal. Thus, the Church of England's unquestioned position as "the one respectable, politically dominant creed with a virtual monopoly of higher education and intellectual life" (Cockshut 9) was slipping away, to the dismay of Dickens and others, who saw the Church, despite its many flaws, as an integral part of the national character, and the last, best defense against extremism. When Dissenters were forbidden to perform marriages and register births outside the parish church, to attend Grammar Schools, to take degrees at Oxford and Cambridge, and to hold public office—as they had been in previous generations—there was little need to worry about their effect on the life of the nation. But when these institutional barriers dissolved, and their numbers grew rapidly—to over four million people, or roughly one-fourth of the population by mid-century—they became, as Gerald Parsons puts it, "a force to be reckoned with" ("From Dissenters to Free Churchmen" 69).

With remarkable consistency, *Bleak House* assigns distinctive physiological traits to Dissenters, as if to suggest by their strange and repulsive appearances and their awkward ways of walking and speaking that theirs was an identity as fundamentally apart from Englishness—as clearly "different"—as a foreign racial identity might be. And one need look no further than Dickens's eager embrace of the ideas of Thomas Carlyle, author of the reactionary treatises *The Nigger Question* (1849) and *Latter-day Pamphlets* (1850), to gauge his attitudes on race. In fact, at times in both his fiction and nonfiction Dickens explicitly aligns the two, positing a kinship between bizarre religious practices in his homeland and the behaviors of those in distant cultures.

The convulsive revivalism that swept Britain in 1859–a kind of "epidemic hysteria"—was, he asserted, of a piece with "the wild excitement of the Dancing Dervish" and the spirit of "the Assassin . . . mad with hachshish and fanaticism" ("Hysteria and Devotion" 31–32). The obsessiveness of a Dissenting Temperance agitator displayed the kind of frenzy seen "when a Malay runs amuck" ("Whole Hogs" 275). Members of Dickens's obscure chapel congregations, who moan, "rock their bodies to and fro, and wring their hands" (*Sunday Under Three Heads* 122); who dance "sacred jig[s]" (*Dombey and Son* 207); who "roar" and "shriek" and roll on the floor ("George Silverman's Explanation" 230–31), must have struck many of his readers as primitives in a kind of native ethnography, one revealing the dark mysteries of a culture as peculiar and backward as any on foreign soil.

Dickens's texts are replete with rough, sweaty, squint-eyed preachers with strong breath and yellow skin; they rant violently and harangue their delirious followers in sermons of enormous length. Their names alone are suggestive: Boanerges Boiler, Jabez Fireworks, Melchisedech Howler, Goosetrap Witness, Verity Hawkyard. In an essay entitled "On the Causes of Methodism" (1815), William Hazlitt had contended that "[i]f you live near a chapel or tabernacle in London, you may almost always tell, from physiognomical signs, which of the passengers will turn the corner to go there" (59). A visit to the country, where he watched a procession of people coming from a neighboring town to the consecration of a chapel, confirmed his proposition: "Never was there such a set of scarecrows. Melancholy tailors, consumptive hair-dressers, squinting coblers, women with child or in the ague, made up the forlorn hope of the pious cavalcade" (59). Dickens may have had this work by Hazlitt in mind (he had a copy of it in his library [Cunningham 223]) when he, too, suggests to his readers that Dissenters can be identified strictly by their appearance:

> It is my first experiment, and I have come to the region of Whittington in an omnibus, and we have put down a fierce-eyed spare old woman, whose slate-colored gown smells of herbs, and who walked up Aldersgate-street to some chapel where she comforts herself with brimstone doctrine, I warrant. We have also put down a stouter and sweeter old lady, with a pretty large prayer-book in an unfolded pocket-handkerchief, who got out at a corner of a court near Stationers' Hall, and who I think must go to church there. . . .
>
> ("City of London Churches" 84–85)

It is hardly unusual, of course, for an author to use outward appearance as a marker of inward character and temperament, but what is extraordinary about Dickens's treatment of Dissenters in this regard is its persistence and consistency over the course of his career: passages from the early polemic *Sunday Under Three Heads* (1836), which protested restrictions on Sunday activities, could be fitted seamlessly into "George Silverman's Explanation" (1868), a short story published near the end of his life that traces the blighting effects of religious fanaticism. This uniformly negative perspective contrasts sharply with the changeableness and inconsistencies of his views on other matters. John Carey notes that "almost any aberration, from drunkenness to wife-beating can be found eliciting at various times both Dickens's mournfulness and his amused toleration" (qtd. in Murray 23). Even his representation of Jews, the traditional outcasts of English literature, underwent drastic change: the despicable Fagin, the "villainous and repulsive" thief of *Oliver Twist*, gave way to the noble Riah of *Our Mutual Friend* (see Harry Stone, "Dickens and the Jews"). But Dissenters are the same, early and late; his hatred of them, as his biographer Edgar Johnson acknowledges, was "lifelong" (1:20). And more often than not, their evident physical degeneracy is counterpoised by healthful, robust, more fully "English" types—in the passage quoted above, the "stouter and sweeter old lady" who bypasses the "brimstone doctrine" of the local chapel for services in the Established Church.

In *Bleak House* the lives of those in the lower reaches of society are plagued by the likes of the Reverend Chadband, the loathsome and endlessly perspiring preacher who ignores the needs of the poor while unctuously pronouncing Christian platitudes. He is, the narrator informs us, a

> large yellow man with a fat smile and a general appearance of having a good deal of train oil in his system. . . . [He] moves softly and cumbrously, not unlike a bear who has been taught to walk upright. He is very embarrassed about the arms, as if they were inconvenient to him and he wanted to grovel.   (274)

Like Stiggins of *Pickwick Papers*, who has a "semi-rattlesnake sort of eye" (327), Chadband's animalism signals not only his physical repulsiveness but his unrestrained appetites. If he is a vessel of the Lord, a Scriptural title he appropriates for himself, he is a "consuming vessel," who gorges himself with food at every opportunity (273). Well-supplied "tea meetings" were part of Dissent's image in mid-Victorian culture and even figured into stage adaptations of Dickens's novels. Completely self-absorbed—Trevor Blount calls him a "moral narcissus" (299)—his attention to his own desires comes at the expense of the young streetsweeper Jo, who when brought into his presence offers an occasion for exercising his other great gift (besides eating): "piling verbose flights of stairs, one upon another" (276). Rather than compassion and pity, Chadband offers Jo a brutal lesson in his own wretchedness:

> A human boy. O glorious to be a human boy! And why glorious, my young friend? Because you are capable of receiving the lessons of wisdom, because you are capable of profiting by this discourse which I now deliver for your good, because you are not a stick, or a staff, or a stock, or a stone, or a post, or a pillar.

O running stream of sparkling joy
To be a soaring human boy!
And do you cool yourself in that stream now, my young friend? No. Why do
you not cool yourself in that stream now? Because you are in a state of darkness,
because you are in a state of obscurity, because you are in a state of sinfulness,
because you are in a state of bondage.   (282)

That Dickens saw this sort of callous religiosity as a significant factor in the
suffering of the underprivileged and in the social disarray of England is made
plain in the novel. And that Dissenters are the great exemplars of this failed
Christianity is evident as well, even if other Christian groups, such as the
Puseyites and Low-Church Evangelicals, also receive blame. Tom-all-
Alone's, the sickening slum Jo inhabits, is visited by clergymen, but apparently they come only to pray and pontificate: "they all mostly sed as the
t'other wuns prayed wrong, and all mostly sounded to be a-talking to their-
selves, or a-passing blame on the t'others, and not a-talkin to us" (653), Jo
confides to his friend Allan Woodcourt. If Jo's fate symbolizes the undeserved
suffering of the working poor—he dies of smallpox in one of the narrative's
climactic scenes—then Chadband and his ilk, whom we see ignoring his
needs, are the prime source of the inhumane and hypocritical religion that
allows such tragedies to occur. The kind of rigidity and willful blindness that
Dissenters displayed, Dickens declared in an 1850 essay on Sabbatarianism,
was "outrageous to the spirit of Christianity, irreconcilable with the health,
the rational enjoyments, and the true religious feeling of the community"
("The Sunday Screw" 186). Monstrous in both appearance and belief, England's sectarians clearly threatened the welfare of the nation's most vulnerable citizens.

But middle class households as well, such as that of Mr. Snagsby the law
stationer, come under Chadband's influence in the novel. It is in Snagsby's
home that the oily reverend engages in his absurd flights of rhetoric ("My
friends . . . to pursue the subject we are endeavouring with our lowly gifts to
improve, let us in a spirit of love inquire what is that Terewth to which I
have alluded" [370]) and his heated verbal assaults on lowly Jo ("We have
here among us . . . a Gentile and a heathen, a dweller in the tents of Tom-all-
Alone's and a mover-on upon the surface of the earth" [368]). While Snagsby
himself is unimpressed with Chadband, his wife is a devoted follower, whose
stern moral rectitude likewise allows no room for genuine compassion. She
terrorizes her timid maid Guster, who is herself under the spell of Chadband's
specious charms, with threats to return her to the notorious orphanage at
Tooting where she grew up. And, not surprisingly, she harbors an intense
distrust of Jo, borne of the ludicrous suspicion that he is her husband's
illegitimate offspring. Fixated on the ideas of sin and corruption—she believes
him "a limb of the arch-fiend" (282)—she fails to see Jo's genuine goodness

and, instead, does her best to make his miserable life even more unbearable. "Mrs. Snagsby, she's always a-watching, and a-driving of me—what have I done to her?" Jo complains at one point in a lament that might be voiced by many others in a nation, in Dickens's view, being overrun by religious zealots.

Like Chadband, Mrs. Snagsby is a strange individual whose body gives outward evidence of her inward deformity. She is severe and sinister in appearance and highly excitable in demeanor; she has a habit of shrieking and swooning and is "liable to spasms" (317). During one sermon at her home she becomes "cataleptic" and "has to be carried up the narrow staircase like a grand piano" (371). Her servant Guster, too, who fancies herself the "handmaid" of the grandiloquent preacher (a term that may have had illicit sexual connotations for a Victorian audience [Macaulay 301]), is feeble-minded, strikingly unattractive, and "subject to fits" (806); during a seizure she can be found "with her head in the pail, or the sink, or the copper, or the dinner, or anything else that happens to be near her" (143). Her mental and emotional instability, which is suggested by her name, turns out to have decisive consequences during an important episode in Esther Summerson's life, when it delays her obtaining information about her mother after she leaves Chesney Wold. If Dickens truly believed, as he announced in *Household Words*, that "Bedlam has often come of indulging in the Bible to excess" (Dickens and Collins, "Doctor Dulcamara, M.P." 626), he may have intended the chaotic Snagsby household as a case in point.

Not even the upper-class world of Chesney Wold is immune from the effects of religious extremism. Dickens suggests that its "deadened," "unhealthy" atmosphere (24), in which "there is not much fancy . . . stirring" (98), is due at least in part to the disruptive influence of a Chadbandian kind of fanaticism. As befitting a family with an ancient lineage, the Dedlocks' experience with spiritual strife dates from the time of the Puritan conflicts of the mid-seventeenth century, as housekeeper Mrs. Rouncewell explains to Mr. Guppy, a visitor to the estate, in chapter 7 of the novel. The latter had asked how the family terrace, ominously called the "Ghost's Walk," came to be named. He is told that during the days of King Charles the First, the owner of Chesney Wold—staunch royalist Sir Morbury Dedlock—was married to a hateful and scheming woman, with "none of the family blood in her veins" (104), who supported the rebellious Puritan side. The rift between them became so great that a violent confrontation ensued, in which the lady was seriously injured. Her dying words were a promise, delivered "fixedly and coldly" to her husband, to haunt the path outside their home "until the pride of [the] house is humbled" (105). Long after this event, Chesney Wold retains a ghostly air, especially during the gloomy weather the area is subject to: "[T]here is a cold, blank smell like the smell of a little church, though something dryer, suggesting that the dead and buried Dedlocks walk there in the long nights and leave the flavour of their graves behind them" (410–11).[3]

This tale from the family's past takes on significance, of course, as the narrative of Esther Summerson and her relationship with Lady Dedlock unfolds (Esther worries guiltily that her illegitimate birth is the fulfillment of the dying woman's prophecy), but it is significant as well in the context of the anti-Dissenting discourse that informs *Bleak House*. A story of a divided household and a haunting by an embittered Puritanical spirit—a specter of judgment amidst a family's material prosperity—would have had special resonance for a mid-Victorian audience, or at least those familiar with Dickens, who saw nineteenth-century Dissenters as direct descendants, both literally and figuratively, of the joyless schismatics who had cast a pall over the nation two centuries earlier. "The Puritans of that time," he asserts in *Sunday Under Three Heads*, "were as much opposed to harmless recreations and healthful amusements as those of the present day, and it is amusing to observe that each in their generation advance precisely the same description of arguments" (137). Present-day enemies of wholesome pleasures are, in the words of a later essay, "Monomaniacs" who are "by their disease impelled to clamber upon platforms, and there squint horribly under the strong possession of an unbalanced idea"; and it is surely the "Ghost of John Bunyan" who ushers them into committee rooms to testify and agitate for their repressive ideals ("The Great Baby" 67, 71).

If the essays cited here (*Sunday Under Three Heads* and "The Great Baby") shed light on the troubled legacy that Puritanism brought to the Dedlocks, these and other nonfiction texts by Dickens illuminate other aspects of *Bleak House* as well. They help demonstrate, for example, the ways in which two of the most memorable characters in the novel, the single-minded philanthropists Mrs. Jellyby and Mrs. Pardiggle, evidence Dickens's anxiety about the inroads Dissent was making in Victorian society. They have become infected with Dissenting ideals and are now carriers of that contagion to other people. Mrs. Jellyby, whom Esther Summerson visits soon after her arrival in London, is, of course, the work's signal example of "telescopic philanthropy"; she is so thoroughly preoccupied with her project of establishing a colony at Borrioboola-Gha in Africa (she once "sent off five thousand circulars from one post office at one time" [57]) that she neglects nearly everything and everyone else, including her children and her dejected husband, who live in a house that is literally coming apart around them. As she sits amidst her voluminous correspondence with a "curious, bright-eyed, far-off look" on her face (340), as if she could see all the way to Africa, her unwashed offspring tumble about the home completely unsupervised. When Esther first arrives, one of them has his head stuck in the iron railings near the front door. After her eldest daughter Caddy leaves home, she employs an "unwholesome" looking boy as her amanuensis.

Dickens's point—that Mrs. Jellyby's primary duty is to her family and those in her immediate surroundings rather than to natives in far-away lands—is obvious enough, but he also uses her to remind readers that this kind of misguided charity is, in his view, particularly characteristic of Dissenters and increasingly common in English life. She is not explicitly religious in her language—the Borrioboolan project, she informs Esther, aims at "cultivating coffee and educating the natives" (53)— but her conduct clearly suggests the direction of her sympathies. For example, at one point in the narrative she attends a "tea drinking" (196) where missions work is discussed, an activity that Dickens ("Whole Hogs" 274) and many others closely associated with Dissent. (Matthew Arnold would later famously skewer Nonconformity as a petty world of "jealousy of the Establishment, disputes, tea-meetings . . . " [*Culture and Anarchy* 58]). And as Norris Pope notes, the very word "philanthropy" had religious connotations at this time (134). Mrs. Jellyby's overseas venture, which includes a colleague's plan to teach the natives how "to turn piano-forte legs" (56), would have reminded readers of the immensely impractical efforts of Mrs. Weller and her fellow Dissenters in *The Pickwick Papers*, who work to provide "infant negroes in the West Indies with flannel waistcoats and moral pocket handkerchiefs" (329).

Perhaps most prominent in a contemporary reader's mind, however, would be the similarity between Mrs. Jellyby's all-consuming project and the disastrous Niger expedition of 1841 led by Thomas Fowell Buxton, which aimed at both spreading the Gospel and suppressing the slave trade. (An act of Parliament seven years earlier, eliminating slavery in the British Empire, had been, as Owen Chadwick points out, a product of "Dissenting fervour and radical liberty" [55]). There was much work to be done in the Dark Continent: Africans, the Evangelical Buxton had declared, needed "to be awakened to a proper sense of their own degradation" (qtd. in Dickens, "The Niger Expedition" 45). The mission received the enthusiastic support of Exeter Hall, but it was aborted after dozens died of fever, and for Dickens and others it stood as a glaring example of a foolish and futile attempt at "the railroad Christianisation" of another country. Critics of *Bleak House* have frequently noted that Dickens probably had Buxton's ill-fated efforts in mind when he created Mrs. Jellyby—he himself had written a memorable denunciation of the enterprise for *The Examiner* in 1848—but what made Buxton an especially apt target for the novelist's abuse is not simply his notorious decision to exercise his philanthropy abroad rather than at home, where one's "natural duties and obligations" lie (*Bleak House* 544), but his reputation as a dangerous fanatic who blurred the distinctions between Anglicans and Dissenters. (Indeed, the same disruptive role might be given to Exeter Hall itself, where, by 1853, the Baptist firebrand Charles Haddon Spurgeon was preaching to vast crowds composed of Anglicans and non-Anglicans alike.) Reared in a religiously hybrid home—he and his brothers were brought up in the Established Church while his sisters were trained as Quakers—Buxton maintained highly public and controversial ties with Dissenters (Metcalfe v); he, and, by extension, Mrs. Jellyby, no doubt represented for Dickens the frightening prospect, in evidence throughout *Bleak House,* of the nation and its church being reshaped in the image of Nonconformity. If Anglicans could so easily "turn Dissenter," transgressing a previously rigid cultural boundary, what remained, one might ask, of the nation's religious identity?

The loud and strong-willed Mrs. Pardiggle, known for her "rapacious benevolence" (115), is another character of somewhat indistinct religious affiliation who at times seems very much like a Dissenter. In chapter 8 Esther accompanies her on a visit to a young brickmaker and his family. Her bull-headed, hectoring tone ("I am incapable of fatigue, my good friend, I am never tired, and I mean to go on until I have done" [119]) links her with Chadband, another itinerant proselytizer ("I say to you that I will proclaim it to you, whether you like it or not; nay the less you like it, the more I will proclaim it to you" [369]). And her friend and colleague Mr. Gusher seems a second Chadband in appearance; he is a "flabby gentleman with a moist surface" (216). "Stationed in a waggon" out of doors, Mrs. Pardiggle tells Esther, Gusher "would improve almost any occasion you could mention for hours and hours!" (118). "Improving an occasion," as an illustrative quotation in the O.E.D. suggests, was at this time a typical Nonconformist way of referring to preaching. While some twentieth-century critics have labeled her a Puseyite because of the saintly names she gives her children, for Victorian readers, the practices of Mrs. Pardiggle and her cohorts—the distribution of tracts to the poor, outdoor preaching, and temperance activity (her youngest son belongs to the Infant Bonds of Joy)[4]—more strongly align her with Dissenters. Like her friend Mrs. Jellyby, she evidences Dickens's uneasiness over the threat of a kind of spiritual miscegenation in England, the dilution of categories of religious difference that were, in his mind, every bit as important as categories of racial difference. In fact, given his "racialized" conception of Dissenters, as distinctive in outward appearance and manner, it is not surprising that at times these two types of alien identity—racial and religious—are, as suggested earlier, conflated in interesting ways. The cover of the monthly numbers of *Bleak House,* for example, contains among other images the figure of a woman—Mrs. Jellyby perhaps—embracing two young black children and standing next to a man wearing a fool's cap and a board reading "Exeter Hall."

Ironically, the religious figure who casts the longest shadow in *Bleak House* is on stage the shortest time—she dies in the first number. She is Esther Summerson's godmother and aunt, the somber Miss Barbary, whose harsh upbringing of young Esther leaves a lasting imprint upon her life; indeed, much of Esther's first-person narrative can be read as her struggle to overcome the harmful effects of her "overshadowed childhood" (615), which she refers to repeatedly throughout the novel. ("I almost always dreamed of that period of my life," she observes in chapter 9 [136].) What Esther labors under is Miss Barbary's dire pronouncement that because of the disgraceful circumstances of her birth, sin had indelibly stained her life: "Submission, self-denial, diligent work, are the preparations for a life begun with such a shadow upon it. You are different from other children, Esther, because you were not born, like them, in common sinfulness and wrath. You are set apart" (33).

It is common for critics to see Miss Barbary as a figure of "coldness and cruelty" (Conlon 90)—as a repressed and repressive spinster who has the audacity to tell a child that it would have been better if she had never been born. But it is less common for critics to comment on her religious identity and practice, which Dickens is careful to call attention to. Indeed, the very first thing we learn about her—after Esther tells us that as a child she thought her a "good, good woman"—is that "she went to church three times every Sunday, and to morning prayers on Wednesdays and Fridays, and to lectures whenever there were lectures; and never missed" (31). This quite specific information, along with what we are told of her severity toward young Esther ("[S]he never smiled. She was always grave and strict" [31]), would have sufficed, for a mid-Victorian audience, to identify Miss Barbary as an evangelical Christian—either a Low-Church Anglican or a Dissenter. The case for the latter would include the fact that at this time it was probably more common for a Dissenter than an Anglican to attend more than one worship service on a Sunday (Chadwick I: 367, 407). (In fact, it was not uncommon for some Dissenters to attend a parish church service in the morning and a chapel service in the evening [Chadwick I:370], a practice Dickens would hardly look kindly upon.) Other aspects of her character, such as her apparent social isolation, her habit of quoting and echoing Scripture in conversation, and the strongly Calvinist bent of her principles, likewise show that in sketching Miss Barbary Dickens drew upon traits thought to be typical of English Dissenters (see Jay 24–25; Cunningham 11–12; Shatto 50). And, for at least this character, the life of Dickens's own sister Fanny, who herself left the Established Church, may have supplied him with vital details. The Reverend James Griffin's memoirs of his ministry to Fanny Dickens Burnett (which note at one point that "she insisted on being three times at worship on the Sabbath . . . " [200]) sound vaguely familiar at times to a reader who remembers *Bleak House*'s Miss Barbary.

The scene in which Miss Barbary suffers a fatal stroke in the presence of young Esther is also significant. That she dies in a chapter entitled "A Progress" suggests something about the author's attitude toward her religious values. (The chapter title perhaps also alludes to John Bunyan's famous allegory of the Christian life, indicating to readers that Esther's story will likewise be a spiritual autobiography.) Esther had just finished reading a passage from the Gospel of St. John, ending with Christ's words to those who were about to stone a woman taken in adultery: "He that is without sin among you, let him first cast a stone at her!" (8:37)—at which point Miss Barbary rises and cries out "in an awful voice" that sounds "throughout the house" (35) as she quotes from a much different passage of Scripture, one concerning the Second Coming of Christ: "Watch ye, therefore, lest coming suddenly he find you sleeping. And what I say unto you, I say unto all, Watch!" (from Mark 13:35–37). These two texts sum up, of course, opposing religious sensibilities: Esther's benevolent, forgiving spirit, which Dickens endorses, and the monitory, judgmental rigidity of Miss Barbary. And given the fact that Esther's mother, Lady Dedlock, is herself guilty of adultery, the verse she cites here underscores in a clear way, although unknown to young Esther, the hard-heartedness of Miss Barbary, Lady Dedlock's sister, who has pointedly refused to forgive her transgression. But in this scene Dickens may have also intended to use the apocalyptic warning of Miss Barbary and her dramatic physical collapse to align her with the teachings of one of the most well-known and controversial of early nineteenth-century preachers, Edward Irving, who was noted for his millenarianism (i.e., the belief that Christ would soon return to set up a thousand-year reign on earth) as well as for the wild, emotional services at his London chapel, in which worshipers, in the words of one historian, "became 'infected'" (Flegg 52) with the gift of speaking in tongues. Among his followers were a number of prominent secessionists from the Church of England. The Presbyterian Church of Scotland, to which Irving once belonged, pronounced him a heretic in 1833. Dickens, of course, held the Irvingites in derision—a poem he composed in 1831 describes an imagined visitor to their chapel as being among "the Maniacs" (qtd. in Winter 46).

Another member of the Barbary household, the widowed servant Mrs. Rachael, likewise suggests a religion that has hardened into a dismal piety and a physical presence that reflects that spiritual malformation. Esther notes her austerity and, significantly, that it was she "who took my light away when I was in bed" (31). In her will the loveless Miss Barbary bequeaths what little property she has to Mrs. Rachael, and the latter bids a cold farewell to Esther (her parting kiss was "like a thaw-drop from the stone porch" [38]), who leaves the only home she has ever known for life at a boarding school. But years later as an adult, Esther once again encounters Mrs. Rachael, who has retained "her old asperity" (356) and who has since remarried—to the Reverend Chadband.

What gives special force to Dickens's depiction of Chadband, Mrs. Snagsby, and the other religious grotesques of *Bleak House* is his counterbalancing portraits of figures like Lawrence Boythorn, John Jarndyce, and Allan Woodcourt, whose wholesomeness, benevolence, and resolutely English identity stand in sharp contrast to the strange and unforgiving ways of Dissenters. In a novel fixated on the nation's physical and spiritual health, they represent soundness of body and mind. Through these characters Dickens creates the binarism that is the fundamental function of discourse—the construction of opposed categories of normality and deviance; of center and periphery; of values intrinsic and extrinsic to a cultural identity. Through them, in short, he defines the Otherness of Dissent.

Dickens uses various means to associate these three characters—all of whom play a vital role in Esther Summerson's development-with an ideal of Broad Church Anglicanism (then taking shape in England) that is liberal in its theology, keenly sensitive to the social imperatives of the Gospel, and nostalgic for a vision of rural communal life untroubled by the divisiveness and ugliness of Nonconformity. Although Dickens could grow frustrated when it seemed that the Church itself was being swallowed up in the sectarian squabbles of the day, and it is possible to find remarks by him that are sharply critical of its leadership, as Humphry House notes he nevertheless returned again and again in his fiction to its "scenes and forms and language" (110). Despite his interest in Unitarianism, his lifelong friend John Forster affirms that "on essential points he never had any sympathy so strong as with the leading doctrine and discipline of the Church of England" (qtd. in Connell 226). For him the Church, despite its faults, was an embodiment of ritual, ceremony, and celebration that gave continuity and stability to English life. It was the Anglican Establishment that his children were christened in, that he attended and contributed money to, and that oversaw his own burial, with the Dean of Westminster Cathedral presiding. Its ancient buildings and by-ways suggested a world of tradition, order, and hierarchy; of "stout young laborers in clean round frocks, and buxom girls with healthy, laughing faces" making their way to Sunday worship through "hedges . . . green and bloom-ing"; of simple psalms and music; of venerable gray-headed ministers who deliver "plain, unpretending" messages and who are "intimately acquainted with the circumstances of [their] parishioners" (*Sunday Under Three Heads* 138–39).

A number of passages in *Bleak House* give expression to this quiet Anglican pastoralism. When Esther travels to Lincolnshire to pay a visit to the warm-hearted Mr. Boythorn, she is a world away from the repressive gloom and confinement of Miss Barbary's household and its soul-destroying preoccupa-tion with human depravity. Here she experiences a world of freedom and natural goodness: "The green corn waved so beautifully, the larks sang so joyfully, the hedges were so full of wild flowers, the trees were so thickly out in leaf, the bean-fields, with a light wind blowing over them, filled the air with such a delicious fragrance!" (256). The small town she arrives in is home to "an ancient, shady solemn little church" with an earthy smell and a subdued light inside (261). The ringing of its bell calls members of the community—rustics and aristocrats alike—to worship, including the Dedlocks, who live nearby. Boythorn himself lives in a pleasant home, "formerly the parsonage house, with a lawn in front, a bright flower-garden at the side, and a well-stocked orchard and kitchen-garden in the rear, enclosed with a venerable wall that had of itself a ripened ruddy look. But, indeed, everything about the place wore an aspect of maturity and abundance" (259). It is in this mature, abundant world—specifically in the little church in the park—that Esther, in a fascinating scene, has her first glimpse of her true mother, Lady Dedlock, during an Anglican worship service. As the priest begins to read Psalm 143:2 from Evensong in the Prayer Book ("Enter not into judgment with thy servant, O Lord, for in thy sight—"), Esther is transfixed:[5]

> Shall I ever forget the rapid beating of my heart, occasioned by the look I met as I stood up! Shall I ever forget the manner in which those handsome proud eyes seemed to spring out of their languor and to hold mine! It was only a moment before I cast mine down—released again, if I may say so—on my book; but I knew the beautiful face quite well in that short space of time.
>
> And, very strangely, there was something quickened within me, associated with the lonely days at my godmother's. . . . And this, although I had never seen this lady's face before in all my life—I was quite sure of it—absolutely certain. (262)

This moment of unaccountable recognition culminates, of course, in the even more dramatic scene several chapters later—again during a visit to Boythorn's estate—when the troubled Lady Dedlock, now aware of her sister's deception (in telling her years earlier that her illegitimate child had died), reveals her true identity to Esther: "Oh, my child, my child. I am your wicked and unhappy mother! Oh try to forgive me!" (516). Esther responds not in judgment or confused anger but with a warm embrace and assurances of her affection: "I told her that my heart overflowed with love for her, that it was natural love which nothing in the past had changed or could change" (517). It is after this stunning turn of events, and the long night of soul-searching that it induces, that Esther finally comes to the point where she rejects Miss Barbary's image of her as a benighted, sin-cursed creature and obtains a new vision of God's goodness and His working in her life:

> For I saw very well that I could not have been intended to die, or I should never have lived; not to say should never have been reserved for such a happy life. I saw very well how many things had worked together for my welfare. . . . I knew I was as innocent of my birth as a queen of hers and that before my Heavenly Father I should not be punished for birth nor a queen rewarded for it. (523)

The working of God in Esther's life had included the care and protection of John Jarndyce, whose country home, Bleak House itself, is likewise given unmistakable religious associations. Located near St. Albans, a provincial town "famous for its ancient church" (Defoe 344), it is, like the environs of Boythorn's house, a realm of natural fertility and beauty. The estate's orderliness and efficiency, "profoundly English" virtues, in Dickens's view (Andrews 5), are especially striking since Esther first arrives there (early in the novel) not long after her visits to the chaotic Jellyby household and to Krook's cluttered rag and bottle warehouse (which is watched over, incidentally, by a vicious cat named after the ultra-Protestant Tudor monarch "Lady Jane" Grey). Her first sight of this shining realm of "perfect neatness" (82) comes during a night journey through open country. From a distance she spies a "light sparkling on the top of the hill" (77)—an echo perhaps of Matthew 5:14, in which Christ enjoins his followers to perform good works: "Ye are the light of the world. A city that is set on a hill cannot be hid." Early the next morning, after a warm welcome from Mr. Jarndyce ("I rejoice to see you!"), Esther finds herself gazing out her bedroom window on, as she describes it, a "cheerful landscape, prominent in which the old Abbey Church, with its massive tower, threw a softer train of shadow on the view than seemed compatible with its rugged character. But so from rough outsides (I hope I have learned), serene and gentle influences often proceed" (107). The reference in this last sentence is, of course, to John Jarndyce, whose occasional ill humor, which sends him to the room specially designated his "growlery," masks a kind and deeply charitable spirit; he is thus a living emblem of the rugged "old Abbey Church" itself—an actual centuries-old building (Shatto 115)—and in Dickens's narrative an exponent of the Social Gospel that he felt was the Church's highest calling.

It is Jarndyce who voluntarily takes on the role of Esther's protector and surrogate father, offering her everything she had lacked during her difficult childhood with Miss Barbary. Years earlier, after Miss Barbary's death, he had proposed, through his representative Mr. Kenge, "to place her at a first rate establishment, where her education shall be completed, where her comfort shall be secured, [and] where her reasonable wants shall be anticipated" (37)—a program of care and practical betterment of the sort Dickens himself advocated for the underprivileged members of Victorian society, who too often, he felt, were subjected to moral scoldings and religious catechizing. (And it is worth noting that both here and elsewhere in the novel the author plays with the word "establishment" in ways that, for contemporary readers, may have subtly called to mind the ongoing debate over the status of the National Church.) After she spends six happy years at a Greenleaf School, Jarndyce receives Esther, along with the orphans Ada Clare and Richard Carstone, into his own home, where she sees firsthand the full extent of his compassion and generosity. A man of considerable means, he is endlessly besieged for aid by committees and philanthropists, including the "Sisterhood of Mediaeval Marys" and the "Ladies of a hundred denominations" (115), whose fevered activity and programs seem quite at odds with his patient and pragmatic benevolence. He rescues the feckless Harold Skimpole from debt, befriends the orphaned Neckett children, gives lodging to the beleaguered Jo, visits Trooper George in prison, oversees and funds the apprenticeship of Richard Carstone, and arranges Esther's marriage to his protege and intimate friend Allan Woodcourt.

And it is Jarndyce who pronounces the text's most conspicuous denunciations of Miss Barbary, from whom he had learned of young Esther's straitened circumstances. He leaves no doubt concerning the motivation behind her cruelty, telling Esther that a "distorted religion" had "clouded her mind," prompting her to assign guilt to a child who was "quite innocent" of offense (249). Esther learns that Miss Barbary and her sister, the later Lady Dedlock, had quarreled and "gone their several ways" (611); the former dropped out of polite society, apparently succumbing to the fanatical religious beliefs that like the contagion of smallpox were circulating widely in Britain. At one time an acquaintance of Jarndyce, she developed an "inflexible heart" (611) and became "estranged from all intercourse with the world" (250), even with Lawrence Boythorn, her one-time fiancé. The "rigid secrecy" (520) in which Esther was reared was broken only by Miss Barbary's death, at which point the much different Christianity of John Jarndyce opened a new way of living for her.

Under his patient tutelage, she learns that true religion concerns itself not with dogma but with the physical, emotional, and intellectual needs of her fellow human beings. Like her Biblical namesake (who is also raised from a life of bondage to a position of importance—and who was construed in Biblical commentary as a type of the Church who "frees her people from danger" [St. Jerome, quoted in Larson 118, n. 8]), she embraces an ethic of self-sacrifice, duty, and nurturing love. While Mrs. Jellyby plans her mission to far-off Africa, Esther reads bedtime stories to her neglected children; while the blaring Mrs. Pardiggle takes the brickmaker and his family "into religious custody" (122), she whispers words of comfort ("what Our Saviour said of children" [124]) to the grieving mother, who has just suffered the death of an infant. She teaches her servant-girl Charley how to read and write, nurses her in illness, and eventually becomes a "godmother" herself—although one much different from the stern Miss Barbary. As Richard J. Dunn puts it, "she pulsates humanity into the disordered world in which she has at last found her true position" (166).

Her "Progress" toward that position is not an easy and direct one, however, involving as it does a long struggle with the shame and feelings of worthlessness that are the legacy of her childhood. Her "mysteriously complex and profound" development as a character (Bloom 5) has received enormous attention in the criticism of the novel, especially, and, not surprisingly, in the work of feminist scholars, who read her odyssey from foundling to household saint as a study in the operations of Victorian patriarchy (e.g., see Moers; Kennedy; Senf; Newton; Gottfried). But much of the voluminous commentary on the dynamics of gender in *Bleak House* has tended to obscure the importance of religious identity in the conflicts Esther faces and in the personality she ultimately develops; Dickens plainly intends her to be not simply an ideal of womanhood and domesticity but a model of "Right Religion," and inasmuch as spiritual issues—not gender—dominated cultural debate at this time, a reader interested in the workings of power in Victorian society does well to focus on the dichotomy of Dissent and Broad Church Anglicanism that the text constructs in such painstaking detail. A reading sensitive to the deployment of these discursive categories finds added meaning in numerous passages in *Bleak House*.

A case in point is Esther's description in chapter 35 of the strange hallucinatory dreams she experienced during her long, disfiguring illness, one of the most arresting episodes in her narrative. For a period of several weeks she lay in her bed, blinded and virtually insensible to her surroundings. "[D]ivisions of time became exceedingly confused with one another"; and "the various stages of [her] life" had "little or no separation" between them (495). She was "[a]t once a child, an elder girl, and the little woman" she had formerly been so happy as, now facing the oppressive task of "trying to reconcile" these different positions. The psychological trauma that Esther is experiencing here seems to arise from her continued preoccupation with Miss Barbary's fearful words to her and the possibility that she has not escaped after all from the awful world of her godmother and her dire threats of divine punishment—a horrible thought that finds expression in a number of nightmare images:

> ... I am almost afraid to hint at that time in my disorder—it seemed one long night, but I believe there were both nights and days in it—when I labored up colossal staircases, ever striving to reach the top, and ever turned, as I have seen a worm in a garden path, by some obstruction, and labouring again. ...
>
> Dare I hint at that worse time when, strung together somewhere in great black space, there was a flaming necklace, or ring, or starry circle of some kind, of which *I* was one of the beads! And when my only prayer was to be taken off from the rest and when it was such inexplicable agony and misery to be a part of the dreadful thing?   (496)

The shifting and incongruous images that inform this remarkable passage—endless stairs, a laboring worm, a flaming necklace in a black void—can all be seen as evidencing in oblique but richly suggestive ways Esther's deep anxiety about her standing before God; indeed here she seems to be reliving the confined and troubled days of her childhood, when the idea of her own unworthiness was a constant presence. By this point in the narrative, it is worth noting, Dickens had used the image of staircases a number of times to suggest the difficulties and impediments that religion, especially religious Dissent, creates in the lives of others: in his preaching, we have learned, Chadband piles "verbose flights of stairs, one upon another" (276), the insensible Mrs. Snagsby must be laboriously carried up the narrow staircase of her home after a fit of religious hysteria, and in the turbulent Jellyby household the stairways are a particular danger—the "stair-carpets, besides being very deficient in stair-wires, were so torn as to be absolute traps" (55–56). A reader might also remember the entryway to a London law office Esther visits, which, she observes, was "up a steep, broad flight of stairs, like an entrance to a church" (44). Her dark vision of a struggle up a "colossal staircase" calls to mind these disordered images and suggests that she has yet to fully come to terms with Dissenting Christianity in her own life.

The worm that she likens herself to implies, of course, the lowliness of her own self-image, but here, too, a religious frame of reference might apply, whether it be "worm" as a term of self-revilement common to religious discourse (it appears, for example, in a famous hymn by the Nonconformist theologian Isaac Watts[6]) or as a symbol of the terrors of hell awaiting the damned, "Where their worm dieth not, and the fire is not quenched" (Mark 10:9). And it is Biblical images of damnation that, more than anything else, seem to lie behind Esther's most bizarre and horrifying apparition, in which she is part of a "flaming necklace, or ring, or starry circle" that is "strung together somewhere in great black space." The terror here is of a loss of control—an understandable fear for someone in the throes of a life-threatening illness—but it seems also, given our knowledge of Esther's childhood trauma, a terror of divine retribution, of the ominous Scriptural edicts that the Godless would be "cast out into outer darkness" (Matthew 8:12), that they would be "wandering stars to whom is reserved the blackness of darkness forever" (Jude 13). It was Miss Barbary, of course, who had implanted such horrors in Esther's mind, telling her that she had been "set apart" (33) as a special object of God's displeasure, and it is scenes like this one on Esther's troubled sickbed that reveal how difficult it is for her to completely disown that imputed image.

But with the help of others, she does move forward, and as she matures, her Puritanical upbringing, "that old time of [her] life" [328] that had been so psychically damaging, becomes an increasingly distant event in both time and influence, until, shortly after her unexpected reunion with her mother, she is able to affirm her faith in God's benevolence and the worthiness of her own life. Like the newly converted Apostle Paul, her blinding is only temporary (her ''sight strengthening and the glorious light coming every day more fully and brightly'' upon her [497]), and like her faithful servant Charley who had nursed her through her illness, she goes forth ''to minister to the weak and sick'' (497). Having obtained a healthy image of herself and her role in the world, she is eventually able to entertain the idea of romantic love, which earlier she had experienced only vicariously through her involvement in the courtship of Ada Clare and Richard Carstone. Her desire for Allan Woodcourt, which John Jarndyce facilitates by stepping aside as a suitor in the most surprising scene of the narrative, finds fruition in the end.

The man that she marries, a selfless and indefatigable physician among the poor and outcast, is perhaps an even greater exemplar than Jarndyce of the Gospel of good works that Dickens sets up in *Bleak House* as the antithesis of the blighting influence of Dissent. His services to the addled Miss Flite, which he carries out ''with much solicitude and compassion'' (210), are performed without charge, as are his efforts on behalf of poor Jo and others. Significantly, when Jo lies on his deathbed, he attempts to comfort him with the words of the Lord's Prayer, which he asks Jo to repeat after him—a gesture that, in the minds of some readers at least, would have linked Woodcourt with the traditional liturgy of the Church. (Liturgical issues were, of course, very much alive in mid-Victorian culture. And by 1850 at least one controversial Evangelical, George Gorham, had been examined by church officials on charges of omitting the Lord's Prayer from its proper place in worship services [Chadwick I: 253]). Here, and at Richard Carstone's deathbed, he is, in the words of Andrew Sanders, ''a transforming presence,'' an example of the ''active Christian involved in mankind'' (157–58).

Woodcourt's stature takes on heroic proportions, when, during a term of service as a naval surgeon he comes to the aid of victims of a shipwreck. Miss Flite describes the event for Esther in stirring terms:

> An awful scene. Death in all shapes. Hundreds of dead and dying. Fire, storm, and darkness. Numbers of the drowning thrown upon a rock. There, and through it all, my dear physician was a hero. Calm and brave through everything. Saved many lives, never complained in hunger and thirst, wrapped naked people in his spare clothes, took the lead, showed them what to do, governed them, tended the sick, buried the dead, and brought the poor survivors safely off at last! My dear, the poor emaciated creatures all but worshipped him. They fell down at his feet when they got to the land and blessed him. The whole country rings with it.   (508)

As a doer of good deeds in foreign lands (his voyage took him to China and India), Woodcourt stands, in Dickens's scheme, as a type of the ''good missionary,'' who brings salvation not in the form of credos and moral crusades but in the form of attention to pressing physical needs. His overseas travels are in the service of humanity. Esther's greeting to him upon his safe arrival back in England—"You have been in shipwreck and peril since you left us" (629)—calls to mind the well-known ordeals of the Apostle Paul as described in II Corinthians 11:25–26 ("Thrice I suffered shipwreck . . . ; In journeyings often, in perils of waters . . .") and underscores the fraudulence of the novel's outrageous pretender to Pauline virtue, the Reverend Chadband, who, as noted earlier, deigns to call himself a "vessel," as Paul himself was known. That Woodcourt's altruism arises out a sense of religious obligation, albeit one quite different from that which motivates Dissenters, is suggested by his response to Esther's request that he befriend the troubled Richard Carstone, whose life had become increasingly consumed by the case before Chancery. "Before heaven," he declares, "I will be a true friend to him! I will accept him as a trust, and it shall be a sacred one!" (631). And his apotheosis at the close of Esther's narrative as a beloved physician ("I never walk out with my husband but I hear the people bless him" [880]) casts him in a spiritual role as well. The home that they inhabit together—literally a second Bleak House—is a "rustic cottage" set in a definitively English landscape "with water sparkling away into the distance, here all overhung with summer-growth, there turning a humming mill; at its nearest point glancing through a meadow by the cheerful town, where cricket players were assembling in bright groups and a flag was flying from a white tent that rippled in the sweet west wind" (858).

If the bodies of Dissenters testify to their corruption, those of the novel's true Christians—a strong, vigorous, and handsome lot—not surprisingly affirm their goodness and normality. Like the clean and pleasant houses they inhabit, their appearances suggest their beneficence and rectitude. Boythorn is a solid and sturdy man "with his head thrown back like an old soldier, his stalwart chest squared, his hands like a clean blacksmith's, and his lungs! . . . Talking, laughing, or snoring, they make the beams of the house shake" (129). These traits, Jarndyce assures Esther, Richard, and Ada, indicate something about the "inside of the man" as well. It is "the warm heart of the man, the passion of the man, the fresh blood of the man" that make Boythorn a tremendous friend (130). Jarndyce himself is a picture of health. He has a "handsome, lively, quick face, full of change and motion"; he is nearing sixty, but is nonetheless "upright, hearty, and robust" (78). The fixed, unpleasant gaze of Dissenters can unnerve those around them—Mr. Snagsby quails beneath his wife's accusing glare—but in Allan Woodcourt's "bright dark eye there is compassionate interest" (633).

What can easily get lost in a cataloguing of the many people and places in *Bleak House*, however, is a sense of its complex unity as a narrative. For the novel is more than just a great mixture of allusive details, a "loose, baggy monster'' (to borrow a phrase from Henry James) ranging widely over the British landscape. Dickens succeeds, rather, in integrating the miscellaneous elements of his work—its sundry settings and personalities, its formal complications, and its abundant topical references—into a coherent whole, a single, albeit multifaceted story. He accomplishes this not simply through recurring images and symbols, such as mud, fog, rust, and disease, which help enforce the novel's serious tone and which have been extensively analyzed in the many formalist treatments of the novel (e.g., see J. Hillis Miller, ''Bleak House''; Rosner), but through an extraordinarily intricate network of connections between characters and an ingenious system of correspondences, doublings, and parallels that link the diverse incidents of the narrative. In this work, says Jacob Korg, ''the art of the particular,'' at which Dickens excels, ''is brought in balance with the art of relationship'' (7).

This reiterative narrative scheme, in which ''characters, scenes, themes, and metaphors return in proliferating resemblances'' (J. H. Miller, ''Interpretation'' 183), obviously lends itself to a work of fiction whose cultural criticism is concerned not simply with discrete and tangible social problems but with the ''endemic mental systems'' (Herbert 135) of that society that help engender and sustain those problems. H. M. Daleski, commenting on the duplications and likenesses of *Bleak House*, speaks of the novel's ''analogical strategy,'' through which seemingly unrelated and peripheral figures and events lead ''straight to the complex of ideas that is at the thematic centre of the novel'' (16).

Dissenters play an important part in this ''analogical strategy,'' which Dickens uses to suggest that their distorted ways of thinking and acting were extending far beyond the chapels and drawing rooms where sweaty preachers gathered to exhort their followers. Their baneful influence was manifesting itself in numerous forms throughout the culture, and it was a major factor, he believed, in the malaise of mid-Victorian society and the dysfunction of British institutions. The dark joylessness of Miss Barbary's home, where not even a birthday party is allowed to pierce the somber gloom (''My birthday was the most melancholy day at home in the whole year,'' Esther observes [32]), is replicated in the dreary Smallweed household, which has ''discarded all amusements, discountenanced all story-books, fairy tales, fictions, and fables, and banished all levities whatsoever'' (299). The Smallweeds ''hover over teacups like a company of ghastly cherubim'' (302). (And the eldest's favorite term of abuse for his now-senile wife [''you brimstone chatterer!''] hints at the influence of religion in the household desolation.) Young Esther's neglected education, which surprises Mr. Jarndyce's emissary Mr. Kenge (36), finds a counterpart in the ignorance of Jo, who is so backward that a coroner's inquest after the death of Captain Hawdon refuses to even consider his testimony. (He doesn't know, for example, that everybody has two names:

"Never heerd of sich a think" [162].) And when (in chapter 54) the Chad-bands, Mrs. Snagsby, and Grandfather Smallweed brazenly attempt, as a group, to blackmail Sir Leicester Dedlock, having learned the secret of Lady Dedlock's past, Dickens even seems to be implicating Dissenters in the grasp-ing commercial ethos of mid-Victorian capitalism.[7]

Even the Courts and Parliament image the moral failings Dickens associ-ated with Dissent; in their endless contention and evasion of responsibility, the practitioners of the law resemble no one so much as the novel's Noncon-formists. The "jar and discord of lawsuits" (531), the novelist seems to be implying, is a natural outgrowth of a culture of endless religious disputes, in which "sects and denominations of Christians quarrel with each other" continuously ("Ignorance and Crime" 100). Indeed, as historian Clyde Bin-field observes, the intertwining of the law and religion was an inescapable fact at this time. (In the Parliamentary session that concluded in early 1854, twenty-six of fifty-four votes were on ecclesiastical topics [116].) Dickens prepares his readers for this analogous relationship from the very beginning of *Bleak House*, not only by using religious language in his references to Chancery (it is the "most pestilent of hoary sinners" [18]) but by giving the Court a distinctly church-like appearance. The Lord High Chancellor sits in front "with a foggy glory round his head" (18); the chamber itself is a dim, "curtained sanctuary" [19] with "wasting candles here and there" [18] (an appearance that corresponds, it might be noted, with contemporary descrip-tions of Irvingite chapels).[8] And as if to underscore the point, it is at the Court of Chancery that Dickens has the adult Esther encounter, in a "chill of . . . unexpected recognition" (357), that harpy of Dissent, Miss Barbary's former servant, Mrs. Rachael, now Mrs. Chadband.

That Dickens saw the divisiveness and intransigence of Dissent as part and parcel of the bureaucratic irresponsibility that had taken hold in England is suggested in his journalism of this period. "There are two public bodies remarkable for knowing nothing of the people, and for perpetually interfering to put them right," he declared in 1855. "The one is the House of Commons; the other the Monomaniacs" ("The Great Baby" 66). The latter group in-cludes Sabbatarians like "the Reverend Single Swallow" and "the Reverend Temple Pharisee," who see public houses open on Sunday as dens of iniquity. In a passage on the same topic from an 1850 essay that anticipates the first chapter of *Bleak House*, Dickens likewise suggests a connection between ineffectual government and the legalistic religion of Nonconformists:

> Move and carry resolutions, bring in bills, have committees, upstairs, down-stairs, and my lady's chamber; read a first time, read a second time, read a third time, read thirty thousand times; the declared authority of the Christian dispensation over the letter of the Jewish law, particularly in this special in-stance, "cannot be petitioned, read or committee'd away."
>
> ("The Sunday Screw" 186)

It is in light of sentiments like these, implying that England's institutional and religious problems spring from the same poisoned well, that Ada Clare's comments in chapter 5–and similar expressions of exasperation in *Bleak House*—have a resonance that reaches far beyond simply the legal satire of the novel: "I am grieved that I should be the enemy—as I suppose I am—of a great number of relations and others, and that they should be my enemies—as I suppose they are—and that we should be ruining one another without knowing how or why and be in constant doubt and discord all our lives" (73).

But, as noted at the outset of this essay, Dickens's attitude toward the troubled institutions and culture of Britain was quite complicated; he was certainly more supportive of existing authority and the idea of a strong, centralized government than his popular reputation as a tireless crusader against bureaucratic bungling and social injustice might lead one to believe. If he was a vocal critic of the Victorian power structure—a "subversive writer" and a "radical," as George Orwell describes him in a notable essay (2)—he was also at times a forceful spokesman *for* it, a staunch defender of the existing British polity at a time when various changes, such as the influx of immigrants, worker unrest, calls for women's rights, and (especially) growing religious sectarianism, threatened to remake the nation in ways he found abhorrent. His image as a champion of the downtrodden has tended to obscure what Humphry House calls the "strong authoritarian strain" (201) in his character, a frame of mind that, on certain issues, could be paternalistic, conservative, and even reactionary (Ackroyd 738–41).

In the end it may be impossible to fully reconcile what Myron Magnet calls "the *other* Dickens" (1), the proponent of authority and aggression who could advocate harsh penal methods and brutal treatment of colonial peoples,[9] with the author who seems so keenly sensitive to human suffering and the abuses of power—who was alive to the "social sin" of Victorian England (G. B. Shaw, qtd. in Ford, *Dickens and His Readers* 234). But two considerations at least partly account for the seemingly contradictory quality of his opinions about and representations of the workings of government. One is his obsession with order and regularity, which, in his private life, manifested itself in a mania for punctuality (and a fastidiousness that extended even to the rearranging of furniture in hotel rooms to suit his liking) (Ackroyd 236, 222). The other is the strongly nationalistic strain in his thinking. *Any* threat to the peaceful and healthy existence of the nation's citizenry, whether from "above" by incompetent leadership or from "below" by crime and insurrection, he reacted to strongly. Bureaucratic negligence was on a par with social agitation as objects of his disdain (even if the latter might help eliminate the former) since both were at odds with his vision of a harmonious, hierarchical community. Time and again in his writings, as this essay has shown, he evokes this ideal of a well-ordered world in his descriptions of quiet provincial villages and cathedral towns. It is not surprising, therefore, that Dickens found so much to dislike about America (which he visited in 1842 and again in 1867–68), especially its chaotic and socially unstratified frontier, which bore so little resemblance to his conception of a civilized and carefully cultivated society.

In short, British institutional authority was a highly problematical matter for Dickens, and his conflicting attitudes toward it influenced his treatment of religious issues in this famously split narrative. The virulence of his anti-Dissenting discourse in *Bleak House* certainly owes something to his belief that the state was proving increasingly incapable of dealing with the threat that Dissent posed, and that his readers, if powerfully convinced of its abnormality, might help limit its role in British life. But at the same time, Esther Summerson's spiritual odyssey, which ends in a rural Yorkshire paradise, reflects his hope that there might yet be an institutional means of containing the threat of Dissent, namely a stalwart Anglican Establishment, reorganized along Broad Church lines. Esther's way-of-the-soul repudiates Dissent and affirms a Christian faith unburdened by questions of sin and judgment. Perhaps it is Dickens's own voice we hear in Inspector Bucket's warm-hearted praise of her: "You're a pattern, you know, that's what you are. . . . you're a pattern" (803).

NOTES

1. For example, the ever-confident Thomas Babington Macaulay described 1851 as "a singularly happy year of peace, plenty, good feeling, innocent pleasure and national glory" (qtd. in Ackroyd 632). Concerning opening ceremonies at the Crystal Palace, one essayist in *The Times* (2 May 1851) wrote, "Some saw in it the second and more glorious inauguration of their sovereign; some a solemn dedication of art and its stores; some were most reminded of that day when all ages and climes shall be gathered round the throne of their maker; there was so much that seemed accidental and yet had a meaning, that no one could be content with simply what he saw . . . all contributed to an effect so grand and yet so natural, that it hardly seemed to be put together by design, or to be the work of human artificers" (qtd. in Thomson 99).

2. In Quiller-Couch's view Dickens was completely aloof from religious controversy: "You must remember that, while Dickens wrote, Tractarian Movements, Unitarian Movements, Positive Movements—Wiseman's claim, Newman's secession, the Gorham judgment, Bishop Colenso's heresies-Darwin's hypothesis, Huxley's agnostic rejection of doctrine, and so on—that all these things were agitating men's thoughts as with a succession of shocks of earthquake. But all

these passed Dickens by, as little observed as felt by him; simply disregarded"
(65–66).

3. There are other texts in which Dickens associates the smell of the dead with
   outworn religion. For example, in "The City of London Churches" (chapter 9
   of *The Uncommercial Traveller*) the narrator visits an obscure place of worship
   in which "rot and mildew and dead citizens formed the uppermost scent" (91).

4. Richard J. Helmstadter notes that the "temperance movement began in the 1830s,
   and from that time most of the temperance leaders were Nonconformists" (81).
   Dickens's "Infant Bonds of Joy" mocks the Band of Hope union, a temperance
   organization for children encouraged by ragged schools and Nonconformist
   churches.

5. As Janet Larson notes, in *Bleak House* Dickens alludes to the Bible and the Book
   of Common Prayer more often than to any other text (99).

6. The first verse is as follows: "Alas and did My Saviour Bleed/ And did my
   Sovereign die/ Would He devote that sacred head/ For such a worm as I?" Watts
   lived from 1674 to 1748.

7. At least Smallweed lacks Chadband's loquaciousness: "I want five hundred
   pound" (735).

8. Dickens's acquaintance and next-door neighbor in Tavistock Square, where he
   lived while composing *Bleak House*, was the one-time Anglican John Bate Car-
   dale, who became first "apostle" of the Irvingite Church (*Letters*, 6:482, n. 4).

9. Dickens was, according to his colleague G. A. Sala, a devoted supporter and
   friend of the Metropolitan Police, who maintained discipline in London's crowded
   streets and neighborhoods—with the novelist occasionally in tow—and throughout his life he advocated stern penal measures, complaining loudly when he
   believed criminals were being dealt with too leniently (as in the so-called Separate
   System of the newly established Pentonville Prison). Law-breakers, he argued,
   should be handled severely, forced to perform work "badged and degraded as
   belonging to gaols only, and never done elsewhere" ("Pet Prisoners" 179). Even
   the danger posed by petty thieves and pickpockets in London, whose disadvantaged backgrounds he was certainly familiar with, provoked a stern reaction.
   "The Ruffian," he declared (in an 1868 essay of the same title) is "the common
   enemy to be punished and exterminated" (308). Dickens himself once saw to it
   that a teen-age girl who had used foul language in public (a punishable if rarely
   prosecuted offense) was arrested and sentenced before a suburban magistrate
   ("The Ruffian" 305–07). The most important study of Dicken's attitudes toward
   the law and punishment remains Philip Collins's *Dickens and Crime*.

It is especially startling for the reader schooled only in the sentiments of
Dickens the social critic and Liberal reformer to encounter his baldly racist pronouncements about the "uncivilized" peoples of other regions of the world and
his forthright approval of violence to suppress challenges to British colonial
authority. During the Indian Mutiny of 1857–58, for example, he told Angela
Burdett-Coutts that if he were Commander-in-Chief in India, he would "do [his]
utmost to exterminate the Race upon whom the stain of the late cruelties rested
. . . with all convenient dispatch and merciful swiftness of execution, to blot it

out of mankind and raze it off the face of the Earth'' (Letter, 4 October 1857, 8: 459). At about the same time, he suggested to a friend that Anglo-Chinese hostilities would be best addressed ''if we struck off the heads of 500 mandarins'' (qtd. in Ackroyd 838). That these vengeful statements were more than just idle remarks on Dickens's part is confirmed by his later public support (along with Thomas Carlyle) of British colonial governor Edward Eyre, who in 1865 dealt with a Jamaican slave revolt by executing over 400 people (and flogging hundreds more). The controversy in England over Eyre's brutality, he felt, was ridiculous: ''So we are badgered about New Zealanders and Hottentots, as if they were identical with men in clean shirts at Camberwell, and were to be bound by pen and ink accordingly''   (qtd. in Adrian 329).

WORKS CITED

Ackroyd, Peter. *Dickens*. London: Sinclair-Stevenson, 1990.

Adrian, Arthur A. ''Dickens on American Slavery: A Carlylean Slant.'' *PMLA*. 67 (1952): 315–29.

Andrews, Malcolm. *Dickens on England and the English*. New York: Barnes and Noble, 1979.

Binfield, Clyde. *So Down to Prayers: Studies in English Nonconformity, 1780–1920*. London: J. M. Dent, 1977.

Bloom, Harold, ed. Introduction. *Charles Dickens's* Bleak House. New York: Chelsea House, 1987. 1–12.

Blount, Trevor. ''The Chadbands and Dickens' View of Dissenters.'' *Modern Language Quarterly*. 25.3 (1964): 295–307.

Brown, James M. *Dickens: Novelist in the Market-Place*. London: Macmillan, 1982.

Butt, John, and Kathleen Tillotson. *Dickens at Work*. London: Methuen, 1957. Chadwick, Owen. *The Victorian Church*. Part I. London: Adams and Charles Black, 1966.

''Charlotte Brontë.'' *Nineteenth-Century Literature Criticism*. 8: 50–51.

Cockshut, A. O. J. *Anglican Attitudes: A Study of Victorian Religious Controversies*. London: Collins, 1959.

Collins, Philip. *A Critical Commentary on Dickens's 'Bleak House'*. London: Macmillan, 1971.

———. *Dickens and Crime*. London: Macmillan, 1962.

————, ed. *Dickens: The Critical Heritage*. New York: Barnes and Noble, 1971.

Conlon, Raymond. "*Bleak House*'s Miss Barbary: A Psychological Miniature." *Dickens Studies Newsletter*. 24.3 (1983): 90–92.

Connell, J. M. "The Religion of Charles Dickens." *Hibbert Journal*. 36 (1938): 225–34.

Coolidge, Archibald C., Jr. "Dickens and Latitudinarian Christianity." *Dickensian* 59 (1963): 57–60.

Cunningham, Valentine. *Everywhere Spoken Against: Dissent in the Victorian Novel*. Oxford: Clarendon, 1975.

Daleski, H. M. "*Bleak House*." In his *Dickens and the Art of Analogy*. New York: Schocken Books, 1970. 156–89. Rpt. in *Critical Essays on Charles Dickens's* Bleak House. Ed. Elliot Gilbert. Boston: G. K. Hall, 1989: 13–40.

Defoe, Daniel. *A Tour Through the Whole Island of Great Britain*. 1724–26. Harmondsworth, Middlesex: Penguin, 1971.

Deen, Leonard W. "Style and Unity in *Bleak House*." *Criticism* 3.3 (1961): 206–18. Rpt. in *Twentieth-Century Interpretations of* Bleak House. Ed. Jacob Korg. Englewood Cliffs, NJ: Prentice-Hall, 1968. 45–57.

Dickens, Charles. *Bleak House*. 1852–53. New York: Signet, 1964.

————. "George Silverman's Explanation." *All the Year Round*. 458 (Feb. 1, 1868): 180–83; 460 (Feb. 15, 1868): 228–31; 462 (Feb. 29, 1868): 276–81.

————. "The Great Baby." 4 August 1855. *Household Words*. Rpt. in *The Works of Charles Dickens: Miscellaneous Papers, Plays, and Poems*. Vol. 2. London: Chapman and Hall, 1908. 66–73.

————. "Hysteria and Devotion." *All the Year Round*. 28 (5 November 1859): 31–35.

————. "Ignorance and Crime." 22 April 1848. *The Examiner*. Rpt. in *Miscellaneous Papers from 'The Morning Chronicle,' 'The Daily News,' 'The Examiner,' 'Household Words,' 'All the Year Round,' Etc. by Charles Dickens*. London: Chapman and Hall, 1914.

————. *The Letters of Charles Dickens*. Ed. Madeline House, Graham Storey, and Kathleen Tillotson. 9 vols. to date. Oxford: Clarendon Press, 1965–.

————. "The Niger Expedition." *The Examiner* 19 August 1848. Rpt. in *The Works of Charles Dickens: Miscellaneous Papers, Plays, and Poems*. Vol. 1. London: Chapman and Hall, 1908. 43–61.

————. "Pet Prisoners." *Household Words* 27 April 1850. Rpt.in *The Works of Charles Dickens: Miscellaneous Papers, Plays,and Poems*. Vol. 1. London: Chapman and Hall, 1908. 165–179.

————. "A Preliminary Word." *Household Words*. 30 March 1850.Rpt.in *The Works of Charles Dickens: Miscellaneous Papers, Plays,and Poems*. Vol. 1. London: Chapman and Hall, 1908. 107–09.

————. "Red Tape." *Household Words* 15 February 1851. Rpt. in *The Works of Charles Dickens: Miscellaneous Papers, Plays, and Poems*. Vol. 1. London: Chapman and Hall, 1908. 243–50.

————. "The Ruffian." *All the Year Round* 10 October 1868. Rpt. in *The Uncommercial Traveller*. Illustrated Library Edition. 1875. Oxford: Oxford UP, 1958.

————. Speech to Administrative Reform Association. London. 27 June 1855. In K. J. Fielding, ed. *The Speeches of Charles Dickens*. Oxford: Clarendon, 1960. 197–208.

————. Speech to Soiree of the Mechanics' Institution. Liverpool. 26 February 1844. In K. J. Fielding, ed. *The Speeches of Charles Dickens*. Oxford: Clarendon, 1960. 52–58.

————. "The Sunday Screw." *Household Words*. 22 June 1850. Rpt. in *The Works of Charles Dickens: Miscellaneous Papers, Plays, and Poems*. Vol. 1. London: Chapman and Hall, 1908. 185–93.

————. "Sunday Under Three Heads." 1836. In *The Writings of Charles Dickens*. Standard Library Edition. Vol. 28. Boston: Houghton Mifflin, 117–43.

————. "Whole Hogs." *Household Words* 23 August 1851. Rpt. in *The Works of Charles Dickens: Miscellaneous Papers, Plays, and Poems*. Vol. 1. London: Chapman and Hall, 1908. 272–78.

————. "Why?" *Household Words* 1 March 1856. Rpt. in *The Works of Charles Dickens: Miscellaneous Papers, Plays, and Poems*. Vol. 2. London: Chapman and Hall, 1908. 96–102.

Dickens, Charles, and Wilkie Collins. "Doctor Dulcamara, M.P." *Household Words*. 18 December 1858. Rpt. in *Charles Dickens' Uncollected Writings from* Household Words: *1850–1859*. Vol. 2. Bloomington: Indiana UP, 1968. 619–26.

Dickens, Charles, and W. H. Wills. "The Doom of English Wills." *Household Words*. 28 September 1850. Rpt. in *Charles Dickens' Uncollected Writings from* Household Words: *1850–1859*. Bloomington: Indiana UP, 1968. 163–72.

Dunn, Richard J. "Esther's Role in *Bleak House*." *Dickensian* 62 (1966): 163–66.

Eliot, T. S. "Wilkie Collins and Dickens." *The Times Literary Supplement*. 4 August 1927: 408–410. Rpt. in *Charles Dickens: A Critical Anthology*. Ed. Stephen Wall. Harmondsworth: Penguin, 1970. 278–80.

Engel, Elliot. Pickwick Papers: *An Annotated Bibliography*. New York: Garland, 1990.

Flegg, Columba Graham. *'Gathered Under Apostles': A Study of the Catholic Apostolic Church*. Oxford: Clarendon, 1992.

Ford, George H. *Dickens and His Readers: Aspects of Novel Criticism Since 1836.* New York: Gordian, 1974.

———. "The Governor Eyre Case in England." *University of Toronto Quarterly.* 17 (1948): 219–33.

Forster, John. *The Life of Charles Dickens.* 1872–74. Ed. J. W. T. Ley. New York: Doubleday, Doran, and Company, 1928.

Gilmour, Robin. *The Victorian Period: The Intellectual and Cultural Context of English Literature, 1830–1890.* London: Longman, 1993.

Gottfried, Barbara. "Household Arrangements and the Patriarchal Order in *Bleak House.*" *The Journal of Narrative Technique.* 24.1 (1994): 1–13.

Griffin, James. *Memories of the Past: Records of a Ministerial Life.* London: Hamilton, Adams, 1883.

Helmstadter, Richard J. "The Nonconformist Conscience." In *Religion in Victorian Britain. Vol. 4: Interpretations.* Ed. Gerald Parsons. Manchester U P, 1988. 61–95.

Herbert, Christopher. "The Occult in *Bleak House.*" *Novel: A Forum on Fiction* 17.2 (1984). Rpt. in *Charles Dickens's* Bleak House. *Modern Critical Interpretations.* Ed. Harold Bloom. New York: Chelsea House, 1987. 121–38.

House, Humphry. *The Dickens World.* London: Oxford U P, 1941.

Jackson, Thomas A. *Charles Dickens: The Progress of a Radical.* New York: International Publishers, 1938.

Jay, Elizabeth. *The Religion of the Heart: Anglican Evangelicalism and the Novel.* Oxford: Clarendon, 1979.

Johnson, Edgar. "The Anatomy of Society." From *Charles Dickens: His Tragedy and Triumph.* Vol. 2. New York: Simon and Schuster, 1952. 769–79. Rpt. in *Twentieth-Century Interpretations of* Bleak House. Ed. Jacob Korg. Englewood Cliffs, NJ: Prentice-Hall, 1968. 21–30.

Kaplan, Fred. *Dickens: A Biography.* New York: William Morrow, 1988.

Kennedy, Valerie. "*Bleak House*: More Trouble with Esther?" *Journal of Women's Studies in Literature.* 1 (1979): 330–47.

Korg, Jacob. Introduction. *Twentieth Century Interpretations of* Bleak House. Englewood Cliffs, NJ: Prentice-Hall, 1968. 1–20.

Larson, Janet L. "The Battle of Biblical Books in Esther's Narrative." *Nineteenth-Century Fiction.* 38.2 (1983). Rpt. in Elliot L. Gilbert, ed. *Critical Essays on Charles Dickens's* Bleak House. Boston: G. K. Hall, 1989. 99–122.

Lecky, William E. H. *Religious Tendencies of the Age.*

Macaulay, Thomas Babington. *The History of England from the Accession of James II.* Vol. 1. 1848. New York: John Wurtele Lovell, n.d.

Machin, G. I. T. *Politics and the Churches in Great Britain:1832–1868.* Oxford: Clarendon, 1977.

Magnet, Myron. *Dickens and the Social Order.* Philadelphia: U of Pennsylvania P, 1985.

Maynard, John. *Victorian Discourses on Sexuality and Religion.* Cambridge: Cambridge U P, 1993.

Metcalfe, G. E. Introduction. *The African Slave Trade and Its Remedy.* By Thomas Fowell Buxton. London: Dawsons of Pall Mall, 1968. iv-xxiv.

Miller, J. Hillis. "Bleak House." In his *Charles Dickens: The World of His Novels.* Cambridge, MA: Harvard UP, 1958. 190–205. Rpt. in *Twentieth-Century Interpretations of* Bleak House. Ed. Jacob Korg. Englewood Cliffs, NJ: Prentice-Hall, 1968. 74–87.

———. "Interpretation in Dickens' *Bleak House.*" In *Victorian Subjects.* Durham, NC: Duke UP, 1991. 179–99. Rpt. of Introduction. *Bleak House.* By Charles Dickens. Harmondsworth, Middlesex: Penguin, 1971.

Moers, Ellen. "*Bleak House*: the Agitating Women." *Dickensian.* 69.1 (1973): 13–24.

Morse, David. *High Victorian Culture.* Houndmills, Basingstoke, Hampshire: Macmillan, 1993.

Murray, Brian. *Charles Dickens.* New York: Continuum, 1994.

Newton, Judith. "Historicisms New and Old: 'Charles Dickens' Meets Marxism, Feminism, and West Coast Foucault." *Feminist Studies* 16 (1990): 449–70.

Orwell, George. "Charles Dickens." In his *Dickens, Dali and Others.* New York: Reynal and Hitchcock, 1946.

O'Toole, Fintan. "The Meanings of Union." *The New Yorker.* 27 April and 4 May 1998: 54+.

Page, Norman. Bleak House: *A Novel of Connections.* Twayne's Masterwork Studies No. 42. Boston: Twayne, 1990.

Parsons, Gerald. "From Dissenters to Free Churchmen: The Transitions of Victorian Nonconformity." In *Religion in Victorian Britain. Vol. 1: Traditions.* Ed. Gerald Parsons. Manchester U P, 1988. 67–116.

———. "Reform, Revival, and Realignment: The Experience of Victorian Anglicanism." In *Religion in Victorian Britain. Vol. 1: Traditions.* Ed. Gerald Parsons. Manchester U P, 1988. 14–66.

Pope, Norris. *Dickens and Charity*. New York: Columbia U P, 1978.

Quiller-Couch, Arthur. *Charles Dickens and Other Victorians*. Cambridge: Cambridge U P, 1925.

Rosner, Mary. "Drizzle, Darkness, and Dinosaurs: Defining the World of *Bleak House*." *Dickens Studies Newsletter*. 13.4 (1982): 99–108.

Routley, Erik. *English Religious Dissent*. Cambridge: Cambridge U P, 1960.

Ruskin, John. "Fiction, Fair and Foul." *Nineteenth Century*. 7 (June 1880): 945. Rpt. in Philip Collins, ed. *Dickens: The Critical Heritage*. New York: Barnes and Noble, 1971: 298–299.

Sanders, Andrew. *Charles Dickens: Resurrectionist*. London: Macmillan, 1982.

Senf, Carol A. *Bleak House*: Dickens, Esther, and the Androgynous Mind." *Victorian Newsletter*. 64 (Fall 1983): 21–27.

Shapiro, James. *Shakespeare and the Jews*. New York: Columbia U P, 1996.

Shatto, Susan. *The Companion to* Bleak House. London: Allen and Unwin, 1988.

Stone, Harry. "Dickens and the Jews." *Victorian Studies*. 2 (1959): 223–53.

Thackeray, William Makepeace. *The Letters of Thackeray*. Ed. Gordon N. Ray. Vol. 2. Cambridge, MA: Harvard U P, 1945.

Thompson, David M., ed. *Nonconformity in the Nineteenth Century*. London: Routledge and Kegan Paul, 1972.

Thomson, David. *England in the Nineteenth Century: 1815–1914*. Harmondsworth, Middlesex: Penguin, 1950.

Walder, Dennis. *Dickens and Religion*. London: George Allen and Unwin, 1981.

Wilson, Angus. *The World of Charles Dickens*. New York: Viking, 1970.

Winter, Mrs. *The Love Romance of Charles Dickens: Told in His Letters to Maria Beadnell*. London: Argonaut, 1936.

Wolff, Robert Lee. *Gains and Losses: Novels of Faith and Doubt in Victorian England*. New York: Garland, 1977.

Wood, Anthony. *Nineteenth Century Britain: 1815–1914*. 2nd ed. London: Longman, 1982.

Woodruff, Douglas. "The Christianity of Charles Dickens." *The Tablet*. 224 (1970): 542–44.

Speculative Plagues and the Ghosts of *Little Dorrit*

Daniel P. Scoggin

Dickens's extended description in Little Dorrit *of the desire to speculate with capital as an unwitting bodily infection touches on a central Victorian concern, one with links to political economy, medical theories of contagion, and evangelical spirituality: the causal connection between liability and subsequent suffering. In the novel, originally titled No-body's Fault, Dickens presents an addition to the catalogue of so-called "social diseases" to compel the reader to reexamine the laissez-faire conception of financial reversal as necessarily rooted in personal short-comings, such as avarice, laziness, and luxuriousness. More specifically, by offering the detailed history behind Arthur Clennam's fall, Dickens constructs a complex pathology of monetary failure, suggesting that there may be mitigating factors that corrupt the individual's relationship to (and perception of) an economy. Furthermore, the novel's presentation of Gothic themes (including imprisonment, domestic tyranny, and the supernatural) is based in a series of mis-speculations regarding the self's role in institutional failure. Dickens extends a long Gothic tradition by having his misguided but true-hearted protagonist carry his sense of personal loss out of a haunted house to the arena of market speculation, to an institution in which the possibility of debt and "relational identity" are approached as an acceptable investment. In the end, the Clennam haunted home is connected, via this idea of plague-ridden speculation, to the Marshalsea debtor's prison; or, put another way, that prime speculator Mr. Merdle and the extremely evangelical Mrs. Clennam are joined in one villainous, corrupted order.*

> *"I am in a very anxious and uncertain state; a state that even leads me to doubt whether anything now seeming to belong to me, may really be mine."*
>
> —Arthur Clennam, *Little Dorrit*

> *" 'There have been at work among us', a Nonconformist preacher told his people, 'three great social agencies: the London City Mission; the novels of Mr. Dickens; the cholera.' "*
>
> —G.M. Young, *Portrait of an Age*

In book two, chapter thirteen, of Charles Dickens's *Little Dorrit* (1857), Arthur Clennam visits the poverty-stricken tenement of "Bleeding Heart Yard" a healthy man, albeit a little "worn and solitary," but returns home infected and replete with "the signs of sickening" (643). More precisely, in this chapter titled "The Progress of an Epidemic," Clennam catches a familiar Victorian strain of the plague, the plague of speculation, from Pancks, who has himself caught it from Casby's desperate tenants. "So rife and potent was the fever in Bleeding Heart Yard, that Mr. Pancks's rent-days caused no interval in the patients. The disease took the singular form . . . of causing the infected to find . . . excuse and consolation in allusions to the magic name" (628). Dickens's plague narrative recalls what an influential economist from the period, J. R. McCulloch, describes as the rage in "imitative speculations," a "dangerous tendency" in which many otherwise fastidious citizens engage in "speculative adventures" not in the spirit of gambling but by the "principle of imitation" (270–71).[1] In *Little Dorrit*, the "magic" person to be emulated by representatives from each of the classes is, of course, Mr. Merdle, the capitalist-king whose inevitable fall ruins Clennam and many others.

I would argue that Dickens's extended description of the spread of speculation as an unwitting bodily infection touches on a central Victorian concern, one with links to political economy, medical theories of contagion, and evangelical spirituality: the causal connection between liability and subsequent suffering.[2] In *Little Dorrit*, originally titled *Nobody's Fault* (Butt and Tillotson 223–27), Dickens presents an addition to the catalogue of so-called "social diseases" to compel the reader to reexamine the laissez-faire conception of financial reversal as necessarily rooted in personal shortcomings, such as avarice, laziness, and luxuriousness. More specifically, by offering the detailed history behind Clennam's fall, Dickens constructs a complex pathology of monetary failure, suggesting that there may be mitigating factors which corrupt the individual's relationship to (and perception of) an economy. Clennam unconsciously develops a propensity to speculate long before he visits Bleeding Heart Yard. Ironically, the seeds of this upright protagonist's illness (a commentary on the distortion of liability) can be found in his flawed upbringing in his parent's "counting-house" and his mother's severe abuse of an evangelical ethos concerning earthly suffering. In fact, *Little Dorrit's* speculative plague is the result of a desire to eschew judgment by passing it on: a flawed search for a material substitute for what should be an internal quest for self-responsibility, atonement, and personal healing.

I would claim, furthermore, that the novel's presentation of Gothic themes (including imprisonment, domestic tyranny, and the supernatural) is based in a series of mis-speculations regarding the self's role in institutional failure. At the center of *Little Dorrit's* extensive appeal to a Gothic tradition (or literature of corruption) is the protagonist's guilty attempt to map a personal debt onto the exorcism of a physical structure, a quest that remains terrifying, we shall see, until possession is properly aligned with what the novelist considers to be a grounded and useful identity. Clennam's misdirected investigation, to be sure, recalls the failed attempt by earlier Gothic protagonists, such as Horace Walpole's Manfred and Ann Radcliffe's Emily St. Aubert, to interpret monetary-genealogical disruptions, either at their own hands or the hands of others, in terms of the haunting of an ancient, decaying castle. Of course, Dickens takes this Gothic dialectic one step further in *Little Dorrit* by having his misguided but true-hearted protagonist carry his sense of personal loss out of a haunted house to the arena of market speculation, to an institution in which the possibility of debt and "relational identity" are approached as an acceptable investment.[3] In the pages to follow, I want to show exactly how the Clennam haunted home is connected, via this idea of plague-ridden speculation, to the Marshalsea debtors' prison, or, along the same lines, how that prime speculator Mr. Merdle and the extremely evangelical Mrs. Clennam are joined in one villainous, corrupted order.

Before clarifying these connections, I would like to point out the obvious reason why Dickens evoked the plague as the central metaphor for social upheaval. "Two hundred years after the Great Plague, England again had to confront disease as a force for decimating significant segments of the population: the death rate by tuberculosis and phthisis rose to almost 20% in 1851, and epidemic outbreaks of cholera and smallpox in 1831, 1848, and 1870 exacerbated the problem of ineffective disease control" (Benton 69). Dickens was deeply concerned with this most pressing of urban problems. Michael Gurney notes the rather extensive medical knowledge the author displays in describing disease in his novels:

> The fictive ills given to his characters are real diseases, not romantic swoons or lingering obscure fevers. The diseases are from Dickens's actual experience, carefully observed and painstakingly reproduced with definite signs and symptoms that progress in a logical sequence. His descriptions of disease are frequently superior to the medical texts of his day. The illnesses are realistic and

challenging enough that Dickensian diagnoses are often the subject of discussion in current medical journals.   (Gurney 80)

Most critics agree that *Bleak House* offers Dickens's most sustained discourse on disease. In this novel (preceding *Little Dorrit* by three years), Jo contracts smallpox from Nemo's corrupt burial site only to pass it on to Charley and Esther, who nearly dies from the illness and is scarred for life. Gurney suggests that Dickens selected smallpox for *Bleak House* as opposed to cholera, which claimed more lives in the mid-nineteenth century, because a cholera infection would have carried with it certain "moral stigmas unsuitable for Dickens's 'good girl'" (90). Cholera was associated with the filth and slums of the lower classes in a way which gave the disease a religious and judgmental quality; many commentators went so far at to connect the disease to intemperance and immoral behavior, even regarding the disease as a token of moral retribution. In contrast, smallpox was perceived as a "democratic disease" because, as Gurney observes, it was passed from person to person across socioeconomic boundaries, "having afflicted Englishmen from Jacob's Island to Buckingham Palace for over a century": "Only smallpox could so effectively lobby for reform, symbolize a major theme, and bring about the transformation of the novel's heroine" (90). Furthermore, as another critic claims, the "encompassing and exhaustive" appearance of smallpox in *Bleak House* helps confirm Dickens's main theme: how individuals are consumed, by no fault of their own, in a corrupt juridical and governmental system, " 'this High Court of Chancery, most pestilent of hoary sinners'" (Benton 70). Or, from a slightly different perspective, the images of chance and randomness Dickens uses to demarcate Chancery's legal pestilence also undercut the popular assessment that contagion was naturally a byproduct of the supposedly corrupt and corrupting lower classes.[4]

In *Little Dorrit*, Dickens returns to the notion of institutionalized corruption. Not only does he offer a sequel to Chancery's governmental incompetence in the form of the "Circumlocution Office"; he describes the mushroom growth of the stock market and incorporation as underwriting a public contagion, a speculative plague. By showing how speculation works as a pastime at all social levels, and by presenting it as the medium by which even aristocrats worship the great wealth of the *nouveau riche*, Dickens subtly refutes the notion that economic woes (or natural tribulations) are based in the class-climbing prognostications (or moral transgressions) of the sick-poor as opposed to the healthy-rich. As one respected Victorian writer on economic issues, David Morier Evans, claims of speculation's key role in allowing the highest level of society to degenerate: "the gambling encouraged through the fictitious value which shares have attained [since 1845] has done much to aggravate the existing evil—the looseness of principle and the sacrifice of probity to secure the golden prize, having been only too freely sanctioned in circles where a higher sense of moral rectitude should have prevailed'' (52). In *Little Dorrit*, Dickens offers a specific example of moral failure, a counter-speculation of sorts, to illuminate how this public trend itself figures as a form of degeneration. Ironically, speculation functions as a type of contagion because its practitioners, in trying to distance themselves from the tenuous position and graspings of the lower class, engage in the very practices they claim to be above. For instance, the speculative disease Clennam contracts, a direct contagion passed from person to person, is only aggravated by his visit to the slum of Bleeding Heart Yard. Clennam, sensing that his parents have established the present family footing in society through a usurpation in an obscure past, seeks to do away with a guilty family history. Yet the method the son chooses to address the family problem of escaping poverty and debt (the family connection to the Dorrits) introduces the specter of poverty and debt itself: his dangerous fascination, via Pancks, with the meteoric rise and fall of Merdle, the ''golden wonder.''

Not only does Dickens's narrator say that ''it is at least as difficult to stay a moral infection as a physical one''; he also asserts that the contagion, ''when it has once made head, will spare no pursuit or condition'' (627). The novelist's description of the magnitude of the problem corresponds to Thomas Carlyle's dramatic vision in his *Latter-Day Pamphlets* (1850): ''British industrial existence seems fast becoming one huge poison-swamp of reeking pestilence physical and moral; a hideous living Golgotha of souls and bodies buried alive'' (430). Likewise, John Ruskin, in *Unto This Last* (1860), offers a similar view, but in terms of an unhealthy circulation:

> Thus the circulation of wealth in a nation resembles that of the blood in the natural body. There is one quickness of the current which comes of cheerful emotion or wholesome exercise; and another which comes of sham or of fever. There is a flush of the body which is full of warmth and life; and another which will pass into putrefaction.
> The analogy will hold down even to minute particulars.   (34)

Ruskin later warns that if wealth is left to ''its own lawless flow'' it will becomes ''the last and deadliest of national plagues: waters of Marah—the water which feeds the roots of all evil'' (47). In general, the rhetoric of both thinkers recalls a connection between disease and economic growth common to the previous century. In an exhaustive study of eighteenth-century medical, economic, and religious discourses, Roy Porter clarifies how ''consumption'' was perceived as the most common disease during the emergence of the first widescale consumer revolution. He argues that political models of society and economy

traded upon key images: of system, balance, cycles, and circulation. Thinking
about the human body likewise predicated notions of exchange, transformation,
process, getting and spending, work and waste. Both involved conceptions of
normality and pathology, health and sickness. And both interacted so sympathetically—through language, metaphor and analogy—that one may rarely be
able to pin down strictly documentable "influence" . . . provoked by the very
obvious rise in wasting diseases in an increasingly commercial society, people
were forced to reflect upon the resonances between the active verb "consuming"
—an act of incorporation—and the intransitive "consuming" or being "consumed"—the condition of wasting.   (70)

Porter suggests that there were essentially two camps in the "consumption"
debate. On the one hand, a number of influential sources counseled that a
reckless attitude towards riches and a new array of possessions was becoming
"the cancer of the commonwealth," especially in regard to the growing "luxury" of the lower classes (59).[5] "Churches preached against the love of lucre
and the sin of unbridled appetite, and civic humanism prophesied that private
enrichment sapped public liberty and virtue. 'Luxury,' warned John Dennis
in 1711, is the 'spreading Contagion which is the greatest Corrupter of Publick
Manners and the greatest Extinguisher of Publick Spirit'" (59). On the other
hand, thinkers such as David Hume, Jeremy Bentham, and Adam Smith
would begin to legitimate possessions, pleasures, and the pursuit of profit
through an "individualist economics which defined 'Consumption' as the
'sole end and purpose of all production'" (65). Still, Porter argues, "if production was the summum bonum for early wealth theorists, consumption was
their headache" (59), the process they spent the most time trying to justify
or explain away.

This debate was revisited with added force in the Victorian period, the
second age of consumption, as even secular or empirical political economists
could point to the downside of growth in the wake of industrialization. Writers
inherited the difficult task of mediating between a condemnation of market
failure and urban blight and the public's fascination with the new "necessities" advertised by a consumer economy. Yet it is important to note that
Victorian social critics, such as Carlyle and Ruskin, were less preoccupied
with the emerging problem of "consumption" (a word which always implies
a person and a body), and more concerned with identifying disease with
institutions and the widespread aftereffects of a capitalist system they saw as
permanent: industrialization, monetary circulation, etc. With this in mind,
Dickens's use of an economic-based plague metaphor can illuminate his
loyalty in the Victorian debate between economists (following Adam Smith)
who thought of the uncertain relation between developing production and
consumption as generally beneficial, linear, and progressive, and others (following Thomas Malthus) who conceived of it as cyclical and retributive.

While Adam Smith argued that a general increase in wealth provided a market for the nation's goods and increased the general circulation of money, Malthus suggested that the more a society seeks the absolute extension of riches, through speculation or the belief "in the abstract equivalencies of monetary value," the more it is "enfeebled" due to overpopulation, disease, and famine (Gallagher 94). In opposition, then, to a free market ideology which imagines the banking-investment system as a healthy body troubled only by an occasional virus,[6] Dickens, with his metaphor of a speculative plague, follows in the Malthusian tradition of conceiving of the intense, non-productive pursuit of wealth as a threat to the long-term well-being of a community. Still, Dickens's extensive compassion for the impoverished, both in his novels and his personal life, serves as a rejection of the Malthusian "politico-economical principle that a surplus population must and ought to starve" (Myers 93). In his increasingly dark fiction of the 1850s, the unsatisfied hunger of the poor becomes the all-consuming greed of morally bankrupt capitalists.

Although economics was increasingly regarded as a science in the nineteenth century, a religious reading of the growths and tribulations of the economy was still widely supported. Boyd Hilton notes that "Even within middle-class Anglican circles, extreme evangelicalism spread rapidly from the mid-1820s onward, thanks to economic alarms, Catholic emancipation, constitutional crisis, cholera, and other 'signs' of an impending divine initiative" (10). Evangelicals presented a strict (and professedly supernatural) reading of public disasters, such as the mid-century return of cholera to England, as a dispensation of providence for both lax individual morality and national economic greed.[7] In the evangelical analysis of these disorders, the notion of "speculation" was positioned as the dividing line between proper and improper conduct; as Hilton remarks, it was the "most pejorative of all commonly used words in the first half of the nineteenth century, in that it implied not merely economic irresponsibility but even philosophic doubt and atheism" (123).[8] Strictly speaking, the expanding causal chain the evangelicals proposed—from spiritual doubt, to monetary speculation, to disease—maintains a defensible logic. After all, according to a popular Victorian theory of contagion, "Disease exists 'in the air': it can not be seen or smelt or heard until one 'catches' it and harbors it, and even then one exhibits *symptoms* of the disease, while the malady itself remains amorphous—dangerous and undetectable" (Benton 71).

In contrast to the extreme variety, moderate evangelicalism provided the terms for many conservatives who sought to deflate an ideology of unreflective progress. The evangelical Thomas Chalmers, for instance, purposefully avoided the apocalyptic language of his pre-millenarian brethren in founding a popular form of "Christian economics" which blended a traditional rhetoric against luxury with a systematic rejection of the uninhibited optimism of

Ricardo and Smith.[9] In his widely-read treatise *On Political Economy, in Connexion with the Moral State and Moral Prospects of Society* (1832), Chalmers constructs a Malthusian-based reply to Adam Smith by suggesting that God has indirectly imposed a "natural check" to economic growth by both limiting the nation's supply of food and ability to back capital up with production. He asserts that over-production "soon meets with its correction in bankruptcies and losing speculations by which some are driven from the trade altogether" (Chalmers 122). The "natural theology" offered in his earlier *Christian and Civic Economy* (1826) sheds a new light on Dickens's comments in *Little Dorrit* concerning the relationship between moral and physical infections:

> "A prevalent physical distemper might seize upon households, and carry off many families. The consequent abundance of provisions will speedily bring forward other families in their room. A prevalent moral distemper, even that of ruinous extravagance, might seize upon merchants, and sweep away many of our capitals. The consequent abundance of profits will construct other capitals, and raise up other capitalists, with a rapidity like that of magic . . . To the mere student of political science, it may wear the air and boldness of a paradox, when we affirm of capital, that too little goes into the stock for immediate consumption, and too much is adventured upon the field of commerce—that the competition for business, and for its profits, is greatly overcrowded—that traders jostle out each other, and so many become outcasts from safe or gainful merchandise—that what disease does with the redundant population, bankruptcy does with the redundant capital of our land; relieving the overdone trade of its excess, and so reducing capital within those limits beyond which it cannot find any safe or profitable occupancy."   (qtd. in Hilton 118–19)

In an application of Malthus's stagnation thesis to business cycles, Chalmers outlines the inevitable (but natural) downside of widespread financial gains. He proposes an "alternative, evangelical, version of Free Trade," one which may be characterized as "static (or cyclical), nationalist, retributive, and purgative, employing competition as a means to education rather than to growth" (Hilton 69–70). But if Chalmers undercuts the positive connotations associated with describing trade as "free," he equally rejects the pre-millenarian gloom of certain evangelical readings of financial-natural crises as a sign of impending apocalypse. Instead, his moderate synthesis is to encourage the full "consumption" of food and commodities (an anti-savings position which extremists would interpret as indulgent) because such a use of resources allows the natural, preventative check to growth to be kept constantly in sight. In his *Political Economy*, Chalmers not only condemns "profuse expenditure" as luxurious; he also speaks of "excessive speculation" as the worst form of "extreme parsimony" (Chalmers 123) in its attempt to save and multiply capital to its own destruction. He describes the severe savings of speculation as a "moral gangrene . . . under the semblance of a benefit and boon" (413), a "mania communicated, as if by infection, . . . of wild and ruinous adventure" (518). According to Chalmers, a plague (especially a speculative one) is based in the natural link between the appetite for gain through self-denial and the appetite for indulgence through expenditure, a "hurtful and vicious combination" which seeks to circumvent the check established by God to ensure private and public happiness (123–24).

An awareness of this moderate evangelical link between "extreme parsimony" and "ruinous adventure" can help us to understand Dickens's characterization of economics and speculation in *Little Dorrit*. In order to present a pathology of monetary and moral failure, Dickens draws a subtle line between the arch-capitalist Mr. Merdle, the center of one type of diseased speculation, and the Calvinistic Mrs. Clennam. Merdle's status as a walking corpse is rather obvious. An issue less clear, but equally important, is how Mrs. Clennam's status as an un-dead, vampiric villain is also based on her desire to speculate, her zealous faith in the possibility of trading (from here to the hereafter) on her strict parsimony in what Arthur variously calls her "luxuriousness" or "liberal delivery of others to judgment" (84, 368). In this sense, Mrs. Clennam figures as the spiritual and female equivalent of what J. R. McCulloch describes in his *Political Economy* as the character of a "successful speculator," one "who has skillfully devised the means of effecting the end he had in view, who excelled his competitors in the judgment with which he has looked into futurity, and appreciated the operation of causes producing distant effects" (260). In *Little Dorrit*, Dickens links Mrs. Clennam's eschatological meditations to the character of the "successful speculator," both in the similar nature of their actions and in the plot, in order to turn the tables on the two foremost Victorian ideologies of autonomy: laissez-faire economics and an extreme form of Calvinism which preached the soul alone before an unremitting God. The novelist thus condemns speculation as a diseased approach to advancement by referring to two of speculation's meanings at once: (1) a business enterprise of a venturesome and risky nature offering the chance of great or unusual gain and (2) abstract or hypothetical reasoning on subjects of a deep, abstruse, or conjectural nature.[10] In the end, by equating spiritual judgment with the period's disastrous economic cycles, Dickens censures the quest for sudden personal gain at the expense of others, be it moral or monetary. Similar to the methods used by earlier Gothic novelists to suggest a proprietary resolution to terror, he eventually presents Arthur Clennam as thoughtfully *working through* a labyrinth of doubt and conjecture before taking lasting possession of the ever-serving Little Dorrit, a more worthy inheritance. In short, this spectral *bildungsroman* proposes an anti-speculative code of "moral worth and personal identity . . . determined on the basis of characteristics whose value resides ultimately in their utility" (Henderson 41).

It is the career of the restless son, then, that most clearly fills out (or suffers from) the link between Mrs. Clennam's spiritual "counting-house" and the market. Originally, Arthur inherits the contagion of speculation through his mother's own strict management of the Clennam family secret, her sinful judgment of the circumstances surrounding his own "abject" birth. "*Bred at first*," Dickens writes, "as many physical diseases are, in the wickedness of men, and then disseminated in their ignorance, these [speculative] epidemics, after a period, get communicated to many sufferers who are *neither ignorant nor wicked*" (640, emphasis added). More precisely, Mrs. Clennam's haunting eschatological meditations concerning one's full payment for sin infect Arthur in his passage from child to adult as he unsuccessfully seeks to distance himself from her by compensating, via a series of secular conversions, for a family crime over which she furtively presides. Arthur's attempt to shore up his own lost origins through one lump payment eventually culminates in his participation in Merdle's secular plague of achieving instant, magical wealth without work.

However, market speculation, with its inherent intangibility and fall, will eventually serve as the ideal site for the son to address and redeem the irreconcilable contradictions surrounding his own position and character; speculation becomes a medium by which one is forced to face the inevitable dissolution of possession in this life. Preparing the way for Clennam's confrontation with a fallen institution and indefinite origin is yet another derivative from the root *specere* (to look, and associated with *speculum*, or mirror),[11] the specter. For specters, with their perceptual split between body and spirit, are the progeny of Arthur's inability to resolve indefiniteness through expectation. Although specters denote a failure in moral judgment, they can compel the remorseful to seek a career of atonement. Not the least of these specters is Little Dorrit who, as anti-body and partial solution to Arthur's past, allows the son to carry his plague of speculation out into the street where he will certainly fail.

Dickens can blend elements of political economy with scraps of evangelical doctrine because, to the Victorian mind, both attempt to explain the role of personal responsibility in relation to a mysterious, higher order. As the novel which stands as Dickens's most "profound" assertion of the "religious aspect" of his imagination" (Walder 144), as well as the work of his most concerned with economic fall and failure, *Little Dorrit* addresses an issue which many Victorians would identify as evangelical: suffering as personal judgment for sin. At least, Dickens asserts that Mrs. Clennam is not unusual in "balancing her bargains" of reparation with God: "Thousands upon thousands do it, according to their varying manner, every day" (89). In response to this conception of debt, Dickens addresses and reevaluates the nature of expiation in what could be interpreted as his *Calvinized bildungsroman*: is suffering the price of personal or communal transgression? Are sins really passed from father to son? How should one pay and make others pay as well? Are Arthur Clennam's dislocation, fall, and eventual imprisonment the just punishment for his own speculations, or is he suffering for Mrs. Clennam's secretive use of wealth to judge others? In short, who is to perform judgment, when, and for how long? As the irascible Flintwinch asks of Mrs. Clennam's rigorous judgments: "Who are you, that you should be appointed to do it?" (851)

However, as soon as we identify Dickens's theme as evangelical, even moderately so, we must recant. Most Dickens scholars would immediately acknowledge this association as an odd one. After all, one of Dickens's favorite satirical targets in his novels is the zeal of evangelicalism's more extreme adherents, types such as Pecksniff in *Martin Chuzzlewit* (1843–44), Chadbrand in *Bleak House* (1852–53), and Mrs. Clennam in *Little Dorrit*. As Norris Pope claims, Dickens's attack on evangelicals serves as a restatement of the eighteenth-century case against Methodism: "it is easily argued that he did more than any other novelist (Mrs. Trollope included) to pass on the eighteenth-century view to the Victorians" (38). Still, while Dickens's most consistent religious position has been defined as progressively Unitarian (Pope 38), a "broad, humanist form of Christianity" emphasizing the New Testament (Walder 179), Dickens attacks something in evangelicalism with which he is intimately connected (18). Dennis Walder considers various aspects of the novelist's thought in the course of a shifting relationship with evangelicalism: the "innocent fall" in *Pickwick Papers* (1836–37), charity in *Oliver Twist* (1837–39), consoling death in *The Old Curiosity Shop* (1840–41), conversion in *A Christmas Carol* (1843), and the "social gospel" in *David Copperfield* (1849–50) and *Bleak House* (1852–53).[12] An indicator of Dickens's deeper consideration of the broad current of evangelical ideas is the increasingly dark tone of his novels of the 1850s, "the first fruits of what one might call Dickens's conversion from a sense of individual to a sense of social sin" (Walder 144). At the center of this complex reaction stands *Little Dorrit*, with its central metaphor of a speculative plague. The novel presents an emphatic rejection of the evangelical zeal of Mrs. Clennam while portraying as admirable, in the story of Arthur's pilgrimage to pay a debt, the connection in evangelical doctrine between conversion and the quest for atonement. "At the heart of 'Evangelical' theology, as at the heart of Methodism, stood the doctrine of conversion, a belief in the intense and dramatic personal change which occurred when, burdened down by a sense of inadequacy, one threw oneself on God's mercy and was regenerated" (Walder 18). Recognizing that Dickens is working through some of the contradictory messages of evangelicalism, I think, helps to explain the contrast in

Little Dorrit between the Clennams' haunted home and the Marshalsea debtors' prison (both structures of atonement), and how Arthur sees the first as a place of zealous repression while he strongly desires to read the latter, for reasons we shall explore, as a focus for material and spiritual recovery.

Boyd Hilton notes how different interpretations of suffering served as the primary distinction between moderate evangelicals and extremists:

> The sequence of sin, suffering, contrition, despair, comfort, and grace—so common in moderate evangelical homiletic—shows that pain was regarded as an essential part of God's order, and as bound up with the machinery of judgment and conversion. ''Everything is exactly proportioned: the degree of suffering corresponds with the measure of offence.'' Pre-millenarian extremists, on the other hand, such as Irving and the Recordites, regarded pain as a sign of ''dislocation'' in God's order. They accepted it as a mark of God's sadistic regard for a nation or a life, and even welcomed it as a sign that the last days were nigh at hand. But they were less confident than the moderates about the world's capacity for inculcating virtue, and they tended to preach resignation rather than the need for discipline.   (11)

According to extremists, suffering could be interpreted as an earthly precursor of final damnation, or, depending on the subject of such suffering, absolute reward, as opposed to the moderate view of penance preceding conversion. In the plot of *Little Dorrit*, Dickens makes full use of this evangelical split by sharply contrasting Little Dorrit's (and later Arthur's) composed acceptance of suffering and discipline with the ''dislocation'' fostered by the sadistic Mrs. Clennam.

Alex Owen has pointed out that the second Evangelical revival of the mid-century, with is central tenet of pre-millennialism, ''was strongly associated with female preaching and saw a significant rise in the number of middle-class women who stood firmly by the right to preach'' (16). Many within this movement were committed to the belief that the second coming was imminent and that the validity of prophecy would accompany the last days (Owen 16). Perhaps serving as his pessimistic appraisal of this female ministry, Dickens describes how a self-proclaimed minister such as Mrs. Clennam might pray for and even extend the trials of one's spiritual enemies in the hope of initiating the imminent fulfillment of apocalypse. While she reads her own seclusion and inactivity as a sign of the merited pain of one of the ''elect,'' she judges the extended suffering of others as a sign of damnation, as a precursor to the millennium during which the faithful will rule over the sinful. As such, a pre-millenarian might pray for God to fulfill her own judgment. Mrs. Clennam turns to the Old Testament with what she feels to be a corresponding spirit of vengeance:

> She then put on the spectacles and read certain passages from a book—sternly, fiercely, wrathfully—praying that her enemies (she made them by her tone and

manner expressly hers) might be put to the edge of the sword, consumed by
fire, smitten by plagues and leprosy, that their bones might be grounded to dust,
and that they might be utterly exterminated. As she read on, years seemed to
fall away from her son like the imaginings of a dream, and all the old dark
horrors of his usual preparation for the sleep of an innocent child to overshadow
him.   (75)

She calls for a plague upon her enemies based on her own conclusions concerning their guilt and her salvation. Although the reader and Arthur are still
uncertain about exactly who her enemies might be, Mrs. Clennam is already
an established speculator who, as McCulloch might suggest, "excell[s] [her]
competitors in the judgment with which [she] has looked into futurity" (260).

For Arthur, Mrs. Clennam's vengeful Bible reading recalls an entire youth
spent on such verses, passages that have left him "with no more real knowledge of the beneficent history of the New Testament than if he had been bred
among idolaters" (69). In this inverted case of the prodigal son, the grown
man returns from his travels to a house whose gloomy spaces evoke imaginative associations of incessant childhood judgments and expiations. Arthur
passes through the labyrinth of the imposing dining room, with its framed
"Plagues of Egypt" and the "old dark closet," a former place of punishment
(72), up the stairs to Mrs. Clennam's stagnant room and the innermost chambers of the Word. In this progression, Dickens seems quite intent on introducing the Clennam house in terms of a number of Gothic criteria: "it is ancient,
uncared for, ruinous, haunted, defended by rusty iron railings, gloomy and
deathly" (Milbank 108). But the key to the structure's imposing status is
Arthur's own catatonic sense of dread which, as Milbank notes, actively
grasps the son of the house "like the trapdoors and tortures of the traditional
Gothic mansion" (108). Similar to Emily St. Aubert's apprehension during
her imprisonment at Castle Udolpho, Arthur is overcome by the confluence
of memory and perception as he descends (and ascends) into the "old dark
horrors" the moment he passes over the threshold. His confrontation with
this fallen institution demonstrates, in Freud's analysis, how an early trauma is
often experienced as a series of symptoms: "although he [man] is sufficiently
grown-up to satisfy most of his needs for himself . . . he nevertheless behaves
as though the old danger-situation still existed, and keeps hold of all the
earlier determinants of anxiety" (*Inhibitions, Symptoms, and Anxiety* 147).

After discussing "family affairs" with his mother in the stagnant, upstairs
room, Arthur visits the chamber his deceased father had occupied for business
purposes and likewise finds it "so unaltered that he might have been imagined
still to keep it invisibly" (95). In this scene, Dickens again borrows from the
early Gothic novel. Reminiscent of the portrait ghost in Walpole's *Otranto*,
the picture of Arthur's father compels one to make right a past wrong: "His
picture, dark and gloomy, earnestly speechless on the wall, with the eyes

intently looking at his son as they had looked when life departed from them, seemed to urge him awfully to the task he had attempted'' (95). The son is thus compelled to face the "earlier determinants of anxiety"; as an adult, he must begin the important process of negotiating for himself between the intentions of two essentially dead parents. According to the Protestant iconography which represents the home as an extension of the soul, the "dark house," the *unheimlich* (Sage 4, 25), will come to serve as the endpoint of Arthur's troubled, moral speculations.

At least initially, the morbid counting-house most clearly connects *Little Dorrit* to a Gothic tradition in which the character of a crumbling castle is often "inextricably associated with the villain, usually a persecuting and usurping parent-figure" (Jarrett 155). Certainly, this proves to be the case in *The Castle of Otranto* and *The Mysteries of Udolpho*, in which Manfred and Montoni respectively seek to shore up their suppression of a true descendant by leaning on the authority implied by an ancient and oppressive structure. Interestingly enough, *Little Dorrit* adds a new twist to this Gothic legacy by not only offering a villain who hopes to shame the son out of the claims of the other parent, but by describing an antagonist who solicits credibility through her own suffering within a system over which she presides. Mrs. Clennam's self-conscious affliction at the hands of a crippling malady corresponds to the house's decaying state, which she seems to consider as a detailed receipt of a debt owed, as Flintwinch says, a "lean[ing] against the dead" (224):

> It was a double house, with long, narrow, heavily-framed windows. Many years ago, it had had it in its mind to slide down sideways; it had been propped up, however, and was leaning on some half-dozen gigantic crutches: which gymnasium for the neighbouring cats, weather-stained, smoke-blackened, and overgrown with weeds, appeared in these latter days to be no very sure reliance.
>
> (71)

The Gothic counting-house is, at heart, a house of debt; its tentative, doubling existence is maintained by an economy of props and supports that can only hold off its inward collapse for so long. Of course, sitting at the center of this structure of debt and purveying its partial solutions (like the Lord High Chancellor at the center of Chancery in *Bleak House*) is the self-elected sufferer. "Smite Thou my debtors, Lord," Mrs. Clennam prays, "wither them, crush them; do Thou as I would do, and Thou shall have my worship: this was the impious tower of stone she built up to scale Heaven" (86). Once again, we should note here that the narrator uses a Gothic, architectural metaphor—"impious tower of stone"—to demarcate Mrs. Clennam's religious dependence on liability and differentiation. As Arthur confesses to the sympathetic Mr. Meagles during their stay in quarantine abroad:

"I am the son . . . of a hard father and mother. I am the only child of parents who weighed, measured, and priced everything; for whom what could not be weighed, measured, and priced, had no existence. Strict people as the phrase is, professors of a stern religion, their very religion was a gloomy sacrifice of tastes and sympathies that were never their own, offered up as a part of the bargain for the security of their possessions. Austere faces, inexorable discipline, penance in this world and terror in the next—nothing graceful or gentle anywhere, and the void in my cowed heart everywhere—this was my childhood, if I may so misuse the word as to apply it to such a beginning of life." (59)

Arthur's "strict" parents had at one time dexterously managed a fund of seemingly irreconcilable spiritual and material commodities. At the core of their anxious political economy was an attempt to overcome monetary indefiniteness with spiritual expectation. They had taken judgment into their own hands by regarding their "inexorable discipline" as a sign of their salvation, an intangible investment that they and their possessions would remain secure into the next world. On Arthur's return, only Mrs. Clennam continues in the family business by hoping to profit from her spiritual enemies: "balancing her bargains with the Majesty of heaven, posting up the entries to her credit, strictly keeping her set off, and claiming her due" (89). In this case, Mrs. Clennam engages in a process of parsimonious savings that both Chalmers and McCulloch would recognize, at least in economic terms, as the first step in becoming a successful speculator, an enemy to a market whose health depends on the individual's desire to spend.

Mrs. Clennam hopes to provide evidence of her own status as one of the "elect" by referring to her holdings in this world, a Calvinistic gesture of investment and "worldly asceticism" which Max Weber claims may have made capitalism possible in the first place. From this perspective, the premillenarian Mrs. Clennam suffers acutely from what Erich Fromm has called the *neurosis of Calvinism*, "an irrational attempt to control the outcome of an event by manipulating the evidence for the event" (qtd. in Welsh 85). McCulloch writes of the skill of anticipation that all speculators try to cultivate: they "must look forward to periods more or less distant, and their success depends entirely on the sagacity with which they have estimated the probability of certain events occurring, and the influence which they have ascribed to them" (759). At the center of Dickens's critique of extreme evangelicalism in *Little Dorrit* is his initial narrative of how such an estimation of probability is all too successful; paving the way for his full pathology of a speculative plague is the example of how a debilitating anxiety which overloads the signs of the present with meaning is passed from one generation to the next. Of course, this domestic speculation (or inheritance) carries with it the inevitable threat of material and moral debt. As Arthur reminds his mother: "Our House has done less and less for some years past, and our dealings have been progressively on the decline . . . we have been left far behind'' (85). The falling off of the House of Clennam is made complete when Arthur, too, begins to read possession as a form of judgment; he has his ''misgivings that the goods of this world'' which his parents have ''painfully got together,'' as they claim, ''early and late, with wear and tear and toil and self-denial,'' are only ''so much plunder'' (89).

The several mysteries at the heart of the novel's plot—from the enigma surrounding the Clennams' haunted home to the presence of the nearly generic Gothic villain, Rigaud—are all grounded in the attempt to absolve one's own accumulation of wealth through a judgment against others. One might say that blackmail is the original sin from which the plot of the novel springs. The exact connections between money, self-appointed vengeance, and Arthur's secret origin only become clear in the dénouement of the novel when Mrs. Clennam justifies her career of abuse against Arthur's *real* mother and his father, specifically her locking-away of the codicil to Gilbert Clennam's will.[13]

> ''Those who were appointed of old to go to wicked kings and accuse them—were they not ministers and servants? And had not I, unworthy and far-removed from them, sin to denounce? When she pleaded to me her youth, and his wretched and hard life (that was her phrase for the virtuous training he had belied), and the desecrated ceremony of marriage there had secretly been between them, and the terrors of want and shame that had overwhelmed them both when I was first appointed to be the instrument of their punishment, and the love (for she said the word to me, down at my feet) in which she had abandoned him and left him to me, was it my enemy that became my footstool, were they the words of my wrath that made her shrink and quiver! Not unto me the strength be ascribed; not unto me the wringing of the expiation!''
>
> (844–45)

As in her reading of scripture, Mrs. Clennam's ''wringing of the expiation'' is based on her personal reinterpretation of a written command, in this case the ''D.N.F.'' (''Do Not Forget'') inscribed on her dead husband's watch. Instead of reading the letters as a just reminder to reverse the suppression of the codicil to Gilbert Clennam's will, she takes them as a reference to the evil-doing on which she has already been exacting vengeance. Clearly, Dickens wants us to think of her self-appointment as both judge and instrument of expiation as a form of witch-like idolatry. In claiming that her own vengeful intentions are divinely inspired and controlled, she turns away from the forgiving God of the New Testament, and the occasionally stern God of the Old, to worship some formulaic divinity of the pagan world. Supporting Sekora's assessment that luxury follows a history of restless conjecture, Mrs. Clennam's religion reflects that ''pagan idolatry which was the basic sin of the peoples of the earlier dispensation, and for which they merited the misery and pain of alienation from God'' (Walder 188). Arthur describes the outside of the dilapidated, ''smoke-blackened,'' former trading-house as a sort of ungodly church, a ''gymnasium for the neighbouring cats'' (70–71); inside, his mother, in ''widow's dress,'' sits incessantly in an airless room with an undying fire, a kettle, little mounds of ''damped ashes'' and a pervasive ''smell of black dye'' (73).

Dickens's scathing characterization of Mrs. Clennam as an evangelical witch culminates in her proud estimation of her own atonement, which, as Arthur notes, she engages in with an ''austere air of luxuriousness'' (84). Her sense of the primacy of her own suffering and savings allows her to savor her possessions all the more:

> But Mrs. Clennam, resolved to treat herself with the greater rigour for having been supposed to be unacquainted with reparation, refused to eat her oysters when they were brought. They looked tempting; eight in number, circularly set out on a white plate on a tray covered with a white napkin, flanked by a slice of buttered French roll, and a little compact glass of cool wine and water; but she resisted all persuasions, and sent them down again—placing the act to her credit, no doubt, in her Eternal Day-Book.   (92)

In sharp contrast to Little Dorrit's constant and quiet renunciations, she later states: ''I take it as a grace and favor to be elected to make the satisfaction I am making here, to know what I know for certain here, and to work out what I have worked out here'' (407). The satisfaction Mrs. Clennam derives from her self-inflicted work of atonement emerges as a luxury of the worst kind, the modern-day equivalent of the Israelites worshipping the Golden Calf instead of dutifully accepting the suffering of exile. In fact, as I have begun to suggest, her attempt to control God by predicting outcomes, her conclusions about the enormous heavenly return she can expect on her proud savings and earthly denial, finds its closest equivalent in *Little Dorrit* in the motivations and excitement surrounding the figure of Merdle. Otherwise known as the ''golden wonder'' (626), Merdle, who also suffers from a nameless ''complaint,'' is the center of a speculative paganism that pervades the entire society beyond the confines of the Clennams' outdated house of business. ''The name of Merdle is the name of the age,'' the newly wealthy William Dorrit tells his family circle, Mrs. General bowing her head ''as if she were doing homage to some visible graven image'' (536–37). The question still to be addressed is precisely how these two spheres of paganism inform one another. How does the dejected son, Arthur, inherit a contagion, both a hidden debt and the desire to strike it clean? How does the son transform solitary judgment into a secular career which culminates in the illusive financial promises associated with Merdle's magic?

As early as the third chapter, titled "Home," Dickens begins to describe the paganism of extreme religiosity as a plague that infects the whole society. Arthur finds his way home on a gloomy Sunday evening in which the sounding of church bells proves to be anything but a consolation: "In every thoroughfare, up almost every alley, and down almost every turning, some doleful bell was throbbing, jerking, tolling, as if the Plague were in the city and the dead-carts were going round" (67). The novelist mocks the deprivation of a supposedly enlightened Christian London by portraying it as a city locked in perpetual spiritual mourning: "No pictures . . . no natural or artificial wonders of the ancient world—all *taboo* with that enlightened strictness that the ugly South Sea gods in the British Museum might have supposed themselves at home again" (67). The city lies in wait, suffering from its self-imposed eschatological expectations to the extent any figure offering relief would be considered welcome. Arthur's sense of dread is given a further impetus as his reflections on returning home—church bells as plague bells, pagan gods and their taboos—naturally remind him of the "morally handcuffed," dreary Sundays of his youth, days passed "with a sullen sense of injury in his heart" (69).

Although still oppressed by feelings of guilt and injury, the mature Arthur searches for a way to circumvent the taboo against earthly expectation by working for the compensation of others, especially those harmed by his family's secretive use of wealth. While his mother is only concerned with performing a private reparation of self-denial for her sins, Arthur, as a priest of sorts, hopes to wash away a public and familial guilt for which he is not technically culpable. "If reparation can be made to any one, if restitution can be made to any one," he exclaims, "let us know and make it. Nay, mother, if within my means, let *me* make it" (88). Yet it is important to note that Arthur is unable to make explicit his forceful charge against his parents. On the one hand, then, Arthur also engages in a speculative form of judgment, a moral conjecture based in his own tentative interpretation of the "D.N.F." inscribed on his dead father's watch. Much like Hamlet, Arthur wants to adhere to his father's instigation of justice from beyond the grave. On the other hand, Dickens clearly separates Arthur's active motives from the stagnant profit-seeking of his mother by showing how he seeks to use his legacy and savings, at a moment's notice, to reverse the family crime. Instead of considering his secure, spiritual position as a victim, Arthur strives to use the money in his possession as a detailed receipt of a debt that must be repaid in this life although it has been obscured by time and mystery. Already setting up the novel's primary conception of the fortune of the capitalist as a state of equivalent exchange and bound loss (Nunokawa 320), the son proclaims: "It [money] can buy me nothing that will not be a reproach and misery to me, if I am haunted by a suspicion that it darkened my father's last hours with remorse, and that it is not honestly and justly mine" (88).

From this perspective, *Little Dorrit's* Gothic plot is based on Arthur's attempt to answer a haunting suspicion through an aggressive reparation. Although he can only dimly sense its presence, he feels he must atone for a buried family crime: the banishment, imprisonment, and death of his real mother, a judgment enacted by Mrs. Clennam which only partially concerns, we must remember, the "D.N.F." and the suppression of the codicil to Gilbert Clennam's will. Arthur, as such, struggles to replace his already-dead origin by paying it off, an impossible (and rather paganistic) transaction or sacrifice that only further obscures his own loss and the foundation of the family guilt. We might think of Arthur's aggressive turn to the broken career of speculation, his *dilectum delectum* (or "commanding sin"), in terms of Freud's understanding of repression as an attempt at flight: "The ego withdraws its (preconscious) cathexis from the instinctual representative that is to be repressed and uses that cathexis for the purpose of releasing unpleasure (anxiety)" (Freud 93). In the novel's most basic, ironic turn, Arthur unsuccessfully seeks to escape the indefinite memory of the first state of anxiety, the separation from his real mother, by engaging in a cathexis of monetary "symptoms" so as to "avoid a danger-situation whose presence has been signaled by the generation of anxiety" (129). Or, as Julia Kristeva might say, Arthur wants to simplify his own recognition of a complex family problem—an awareness prompted by his return to the decayed but womb-like conditions of the Gothic family house—by working "to feel separated."[14] In her study of the role of birth and mothering in the construction of identity in the late eighteenth and early nineteenth centuries, Andrea Henderson suggests that it was increasingly understood that

> a child, must of necessity, resist a strong connection to its mother in order to establish itself as a self-made subject, "one that is capable of the limitless self-improvement" valorizing and valorized by an "open" society and a "free economy." The child that does not resist possession by the mother finds itself unable to become a complete subject precisely because it is positioned as an object, as a possessed being, in both the economic and gothic sense. Like the abject characters of the gothic novels of the period, such a child becomes nothing more than, in Kristeva's words, an empty castle, haunted by unappealing ghosts—"powerless" outside, "impossible" inside.   (37)

Although the novel never describes a birth, the issue underwriting much of the Gothic plot of *Little Dorrit* concerns the complex (and haunting) relationship among mothering, memory, and self-possession.[15] Arthur's career, for instance, doubly confuses the physical and moral link typically traced between parent and child. As the victim of a fallen family that borders on a fallen economy, he resists possession (by an unknown mother) by speculating on his origins through possessions. Hence, in the hope of positioning himself as a subject, he only becomes a condition of the house he fears: "powerless outside" and "impossible inside."

Of course, Dickens indicates that Arthur is not liable for his (hereditary) contraction of the desire to speculate and advance. If a laissez-faire economy was thought to depend on the notion of a free and self-made subject, Arthur's case goes to show that there may be competing sub-institutions which threaten the supposed benefits guaranteed to all by the honest pursuit of worldly riches (as Adam Smith would propose). In trying to enter an "open society" and a "free economy" before fully examining the underlying symptoms of domestic debt, he only sets himself up for a fall. The novelist presents the early scenes in the dark and decaying counting-house—in which the son questions his false mother about "the moving power of all this machinery before [his] birth" (88)—as a pessimistic commentary on an ingrained economy against which individual agency is futile, no matter how noble. Arthur's attempt to get a direct answer from Mrs. Clennam only further exacerbates the tension between what he already knows and what he cannot admit: "But I [Mrs. Clennam] only tell you that if you ever renew that theme with me, I will renounce you; I will so dismiss you through that doorway, that *you have better been motherless from your cradle*" (90, emphasis added). In response to the anxiety generated by this interview, Arthur works to feel separated but only complicates his condition. In the ultimate failure of credit, he struggles incoherently to redeem a debt to a mother who no longer physically exists while distancing himself from the living representative of parenting, Mrs. Clennam, who will never reveal how much he owes.[16] His horrors arise "from the sense of the gap, the abyss, between power and powerlessness . . . in abjection, we glimpse a constellation in which it is impossible to separate childhood from 'childing'" (Punter 2: 211).

The fact the Arthur tries to redeem his past by leaving the counting-house behind and following his own career only further confuses him concerning his abjection of self, "that experience of the subject to which it is revealed that all its objects are based merely on the inaugural loss that laid the foundation of its own being" (Kristeva 5). While Arthur appears to sense dimly that his inheritance is partially a sign of the crime against (and obliteration of) his origin, he hopelessly fails to recognize that his gift-giving to another, such as the maternal surrogate Little Dorrit, can never overcome his debt or the debt of his family. After all, "the abject is the violence of mourning for an 'object' that has always already been lost" (15). In *Powers of Horror*, Kristeva writes:

> The one by whom the abject exists is thus a deject who places (himself), separates (himself), situates (himself), and therefore strays instead of getting his bearings, desiring, belonging, or refusing. . . . A tireless builder, the deject

is in short a stray. He is on a journey, during the night, the end of which keeps receding. He has a sense of the danger, of that loss that the *pseudo-object* attracting him represents for him, but he cannot help taking the risk at the very moment he sets himself apart. And the more he strays, the more he is saved.

(8)

Arthur is always ready to consider himself a "nobody," an "exile," one older than he really is. As he asks of himself and his romantic rival Henry Gowan: "Where are we driving, he and I, I wonder, on the darker road of life? How will it be with us, and with her [Minnie], in the obscure distance?" (367). In both a process of abjection and "work of mourning,"[17] the dejected Arthur distances himself from his rebuff by the beloved Minnie Meagles by investing his energies in his partnership with the paternal Daniel Doyce, becoming a "tireless builder" who is also a "stray." In the "little counting-house reserved for his own occupation" (312), Arthur works out his own self-inflicted atonement for having desired and hoped for belonging in this life. Outside of his zealous efforts at his counting-house, Arthur labors incessantly on one other project: to restore the fortune of Little Dorrit and her father. In effect, Little Dorrit becomes the focus of Arthur's sad work because this "little mother" serves as the *pseudo-object* which attracts him, a focus for his cathexis or monetary replacement for his own lost mother. Eventually, Arthur must work all the harder as Little Dorrit's family fortune is restored by Pancks's meddling "fortune-telling" and as her status as pseudo-mother/daughter for him is challenged by repressed romantic intentions; indeed, he will even speculate with the savings of Clennam and Doyce, as Kristeva writes, "taking the *risk* at the very moment he sets himself apart" (8).

As I have been implying all along, Arthur's tendency to translate his abjection into compensation is a skill he learns at home. In that strange cycle of judgment and luxurious self-atonement described above, Mrs. Clennam swears a plague upon her house which is, in turn, passed on to the son she has stolen. Instead of acknowledging the consequences of her suppression of the codicil—in this case, the present imprisonment of the Dorrits—Mrs. Clennam nostalgically savors her guilt in the oppressive environment of her room and bleak surroundings. As a result, Affery and Arthur naively search for the material sign of a secret among the corridors of the house itself, although they can never get at the crime underwriting this complex case of self-atonement. Affery's constant state of expectation for "some dark form to appear" from behind a door and make the party "one too many" (230) feeds Arthur's hopes for a more detailed illumination of evidence. "Affery," Arthur demands, "I want to know what is amiss here; I want some light thrown on the secrets *of this house*" (753, emphasis added). In a contagious form of guilt projection, Arthur seeks to shore up his already-broken origin by speculating on the secrets of the haunted house as a riddle to be solved and even reversed. He longs to become a traditional Gothic hero for whom the finding of a hidden manuscript or the experience of a supernatural event will suddenly reveal the secret of his birth, as was the case in such early Gothic novels as Horace Walpole's *The Castle of Otranto* and Clara Reeve's *The Old English Baron*.[18] In what also turns out to be an important revision of Radcliffe's use of the "explained supernatural," Dickens presents his hero (and Affery) as discovering that the house's specters were *only* the groanings of a failing structure after the house has already collapsed.

Part of Arthur's failure as a pseudo-Gothic protagonist stems from his simplistic belief that the family crime can be approached as a tableau or self-contained system. Unfortunately, his equally nostalgic attempt to uncover a bound sign of obligation and payment within the haunted home itself is defeated by a series of spectral *counterfeits* that spread beyond its crumbling walls.[19] For instance, on the night of Arthur's return, Flintwinch (against his mistress's will) replaces the codicil hidden in the basement with a fake in order to ship it off in an iron box with his twin brother. This hiding-away of the original (by a duplicate Flintwinch) figures as the substance of the first of Affery's ghost-dreams (Dickens 82). The next morning, Flintwinch makes a "little exchange" before Mrs. Clennam, like a "conjurer," and burns the fake codicil and letters accordingly (852). On the same night as Flintwinch's counterfeiting, Arthur suffers from his own doubling as he notices the small girl "almost hidden in the dark corner" of his mother's room and immediately begins to think of her as a sign of the family crime (80, 92). And in the final move of this "regression towards/distancing of the past" (Hogle, "*Frankenstein as Neo-Gothic*" 33),[20] Little Dorrit herself burns the real codicil in the Marshalsea before Arthur, who, still ignorant of its real contents, thinks it only a "charm" (893).

We might think of ghosts in *Little Dorrit*, then, as the progeny of speculative uncertainty, progeny that, in turn, keep such uncertainty firmly in place.[21] Arthur's meditations on Little Dorrit herself exemplify how the ghost of an unbearable origin is given life only to take on a life of its own. Just as Mrs. Clennam tries to settle the score with Arthur's real mother by hiring Little Dorrit as a domestic (both as an act of compensation and vengeful judgment), Arthur employs Little Dorrit as the end point of his own conjectures on coming clean. Not only does Little Dorrit emerge from the shadows (80) or miraculously appear (229) when Arthur's "old dark horrors" afflict him most severely; she serves as the catalyst for the adult son in his characteristic repression of memories through imagination.[22] After hearing the briefest of stories concerning Little Dorrit from Affery on the night of his return home, Arthur indulges in his familiar "fancy":

> He leaned upon the sill of the long low window, and looking out upon the
> blackened forest of chimneys again, began to dream; for it had been the uniform
> tendency of this man's life—so much was wanting in it to think about, so much
> that might have been better directed and happier to speculate upon—to make
> him a dreamer after all.   (80)

As Arthur leaves the house, only to return periodically for business-dealings,
his manifold impulse to fantasize and unravel the family secret is given a
new and powerful focus; his mother's quiet servant acts as a host of sorts
who carries the burden of Arthur's disease-ridden desire to speculate to the
outside world:

> His original curiosity augmented every day, as he watched for her, saw or did
> not see her, and speculated about her. Influenced by his predominant idea, he
> even fell into a habit of discussing with himself the possibility of her being in
> some way associated with it [the family crime]. At last he resolved to watch
> Little Dorrit and know more of her story.   (96)

At the scene of the family crime, Arthur begins to assuage a guilty incertitude
by projecting it onto the slight and shadowy figure of Little Dorrit, the only
one to enter the house and bear her service silently. Only much later, after
his move into the Marshalsea, does Arthur fully reflect on the extent to which
Little Dorrit has served as his guide and goal: "Looking back upon his own
poor story, she was its vanishing point. Everything in its perspective led to
her innocent figure. He had traveled thousands of miles towards it; previous
unquiet hopes and doubts had worked themselves out before it; it was the
centre of the interest of his life" (801). Ironically, then, Arthur is only able
to praise Little Dorrit's role in his life from the tragic perspective of speculative failure, an irony reinforced by his perception of her person as a "vanishing point," a "figure," just an "it."[23] The double role played by this
captive heroine and beloved servant stands as another expression of the novel's appeal to its Gothic roots. As David Jarrett has noticed: "She in her
modesty, her vulnerability, her quiet generosity and, of course, in her littleness, is clearly a reworking of the 'orphan of the castle' Gothic heroine"
(161).[24]

In the most unifying gesture of the novel, Dickens not only links the fissured
Clennam house to the debtors' prison via Little Dorrit's daily passage between
them but also through their mutual identity as sites of luxurious mis-atonement. Both are crumbling institutions occupied by inmates who dramatically
draw attention to their suffering. A whole study could be done comparing
the gateways of the two pseudo-prisons and who chooses to pass freely and
who is freely confined. Much like Mrs. Clennam, a smug Mr. Dorrit approaches his confinement as the member of an "elect" group (in his case, as

a gentleman) in order to establish himself as the head of an ethical system of payments and obligations. In contrast to Mrs. Clennam's solitary, Calvinistic system of personal suffering and vengeance, however, Mr. Dorrit incorporates a deeply social hierarchy of false humility, indulgence, and penance, evoking, according to the Protestant imagination, images of Roman Catholic Papal authority. Arthur notices that Mr. Dorrit stands at his window in the Marshalsea "with the air of an affable and accessible Sovereign, and that, when any of his people in the yard below looked up, his recognition of their salutes just stopped short of a blessing" (426).

But as opposed to his depiction of the suffocating environment of the counting-house, Dickens constructs a scathing critique of Mr. Dorrit's luxuriousness by describing his unbroken arrogance both within the wall of the debtors' prison and in his travels abroad. From this perspective, Dickens powerfully blends an eighteenth-century novelistic attack on luxury, best represented by Tobias Smollett (in, for example, *Ferdinand Count Fathom*),[25] with a Victorian one, largely grounded in Thackeray's denunciation in *Vanity Fair*. Sekora writes:

> For the one man [Thackeray], luxury as a vice could not, by definition, reach down to the lower levels of English society; it was a vice of the rich. For the other [Smollett], luxury had nothing to do with the idleness of a Carlisle or the sycophancy of a Varner. It could not, by definition, directly touch the behavior of royal, noble, or gentle society; it was a vice of the middling and poorer sort of Englishman. Between their respective uses of the same concept there is not only logical contradiction, but also social tension. Between 1771 and 1856 one of the basic principles for understanding the relationships within a society underwent fundamental transformation.   (19)

While to Smollett the vice of luxury was denoted by the tawdry and shameless fabrications of the lower classes for the sake of show, to Thackeray, the presence of luxury was indicated by the conspicuous consumption and outlandish abuses of the upper echelon. The class source of luxury underwent such a powerful revision between the two periods due to the emergence of a middle-class reading of the dissolute habits of the wealthy as largely to blame for the upheaval of the French Revolution and the convulsions and cycles of the first age of capital. Yet by the mid-nineteenth century Dickens could turn this middle-class reading back on itself, for even his moderately well-off readers would increasingly be able to venture their wealth in the market and partake of the solicitudes, quiddities, and dangers of a consumer economy. "During the 'excitement' phase of a business cycle whole communities became 'crazed,' and even in ordinary times a widespread 'passion for cheapness' betokened degradation on the part of producers as well as consumers" (Hilton 136). In the story of the spectacular debt and windfall of Mr.

Dorrit, Dickens constructs a double attack on luxury by describing how the tawdriness of the Marshalsea can be infinitely extended beyond its walls (like, some might say, a plague from the slums) while sumptuous behavior can equally penetrate the prison's innermost recesses. In the case of either the vice of the rich or the cheapness of the poor, luxury is defined as the desire to forget that wealth and possession are based in another's (say nobody's) ongoing sacrifice and labor.

Even before Arthur returns from abroad, a thread of service exists between the debtors' prison and the Clennams' decaying counting-house. Mrs. Clennam's continued moral and monetary debt to the Dorrits is fueled, with interest, by Little Dorrit's silent service in both outdated financial institutions. The maintenance of the debt is passed on to the "Father of the Marshalsea" and his offspring as their denial of, but dependence on, Little Dorrit's work keeps the floating walls of the prison firmly in place. In time, the youngest daughter's ubiquitous presence functions as an extension of credit, as both families are given the deferential option to "work-out" wrongfully their respective atonements: "This family fiction was the family assertion of itself against her services" (280). As such, the decaying home and shabby prison are further united as Gothic through Little Dorrit's ghostly labor as a pseudo-mother for dependent children in both. Only this "solitary girl" is able to see together both places for what they really are: "two ruined spheres of suffering and action" (671).

Arthur himself solidifies the connection between the counting-house and the debtor's prison that Little Dorrit's quiet work has implied all along, moving out of one only to take up a mournful residence in the other. Ironically, in Dickens's final pathology, Arthur will obtain what he so strongly desires, a material connection between the place of usurpation and the place of debt, even if it is through his own diseased failure. As suggested earlier, the tragic outcome of Arthur's contradictory *work of speculation* is set up long before he hears the name of Merdle. The inherent miscarriage of the son's desire to reverse the constant recession of the signs of his lost origin, through a career-based cathexis of such signs, naturally leads to that other "sphere of action," the speculative search for a monetary replacement via an instant reproduction of wealth. In looking back, we should note how from an early stage Arthur's "uniform tendency" to dream leads him to confuse speculation with work:

And whether the attainment of that object [the story of the Dorrit's] by Mr. Pancks's industry might bring to light, in some untimely way, secret reasons which had induced his mother to take Little Dorrit by the hand, was a serious speculation.

> Not that he ever wavered in his desire or his determination to repair a wrong
> that had been done in his father's time, should a wrong come to light, and be
> reparable. The shadow of a supposed act of injustice, which had hung over him
> since his father's death, was so vague and formless that it might be the result
> of a reality widely remote from his idea of it. But, if his apprehensions should
> prove to be well founded, he was ready at any moment to lay down all he had,
> and begin the world anew.... Duty on earth, restitution on earth, action on
> earth; these first, as the first steep steps upward. Strait was the gate and narrow
> was the way; far straiter and narrow than the broad high road paved with vain
> professions and vain repetitions, motes from other men's eyes and liberal deliv-
> ery of others to judgment—all cheap materials costing absolutely nothing.
>
> (367–68)

Arthur ends with an attack on his mother that clearly equates her "cheap"
judgments and "vain repetitions" with other forms of luxurious profit-seeking. Yet Arthur savors a luxury of his own as he imagines his work and
wealth as only lying in wait to "repair a wrong," as a willful extension to
any determined speculation that might arise. He concludes that if he can only
define his "apprehensions" as "well founded," he will be able to reverse,
"at any moment," a hidden transgression and "begin the world anew."

In this sense, Arthur's later inclination to speculate imitatively with Merdle
grows out of Pancks's initial success with his research concerning the Dorrits.
Arthur increasingly adheres to Pancks's view that "fortune-telling" is the
"charm" which will make all the Dorrit family problems vanish. Although
Dickens has already detailed Arthur's strong propensity to the disease, the
confusion between fact and "fortune-telling" officially takes on a life of its
own amidst the mildly coercive relationship between Pancks and Little Dorrit,
and then spreads outward. Affery notices that certain natural portents coincide
with the "enigma" of Pancks confronting Little Dorrit immediately outside
the door of the Clennam house. (One should recall the natural portents that
coincide in *Bleak House* to Jo taking Lady Dedlock to the diseased burial site
of Nemo.) The wind rushed "round and round a confined adjacent churchyard
as if it had a mind to blow the dead citizens out of their graves.... the sky
at once seemed to threaten vengeance for this attempted desecration, and to
mutter, 'Let them rest! Let them rest!'" (392).

Later, in the chapter titled "The Progress of an Epidemic," the true "sign
of sickening" proves to be Arthur's absolute trust in Pancks's research and
empirical approach to monetary gain. Although suffering as a "deject" (Kristeva), Arthur is not necessarily ruined by his initial desire to back up his
speculations with solid facts; his downfall springs from his longing to reach
the endpoint of the cognitive labyrinth of the family crime by confusing the
process of his renunciatory career with an alternative form of accumulation
associated with the meteoric rise of Merdle. As Chalmers would say, in
moving from an occasionally justified parsimony to "excessive speculation,"

one contracts a "moral gangrene . . . under the semblance of benefit and boon." The craving to convert quick action into restitution is the "dangerous infection" with which Pancks's speech is "laden" (*Little Dorrit* 640): the way Pancks is able to assist in Arthur's replacement of his definition of speculation as a "venture" with the term "investment" amidst his anxiety concerning the events at his mother's house and his dull career with Doyce. Arthur will work to circumvent the question he has been asking all along concerning Pancks's "fortune-telling": " 'Does it implicate any one? . . . In any suppression or wrong dealing of any kind?' " (439). In ignoring the solution to the family crime in trying to solve it, Arthur finally sets up his own failure. Arthur's participation in Merdle's "apocalypse of absence"[26] becomes, in a series of full confidences, psychological divestment, indicating how speculations are doomed to fall short in the end because they are based on only an imaginative and anxious exchange of wealth and value. As David Morier Evans writes of the inevitable flip side to expectation: "Gaunt panic, with uncertain gate and distorted visage stalks hurriedly through the land . . . The slightest blast from his lividly scorching breath remorselessly crumples up credit, and destroys, as by the fell wand of the necromancer, the good fame and fortune acquired by long years of toil and steady accumulation" (36).

The form of Arthur's subsequent punishment for a "commanding sin" recalls an important literary influence on *Little Dorrit*, Daniel Defoe's deeply Protestant *Robinson Crusoe*. Rather like Crusoe, who tragically neglects his father's advice not to leave land or the middle state of life, Arthur disregards Doyce's sound, paternal caution "against speculating." Although he states his agreement with Doyce that "to travel out of safe investments is one of the most dangerous, as it is one of the most common, of those follies which often deserve the name of vices" (736), Arthur, against his better sense, is tempted to "venture" not only his entire inheritance but also the savings of his partner. In a natural and spiritual cycle that also recalls Crusoe's vicissitudes at sea, "inevitably the crash occurs, and, as if to emphasize the transitory nature of all temporal wealth, business failure brings immediate oblivion" (Hilton 145).

From an evangelical perspective, Arthur's unequivocal response to the suffering which follows his sin of speculation offers the hope of salvation. Tearfully, the bankrupt expresses his wishes to Pancks:

> "My course . . . must be taken at once. What wretched amends I can make must be made. I must clear my unfortunate partner's reputation. I must retain nothing for myself. I must resign to our creditors the power of management I have so much abused, and I must work out as much of my fault—or crime—as is susceptible of being worked out in the rest of my days." (779)[27]

Arthur, forlorn and desolate, immediately resigns himself to the worst financial and physical punishment possible, exile to the Marshalsea, claiming that imprisonment there serves as a "better atonement" for him than it would be to many others (782). His desire to spare his partner, Doyce, and "work out" his crime both in body and in money corresponds to an evangelical argot which expressed that "a state of debt was always sinful, but an honorable bankruptcy—one in which the bankrupt strove to ensure that no one but himself suffered—was, of course, more than compatible with Christian virtue" (Hilton 146). The description of the minute particulars of Arthur's suffering expresses an understanding of "innocent bankrupts as sacrificial offerings, beloved of God, and atoning vicariously for the sins of a commercially fallen world" (138). In contrast to a secular interpretation of bankruptcy as largely unforgivable, moderate evangelicals tried to imply that seemingly irreversible financial failure "would yield not material but moral and spiritual benefits, would engender remorse, which in turn would foster self-denial, the latter being the hinge on which evangelical economics turned" (32).

Yet, unlike Crusoe, Arthur is not left to "work out" his sickness alone. Amidst his laborious, incoherent dreams, Little Dorrit suddenly appears in her "old, worn dress" (a lasting vision) to resume her long-standing work of nursing a debtor back to health (825). As such, this "little mother" again assumes the role of anti-body, not destroying sickness altogether but at least reducing its most acute symptoms. In one sense, then, Dickens complicates the moderate evangelical notion that the supreme virtue, charity, could serve as an answer to the supreme sin, speculation, by describing how Little Dorrit's gifts to Arthur in prison figure as the final commitment to (and commitment for) a still hidden debt.

We might think of Little Dorrit's generous pledge to serve a bankrupt as once again interrupting, at the price of saving his life, the son's clearest, albeit troubling, confrontation with that "otherness" or "maternal blackness" described above, as Kristeva puts it , as "a burden both repellent and repelled, a deep well of memory that is unapproachable and intimate: the abject" (6). In contrast to the generic Gothic villain Rigaud, who will only keep the secret from Arthur for a price, Little Dorrit offers the gift of her savings and self in order, one might say, to re-abject the abject. Just as she attempts to pay Arthur's debts for him with a fortune which has already been lost, Little Dorrit secretly prevents Arthur from confronting the buried family crime, cutting short the atonement he had planned to "work out" with his remaining days. In this sense, her silent gift of service is an example of how Victorian women "were conceptually linked to the anxieties generated by the new market economy and to the symbolic solutions formulated to resolve these anxieties" (Poovey 61). *Little Dorrit* closes with the powerful, symbolic solution of the marriage between the fallen debtor and the daughter of the Marshalsea. In this union, at least one of the noble son's long-term speculations about a hidden value will bring back a return beyond all expectation.

Although still within the prison walls, Arthur finds that his perception of the future is now supported by the statement of a mutually beneficial (or debtless) possession, an inheritance and home he need not renounce: "Never to part, my dearest Arthur; never any more, until the last! I never was rich before, I never was proud before, I never was happy before, I am rich in being taken by you, I am proud in having been resigned by you, I am happy in being with you in this prison, as I should be happy in coming back to it with you" (886).[28]

Various debts are signed over in the novel's final pages. Taking over the role of specter herself (856), Mrs. Clennam petitions Little Dorrit within the prison walls not to tell Arthur the secret of his birth. As her last maneuver around an expiation, the widow prays to be spared until her own death (858). Little Dorrit gives in to the widow's demands and thus continues silently to serve Mrs. Clennam in her luxurious career of mis-atonement. Even though her secret has passed from house to prison, Mrs. Clennam justifies her career once more:

> "I was stern with him, knowing that the transgressions of the parents are visited on their offspring, and that there was an angry mark upon him at his birth. I have sat with him and his father, seeing the weakness of his father yearning to unbend to him; and forcing it back, that the child might work out his release in bondage and hardship. I have seen him, with his mother's face, looking up at me in awe from his little books, and trying to soften me with his mother's ways that hardened me." (859)

Sin is a hereditary disease in *Little Dorrit* precisely because Mrs. Clennam is always ready to force someone else to work it out, be it the son she never had or his dead mother's replacement. Mrs. Clennam, as a false mother, has spent her life trying to suppress the soft traces and sins of a dead mother, fulfilling, through her severe career, her own prophecy that the "transgressions of the parents are visited on their offspring." In contrast, Little Dorrit knows that the best way to stop the spread of a hereditary, speculative contagion is to replace judgment with a healing form of silence. Little Dorrit's final management of the iron box (holding the codicil to Gilbert Clennam's will) demonstrates that the most effective forms of quarantine are backed up by the claims of self-justified possession:

> ... and Little Dorrit came in, and Mr. Meagles with pride and joy produced the box, and her gentle face was lighted up with grateful happiness and joy. The secret was safe now! She could keep her own part of it from him; he should never know of her loss; in time to come he should know all that was of import to himself; but he should never know what concerned her only. That was all passed, all forgiven, all forgotten. (880–81)

NOTES

1. Likewise, as an anonymous writer pointed out in *The Economist* shortly after the failure of the Royal British Bank in 1856: "The career of this bank is an extraordinary example of the little trouble the public take to think for themselves, and of the incautious manner in which they trust their money" (Anderson and Cottrell 300).

2. I purposefully use the term "liability" here in order to call to mind N.N. Feltes's and Timothy Alborn's important work on the economic context of *Little Dorrit* and the passage of the Limited Liability Act in 1855.

3. Andrea Henderson observes that the choice of the capitalist class between supporting a genealogy-based notion of identity or accepting increasingly fluid market relations brought with it a crisis of "measuring human value" and "a cluster of metaphoric associations that played their part in creating the ghostly world of gothic character" (5). Henderson suggests that the early Gothic novel, as opposed to the Romantic model of interior depth, focuses on "relational identity" by presenting character as "a matter of surface, display, and 'consumption' by others." Much of what I propose below about Dickens's appeal to a Gothic tradition in order to interpret a contemporary economic crisis will follow Henderson in suggesting that "the mystery and violence of the gothic . . . arises from its vision of a world of what could be called 'commodities among themselves'" (39).

4. "A public outcry for legislative reform focused attention on the urban slums of London as a primary contributor to contagion and social blight: The Report on the Sanitary Condition of the Laboring Population of 1842 cited working class neighborhoods, with their 'broken panes in every window frame, and filth and vermin in every nook . . . with stagnant puddles here and there with their foetid exhalations, causeways broken and dangerous, ash-places choked up with filth, and excrementitious deposits on all sides,' as areas that not only bred disease, but also instilled within its inhabitants a 'moral degradation . . . and vicious habits and criminal propensities'" (Benton 69).

5. See McKendrick et al.

6. Alborn indicates that "Books with titles like *The Anatomy and Philosophy of Banking, The Physiology of the Joint Stock Banks,* and *The Physiology of London Business* compared the banking system to a healthy body" (207). Dickens, for instance, might agree with one writer from an 1857 edition of the *Banker's Magazine* who claimed of the Royal British Bank (the company on which Dickens at least partially based his so-called "extravagant conception" of Mr. Merdle [Dickens 35]), it cannot "'be regarded merely as one of those monstrosities which will occasionally arise in the social system'" because " 'the virus is more widely spread than our regard for the national reputation would otherwise induce us to admit'" (Alborn 211). Also see Barbara Weiss ("Secret Pockets") for a detailed discussion of the connections between Merdle and the notorious career of the banker-swindler John Sadlier, who committed suicide in 1856 when his frauds were exposed.

7. See Hilton 123–155.

8. John Sekora notes that commentators from Herodotus (and later Augustine) on considered luxury as a "generic vice," "using some metaphor like contagion to

describe the movement of its corruption from the one to the many'' (49). In the recurring analysis of luxury as the cause of a spectrum of social ills, moralists often dwelled on one symptom in particular: intellectual restlessness, the forerunner of a breach of faith: "from the Hebrews through the Protestants, luxury represents the starting point of historical or philosophical speculation . . . In the social realm it is an index of chaos and irrationality in the workings of public affairs, calling forth the demand for order, discipline, authority, and hierarchy (and implicitly, self-surrender and sacrifice)'' (49).

9. See Hilton (66–162) for a discussion of Chalmers's influential career and important role in establishing a moderate evangelical reading of British capitalism from 1820 to 1845.

10. *Oxford English Dictionary*, entries eight and six respectively. This two-fold use of the term was firmly established by Edmund Burke in his *Reflections*. He simultaneously condemns French philosophy and the failure of French credit by describing the revolution as one unfounded process of "airy speculation," as opposed to the soundness of English reflections on the natural order. Likewise, David Morier Evans later plays with the double meaning of the term by titling his popular book on the economic conditions of the time *Speculative Notes and Notes on Speculation* (1863).

11. See Holway 103–04.

12. See Walder 17, 44, 113–14, 140–69.

13. The denouement of *Little Dorrit* is extremely complex. A helpful summary of the events occurring before the novel opens can be found in Appendix A of the Penguin Special Film Edition (1987).

14. See Hogle ("The Gothic and the 'Otherings'") for a detailed discussion of the connection between Kristeva's notion of abjection and the original themes of Gothic fiction.

15. In his biography of Dickens, Fred Kaplan notes that author's "need to be recognized by his mother seems always to have been unfulfilled" (20). For the young Dickens, this perceived lack of good mothering came to a crisis when his father was arrested for debt and sentenced to the Marshalsea. Over twenty years later, the grown man would write of his being sent to work in Warren's Blacking Factory and his mother's wish not to offend his employer even after his father's release: "I know how all these things have worked together to make me what I am: but I never afterwards forgot, I never shall forget, I never can forget, that my mother was warm for my being sent back [to the factory]'' (44). Kaplan suggests that the novelist "created many variations on this experience in his fiction, dividing his pain into the two women of his fantasy life, the oppressive, witch-like, or carelessly self-indulgent mother he felt he had, and the idealized, loving antimother of wish fulfillment" (44).

16. H.M. Daleski observes: "It is because Clennam guiltily regards himself as owing two debts that he cannot pay—the debt to his mother, and the mysterious family debt that he intuits and wishes to make restitution for but does not know to whom or for what—that he is shackled . . . '' (134).

17. See Derrida 97.

18. In the light of Arthur's desire to emerge as a hero within an ingrained economy, we might think of him as a representative middle-class subject who attempts to escape and repress the usurpation of wealth that makes his position possible "by recasting such anomalies into the horrors of old and seemingly alien specters, building, and crypts" (Hogle, "The Gothic and the 'Otherings'" 822). Also see Punter (2: 418–19) and Fiedler (27–31, 134).

19. I am indebted here to Jerrold Hogle's notion of the "ghost of the counterfeit." As he says of the Walpolean Gothic and later of *Frankenstein*: "Abjected half-inside/half-outside conditions can be 'thrown' into ghosts of counterfeits because the counterfeit and especially its ghost, as process of signification, are already betwixt-and-between interactions of regression towards and distancings of the past. The counterfeit, at its earliest point, offers a belated nostalgia of a self 'bound' to its others (its statuses) that is like the child's 'outside' longing for oneness with the 'inside' of its primordial mother" ("Frankenstein as Neo-Gothic" 33).

20. In his discussion of the "ghost of the counterfeit" from the Renaissance on, Hogle suggests that Walpole's Gothic novella is exceptionally concerned "with signs divorced from substance," but that Walpole, too, borrows from an older literature of the counterfeit, namely Shakespeare's *Hamlet*. *Otranto's* portrait ghost refashions the scene in which Shakespeare's Prince asks the Queen "to compare portraits of his kingly father and his usurper-uncle Claudius, playing out the premise that Claudius is the false and fallen image of the true king, among other corruptions." But the fact that Hamlet describes the picture itself as a "counterfeit" also suggest that the son has "doubts about his father's ghostly form and his very early sense that Claudius is similarly suspect" (Hogle, "Ghost of the Counterfeit" 27–29). Like Hamlet, Arthur Clennam can only respond to a prior counterfeiting with further counterfeiting; he turns to an accelerated form of monetary fakery—market speculation—to answer the machinery set in place before his birth. "It is this identity based on the need to accumulate fragmentary counterfeits, and to recounterfeit them endlessly to shore up an unstable base of funds and social positions, out of which the first gothic novel most immediately emerges" ("Ghost of the Counterfeit" 33), and, I think, *Little Dorrit's* plot of a speculative plague as well.

21. In similar fashion, Marc Redfield writes of the oedipal plot of Goethe's *Wilhelm Meisters Lehrjahre*: "The tension in this narrative is between an initial 'incertititude,' on the one hand, and a dialectical passage from 'loss' to 'gain,' on the other: uncertainty is not quite the same as loss, and though the dialectical narrative tells the story of the father's 'undiminished' survival, the uncertain status of the father renders him 'a ghost, a shadow,' precisely because this uncertainty can never be entirely stabilized as a loss" (83).

22. Brian Rosenberg discusses at length the centrality of the shadow image in *Little Dorrit*. He suggests that "it emerges as the clearest physical manifestation of Dickens's special concern with contradiction and the problems of seeing and understanding" (42). Rosenberg goes on to point out that "Many characters, good and bad, emerge from and melt back into shadowy corners" as quickly in

the novel "the shadow expands from a literal to a metaphoric image that reinforces again the sense of confusion, blindness, and self-division" (43).

23. Janet Larson points out the novel's commitment to "visionary and speculative language": its "wide use of conditional clauses, 'as if' constructions, subjunctive mood verbs, rhetorical questions treated as real questions, and all the ways the characters revise present reality by projecting alternate worlds in language. They envision conditions contrary to fact, they make threats or promises unlikely to be carried out, they propose hypotheses, they construct images and stories, they hope and imagine futures. In short, they speculate" (45).

24. Also see Milbank (102–20) for a comparison between Little Dorrit and Emily St. Aubert, especially in regard to their excursions on the Continent.

25. I chose *Ferdinand Count Fathom* (1753) here as opposed to more popular Smollett novels such as *Roderick Random* and *Humphrey Clinker* because the former is cited by some critics as an important precursor of the Gothic novel (see Varma 38–40, and Baker 4: 218). Not only does *Fathom* contain some detailed descriptions of supernatural events (which are explained by the end of the plot along the lines of Radcliffe); the plot outlines the adventures of a luxurious villain and bastard, Fathom, who uses a series of deceptions to justify the highest social pretensions.

26. Nunokawa writes: "Merdle's ruin is an apocalypse of absence, a revelation of the loss inherent in the fortune of the capitalist when he is bound, as the novel conceives him to be, to the requirement of equivalent exchange. Property that is acquired must be relinquished; property that acquires is already relinquished. In *Little Dorrit*, the estate of the capitalist is a form of loss" (320).

27. Arthur exhibits a sense of honesty uncharacteristic of the bankrupt in the Victorian period. "The ways of defrauding one's creditors were apparently numerous: one could declare bankruptcy with the deliberate intention of evading debts; one could make a gift of all one's assets and then declare bankruptcy; one could conspire with one's creditors to defraud the others, etc." (Weiss, *Hell of the English* 34).

28. Nunokawa observes: "The domestic estate in the novel represents the formation of, rather than a flight from something like capital. Its security depends on the same separation that enables the accumulation of capital, the temporal disjunction which separates it from the terms of exchange. This similarity between the provenance of the capitalist in Marx's account and the lover's fortune in *Little Dorrit* becomes dramatic when Little Dorrit reveals her love to be labor-power" (329–30).

WORKS CITED

Alborn, Timothy L. "The Moral of the Failed Bank: Professional Plots in the Victorian Money Market." *Victorian Studies* 38.2 (1994): 199–226.

Anderson, B.L., and P.L. Cotrell. *Money and Banking in England: The Development of the Banking System, 1694–1914.* London: David and Charles, 1974.

Baker, Ernest A.. *The History of the English Novel*. 2nd ed. 10 vols. London: Witherby, 1934–57.

Benton, Graham. "'And Dying Thus Around Us Every Day': Pathology, Ontology, and the Discourse of the Diseased Body. A Study of Illness and Contagion in *Bleak House*." *Dickens Quarterly* 11.2 (1994): 69–80.

Butt, John, and Kathleen Tillotson. *Dickens at Work*. London: Methuen, 1958.

Carlyle, Thomas. *Latter-Day Pamphlets*. in Carlyle: *Selected Works, Reminiscences, and Letters*. Ed. Julian Symons. Cambridge: Harvard UP, 1970.

Chalmers, Thomas. *On Political Economy in Connexion with the Moral State and Moral Prospects of Society*. 1832. New York: Kelley, 1968.

Daleski, H.M.. "Large Loose Baggy Monsters and Little Dorrit." *Dickens Studies Annual* 21 (1992): 131–42.

Derrida, Jacques. *Specters of Marx: The State of the Debt, the Work of Mourning, and the New International*. Trans. Peggy Kamuf. London: Routledge, 1995.

Dickens, Charles. *Little Dorrit*. Special Film Edition. London: Penguin, 1987.

Evans, D. Morier. *Speculative Notes and Notes on Speculation*. 1864. New York: Burt Franklin, 1968.

Feltes, N. N.. "Community and the Limits of Liability in Two Mid-Victorian Novels." *Victorian Studies* 17 (1974): 355–69.

Fiedler, Leslie A.. *Love and Death in the American Novel*. New York: Stein and Day, 1966.

Freud, Sigmund. *Inhibitions, Symptoms, and Anxiety*. Trans. James Strachey. London: Hogarth, 1959.

Gallagher, Catherine. "The Body Versus the Social Body in the Works of Thomas Malthus and Henry Mayhew." *Representations* 14.2 (1986): 83–97.

Gurney, Michael S.. "Disease as Device: The Role of Smallpox in *Bleak House*." *Literature and Medicine* 9 (1990): 79–92.

Henderson, Andrea. *Romantic Identities: Varieties of Subjectivity, 1774–1830*. Cambridge: Cambridge UP, 1996.

Hilton, Boyd. *The Age of Atonement: The Influence of Evangelicalism on Social and Economic Thought, 1795–1865*. Oxford: Clarendon, 1988.

Hogle, Jerrold E.. "The Ghost of the Counterfeit in the Genesis of the Gothic." *Gothick Origins and Innovations*. Ed. Allan Lloyd Smith and Victor Sage. Amsterdam: Rodopi, 1994. 23–33.

————. "*Frankenstein* as Neo-Gothic: From the Ghost of the Counterfeit to the Monster of Abjection." *Romanticism, History, and the Possibilities of Genre: Reforming Literature, 1789–1837.* Ed. Tilottama Rajan and Julia W. Wright. Cambridge: Cambridge UP, 1998. 176–210.

————. "The Gothic and the 'Otherings' of Ascendant Culture: The Original *Phantom of the Opera.*" *South Atlantic Quarterly* 95.3 (1996): 821–46.

Holway, Tatiana M.. "The Game of Speculation: Economics and Representation." *Dickens Quarterly* 9.3 (1992): 103–14.

Jarrett, David. "The Fall of the House of Clennam: Gothic Conventions in *Little Dorrit.*"*Dickensian* 71.3 (1975): 155–61.

Kaplan, Fred. Dickens. *A Biography.* New York: William Morrow, 1988.

Kristeva, Julia. *Powers of Horror: An Essay on Abjection.* Trans. Leon S. Roudiez. New York: Columbia UP, 1982.

Larson, Janet. "Apocalyptic Style in *Little Dorrit.*" *Dickens Quarterly* 1 (1984): 41–49.

McCulloch, John R.. *The Principles of Political Economy.* 1864. New York: Kelley, 1965.

McKendrick, Neil, John Brewer, and J.H. Plumb. *The Birth of a Consumer Society.* Bloomington: Indiana UP, 1982.

Milbank, Alison. *Daughters of the House: Modes of the Gothic in Victorian Fiction.* New York: St. Martin's, 1992.

Myers, William. "The Radicalism of Little Dorrit." *Literature and Politics in the Nineteenth Century.* Ed. John Lucas. London: Methuen: 1971.

Nunokawa, Jeff. "Getting and Having: Some Versions of Possession in *Little Dorrit.*" in *Charles Dickens: Modern Critical Views.* Ed. Harold Bloom. New York: Chelsea House, 1987.

Owen, Alex. *The Darkened Room: Women, Power, and Spiritualism in Late Nineteenth Century England.* London: Virago, 1989.

Poovey, Mary. "Reading History in Literature: Speculation and Virtue in *Our Mutual Friend.*"*Historical Criticism and the Challenge of Theory.* Ed. Janet Levarie Smarr. Urbana: U of Illinois P, 1993. 42–80.

Pope, Norris. *Dickens and Charity.* New York: Columbia UP, 1978.

Porter, Roy. "Consumption: Disease of the Consumer Society?" *Consumption and the World of Goods.* Ed. John Brewer and Roy Porter. London: Routledge, 1993. 58–84.

Punter, David. *The Literature of Terror*. 2 vols. New York: Longman, 1996.

Redfield, Marc. *Phantom Formations: Aesthetic Ideology and the Bildungsroman.* Ithaca: Cornell UP, 1996.

Rosenberg, Brian. *Little Dorrit's Shadows: Character and Contradiction in Dickens.* Columbia: U of Missouri P, 1996.

Ruskin, John. *Unto This Last: Four Essays on the First Principles of Political Economy.* Lincoln: U of Nebraska P, 1967.

Sage, Victor. *Horror Fiction in the Protestant Tradition*. London: Macmillan, 1988.

Sekora, John. *Luxury; The Concept in Western Thought, Eden to Smollett*. Baltimore: Johns Hopkins UP, 1977.

Varma, Devendra Prasad. *The Gothic Flame: Being a History of the Gothic Novel in England; its Origins, Effloresence, Disintergration, and Residuary Influences.* New York: Russell and Russell, 1957.

Walder, Dennis. *Dickens and Religion*. London: George Allen and Unwin, 1981.

Weber, Max. *The Protestant Ethic and the Spirit of Capitalism*. Trans. Talcott Parsons. New York: Charles Scribner's Sons, 1958.

Weiss, Barbara. *The Hell of the English: Bankruptcy and the Victorian Novel*. Lewisburg: Bucknell UP, 1986.

———. "Secret Pockets and Secret Breasts: *Little Dorrit* and the Commercial Scandals of the Fifties." *Dickens Studies Annual* 10 (1982): 67–76.

Welsh, Alexander. *The City of Dickens*. Oxford: Clarendon Press, 1971.

Young, G.M. *Portrait of an Age: Victorian England*. New York: Oxford UP, 1977.

Desire and Deconstruction: Reclaiming Centers

Karen C. Gindele

This essay argues against constructs of lack as they inform desire, subjectivity, and meaning in two sections: one on theory, and one on Dickens's Our Mutual Friend. *The first section argues that we can locate positive models of desire based on energy both before and after the investment in ideas of lack theorized by Freud, Lacan, and Derrida. We can find them not only in literary and cultural theory, but in the discourses of biology and physics. Relativity theory in fact reveals that there were relational models before Einstein, namely in Darwin's work, which implicitly situates within human subjects the energy of desire to reproduce and compete while subjects are also shaped by interaction with other beings and the environment. The essay proceeds by examining the conjunction of capitalism and theories of lack, arguing especially against Lacan and Derrida, and speculating about positive models for desire as the conscious forming of relationships. It then examines works in literary criticism and cultural theory from Coleridge, Shelley, and Pater to Foucault to trace this alternative line of thinking. The second half of the essay uses Dickens's response to Darwin's* Origin of Species *and refers to the prototypical concept of a force field in Mesmer's "animal magnetism." The essay argues that in Bradley Headstone, Eugene Wrayburn, and Lizzie Hexam, there are three models of desire based respectively on lack, the exercise of power, and a more socially responsible and imaginative relationality. Lizzie's desire is the most complete and demonstrates that human "nature" is its origin, while Lizzie also responds morally and imaginatively to other*

Dickens Studies Annual, Volume 29, Copyright © 2000 by AMS Press, Inc. All rights reserved.

people in her environment and wants to learn how to read in order to connect herself to the world.

I. Stellar Subjects

Theories positing lack have had substantial influence on psychoanalytic and philosophical models of the human subject, desire, and meaning. Although we need to acknowledge this history, we do not need to accept it. In fact, we can locate a series of positive models of desire to help counteract the influence of more recent work which proclaims lack a constitutive but negating part of human subjectivity. These models are available not only within literary and cultural theory but in works of literature themselves. In this essay I will make two theoretical claims and then argue that Dickens's *Our Mutual Friend* demonstrates them because nineteenth-century novelists especially after Darwin began to think of desire as originating from energy rather than lack, although a model based on energy was available earlier. I will argue first that desire and therefore subjectivity are founded on plentitude rather than lack, and second, correspondingly, that meaning is not founded on lack or absence. Rather, meaning is productive, as Foucault argues power is productive, and it organizes language in centers of interest that reflect energy. I will necessarily be arguing against Freud, Lacan, and Derrida. I even hope to show that deconstruction, sounding as if it is a process that dismantles constructions of meaning, is unwittingly, and in spite of itself, positive.

The theory that I propose here derives from an argument grounded in physics, which has taught us that space is not nearly as empty as people had thought, and that solid objects not only have internal spaces, so that smaller parts move in relationship to each other, but that they hold together by means of immense energy.[1] Theories of energy (a word Aristotle coined from the word for "work") concern both matter and mind, and by means of them I believe we can argue that selves have centers. Freud's theory of the unconscious formally "decentered" the subject by removing a person's motives from knowledge and control; deconstruction disallows a center altogether and does not account for motivation which gives energy to characters both real and fictional. Relativity theory has shown us at the very least that we are entities acting within fields and that no observer can remain apart from the field he or she observes. Broadly speaking, psychoanalytic and social relational theories, which seem clearly to have been shaped by relativity theory, in fact owe significantly to Darwin's *Origin of Species,* so that their own origins can be situated earlier than relativity theory. I believe that literary and psychoanalytic critics can apply physical models of how the world works not as the only, therefore reductive explanation of language and minds, but as a ground for them, possibly sharing ways of behaving. I maintain that Darwin provided a framework in which Dickens could articulate his interset in the energy and desire of human beings in their interactions in the social environment with the conception of a universe partly governed by physical forces. Although social Darwinism, concerned especially with human progress, did not spontaneously appear immediately after the *Origin,* Dickens was quick to apprehend the *Origin*'s implications for human beings. In July 1860 he wrote an article for *All the Year Round* praising Darwin, recognizing how important his theory of natural selection was, and closing with the witty if too optimistic analogy that "for theories, as for organised beings, there is also a Natural Selection and a Struggle for Life. Those theories only survive which are based on truth . . . if Mr. Darwin's theory be true, nothing can prevent its ultimate and general reception, however much it may pain and shock those to whom it is propounded for the first time. If it be merely a clever hypothesis . . . to which a very industrious and able man has devoted the greater and the best part of his life, its failure will be nothing new in the history of science" (299).[2]

Another contribution by Darwin, and incidentally by Marx, was the increasing interest in theories of identity, especially sexual identity. With so much emphasis placed on reproduction to guarantee the survival of a species, it was perhaps inevitable that people would feel an urgency about the sexual and gender roles of human beings. Darwin comments on the seemingly unrelated subject of male and female holly flowers: "No naturalist doubts the advantage of what has been called the 'physiological division of labour; hence we may believe it would be advantageous to a plant to produce stamens alone in one flower or on one whole plant, and pistils alone in another flower or on another plant . . . as a more complete separation of the sexes of our plant would be advantageous on the principle of the division of labour, individuals with this tendency more and more increased, would be continually favoured or selected, until at last a complete separation of the sexes would be effected" (141). At least biologically, then, it seems to have been more efficient to specialize in labor—to use resources or energy to perform only one function—although this specialization also makes the two sexes more dependent on each other.

As there was increased awareness of competition among men for work in the social world, there was anxiety about the possibility that women might also compete with men in this sphere. Efforts to exclude women from the work force relied on arguments either about women's natural inferiority in body and mind or about their natural role as mothers.[3] From Darwin's perspective, any innate capacities were selected from existing beings, but they might appear as characteristics and features inheritable and transmissible, therefore metaphorically "owned" or lacked. Anxieties about survival thus help to explain those about the ownership or lack of attributes as well as resources and even partners. At the same time, feminists argued against "natural" essential identities as the interiority of the subject developed in importance with the rise of the individual in political, private, and experiential terms in the late eighteenth century and especially after the Romantics.[4] Michel Foucault has argued that sexual categories became identities in the nineteenth century when what had been practices or acts were attributed to essential subjectivities.[5]

The concept of lack in identity (not lack itself) and lack as the origin of desire has been historically highly productive, but we should distinguish between lack, especially as it refers to the failure to meet basic needs, and desires, which are a quite different phenomenon. It is interesting that Freud and Lacan, both so determined to read having and not having a penis, the phallus, fetishized objects, or the "objet petit a," developed their theories of lack at the historical moment of advanced capitalism, where having is everything, and having is being. John Berger, in *Ways of Seeing,* has shown how advertising depends on the idea of a fundamental lack to promote unsatisfiable desires requiring the constant acquisition of new commodities in order to create an image of the self that presents plenitude (131–32). My argument will focus on lack only as it has informed subjectivity and desire. If we can rethink how desire works, we might be able to desire differently and to choose more satisfyingly. We might, refusing the exigencies of lack, transform a theory of desire into something "rich and strange."

The theory of desire that I propose is that to desire something, someone, or a state of being, is to imagine and have an idea of it and try to form a relationship with it. I certainly owe part of this statement to object relations theory, first developed by Nancy Chodorow in a feminist context in *The Reproduction of Mothering,* and based on D. W. Winnicott's theory that drives are not innately and independently determined but demonstrated a subject's effort to form relationships with objects, including other subjects, in its world. More recently Barbara Schapiro has applied Stephen Mitchell's exposition of relational psychoanalysis to literary analysis to show especially how writers affirm these relations.[6]

Desire begins by assenting to, affirming, and choosing an array of possibilities, material and mental, actual and imagined; we affirm some and not others, but I want to emphasize that desire is already a bestowing of energy on some project or being. The effort to form relationships means that desire is work, but the character of desire is to expend energy precisely so that it does not feel like work. Lacking an object and wanting to have it are to want continuous relationship with it, and that means keeping it near. For those who argue that *not* attaining the object maintains desire, so that desire requires lack, I would say first, that such nonsatisfaction retains a desired ideal relationship which allows a subject to be completely centered on the object, and this complete centering is a desired state; second, that a plenitude in the desiring sub-ject—too much feeling without outlet—accounts for the intensity of desire. Freud writes constantly about "excitation" or libidinal or psychic energy, which needs to find form and be released, and John Kucich has argued specifically that Victorian writers sought to intensify interiority by means of repression—in his analysis, not getting the object. He astutely notes the productive effect of this nonsatisfaction. However, I will argue that the energy of desire concerns the subject's intensity and plenitude regardless of whether one gets the object. Once a desire is satisfied, that intense energy is expended, so the relation changes, and that is what people are unprepared for. We need to connect ourselves to other beings and our environment, but it is as im-portant to be aware of those relationships as to form them. We intensify consciousness of our relations to chosen beings in our worlds or to beings that we imagine by being interested in them, by investing energy in them.

For Freud, any number of texts would serve to discuss the lack of the female body, but for many feminists, the issue does indeed come down to anatomy and how the subject negotiates his or her perceptions. Since much depends on having a penis, it is odd that Freud does not propose two *entirely* different models of desire, but in any event, he only elaborates some differ-ences. Significantly, these have to do with how one is regarded and treated in the world as often as with some inexorable condition and response. In "Some Psychological Consequences of the Anatomical Distinction between the Sexes" (1925), Freud argues that a boy's perception of a girl's genitalia will "permanently determine the boy's relations to women: horror of the mutilated creature or triumphant contempt for her. . . . A little girl behaves differently. She makes her judgment and her decision in a flash. She has seen [the penis] and knows that she is without it and wants to have it" (177). Somehow the problem seems to be hers rather than his.

Whatever one thinks of the theory, it is important that there is a range of responses. The little girl might hope some day to have a penis and become "like a man," or she might go through a process of "denial" and "refuse to accept *the fact* of being castrated" (178; my italics). There is a telling slippage between perception and "fact" for Freud—he speaks as if the girl really has been castrated—and it is amazing how certain he is. The little girl may alternately discover "the inferiority of the clitoris" (179). Freud says, "After a woman has become aware of the wound to her narcissism, she develops, like a scar, a sense of inferiority" (178). With all the negative cultural reinforcement she gets, it is unlikely she could escape until she is a woman, but again, there is no uniform innate response to recognition that a boy has a penis. In "Female Sexuality" (1931), Freud expands his notion to allow that the male "has only one principal sexual zone—only one sexual organ—whereas [the female] has two: the vagina, the true female organ, and the clitoris, which is analogous to the male organ" (187). Luce Irigaray elaborates positively on the multiplicity of female erogenous zones while she also critiques Freud's continual reference of the female body and its correct, "true" pleasures to analogy with, and their function for, the penis (TS 23, 26–28). Irigaray also cites Karen Horney's argument that any concept of female sexuality ought to have taken into account "determining sociocultural factors" rather than an inevitable and innate response to male anatomy (PT 51). Freud had earlier argued for a plenitude, if a negative one, in "On Narcissism" (1914), where he claimed that "the purest and truest feminine type" of narcissist has "a certain self-sufficiency (especially when there is a ripening into beauty) which compensates her for the social restrictions upon her object-choice" (70). Here any lack seems to lie in the range of object-choices, not in her. Finally, that a girl comes to her wish for a child as a substitute for her wish for a penis (FS 187) seems exactly to reverse the actual priority, which is to create life. Whether this should be so is debatable, but biologically, sexual drive is the means to the end that is reproduction. The female body is the site of this creative activity, whether men might actually envy women or not. Perhaps Freud's greatest achievement in this context is that he actually grants women desire, although he also says in *Jokes and Their Relation to the Unconscious* that they are more civilized than men because they are better able to repress their desires.

What Freud could posit as an anatomical lack, Lacan and Derrida transform into an existential one, inventing an absence where it did not exist. This invention turns on the distinction between the penis and phallus. Lacan says Freud made this distinction, but it is in fact his own. Lacan's analysis is riddled with contradictions and downright impossibilities: the libido is both an organ and not an organ; the phallus both exists and doesn't. A similarity in response to anatomy between a boy and a girl indicates that "equally for the girl, the only organ or, to be more precise, the only kind of sexual organ which exists is the phallus—which, as Freud makes clear, does not mean the penis" (FS 124). On the same page, Lacan says that "the idea of an organ is glorious, monadic isolation, . . . must refer to an essentially *imaginary* organ, even if this image is that of a real organ, namely the penis . . . in its privileged state of tumescence and erection" (124). The phallus exists but it's not the penis; it's also imaginary. Since the phallus doesn't exist, no one can have it, and everyone therefore lacks it.

Although Lacan acknowledges that both men and women, therefore, are lacking, in part because they must get their desire from the symbolic and sociocultural orders which teach them how to desire, regulate their desires, and alienate them from their desires, Lacan's model of desire is for a missing part of and complement to the self, conceived of in three ways: the part of the self which Lacan rewrites from Aristophanes' myth of one's missing "sexual other half" (FFC 205), the "central defect around which the dialectic of the advent of the subject to his own being in relation to the Other turns" (FFC 204–05), and the earlier "real lack" that is the result of the subject's "being subject to sex . . . [by which he] has fallen under the blow of individual death" (FFC 205). Lacan further states that this "myth of the lamella . . . is new and important because it designates the libido *not as a field of forces, but as an organ*" (FFC 205; my italics). To define the libido "not as a field of forces, but as an organ," while he also claims that the only organ is the phallus, is a crucial act of appropriation on Lacan's part, which allows him to align the libido itself with masculinity. While Lacan might seem to allow for relational theory in his location of desire in the field of the Other, he locates desire so exclusively there that he makes no allowance for actual bodies as the ground of desires.

The most crucial failure on Lacan's part is to oppose being and meaning and to imagine them in a closed economy, so that the more we mean, the less we can be, and we are always looking for substitutes for a prohibited object we eternally lack. Being, for Lacan, means some unalienated continuity of the self—its "libido, *qua* pure life instinct, life that has need of no organ, simplified, indestructible life" (FFC 198). Ideally he would like this self to be "joined" to "the subject as he appears in the field of the Other" (199). But "the sexual relation is handed over to the hazards of the field of the Other. . . . It is handed over to the old woman of whom—it is not a pointless fable—Daphnis must learn what one must do to make love" (199). It is impossible to imagine what Lacan would have liked to see instead—Daphnis untaught? Knowing instinctively? The fable might have a point, but presumably there was some distant era in evolution when human beings figured sex out by themselves, were taught, or didn't survive. How could we be here otherwise? Lacan seems to despair at any dependence on other human beings; perhaps he wanted to live "in glorious, monadic isolation" himself? Whatever it is that the social order manipulates, that energy or force must originate in the subject; it is Lacan's construction of the social order that teaches us we are lacking. But it does *not* seem an entirely negative proposition that humans beings (need to) learn things from each other, including how to love, and even how to have sex. And if the social order gives us back the forms of our desires, do we not want, precisely, *forms*? If what we learn constrains, it also enables. Language gives us forms; could we not think that language proliferates and multiplies desires, exactly in different forms? That it adds rather than substitutes? How does our making meaning in fact signify either that we are less or that the object about which we are making meaning is somehow less? One of the problems here is that imagined beings, objects, or worlds are usually conceived of in opposition to the real, and it is easy to see how imagining something that does not exist (and which we might like to exist) implies that something is missing, or lacking, from the real world. There are at least two results: the real world seems to lack the imagineed being, and the imagined being lacks reality or substance. But we might reject the assumed opposition and claim rather that imagined beings add to our real world. We might rearticulate the relationship of the imagined and the real. Even if we think of invention as supplying a thing previously lacking, we might also conceptualize that invention as a response to conditions that exist.

Desire includes not only imagination and choice but also organization—the interaction of our own organization with a thing outside that motivates and directs our energies. I propose five main ways in which we want to be organized in order to form relationships: (1) in some ways the first, physiological form is the most difficult to characterize, but it is to renew the self (and occasionally the species) by means of sexual relationships (along with sexual pleasure, touch makes us conscious of our embodiment, of our surfaces and limits, while we also touch another's surfaces, towards which we are sensitively responsive and active); (2) we also love other beings, and that companionship encompasses physical relationship; (3) we form other social relationships and (4) use language to make these relationships; (5) we also make statements about the world by seeing and forming relationships in language.[7] Language, it is not new to say, maintains its internal sets of relations in a closed system but also establishes relations, however, tenuous and relative, to the real world. It can move between referentiality and abstraction, but not be exclusively either. The only gap I can understand is that a word is not the same thing as the object to which it refers. But a gap can mean distance; it does not have to mean lack or absence. We cannot have relationships without separation, but there can also be a continuum. Language and its real world referents are different systems of plenitudes that do not entirely coincide. "Had we but world enough, and time," we might bring them in closer relation. But we can only establish relationships, real or imagined, out of things that exist. Not being gods and goddesses, people do not produce anything *ex nihilo*.

The relation that we perhaps most characteristically as human beings desire to form is to materialize ideas, to try to make them real, as we understand "realness," and thus secure the link between thinking and the real world. This process seems to me to be adding *dimension* in two directions: first, to take something that is in a manner of speaking flat or two-dimensional (an idea or a desired relation) and to make it solid, give it substance, because we want to be in physical relation to it; and second, to proliferate and transform the real world, including ourselves, in systems of representation so that we can enrich that world and in turn multiply our own existence and experience.

Allison Weir has also contributed to the critique of lack regarding subjectivity in Lacan and Derrida by building on Julia Kristeva's work. Weir's main project in *Sacrificial Logics* is to theorize the identity of the self and of a collectivity as not necesssarily difference(s) and not mutually exclusive in relation to difference. She argues that identity is necessary in order to take ethical positions. I would add that identity is necessary in order to act meaningfully at all; one needs to be organized; one's internal differences still have to work together as a self. Showing the influence of field theory, Weir uses Kristeva's work to argue that a subject's use of language shows a dialectical interaction between the system (language) and the practices of subjects, so that the system is continually transformed and therefore reflects subjects' influence and agency. For Lacan, "self-identity is achieved only through an acceptance of lack" (Weir 11), but again Weir uses Kristeva to argue that the separation of the subject from the object and other subjects can be pleasurable and does not require lack. Furthermore, the infant does not lose the mother; rather, the mother connects the infant to other beings: "It is the mother's position within a social world which provides the child with a mode of investment in that world. The mother's relation to the symbolic provides a means of reconciling differentiation and identification for the child: the child is able to identify as a self by identifying with the mother's investment in the socio-symbolic order" (182). To translate into my own terms, the mother-figure's interest in other beings brings them into close relation with the child, and the child's circle of interest expands, adding relationships. To be a bounded self does not mean in any useful way that one is without something. It means one is separate from and not the same as other beings. Separation is different from lack; separate means separate.

"Poststructuralist feminists," Weir says, "on the side of Derrida argue that the ideal of the identity of the self must be subverted in favor of an affirmation of nonidentity and multiplicity" (7). Why is it more ethical simply to choose the other side of the opposition identity/difference? The Derridean privileging of absence and difference at the expense of identity works as a kind of repression. The ethical aim I see is not to have or be everything else, although certainly we should recognize our internal differences and discontinuities; it is rather to exist as little as possible at someone else's expense; to let others determine themselves; and to enrich one's experience of other people while taking responsibility for being alive and imagining one might also contribute positively to someone else's experience. I contend that we cannot afford to keep thinking in terms of the opposition between the self and others, within or outside the self. We might encourage some differences rather than others in ourselves, but we cannot be just anything, psychologically or physiologically. Weir also cites Kristeva's argument that "the body, as site of drives and desires, aggression and pleasure, has to be included in any theory of motivation for change" (167). The body is a source of energy that both supports desire and is the means of carrying it out.

I have briefly sketched what I hesitate to call a "neopositivist" theory of desire, since nineteenth-century positivism has received such bad press. As for deconstruction, regarding language as well as subjects, the absence of an identity or of a center if meaning works like lack. Derrida and Lacan cross-fertilize each other. Derrida, indeed, identifies lack as the cause of the "over-abundance of the signifier" in a strangely Freudian construction (since in the short piece "Medusa's Head" the multiplication of snakes indicates lack). "The *overabundance* of the signifier, its *supplementary* character, is thus the result of a finitude, that is to say, the result of a lack which must be *supplemented*" (290); his italics; he is reading Lévi-Strauss). One can only say what is missing if one has an idea (1) of what should be there, but a finitude only signifies lack if one considers "being" to mean "having." If for Derrida the glass is half empty rather than half full, it is an imaginary whole glass, and the emptiness has been deduced from the presence. But presence *is*; we might abandon the idea that it has a necessary opposite in absence. I might have differing degrees and kinds of awareness of presence, but I exist. Subjects are the ones who impose lack on the systems of world and meaning. Derrida admits that the "movement of signification adds something," but says the sign does *not* "replace the center"; it does not take the center's place in its absence."[8] Nor does it. The sign and the center coexist. We might surely consider the overabundance of the signifier to be a sign of energy, not absence. This overabundance does not substitute for a void; it adds versions. It is human beings who either provide many meanings for one word or use many words and perhaps metaphors to characterize a thing in which they are interested. Similarly, examining his statement, "Play is the disruption of presence," we might see play as the sign of presence. "Play" *is* the center; it is not around nothing. Play is the changing relationships of parts, of interactions. If Derrida takes his toys apart, how can he play with them?

While deconstruction is indispensable in examining and critiquing classifications that reinforce oppression, such as gender, race, and class, it does not accurately describe itself as the principle of deconstructing, or the failure of categories to hold. Instead, it is an activity of adding to and constructing a functional plenitude. By "functional plenitude" in language I mean a bounded multiplicity, a constellation of meanings that might concern power and hierarchies, but also concerns richness of meaning. By "functional plenitude" in subjects I do not mean satiety but capacities we exercise and fundamental energies we can bestow and channel. There are many areas to which we might direct our energies in ways that give pleasure to others and ourselves—whether our world offers the chance to develop them is another question entirely.

Furthermore, in the process of making meaning, we may indeed perceive and classify objects within categories based on oppositions, but the *différance* which Derrida believes he is describing is not the result of substituting new pairs of opposites endlessly, none of which will hold. I do not agree that language is only built on oppositions, which can be shown to collapse. Not every word has a given and fixed opposite, and opposition is only one narrow form of relationship.[9] Making meaning, and particularly complex meaning, is a matter of seeing many relationships. Opposition or contrast is a fundamental process, but not the only one. What we did is more like assigning coordinates between oppositions, thus constructing meaning by addition, amplification, qualification. Even those processes that qualify a given meaning (that constrain it) do not simply erase it or undo it; rather, they add complexity and dimension, refining it and making it more precise, filling in details. Ordinarily, deconstructive readings do make categories complex, but the practice is richer than the theory. The error lies in the notion of substitution—that a new set of terms (oppositions) replaces an old. Derrida's sense of language is amazingly both machine-like and negating. It is only useful to deconstruct a statement so far (which must be determined by the readers involved), even if it can be done infinitely until it is nothing and means nothing, as if entropy were to set in, causing energy to cease. But we do not exist in a vacuum, and our thought slows with resistance. We are interested in and respond to interest, the signs of other intelligences and energies in the universe; we need to see signs that some energy has been at work.

The major critique of lack in Lacan and Derrida can be found in the work of Michel Foucault. *The History of Sexuality* describes relations of power in terms of an electromagnetic field:

> [S]till others [i.e., resistances] . . . are quick to compromise, interested, or sacrificial; by definition, they can only exist in the strategic *field of power relations*. . . . [T]he points, knots, or focuses of resistance are *spread over time and space at varying densities, at times mobilizing* groups or individuals in a definitive way, *inflaming* certain points of the body, certain moments in life, certain types of behavior. . . . Just as the *network of power relations* ends by forming a *dense web that passes through* apparatus and institutions, without being exactly localized in them, so too the swarm of *points of resistance traverses* social stratifications and individual unities. . . . It is in this sphere of *force relations* that we must try to analyze the *mechanisms of power*.   (96–97; my italics)

The metaphors that Foucault borrows from physics and field theory to characterize a subject's resistance prepared me to notice similar constructs transmitted in a literary history that can be traced from Coleridge and Shelley to Pater. It is interesting that the Romantics provide both a rearticulation of metaphysical, neoplatonic lack, and a materialist means of dismantling its later appearance in Freud, Lacan, and Derrida. Although Foucault argues that power, productive rather than repressive, shapes the ways in which we experience our desires and pleasures as *resistance* to repression and power, and although he talks of the mutually determining relation of power and pleasure, nowhere does he speak of desire as a similar field of force or energy, arising from the subjected, and this is precisely what is significant. The gains from such a conception of desire are twofold: first, a subject can be thought of as mass and density capable of mobilizing energy and being motivated and charged in order to act and move, which means subjects are not locuses of lack; and second, the capacity to be so motivated implies an organization or reorganization by and in this field of relations, whether of power or desire. I have said that desire is fundamentally a state of being organized in relation to an object. Our desire to desire is for this state or organization that lets us do things, and above all to make meaning. The things which can effect this organization are not infinite, but they are varied and incessant as long as we are alive.

Coleridge provides a model in the *Biographia Literaria* for how to think about desire in terms of energy: he talks about the poet's activity that organizes a "whole soul," and about a poem as a finely organized instance of language: "The poet, described in *ideal* perfection, brings the whole soul of man into activity, with the subordination of its faculties to each other, according to their relative worth and dignity.... This power [the imagination] ... reveals itself in the balance or reconciliation of opposite or discordant qualities: ... a more than usual state of emotion, with more than usual order" (ch. XIV, 12; his italics). Coleridge's statement that the poet brings his own "whole soul" into activity might also apply to the reader, but what interests me is the "more than usual state of emotion, with more than usual order." Coleridge sees emotion and order as opposed or "discordant," but I think they are mutually determining. I believe we can use this statement to describe desire itself. Emotion *is* a kind of ordering; that is to say, it orders or organizes the person who feels it. Emotion is not something that exists first and is then ordered; it already organizes a person. Desire is the fundamental organizing emotion, which incites, moves, or stimulates one *to* motion, therefore directs one's activity, and organizes that activity in relation to an object, usually what one wants to "get" or "have."

The concept of the Aeolian harp or lyre that Wordsworth, Coleridge, and later Shelley developed makes the human subject, and particularly the poet, an "instrument" that is itself finely organized, and therefore can respond or "correspond" to the most delicate and subtle "breezes," stirrings, or something that might be spirit but can also be thought of as energy or desire. It is not an accident that the subject, as instrument, then produces a music—language—which is emotion ordered, but the important aspect for me is that the subject is in part passive. He or she is acted on by means of this sensitivity and responsiveness to and with the environment, as if in a field of energy, and this passivity has been valued. It is crucially not inertness, but it allows one not always to be in command, while one is still responsively connected to one's environment. In Enlightenment terms it allowed one to feel sympathy, to be moved to respond to one's fellow being, and it continued in the Romantic period and afterwards to describe the creative process by which one was an impassioned, possessed agent, as Mary Shelley and Charlotte Brontë sometimes regarded themselves. Conscious rational production was underplayed so a writer could claim to be written by the work rather than to write the work. This relationship was a sign of passion, inspiration, and spontaneity—genius rather than laborious workmanship. Thus desire appeared to erase the fact of work, but it is work.

We as readers (if ideal) presumably also respond by resonating and being moved, at least at the moment in which we are reading. To think of being momentarily organized by the text could help explain how we assume the positions it creates and take up its values until we have reason to critique them—until there is something "discordant." Furthermore, we as reading subjects are clearly differently organized beings wanting the kind of organization that reading (poetry) gives. So the act of desiring is the act of organizing oneself to maintain a relationship with the object that enables it. There may be shapelessness, but not a void, not a lack. This organization gives us purpose, so that we may direct our energy. We need something from the outside to organize us, but we cannot be said to lack that stimulus; we are always getting stimuli. And we are entities to be so moved. We need texts to organize experience, language, and ourselves *so that* we can make meaning. Percy Shelley, perhaps the most actively desiring instrument, as one sees in "Ode to the West Wind," thought that the poet's chief ability was to see "the before unapprehended relations of things," which language marks (Defence 111). His desire was to find a pattern and transmit it, and he affirms human need for the consciousness of relationality.

By 1867, only three years after *Our Mutual Friend,* and showing the influence of Darwin as well as physics still predating Einstein, Walter Pater was writing about "natural law" as the transformation of the earlier constructs of necessity and fate in terms very similar to Foucault's conception of power, but he did so in the context of a discussion of literature. In the closing pages of "Winckelmann," Pater asks what purpose modern art (in its generic sense) might serve:

> The chief factor in the thoughts of the modern mind concerning itself is the intricacy, the universality of natural law, even in the moral order. For us, necessity is not, as of old, a sort of mythological personage without us, with

whom we can do warfare. It is rather *a magic web woven through and through us, like that magnetic system of which modern science speaks, penetrating us with a network, subtler than our subtlest nerves, yet bearing in it the central forces of the world.* Can art represent men and women in these bewildering toils so as to give the spirit at least an equivalent for the sense of freedom?

(230–31; my italics)

Necessity is "woven through and through us" and it bears "the central forces of the world." It may seem opposed to freedom, yet I would say that desire may be as close as we get to freedom because it is motion, the use of energy, and play in our relation to our field of action. It is possible to think of desire in these terms, as "woven through and through us" like a magnetic system with its network "subtler than our subtlest nerves." The metaphor of the web and network, or the "dense web"—the field of force—as Foucault picks it up, was prevalent in the nineteenth century, most often used to understand and describe the complex relationship of individuals to each other within the social "fabric," as well as general human connectedness.

The web was also Darwin's metaphor for the affinities among species in his theory of evolution. Later, the web became a metaphor for the organizing principle of the new physics, as Katherine Hayles argues in *The Cosmic Web: Scientific Field Models and Literary Strategies in the Twentieth Century.* Hayles shows primarily that the field model, which included the observing subject as acting in and upon the field which appears to be only the perceived object, helped to account for the decentering of subjects and truths in favor of relativity and relationality. Surely it also helped shape structuralists' ideas of the relationality of linguistic positions such as "I" and "you" and a system of meaning built on differences, but the late Victorians were already thinking of desire and imagination as energy that connects. It has seemed fitting to find a theory of desire that has to do with light and energy: "to consider" derives from CON + SIDERA, "with the stars," and "to desire" derives from DE + SIDERA, "from the stars." They compose our bodies and minds; we do not have to wait for anything, wanting. To read Dickens in this light is to see how much he contributed to the later theories that have shaped us.

II. Fiction as Strange as Truth

Our Mutual Friend, which started serial publication in 1864, marks the beginning that I see of the shift toward models of desire that qualify concepts of lack. Althought *Great Expectations* began to appear in 1860 and Wilkie Collins published *The Woman in White* in 1859, *Our Mutual Friend* is the first major novel to register fully the effects of Darwin's *Origin of Species*

(1859). Darwin provides the strongest case against the lackers by positing in all living things a physical instinct or drive to survive and reproduce that resituates its energy and life force within living beings, not as a gift from God, while he also develops a theory of complex relationality of beings to each other and to their environment.

Dickens certainly held a belief in God, and he goes so far as to suppose that Darwin did, too: the commonality that Darwin saw among life forms that linked them to a single progenitor, an organized cell, led Dickens to conjecture, "Therefore, Mr. Darwin would infer from analogy that, probably, all the organic beings which have ever lived on this earth have descended from one primordial form, into which life was first breathed by the Creator" (NS 294). However, Dickens removes God farther from the world in *Our Mutual Friend*. Lizzie, Jenny, Riah, and Betty Higden might believe in Him but do not feel His presence in the social world; they try to approach Him by escaping from the world, as when the first three go up on the roof, which is a replication of paradise but also means death.[10] Dickens eliminates omniscient perspectives from this novel, including even the narrator's, that might direct human energy wisely and morally. Characters in *Our Mutual Friend* are severely limited in their capacities to make sense of a whole; left largely to themselves, they struggle in a barely intelligible world. One problem that they do not really see is actually how to get rid of accumulated stuff—garbage and history, in the form especially of the dustheaps, which, along with wealth and filth, signify much uselessly spent energy. In *Great Expectations,* Dickens had plotted the quest for entry into history, identity, and origins; in *Our Mutual Friend,* characters try to get out—not by trying to escape from prisons, as in *Little Dorrit,* but by creating spaces of temporary sanctuary within the existing world that they have to reenter.

This world is starkly elemental, with some emphasis on light that looks like fire, but mainly on darkness and water. It is post-Darwinian in its emphasis on the difficulty of sheer survival in the context of vicious competition in the social order, and on the obscurity that prevents any sure answer as to whether humankind is evolving or redescending to primordial water forms. There had always been exploiters and exploited in Dickens's worlds, but competitive relations are sharper and more intense in this one. Gaffer Hexam is "half savage" (44); his son Charley has "a curious mixture . . . of uncompleted savagery, and uncompleted civilization" (50) and leads Mortimer and Eugene "down by where accumulated scum of humanity seemed to be washed from higher grounds, like so much moral sewage, and to be pausing until its own weight forced it over the bank and sunk it in the river" (63). There is continual reference to the Thames bank as a swamp, and "birds of prey" keep appearing figuratively along with other metaphors of trapping to represent hunting and hunted people. The weight and mass of human productions—objects and social and historical experience that are figured in the dustheaps that make fortunes, or the waterside buildings that are damp and have "a look of decomposition" (84)—are contrasted with the spareness of a few gleams of light and warmth by which characters huddle in physical and sometimes metaphysical darkness and which also inform their own beings. Although the novel opens with the "red light" of sunset that seems to color a dead body "as though with diluted blood" (44), the light quickly fades. Most of the scenes in the novel take place in the dark ("In the Dark" is a chapter title) or when the sun is going down. "Here's my father's, sir; where the light is," directs Charley, and Gaffer is looking into a red fire while Lizzie is doing needlework by its light (63). Eugene Wrayburn, ready to kindle, has nonetheless recently said that he abominates energy, because it would require him to collar clients to engage him as their lawyer (62). He thus neatly applies to himself the thermodynamic principle of the conservation of energy, maybe because he is no more than a "ray." Mortimer Lightwood, the better lawyer, replies, "But show me a good opportunity, show me something really worth being energetic about, and *I'll* show you energy" (62–63). Lizzie's friend Jenny Wren, with a mass of radiantly shining hair, provides another point of light that symbolizes not only imagination and moral good (the little that can be found in the novel) but also energy. Thus the long-standing metaphor of light for goodness and wisdom becomes increasingly literal and material in a physically perceived universe; it also becomes active.

Desires and passions, too, are elemental in this world of attractions and repulsions with its atmosphere of an urban Victorian *Waiting for Gadot*. Although the principals are immediately and mysteriously attracted to each other, their fascination is not love at first sight, nor is it given with the self's whole consent: not actively willing connection, they are almost helpless in being moved by and towards and away from each other, as if by the contingency of physical laws that they cannot understand, let alone govern. They are as perplexed by competition as by desire. Lizzie is disturbed but attracted by Eugene's interest and frightened at Bradley Headstone's; Eugene won't commit himself to her but finds his power over her and Bradley something new; and Bradley, drawn to Lizzie in spite of himself and used to struggling all his life, is crushed by Eugene's victory over him. Characters are also repelled from each other by an equally mysterious force that can only be known as instinct. Dickens had paid much attention to instincts in Darwin, noting the acquisition of a complex instinct "by the slow and gradual accumulation of numerous slight, yet profitable, variations" (NS 295), and also misconstruing Darwin concerning progress by seeing that "as Natural Selection works solely by and for the good of each being, all corporeal and mental endowments will tend to progress towards perfection. Thus, from the war of nature, from famine and death, the most exalted object which we are capable of conceiving, namely, the production of the higher animals, directly follows'' (299).

These forces are unknown to the characters, however. Eugene thinks of himself as a ''conundrum'' and does not know what his desires are, let alone his ''designs.'' Although he, Bradley, and Charley go to and from wherever Lizzie is, it is as if they are both magically drawn to each other *and* meet by chance, as if in some large and unknowable pattern. Other characters, too, feel themselves subject to desire and try to resist it. John Harmon dislikes but is attracted to Bella, and will both test and transform her; Bella in turn thinks him not good enough for her though he is critical of her desire for money; Jenny is hostile towards a future imagined husband and meanwhile adores Lizzie. Forces seemingly outside characters, while not locatable in God or fate, are stronger than characters themselves. This is new in Dickens. Also, while there is metaphysical darkness, the villains are no longer metaphysically evil: Headstone is pathetically desperate; Wegg and Rogue Riderhood are small folk, self-interested scum, less adept in language and less educated than, for example, Rigaud in *Little Dorrit* or Quilp in *The Old Curiosity Shop*. They have sunk in class a long way from Milton's intellectual Satan. The absence of a metaphysical villain shows that evil has disappeared as an external entity; it is located in human beings and therefore works on a smaller scale.

Dickens presents three models of desire in Bradley, Eugene, and Lizzie. Bradley represents the model of lack; Eugene's desire begins by the exercise of power; and Lizzie's desire is imaginative, connecting her not only to a lover but to the world. She is the clearest center of attraction, an embodied woman of warmth and energy,[11] who draws the two opposed men towards her by the spell or ''hex'' that is good because she is good, but that cannot be explained by reason. Her desire is harder to know than theirs.

Bradley is heavy, massive, and forceful; his earnestness is often termed ''gravity''; and his jealous passion is bound for destruction. Eugene's and his own (he is grave-bound, to judge from ''headstone''). Eugene is light, careless, and uncommitted, always joking at anyone's expense both ''airily'' and ''lazily''; he is not grave at all but spirited in his witty sallies. Physical mass and mental energy are thus opposed; the latter is socially valued and gives Eugene the upper hand. The laborious effort that might serve Bradley in another context has not helped him enough in the social world of middle-class labor in which he can never be secure. Bradley has great physical energy, but he can barely restrain his emotion when he is taunted by Eugene. He must always find a physical outlet such as wrenching an object because his mental strain is so great. In Eugene's success and Bradley's failure, Dickens affirms the efficacy of mental ability in the struggle for survival, both as an aid to the individual and as an attractive capacity that might be ''selected.''

Bradley's sense of lack is so extreme and drives him so obsessively that the contradiction between a concept of lack and the actual workings of desiring energy show this concept to be false. Bradley is a driving force, but his mistake is to think of himself in terms of ownership and lack. Since he doesn't own, by his own logic he has to lack. If he had been able to think in terms of force and energy, he might have saved himself. Dickens of course attacks the increasingly materialistic and acquisitive bent of the middle class, but he also critiques the underclass's desire to own what the middle class does while he tries to separate the ownership of material things from the definition of class. This effort on his own part lets him attack materialism but still value class-developed capacities and talents, above all education.

Bradley has constructed his own lack of social class, power, and even rudimentary effectiveness in his world. He has labored to educate himself and become a teacher so that he can "raise [himself] in the scale of society" (343), but nothing comes easily or can be secured. Working so hard for so little, Bradley is described as always "uneasy lest any thing acquired should be missing from his mental warehouse, and taking stock to assure himself" (267). His "slow or inattentive intellect" makes this acquiring and storing difficult, but he works hard at it. As I argued earlier, the idea of lack has historically exerted a productive force, but it should not be translated into theories of identity. For Bradley, lack signifies what he believes everyone else has but he has not yet attained, and he has translated lack into his identity at the most fundamental level. He feels that Lizzie can "[draw] the light out of his eyes" (450)—even his body can lose its integral capacities. His location of all power outside him also causes him to project responsibility for his obsessive desire onto her, and he sees the virtue of her power only in relation to himself:

> Yes! you are the ruin—the ruin—the ruin—of me. I have no resources in myself, I have no confidence in myself, I have no government of myself when you are near me or in my thoughts. And you are always in my thoughts now. I have never been quit of you since I first saw you. Oh, that was a wretched day for me! That was a wretched, miserable day! . . .
> You know what I am going to say. I love you. What other men may mean when they use that expression, I cannot tell; what I mean is, that I am under the influence of some tremendous attraction which I have resisted in vain, and which overmasters me. You could draw me to fire, you could draw me to water, you could draw me to anything I have most avoided, you could draw me to any exposure and disgrace. This and the confusion of my thoughts, so that I am fit for nothing, is what I mean by your being the ruin of me. But if you would return a favourable answer to my offer of myself in marriage, you could draw me to any good—every good—with equal force. . . . I don't know what I could say more if I tried. I might only weaken what is ill enough said as it is. I only add that if it is any claim on you to be in earnest, I am in thorough earnest; dreadful earnest.   (452, 454–455)

The language of physical energy, along with an older notion about the elements of the universe, is certainly present in words such as "influence," "tremendous attraction," "draw me to fire, . . . to water," "equal force." Less explicitly it appears in Lizzie's effect on him when she is near him. When she enters into his sphere, she seems to reduce and confuse him, almost as if there were a transfer of mass (as energy) between them. He sees himself as having or not having things; he sees her as exercising power. The proximity of bodies generates energy which she feels too, although negatively. The language of lack, powerlessness, and social surveillance is apparent in "no resources," "overmasters," anxiety about potential "exposure and disgrace," mental "confusion," and the blame Bradley unintentionally, unskillfully heaps on Lizzie while confessing his passion. Dickens does not argue that love and hate are necessarily yoked in passion, I think; rather, he reveals the problem with the model that yokes them: Bradley does not show any love for Lizzie, nor does he even seem really to desire her physically in some relationship. He feels her force, which prevents him from doing his work. He feels he will not be able to raise himself higher and more visibly in the social order unless he has a wife, but he has to overcome anxiety about Lizzie's inferior social standing. He seems simply to want her, and if he can possess her, he can stop wanting her. He clearly does not want to keep desiring.

Bradley has reified power and cultural and social presence to such an extent that he sees himself as lacking even personal energy. He might seem to demonstrate in a Lacanian mode how thoroughly one's identity rests outside one and is shaped by the social order, and Dickens might seem to be saying that lack provides energy; but Bradley implicitly shows that *thinking* one is lacking is the source of this desperate energy, and this sense of lack has a negative but real effect on other people. Bradley fails to recognize the violent force he wields exactly because he sees power as something he must but cannot securely acquire rather than what he might exercise.

The intensity of Bradley's and Lizzie's relationship is second only to Bradley's and Eugene's, which of course is its result. The charge of physical "magnetic" forces is at its greatest in this triangle. As Fred Kaplan has shown, Mesmer envisioned something very like a force field, although he thought of it in terms of a fluid, "universally distributed and continuous . . . of an incomparably rarefied nature, and which by its nature is capable of receiving, propagating and communicating all the impressions of movement" (Mesmer 67). This fluid, working in an "ebb and flow," registers the "mutual influence between the Heavenly bodies, the Earth and Animate bodies," some of whom can make use of "animal magnetism" more than others, as distinct from the "mineral magnetism," which inheres in actual metals. Through the medium of this fluid, magnetism affects primarily the nerves, and it is exercised by "the communication of will," especially conveyed by sight, by a gaze, which creates a "rapport" or "covenant" between two beings (Mesmer 121). Mesmer insists continually on the medical, healing power of this energy, especially to cure nervous disorders, but Dickens, as Kaplan convincingly argues, saw how such an exercise of will was bound up with the expression of power in sexuality. Dickens locates this power mainly in men and mainly for egocentric ends, exactly as an expression of power (Kaplan 196).

Bradley, as Kaplan also rightly observes, accuses Lizzie of having mesmeric power: "She is like the magnetic loadstone that he has concentrated within it all the focused mesmeric force of the universe, irresistible and undeniable" (209). Lizzie does not use this power, however, even though she "attracts" both Bradley and Eugene, so what is new in this novel is how a character—Bradley—can imagine the power and even use it himself while also attributing it entirely to the other person. To Bradley, awkward newcomer within the sphere of watching (on which I will shortly elaborate), being snubbed by his rival Eugene, who is so highly visible, "as if unaware of [Bradley's] existence," is the ultimate rejection, and an estimation precisely of what he understands as lack. If his physical being, his material presence, cannot even be acknowledged, he seems to be absent from the world. It is true that this perception drives him. He suffers for his inability to be recognized and valued by his social world. Eugene even refuses to call him by his name, which gives social substance and position.

Eugene, in contrast, has a sort of plenitude that is defined as much by power as by actual ownership of things. Careless, with a "lazily arrogant air," holding possession of twice as much pavement as another would have claimed" (279), extending a kind of personal space as if by ownership, he more importantly has "self-possession." This is not a facade covering a lack.

> He knew his power over [Lizzie]. . . . For all his seeming levity and carelessness, he knew whatever he chose to know of the thoughts of her heart.
> And going on at her side, so gaily, regardless of all that had been urged against him; so superior in his sallies and self-possession to the gloomy constraint of her suitor and the selfish petulance of her brother; so faithful to her, as it seemed, when her own stock was faithless; what an immense advantage, what an overpowering influence, were his that night! [Where was] the wonder . . . that his lightest touch, his lightest look, his very presence beside her in the dark common street, were like glimpses of an enchanted world, which it was natural for jealousy and malice and all meanness to be unable to bear the brightness of, and to gird at as bad spirits might. (464–65)

Between two paragraphs we shift almost imperceptibly between Eugene and Lizzie, attached, yet also in their separate worlds—his of imagining power, hers of imagining connection and a better world. Eugene has tangible and intangible things, including a self. Even though he has no clients, and has not chosen his profession anyway, his father having predetermined the vocations of all his children, he nonetheless has social position, education, and immense verbal skill. Not given to feeling emotion or even interest until he meets Lizzie, he has "himself" because nothing else organizes his desire or elicits more than minimal energy. Eugene does not pretend to a plenitude; he knows himself to be superior in Lizzie's eyes. He also has some money and connections, therefore resources, but doesn't use them until he meets Lizzie, and he wants exactly to use them, to spend them, in order to teach her to read, a bit as she has paid for Charley's education.[12] This desire to expend the self's energy shows Dickens's sense that a capacity in fact increases by its use; it is not depleted, although Eugene is certainly spending money at someone else's expense. But as far as Eugene's effort is concerned, he is developing a faculty by exercising it. The idea that strength increases by use supports a Darwinian reading of the "natural selection" of faculties, especially ones that give Eugene an "advantage," a word often used by Darwin. Eugene's initial difficulty is that he is bored; he cannot interest himself in work or in connection to people except for his long friendship with Mortimer, who seems to work harder at the relationship and who calls Eugene his "foundation." This foundation is like a center, but there is no single center for all the characters; there are plural ones, indicating relative, not absolute, importance within small constellations that act in relation to each other.

Eugene claims his proposal to educate Lizzie is stirred by a "disinterested" desire finally to be of use to someone, but he makes the most claim when he says he is claiming nothing. The actions that characterize "disinterested" behavior, which means being interested in others rather than the self, do not show lack of interest. His motives may be generous and not demand return, but they are interested by virtue of deciding on the very person from whom they ostensibly demand nothing. Eugene cannot be alive and not be interested; even wishing Lizzie well shows interest, and in fact he wants the return of her interest in him.

Of the two central marriages in the novel, Lizzie's and Eugene's carries more significance than does Bella's and John's because it crosses wider class boundaries. The symbolic marriage of the middle to the laboring class shows that the middle class, so long trying to secure itself by marrying upwards, then finds that it cannot renew itself because it thinks in terms of acquisition of goods rather than how to use its own energy.[13] The stimulus must again come from outside, but this time from the working class, which doesn't have things but does have energy. Furthermore, while exogamy might once have seemed mainly defensible in theory, Darwin had shown that "with animals and plants a cross between different varieties, or between individuals of the same variety but of another strain, gives vigour and fertility to the offspring" (143). Exogamy in this social context refers to marriage not just out of family but out of class.

It is possible to read Eugene cynically as a bourgeois exploiting Lizzie's energy and labor by constructing this exploitation as love, but Eugene also rejects predominant bourgeois strictures and snobbery in order to marry her. If lack were Dickens's only model of desire, then Eugene should be given lack if he is to desire, so as to correct his physical, emotional, and moral inertia—but he isn't; he is given energy. He pursues Lizzie, wants to exert influence on her, even ruthless force, and finally must choose whether to marry or abandon her, but he never feels (or is) incomplete without her. Robert Kiely uses Carl Jung's reliance on the primacy of the "life instinct," regardless of "conscious will," to describe not only literal efforts—"energy and . . . a powerful will" to survive, but "inventive manipulation or design" (381, cited in Kiely 276).[14] Eugene begins to form designs, even though he tells Mortimer he has none.

Rather, Lizzie creates a field for his energies, and his desire moves him to act, so she connects him to the world. Eugene "has failings," in Lizzie's words, that "have grown up" from "the want of something to trust in, and care for, and think well of" (405), but these failings have presence. The "want of something to . . . care for" is written in the language of lack, and alarmingly of a "thing" which Lizzie ought to think of as a person (but which might also be an ideal or principle), but the lack is not within Eugene. What looks like an emptiness is a failure of stimulation and connection. He himself has been "like one cast away"—*not* wanted; he has been superfluous. He has failed because there was not someone for him to be interested in and centered about. "Only put me in that empty place [of the lady]", Lizzie says, and Eugene will be better. Places are empty, but people are not.

Eugene's ownership even of "pavement," let alone his pursuit of Lizzie, is therefore, in Bradley's eyes, a demonstration of his power—his means to arrange and dominate his world. He claims a field and the ability to act in and upon it; will, efficacy, and autonomy are power made visible and present. Eugene also really works at tormenting Bradley and emotionally blackmailing Lizzie, even though his best demonstration of power lies in the apparent ease and grace of using it, as if it were an innate, customary skill and knowledge, not needing to be learned or acquired. Such a power erases the historicity of its struggle and its own labor of acquisition.

The demonstration of power is a necessary function of power itself. The link between power and vision has of course enabled the complexity and usefulness of Foucault's analyses of the panopticon, the asylum, and the confessional—the specific mechanisms of surveillance. Stuart Ewen had observed that the middle class in the United States consumes and produces images of itself and its power (62–66), and this argument seems to apply to Victorian Britain as well. Someone else's possible vision of oneself operates as a presence; it is a power and force, even if, as Foucault has argued, no real person is present to do the watching. The images that repeatedly perform ownership show the effects of power for two audiences—those who have and those who do not.

The sight of people—as well as the looking done by them—also works like contact that establishes oneself as well as the world and beings in it as real. Sight establishes relationship immediately by nearness or distance and by quality of response, and the middle class, unlike either the working class or the very rich, has developed an acute sensitivity and capacity to see how it is being seen. In *Our Mutual Friend,* it is evident that the middle class must not only have the power to survey but must itself be surveyed, so it turns its acquisition of goods into proof of ownership. The relation of power to ownership and looking helps account for *Our Mutual Friend's* intent focus on the gaze. The need of the middle class to demonstrate its power can of course be interpreted as a quintessential lack, but it is certainly not one that can be fulfilled, and this fact shows more its need to expend energy than to get things. Lacan's concepts of lack and the mirror, including the social order as mirror, go hand in hand. The social order tells one what one has or does not. If we reformulate ideas concerning lack and the gaze (which have seemed to be fundamental, existential, and a historical truths about subjectivity) as *ownership* and the gaze, placing Lacan's theories solidly in late capitalism, we can see how the gaze works both as a capacity and as the sign of how we fit into a social and cultural order that values possessions. John Berger's arguments that oil paintings reflect to an owner what he owns and that publicity projects images of who we would be were we to own particular things support the idea. The mirror itself seems to be a particularly middle-class object, situating an ideal image in a thing,[15] which like the social order reflects one to oneself. Thus the content of Bradley's perception repeatedly shows him what things and powers others have and he does not, whereas Eugene sees that he has effects.

How do we think about Lizzie's desire in this network of objects and performances, ownership and power, if Bradley is trapped in the desire to own objects and Eugene has made the questionable progress of translating ownership into the demonstration of power over other people? I will argue that Lizzie acts without consciousness of performing and links desire far more to being than to owning. She is not used to owning or performing; she is not even used to being seen. Eugene's notice and attention at first make her uncomfortable. Explaining to Charley why she "went out in the dark," she says that Eugene "looked hard at me," and she is afraid he will be able to read her expression. Unused to being seen even as an object of desire, Lizzie becomes simultaneously a subject and object of desire because Eugene starts to make her feel visible. Bradley's attention actually alarms her; early on she also avoids her father's predatory gaze at the river and the bodies he hopes to find there. Unconscious of her presence, she nonetheless exerts it. In this novel which much more than Dickens's other work minutely describes bodies and physical gestures, she has density, mass, energy, and light, which we find out by degrees, as if she were becoming more material. She is physically strong and "lithe in her movements," and this strength alone is unusual for a Dickens woman who is not caricatured. What aristocratic and middle-class men do for sport, Lizzie does as labor; she rows her father's boat. She is "dark" of hair and complexion but her face reflects both light and outdoor labor in her sunburn; her skin is a "rich brown" color (70). In the prevalent nighttime scenes the light reflected on her face comes from the fire into which she gazes. This gazing "in the hollow down by the flare" (404) creates imaginative space for her desire, first for Charley (she wants and pays for his education) and later for herself. In contrast to Charley's calculation, Lizzie's thinking and desiring, which might seem to make her absent and inaccessible not only to us but to any character, since we do not know what she is thinking if she does not tell someone, nonetheless give her presence; they add dimension and substance to her; she has an inner life because she imagines, but this imagination also creates possibilities in the world.

Mary Poovey situates Lizzie between Dickens's recuperation of a naturalized virtue guaranteed by the female body and her figurative status as a man, a "female waterman" (65). I do not agree that "the combination of Lizzie's ambiguous 'purity' with such stereotypically 'masculine' traits as economic autonomy and muscular strength suggests her assimilation to men" (60) rather than independence from men. Jenny Wren has more economic autonomy than Lizzie, and Lizzie's work is something she does, not who she is except as it makes her physically strong. We can read Lizzie as a strong rather than masculine woman.

Perhaps the most troubling question about Lizzie's desire is why she desires Eugene. Dickens understood the difficulty of having the moral center of his novel attracted to a man who is not her moral equal. When Dickens had let "bad" men dazzle "good" women, the women usually did not know the men well enough (Cherry Pecksniff in *Martin Chuzzlewit* and Pet Meagles in *Little Dorrit*). Lizzie is not fooled by Eugene, however, and she is one of few Dickens heroines to fall in love because of sexual attraction rather than perceived character. Eugene is handsome and witty; he has presence and social position; and he is interested in her. Lizzie might also have the same kind of intuitive sense of Eugene's worth, in spite of his failings, that prompts her fear of, and repulsion from Bradley, confirmed in her extraordinarily sensitive touch when Bradley shakes her head. But Lizzie does not assert Eugene's goodness; only his social distance from her makes him dazzling and gives him some undefined "worth" that she also recognizes as socially determined rather than an innate moral quality. She feels herself "so far below him and so different" that she cannot believe he values her (286). Jenny asks her what she would think of him if she were a lady. "I a lady!" Lizzie muses; "I, who was made so timid by his looking at me. . .! (404).

While Lizzie cannot explain her attraction to Eugene, she imagines in their relationship a possible agency for herself. In the passage cited, continuing in the third person as if she were this imaginary lady (but slipping into conversation with him, which makes him present), she says.

> She would joyfully die with him, or, better than that, die for him. She knows he has failings, but she thinks they have grown up through his being like one cast away, for the want of something to trust in, and care for, and think well of. And she says, that lady rich and beautiful that I can never come near, "Only put me in that empty place, only try how little I mind myself, only prove what a world of things I will do and bear for you, and I hope that you might even come to be much better than you are, through me who am so much worse, and hardly worth the thinking of beside you."   (404–05)

The concept of agency through self-sacrifice and the hope of largely transforming a person's character are of course dubious and problematic, especially as they are ideologies offered to women to maintain the family and regenerate a fallen world, but they give more agency than Dickens usually grants his heroines, especially in their own consciousness. The problem in Dickens's work is that he so often separates energy and desire from goodness, thinking them incompatible. Evil had historically been construed as active and desiring; goodness, certainly in women, as passive, inert, static, and undesiring because desire had seemed to characterize a selfish self. Self-sacrifice in Dickens's work often has the aspect of negating desire rather than desiring something for someone else even if at cost to oneself. When Dickens makes goodness the absence of desire, ironically he reemploys the older model of desire as organized around lack. But Lizzie's goodness at its best is active, not self-sacrificing. She risks danger to pull Eugene from the river but does not relinquish herself; she uses her strength.

It is possible to read Lizzie as wanting precisely things: to be rich and beautiful as a reified object herself. While she wants the presence that a lady has, which in part comes from being used to being looked at, and feels "below" Eugene, one cannot conclude that she feels lacking just because she wants to be different. She wants to "come near" this ideal in order to be Eugene's equal. Her desire to learn to read, which she recognizes as a step towards becoming a different person (who can no longer be alienated from her father by this education, because he is dead), would also connect her to the world around her that in this novel ubiquitously presents itself in texts (*Decline-And-Fall-Off-The-Rooshan-Empire* [96], which misrepresents the world; a notice advertising John Harmon's disappearance; Charley's books). This desire therefore creates stronger relationships and cannot fairly be interpreted except as the acquisition of power and position that it would be for Charley. Her "library of books is the hollow down by the flare" (73).

She tells stories to maintain the connections she can—to hold onto shared experience and imagine better possibilities; one might see in her an earlier historical form of recording—an older, oral tradition—while writing exists all around her.

Our lack of knowledge about Lizzie is in some ways in keeping with formal methods of the novel. Dickens causes much information to come piece by piece from the characters themselves in admissions they choose or are driven to make to other characters. In contrast to the narrator's painstaking record of communities and their histories in *Little Dorrit,* together with the awareness that no one narrative can make sense of the whole, as Nancy Aycock Metz argues, the narrator of *Our Mutual Friend* reveals the accidentalness not only of each fragment's expression but also of any whole picture. Dickens had long been interested in the secret connections of characters across class divisions and moral boundaries that are revealed to us in the course of the plot,[16] but in *Our Mutual Friend* the characters themselves construct these relations and comment on them even if they do not understand them. As I have argued, this consciousness is as crucial as the fact of relationship. It is not just the interweaving of plots that is demonstrated, as in *Bleak House,* but the dependence of this interweaving on language, on explanation of characters to each other. Relationships can only be revealed by language, and the delicate dependence of any understanding of relations upon social connection in conversation is made even more fragile by the necessity that characters have to *want* to say things. Dickens has an increasing sense of the materiality of human beings that makes them opaque—not able to be seen into and known—and of the greater necessity for candor and expressiveness in language as well as its greater (in his own developing sense of things) fallibility. There is therefore a great sense of the accidentalness of any communication at all—a particular, contingent, random interaction of forces.

In some ways, as a result, characters in *Our Mutual Friend* have less autonomy, and can control their destinies less than other Dickens novels' characters; in some ways they are granted more independence from the narrator's knowledge and control, and even a kind of integrity, because interiors are *not* easily known; they are less subject to manipulation if they cannot be read. This might be a step nearer the recognition that a narrator is a limited subject, too; he is bound by the same terms as are the characters in the field he observes. Perhaps the awareness also shows a move towards a more dialogic sensibility, not only in Bakhtin's sense, by which characters speak from different philosophical positions that a writer more fully and independently imagines even if unlike his own, but also simply by virtue of their occurrence in dialogue.

In keeping with the disclosures about feelings that characters make in conversation, so that identity itself is constructed in the act of speaking and formed by social and affective relationship, Eugene is the one who discovers qualities in Lizzie that we might not have known otherwise. We see him thinking about her, able to read her expressiveness: he recognizes her earnestness in passion and her inability to choose not to love him: "She cannot choose for herself to be strong in this fancy, wavering in that, and weak in the other. She must go through with her nature, as I must go through with mine. If mine exacts its pains and penalties all round, so must hers, I suppose" (765). Unlike Bradley, he also grants her an existence independent of her effects on him. And he himself must come to the point of choosing her—of committing himself to a relationship imaginatively and in language, showing he desires her to be his wife.

To think in terms of a "nature" might rely either on an idea of essential character, as if it is unshaped by the social world, or on something akin to a drive and the unconscious, but it is also to recognize a pattern of acting that is one's own and material even if also uninterpretable and intractable. To "go through with" is not the same as to yield to something as if given one from the outside. To think of "going through with" one's nature suggests response to an internal source of energy, and it makes of the unconscious a presence, a center of energy even if it is unavailable to control, even while "going through with" it might imply a unified action and some resulting integrity. Rigaud in *Little Dorrit* keeps talking about his "character," which is wholly his manipulation of self-presentation; Lizzie and Eugene enact their "natures." We cannot say what they are but we see their effects. This nature does not seem fixed, requiring a specific result or object to be gotten; rather, Lizzie feels and thinks certain things and must act on them; she must respond. I believe that Dickens's sense of this "nature" is on a continuum with Pater's concept of a universal "natural law," even though Pater wrote three years later. As Pater says, this is not locatable outside us in a being or system that we can confront: "[Necessity] is rather a magic web woven through and through us, like that magnetic system of which modern science speaks, penetrating us with a network, subtler than our subtlest nerves, yet bearing in it the central forces of the world." The universal law acts both within and upon one's nature, yet connects us with the world not only by its "universality," but by its force as desire, which itself connects. This concept of necessity does not have a specific content; it is perhaps only a law of interaction and relationship.

Finally, there is the concept of opposition. Bradley's initial verbal attack and his later physical attack on Eugene clarify and simplify Lizzie's feelings to herself and make her choose one side of an opposition, for she defends not only herself but Eugene from Bradley's charge of ignoble behavior and finally also rescues Eugene. Bradley's negative charge—Lizzie's aversion to him—propels her towards Eugene. There is no space in the novel safe from pressure, persuasion, or influence; no position of neutrality; no condition of the absence of such forces and influences. There is only more or less choice as to where and how to move in response, and characters have to choose between opposite poles and what turn out to be mutually exclusive positions. Lizzie does compare Eugene and Bradley, and Eugene knows Lizzie is at the center of the "secret, sure perception between them, which set [the men] against one another in all ways" (341). One sees the force of Eve Sedgwick's argument that the men's homoerotic relationship is mediated by Lizzie (168). Certainly class opposition is already in place, which might seem to have structured the choices and even determined the choice. Bradley sees the opposition as based on plenitude and lack, but his lack is actually not part of the equation, even though it indirectly results in Eugene's commitment to Lizzie. However, Lizzie would have chosen Eugene whether Bradley was there or not because she desired him and had to act. This is the human predicament: people imagine, and then must make choices because they must act. If we have any capacity to choose, even the illusion of choosing, we have the capacity to act. Our world presents us with choices; we make them into oppositions or other relationships, and actual relationships, constantly changing, will always stimulate a reader/interpreter/actor to think more, to have something more to say—not because we can never close on the object or process of knowing (although it is true that we cannot), but because we keep relating ourselves and responding to what continues to change. If we really want to know a thing, we keep bestowing interest and imagination on it and adding, making the idea denser and richer, like a dark star. We can only use this energy from our own positions. And if we can take positions, we must *be* somewhere.

NOTES

I thank Paul Kinzele for his thoughtful reading of a different version of the theory part of this essay presented in the session "Literary Criticism and Theory: Literature and Psychoanalytic Theory" at the Midwest MLA in November 1997. I am also grateful for the interested response of colleagues, not all of whom I could meet, but to whose comments I have tried to respond.

1. Elizabeth Grosz provides partial support for one argument in *Volatile Bodies:* desire can be thought of as "what produces, what connects, what makes machinic alliances. Instead of aligning desire with fantasy and opposing it to the real, instead of seeing it as a yearning, desire is an actualization, a series of practices, bringing things together or separating them, making machines, making reality. . . . It moves; it does. . . . But the surpassing of the model of lack does not, should

not, return us to the affirmation of pure plenitude or presence. Presence and absence are coupled in and to the same framework. In place of plenitude, being, fullness or self-identity is not lack, absence, rupture, but rather becoming" (165). Grosz uses the work of Dominique Grisoni, Gilles Deleuze and Felix Guattari, and Baruch Spinoza. I disagree with her rejection of presence and strenuously resist the Deleuze-Guattari model of the machine, which does not include consciousness or intention, while I like their emphasis on "intensities and flows." Grosz's project to "displace the centrality of mind, the psyche, interior, or consciousness (and even the unconscious)... through a reconfiguration of the body," from a belief that "[a]ll the effects of depth and interiority can be explained in terms of the inscriptions and transformations of the subject's corporeal surface" (vii) is admirable for its new direction of thought but finally both undesirable and impossible, in my judgment. Desire concerns the mind as well as the body, and the body Grosz imagines seems quite unconnected to anybody or thing around it. "Becoming" does not explain desire or the effort to form relations, and to rewrite interiority as corporeal fails to account for dimensions of experience I want to hold on to, including consciousness and the imagination.

2. Edgar Johnson remarks that Dickens had faith in the general British public's intelligence, saying in a speech that they applauded the discoveries of John Herschel and Michael Faraday. See *Charles Dickens: His Tragedy and Triumph*, vol. 2 (New York: Simon and Schuster, 1952), 757; citation of a speech given by Dickens 1/6[18]53 in *Collected Papers* II, 400–06. New models of the universe, including the vast distances among stars and the multiplicity of galaxies which decenter our own, contributed by both William and John Herschel, are embedded in Dickens's work, although not much work has been done on this relation.

3. Mary Poovey argues that as early as the census of 1851 it was evident that there were too many women to marry and too many governesses competing *with each other* for jobs that paid what was supposed to be freely given work determined by natural, maternal "instinct"—which also showed that the "commodification of labor" did not "[stop] at the door of the home" (UD 144). Walter Besant stated in 1897 that women had "invaded" and "taken over" the professions (56, 58).

4. Mary Wollstonecraft had already argued against an inherently inferior nature in women in her *Vindication of the Rights of Woman* (1792). John Stuart Mill in 1860 wrote his essay *The Subjection of Women* (not published until 1869), in which he argued that "What is now called the nature of women is an eminently artificial thing" (451) and urged that the only means to know about "the natural differences between the two sexes" was "an analytic study of the most important department of psychology, the laws of the influence of circumstances on character" (453). He was well aware how difficult it would be to ascertain anything about "natural differences" since all identities are shaped by the social world.

5. "The nineteenth-century homosexual became a personage, a past, a case history, and a childhood, in addition to being a type of life, a life form, and a morphology, with an indiscreet anatomy and possibly a mysterious physiology.... [T]he homosexual was now a species" (43).

6. Schapiro, in her strictly psychoanalytic framework, nonetheless points out what object relations theory owes to physics: it "corresponds with current models in the natural sciences, with quantum mechanics and systems and field theories. . . . [I]dentity is observer dependent; so too in the psychological universe, . . . identity at the core level of the self is other dependent, and inextricably bound up with human recognition. . . . [N]othing is more fundamental than dynamic, interactive patterns and relationships" (2).

7. According to David Hume, in *Enquiry Concerning Human Understanding,* there are only three forms of "connexion between ideas": causality, resemblance, and contiguity. The last two of course bear relation to metaphor and metonymy, and causality is the stuff of narrative, but they are all positive forms of relationship. Par. 19 cited in Scholes 18.

8. How can there be "movement of signification" without a center from which to move? Derrida rejects energy in a long list of undesirable metaphysical ideas: "It could be shown that all the names related to fundamentals, to principles, or to the center have always designated an invariable presence—*eidos, arche, telos, energeia, ousia* (essence, existence, substance, subject), *alatheia,* transcendentality, consciousness, God, man, and so forth" (279–80). This is quite a list containing largely antimaterialist elements vastly different in their ability to be demonstrated. *Energeia* is of interest to me here, and I do not see how it can be denied.

9. Robert Scholes suggested, in a seminar at Brown University in 1989, that a given word has many opposites; I am suggesting that the relationship is not always opposition.

10. In *Darwin and the Novelists,* George Levine argues that Darwin foregrounded and problematized the relation of the observer to what he was observing. In his analysis of *Our Mutual Friend,* Levine argues that all the spying shows that characters "believe that truth is hidden from social view. Peace comes only outside the world of spying and being spied upon . . . the only safety is an obliteration of selfhood so complete as to become a literal death" (224). He concentrates on John Harmon, who "can observe without distorting" because people think he is dead. Levine states parenthetically, "We needn't explore the complexities of the way the apparently separate observer is, inevitably, shaping and therefore changing the observed" (223). He is right to connect selfhood with being watched, although he is not interested in pursuing this line. Important for my own purposes, Levine documents Dickens's increasingly secular account of personality based on theories of thermodynamics apparent in the expenditure of energy and warmth in *Little Dorrit;* this interest is even more apparent in *Our Mutual Friend.*

11. I disagree with Helena Michie's assessment that women are particularly invisible and not embodied in this novel; everyone is more embodied here than in other Dickens novels. We see many details about the position of bodies and the expression of faces that continually comment on characters' relations to each other in physical space and emotional attitude—Harmon's arm around Bella's waist, or Jenny looking at Lizzie through the fine mesh of her hair.

12. Bella, like Eugene, wants money not for itself but for what it can do; most unfortunately she has to give up her wonderful angry humor and rebelliousness,

along with her desire for money and independence, before she is given back the money only and is transformed into a dutiful housewife. All the energy of John Harmon's and Noddy Boffin's efforts goes into the sharp containment of her own.

13. *Our Mutual Friend* surprisingly owes to *Pride and Prejudice* in its dynamics of interclass marriages based on renewal that a lower-class woman can provide an upper-class man. Lizzie owes to Lizzy Bennet; Bradley's proposal sounds remarkably like Darcy's in acknowledging how he has struggled against his feelings and "considerations" of her poverty (455); there is also a Georgiana who is temporarily seduced by a cad (Fascination Fledgeby in place of Wickham). But in Austen's novel, the middle-class Lizzy brings wit and freedom to Darcy that make the match aesthetically right, whereas Eugene depends on Lizzie for his very life, and it is her physical strength that saves him.

14. Coincidentally, Kiely begins his essay by arguing how concepts of "design" had changed from Austen's *Pride and Prejudice* to Dickens's *Our Mutual Friend.*

15. Lacan's "imaginary" might seem to situate mirroring partly in human beings, but D. W. Winnicott does this better, seeing the mother herself as mirroring the child; he does not situate identity in the object but uses it as a metaphor to describe the mother's active relation to the child.

16. Gillan Beer makes this argument in *Darwin's Plots,* where she also notes how much Darwin and Dickens read each other (8, 47).

WORKS CITED

Beer, Gillian. *Darwin's Plots: Evolutionary Narrative in Darwin, George Eliot and Nineteenth-Century Fiction.* London: ARK/Routledge & Kegan Paul, 1985.

Berger, John. *Ways of Seeing.* London: British Broadcasting Company and Penguin Books, 1972.

Besant, Walter. *The Queen's Reign and Its Commemoration: a Literary and Pictorial Review of the Period: the Story of the Victorian Transformation.* London: The Werner Co., 1897.

Chodorow, Nancy. *The Reproduction of Mothering: Psychoanalysis and the Sociology of Gender.* Berkeley: U of California, P. 1978.

Coleridge, Samuel Taylor. *Biographia Literaria.* Ed. with his aesthetical essays by J. Shawcross. Vol. II. London: Oxford UP, 1907.

Darwin, Charles. *The Origin of Species by Means of Natural Selection, or the Preservation of Favoured Races in the Struggle for Life.* Ed. J. W. Burrow. 1859. London: Penguin, 1968.

Derrida, Jacques. "Structure, Sign, and Play in the Discourse of the Human Sciences." *Writing and Difference.* Trans Alan Bass. Chicago: U of Chicago, P, 1978.

Dickens, Charles. "Natural Selection." *All the Year Round* July 7, 1860:293–99.

——— *Our Mutual Friend.* Ed. Stephen Gill. 1864–1865. London: Penguin, 1971.

Ewen, Stuart. *All Consuming Images: the Politics of Style in Contemporary Culture.* New York: Basic Books, 1988.

Foucault, Michel. *The History of Sexuality.* Vol. 1. New York: Pantheon, 1980.

Freud, Sigmund. "Female Sexualilty." *Sexuality and the Psychology of Love.* Ed. Philip Rieff. New York: Collier/Macmillan, 1963.

——— "Medusa's Head" (1922). Op. cit.

——— "Some Psychological Consequences of the Anatomical Distinction between the Sexes." Op. cit. Grosz, Elizabeth. *Volatile Bodies: Toward a Corporeal Feminism.* Bloomington: Indiana UP, 1994.

Hayles, N. Katherine. *The Cosmic Web: Scientific Field Models and Literary Strategies in the Twentieth Century.* Ithaca: Cornell UP, 1984.

Irigaray, Luce. "Psychoanalytic Theory: Another Look." *This Sex Which Is Not One.* Trans. Catherine Porter with Carolyn Burke. Ithaca, NY: Cornell UP, 1985. 34:67.

——— "This Sex Which Is Not One." Op. cit. 23–33.

Johnson, Edgar. *Charles Dickens: His Tragedy and Triumph.* Vol. 2. New York: Simon and Schuster, 1952.

Jung, C. G. *Memories, Dreams, Reflections.* London: Collins and Routledge and Kegal Paul, 1963.

Kaplan, Fred. *Dickens and Mesmerism: the Hidden Springs of Fiction.* Princeton: Princeton UP, 1975.

Kiely, Robert. "Plotting and Scheming: The Design of Design in *Our Mutual Friend*" *Dickens Studies Annual: Essays on Victorian Fiction* 12 (1983): 267–83.

Kucich, John. *Repression in Victorian Fiction: Charlotte Brontë, George Eliot, and Charles Dickens.* Berkeley: U of California P, 1987.

Lacan, Jacques. "Feminine Sexuality in Psychoanalytic Doctrine." *Feminine Sexuality.* Jacques Lacan and the *école freudienne.* Ed. Juliet Mitchell and Jacqueline Rose. Trans. Jacqueline Rose. New York: Norton, 1982.

——— *The Four Fundamental Concepts of Psycho-Analysis.* Ed. Jacques-Alain Miller. Trans. Alan Sheridan. 1973. New York: Norton, 1981.

Levine, George. *Darwin and the Novelists: Patterns of Science in Victorian Fiction.* Cambridge, MA: Harvard UP, 1988.

Marx, Karl, and Frederick Engels. *Manifesto of the Communist Party.* 1848. New York: International Publishers, 1969.

Mesmer, Franz Anton. *Mesmerism: A Translation of the Original Scientific and Medical Writings of F. A. Mesmer.* Trans. George Bloch. Los Altos, CA: William Kaufmann, 1980.

Metz, Nancy Aycock *"Little Dorrit's* London: Babylon Revisited." *Victorian Studies* 33:3 (Spring 1990): 465–86.

Michie, Helena. " 'Who is this in Pain/': Scarring, Disfigurement, and Female Identity in *Bleak House* and *Our Mutual Friend." Novel* 22:2 (Winter 1989): 199–212.

Mill, John Stuart. "The Subjection of Women." *On Liberty: Representative Government; The Subjection of Women: Three Essays.* With an introd. by Millicent Garrett Fawcett. 1869. London: Oxford UP, 1912.

Pater, Walter. "Winckelmann," *The Renaissance: Studies in Art and Poetry,* Ed. Donald L. Hill. Berkeley: U of California, P. 1980.

Poovey, Mary. "Reading History in Literature: Speculation and Virtue in *Our Mutual Friend. Historical Criticism and the Challenge of Theory.* Ed. Janet Levarie Smarr. Urbana: U of Illinois P, 1993. 42–80.

——— *Uneven Developments: The Ideological Work of Gender in Mid-Victorian England.* Chicago: U of Chicago, P, 1988.

Schapiro, Barbara Ann. *Literature and the Relational Self.* New York: New York UP, 1994.

Scholes, Robert. *Protocols of Reading.* New Haven: Yale UP, 1989.

Sedgwick, Eve Kosofsky. *Between Men: English Literature and Male Homosocial Desire.* New York: Columbia UP, 1985.

Shelley, Percy Bysshe. *"A Defence of Poetry." The Complete Works.* Ed. Roger Ingpen and Walter E. Peck. 10 vols. Vol. VII, *Prose.* New York: Gordian Press, 1965. 109–40.

Weir, Allison. *Sacrificial Logics: Feminist Theory and the Critique of Identity.* New York: Routledge, 1996.

Winnicott, D. W. *Playing and Reality.* 1971. London: Routledge, 1991.

Doing the Police in Different Voices: The Search for Identity in Dust Heaps and Waste Lands

Keith Hale

Even before the recovery of T. S. Eliot's "lost" manuscripts identified his working title for sections of The Waste Land *as "He Do the Police in Different Voices, Parts I and II" (a reference to Sloppy found in* Our Mutual Friend*), two critics had noted similarities between the words. Edgar Johnson referred to* Our Mutual Friend *as "The Waste Land of Dickens's work," and Lionel Trilling wrote of similarities he and his students discovered. The most extensive comparison was undertaken in 1977 by Peter Lewis in the* Durham University Journal. *Lewis found a number of interesting parallels, but the most notable similarity of all—how the manner in which Dickens and Eliot address the question of identity makes* Our Mutual Friend *Dickens's most "modern" novel and* The Waste Land *Eliot's quintessential "modern" poem—went undiscussed.* Our Mutual Friend *is a modern text in both its central theme of maintaining one's identity amid modern disintegration and its focus on the narrative as a means of telling one's own story and thereby escaping the fate of having one's story told by others. The characters in* Our Mutual Friend *are forever asking, "Who am I?"—often not liking the reflected answers. Their lost identities, false identities, and mistaken identities form the crux of the novel.*

Even before the recovery of T. S. Eliot's "lost" manuscripts identified his working title for *The Waste Land* to be "He Do the Police in Different Voices,

---

Dickens Studies Annual, Volume 29, Copyright © 2000 by AMS Press, Inc. All rights reserved.

Parts I and II," two critics had noted similarities between *The Waste Land* and Dickens's *Our Mutual Friend.* Edgar Johnson, in volume two of the first edition of his *Charles Dickens: His Tragedy and Triumph* (1952), referred to *Our Mutual Friend* as "*The Waste Land* of Dickens's work" (Brattin and Hornback 73). Unfortunately, the pages were deleted from the revised and abridged edition published in 1977. In Lionel Trilling's 1956 *A Gathering of Fugitives,* Trilling reports asking a class to point out similarities between *Our Mutual Friend* and *The Waste Land.* The students noted that both works had in common

> the great oppressive images of London, and the dominating symbols of waste and decay, and the extreme representations of boredom and *taedium vitae,* and the scenes in lower-class bars, and the River Thames that cannot wash the city clean but becomes itself soiled and foul, and the deaths by water and the hope of rebirth, and the drowned sailors, and the bridges and the omnipresent financial transactions; and one student said that, as to the lost consignment of figs in *The Waste Land,* it was worthy of note that Mr. Podsnap was in the Marine Insurance business.   (42–43)

Once the Eliot manuscripts were discovered, Donald Gallup noted in the *Times Literary Supplement* (1968) that the original title of "The Burial of the Dead" and "A Game of Chess" was "He Do the Police in Different Voices, Parts I and II," respectively, but he failed to give *Our Mutual Friend* as the source (1238). However, Thomas and Brian Kelly identified *Our Mutual Friend* as the source and noted similarities between Eliot's Unreal City and Dickens's London, particularly the way in which the Thames "is dead in both Londons." The Kellys also claimed that both Sloppy and Tiresias were "interpreters of myth" (9 Jan. 1969:38). Their letter was followed by eight others in *TLS* debating the connection between the two works. Douglas Hewitt claimed that "The most likely interpretation . . . is surely that the rejected title was in the nature of a private joke," and might, therefore be "downright frivolous" (23 Jan. 1969:86). D. A. N. Jones more or less sided with the Kellys, noting that Eliot's use of London speech is not so very different from Dickens's and commenting on the way "both writers express their troubled feelings about sex, death, and money, the way they use Dust and Water as symbols" (30 Jan. 1969:110). Hewitt responded that he was

> appalled at the thought of all those forthcoming theses which will labour every parallel between the two works and misrepresent Dickens where he does not fit in with Eliot's vision. I did Sloppy less than justice; at least I didn't try to turn him into Tiresias.   (13 Feb. 1969:158)

Of course one could not argue that Sloppy is Tiresias, for Tiresias is merely one of Eliot's several ventriloquial voices in the poem. The Kellys responded that the " 'jocular' Douglas Hewitt has ceased to be funny" (6 Mar. 1969:242), but the last word (or, in any case, the last *TLS* was willing to print) went to Hewitt, who restated his contention: "We should not be in such a hurry to fit new evidence into old patterns" (20 Mar. 1969:229).

In 1977, Lyndall Gordon wrote that "He do the Police in Different Voices" refers "to the experimental method of *Our Mutual Friend*, Dickens's apparently disconnected anecdotes and panoramic reportings which gradually cohere as the hard manipulative tone of society (107). Gordon left it at that, but in the same year, what seems to be the most extensive comparison of the works was undertaken by Peter Lewis in the *Durham University Journal*. Lewis found a number of parallels, including "gloominess, disjunctive technique, symbols of sterility, river imagery, dehumanization, and an equation of life with death" (Brattin and Hornback 146). Other themes common to both books include mirrors, surfaces, reflections, "society," and identity.

It is this last item—the question of identity—that seems most important in both works. Too, it is the way in which Dickens and Eliot deal with this question that makes *Our Mutual Friend* Dickens's most "modern" novel and *The Waste Land* Eliot's quintessential "modern" poem.

However, the parallel between the two works regarding identity seems to have gone undisclosed. Perhaps Hewitt's foreboding made further comparison of the works unappealing to many. But a comparison can certainly be made without misrepresenting Dickens "where he does not fit in with Eliot's version," as Hewitt feared.

We know, in any case, that Eliot read Dickens. In a letter to his mother, 6 February 1918, he wrote of an upcoming teaching assignment: "I am looking forward to lecturing on Dickens" (*Letters* 219). We also know that Eliot had *Our Mutual Friend* in mind not only as he penned section headings for *The Waste Land,* but also as he wrote *Practical Cats*, which drew off Podsnap (*Facsimile* 125).

As Robert Newsom has noted:

> No novel of Dickens has so impressed and perplexed twentieth-century readers with its appositeness to our own sense of the difficulty and unsatisfactoriness of existence and in particular with the difficulty of maintaining an existence that is not hollow or inauthentic [as *Our Mutual Friend*].　　　(39)

Whether hollow or solid, authentic or false, the characters in *Our Mutual Friend* seems forever to be asking, "Who are we?"—often not liking the reflected answer. Their lost identities, false identities, and mistaken identities form the crux of the novel from the outset. Likewise, the importance of identity in *The Waste Land* is seen in Calvin Bedient's summary of a passage in Julia Kristeva's *Powers of Horror:* "Eliot's protagonist negotiates a passage from unbearable identity to the unapprehensible" (51).

The theme of identity is first established in both *Our Mutual Friend* and *The Waste Land* as if identity is little more than a parlor trick; that is, in both instances, the author makes use of mirrors. In *The Waste Land,* everything on which the narrator's eyes fall

> is bewilderingly referred, or refers itself, to something outside its own physical confines. Begging attention from other things, it seeks reflection, but the maddening quality of reflection is to give itself up again, in an elusive, unreal bid for conclusion.   (Bedient 88)

These reflections, only hinted at in part one, "The Burial of the Dead," come to the surface in part two, "A Game of Chess," in which the Chair is "displaced by its own reflection," and in which "the flames only appear to be in the glass; at the same time, as the doubles of real flames, they are in some sense a real if fugitive part of the mirror" (Bedient 88–89). The candelabras reflect light upon the table. Jewels, ivory, and colored glass reflect—"objects flatter and prolong one another (reflecting mirrors do so, and shiny table tops, and jewels, and flame-feeding odors)" (91).

The importance of the mirror imagery in *The Waste Land* was obvious to early critics. Conrad Aiken wrote, "We are invited into a mind, a world, which is a 'broken bundle of mirrors,' a 'heap of broken images' " (17). Harriet Monroe said the poem "gives us the malaise of our time, its agony, its conviction of futility, its wild dance on an ash heap before a clouded and distorted mirror" (20).

Mirrors and reflections have a great deal to do with the question of identity in *Our Mutual Friend,* as well. Chapter one opens with an air of mystery, the action reflected in the waters of the Thames. Characters' identities in this chapter are sketched out over many paragraphs—if they're completed at all. Just as Tiresias is not named until part three of *The Waste Land,* Riderhood isn't given a name until the fourth chapter of *Our Mutual Friend.*

The second chapter is quite the opposite, with characters immediately identified as they are reflected by the Veneering's mirror. After the Veneerings are introduced as "bran-new People in a bran-new house in a bran-new quarter of London," their guests are, in fact, introduced by the word *reflects.* This is consistent with the existences they lead, for they are shallow people representing a hollow and inauthentic society. These people have no pasts. There is no reason to surround them with mystery for there is nothing really there. While all manner of objects below the surface of the Thames and the characters of the first chapter, the characters in the Veneering social circle are only surface, with no depth.

Reflections also play a part in the way most characters in the novel view themselves. The Lammles, for instance, act one way in front of the mirror and another way when they can't see their reflections. Because one and all seem in search of identity, they search each other for clues or affirmation. As John Robson put it,

> In the absence of inner definition, all fall back on their reflections in the eyes of others, and vanity ensures that 'respectability' will make the largest claims. And in a world floated on evanescent dreams, the search for defining buoyancy is inevitably without end. (211–12)

Dickens uses many devices that obfuscate the identities of his characters. One such device is the use of multiple names and nicknames. Dickens as narrator is usually left out of these identifications, however, as the nicknames are supplied by his characters for themselves and for each other. John Harmon is called at least fifteen different names. Often, the nicknames given characters border on the fantastical. Jenny calls Riah "godmother" and insists that he was brought up by the fairies. These obfuscations seem to be a means of showing that identity is not entirely uniform or homogeneous—except when it is fully externalized. Indeed, the exceptions to these multiple-named characters are the Veneerings' and Podsnaps' social circle. These characters are more or less interchangeable with their paper cards, and often with each other; thus, multiple names for them would be defeating the purpose of their singular existences.

In *The Waste Land,* Eliot, too, uses various identities and voices to complicate the protagonist's self-portrait, which "is scribbled over with multiple fugitive disguises" (Bedient 59). "Sometimes the identity of a 'speaker' changes in the middle of a sentence, with some overlap, so that part of it could be spoken by either one of two people" (Harvey 2).

In *The Waste Land,* too, cards are used to identify. The fortune-teller draws cards from the Tarot. Bedient says the Tarot cards "drape identity on a hook of circumstance" (54): "Eliot introduces through Madame Sosostris's card language a sort of allegorical kit, an unassembled allegory of the protagonist's future story. If the cards fortell his life, it is in a choked, nonnarrational manner" (59).

Another question of identity arises in *Our Mutual Friend* because of Dickens's frequent references to his characters as objects. Twemlow is introduced as a piece of dinner furniture that can be expanded to fit any occasion. Silas Wegg puts forth the question, not "Who am I?" but "Where am I?" in Venus's shop, with the answer being that he is partially (in the form of his amputated leg) in the back of the shop. Mr. Boffin thinks Rokesmith's desire to be his secretary means the young man has some inclination to be "a piece of furniture, mostly of mahogany, linted with green baize or leather, with a lot of little drawers in it" (I, 15). Eugene Wrayburn is initially described as "buried alive in the back of his chair"—not exactly an object, merely embed-ded in one—then later referred to as "the wretched object" (III, 10). Rid-erhood is called, ironically, "the piece of honesty" (II, 12), and later, when he is nearly drowned, "this flabby lump" which "yields no sign of you" (III, 3). Sloppy, too, is called a "piece of honesty," but Dickens apparently is sincere in this case, for the one chance Sloppy has to be deceitful—when Mrs. Boffin inquires after Johnny's health—he cannot bring himself to lie. Mrs. Wilfer is "like a frozen article on sale in a Russian market" (III, 16). Her daughter Lavinia is stared at "as if she was a clock" (III, 16). Mr. Beneering becomes "mere vacant space" (III, 17) at his own dinner table. The Podsnaps' footman is, of course, an object—a six-foot-one "article" (II, 4).

This habit of referring to characters as objects is particularly evident when characters are dead or near death. Then, there is also a confusion of person. Jenny Wren's father becomes an "it" (IV, 9). For Harmon, narrating his near-drowning, the question of which person to use plays an important part in his finally coming to terms with himself. He describes the event in third-person until a critical moment when he realizes "I cannot possibly express it to myself without using the word I. But it was not I. There was no such thing as I, within my knowledge" (II, 13). While the old Harmon is passive, his new-found "I" tried to gain control of the situation. Having found his true nature, he later walks the streets of London "piling mounds of earth over John Harmon's grave" (II, 13). While this passage refers more to his wanting to protect the Boffins than his desire to dispense with his old self, another line in the same chapter obviously refers to his desire no longer to be the passive victim: "The late John Harmon . . . would probably have remained silent."

Identity is also blurred when people are referred to in the third person, as when Eugene's belligerence forces Charley to address him in the third person, or when Jenny Wren humbly refers to herself as "the third party." Interest-ingly, whereas Harmon switches from the third person to the first when he unravels his identity, Wrayburn becomes an "it" when he finds him.

That the name of Wrayburn should so often crop up in these passages concerning people as objects or third person references is no coincidence, for Wrayburn above all characters is a man in search of identity, as he readily and repeatedly admits. Eugene recites the nursery rhyme, "Riddle-me, riddle-me-ree, perhaps you can't tell me what this may be?" while tapping on his chest, then answers, "No, upon my life I can't. I give it up!" He confesses, "I know less about myself" than anyone he might meet, for "I bored myself to the last degree by trying to find out what I meant" (II, 6).

Identity is hard to establish, of course, when characters keep disappearing. Harmon disappears in a rather literal sense, although he did not really disap-pear at all. But in describing the embracing of John and Bella, Dickens has

Bella "disappearing" several times and John "disappearing" once in some other sense, one that seems to reflect the approaching change in their identities.

More identity confusion occurs when Dickens has his characters switch roles. Jenny calls her father her "child," and refers to herself as "the person of the house." Lizzie Hexam and Pleasant Riderhood also seem more the protectors than the protected in their relationships with their fathers, although in each case the daughter suffers at the hands of the father: Pleasant is physically beaten; Lizzie is prevented from acquiring an education. There is also Dickens's habit of giving his characters sarcastic descriptions, such as referring to Riderhood as "the piece of honesty" and "the honest man" (the latter a description used by both the narrator and Riderhood himself).

In *The Waste Land*, "the human engine waits / Like a taxi," and the protagonist's wife "is not so much displaced by her possessions as expressed by them" (Bedient 87). Bedient says

> the original working title, "He Do the Police in Different Voices," implies the presence of a single speaker in the poem who is gifted at "taking off" the voices of others . . . [and] an all-centering, autobiographical protagonist-narrator . . . explains the confident surfacing . . . of an unmistakable religious pilgrim. Unless this pilgrim can be shown to develop . . . out of a waste land that is, or was, himself, the poem splits apart into two unequal sections, a long one constituted by what Lyndall Gordon calls "the Voices of Society" and a shorter one on a lone pilgrim to elsewhere. (73)

Eliot's voices change to other voices, but no one really "disappears" in *The Waste Land*. Even Phlebas is on his way back to life.

Some of Dickens's devices for establishing or re-establishing identities are hard to classify. For instance, as Bradley Headstone's identity changes from semi-respectable schoolmaster to tormented wreck, Dickens describes the door of Eugene's office closing behind Headstone "like a furnace-door." One might think he has entered hell, as indeed he has; the pursuit of Lizzy and then of Eugene will be his torment and damnation.

Another problem of identity is pointed out by Lawrence Frank, who notes that when Silas Wegg says, "I shouldn't like . . . to be what I may call dispersed, a part of me here, a part of me there" that he has indicated a problem for all the novel's city-dwellers, that "the dispersal of the self seems the inevitable fate for the inhabitants of London" (167). While Wegg and other characters try to find the pieces of their lives, Betty Higden tries to keep herself whole. In the end, however, she must leave London in order to keep faith with herself. Living in the city plays an important part in identities, especially for the members of Society, for their society is in decline and fall. Dickens accentuated the decline and fall by having Wegg read to the Boffins

Gibbon's *Decline and Fall of the Roman Empire*. (It is worth noting that in a line of *The Waste Land* cancelled by Ezra Pound, the woman in "The Fire Sermon" "explores a page of Gibbon as she eats"—see *Facsimile* 22–23).

The characters of *Our Mutual Friend*, in making the pursuit of money their foremost concern, find themselves living "in the barren landscape of the urban desert," observes Frank (159). The city itself represents corruption. When Betty Higden leaves London, she is said to be walking "away from paralysis and pauperism," because she, at least, knows who she is and knows what she is trying to escape. Others, like Wegg, stepping from among the dead things in Venus's shop into the streets of London, "a world dying or already dead," remain in the city unable to withstand its corrupting influence. The ability to withstand corruption becomes a litmus test of identity. Wilfred Dvorak put it like this:

> In *Our Mutual Friend*, Dickens depicts human beings as emerging from the primordial slime, with some, like the Boffins, young Harmon, Bella Wilfer, Eugene Wrayburn, and Lizzie Hexam, finally learning to work together to build a civilized moral community, while others, like Fledgeby, the Podsnaps, the Veneerings, Bradley Headstone, Charlie Hexam, Rogue Riderhood, and Wegg, continue to thrash about in the dismal swamp of avarice.   (128)

In *The Waste Land*, remarks Robert Crawford, "The 'city' is not simply London with its metropolitan sophisticate and its City financial district, but also the drab urban landscape which Eliot annexed as his poetic territory from his first book onwards" (3). It is interesting that although Crawford noted that "Eliot in 1932 wrote that 'some of Dickens' novels stand for London,' " he believed that "essentially [*The Waste Land*'s] city owes more to Kipling and Victorian poetry [than to Dickens]" (3). Crawford points to Eliot's influences—ranging from Dante, Baudelaire, and James Thomson's *The City of Dreadful Night*—but fails to mention *Our Mutual Friend* (39–60). It is a curious omission, for the city is described similarly in both works and acts as the same type of symbol: a corrupting force that creates a multiplicity of false identities.

Gordon writes, "All the violent fragments written during Eliot's early years in London . . . foretell the need, eventually realized at the end of *The Waste Land*, to declare civilization 'unreal' and so escape" (100). The *Waste Land* pilgrim "acts rationally—before he escapes he accumulates evidence against civilization and makes his categoric judgement: 'Unreal' " (Gordon, 109).

Inauthentic existences producing false identities come into play in *Our Mutual Friend* particularly with the Veneering and Podsnap circles, as one might expect. These characters create facades of identity, every one a lie. The Lammles are neither happily married nor wealthy. The house they talk of building is only a pipe dream, a cover for their poverty. Lady Tippins invents lovers. The Veneerings and Podsnaps pretend they are the oldest of friends. Most telling of all, people in society scurry about the streets of London in cabs, going nowhere. No wonder then, that they refer to Harmon as the "Man from Somewhere." If Dickens's decision to have Wegg read Gibbon's *Decline and Fall of the Roman Empire* to the illustrious Mr. Boffin lends stress to the idea of a London society in decline and fall, then the upper crust of London society would appear to have declined and fallen into near imbecility. The characters gathered around the Veneerings' table and the Podsnaps' parlor are laughable in their pettiness, but they are also tragic—for their corruption, greed, and selfishness have turned their lives into farce—and, for the most part, deplorable—for they are enjoying (if that is the word for it) their positions at the expense of others who suffer greatly.

The theme of greed is represented in *Our Mutual Friend* by dust. Dust is money. Or rather, dust is garbage is dung is money, for scavengers search through garbage collecting "night-soil," and chamber-pot contents are put into vats and turned into fertilizer (thus, the equation is not merely symbolic). It is a society obsessed with dust that Dickens indicts. Money in another form is worshipped as Shares—"the one thing to have to do with in this world" (I, 10). It is the pursuit of money in either form that leads Dickens to describe London as "unpromising enough . . . the newly-stopped whirling and grinding on the part of the money-mills seemed to linger in the air, and the quiet was more like the prostration of a spent giant than the repose of one who was renewing his strength" (III, 16).

It is, in any case, a London in which Mr. Veneering can buy a seat in the House of Commons ("the best club in London," Twemlow calls it) without ever seeing the constituents of Pocket-Breaches.

"Society" in *The Waste Land* is portrayed in much the same way. After the transition to the Starnbergersee "we are among a group, seemingly representing the 'best' society of modern Europe, and listening to their vapid conversation" (Harvey 9). These people are wealthy, leisured, and snobbish. C. J. D. Harvey says the passage is about Countess Marie Larisch: "It is clear that her life had appalled [Eliot] by its pettiness, its emptiness and its faded pretentiousness and came to represent the ashes and dust of a once vigorous aristocrat civilization" (10). It is interesting that Harvey uses "ashes to dust" to describe the decayed aristocracy. He notes that the next "abrupt transition" in the poem deals with stony rubbish, representing much the same thing: "The stony rubbish, dry and sterile, is, of course, the society represented by Marie and her friends' (11). It could be argued, as well, given Eliot's increasing conservatism, that he saw in the decayed aristocracy a betrayal of aristocratic function in stabilizing society. It is likely that in Eliot's view Marie Larisch had abdicated her social and political function and had only snobbery and memories remaining.

In *Our Mutual Friend,* the search for "defining bouyancy," the desire to stay afloat, plays a role in the quest for identity, as well. Some characters—the Lammles, the Veneerings, Silas Wegg, Rogue Riderhood, and others—try to stay afloat by using others, but their schemes inevitably fail. Other characters—Lizzie Hexam, Eugene Wrayburn, John Harmon, and the Boffins, to name five—forget themselves in attempts to keep others afloat but are themselves made the better for it. Lizzie and Eugene act selflessly to protect each other and end up getting what they want—each other. Mr. Boffin renounces the Harmon property twice—first when he buries the Dutch bottle with the latest will, then when he reveals it only if John agrees to take the property—and comes through it all a happy man. John Harmon is willing to renounce his inheritance to keep the Boffins happy, but he gets his due in the end. This sense of justice is, of course, not a very modern idea. It is probably one of the things Hewitt had in mind when he feared that trying to find parallels between *Our Mutual Friend* and *The Waste Land* would lead to the misrepresentation of Dickens.

Chapter two of *Our Mutual Friend* shows us the Veneering circle creating a death-in-life. In a corrupt city where living is death-in-life, the ability to escape through fantasy becomes life-in-death. Thus, Jenny, free and alive with her rooftop fantasies, describes the sensation as feeling "as if you were dead." She fancies Riah as "called back to life," tells Fledgeby to, "Get down to life," and beckons Riah to "Come back and be dead" (II, 5). In her delightful death, Jenny smells flowers when there are no flowers and sees children playing in dresses she could never imitate, dolls' dress-maker that she is. Her imagination is shown to be important in forming her own identity, but the message seems to be either that life or reality can be glimpsed only through imagination, or that reality, and art, can never measure up—that imagination is purer than life. In Jenny's world of fantasy, truth is even represented by a doll (II, 11).

Jenny's theme is particularly striking when she says from the rooftop of St. Mary Axe: "You can see the clouds rushing on above the narrow streets, not minding [the people below], and you can see the golden arrows pointing at the mountains in the sky from which the wind comes, and you feel as if you were dead" (II, 5). How does it feel to be dead? "Oh, so peaceful and so thankful! And you hear the people who are alive . . . down in the close dark streets, and you seem to pity them so!" Clearly, if living has become death for this child, death represents resurrection.

Just as, for Jenny, the invitation to come up and enter a purer world of fantasy is to "come up and be dead," to Fledgeby, the desire to make money is "coming out and looking alive" (IV, 8). This contrast is even more striking than that between Jenny's invitation and the melancholy retainer's imagined biddance to "Come down and be poisoned, ye unhappy children of men" (I, 2).

Life-in-death, and death-in-life, is clearly a central theme of *The Waste Land*. Bedient says that, contrary to what the fortune teller instructs, "the death the protagonist should fear is the one he dully takes part in as he flows with the crowd through the City" (68). Harvey says the line "I will show you fear in a handful of dust" reflects a fear of returning to dust "and fear of being more than that, too, perhaps—fear of being truly alive" (12). Brooks says, "Life devoid of meaning is death; sacrifice, even the sacrificial death, may be life-giving, an awakening to life" (38) and points out that "The first section of 'The Burial of the Dead' develops the theme of the attractiveness of death, or of the difficulty in rousing oneself from the death in life in which the people of the waste land live . . . Men dislike to be roused from their death-in-life" (39). This theme of "the life which is death is stated specifically in the conversation between the man and the woman. She asks the question, 'Are you alive, or not?' " (47).

In both works, the life-in-death motif is linked with themes of drowning and resurrection—and all three are explored with images of fishing and the Thames. Calvin Bedient, among others, has noted the comparison of the naked bodies from drowning in *The Waste Land* and the "corpse-haunted Thames of Dickens's *Our Mutual Friend*" (117). In the opening chapter of *Our Mutual Friend*, Lizzie Hexam is with her father "fishing-for-men" upon the Thames. Lizzie hates the evil (death, murder) of the river but is drawn to it nonetheless. The river furnishes her with a living, she uses its driftwood, for fire, and as a baby she slept in a basket that it washed ashore. The sixth chapter of the first book finds her on the bank of the Thames "unable to see into the vast blank misery of a life suspected." She feels, whatever her future, it is tied to the river. That she should look into it for a clue to her very life comes as no surprise, even when it is "stretching away to the great ocean, Death." Later, when Charley wants to remove her from her dwelling by the river, she tells him she cannot turn her back on it (when he is so cruel as to disown her for not following his dictates, even her heart is described as a "breaking up of waters" (II, 15]). When Lizzie is removed to the country, she lives and works beside the Thames. In the end, although the river nearly kills the man she loves, it gives her a new life as his rescuer. Lizzie and Eugene are married as the river outside flows on to the ocean. Death? Well, Lizzie Hexam is dead, and Eugene the Perpetually Bored is dead. The river has played a part in giving them new identities.

The river takes its place in establishing the identities of other characters, as well. Of particular importance is the idea of baptism and resurrection, as character after character is submerged in the depths of the Thames, then retrieved (the idea of being "baptized unto Death" is a corruption of Romans 6:3–5, "We are buried with Christ by baptism into death"). Gaffer Hexam makes his living fishing bodies from the Thames (life in death). Harmon is believed to be drowned, but drowns his identity instead, coming back to life as a new man with a new name. Radfoot, Gaffer, Rogue Riderhood, and Bradley Headstone are all drowned and retrieved. Prior to his final encounter with the river, Riderhood is run over by a river steamer then resuscitated. Prior to *his* final encounter, Bradley Headstone throws his identity—in the form of his clothes—into the river, but the items are retrieved by Riderhood. Other references to the theme of resurrection include Mr. Boffin's Christian name, which is, indeed, a Christian name; Nicodemus, in John 3:1–6, is a Jewish ruler with whom Jesus discusses being "born again": "Except a man be born of water and of the Spirit he cannot enter the kingdom of God" (Cotsell finds sixty biblical references in *Our Mutual Friend.* Bedient notes several in *The Waste Land,* as well, including allusions to Psalms 63, Jeremiah 2:13, John 3:5, and John 4:14). That the reference refers not only to rebirth, but rebirth through water, makes it unlikely Dickens chose the name by accident. Likewise, Charley Hexam's describing the supposed Harmon body as Lazarus is hardly haphazard, for Harmon, like Lazarus, will return to life.

Other identity-forming events pertaining to the river include John and Bella floating downstream to Greenwich to be married, Betty Higden taking "the upward course of the river Thames" to escape London and start a new life (brief though it is), the river whispering "come to me" when Betty is near death, Betty (again) being buried in a churchyard near the river, Bella and Lightwood crossing the river on a train in a passage that seems to relate both the river and the train to Father Time and eternity (IV, 11), and Bella reflectively looking into the Thames outside of London. This last passage goes back to the theme of reflections, contrasting the river to man-made mirrors:

> Perhaps the old mirror was never yet made by human hands, which, if all the images it has in its time reflected could pass across its surface again, would fail to reveal some scene of horror or distress. But the great serene mirror of the river seemed as if it might have reproduced all it had ever reflected between those placid banks, and brought nothing to the light save what was peaceful, pastoral, and blooming.   (III, 9)

This is important, for the river serves to illustrate the opposite worlds of city and country. While the city is steeped in corruption, the upper reaches of the Thames are described in pastoral terms. At one point, Dickens even compares the "young river" upstream from London to a young child "unpolluted by the defilements that lie in wait for it on its course" (III, 8).

Annabel Patterson has pointed out several similarities between *Our Mutual Friend* and Isaak Walton's *Compleat Angler.* In doing so, Patterson describes the deeper theme of the "pastoral epic" being one of "fishing-for-men." In *Our Mutual Friend,* of course, we have several characters literally fishing for men, beginning with Gaffer Hexam in chapter one. However, as Patterson says, "Their activity is the darkest antithesis possible to the true act of fishing-for-men in its scriptural sense and in the sense of Walton's 'Anglers Song' "

(258). The scriptural reference, of course, is Matthew 4:19 (also Mark 1:17), in which Christ says, "Follow me, and I will make you fishers of men." Patterson also notes that in the world of Podsnap, fishing-for-men means fishing for wealthy associates.

In summary, then, the role of the river in this question of identity takes several forms: as establishing the contrast between the pastoral countryside and the corrupt city, as the element in which characters become "fishers-of-men," as the element of baptism and resurrection, as a common thread running through the characters' lives, as an element of Time in which characters can lose their pasts and gain new futures, as a mirror, as an element to illustrate surfaces and what may or may not lurk below them, and as a source of life itself. Related to this water theme, we find the "children of Podsnappery" made to skate on ice—frozen water—while performing their ridiculous social rites, or "ice-exercises" (II, 8).

In *The Waste Land*, these fishing, drowning, and resurrection motifs begin with the Fisher King of the Grail legend. According to Brooks, "The castle of the Fisher King was always located on the banks of a river or on the sea shore. The title 'Fisher King,' Miss [Jessie L.] Weston shows, originates from the use of the fish as a fertility or life symbol" (50). In the legend, the Fisher King and his kingdom are both infertile, and the land the Fisher King rules over "has become a Waste Land" (Harvey 4). Thus, says Gilbert Seldes, *The Waste Land* tells us "that life has become barren and sterile, that man is withering, impotent, and without assurance that the waters which made the land fruitful will ever rise again" (9). It is into this setting, in the third party of *The Waste Land* amid the Unreal City, that "the Fisher King appears fishing in the first person behind the gashouse" (Lucas 30). Bedient says, "The protagonist fishes in himself and shortly brings up, among others, Spenser" (113) and that, given the Fisher King in the Grail legend, "it seems reasonable, then, to assume that fishing in Eliot's poem figures a hunger for the Mystic Meal, for proof of purity" (117). Gordon shares a similar opinion, saying, "Eliot thinks of the fisherman as a concentrated will confronting the sea, 'something inhuman, clean and dignified' " (112). "Fishing," according to Bedient, "proves an optimal closural image in its fusion of quietness with quest" (210). He maintains that Eliot's calling the London women "nympha" implies that they have not only abandoned the river banks but abandoned pastoral innocence—"they were seduced by the antipastoral heirs of city directors. They are after mythology and the pastoral" (111). This interpretation calls to mind Annabel Patterson's belief that the "fishing-for-men" motif of *Our Mutual Friend* reflects the essence of the pastoral tradition. As in the novel, the protagonist of the poem "abandons the city" and "moves out of 'unreal' or dead history into a bracing atmosphere of stirring grass and gusts of wind" (Gordon 113).

As in *Our Mutual Friend,* water holds the key to resurrection in *The Waste Land.* Harvey says drowning is used in the poem as a symbol of letting go, "a dissolution of the old self leading, perhaps, to a transformation 'into something rich and strange.' " He notes that

> The Phoenicians were great merchant-sailors to whom drowning was the greatest occupational hazard, but reference to *The Golden Bough* reminds us that it was also among them that an image of Adonis was thrown into the sea every year to symbolise the death of summer and ensure resurrection in the spring.
> (14)

In "Death of Water," Phlebas, "clearly a merchant sailor," is identified with the drowned Phoenician sailor of the Tarot pack. Harvey says that since the fortune teller told "the protagonist that this was *his* card (line 47) it confirms that he is, indeed, the prototypal Waste Lander for whom 'death by water' is the only 'solution.' " Harvey also points out that the Phoenicians were famous throughout the ancient world not only for their seamanship but also "for their feverish desire for commercial gain—'profit' " (37). The dust heaps, of course, symbolize profit in *Our Mutual Friend.* Consider, then, the threat in *The Waste Land*'s "I will show you fear in a handful of dust," and Phillip Collins's statement in his *Dickens and Crime* that " 'Fear death by water' might be the epigraph of *Our Mutual Friend*" (Jones, 185). It is dust as profit that should be feared, not water as resurrection. Brooks says the fortune teller warns the protagonist "against death by water, not realizing any more than did the other inhabitants of the modern waste land that the way into life may be by death itself" (43). The protagonist of *The Waste Land,* anxious about the corpse in the garden, wonders, "What is the good of rising, and sinking, and rising again . . . in a mad, libidinous, profitless cycle" (Bedient 66). It might not be far off the mark to suggest that as long as his interest is in "profit," he likely will miss the chance for life-in-death. Harvey says the inhabitants of the Waste Land "do not want to live and yet they will not die and 'let go' of their individual identities, the only things they can attach value to" (7). Dying and being reborn "to a fuller more intense life" are what the people fear most and seek to avoid (8).

Gordon says

> The drowning at the end of "Death by Water" reinforces the authority of the dream even while it falls short of enlightenment. For the death that follows a life of honest endeavour is not conceived as a disaster but as a stage of purification and metamorphosis.
> (112)

To partake, he must surrender, for "Death by Water" is "a symbol of surrender and relief through surrender" (Brooks 55), and the "Full Fathom Five" song is "used as a vision of life gained through death" (58).

Unpublished sections of *The Waste Land* strengthen the water motif. One section does it partially through the words of Christ, which also reflect the resurrection theme: "I am the Resurrection and the Life / I am the things that stay, and those that flow" (*Facsimile* 110–11). Another deals with surfaces: "Like a blind man swimming deep below the surface / Knowing neither up nor down, swims down and down / In the calm deep water where no stir nor surface" (*Facsimile* 114–15).

But is drowning, or near-drowning, really the answer? It could be argued that in *Our Mutual Friend* Harmon's near drowning gave him a new identity, but not self-knowledge. In assuming the identity of Rokesmith, Harmon frees himself from the baggage of his family name and his role as victim—having his life plotted for him even from beyond the grave—by taking on an identity closer to his true self. But Harmon does not truly discover who he is until he describes the event to himself. It is during the act of narrating his near-death that he comes to realize who "I" is. Dickens has presented John Harmon's life as a fiction within a fiction, representing the lies that surround all our lives and make the tombstones want to tilt "ashamed of the lies they told" (II, 15). But here Dickens has provided a tool for establishing one's identity: telling one's own story.

A second example of telling one's own story can be found in Blight the clerk, who seems to illustrate in a nutshell the pervasiveness of the identity problem. Given only two paragraphs in the nine-hundred-page novel, Blight nevertheless establishes an identity for himself simply by insisting he have one. As Blight makes a show of staffing a busy office, Mr. Boffin observes, "strict system here, eh, my lad?" Blight replies, "I couldn't get on without it," to which the narrator supposes, "By which he probably meant that his mind would have been shattered to pieces without this fiction of an occupation." Robert Kiely says that author, reader, and every character are implicated by this passage because of "the universally shared dread of no story at all. If individuals do not provide their own version of things, they risk being left out of the design altogether or being pawns in other people's plots" (283).

Although fragmentation and dispersal can seemingly destroy one's identity, it should also be noted that some characters use these very tools to find an identity that assumes a wholeness. While it is true that the Veneerings, through their calling cards, endlessly repeat themselves and sow themselves in the fields of fashionable dining and drawing rooms, it seems equally true that only those characters who come to see themselves as riven in some way also find themselves. There is Harmon, of course, but also the broken and disfigured Wrayburn and, more comically, the benevolent pretended miser Boffin. It is as if the breaking up of identities is a necessary first step in being reborn. It may be that the multiplicity of human life must face itself through the controlled social surface in order for characters to confront themselves in ways that allow them to tell their own stories. When not telling their stories, they are using stories to find out what the stories leave untold. That is, they live lives with their eyes slightly aslant, like Jenny Wren's, to see what can only be seen if they know, unlike Wegg and Headstone, that stories open onto truths that the stories shape but can never tell.

This emphasis on the narration itself would have appealed to Eliot, one would think. Certainly, the narration of *The Waste Land* calls attention to itself as being one of the more important elements of the poem.

If Eliot had *Our Mutual Friend* in mind as he wrote *The Waste Land*, it seemingly would make ironic Cooper's statement that the poem "is designed to knock out of our heads and hearts the moral and spiritual ruins of a decayed and corrupted inwardness inherited from the Victorians" (3). Or, maybe not. It can be argued that *Our Mutual Friend* has as much, or more, in common with the "moderns" than with the Victorians of its time. Banerjee points to a pre-war trend in English poetry "towards dealing with suffering, violence and a general sense of disintegration in modern life. This was the trend which, having been established by the war poets, became the central preoccupation of poets like Pound, Yeats, and Eliot, who immersed themselves in the "destructive element" (15). This disintegration of identity in London society was clearly on Dickens's mind when he wrote *Our Mutual Friend,* as well.

Of greater difficulty, however, is Eliot's clearly anti-humanist view of the world when he wrote the poem. Cooper says that, "In the period of *The Waste Land* Eliot consistently characterized people from the lower classes and other marginalized groups either as subhumans or nonhumans" (30). Cooper says, "As Eliot always insisted, *The Waste Land* was not simply an attempt to mirror post-Great War European society . . . it was his attempt to knock liberal-humanist sentimentality and weakness . . . right out of his readers' heads" (48).

Our Mutual Friend is, if nothing else, a humanist work, and it would provide a curious and unwilling model for anyone who "marginalized" the lower classes. But it is also a very "modern" test in both its central theme of maintaining one's identity amid modern disintegration and its focus on the narrative as a means of telling one's story and escaping the fate of having one's story told by others. The similarities between *Our Mutual Friend* and *The Waste Land*, especially concerning the question of identity, make it likely that Eliot's use of "He Do the Police in Different Voices" as a working title for the first two sections of *The Waste Land* was something more than "downright frivolous."

WORKS CONSULTED

Ackroyd, Peter. *T. S. Eliot: A Life.* New York: Simon, 1984.

Aiken, Conrad. "An Anatomy of Melancholy." Gunter 13–18.

Banerjee, A. *Spirit Above Wars: A Study of the English Poetry of the Two World Wars.* New Delhi: Macmillan, 1976.

Bedient, Calvin. *He Do the Police in Different Voices:* The Waste Land *and Its Protagonist.* Chicago: U. of Chicago P, 1986.

Bergonzi, Bernard. *Heroes' Twilight: A Study of the Literature of the Great War.* London: Constable, 1965.

Brattin, Joel J. "Dickens' Creation of Bradley Headstone." *Dickens Studies Annual: Essays on Victorian Fiction* 14 (1985): 147–65.

———— and Bert G. Hornback. *Our Mutual Friend: An Annotated Bibliography.* New York: Garland, 1984.

Brooker, Jewel Spears, and Joseph Bentley. *Reading* The Waste Land: *Modernism and the Limits of Interpretation.* Amherst: U. of Massachusetts, P, 1990.

Brooks, Cleanth. "*The Waste Land:* Critique of the Myth." Gunter 37–66.

Canary, Robert H. *T. S. Eliot: The Poet and His Critics.* Chicago: ALA, 1982.

Carey, John. *The Violent Effigy: A Study of Dickens' Imagination.* London: Faber, 1973.

Cooper, John Xiros, *T. S. Eliot and the Politics of Voice: The Argument of* The Waste Land. Ann Arbor: UMI Research P, 1987.

Costell, Michael. "The Book of Insolvent Fates: Financial Speculation in *Our Mutual Friend.*" *Dickens Studies Annual: Essays on Victorian Fiction* 13 (1984):125–42.

————.*The Companion to* Our Mutual Friend. London: Allen, 1986.

Crawford, Robert. *The Savage and the City in the Work of T. S. Eliot.* Oxford: Clarendon, 1987.

Davis, Earle. "Dickens and Significant Tradition." *Dickens Studies Annual* 7 (1978): 49–67.

Dickens, Charles. *Our Mutual Friend.* New York: Scribner's, 1926.

Dunn, Richard J. "Far, Far Better Things: Dickens' Later Endings." *Dickens Studies Annual* 7 (1978): 221–36.

Dvorak, Wilfred P. Charles Dickens' *Our Mutual Friend* and Frederick Somner Merryweather's *Lives and Anecdotes of Misers.*" *Dickens Studies Annual: Essays on Victorian Fiction* 9 (1981): 117–41.

Eliot, T. S. *The Letters of T. S. Eliot.* Ed. Valerie Eliot. Vol. 1:1898–1922. San Diego: Harcourt, 1988.

————.*The Waste Land: A Facsimile and Transcript of the Original Drafts Including the Annotations of Ezra Pound.* Ed. Valerie Eliot. New York: Harcourt, 1971.

Frank, Lawrence. "The Intelligibility of Madness in *Our Mutual Friend* and *The Mystery of Edwin Drood.*" *Dickens Studies Annual* 5 (1976): 150–95.

Fussell, Paul. *The Great War and Modern Memory.* New York: Oxford UP, 1975.

Gallup, Donald. "The 'Lost' Manuscripts of T. S. Eliot." *Times Literary Supplement* 7 Nov. 1968: 1238–40.

Ganz, Margaret. "The Vulnerable Ego: Dickens' Humor in Decline." *Dickens Studies Annual* 1 (1970): 23–40.

Gomme, A. H. *Dickens.* London: Evans, 1971.

Gordon, Lyndall. *Eliot's Early Years.* Oxford: Oxford UP, 1977.

Gunter, Bradley, Comp. *The Merrill Studies in* The Waste Land. Columbus, OH: Merrill, 1971.

Harvey, C. J. D. *A Complete Guide to T. S. Eliot's* The Waste Land. Cape Town: Juta, 1978.

Hewitt, Douglas. "He Do the Police in Different Voices." Reply to letter of Thomas and Brian Kelly. *Times Literary Supplement* 9 Jan. 1969:38.

——.Reply to letter of D. A. N. Jones. *Times Literary Supplement* 13 Feb. 1969:158.

——.Reply to Thomas and Brian Kelly. *Times Literary Supplement* 20 Mar. 1969:299.

Hutter, Albert D. "Dismemberment and Articulation in *Our Mutual Friend.*" *Dickens Studies Annual: Essays on Victorian Fiction* 11 (1983): 135–75.

Hynes, Samuel. *A War Imagined: The First World War and English Culture.* New York: Atheneum, 1991.

Johnson, Edgar. "The Art of Biography: An Interview with Edgar Johnson." *Dickens Studies Annual: Essays on Victorian Fiction* (1980): 1–38.

Jones, D. A. N. "He Do the Police in Different Voices." Reply to letter of Douglas Hewitt. *Times Literary Supplement* 30 Jan. 1969:110.

——.*Times Literary Supplement* 20 Feb. 1969:185.

Kelly, Thomas, and Brian Kelly. "He Do the Police in Different Voices." Letter. *Times Literary Supplement* 9 Jan. 1969:38.

—— ——.Response to letter of Douglas Hewitt. *Times Literary Supplement* 6 Mar. 1969:242.

Kiely, Robert. "Plotting and Scheming: The Design of Design in *Our Mutual Friend.*" *Dickens Studies Annual: Essays on Victorian Fiction.* 12 (1983): 267–83.

Lucas, F. L. "*The Waste Land.*" Gunter 28–36.

Maxwell, D. E. S. *The Poetry of T. S. Eliot.* London: Routledge, 1952.

Menand, Louis, *Discovering Modernism: T. S. Eliot and His Context.* New York: Oxford UP, 1987.

Monroe, Harriet. "A Contrast." Gunter 19–22.

Newsom, Robert. " 'To Scatter Dust': Fancy and Authenticity in *Our Mutual Friend.*" *Dickens Studies Annual: Esssays on Victorian Fiction* 8 (1980): 39–60.

Patterson, Annabel M. "*Our Mutual Friend:* Dickens as the Compleat Angler." *Dickens Studies Annual* 1 (1970): 252–64.

Reed, John R. "Confinement and Character in Dickens' Novels." *Dickens Studies Annual* 1 (1970): 41–54.

Robson, John M. "*Our Mutual Friend:* A Rhetorical Approach to the First Number." *Dickens Studies Annual* 3 (1974): 198–213.

Ross, Robert. *The Georgian Revolt: Rise and Fall of a Poetic Ideal, 1910–1922.* Carbondale: Southern Illinois UP, 1965.

Sanders, Andrew. *Charles Dickens: Resurrectionist.* New York: St. Martins, 1982.

Seldes, Gilbert. "T. S. Eliot." Gunter 5–12.

Symons, Julian. *Makers of the New: The Revolution in Literature, 1912–1939.* New York: Random, 1987.

Trilling, Lionel. "The Dickens of Our Day." *A Gathering of Fugitives.* Boston: Beacon, 1956. 41–48.

Tracy, Robert. "Reading Dickens' Writing." *Dickens Studies Annual: Esssays on Victorian Fiction* 11 (1983): 37–59.

Whipple, Edwin Percy. *Charles Dickens: The Man and His Work.* 1912. Boston: Houghton, 1975.

Beauty is as Beauty Does: Action and Appearance in Brontë and Eliot

Carol-Ann Farkas

In Jane Eyre *and* Villette, *and* Middlemarch *and* Daniel Deronda, *Charlotte Brontë and George Eliot chart the personal and moral development of several women characters. Both writers explore the effects of social context on the course of this development, as the heroines either learn and grow within, or without, the boundaries of what is approved and expected within their social milieu. Brontë's heroines tend to follow an unconventional course: they start out as outcasts, which then allows, or requires, them to live unconventional lives. By contrast, Eliot's heroines frequently find themselves to be living conventional lives, which nevertheless fail to satisfy them; custom and complacency are the major threats to their development as fulfilled human beings. In both cases, appearance plays a central role in determining the degree to which these characters rebel, conform, or compromise, as social expectations about what constitutes acceptable behavior are revealed to be quite different for the poor, plain woman and the woman of status and beauty. Moreover, for both Brontë and Eliot, appearance serves as a marker of moral potential: either characters grow into beauty as they become more beautiful morally (Brontë), or they justify the privilege of beauty by going beyond an admirable appearance to act admirably as well (Eliot).*

Dickens Studies Annual, Volume 29, Copyright © 2000 by AMS Press, Inc. All rights reserved.

" . . . the most powerful of all beauty is that which reveals
itself after sympathy and not before it"

Daniel Deronda, 281

Regardless of what the world may have thought, both Charlotte Brontë and
George Eliot considered themselves to be physically unattractive by the standards of the day. Both women, to varying degrees, found their looks to be
cause for serious reflection, if not actual anxiety; Charlotte Brontë in particular, was known to be especially hard on herself in regards to her plain appearance: "Perhaps few women ever existed more anxious to be pretty than she,
or more angrily conscious of the circumstance that she was not pretty"
(George Murray Smith, qtd. in Lambert, 96). But at the same time, being
unconventionally attractive—because both these women were attractive to
those who loved and admired them—meant that they could never take appearance for granted in a society which, like our own, placed considerable value
on both conventional looks and behavior. Consequently, in art, as in life,
both Brontë and Eliot reveal a notable consciousness of the connection between action and appearance in the portrayal of many of their literary heroines
(Lambert 96–97).

In *Jane Eyre* and *Villette*, and *Middlemarch* and *Daniel Deronda*, Brontë
and Eliot chart the personal and moral development of several women characters. In these novels, both writers explore the effects of social context on the
course of this development: the conventions of society form the background
of the narrative and the heroines either learn and grow within, or without, the
boundaries of what is approved and expected in their social milieu. Brontë's
heroines tend to follow an unconventional course: they start out as outcasts,
which in turn allows, or requires, them to live unconventional lives. By
contrast, Eliot's heroines more frequently find themselves to be living conventional lives, which nevertheless fail to satisfy them; custom and complacency
are the major threats to their development as fulfilled human beings. In both
cases, appearance plays a central role in determining the degree to which
these characters rebel, conform, or compromise, as social expectations about
what constitutes acceptable behavior are revealed to be quite different for the
poor, plain woman and the woman of status and beauty. Moreover, for both
Brontë and Eliot, appearance serves as a marker of moral potential: either
characters grow into beauty as they become more beautiful morally (Brontë),
or they justify the privilege of beauty by going beyond an admirable appearance to act admirably as well (Eliot). As a result, "because the heroine
embodies desired virtues, beauty is . . . reinforced as the ultimate symptom
of virtue. The body becomes a repository for those values which characters
and readers want to possess . . . That which is beautiful is loved and that
which is loved appears beautiful" (Lefkovitz 19–20).

The analysis which follows, then, will consider the personal and moral development of a selection of heroines from both Brontë and Eliot, concentrating not only on the portrayal of the characters' actions, but on the portrayal of their physical presence in the narrative as well. As Lefkovitz points out, "physical description functions as a strategy of characterization" (1); and Brontë and Eliot were certainly not the only nineteenth-century writers to incorporate appearance into the delineation of character in their works. In fact, as Jeanne Fahnestock suggests, the action-appearance link was practically a generic convention of mid-Victorian fiction, reflecting the assumption, articulated and popularized by the pseudo-sciences of phrenology and physiognomy, that moral and mental traits manifested themselves physically through a vocabulary of characteristics that could be read by others. Such a vocabulary lent itself particularly well to the representation of character and personality in fiction, which, like other art forms, already relied heavily on creating internal symbolic economies to create meaning—using images to render the abstract into the concrete, both to enrich the reader's experience, and better to guide him or her through the narrative's moral world view. A writer like Dickens was working in the same tradition as an artist like Hogarth—despite their different historical moments, both employed their own systems of iconography to make the connection between deed and consequence, action and appearance, clear and unavoidable for the reader/viewer.

But during the mid-nineteenth century, this iconographic and physiognomic approach to delineating character was complicated, and sometimes challenged, by new ideas about morality, psychology, and the representation of reality. The novels of both Brontë and, later, Eliot, bear the traces of two converging ideas about the relation of appearance and action in fiction. One, the older, iconographic view, was based on an assumption of what Elizabeth Deeds Ermarth describes as a providentially ordered universe, ruled by simple truths, imposed irrevocably on the individual from without by social or divine forces; the other, newer view, was more local, democratic and contingent. In this case, the only simple assumption was that there were no longer any simple assumptions: truth and understanding were created from within, earned through the hard work of self-examination and self-restraint. Moreover, character was seen as far more fluid and subjective than in the past, the product of both internal struggles and negotiation with external social conditions: verisimilitude came from complexity.[1] Consequently, the elements of character as represented in art—in fiction—were no longer straightforward; the heroine was not straightforwardly heroic, good, or noble, and the relation of her personality and behavior to her appearance came to reflect this preference for, or belief in, complexity. The harmony of moral and physical traits could no longer be assumed: for writers like Brontë and Eliot, committed to capturing the realistic moral struggles of flesh-and-blood humans, such physical and psychological harmony was achievable for their heroines only as a result of an unsettling, but more honest, evolutionary process within the fictional world of the narrative.

I

In both *Jane Eyre* and *Villette*, Charlotte Brontë presents central characters who are young, female, utterly alone in the world—and plain. Their lack of family, status, and wealth is reflected in a lack of physical presence and approved beauty; it is only when the characters grow into independence and self-awareness, and start to forge meaningful connections with other characters (especially male ones) that their appearance and presence begin to be felt more strongly and positively. When they are socially secure and loved, they become beautiful both to themselves and to their readers; moreover, the fact that these heroines triumph in their moral and personal development in spite of what society expects from their origins and appearance implicitly critiques that society for its amoral emphasis on superficial conformity.

When we are first introduced to Jane Eyre, we are presented with a character who is, by her own admission, "a heterogeneous thing . . . a useless thing . . . a noxious thing" (47):

> I know that had I been a sanguine, brilliant, careless, exacting, handsome, romping child—though equally dependent and friendless—Mrs Reed would have endured my presence more complacently; her children would have entertained for me more of the cordiality of fellow-feeling; the servants would have been less prone to make me the scapegoat of the nursery.   (47)

The young Jane has control over neither her appearance nor her personality, but the Reed family offers her no sympathy, even though "as a plain child she is all the more deserving of . . . compassion, because she is all the more deprived" (Lambert, 99). For the Reeds, affection is reserved only for others like themselves, who are spoiled by their privileged position in society, and who have the luxury of a conventionally pleasing appearance. As a result, although she is only a child, Jane is made to feel unwanted and unloved because of who and what she is, and because of her inability to match up with externally imposed social standards; she has even internalized these judgments to such a degree that she begins to believe them herself: "All said I was wicked, and perhaps I might be so" (48). Jane has already begun to learn that because of her looks, her disposition, and her status, society will judge her, and place her outside of itself.

This message is reinforced by her experiences at Lowood. There Jane, like all the other students, discovers the expectations society holds in regard to girls who come from nowhere and who have no prospects ahead of them but work and dependence. Because they are considered as nothing, they receive almost nothing in terms of food, enjoyment, comfort, and self-respect—unlike Mr. Brocklehurst's own daughters, well-to-do young ladies who are being groomed and fattened for the marriage market, and who thus are deemed to be worth an investment of money and attention. By contrast, the pupils at Lowood are not even allowed the simple indulgence of their own natural attractiveness; even that must be stripped away, in the name of suppressing useless vanity: "[W]e are not to conform to nature," says Mr. Brocklehurst. "My mission is to mortify in these girls the lusts of the flesh, to teach them to clothe themselves with shamefacedness and sobriety" (96). In other words, beauty, and one's own enjoyment and cultivation of it, is reserved only for those young women with wealth and status enough to use it for the advancement of middle-class interests; girls whose lives will be hidden, as teachers or servants, can have no claim to superfluous aesthetic pleasures.

As a result, while Jane's days at Lowood make her accomplished in many things, appearance is not one of them; in fact, the only lesson she can learn in this subject is that beauty is very much a marker of economic privilege, and plainness is a marker of want: when girls are withered and pinched by poverty and narrowness of prospects, by lack of air, scenery, and exercise, by the constant weight of illness and overwork—how can they possibly come to blossom the way that middle-class young women would be able to do? The deprivations of Jane's childhood experiences seem to be the source for a more general skepticism toward beauty that Brontë demonstrates throughout both *Jane Eyre* and *Villette:* indeed, "as a novelist and as a woman [Brontë] felt it her responsibility to alert readers to the arbitrary standards of beauty in her society, and to dominant attitudes—political attitudes based as much upon class as upon sex—that either limit or privilege women's potential for self-actualization" (Federico 29).[2]

Women such as Georgiana Reed, Blanche Ingram, and Ginevra Fanshawe are all beautiful, and they are all treated with dislike and contempt by Jane and Lucy. Both of these protagonists seem strongly to resent these other women for their good fortune in terms of both status and appearance; resentment then turns to condemnation when Jane and Lucy realize that the privileges enjoyed by the Blanches and Ginevras of the world are not earned by moral worth, or appreciated with humility and gratitude. "Beauty is power . . . for it can bring a woman effortless achievement" (Federico 30); but nevertheless, the women with the most attainments are the most empty, a connection which in turn makes the attainments themselves seem devoid of value.[3]

By contrast, Jane learns that real, valuable beauty must be earned, as one earns self-respect and independence; earned beauty then becomes a marker for moral worth and love. For example, Miss Temple, and later the Rivers sisters, both exhibit a combination of attractiveness and generosity of spirit that clearly illuminates them from within. Even sickly Helen Burns becomes attractive when the true force of her intellect and faith is allowed to shine forth:

> [Helen's powers] woke, then kindled . . . then they shone in the liquid lustre of her eyes, which had suddenly acquired a beauty more singular than that of Miss Temple's—a beauty neither of fine colour nor long eyelash, nor pencilled brow, but of meaning, of movement, of radiance. Then her soul sat on her lips, and language flowed, from what source I cannot tell.   (105)

The beauty of such women is not based on superficial accomplishments or wealth; rather, it is an inner quality that makes possible the attainment of meaningful accomplishments, and the merit of personal happiness. This inner beauty is the goal that Brontë sets for Jane as well: Jane's plainness of person and prospects will be transformed as she successfully completes her journey towards personal fulfillment and self-realization.

While the end of this journey has other, conventional rewards—marriage and motherhood—the means Brontë employs to accomplish them are notably unconventional. Jane's formative childhood experiences lay the groundwork for a personality that is unique and self-contained; when one is perceived as other, or outside, not only is one able to act against the status quo, such unconventional behavior becomes necessary for survival. For example, as Jane contemplates "a new servitude" (117) she expresses ambitions that are outside those traditionally reserved for the more typical, upper-middle-class novel heroine—that is, romance and marriage. These things, she has learned, are not to be desired by poor, outcast, dependent young women, who are instead forced, by circumstances, to set their sights elsewhere, on other goals. However, Jane quickly realizes that being dependent on others for work actually requires her to be independent—dependent on herself; she must act in an assertively self-reliant way that would never be contemplated by, or approved in, a more conventional or privileged young woman whose interests are looked after by a mamma and papa: "How do people do to get a new place? They apply to friends I suppose. I have no friends. There are many others who have no friends, who must look about for themselves and be their own helpers; and what is their resource?" (116). The answer to Jane's question is not simply advertising, but a taking in hand of her own destiny.

Jane's developing relationship with Rochester is similarly unconventional, even scandalous by "polite" standards. She is young, single, living in his house, and yet supposedly beyond the pale in terms of desirability because of her lack of status; nevertheless, it is the very lack of conventional ties to family and security that allows her to act in an unconstrained way with little concern for reputation (morality, of course, is another matter). Dressed neatly in her Quakerish, nonconformist, fashion, she trades ripostes with Rochester with a degree of candor and frankness that would be quite beyond the scope of an ordinarily respectable young lady, but which is nevertheless scrupulously virtuous. And it is this unconventional appearance and conduct that attract Rochester to Jane, and her to him. What makes these two plain protagonists attractive to one another is their mutual isolation from the polite world—unattached, they can be unreserved, and, free from the constraints and deceptions of fashionable society, they can each *see* the other for what they truly are.[4] Under this kind of regard—being looked at, being measured and found worthy—both Jane and Rochester become beautiful to one another:

> I looked at my face in the glass and felt it was no longer plain: there was hope in its aspect and life in its colour; and my eyes seemed as if they had beheld the fount of fruition, and borrowed beams from the lustrous ripple. I had often been unwilling to look at my master, because I feared he could not be pleased at my look: but I was sure I might lift my face to his now, and not cool his affection by its expression. (286)[5]

Nevertheless, Rochester has some residual assumptions about conventional women that he must shed—along with his eyesight, a conventional way of seeing—before he and Jane can be fully united:

> "I will make the world acknowledge you a beauty, too," he went on, while I became really uneasy at the strain he had adopted, because I felt he was either deluding himself or trying to delude me. . . .
> "And then you won't know me, sir; and I shall not be your Jane Eyre any longer, but an ape in an harlequin's jacket—a jay in borrowed plumes." (288)

Jane realizes that the standards of external beauty which apply to women of fashion and wealth can never apply to her; such trappings as Rochester would bestow on her would only suppress her individuality, and would make her more of a mistress than an equal companion, the very kind of slave which Rochester himself claims to despise (339). Furthermore, while Jane's growing sense of self-respect and integrity may have been shaped by her unconventional life, her choice to resist Rochester's flattery and his later temptation to live—unconventionally—in sin, reveals that some aspects of conventional morality are still of great value to her. There is much in society which is superficial and must be rejected, but there is much that is also worthwhile, and fashionable or otherwise, she cannot turn her back on what is, to her, morally correct, without also losing her very identity:

> *I* care for myself. The more solitary, the more friendless, the more unsustained I am, the more I will respect myself. I will keep the law given by God; sanctioned by man. I will hold to the principles received by me when I was sane . . . Laws and principles are not for times when there is no temptation: they

are for such moments as this, when body and soul rise in mutiny against their rigour . . . If at my individual convenience I might break them, what would be their worth? . . . Preconceived opinions, foregone determinations are all I have at this hour to stand by; there I plant my foot. (344)

As Paul Schacht points out, in this case "[r]especting herself . . . does not mean following the dictates of private conscience in defiance of convention, but relying on public canons of acceptable conduct" (444). This moral sense based on "preconceived opinions" compels Jane to flee Thornfield—and lands her right in the midst of temptation of a different sort, in the person of St. John Rivers.[6] She is strongly attracted, even against her own will, by his offers of a conventional life as a wife and missionary; while she is repelled by the idea of marrying a man who neither loves her, nor finds her attractive or desirable, she does believe in the merits of duty and self-sacrifice, in accordance with conventional notions of female piety and morality. Consequently, her decision to return to Rochester and be his wife, his nurse, and the mother of his children is actually not quite the conventional ending it seems to be; nothing could be more unconventional than rejecting the life of service St. John offers her, to seek out, and propose (for a second time) to a man with a past that defies society's normal definition of "respectable."

In the end, although Rochester cannot even see her physically, Jane has achieved beauty because she is living what is, for her, a beautiful life. And while the end of *Jane Eyre* possesses undeniably conventional elements—she does take on the expected roles of wife, nurse, and mother—that is of less significance than the process by which that end is achieved. Jane's conventional rewards have been earned by unconventional means: in the mind's eye of Rochester, the reader, and herself, she has come to be beautiful, and despite all the disadvantages and want of privilege in her life, she has demonstrated to the reader that the conventional is not the only path to happiness; it may not even be the right path at all. If the conventional model for female behavior in the traditional novel is a young woman who is beautiful, well-to-do, loved by friends and family, then perhaps, Brontë seems to be suggesting, this notion of convention is unrealistic. For every privileged young woman who fits such a fictional model, there must be many in real life who have no prospects in the conventional sense, who are isolated, without privilege, and without the means to cultivate an idealized physical appearance and personal demeanour. But it is exactly this latter model that Brontë presents to her readers; she offers us a heroine who can *earn* beauty, love, and comfort, forged by her own efforts out of next to nothing (with a little help from a narrator with good timing), whose story can still satisfy readers, and offer them a protagonist to identify with—all in defiance of accepted notions of convention.

The life of Lucy Snowe parallels that of her predecessor, Jane Eyre, in many respects, but ultimately Lucy's fate, and the ending of *Villette*, conform even less to the expected or the customary. Like Jane, Lucy is also an orphan, a young woman who is completely cast adrift in life, and who can only rely on her own inner resources to supply the want of family, friends, status, and attractiveness. In Lucy's narrative, however, Brontë makes a more striking point about some of the underlying social causes for Lucy's outcast state: the want that Lucy suffers is due as much to others' perceptions of her as disadvantaged and outcast as it is due to quantifiable deficits, particularly when it comes to the appearance of plainness and poverty: "How could inn-servants and ship-stewardesses everywhere tell at a glance that I, for instance, was an individual of no social significance and little burdened by cash? They *did* know it, evidently: I saw quite well that they all, in a moment's calculation, estimated me at about the same fractional value" (54). When we think of Lucy's appearance, we might be thinking "plain," but that impression comes from only a few mentions in the text. Nowhere does Lucy describe exactly how tall she is, what colour her eyes are or what state her teeth are in; Jane is guilty of this as well—instead of providing details about their appearance that would enable readers to form more objective notions about what they look like, both Jane and Lucy provide only vague hints. Jane is very conscious of her plainness; and Lucy also seems to think that she is plain and unremarkable: but how accurate are these impressions? In Jane's case, we have seen that these impressions change based on her own sense of self-worth, which is in turn strongly tied to the relationships she has: the more isolated and rejected she is (especially as a child) the more likely she is to see herself as plain, and flawed; maturity and love bring her self-acceptance and even self-satisfaction. Lucy's awareness of herself depends similarly on her relationships with others; in fact, as she herself seems to acknowledge, "Lucy" is a different person to almost everyone she meets.

Moreover, Lucy's own perceptions of herself seem almost to be dormant, or suppressed, compared to her observations of others' appearance and behavior; there are times when Lucy is present as a narrator, but hardly there at all as a character in the narrative. But perhaps there is a point to this; perhaps Lucy places so little emphasis on her own appearance and presence, as she sees it, because whatever she may think of herself, in the eyes of the world—if it thinks at all about single, friendless women—she is at most a pitiable curiosity, and at the least an inconsequential nobody. The world—the one within which Lucy struggles—is apparently much more interested in those who are fortunate enough to conform to its expectations and ideals.

Such seems to be the motivation behind the first three chapters of *Villette*. Although narrated by Lucy, these chapters do not seem to contain her: she makes observations on the life of the Bretton household, but represents herself as being aloof and removed from the action. She is there by inference, felt through her silence, self-restraint and distance, rather than through her presence: "I, Lucy Snowe, was calm" (19). Instead, the subject of the novel seems in fact to be Paulina Home,[7] a little doll-like creature whose acute sensitivity and suffering make Lucy extremely uncomfortable even while they fascinate. In fact, everyone is fascinated by Paulina's poignant, childish beauty, and it is exactly this tendency to dominate the attentions of others which in many ways *does* make her the subject of the novel. Her privileged existence throws Lucy's deprived life into stark relief; and just as Paulina's childhood presence in the Bretton household displaces Lucy—apparently willingly—from her own narrative, the whole course of life for a Paulina makes the life of a Lucy seem insignificant, unrewarding, and displaced by comparison. Paulina has all that Lucy, for the longest time, does not: the comfort of wealth, a loving parent to protect her, the luxury of health and leisure, which allow beauty—at least in the conventional sense—to flourish. And Paulina's life—like Dr. John's—demonstrates that privilege is self-propagating; happiness and success guarantee more happiness and success, at least by the world's standards, and beautiful people are meant to be with other beautiful people:

> I *do* believe there are some human beings so born, so reared, so guided from a soft cradle to a calm and late grave, that no excessive suffering penetrates their lot, and no tempestuous blackness overcasts their journey. And often these are not pampered, selfish beings, but Nature's elect, harmonious and benign; men and women mild with charity, kind agents of God's kind attributes. (419)

Lucy, like Jane before her, quickly learns this lesson, and learns also that this conventional system of success is closed to those who lack even one of the variables—wealth, status, charm, looks—involved in the formula. Whatever system Lucy is to follow, she must invent it for herself: "I know not that I was of a self-reliant or active nature; but self-reliance and exertion were forced upon me by circumstances, as they are upon thousands besides" (31). Moreover, as Jane also discovered, when one is outside the preferred course of life, hardship leads to hardship, and long before Lucy's life comes together, it first has to disintegrate entirely; she loses her family, her friends, her money—her looks: "I grant I was not looking well, but on the contrary, thin, haggard, and hollow-eyed; like a sitter-up at night, like an over-wrought servant, or a placeless person in debt" (38–39). However, Lucy's triumph is that she does assemble a life for herself—again, like Jane, in spite of conventional notions about female behavior and dependence. As Jane learned, all the hardships aside, being outside of the accepted order of things allows one to order things for oneself: Lucy is able to gain success, independence, and love—outside of what society would consider customary, it is true, but acceptable to herself nevertheless.

Brontë has made Lucy much weaker, in many ways, than Jane; whereas Jane always has ample to say in defense of her own desires, Lucy is more often than not gripped by a "moral paralysis" (426) that prevents her from asserting herself, with M. Paul in particular. But while this weakness would seem to destine Lucy for a more conventional life than Jane achieves, Lucy nevertheless clings to independence and isolation in preference to conformity for its own sake. For example, she has the opportunity to become Paulina's companion—a position that would possibly raise her social status, and would definitely allow her to enjoy a life of leisure and the pursuit of personal interests. But Lucy turns it down, preferring to work instead; while obscurity seems to be her portion, she prefers to inhabit that role on her own terms, rather than have her obscurity made more plain by immediate contrast with Paulina:

> I was no bright lady's shadow—not Miss de Bassompierre's. Overcast enough it was my nature often to be; of a subdued habit I was: but the dimness and depression must both be voluntary . . . my qualifications were not convertible, not adaptable; they could not be made the foil of any gem, and adjunct of any beauty, the appendage of any greatness in Christendom.   (286)

Not that Lucy begrudges Paulina her good-fortune; in fact, Paulina is one of the few women that Lucy actually admits to liking. As in *Jane Eyre*, Brontë seems to assert in *Villette* that true beauty must be earned, and although Paulina has not come by her wealth and natural endowments through her own efforts per se, Lucy does seem to believe that her good nature and generosity entitle her to the enjoyment of what she has:

> In Paulina there was more force, both of feeling and character, than most people thought . . . than she would ever show to those who did not wish to see it. To speak truth, reader, there is no excellent beauty, no accomplished grace, no reliable refinement, without strength as excellent, as complete, as trustworthy. . . .For a little while, the blooming semblance of beauty may flourish round weakness; but it cannot bear a blast: it soon fades, even in serenest sunshine.
> (301)

Paulina's life has not corrupted her because she has not tried to use any of her privileges selfishly. That fate has been reserved for Ginevra Fanshawe; like the Reed sisters and Blanche Ingram before her, she is the tainted beauty of this story, the woman who deserves only contempt because she seeks to pay her way in life with superficial accomplishments, instead of working to develop her potential as a moral being. In contrast to the approbation with which she regards Paulina, Lucy's exasperated and disgusted assessment of

Ginevra's conduct serves as a critique of a society that appears to reward such behavior, and prefers surfaces over depth.

Lucy's story, on the other hand, is a triumph of depth over surfaces. Like Jane Eyre, Lucy maintains her integrity; like Jane, she discovers that integrity and self-respect in others are what attract her the most, and what make her in turn, the most attractive. M. Paul does not realize Lucy's merits right away; it takes some time indeed before he can accept her as a superior compromise between those two extreme images of female appearance and behavior, the "Cleopatra," and the subject of "La vie d'une femme."[8] Nevertheless, through their almost antagonistic relationship, the two do penetrate through exterior defenses and the boundaries of custom, manners, and religion, to the true individuals underneath. Lucy comes to see M. Paul's generosity and kindness; and beneath her quiet, self-effaced demeanour, he sees her for the passionate self-possessed young woman she has the potential to become, despite her preliminary denials to herself: "You are well habituated to be passed by as a shadow in Life's sunshine: it is a new thing to see one testily lifting his hand to screen his eyes, because you tease him with an obtrusive ray" (321).

In the end, M. Paul gives Lucy two essential gifts that complete her development as an individual, and allow her to view her life as a success, even though it ultimately bears little resemblance to the conventional happy ending traditionally reserved for worthy novel heroines. The gift of the school gives Lucy the opportunity to be an independent businesswoman, with complete power over her fate—just like Madame Beck, but with the improvement of a moral conscience. And the gift of M. Paul's love, which she happily reciprocates, allows her to see that independence does not need to mean isolation or solitude, and that unconventional does not mean unattractive. To M. Paul, the interior and the exterior are the same—beautiful and worthy of love—and through him, Lucy begins, hesitatingly to see herself as he does:

> . . . I never remember the time when I had not a haunting dread of what might be the degree of my outward deficiency; this dread pressed me at the moment with special force . . .
> " . . . Do I displease your eyes much?" I took courage to urge: the point had its vital import for me.
> He stopped and gave me a short, strong answer—an answer which silenced, subdued, yet profoundly satisfied. Ever after that, I knew what I was for him; and what I might be for the rest of the world, I ceased painfully to care. Was it weak to lay so much stress on an opinion about appearance? I fear it might be—I fear it was; but in that case I must avow no light share of weakness. I must own a great fear of displeasing—a strong wish moderately to please M. Paul.   (463)

Lucy may only be able to please one person in all the world, just as he pleases only her, but the mutual attraction between M. Paul and Lucy is based on sympathy and complete understanding, not superficial attraction, and for this reason it matters more than anything.

It matters, in fact, more than whether M. Paul ever returns to Lucy. That would be the expected, conventional happy ending; but in *Villette*, Charlotte Brontë has come to terms with the fact that for many people—many women—in her world, conventional happy endings just never happen. The fate of Lucy Snowe is an assertion that while the conventional is desirable (if it were not, we would not be sensible of the great sadness of the novel's ending), it is not the only satisfying outcome available for women: for the woman who finds fulfillment and self-respect, love of others, and love of oneself, can be found anywhere; privilege and beauty can be earned, and can be brought to illuminate the most shadowy recesses of life.

II

In the novels of George Eliot, the combination of idealized, fashionable beauty and behavior reveals itself to be a dangerous trap for young women. While Eliot does not go as far as Brontë in condemning this model of conventional feminine beauty (she can even be said to give it a second chance at redemption, in the person of Gwendolen Harleth), there is nevertheless a strong critique implicit in her description of those characters who take a life of surfaces for granted. Most Eliot heroines are beautiful, and Eliot does not share Brontë's instinctive suspicion of beauty; nevertheless, Eliot does see great potential for moral harm to be done by the temptations which beauty offers. While Brontë will portray heroines who become beautiful through the process of self-realization, Eliot's heroines tend to start off as beautiful, and then become more or less so in accordance with how responsibly and ethically they work to become more beautiful *internally*. The heroine who fails to use her talents, and learn from her mistakes, may not necessarily be punished by society—Rosamond Vincy, does, after all, end up living a conventionally prosperous life—but she is punished by the narrator, by being made to look *less* in the eyes of the reader.

While Charlotte Brontë portrays characters who suffer and are then rewarded with more than they ever expected, many of George Eliot's characters begin their lives with the greatest of expectations, but then realize that in order to achieve growth and moral development, they must settle for less. Like Brontë, Eliot uses the struggle of her heroines to critique society;[9] but unlike Brontë, who questions society's values by placing her characters outside of the approved order, Eliot prefers to challenge the behavior of both communities and individuals from within. Her characters live far more conventional lives than those of Brontë; and the relationship between action and appearance is premised on more traditional notions of beauty. Moreover, by making her heroines beautiful, Eliot is also creating certain accompanying standards of conduct which they must live up to if they are to be respected by the reader, or other characters; Eliot's heroines "become exceptional not by defying conventional roles but by excelling in them" (Foster 197), and there is little sympathy for those characters who do not exert themselves to this end. So that while the central female characters of *Middlemarch* and *Daniel Deronda*—Rosamond Vincy Lydgate, Dorothea Brooke, and Gwendolen Harleth—are all the kind of beautiful, well-to-do women that might initially arouse suspicion and possibly contempt in Jane Eyre or Lucy Snowe, these Eliot heroines would no doubt eventually elicit sympathy from their counterparts in Brontë, once it became apparent that conventional looks and luxury offer their own pitfalls.

The disadvantages of beauty and status are perhaps most clearly seen in the portrayal of Rosamond Vincy Lydgate. Rosamond is the quintessential conventional young lady, having mastered "all that was demanded in the accomplished female" (86). Rosamond has been shaped into exactly the ideal of the young bride, the better to make a match which could improve the Vincy family's efforts to rise in the world. Her natural beauty and good nature have been cultivated, directed, and indulged, in order that she might live up to the upper- and middle-class standards of that show-piece of economic and social success, the lady of leisure. But while she has learned accomplishments, she has not been educated: sheltered by middle-class prosperity, comfort and complacency, she has never learned much about real life, sacrifice, or generosity. Lucy Snowe, or Jane Eyre, for all their social isolation, are in fact less isolated from the immediacy of life because they have been forced to immerse themselves in it; Rosamond, by contrast, possesses a species of ignorance, complacency, and passivity that can only come from a life of too much sheltered ease.

But while Rosamond may not have the slightest ideas about economics, politics, or philosophy, she can compensate by making a pretty and flirtatious spectacle of herself. Like Madame Laure, Lydgate's first love, Rosamond is a consummate actress and mistress of illusion: "Every nerve and muscle in Rosamond was adjusted to the consciousness that she was being looked at. She was by nature an actress of parts that entered into her physique: she even acted her own character, and so well, that she did not know it to be precisely her own" (106). Accordingly, she captures Lydgate on the first try, and, appropriately, believes herself to be in love with him also since "she did not distinguish flirtation from love, either in herself or in another" (243). Unfortunately, the same childish ignorance of practical matters that makes her so adorable to Lydgate is also responsible for all the difficulties in her life which follow. Since she does not understand the comings and goings of money, and since no one has ever thought to trouble her with an explanation, she is not able to make an accurate assessment of Lydgate's prospects; but since her family has made her into the kind of spoiled and willful woman who expects always to have her way, she does.

As she proceeds to make both her life, and Lydgate's, miserable, it is difficult for the reader not to find her exasperating and contemptible. Eliot's narrator tries to be sympathetic, referring to Rosamond as "poor Rosamond" (the narrator finds many of her characters "poor" creatures), but the reader feels herself to be a very Lucy Snowe in her impatience with Rosamond's absolute inability to perceive any fault within herself, or take responsibility for any part of her life. However, although one cannot absolve Rosamond of all obligation to understand and act, since it is one of the imperatives for an Eliot heroine to learn and grow into a fully developed human being, to be fair, she is only partly to blame. After all, other than choosing a man with uncertain professional prospects, what has she done wrong? A plan of behavior and conduct was laid out for Rosamond long before this part of her life began, wherein she was instructed to use her innate beauty and vivacity for personal and familial gain; and all the comforts of her life were designed to help her capitalize on and perfect these charms at the expense of a more profound instruction in morality and self-realization. She was bred to offer conventional beauty and accomplishments to her husband, in return for which he would offer support and advancement: Rosamond follows this conventional plan to the letter, never having the need to follow any other kind, until she is married and "real life" starts to impose itself on her. Lydgate is made to seem the victim of her ensuing selfish obstinacy and ignorance, but he is far from innocent: it is his acceptance and encouragement of Rosamond's brand of conventional and superficial charm that keeps finishing-schools like Mrs. Lemon's in business, churning out more of the same.

The limitations of Rosamond's life are further emphasized by their contrast with the example of Dorothea, the would-be Saint Theresa of the novel. Dorothea, like Rosamond, is also portrayed as a conventionally beautiful and privileged woman (that she is privileged compensates for any idiosyncrasies in her appearance, such as dressing plainly), living among the expectations of conventional society: and although she is far removed from the social sphere of women like Rosamond, she is threatened by the same trap. However, Dorothea herself yearns to be more than just the sum of person and property. Throughout the novel she struggles with her own desires and ambitions for a more unconventional life, one that would allow her to act, to learn, and to make a difference in the world, rather than settle for using her physical charms and attractions to win a comfortable, and suffocating, life for herself as someone's wife and mother. And when Dorothea first appears in the narrative, there is no reason to expect that she will not achieve her goals—unless we are made alert by the warning of the novel's prelude:

Many Theresas have been born who found for themselves no epic life wherein there was a constant unfolding of far-resonant action; perhaps only a life of mistakes, the offspring of a certain spiritual grandeur ill-matched with the meanness of opportunity; perhaps a tragic failure which found no sacred poet and sank unwept into oblivion. . . . these later-born Theresas were helped by no coherent social faith and order which could perform the function of knowl-edge for the ardently willing soul. Their ardour alternated between a vague ideal and the common yearning of womanhood; so that one was disapproved as extravagance, and the other condemned as a lapse . . . Some have felt that these blundering lives are due to the inconvenient indefiniteness with which the Supreme Power has fashioned the natures of women. . . .   (1–2)

In other words, an ardent nature like Dorothea's literally burns with the desire to lead a life of significance; but while well-intentioned ambition meets with many obstacles amidst obstinate society (as Lydgate could attest), the ambi-tions of women are countered with special resistance due to the double stan-dard which demands that they be models of virtue and self-sacrifice at the same time as they are to be passive and dependent. Such a system does not permit women—especially beautiful upper-middle-class women like Doro-thea—to pursue the kinds of education and experience that would make them capable of judgment and action; and yet, because such a system claims to prize virtue—or at least the appearance of it—women like Dorothea cannot help but find themselves in the position of longing to do right, without the means or specific practical knowledge really to do so. Thus, throughout the novel, Dorothea frequently refers back to her plans for the tenants' cottages; but these plans are as frequently deferred because some other female obliga-tion, or male objection, demands attention instead. By the end of the novel, Dorothea has managed to use some of her money for the hospital, but her cottages have long since fallen by the wayside, thanks, as Dorothea puts it, to "the unexpected way in which trouble comes, and ties our hands, and makes us silent when we long to speak. I used to despise women a little for not shaping their lives more, and doing better things. I was very fond of doing as I liked, but I have almost given it up" (496).

Dorothea starts off wanting to be the kind of woman who "shapes her life more," the kind of woman who does not easily conform to the course of indolence and passivity expected from beautiful women of leisure. Hers is a constant battle to push past the inertia of life lived on the surface of things, to find within herself a deeper store of understanding and action. In some ways, she does succeed in this struggle; she grows more mature, thoughtful and wise, transcending her own naiveté and self-centeredness to become an awe-inspiring force of morality and forgiveness in the lives of others. And as this process of growth takes place, her appearance also seems to change: the narrative provides fewer specific details about her looks and those that are provided serve only to illuminate and intensify her inner qualities of purity, grandeur, and love of life. Again, the contrast with the hopelessly shallow, because infantile, Rosamund, is striking: descriptions of her dwell most often on the physical—her fingers, her hair—in the absence of any deeper feelings or awareness. Dorothea's greater capacity for generosity and love allow her to be more than just a pretty face, whereas Rosamund is incapable of such inner growth. Nevertheless, Dorothea's ability to achieve such rare harmony, where the beautiful exterior communicates an inner understanding, comes at the cost of constricted ambitions within a more narrow sphere of influence (Lambert 143). The same saintly quality that compels Lydgate to think, reverentially, that "this young creature has a heart large enough for the Virgin Mary" (703), is only achieved through the personal sacrifice of her grander plans, and a gradual, martyred resignation to the limitations imposed on her life by custom and habit.

Eliot's psychological portrayal of Dorothea, and the narrator's sometimes ironic comments about the character's thought-processes, make it quite clear that part of what holds her back comes from within—unlike her sister Celia, Dorothea has a deficiency of common sense, and an excess of unfashionable enthusiasm, which impedes her ability to be realistic: "You always see what nobody else sees," Celia insists. "[I]t is impossible to satisfy you; yet you never see what is quite plain" (30). Dorothea's combination of education and worldly ignorance, mixed with a partial acceptance of conventional values, has given her a confused notion of what she requires to be happy: Celia's version of domestic bliss—the companionate marriage with many children—is not quite the thing; but neither is independence and self-assertion. What she settles on is marriage to Casaubon, wherein she mistakenly sees the opportunity for education, activity, the fulfillment of duty, and the denial of shallow physical vanity, all guided by a superior male father-figure:

> It was this which made Dorothea so childlike, and according to some judges, so stupid, with all her reputed cleverness; as, for example, in the present case of throwing herself, metaphorically speaking, at Mr. Casaubon's feet, and kissing his unfashionable shoe-ties as if he were a Protestant Pope. She was not in the least teaching Mr. Casaubon to ask if he were good enough for her, but merely asking herself anxiously how she could be good enough for Mr. Casaubon. (44)

Despite Dorothea's blindness to her own situation, however, she is not solely to blame; although she is unlike Rosamond in so many other respects that their paths almost never cross, the two are linked in that their flaws are due to a faulty education, which is in turn due to a fault in society which makes it unacceptable for conventionally-minded people such as the Brookes and Vincys to educate their pretty female charges in any way other than what is designed to make them into unobjectionable wives and mothers—or at least, charming fiancées—and no more. Everyone assumes that because Dorothea is wealthy and beautiful her only concerns are to become more so by making a good match, "decided according to custom, by good looks, vanity, and merely canine affection" (4); her desire to go beyond this narrowly defined role, to become morally beautiful by cultivating judgment and practical knowledge, is seen as a needless waste of feminine energy.

These customary attitudes have prevailed in such societies as Middlemarch's partly through their acceptance and support by many of its women. Celia Brooke, as we have already seen, plays out her conventional role as pretty young lady—and later, pretty young mother—quite cheerfully; not only does she not feel any need to examine into her situation, she is exasperated by Dorothea's chronic dissatisfaction, and bewildered by her sister's failure to see the obvious benefits of doing the done thing. Mary Garth is perhaps an even more striking example, if not for Dorothea, then for the readers, of the power of normative influences. One of her principal functions in the novel is to act as a moral conscience for Fred Vincy, compelling him to set aside selfishness and immaturity, to act like a sober, mature, contributing member of society, just like her father. Mary is plain, and not conventionally passive and acquiescent; if she were a Brontë heroine, her strong personal integrity and work ethic might have been made to dominate this novel. However, plainness in Eliot does not seem to be a special marker for nonconformity as it is in Brontë; rather, Mary's appearance and behavior, while exemplary, serve rather to signify an approved combination of conformity with common sense. Both Mary's looks and values are perfectly in keeping with her place in society, and make her the one woman in this narrative who is most qualified for success in the "home epic."

By contrast, although Dorothea would seem to be *the* heroine of this novel, her ending is not clearly heroic; nor does she appear to be completely triumphant in her progress through that same home epic. Her ardent inner nature, so out of proportion to convention and expectation, is nevertheless not enough to release her from their pull. Even freedom from her marriage to Casaubon does not make her free. His death would seem to be permission for her to pursue a relationship with Ladislaw, but, even disregarding the strictures of Casaubon's will, both Dorothea and Ladislaw are severely constrained by the conventional codes of behavior between men and women which hinder openness for the sake of decorum and propriety. Dorothea wants to make more of her life; Will wishes to do what he pleases; they both claim to love what is good and beautiful (357)—but it takes them several hundred pages to overcome the false assumptions and pride prompted by the kind of social conventions to which they would otherwise claim immunity.

They do end up living happily ever after, "bound to each other by a love stronger than any impulses which could have marred it" (763); but, thanks once again to the power of conventional behavior, their married life becomes less and less extraordinary as it goes on. Or rather, it is extraordinary that they are happy, when the novel has taught us how rare and precious the mutually satisfying union is; but this extraordinary outcome is only possible by giving up other, less ordinary rewards—at least in Dorothea's case. We are told that her life is "filled . . . with a beneficent activity which she had not the doubtful pains of discovering and marking out for herself" (763)—but this activity seems to center on supporting her husband in his more active contributions to the world:

> Dorothea could have liked nothing better, since wrongs existed, than that her husband should be in the thick of a struggle against them, and that she should give him wifely help. Many who knew her, thought it a pity that so substantive and rare a creature should have been absorbed into the life of another, and be only known in a certain circle as a wife and mother. But no one stated exactly what else that was in her power she ought rather to have done. . . .   (764)

There is a sense here that a person such as Dorothea could have done greater things; exactly what specific great things she could have done, however, will never be known because she has sacrificed her unconventional ambitions for more conventional ones. But I do not believe that Eliot means this as a punishment for Dorothea: she has lived up to the promise of her physical beauty by realizing an equally beautiful inner self, and she is rewarded for it with personal happiness. That she has achieved this state of beauty and harmony within the bounds of convention would no doubt be disappointing to some—I think Brontë would be somewhat irked by Dorothea's story—and the narrator herself admits that Dorothea's life is, to a degree, a sad sacrifice (766) to the limitations of social conformity: "there is no creature whose inward being is so strong that it is not greatly determined by what lies outside it" (766). But there is another level of meaning at work in her fate that does something to redeem it.

In *Middlemarch*, Eliot is not simply portraying the progress of individuals; also of great interest to her is the individual's involvement in the life of the community, and the contribution he or she might make to social harmony by exerting a positive influence on others. Consequently, when we are presented with a heroine like Dorothea, whose external beauty offers the potential for inner goodness and growth, we must consider that her successful realization of that potential will result not simply in the development of that heroine as a more complete human being, but also in her participation in the development of others. For Eliot, the customs of society are often seen as being limiting and harmful, perpetuating repression and injustice; nevertheless, bending to these customs is sometimes necessary to achieve the larger goal of doing good for others: "Both love and duty, family and vocation, are insisted upon throughout the George Eliot canon as being essential to happiness, but whereas the most mediocre and talentless of men can find fulfillment in both, the most exceptional women have to choose one or the other, and lesser women are not given the choice"(Barrett, 168). This ability to work for the greater good by "holding up an ideal for others in her believing conception of them" (706) means that Dorothea does not achieve the kind of independence and self-fulfillment that a Brontë heroine might do. Nevertheless, acting as the inspiration in the lives of others in no way diminishes her; on the contrary, the role—"one of the great powers of her womanhood" (706)—not only satisfies her, it beatifies her, making her truly beautiful because she is beautifully true to those who need her most. Her success in achieving this great goal of essential womanhood, is, to Eliot, the most beautiful thing Dorothea can do for herself and for others, and is its own reward: "for the growing good of the world is partly dependent on unhistoric acts; and that things are not so ill with you and me as they might have been, is half owing to the number who lived faithfully a hidden life, and rest in unvisited tombs" (766).

"Essential womanhood" is a somewhat more problematic concept for *Daniel Deronda*'s Gwendolen Harleth.[10] When we are first introduced to her at the beginning of this novel, we soon learn that her ideas of womanhood, of womanly power, are based on her being able to "do what was pleasant to herself in a striking manner; or rather, whatever she could do so as to strike others with admiration and get in that reflected way a more ardent sense of living, seemed pleasant to her fancy" (69). Gwendolen seems at first to be much more like Rosamond Vincy than Dorothea Brooke; like Ginevra Fanshawe, or Blanche Ingram, rather than Lucy Snowe or Jane Eyre. Gwendolen is loved and spoiled by her family, and while money is a problem—*the* problem in many respects—social status is not: she is one of those special creatures who are born to ease and privilege, or so Gwendolen thinks at the start of the novel. As other examples from Brontë and Eliot have suggested however, the fact that such a creature is beautiful and charming—and willing to exploit her own desirability as a result—signifies a high risk of moral bankruptcy. And our first encounter of Gwendolen, as a spectacle seen through Daniel Deronda's eyes, does indeed employ her appearance to establish the problem of her moral jeopardy as a theme for the novel: "Was she beautiful or not beautiful? and what was the secret of form or expression which gave the dynamic quality to her glance? Was the good or evil genius dominant in those beams? Probably the evil; else why was the effect that of unrest rather than of undisturbed charm? " (35)

The description is ostensibly about Gwendolyn's looks, about the quality of her beauty—and yet, the evil and unrest that Deronda observes are moral and psychological characteristics that Deronda is detecting as distortions in what should otherwise appear as a smooth surface: right away, the readers are being instructed that Gwendolyn's is a character of flaws, which contaminate her from the inside out. Other spectators notice this troubled, and troubling, quality to her appearance, describing her as "a sort of serpent" (40), possessing a "sort of Lamia beauty" (41): her physical desirability is agreed upon by all, but the comparisons to serpents and soul-destroying demons suggests that her personal desirability—and more importantly, her humanity—is not a foregone conclusion. In Eliot's world, however, while Gwendolen's beautiful exterior signifies moral peril, it also offers the potential for the development of the inner beauty of moral understanding and self-knowledge. Gwendolen's vanity and selfishness would be the subject of disgusted critique in Brontë—to that writer, the Gwendolen of chapter one of the novel would already be guilty of squandering her natural gifts; Eliot, on the other hand, gives her flawed heroine the chance to redeem herself throughout the course of the novel, to turn the discord of her *self* into a harmonious complement to her *person.*

Like her predecessor, Rosamond, Gwendolen has been well-educated for the profession of "lady": she is beautiful, accomplished, and can speak engagingly on a variety of appropriate drawing-room subjects. However, her education has been based on the assumption that she might use it to make a good match with a wealthy husband who would raise her social and economic status, along with that of her entire family; the possibility of Gwendolen ever having to work, or be independent in any way has been completely overlooked, as has the need to instruct her in practical considerations of daily living. In short, she is not only conventional, but a near perfect realization of the ideal young lady whose thoughts and ambitions are remarkable only in their ordinariness:

> her horizon was that of the genteel romance where the heroine's soul poured out in her journal is full of vague power, originality, and general rebellion, while her life moves strictly in the sphere of fashion. . . .Here is a restraint which nature and society have provided on the pursuit of striking adventure; so that a soul burning with a sense of what the universe is not, and ready to take all existence as fuel, is nevertheless held captive by the ordinary wirework of social forms and does nothing in particular. (83)

Unfortunately, this ideal of the young lady presupposes—risks everything for—a correspondingly ideal life. Consequently, when the ideal fails to happen and financial disaster strikes, Gwendolen discovers that she is completely unprepared to care for either herself or her family in any way other than through a profitable marriage: indeed, so committed to this ideal are they, her whole family expects her to do no more than market herself aggressively to the first available bachelor with a decent income. And once Klesmer has opened Gwendolen's eyes to the impossibility of her ever achieving success elsewhere, that is what she resigns herself to do.

Like Rosamond, Gwendolen marries less for love than for love of money, status, and comfort; and like Rosamond, all that Gwendolen is able to offer her husband in return is a pleasing display of beauty, charm and dependence, once Grandcourt has done breaking her will. Odious as Grandcourt is, we cannot help holding Gwendolen responsible for her own actions. The narrator makes it quite clear that Gwendolen chooses to do the done thing for its own sake, to trade on her looks rather than endure the inconvenience and discomfort of self-assertion and principled, independent action. But what else could Gwendolen do instead? "In the characterization of Gwendolen there is a suggestion that any woman of personal power is bound to be bad; the conflict between her potential and the paucity of opportunity will inevitably result in evil" (Barrett, 155). Marrying a wealthy man is all that Gwendolen's beauty and charms have qualified her to do—just like Rosamond, or Ginevra, or Blanche, or even Paulina before her—so thoroughly has society trained her to conceive of herself in that conventional way. Having been inculcated with a sense of privilege appropriate to her looks and expectations has made it virtually impossible for Gwendolen to humble herself to governessing (humility is not part of the upwardly mobile young lady's curriculum), even though governessing is the only non-marital solution society provides for these situations.

This then is the trap into which Gwendolen—"poor thing"—has stumbled: the world expects her to act as conventionally as she looks; but when this is not possible, due to society's own way of ordering things, society washes its hands of her. The absurdity and pathos of this predicament does lead us to judge Gwendolen, but the narrator portrays her sympathetically enough that we go further and judge Gwendolen's world as well: there is an implicit critique being made here of society's treatment of women. At issue: the inappropriateness of a fashionable education for young women and the need to offer knowledge and independence to girls so that they do not become a burden either to their families, or their husbands—and more importantly, so that they are not forced to compromise their integrity out of gratitude or obligation to those who support them. Furthermore, as in *Middlemarch*, Eliot appears to be criticizing marriage as well (and well-qualified she is, too). The manners of society insist on reserve and modesty between men and women before marriage; consequently they never know each other well enough to realize just who and what they are marrying; then, because of idealized, romantic notions of marriage, they are trapped with one another, literally for the rest of their lives: "What possible release could there be for her from this hated vantage-ground, which yet she dared not quit, any more than if fire had been raining outside it? What release, but death?" (668)

If Gwendolen's conventional life has become a trap, whether as a result of societal forces or her own selfishness, it is up to her to get herself out. If she wastes her life—or allows others to waste it, which is just as bad—she will not be redeemed; failing to make something of her situation, of herself, will result in her being made physically and psychologically abhorrent to herself and to the readers of her story. But the promise of beauty is not wasted in her; unable to find a conscience within herself, she finds one in Daniel Deronda, and eventually she learns from the advice he gives her: "Look on other lives besides your own. See what their troubles are, and how they are borne. Try to care about something in this vast world besides the gratification of small selfish desires. Try to care for what is best in thought and action—something that is good apart from the accidents of your own lot" (501–02). This lesson could as easily be voiced by Dorothea: as she learns in *Middlemarch*, individual satisfaction is not enough if it does nothing for the larger good of the community. But when an individual has been taught to value nothing but his or her own satisfaction, when one has never been required or accustomed to do otherwise, this is easier said than done: "There is no escaping the fact that want of sympathy condemns us to a corresponding stupidity" (658). This last remark is made by the narrator in reference to Grandcourt, but it could just as well apply to Gwendolen (and a great many other Eliot characters). And the only way for Gwendolen to be edified by sympathy is to be brought to such a crisis of suffering that, desperate for sympathy herself, she can finally identify with others—like Lydia Glasher—in situations just as desperate.

This crisis—her supposed murder of Grandcourt—strips her of her reliance on conventional behavior, and conventional acceptance of the right of beautiful girls to be selfish and self-absorbed. She is willing to pay for her mistakes, and to earn back her self-respect; with the addition of Grandcourt's punitive will, she is given the means to help both her own family and that of Lydia Glasher. Moreover, she is brought to the realization that her privileged status in life does not in any way entitle her to happiness, or success, or recognition: "She was for the first time feeling the pressure of a vast mysterious movement, for the first time being dislodged from her supremacy in her own world, and getting a sense that her horizon was but a dipping onward of an existence with which her own was revolving" (876). Materially reduced to nothing, she is ready to become something spiritually, to be one of Dorothea's admirable women who "shape their lives more, and do better things" (496).

As a result, Gwendolen's destiny lies more in the direction of a Dorothea—a later-born St. Theresa—rather than that of a Rosamond. Her suffering has already made her "more fully a human being" (741); the Lamia-like taint of evil—selfishness, want of sympathy—which had been encasing

Gwendolen like a beautiful, but poisonous shell, is gone, and, free of superficial ambitions after pleasure and admiration, she has achieved a "sober gladness which [gives] new beauty to her movements" (880). Like Dorothea, Gwendolen—if she has truly learned her lessons—will be fated to a life of obscurity, where her greatest triumphs will come from what she can do for others, rather than for herself: once again the individual life is only made beautiful through its involvement with other lives. Eliot has given her heroine this conventional ending (if convention demands either marriage or penance) not out of a slavish obedience to custom, but in order to critique society from within, using as her agent one of conventional society's own. Gwendolen's life, like Dorothea's, has been used to highlight the limitations of conventional society; now, her life will be added to the ranks of conventional lives, to work its changes quietly but profoundly.

III

George Eliot's heroines are made to sacrifice a great deal in exchange for peace and fulfillment; even then there are no guarantees of a perfect happy ending because, in Eliot's world, not even beautiful, wealthy women are allowed a respite from the process of moral growth. As we learn from the examples of Gwendolen, Dorothea, and even Rosamond, beauty is a goal in life well worth pursuing, but there is no greater mistake to be made than to settle for the world's conventional definition of beauty as a quality of exteriors. It is the fully realized inner life, and its dedication to the good of the larger world, that confers true beauty on an Eliot heroine, and allows her to enjoy the best of society's conventions, while transcending the worst. For Charlotte Brontë, on the other hand, the conventional is almost immaterial; goodness and beauty will emerge out of one's own efforts, in spite of what the world would have. Indeed, the expectations of the world tend rather to suppress individual integrity and inner beauty in favor of conformity and emptiness, leaving a creature who can be of no use to herself, or to anyone else. But while Brontë and Eliot each approach the issue of their heroine's moral development from slightly different angles, they both make the physical life inseparable from the psychological or spiritual: no matter what the larger world may desire in a woman, the women of these novels are neither ethereal, bodiless saints, nor mindless, soulless dolls. Their heroines, all beautiful in their own way, are an expression of the belief that both Brontë and Eliot seem to share, that the full development of the individual—the individual woman—must involve the bringing together of matter and spirit, to make one beautifully whole being who can serve as a worthy example to others.

NOTES

1. For a more detailed analysis of the social, economic, and philosophic motives behind this shift, see Elizabeth Deeds Ermarth's *Realism and Consensus in the English Novel*, and *The English Novel in History 1840–1895*. I also find Nancy Armstrong's *Desire and Domestic Fiction* useful for its description of the female heroine as the embodiment of middle class values; in particular, she argues that the replacement of aristocratic values with those of the middle class, as the latter became a dominant cultural force, resulted in a preference, in fiction and in "real life," for depth over surfaces—for self-awareness and self-restraint over self-indulgence and empty and superficial display. According to Armstrong, these values resulted in the shaping of the first modern individual as a woman (8)—specifically, the woman protagonist of domestic fiction. Because the middle-class capitalist system created an equation of world=surface (male), home/refuge= depth (female), the female character in domestic fiction—the novel—is placed in a situation which demands depth of character, achievable only through moral and psychological negotiation with internal and external—personal and societal—influences.

2. Charlotte Brontë's own horrible experiences at a charity school have been well documented by her biographers (cf. Mrs. Gaskell's *Life of Charlotte Brontë*), and it is quite possible that her own plainness was in part due to the hardships she endured as a child; as Lambert suggests, smallness and plainness are associated in Brontë's mind "with a lack of essential nurture in her formative childhood years" (102).

3. Rosamond Oliver, while hardly a paragon like the Rivers sisters, does not quite fit into the category of contemptible beauties like, say, Georgiana or Blanche. Rosamond is beautiful and spoiled, but essentially harmless, and does have some redeeming qualities that justify her existence in Jane's eyes: "She was very charming, in short, even to a cool observer of her own sex like me; but she was not profoundly interesting or thoroughly impressive" (394). Jane goes on to compare Rosamond to Adèle, an interesting case that must not be overlooked. When we first meet Adèle, she seems to be almost hopelessly and disturbingly corrupted by her early training as a coquette, but it is one of Jane's triumphs that, in the end, as Adèle's adopted mother, she is able to save Adèle from becoming another Ginevra Fanshawe: "As she grew up, a sound English education corrected in a great measure her French defects; and when she left school, I found in her a pleasing and obliging companion—docile, good-tempered, and well-principled" (475). But even redeemed and domesticated, Adèle is nevertheless, significantly, kept at a distance from Jane's new family (475).

4. The ability to see others clearly is a central idea in Brontë; the characters who are most moral and good are the ones who are the most observant, and the least distracted by surfaces. Overcoming varieties of blindness—the inability to see into the souls of others, and oneself—is crucial to the full development of Jane and Lucy, and their beloved Rochester and M. Paul.

5. Brontë apparently took the subjects of phrenology and physiognomy far more seriously as explanatory models of character than did Eliot, who was an admitted

skeptic (Fahnestock, 349). Both Jane and Rochester assess one another's characters partly on the basis of the set of the chin, the shape of the forehead, the line of the nose. But while the physiognomic is only one measure of two very complex characters, it becomes *the* measure when applied to characters portrayed as having a more basic nature—namely Bertha Mason. Because Brontë sees Bertha as simply depraved and reduced to a bestial condition (if, indeed, she was ever fully human and English), her physiognomy is portrayed as simply bestial also. Her features are wild, distorted, and indistinct, representing the blurring of her human mind, and, presumably, soul.

Both St. John and Dr. John are gorgeous men—but the same wariness with which Brontë regards female beauty is applied to the beautiful man as well. Brontë can sometimes accept the possibility of the neo-classical ideal—that external perfection must imply harmony with inner perfection—but she does not take the ideal for granted, recognizing that the psychological complexity of individuals problematizes the relation between character and appearance, as often as not. So that St. John and Dr. John can appear to be "Nature's elect," combining beautiful looks with intelligence, strength and nobility—but at the same time, beauty can hide flaws, or provide obstacles to achieving the more vital perfection of character: Dr. John can be thoughtless, and St. John can be cold and unforgiving. As both Jane and Lucy discover, the appearance of divinity in men is just that—an appearance, a superficial display; real perfection is to be found only through love that transcends the visual and physical, to forge deeper spiritual and emotional connections.

7. I can't help but think that the surname Home is not a random choice: it seems rather to embody all that Paulina has, and Lucy has not, until the end of the novel.

8. As Helena Michie points out, Lucy's encounter with Cleopatra and La Vie d'Une Femme is reminiscent of Jane's penitential drawings of herself and Blanche Ingram. In the latter case, "Jane has replicated two bodies that served as alternatives for Victorian women . . . [but] . . . Jane fits into neither portrait, neither body." She is "not completely a dependent" nor is she a "leisure-class heroine" (50). Similarly, when Lucy confronts the opposing images of female decadence and female self-sacrifice, she is unable to identify with either. The struggle for both protagonists is to find a compromise between the two extremes, without compromising their own values and individuality.

9. While the use of the word "heroine" as synonymous for "central female protagonist" is relatively unproblematic in Brontë's novels, where Jane and Lucy really do enjoy a species of triumph in the end, the case is not so straightforward with Eliot's novels. Neither Dorothea, Rosamond, or Gwendolen "triumphs" at the end of their stories; in fact, in some instances, the word "anti-heroine" might even be a more appropriate term. But these characters are nevertheless the central female protagonists of the novels, and "heroine" is a less cumbersome description, even if it does become as complicated as the characters it describes.

10. I have chosen to focus on Gwendolen, but not Mirah, because the latter is arguably not a central character in *Daniel Deronda*—or rather, I would argue that she is not. Her storyline revolves around Deronda, and seems to function more as a way of elucidating his character than as a plot-line in its own right. Compared

to Gwendolen, Mirah simply does not seem to be as central or as complicated a female character as I would like to consider in this analysis. Her lack of complexity, like that of *Villette*'s Paulina, is a result of a near-perfect combination of beauty and goodness; although Mirah has a "difficult" life, she herself does not seem to be really touched by the same sorts of inner conflicts and turmoil that make characters like Gwendolen so interesting.

WORKS CITED

Armstrong, Nancy. *Desire and Domestic Fiction: A Political History of the Novel.* New York: Oxford UP, 1987.

Barrett, Dorothea. *Vocation and Desire: George Eliot's Heroines.* London: Routledge, 1989.

Brontë, Charlotte. *Jane Eyre.* London: Penguin, 1966.

———. *Villette.* Toronto: Bantam , 1986.

Eliot, George. *Daniel Deronda.* Harmondsworth: Penguin, 1974.

———. *Middlemarch.* New York: Bantam, 1985.

Ermarth, Elizabeth Deeds. *Realism and Consensus in the English Novel.* Princeton: Princeton UP, 1983.

———. *The English Novel in History 1840–1895.* London: Routledge, 1997

Fahnestock, Jeanne. "The Heroine of Irregular Features: Physiognomy and Conventions of Heroine Description." *Victorian Studies* 20 (Spring 1981): 326–50.

Federico, Annette. "'A Cool Observer of Her Own Sex Like Me': Girl-Watching in *Jane Eyre*." *Victorian Newsletter* 80 (Fall 1991), 29–33.

Foster, Shirley. *Victorian Women's Fiction: Marriage, Freedom and the Individual.* London: Croom Helm, 1985.

Lambert, Ellen Zetel. *The Face of Love: Feminism and the Beauty Question.* Boston: Beacon, 1995.

Lefkovitz, Lori Hope. *The Character of Beauty in the Victorian Novel.* Ann Arbor: UMI Research, 1987.

Michie, Helena. *The Flesh Made Word: Female Figures and Women's Bodies.* New York: Oxford UP, 1987.

Schacht, Paul. "*Jane Eyre* and the History of Self-Respect." *Modern Language Quarterly* 52 (Dec. 1991): 423–53.

"Three Leahs to Get One Rachel": Redundant Women in *Tess of the d'Urbervilles*

Lisa Sternlieb

After carrying three other dairymaids across a flooded lane, Angel Clare finally gets his chance with Tess Durbeyfield. "Three Leahs to get one Rachel," he whispers. This essay argues that the unwanted dairymaids, the duped husband on his honeymoon, and the younger sister who replaces the elder find their origins in the story of Jacob and his wives. This biblical tale of sexual selection works in dialogue with Darwin's theory in Hardy's novel. The essay seeks to show that Hardy's concern is not only for the beautiful and beloved Tess, but for Marian, Izz, and Retty, redundant women who would have fared better in biblical times than in late Victorian England. One of the last great Victorian novels destroys the nineteenth-century marriage plot by exposing it as a statistical lie.

Walking to church one Sunday, Tess Durbeyfield and her three fellow dairymaids come across a flooded lane. The young women are rescued by the man each adores, Angel Clare, who carries first Marian, then Izz, then Retty across the pool. When a shy Tess protests that she can climb along the bank without being carried, Angel quickly grabs her. "Three Leahs to get one Rachel," he whispers.[1] This has been a strangely forgotten line in a memorable scene. While much has been made of Hardy's constant comparisons between Tess and Eve, I have found no critics referring to this other crucial story from

---

Dickens Studies Annual, Volume 29, Copyright © 2000 by AMS Press, Inc. All rights reserved.

Genesis. Yet in Angel's off-hand remark Hardy suggests a key to understanding how *Tess of the d'Urbervilles*'s interests in ancient origins, sexual selection, naïve husbands, unmarriageable women and conveniently replaceable sisters converge.

For many years discussions of sexuality in *Tess* focused on the heroine's purity, on Hardy's critique of the double standard and "the social emphasis on virginity."[2] This criticism concentrated on male hypocrisy and men's objectification and victimization of Tess. More recently criticism has implicated Hardy himself in his portrait of Tess. Feminist psychoanalytic critics have shown how Hardy turns Tess into a spectacle, how he betrays his own fascination with her as a sexual being by making her sexuality available to the assumed male reader.[3] What unites this criticism is its emphasis on the male spectator and the male seducer, on masculine prerogative in the mating game. An examination of the Rachel and Leah story, however, shows how *Tess* is equally invested in a feminine perspective and in a consideration of women's sexual prerogative. Since Gillian Beer's *Darwin's Plots*, critics have tended to study the influence of Darwin's theories of origin on Hardy and to ignore competing myths of origin. But as Hardy's biographer, Martin Seymour-Smith argues, "When in his early 20s he discovered himself to be an unbeliever after reading much including *Origin of Species*, this was 'in a purely intellectual sense.' He never would part from what the church service meant to him in emotional terms, and could never contemplate any notion other than that the survival of humanity depended on the survival of religion. . . . One side of him, the emotional, was (and always would be) in need of religious ritual" (Seymour-Smith 30, 77). We might say that *Tess*'s engagement with Genesis and with Darwin illustrates this emotional/intellectual divide in Hardy. His sense of both hopefulness and hopelessness in the light of Darwin is illuminated by his use of the Rachel and Leah story. He chooses this competing myth of origin that comfortingly refutes Darwin's theory of sexual selection while simultaneously affirming the unfortunate evolution of the human species.

In Genesis (29) Jacob journeys from his home to Paddan-aram where he meets and falls in love with Rachel. After laboring for her father, Laban, for seven years, he is allowed to marry her. Jacob wakes the morning after his wedding to find that his father-in-law and veiled bride have duped him, that he has married Rachel's older sister, Leah. Only now that he has consummated his marriage to Leah and promised to labor another seven years for Laban is he allowed to marry Rachel as well. Angel is clearly referring to Jacob's fourteen years of labor. (In a clever but insulting pun Angel associates the three dairymaids with the name Leah [meaning "cow"] while naming his bashful beloved Rachel [meaning "ewe"].) But his words come back to haunt him on his wedding night when he too finds that he has married the "wrong" woman: "You were one person: now you are another," he tells Tess. "The woman I have been loving is not you. . . . [but] another woman in your shape"(179).

Biblical scholars have generally agreed about the meaning of the story of Laban and Leah's deception. Jacob, the younger son who successfully deceives his blind father through the sense of touch, gets his comeuppance in the darkness when his sense of touch deceives him as well.

> The Midrash Bereishit Rabba vividly represents the correspondence between the sin Jacob perpetrates against Isaac and Esau and the wrong Leah and Laban do to Jacob: "And all that night he cried out to her, 'Rachel!' and she answered him. In the morning, 'and, look, she was Leah.' He said to her, 'Why did you deceive me, daughter of a deceiver? Didn't I call out Rachel in the night, and you answered me!' She said, 'There is never a bad barber who doesn't have disciples. Isn't this how your father cried out Esau, and you answered him?'⁴

Hardy takes pains to show that Angel's own dishonesty prior to his marriage results in the bad timing of his confession: "I was going to tell you [about my sexual relationship] a month ago . . . I thought it might frighten you away from me . . . then I thought I would tell you yesterday, to give you a chance at least of escaping me. But I did not. And I did not this morning, when you proposed our confessing our faults on the landing—the sinner that I was!"(176)

From its beginning the story of Jacob and Rachel is highly unusual, for when Jacob first meets Rachel he immediately kisses her and within several lines declares his love for her. The Bible never tells us that Adam loves Eve or that Abraham loves Sarah, yet Jacob loves Rachel. And this kiss has troubled biblical scholars for centuries, for while brothers kiss brothers, parents kiss children, God kisses Moses at his death, and even heaven and earth kiss, men and women in the Bible do not kiss (Dresner 32). Thus, Hardy alludes to a particularly suggestive biblical account of a man who deeply loves a beautiful woman, yet who willingly agrees to father children with three other women as well.

"The covenant God made with Abraham promised blessing to all humanity through the people that would come from Abraham and Sarah," the biblical scholar Samuel Dresner writes. "So fragile was the chain of the covenant in those early years that it might have broken" had women been forced to remain childless (46). So after Leah gives Jacob four sons and Rachel remains barren, the younger sister gives Jacob her maid Bilhah to mate with. Bilhah gives Jacob another two sons. When Leah thinks her childbearing days are over, she gives Jacob her maid, Zilpah. By Zilpah Jacob has another two sons. Despite the competition between the sisters, Rachel willingly gives her husband back to Leah in exchange for Leah's son Reuben's mandrakes or love apples. Leah bears Jacob two more sons and a daughter. Finally, after watching her husband father eleven children by other women, Rachel is "remembered" by God and she bears him two sons before dying. What are we to make of this strange domestic arrangement?

Many biblical scholars argue that this is a tale of cruel sibling rivalry and that the sour note on which these marriages begin causes terrible divisions for many generations. With the birth of each of her sons Leah expresses her bitterness and jealousy against her favored younger sister. She names her eldest Reuben (Behold a Son!) and declares, "Yes, the Lord has seen my suffering, for now my husband will love me"(29:32). When Jacob continues to despise her, she names her second Simeon (Hearing) and says, "Yes, the Lord has heard I was despised and He has given me this one, too" (29:33). Each son's name bears the mark of her desperation and each comes to despise Joseph, Rachel's firstborn and Jacob's favorite (Armstrong 85–86). Although Rachel has Jacob's love, the first words she speaks emphasize her desperation and envy, his response to her his own ineffectuality as a husband: " 'Give me sons, for if you don't, I'm a dead woman!' And Jacob was incensed with Rachel, and he said, 'Am I instead of God, Who has denied you fruit of the womb?' "(30:1–2).

Yet many other scholars argue that the sisters love each other, that Rachel may have helped Leah disguise herself on her wedding night and that she may have slept underneath the marriage bed so that her voice would help with the impersonation (Dresner 46). In turn, other scholars argue that Leah sacrifices herself for Rachel. Leah, according to an ancient rabbinic legend which is part of the liturgy of the Jewish New Year, becomes pregnant with Joseph and prays to God to switch the male embryo in her womb for the female embryo (Dinah) in her sister's so that Rachel can finally bear as many sons as Bilhah and Zilpah. This bizarre interpretation fits neatly into the substitution motif (Jacob for Esau, Leah for Rachel, Joseph for Dinah) so crucial to Jacob's story (Dresner 59–60, 86–88). The scholar Levi Yitzhak has gone so far as to argue that Jacob loves Rachel all the more for giving him so pious a wife as Leah. Samuel Dresner writes that in Yitzhak's interpretation:

> All family conflict vanishes. . .the matriarchs are models demonstrating how to overcome family unhappiness through the power of love and the example of piety. Far from Rachel's envying Leah, she was responsible for her marriage; far from Jacob's resenting the deception, he only loved Rachel more. Human kindness and nobility of character conquer society's flaws. The tale is no longer one of sibling tragedy but a record of the trial and victory of Leah's piety, Rachel's compassion, and Jacob's respect for the one and love for the other.
>
> (72–73)

Hardy was well-acquainted with the Bible, and while he may have known little about these arcane discussions, I would like to argue that he too was attracted to the rather strange success of this domestic arrangement.

After all, the twelve sons of these four different women are the patriarchs of the twelve tribes of Israel, according to Genesis, the fathers of the Jewish people. (Although the slavegirls ostensibly bear sons for their mistresses, Bilhah and Zilpah are always given credit for being the mothers of their own sons and are frequently referred to as Jacob's wives. When Jacob and Esau are reunited, for example, Jacob places the slavegirls and their children together, Rachel and Leah and their children together.) Tess and the three other dairymaids are possible descendants of these four women. Steeped in his reading of Darwin, Hardy looks back to a story that contradicts both our understanding of sexual selection and survival of the fittest. He looks to a story in which neither God nor nature is "careless of the single life."[5]

The demands made on Jacob by his father-in-law and four women suggest that he has stumbled into a land devoid of men. Rather than pleading exhaustion, Jacob gives into the demands of all five. He loves only one of these people, yet he manages not to reject any of them. As Robert Alter has written,

> In his transactions with these two imperious, embittered women, Jacob seems chiefly acquiescent, perhaps resigned. When Rachel instructs him to consort with her slavegirl, he immediately complies ('Here is my slavegirl, Bilhah. Come to bed with her, that she may give birth on my knees, so that I, too, shall be built up through her.' And she gave him Bilhah her slavegirl as a wife, and Jacob came to bed with her. And Bilhah conceived and bore Jacob a son" (30:3–5), as he does . . . when Leah tells him it is she who is to share his bed this night. 'With me you will come to bed, for I have clearly hired you with the mandrakes of my son.' And he lay with her that night. And God heard Leah and she conceived and bore Jacob a fifth son. In neither instance is there any report of response on his part in dialogue.   (159–60)

Rachel, Leah, Bilhah and Zilpah are allowed to fulfill the promises of the covenant for the simple reason that Jacob doesn't take the prerogative of sexual selection. He doesn't choose among them. Instead, they choose among themselves. Jacob's wedding night with Leah sets up a sexual pattern throughout his story. Each time we are told about his specific bed partner she has been chosen by another. Laban gives him Leah, Rachel gives him Bilhah, Leah gives him Zilpah, Rachel gives him Leah. Hardy may have seen in this story an alternative to both the societally imposed sexual selection of his own era and a Darwinian model of sexual selection in which many die out that one may procreate. He may have found that Jacob's extraordinary capacity not to make choices allowed him to include, even satisfy more than one woman. So when he begins his novel by posing the same question asked in Genesis (29)—What happens when there are not enough men to go around?—he immediately signals that his own version of the Jacob and Rachel story will be about choice and exclusion, *selection* and rejection.

Angel enters the novel as the only man available to partner many women. " . . . what's one among so many!" he asks the members of the dancing club. "Better than none. . . . Now, pick and choose," replies the boldest young woman (9). Once we accept the improbabilities of Hardy's plot in which Tess continually runs into both Alec and Angel, in which Angel is equally attractive to every woman who meets him, from the dancers, to Mercy Chant, to the dairymaids, to Liza Lu, we must notice that Hardy has created a world in which there are essentially two men to accommodate all women. In this agrarian community in which machines have taken their place, men have fled to the cities, leaving the women behind to compete among themselves for the little that is left.

Hardy is making the vexed question of redundant women the very subject of his novel. (The 1851 Census had shown that there were half a million more women than men in Britain. It also revealed that a million women remained unmarried. By 1911 this number rose to nearly one and a half million.) In 1862, the well-known journalist, W. R. Greg, advised that single women over the age of thirty be shipped off to the colonies where they would find a surplus of men. His ideas remained popular throughout the century (Perkin 153–62). Hardy is not proposing bigamy or incest as alternatives to Greg's schemes; he is merely exposing the *lie* of the Victorian marriage plot which has always ignored these statistics, which has structured its narratives around the pairing off of all men and women. Tess is punished not simply because Angel chooses unwisely at the dance, but because in her community the choice of any woman is the rejection of every other.

Tess, like Rachel, becomes the favorite among four women. But Angel is not in the position of Jacob. He has no power to treat kindly his three "Leahs." On his wedding night Retty tries to drown herself, Marian is found "dead drunk,"(175) and Izz is "very low in mind"(175). Izz finds life so dismal at the dairy without Angel that she leaves her job and goes off to visit him on his "honeymoon." Retty, she tells him, is "so thin and hollow-cheeked. . . . Nobody will ever fall in love wi' her any more"(210). Marian, too, is out of the marriage market. Now that she is a heavy drinker, her boss has gotten rid of her, and it is feared that "she would come to no good"(198). When Izz declares her love for Angel, he asks her to go off with him, and Hardy's novel would have ended in Brazil had Izz not uttered the fatal words, " . . . nobody could love 'ee more than Tess did! . . . She would have laid down her life for 'ee. I could do no more!"(212).[6] Angel's brutal fickleness has been foreshadowed on his last night with Tess. While sleepwalking, he carries her across a railless, narrow footbridge below which Tess hopes he will drown her. But Tess has not been brought to the river to suffer the fate of countless other fallen women, but to relive the fateful moment of selection, to compare herself to her competitors: "Ah—now she knew what he was dreaming of; that Sunday morning when he had borne her along through the water with the other dairymaids who had loved him nearly as much as she. . . ."(194). While Angel seems ready to reexamine his decision, to forsake his wife for rivals he has already rejected, the women remain loyal to each other.

Despite the unhappy destiny to which she and her fellow dairymaids are fated, Izz's selfless honesty typifies the behavior of all four women. When Tess announces that she will marry Angel, Marian speaks for the three rejected ones: "You will think of us when you be his wife, Tess, and of how we told 'ee that we loved him, and how we tried not to hate you, and did not hate you, and could not hate you, because you was his choice, and we never hoped to be chose by him"(157). Tess, of course, has insisted that "he ought to marry one of you . . . you are all better than I"(156). She resolves to tell Angel her history, for her silence "seemed a wrong to these"(157). Tess last sees Marian and Izz as they journey "in the direction of their land of Canaan"(287). Angel and Tess are finally able to consummate their marriage because the letter the would-be Bilhah and Zilpah write after arriving at their destination implores the wayward husband to seek his wife. Each woman's intense desire for Angel is complemented by an honest urge to give him to another. The dairymaids' relationship is probably as close as Hardy could have come to imagining a situation in which one man is *shared* among four women. Yet while the women in Genesis share Jacob only in support of their own interests, Tess and the dairymaids have little capacity to do anything on their own behalf. The dairymaids never make their own sexual decisions, but rely wholly on Angel's. They make sure never to get in another dairymaid's way. Their selflessness and passivity ensure that all will die without progeny.

Why are the dairymaids so different from their biblical progenitors? Hardy seems to blame their behavior on his readings in Darwin as well. In his notebooks Hardy argues that man has evolved too far for the imperfect environment in which he is placed. Human emotions, the capacity to feel and therefore to suffer are "a blunder of overdoing" in the evolutionary process, "the nerves being evolved to an activity abnormal in such an environment."[7]As Roger Robinson argues so persuasively in his discussion of *Jude the Obscure*:

> Living entirely for the present, mating, separating, bearing and discarding offspring, re-mating, all without compunction, Arabella accepts the reality of the struggle for survival with matter-of-fact self-interest. In Jude and Sue, however, Hardy takes one stage further his concept of the over-evolution of sensitivity. The especial pathos of their situation is that they not only suffer themselves, but suffer with others' sufferings. . . . Hardy makes clear that their sensitivity

is part of a still-continuing evolution towards yet greater pain. "Everybody is getting to feel as we do. We are a little beforehand, that's all. In fifty, a hundred, years the descendants of these two children will act and feel worse than we. They will see weltering humanity still more vividly than we do now."

(132–34)

Using clearly biblical language, Hardy shows how dangerously far Tess has evolved beyond the instinct of self-preservation, how many generations she is removed from the Rachel who saw Jacob's love as her entitlement, his children as her birthright: "They were simple and innocent girls on whom the unhappiness of unrequited love had *fallen*: they had deserved better at the hands of fate. She had deserved worse; yet she was the *chosen one*. It was wicked of her to take all without paying. She would pay to the uttermost farthing: she would tell, there and then"(175) (emphasis added).

Women's hypersensitivity coupled with another accident of "overevolution," men's sexual dominance, creates absolute disaster in *Tess*. As Gillian Beer has noted: "[Darwin] makes it explicit . . . throughout *The Descent* that, in contrast to all other species (where the female most commonly holds the power of selection), among humankind the male dominates choice. This reversal creates crucial difficulties: 'man is more powerful in body and mind than woman, and in the savage state he keeps her in a far more abject state of bondage than does the male of any other animal: therefore it is not surprising that he should have gained the power of selection.'"[8] Both Alec and Angel demonstrate this power at every opportunity. Although Alec's former mistresses, the Queen of Spades and the Queen of Diamonds "unite . . . against the common enemy,"(52) Tess, they have no physical or emotional power to sway their boss when he swoops down among them to claim Tess for himself. Alec commonly reminds his mistress that he has picked her out from among many: "There was one petticoat in the world for whom I had no contempt; and you are she"(253). When Tess sees her three fellow dairymaids across the flooded lane and faint with love for their rescuer, she tells Angel that "They are better women than I," but the argument is over before it has begun, "Not to me," Angel replies (113). After this scene, Hardy frequently writes of the dairymaids as a unity: "The air of the sleeping-chamber seemed to palpitate with the hopeless passion of the girls. They writhed feverishly under the oppressiveness of an emotion thrust on them by cruel Nature's law. . . . The differences which distinguished them as individuals were abstracted by this passion, and each was but portion of one organism called sex"(115). Yet Angel sees it as his prerogative to choose from among them:

All the girls drew onward to the spot where the cows were grazing in the further mead, the bevy advancing with the bold grace of wild animals—the reckless, unchastened motion of women accustomed to unlimited space—in which they abandoned themselves to the air as a swimmer to the wave. It seemed natural enough to him, now that Tess was again in sight, to choose a mate from unconstrained Nature, and not from the abodes of Art. (136)

Even at Flintcomb-Ash it is Farmer Groby who has the power to choose which woman will have the most laborious task and Tess who is "selected" from among the many (257).

It is difficult to think of the work of another Victorian novelist in which the laws of sexual selection are so starkly set forth. The Victorian marriage plot generally shows both men and women negotiating themselves into a partnership. Rather than arguing that Rochester *selects* Jane, Hareton Catherine or Will Dorothea, we think of how these characters independently and mutually learn to come together. Hardy affords his characters in *Tess* no such luxury. His novel is too conscious of the extent to which his men's and women's needs and desires are at odds with each other. When Angel identifies himself with Jacob, he does so with an assured sense of his male advantage. He refers to a cocky Jacob who chooses the woman he wants and must dispense with her sister before getting to her. But if Angel associates Tess with the young, beloved Rachel, Tess has already identified herself with the older, embittered wife, who waits too long for the fulfillment of her dreams. Asked what she will christen her son the night of his baptism and death, Tess "had not thought of that. But a name suggested by a phrase in the book of Genesis came into her head as she proceeded with the baptismal service, and now she pronounced it: SORROW. . . ."(74). The biblical reference is to Rachel, who, on her deathbed names her newborn son Ben-oni (son of sorrow); Jacob calls him Benjamin instead. Rachel had named her long-awaited firstborn Joseph (May the Lord add me another son). Rachel "remains true to the character of her initial speech to Jacob, where she demanded of him not a son but sons. She will be granted the second son she seeks, but at the cost of her life."[9] Throughout her relationship with Angel Tess perceives herself as a woman for whom time has run out: "Why didn't you stay and love me when I was sixteen; living with my little sisters and brothers, and you danced on the green—O why didn't you, why didn't you!"(154) she implores him during their courtship. Looking into the future of their marriage, she knows it cannot bring happiness; time cannot heal the wounds of their wedding night: "if we should stay together, yet somewhen, years hence, you might get angry with me for any ordinary matter, and knowing what you do of my bygones, you yourself might be tempted to say words, and they might be overheard, perhaps by my own children. O, what only hurts me now would torture and kill me then! I will go—to-morrow"(192). And when Angel finally returns to claim Tess, her first words are "It is too late! Too late, too late!"(298)

Thus, Hardy sets up the primary narrative conflict by endowing his protagonists with the same characteristics as Jacob and Rachel. Angel identifies himself with the Jacob who can easily labor seven years for Rachel for "they seemed in his eyes but a few days in his love for her"(29:18). In the jungles of Brazil Angel seems to lose all sense of time; in his pursuit of moral truths he forgets about the material concerns that are claiming Tess's patience. Tess remembers the frustrated, impetuous woman who demands of her husband, "Give me sons, for if you don't, I'm a dead woman!" (30:1) The conflict is between a man who has time on his hands and a woman who is always conscious of the approach of death. Like Rachel, Tess has little time to savor what she has desired; like Jacob, Angel seems poised to endure for many years without the woman he loves.

By naming her child Sorrow, Tess acknowledges that she will produce no more progeny and foreshadows her own premature death. Hours before being captured and certain of her imminent execution, she begs Angel to marry her younger sister, Liza-Lu. Angel has protested that he cannot marry her; she is his sister-in-law. Yet, in the novel's final paragraphs as his would-be Rachel is hanged, Angel stands and watches for a sign of her death with Liza-Lu. As John Sutherland writes,

> No Victorian would have missed the cue: with the hoisting of the black flag Liza-Lu becomes Angel's "Deceased Wife's Sister"—a phrase heavy with legal baggage. Ever since the Act of 1835, marriage with a deceased wife's sister had been determined by the law of England to be within the degrees of incest. . . . There were some twenty-six abortive initiatives [to overturn the law] between 1850 and 1896. (190)

The Wife's Sister's Bill finally passed in 1906.

Sutherland argues that because of this law, Angel has several possible options. He can emigrate with Liza-Lu to one of the colonies which has overturned the deceased wife's sister legislation; he can remain in England, enter into an "open sexual union" with Liza-Lu and risk being prosecuted for incest; or he can, as Sutherland finally argues, love Liza-Lu spiritually: "Angel will nobly undertake not to impose his animal appetites on the woman he worships, fulfilling himself with a 'higher' spiritual and intellectual union" (191). It is an odd leap Sutherland has made. Three days after Angel rejects Tess, Hardy writes of him: "Some might risk the odd paradox that with more animalism he would have been the nobler man. We do not say it. Yet Clare's love was doubtless ethereal to a fault, imaginative to impracticability"(191–92). As Sutherland himself reminds us, the novel's closing lines, "As soon as they had strength they arose, joined hands again, and went on" (314) evoke the end of *Paradise Lost*: "They hand in hand with wandering steps and slow/Through Eden took their solitary way." In the end Hardy again returns to the very beginning. And as in his earlier evocations of Genesis he is clearly concerned neither with legal sanctions nor with purity. As a man raised on the Bible, as a follower of Darwin, Hardy surely sees no value in making of Liza-Lu another redundant woman. For Angel to admire Liza-Lu purely and spiritually would be, according to both God's and Darwin's laws, to abandon her. Angel has learned the hard way the dangers of idealizing and holding back from women. There is no evidence that this is "the woman he worships." But he is finally in a position to make a woman happy whether she is the woman he loves or the sister who equally deserves love. He has come a long way since he "picked and chose" without insight or discrimination at the Marlott dance. He has finally abdicated the role of selector entirely. Adam took the Eve God made for him, Abraham the Hagar Sarah gave him, Jacob the Bilhah Rachel shared with him. Legally or illegally Angel will take the woman Tess has left for him.

While he returns to Genesis, Hardy takes a Darwinian approach to the conclusion of his novel. Four women have been sacrificed so that Liza-Lu can be a lover and mother. *Tess of the d'Urbervilles* signals the imminent demise of the Victorian marriage plot. Within a few years George Gissing would write *The Odd Women* which asks even more blatantly than *Tess*—what becomes of the novel when it can neither kill off nor marry off all of its female characters? The Victorian marriage plot often toyed with characters' and readers' desires. Dickens taught Arthur Clennam how to get over Pet Meagles and fall in love with Little Dorrit; George Eliot showed her readers why Daniel Deronda must marry Mirah rather than Gwendolen. But Hardy has done something quite unprecedented to our narrative desires and expectations. We cannot easily imagine Angel choosing Marian, Izz, or Retty, yet we are stunned to see him go off with the non-character, Liza-Lu, a woman neither the reader nor Angel has grown to love. That this non-character is, of course, the long-anticipated Rachel, the beautiful, flawless, younger sister of male fantasy, "a spiritualized image of Tess," (313) with "all the best of [Tess] without the bad of [Tess]"(311) is still shocking. For in Genesis she was Jacob's reward; in *Tess* she is Angel's punishment.

At different times in her story we can identify Tess with each of Jacob's lovers. From the birth of her son through her courtship with Angel, she can be seen as Rachel. On her wedding night she becomes Leah. Through the desperate letters she writes her estranged husband we can see her identification with Bilhah and Zilpah: "I would be content, ay glad, to live with you as your servant, if I may not as your wife; so that I could only be near you, and get glimpses of you, and think of you as mine"(265). I would like to conclude by briefly considering Tess's relationship to Jacob's only daughter, Dinah.

The story of Jacob's extraordinary sexual passivity is quickly followed by one of the most brutal tales in the Old Testament. Leah's daughter, Dinah, is raped by Shechem. When Jacob hears of the crime committed against his only daughter, he "[holds] his peace"(34:6). Instead, Leah's sons express their outrage. They agree to let Shechem marry Dinah if he and the rest of the men of his tribe agree to be circumcised. While the men are still incapacitated, Simeon and Levi attack Shechem's town unopposed, slaughter all the men, and liberate their sister. Their brothers join in by looting the town and taking all the women and children captive. This is the "first major crime of the people of Israel" (Armstrong 96). Yet despite his sons' brutality, it is Jacob himself who has often been criticized for his non-responsiveness and "puling self-pity" (97). "You have stirred up trouble for me, making me stink among the land's inhabitants, among Canaanite and Peruzite, when I am a handful of men. If they gather against me and strike me, I shall be destroyed, I and my household" (34:30).

> At last, at the end of the massacre and the plunder, Jacob broke his long, shameful silence. Did he express horror at the cruelty of the crime? Did he finally lament the outrage suffered by his daughter? Did he grieve for the slain? Apparently, these considerations weighed little with the patriarch of Israel. He simply regretted the danger that Simeon and Levi had brought upon the family and—above all—upon himself.   (Armstrong 97)

Jacob's sons have the last words in this story: "Like a whore should our sister be treated?" (34:31) The strong implication of their response, as Karen Armstrong has noted, is that not only Shechem but Jacob himself has treated Dinah as a prostitute; "by doing nothing, he had tacitly suggested that the rape of his daughter was acceptable to him" (98).

In Tess's case, of course, both of her parents are eager to forgive their daughter's rapist and quick to blame Tess herself for leaving him prematurely. Tess is forced to baptize her own child because her father is so ashamed of his daughter and grandson:

> It was nearly bedtime, but she rushed downstairs and asked if she might send for the parson. The moment happened to be one at which her father's sense of the antique nobility of his family was highest, and his sensitiveness to the smudge which Tess had set upon that nobility most pronounced, for he had just returned from his weekly booze at Rolliver's Inn. No parson should come inside his door, he declared, prying into his affairs just then, when, by her shame, it had become more necessary than ever to hide them. He locked the door and put the key in his pocket.   (73)

If Jacob plays no part in liberating Dinah, this travesty of the proud patriarch actually locks his daughter up. When Tess is raped, Hardy's narrator asks "where was Tess's guardian angel? where was the Providence of her simple faith?''(57) and concludes that, perhaps like the God Elijah spoke of, he "was sleeping and not to be awaked''(57). But it is never a divinity who rescues or avenges raped women in the Bible. That job is always reserved for their kinsmen. (See, for example, the story of Tamar and Amnon [II Samuel 13].) It is doubly ironic that Hardy here reminds us of "the sins of the fathers''(57), "some of Tess d'Urberville's mailed ancestors,'' who doubtless "rollicking home from a fray had dealt the same measure even more ruthlessly towards peasant girls of their time,''(57) when her own living family—father, brothers, and finally and most tragically husband—is absent during and after every crisis of her life.

Lest we had forgotten, the horrible massacre perpetrated by Jacob's sons reminds us that the powerful, controlling women of Genesis lived under a patriarchy. Tess, of course, does as well, but it is a patriarchy largely devoid of men. During the course of the novel, this "visionary essence of woman—a whole sex condensed into one typical form'' (103) takes on many roles normally reserved for men; she baptizes her baby, performs the most difficult labor in the field, and becomes her family's sole breadwinner. Throughout the novel she defends and protects herself and inevitably as her ineffectual husband leaves her home and somehow "[finds] himself in the street, ''(299) avenges herself. In the eerie scene at Stonehenge, Hardy suggests that Tess must murder a man in order for other men to appear on the horizon:

> The figure came straight towards the circle of pillars in which they were. [Angel] heard something behind him, the brush of feet. Turning, he saw over the prostrate columns another figure; then, before he was aware, another was at hand on the right, under a trilithon, and another on the left. . . . "It is no use, sir,'' he said. "There are sixteen of us on the Plain; and the whole country is reared.'' (312)

In an exquisitely ironic gesture Hardy ends his novel about the abandonment of women with men arriving in droves to punish a woman—for having been left alone.

NOTES

1. Thomas Hardy, *Tess of the d'Urbervilles* (New York: Norton, 1991), 113. All further references are to the same edition.
2. Gillian Beer, *Darwin's Plots* (London: Ark, 1985), 214. See, for example, Mary Jacobus, "Tess's Purity,'' *Essays in Criticism* 26 (1976): 318–38 and for a summary of some of the history of this criticism Margaret Higgonet's introduction

to and essay "A Woman's Voice: Tess and the Problem of Voice," in *The Sense of Sex*, ed. Margaret R. Higonnet (Chicago: Illinois, 1993), 1–31.

3. See, for example, Dianne Fallon Sadoff, "Looking at Tess: The Female Figure in Two Narrative Media," *The Sense of Sex*, 149. "Women readers suspect such adoration. For Kaja Silverman, Tess is *not* desirable and so seduced but mastered by the masculine gaze as figuration, split as subject, and submitted to the oscillation such instability produces; for Penny Boumelha, the narrator's fantasies of penetration and engulfment violate Tess as fully as do Alec's actions. Indeed, Hardy feels ambivalent toward the image of woman and the destiny to which he consigns her; complicit in Tess's violation, Hardy and his narrator, like Angel, participate in killing her."

4. Robert Alter, *Genesis: Translation and Commentary* (New York: Norton, 1996), 155. I will be using Alter's translation of Genesis throughout the article.

5. Alfred, Lord Tennyson, *In Memoriam* (LV) in *The Plays and Poems of Alfred, Lord Tennyson* (New York: Random House, 1938), 323.

6. Izz is later briefly (and apparently unsuccessfully) courted by another man, Amby Seedling (246).

7. See Roger Robinson's discussion in "Hardy and Darwin" in *Thomas Hardy: The Writer and his Background*, ed. Norman Page (London: Bell & Hyman, 1980), 132. Hardy's journal entries from 1881 and 1889 are quoted in their larger context by Lionel Stevenson, *Darwin Among the Poets* (New York: Russell & Russell, 1963), 266.

8. Beer, 211. See Charles Darwin, *The Descent of Man and Selection in Relation to Sex* (London, 1871), 911.

9. See Alter, p.194 for a discussion of Jacob's non-response.

WORKS CITED

Alter, Robert. *Genesis: Translation and Commentary*. New York: Norton, 1996.

Armstrong, Karen. *In the Beginning*. New York: Knopf, 1996.

Beer, Gillian. *Darwin's Plots*. London: Ark, 1985.

Darwin, Charles. *The Descent of Man and Selection in Relation to Sex* London, 1871.

Dresner, Samuel. *Rachel*. Minneapolis: Fortress, 1994.

Hardy, Thomas. *Tess of the d'Urbervilles*. New York: Norton, 1991.

Higgonet, Margaret R., ed. *The Sense of Sex*. Chicago: Illinois, 1993.

Page, Norman., ed. *Thomas Hardy: The Writer and His Background*. London: Bell & Hyman, 1980.

Perkin, Joan. *Victorian Women*. New York: New York UP, 1993.

Seymour-Smith, Martin. *Thomas Hardy*. New York: St. Martin's, 1994.

Stevenson, Lionel. *Darwin Among the Poets*. New York: Russell & Russell, 1963.

Sutherland, John. *Can Jane Eyre Be Happy?: More Puzzles in Classic Fiction* Oxford: Oxford UP, 1997.

Tennyson, Alfred, Lord. *The Plays and Poems of Alfred, Lord Tennyson*. New York: Random, 1938.

Near Confinement: Pregnant Women in the Nineteenth-Century British Novel

Cynthia Northcutt Malone

While eighteenth-century British novels are peppered with women "big with child"—Moll Flanders, Molly Seagrim, Mrs. Pickle—nineteenth-century novels typically veil their pregnant characters. Even in nine-teenth-century advice books by medical men, circumlocution and euphe-mism obscure discussions of pregnancy. This essay explores the changing cultural significance of the female body from the mid-eigh-teenth century to the early Victorian period, giving particular attention to the grotesque figure of Mrs. Gamp in Martin Chuzzlewit. *Through ostentatious circumlocution and through the hilariously grotesque dou-bleness of Mrs. Gamp, Dickens both observes and ridicules the Victo-rian middle-class decorum enveloping pregnancy in silence.*

> And now one of the new fashions of our very elegant society is to go in perfectly light-coloured dresses—quite tight —without a particle of shawl or scarf . . . and to dance within a fortnight of their confinement and even valse at seven months!!! Where is delicacy of feeling going to? Sybil St Albans danced a quadrille under these circumstances.
> —Queen Victoria, March, 1870 (qtd. in Perkin 66)

Smack in the middle of *Martin Chuzzlewit*, Dickens introduces the unforgetta-ble Mrs. Gamp in a circumlocution so exaggeratedly delicate that it draws attention to the very subject it tiptoes around. Pecksniff has just arrived at

Dickens Studies Annual, Volume 29, Copyright © 2000 by AMS Press, Inc. All rights reserved.

Mrs. Gamp's lodging, seeking that "performer of nameless offices about the persons of the dead" (374). The novel discreetly avoids naming the tasks of preparation for burial—washing and dressing the corpse—but how much greater is the ostentatious, excessive politeness that averts mention of Mrs. Gamp's other professional function: "It chanced upon this particular occasion, that Mrs Gamp had been up all the previous night, in attendance upon a ceremony to which the usage of gossips has given that name which expresses, in two syllables, the curse pronounced on Adam" (374). Compare this scene, peopled by Pecksniff and "whole troops of married ladies (some about to trouble Mrs Gamp themselves very shortly)" (375) with the numerous references to Molly Seagrim "big with child" in Fielding's *Tom Jones*, published in 1749, nearly a hundred years before *Martin Chuzzlewit* (1843–44). These two comic treatments of pregnancy and birth, separated by a century, mark a significant shift in literary decorum.

Compare, for example, Tobias Smollett's *Peregrine Pickle* (published in 1751) and Eliot's *Middlemarch* (published in 1871–72). First, *Peregrine Pickle*: Mrs. Pickle "had not been married many months when she exhibited evident symptoms of pregnancy" (21); the narrator later refers to her as "the big-bellied lady" (24). Now, *Middlemarch*: "It was Sunday, and [Dorothea] could not have the carriage to go to Celia, who had lately had a baby" (329). The only hint of Celia's pregnancy came 62 pages before, when Sir James Chettam forms the plan "to plead Celia's indisposition as a reason for fetching Dorothea by herself to the Hall" (267).

Of course, Eliot treats Rosamond's pregnancy much more directly than Celia's. Focusing on Lydgate, a medical man, allows a straightforward approach to Rosamond's condition: "Rosamond was expecting to have a baby, and Lydgate wished to save her from any perturbation" (323). Later, after Rosamond ignores Lydgate's cautions and suffers a fright while riding, the narrator reveals that "[h]er baby had been born prematurely, and all the embroidered robes and caps had to be laid by in darkness" (401). While the novel marks clearly Rosamond's pregnancy and miscarriage, the fate of those tiny caps and clothes gets more detailed attention than the experiences of the body; we hear only that Lydgate found Rosamond to be "mildly certain that the ride had made no difference, and that if she had stayed at home the same symptoms would have come on and would have ended in the same way, because she had felt something like them before" (404). In the narrative zone of this doctor-husband, Eliot permits herself direct speech; even then, however, her novel avoids unseemly bodily details.

Smollett, on the other hand, highlights the big belly of the pregnant matron. Admittedly, Smollett will say *anything*. In this case, though, his candor resembles that of his contemporaries. Eighteenth-century novels are peppered with women "big with child": Moll Flanders, Molly Seagrim, Mrs. Pickle. Nine-teenth-century novels typically veil their pregnant characters. What accounts for this shift?

In *Martin Chuzzlewit*, of course, veiling serves the particular narrative ends of comedy and social satire. Dickens exploits in this scene the comic possibilities of extravagant circumlocution. This histrionic tiptoeing around "labor" has the effect of whispering in a crowded elevator: we strain to hear what the whisper pretends to hush. Surely Dickens is snorting here at the ridiculous bourgeois etiquette that blushes to name a condition so remarkably hard to miss. After all, pregnancy was a harassingly present reality for Dickens; he must have felt he was sharing his dinner table with an almost always pregnant Catherine. Who could be more likely than Dickens to milk that absurd middle-class delicacy for all its humorous potential? Evidence for this reading lies in the delicious pairing of Dickensian circumlocution with Hablot K. Browne's illustration of the scene. Among the "whole troops of married ladies (some about to trouble Mrs Gamp themselves very shortly)" is one "lady (with her arms folded)" who "said she wished he had chosen any other time for fetching Mrs Gamp, but it always happened so with *her*" (375). Phiz makes visible the reason for her objection by giving those folded arms a prominent resting place (fig. 1).

The comic absurdity of visual spectacle paired with narrative circumspection in *Martin Chuzzlewit* points to a cultural phenomenon so obvious that readers generally pay no attention to it. For most of the nineteenth century, in the novel and in bourgeois culture, pregnancy was visible but unspeakable. "In middle-class circles," as Joan Perkin observes, "pregnancy was too indelicate a subject to discuss" (66). Despite the delicate silence of respectable people, pregnancy must have been part of daily life.[1] The etiquette of public appearance during pregnancy was, of course, inflected by class. Middle-class women, according to Perkin, concealed their pregnant bodies: "Voluminous clothes hid the increasing size of the mother-to-be, who tended to stay in virtual hiding until after the birth" (66). But Judith Schneid Lewis contends that, for aristocratic women, "at no time during the century 1760 to 1860 does there appear to have been any social taboo against appearing visibly pregnant in public, contrary to popular myth" (124; see also Perkin 65–66). Certainly the epigraph to this essay supports the contention that upper-class women, at least, participated fully in social life until their confinements. And working-class women typically continued to work until the births of their babies (Davies; Perkin 66). Thus, people in every stratum of British life must have encountered pregnant women, either family members confined at home, or aristocratic women "valsing" without a particle of shawl, or working women going about their daily rounds; yet the treatment of pregnancy in bourgeois culture brings to mind the story of the emperor's new clothes.

The concealment of pregnancy in the nineteenth-century British novel is an intriguing subject. How did novelists manage to veil a condition at once so common, so necessary to the machinery of plot, and so spectacularly visible? One way to address the question is by looking briefly at several novels spanning the first half of the nineteenth century. But the deeper, more intriguing question, of course, is *why* it became not merely impolite but virtually impossible to speak clearly and directly about pregnancy at this time. *Martin Chuzzlewit* deserves particular attention; in this novel, Dickens deploys the mode of grotesque representation to register the anxieties surrounding pregnancy

Veils and Vulgarity

Between *Tom Jones* and *Martin Chuzzlewit*, between the raucous eighteenth-century comic figures of pregnancy and Dickens's spoof on ladies in what Mrs. Gamp would call "a interesting state," Austen's *Sense and Sensibility* and *Persuasion* serve as a kind of fulcrum (Forster 377). In *Sense and Sensibility*, written in 1797–98 and published in 1811, Austen uses pregnancy to point the contrast between Lady Middleton's coldly elegant manners and the decidedly inelegant manners of her mother, Mrs. Jennings, "a good humoured, merry, fat, elderly woman, who talked a great deal, seemed very happy, and rather vulgar" (29). In Austen's allegory of manners, no conduct is more certain to mark a character as "rather vulgar" than candid discussion of pregnancy. When Charlotte Palmer, Mrs. Jennings's other daughter, appears at the Dashwood's cottage, Mrs. Jennings confides across the room to Elinor Dashwood that Charlotte should not have undertaken an exhausting journey: "it was wrong in her situation" (93). Lest anyone fail to catch her meaning, she elaborates. "She expects to be confined in February," Mrs. Jennings hisses, yet Charlotte refused to stay home and rest this morning. Lady Elegant shrinks in horror from Mrs. Vulgar; the narrator observes that "Lady Middleton could no longer endure such a conversation, and therefore exerted herself to ask Mr. Palmer if there was any news in the paper" (93). The pointed contrast in manners underscores difference in social rank, of course: the late Mr. Jennings made his money in *trade,* and Mrs. Jennings embarrasses Lady Middleton not only by acknowledging frankly her daughter's pregnancy, but also by maintaining friendships with tradespeople in unfashionable quarters of London. A few chapters later, Mrs. Jennings offends again. She asks about Charlotte and her family when Colonel Brandon reports that he has just dined with the Palmers. "I warrant you she is a fine size by now," comments Mrs. Jennings, and an impeccably polite Colonel Brandon responds only that "Mrs. Palmer appeared quite well" (137). No one except Mrs. Jennings refers explicitly to Mrs. Palmer's pregnancy, and at last it is the newspaper that brings word that "the Lady of Thomas Palmer was safely delivered of a son and heir" (207).

In *Persuasion*, pregnancy is more completely veiled. The reportedly beautiful wife of Colonel Wallis never appears because "she was in daily expectation of her confinement" (155). In this novel, the pregnant woman remains discreetly just out of view. Mrs. Wallis does takes part in the circulation of important information, however; her monthly nurse, Mrs. Rooke, also attends Anne's school-friend, Mrs. Smith. As the nurse passes in and out of Mrs. Walli's rooms, taking in "little thread-cases, pin-cusions, and card-racks" and bringing out the money for those dainty niceties, she also—and more importantly—brings out revelations crucial to the plot (167). As I will show, Dickens makes astonishing comic turns twenty-five years later, in *Martin Chuzzlewit*, on the figure of the monthly nurse shuttling in and out of the invisible place where pregnant women are confined in nineteenth-century fiction.

Circumlocution

Dickens's periphrastic treatment of "labor" may ridicule bourgeois delicacy, but it also preserves it. Certainly *Martin Chuzzlewit* seems proof against the charges leveled at *Adam Bede* ten years later. As Jill Matus points out in *Unstable Bodies*, the unsigned review of Eliot's novel in *Saturday Review* reproved the author for "his" indecent treatment of pregnancy:

> The author of *Adam Bede* has given in his adhesion to a very curious practice that is now becoming common among novelists, and it is a practice that we consider most objectionable. It is that of dating and discussing the several stages that precede the birth of a child. We seem to be threatened with a literature of pregnancy. We have had *White Lies* and *Sylvan Holt's Daughter*, and now we have *Adam Bede*. Hetty's feelings and changes are indicated with a punctual sequence that makes the account of her misfortunes read like the rough notes of a man-midwife's conversations with a bride. This is intolerable. Let us copy the old masters of the art, who, if they gave us a baby, gave it us all at once. A decent author and a decent public may surely take the premonitory symptoms for granted.   (28 February 1859, vii, 250–51, qtd. in Carroll 76)

We might wonder which "old masters" this reviewer had in mind, though we can safely rule out the writers of the Hebrew and Christian scriptures, Shakespeare, Defoe, Smollett, and Fielding. But if these "old masters" are open to the charge of representing "the premonitory symptoms" of childbirth, was the author of *Adam Bede* also open to this charge? Evidently these remarks drove Matus back to Eliot's novel. "We are hardly likely to think of *Adam Bede* as a novel that breaks new ground in its treatment of pregnancy,'' Matus comments: "Reviews such as this mark as contentious what we would surely bypass as insignificant, or perhaps even experience as evasive. The narrative offers but a few details and symptoms of Hetty's pregnancy, and those are euphemistically expressed" (2).[2]

Closer investigation of this reviewer's charges leads to the hypothesis that circumlocution is the only available locution for the discussion of pregnancy in the British novel by mid-century. Without that hypothesis, Charles Reade's *White Lies* and Holme Lee's (Harriet Parr's) *Sylvan Holt's Daughter* certainly provide no fuller explanation of this reviewer's disgust. In *White Lies*, Josephine de Beaurepaire, secretly married after her family receives news that a man with her husband's name and title has been killed in battle, loses her appetite, faints once, and then regains her health:

> Her hollow cheeks recovered their plump smoothness, and her beauty its bloom, and her person grew more noble and statue-like than ever, and within she felt a sense of indomitable vitality. Her appetite had for some time been excessively feeble and uncertain, and her food tasteless; but of late, by what she conceived to be a reaction such as is common after youth has shaken off a long sickness, her appetite had been not only healthy but eager.   (249)

Josephine herself fails to grasp the significance of these premonitory symptoms. A trusted servant must break the news: "'My poor young mistress, you are but a child still. You have a deep water to wade through,' said Jacintha, so solemnly that Josephine trembled. 'A deep water, and do not see it even. You have told me what is past [the secret marriage], now I must tell you what is coming.'" After asking whether Josephine has any "misgiving," Jacintha goes on: "'Then turn your head from me a bit, my sweet young lady; I am an honest woman, though I am not so innocent as you, and I am forced against my will to speak my mind plainer than I am used to'" (253). A reader hoping for plain speech here must endure disappointment: Jacintha's explanation is elided.

Like *Adam Bede*, *White Lies* depends on ellipsis, euphemism, and oblique reference to represent pregnancy. A respectable novelist teaches nothing about "the facts of life"; only those who already know the code understand the import of "plump cheeks," "bloom," and "indomitable vitality." If not from the works of respectable novelists, where would a young woman learn the reference of such delicate allusions? What other texts or sources of information supplied the information that the bourgeois novel hushed? The documentary evidence suggests the delicate avoidance of pregnancy-talk may have left many young women ignorant.

While Josephine's ignorance serves the specific narrative end of emphasizing her "innocence" in *White Lies*, it also points to the obvious consequence of polite silence. A sizeable number of young women—even married wo-men—evidently knew nothing about sex or pregnancy. The ignorance of young working-class women shows up in several heartbreaking letters gath-ered by the Women's Co-Operative Guild and published in *Maternity*. One of the most poignant letters begins:

> My first girl was born before I attained my twentieth year, and I had a step-mother who had had no children of her own, so I was not able to get any knowledge from her; and even if she had known anything I don't suppose she would have dreamt of telling me about these things which were supposed to exist, but must not be talked about. About a month before the baby was born I remember asking my aunt where the baby would come from. She was astounded, and did not make me much wiser. (30)

This young woman's experience was not anomalous; letter after letter empha-sizes the suffering that resulted from ignorance. Another writer notes,

> I should tell you I was twenty-eight years old when I was married, and I had been married eleven months when my first baby was born, and I can truthfully say I was ignorant of anything concerning married life or motherhood when I was married. In fact, when the midwife came to me when I was in such pain, I had not the slightest idea where or how the child would come into the world. (187)

(As an aside, let us pause to note that a pregnant woman in her situation would be likely to find the answer, be it ever so plainly spoken, barely comprehensible and nearly unimaginable. I suspect that many and many a well-read, clinically instructed late-twentieth-century woman has sat through prepared childbirth classes in secret certainty that *this is not going to work*. We all learned the lesson of relative size in toddlerhood, when we tried laboriously and repeatedly to pass large objects through small holes. It is late in the day to unlearn that lesson. Surely any pregnant women could echo Louise Erdrich's rueful remark in *The Blue Jay's Dance:* "I fear I've made a ship in a bottle" (9).)

Working-class women may have had fewer resources than middle- or up-per-middle class women for learning about sex and pregnancy; Ross argues that "upper middle-class mothers and daughters exchanged reasonably infor-mative letters and conversations about sex and the female body," but "such sexual talk rarely passed between working-class generations" (107).[3] But ignorance about these matters was also common among young women in the higher ranks. "Women grew up with widely differing knowledge about sex," Perkin suggests, "and it was not simply a matter of class, though upper- and middle-class daughters were more strictly guarded." She goes on to illustrate with the case of "Annie Besant, the birth-control activist," who "said when she married in 1866, 'My ignorance of all that marriage meant was as profound as though I had been a child of four instead of twenty. My dreamy life . . . kept innocent of all questions of sex, was no preparation for married existence' '' (Perkin 57).

Of course, it is dangerous to generalize broadly about the distribution of and access to information. John Hawkins Miller quotes one ladies' magazine story, published in 1828, which reminds readers that some young girls surely knew more than their elders imagined: Two girls are talking in a corner: '''So, Rosa, I see Mrs Buckle is in the family way again.' 'Hush, Laura, pray speak lower, for Mama thinks I don't know anything about it. Our old Nurse and Sally always tell me everything, but Mama would be so very angry if she knew''' (qtd. in Miller 33; qtd. from Cunnington 64–65). Still, we can reasonably conclude that bourgeois delicacy must have left many young women in the dark about these matters.[4]

Women with sufficient leisure and means could consult advice books like Dr. Thomas Bull's *Hints to Mothers*, "the first book devoted to antenatal care," according to Jenny Carter and Therese Duriez. Dr. Bull's *Hints* was published first in 1837 and then in twenty-four subsequent editions (48). In the brief preface to the 1841 edition, Dr. Bull approves the delicacy that silenced direct speech about pregnancy and childbirth even as he acknowledges women's need for information. His work, of course, enters the world to solve their dilemma—in the discreet form of *Hints* rather than, say, *Advice*:

> In the minds of married women, and especially young females, those feelings of delicacy naturally and commendably exist which prevent a full disclosure of their circumstances, when they find it necessary to consult their medical advisers. To meet this difficulty, and to counteract the ill-advised suggestions of ignorant persons during the period of confinement, is the chief aim of the following pages.
> While it is believed that much of the information contained in this volume is highly important to the comfort and even to the well-doing of the married female, much of it is, at the same time, of a character upon which she cannot easily obtain satisfaction. She will find no difficulty in *reading* information, for which she would find it insuperably difficult *to ask*. (3)

The published notes of a man-midwife to a prospective bride, then, are intended to mediate between the insuperable difficulties of clear speech and the perils of ignorance—and, of course, to shore up the medical men's authority as the only reliable writers and resources of information for pregnant women.

At least some of the published instruction about pregnancy, however, used language that was nearly as coded and highly figurative as that of *Adam Bede* or *White Lies*. Consider Dr. Pye Henry Chavasse's *Ladies' Family Physician: Advice to a Wife and Mother*, reprinted several times in the nineteenth century. In the section titled, "Signs of Pregnancy," Chavasse informs women: "The first sign that leads a lady to suspect that she is pregnant is her *ceasing-to-be-unwell*":

> This, provided she has just before been in good health, is a strong symptom of pregnancy; but still there must be others to corroborate it.
>
> A healthy married woman, during the period of child-bearing, suddenly *ceasing-to-be-unwell* is of itself alone almost a sure and certain sign of pregnancy—requiring but little else besides to confirm it. This fact is well known by all who have had children—they base their predictions and their calculations upon it, and upon it alone, and are, in consequence, seldom deceived.
>
> But as *ceasing-to-be-unwell* may proceed from other causes than that of pregnancy—such as disease or disorder of the womb, or of other organs of the body—especially of the lungs—it is not by itself alone entirely to be depended upon; although, as a single sign, it is—especially if the patient be healthy—*the* most reliable of all the other signs of pregnancy.   (108; italics in original)

Chavasse seems not to notice the linguistic peculiarity that his unvarying use of euphemism, "ceasing-to-be-unwell," creates: throughout this passage, readers are assured that a *healthy* woman who *ceases to be unwell* is almost certainly pregnant. Being "unwell," of course, is a euphemistic phrase for menstruating; but this passage suggests that even a woman knowledgeable and resourceful enough to seek information from a physician's advice book might find the language a tad murky. Even Dr. Bull's more direct *Hints* could certainly lead to perplexity. Bull begins, as Chavasse does, with "ceasing to be unwell," but he goes on to use the plainer language of "menstruation." However, he also treats the disappearance of menstrual periods as a far more dubious symptom, listing four exceptions to the general rule that a woman who misses her periods is probably pregnant, so that the gains of clear language are offset by the uncertainty he attributes to bodily signs. These men-midwives' counsel to brides was unlikely to enlighten them much about the signs or symptoms of pregnancy.[5]

Labor

If medical advice books must negotiate ways to give information while showing respect for "those feelings of delicacy" which "naturally and commendably exist" in bourgeois women, of course, it is hardly surprising to find the representation of pregnancy in the nineteenth-century bourgeios novel to be far more constrained. From Austen to mid-century, discreet allusion, euphemism, and periphrasis artfully conceal the pregnant woman in the British novel. The question remains: *Why* must the bourgeois novel—or advice book—use such voluminous sentences to hide the condition of the mother-to-be? *Why* can't these women appear, like Sybil St. Albans, without a particle of scarf?

The most obvious answer is that pregnancy served as an incontrovertible marker of sex, both in the novel and in the semiotics of everyday life. Whether a particular woman's "innocence," so carefully preserved by the mid-century bourgeois novel, was genuine or feigned, her pregnant body testified to carnal knowledge. No wonder bourgeois culture found means of artful concealment; the pregnant body threatened to shatter the culturally defined role for middle-class women.[6] Let her speech be as delicate as may be, if the pregnant woman appeared in public, she might just as well semaphor "sex."

But surely this answer is incomplete. Recent works in the history of sexuality, including Mason's *The Making of Victorian Sexuality*, Barrett-Ducrocq's *Love in the Time of Victoria*, and Anderson's *When Passion Reigned*, have refracted the notion of Victorian prudery. While many works in this area of social history have reminded us to distinguish middle-class mainstream culture from other segments of Victorian life, the wide range of social and sexual practices these works document in the Victorian period should make us cautious about offering simple answers even to questions about middle-class life.

In this essay, I want to complicate that answer. Ruth Perry traces the "desexualization of women" in the second half of the eighteenth century, examining "the double, interlocked, mutually exclusive relationship between sexuality and maternity as it was reconstructed in the middle of the eighteenth century." She argues that, "in a remarkably short span, the maternal succeeded, supplanted, and repressed the sexual definition of women, who began to be reimagined as nurturing rather than desiring, as supportive rather than appetitive" (116). I want to focus on two points in her argument. She documents policy decisions from 1756 to 1760 that situated "reproductive service" first as labor in service to the nation—making new citizens—and then firmly in "the private sphere" (111). By examining "novels dealing with breast disease" and "medical treatises advocating maternal breast-feeding," she highlights "the new cultural discourse constructing women's bodies as maternal rather than sexual" (136–37). By confining and concealing the pregnant woman, I am suggesting, the nineteenth-century novel confirms both the reconstruction of the woman's body as maternal and the containment of that body in the private sphere of the family.

As Sally Shuttleworth observes, "Motherhood was set at the ideological centre of the Victorian bourgeois ideal" (31). While maternity has come to be equated with femininity—understanding "femininity" as a distinctly, if tacitly, middle-class construct—by the nineteenth century, pregnancy troubles this equation, suspending the woman's body between sexuality and maternity. Not only does pregnancy bear clear witness to a woman's sexual relations, defining her simultaneously as sexual being and as mother-in-the-making, but the swelling of the breasts in pregnancy also connoted both preparation for nursing and sexual attractiveness. "According to one scientific commentator of the era," Shuttleworth notes, "woman was most pleasing to man during 'the period of activity of the reproductive organs,' and her 'greatest beauty of form' was to be found in 'those parts peculiar to her organization': the bust and the pelvis'" (41).[7]

Confining the pregnant body, then, conveniently locates both maternity and sexuality in the private sphere. As we've seen already, that confinement—both as a representational practice, in nineteenth-century bourgeois novels, and as a social practice—is largely, at least, a middle-class phenomenon. To understand why women in some ranks are visible while those in other ranks are invisible, we need only return to the word that Dickens avoided with such relish, "labor," and ask: Who owned their labor? Perry suggests that women's reproductive labor was positioned decisively in "the private sphere" in the eighteenth century, and social historians have documented thoroughly the nineteenth-century bourgeois ideal of the maternal woman tending her children and tending the hearth. Her domestic and reproductive labor, like her legal identity, were wholly subsumed in husband, family, and home. Tightening up the constraints when she was pregnant, confining her to the private space of the home, signalled even more clearly that the full range of this sexual-maternal woman's energies and capacities belonged there. While working-class women's reproductive labor presumably belonged to their husbands, the different ownership of reproductive and other forms of labor meant that they couldn't be confined to "the private sphere": their employers also directed and owned their labor.[8] In the ranks above the middle, the structure of financial settlements tended to give women a greater measure of autonomy, and with greater independence from their husbands evidently came greater freedom during pregnancy (see Lewis 124–27). The greater visibility of pregnant women in the ranks above and below the middle serves as a foil, highlighting the complete absorption of a middle-class woman's sexual, maternal, and domestic labor in the private space of the family.

At one level, then, the invisibility of the middle-class pregnant woman signalled the control of her body and her energies. At another, the confinement of that body may have been a strategy intended to contain a less obvious threat: the ways in which pregnancy undermines the notions of self-possession and coherence central to the notion of the bourgeois self. As Donna Haraway observes:

> Pregnant women in Western cultures are in much more shocking relation than men to doctrines of unencumbered property in the self. In "making babies," female bodies violate Western women's liberal singularity during their lifetimes and compromise their claims to full citizenship. For Western men in reproduction, setting aside the "problem" of death, the loss of self seems so tiny, the degrees of freedom so many. Ontologically always potentially pregnant, women

are both more limited in themselves, with a body that betrays their individuality,
and limiting to men's fantastic self-reproductive projects.   (143)

In the case of Victorian culture, we can move from the ontological condition
of perpetual potential pregnancy to the reality: many women of all social
classes were pregnant much of the time for a period of many years. Patricia
Branca concludes that "more than a quarter of the Victorian woman's life
was spent in either pregnancy "or in nursing and recovering from pregnancy"
(75). Think of Catherine Dickens. . . .[9]

As Amanda Anderson has shown, the figure of the "fallen woman" in
Victorian culture registers the threatening opposites of the characteristics that
define "normative masculine identity" (13). But at least a man could close
the door on the importunate fallen woman. The pregnant woman in his own
home, a weirdly double and single body, both herself and not herself, undeniably sexual and visibly maternal, ate at the same table and slept uncomfortably nearby. Small wonder, then, that the fallen woman can parade around
the Victorian novel making a spectacle of herself while the more threatening
figure of the pregnant woman is kept in representational confinement.

"A Interesting State"

In *Martin Chuzzlewit*, Dickens employs a mode of representation that simultaneously observes middle-class decorum and registers the anxieties that
muffle nineteenth-century discussions of pregnancy. He draws Mrs. Gamp as
a grotesque figure, one that brings to mind Bakhtin's musings on the "senile
pregnant hags" in the Kerch collection of terracotta figurines (Bakhtin 25).
Like a Möbius strip, Mrs. Gamp dissolves the distinction between the singular
and the dual. This apparently singular body dresses in voluminous clothing
that blazons doubleness. Furthermore, she speaks as one occupied by another:
that ardent admirer whom "a fearful mystery surrounded," Mrs. Harris (472).

At the most obvious level, of course, Dickens's satirical portrait of Mrs.
Gamp fits within a larger contemporary frame of attacks on midwives. In
professional medical circles, these attacks served to heighten the prestige of
"medical men" and erode the traditional role of midwives (Poovey 39–40).
But the letters in *Maternity*, along with other contemporary evidence, make
it clear that the dirty, drunken, ill-educated nurse-midwife was not simply a
satirical figure which physicians invented for professional gain.[10] One woman
complains of a birth attended by "a woman who did not know her work"
(Davies 83). Another writes, "I have not had a doctor to any of my confinements, but nearly lost my life and child's through the first one. The midwife
was a qualified woman, but addicted to drink (which I found out afterwards)"

(Davies 83, 186). Another describes reports that "the midwife I had [for the first birth] had started drinking," and another observes: "I know from one or two of my friends and from my own experience we were all greatly worried at not being able to secure good nurses. As you are aware, many of them drink" (13, 149). Such dreadful stories should come as no surprise, given the extreme laxity of licensing for midwives. As Patricia Branca notes, the licensing requirement instituted in the eighteenth century required only that "the woman had to be recommended by a few matrons, take a formal oath, and pay a fee of 18s.4d. The oath stated that the would-be midwife foreswore child substitution, abortion, sorcery, and over-charging" (78). Thus, the horrors registered comically in Mrs. Gamp include the usual failures attributed to bad nurses and midwives—tippling, ignorance, brutal treatment of patients—but those horrors run deeper.

The peculiar suggestions that Mrs. Gamp is somehow both dual and singular provoke this deeper horror and anxiety. As a pregnant woman's body does, Mrs. Gamp's body calls into question the distinction between double and single; she embodies an insult to bourgeois notions of selfhood and individuality. As a monthly nurse and midwife, furthermore, Mrs. Gamp is associated with the scenes of birth and death, those liminal moments of human life associated, as Bakhtin points out, with the grotesque (Bakhtin 318): "setting aside her natural predilections as a woman, she went to a lying-in or a laying-out with equal zest and relish" (Dickens 378). Through that unseen creature, Mrs. Harris, Dickens heightens this sense of liminality and duality. When Mrs. Gamp speaks, the words of another issue from her mouth: Mrs. Harris's obliging commendations. Thus, when the loquacious Mrs. Gamp pauses for breath, the narrator notes:

> advantage may be taken of the circumstance, to state that a fearful mystery surrounded this lady of the name of Harris, whom no one in the circle of Mrs Gamp's acquantance had ever seen; neither did any human being know her place of residence, though Mrs Gamp appeared on her own showing to be in constant communication with her. . . . the prevalent opinion was that she was a phantom of Mrs. Gamp's brain . . . created for the express purpose of holding visionary dialogues with her on all manner of subjects, and invariably winding up with a compliment to the excellence of her nature.   (472)

Mrs. Gamp conceives an invisible other with whom she is "in constant communication," but the tracking device that might consolidate the identity and existence of Mrs. Harris, her "place of residence," turns out to be the person of Mrs. Gamp. Dickens registers here the puzzling arithmetic that continues to vex the discourses of pregnancy: here is one self, Mrs. Gamp, but the possibility of an equation hangs in the air—one possibly plus something equals goodness knows what.

Even if we share the "prevalent opinion" which the narrator reports, "that [Mrs. Harris] was a phantom of Mrs Gamp's brain . . . created for the express purpose of holding visionary dialogues with her on all manner of subjects, and invariably winding up with a compliment to the excellence of her nature," the argument holds. Even if she is a chronically soused lunatic, her belief in her duality supports the point: an 1858 *Manual of Psychological Medicine* lists among the primary "Moral and Physical" causes of insanity not only "Intemperance" but also "Uterine and Childbearing" (Bucknill and Tuke 256).

But the grotesque doubleness of Mrs. Gamp is also emphatically physical. If "grotesque imagery constructs what we might call a double body," as Bakhtin suggests, if "the image consists of orifices and convexities that present another, newly conceived body," then Mrs. Gamp is surely a latter-day example of the grotesque (318). Her alcohol-reddened nose and her insatiable appetite are common features of the grotesque body (319). And Dickens complicates the topography of this grotesque body by turning it into a stunning construction of "orifices and convexities" when Mrs. Gamp settles down for the night: "she produced a watchman's coat, which she tied round her neck by the sleeves, so that she became two people; and looked, behind, as if she were in the act of being embraced by one of the old patrol" (481). This "fat old woman" who drinks and overeats becomes "two people" in a moment that collapses the sexual embrace and the doubleness of pregnancy (378). The mode of representation, the grotesque, exaggerates the threatening anxieties of pregnancy—evidence of female sexuality and vexing relations of singularity and doubleness—and displaces them from the young women in the novel. Just as circumlocution allows Dickens to speak the unspeakable, so embodying the troubling features of pregnancy in the "senile hag," Mrs. Gamp, allows him to emphasize and defuse the anxieties that attend pregnancy.

In a social world governed by "delicacy of feeling," as Queen Victoria put it, Dickens whisks the troubling figure of the doubled, bulging female body out of representational confinement. His deployment of the grotesque allows him to figure pregnancy obliquely. Crossing out of the veiled scene of pregnancy and childbirth into the action of *Martin Chuzzlewit*, Mrs. Gamp brings into spectacular visibility the deeply unsettling meanings of the pregnant body.

Fig. 1. Hablot K. Browne's *Mr. Pecksniff on his Mission*

NOTES

1. In *Love and Toil*, Ellen Ross argues: "though ubiquitous, pregnancy was also invisible" (107). George Moore's novel, *Esther Waters*, seems to support the point; when Esther Waters is dismissed from service because she is "seven months gone" and unmarried, her mother fails to notice her pregnancy (116). A few pages later, her mother comments, "'I haven't told yer, but I daresay you have noticed that nother [child] is coming;'" it isn't clear from the narrative whether Esther has noticed (118). Does her silence indicate polite avoidance of the subject or failure to notice her mother's pregnancy? In general, Ross' assumption that silence marks invisibility seems questionable.

2. Matus goes on to note: "At one point, the narrator hints that there is 'a more luxuriant womanliness about Hetty of late'; a bit later we learn that 'after the first on-coming of her great dread, some weeks after her betrothal to Adam, she had waited and waited, in the blind vague hope that something would happen to set her free from her terror'; finally, on her flight from Hayslope a stranger's eyes wander to her figure and detect 'what the familar unsuspecting eye leaves unnoticed'" (2). Matus uses the edition edited by S. Gill, Harmondsworth: Penguin, [1859] 1980) 405, 411, 422.

3. "The word *pregnant* . . . was not used outside medical settings," according to Ross (107).

4. In an 1859 letter to Princess Frederick William, Queen Victoria recalls the princess's wedding and casts a stark light on the position of mother, father, and daughter in relation to secrecy and silence: "That last night when we took you to your room, and you cried so much, I said to Papa as we came back 'after all, it is like taking a poor lamb to be sacrificed'. You now know—what I meant, dear. . . . It really makes me shudder when I look around at all your sweet, happy, unconscious sisters—and think that I must give them up too—one by one!!" (10 April 1859; Hibbert 111).

5. As Lorna Duffin argues in "The Conspicuous Consumptive: Woman as Invalid," the murkiness of these advice books served a strategic end. She notes that "a steady stream of popular literature appeared on the subject of female health" in the nineteenth century: "It revealed little however; to provide women with knowledge of their bodies would have removed the experitise of the doctor and undermined the woman's dependence on him" (31).

6. I am speaking here, of course, about the cultural role assigned to middle-class women, not about individual women's relationships to their own sexuality. As Perkin notes, we do have documentary evidence of married women's enjoyment of sex—notably Fanny Kingsley's—we can't draw general conclusions because, of course, most women didn't comment. But we can say with assurance that "an ideology about women emerged in the 1840s and 50s which virtually denied women's sexuality, and the majority of women accepted the judgment" (64).

7. Shuttleworth goes on: "The descriptions of the bosom, 'on which the organs for nutrituion of the tender offspring are developed' spirals off into ecstatic, sexual contemplation: 'It is to her bosom that woman instinctively clasps all that she

rightly loves—her bosom, remarkable for the unsurpassable beauty of its voluptuous contours and graceful inflexions, the white transparent surface of which is set off with an azure network, or tinged with the warm glow of the emotions and passions that make it heave in graceful undulations (Anon. 1851: 19–20) (41–42). See also Anderson on sexualizing maternity (34).

8. See Duffin 29–31 on the crucial differences between middle- and working-class women's social roles.

9. Dickens's letters show his bemusement at the frequency with which children joined his family: His letter to W. H. Prescott, dated 10 November 1843–during the writing of *Martin Chuzzlewit*—serves as an example: "Mrs. Dickens sends her love and best regards. We think of keeping the New Year, by having another child. I am constantly reversing the Kings in the Fairy Tales, and importuning the Gods not to trouble themselves: being quite satisfied with what I have. But they are so generous when they do take a fancy to one!" (House, Storey, and Tillotson, vol. 3, 597).

10. As Anthony Wohl points out in *Endangered Lives: Public Health in Victorian Britain*, physicians' delivery practices were also appalling (15). All in all, he notes, "the great wonder is that so many babies survived" (14).

WORKS CITED

Anderson, Amanda. *Tainted Souls and Painted Faces: The Rhetoric of Fallenness in Victorian Culture.* Ithaca, NY: Cornell UP, 1993.

Anderson, Patricia. *When Passion Reigned: Sex and the Victorians.* NY: Basic Books, 1995.

Austen, Jane. *Sense and Sensibility.* 1811. Ed. Ros Ballaster. Penguin, 1995.

———. *Persuasion.* 1818. Ed. D. W. Harding. Harmondsworth: Penguin, 1965.

Bakhtin, Mikhail. *Rabelais and His World.* 1965. Trans. Helene Iswolsky. Bloomington: Indiana UP, 1984.

Barrett-Ducrocq, Françoise. *Love in the Time of Victoria: Sexuality, Class and Gender in Nineteenth-Century London.* Tr. John Howe. London: Verso, 1991.

Branca, Patricia. *Silent Sisterhood: Middle Class Women in the Victorian Household.* Pittsburgh: Carnegie Mellon UP, 1975.

Bull, Thomas. *Hints to Mothers for the Management of Health During the Period of Pregnancy* . . . NY: Wiley and Putnam, 1842.

Carroll, David, ed. *George Eliot: The Critical Heritage.* NY: Barnes and Noble, 1971.

Carter, Jenny, and Therese Duriez. *With Child: Birth Through the Ages.* Edinburgh: Mainstream, 1986.

Chavasse, Pye Henry. *Ladies' Family Physician: Advice to a Wife and Mother*. Chicago: Donohue, Henneberry, 1890.

Cunnington, Cecil W. *Feminine Attitudes in the Nineteenth Century*. New York: Macmillan, 1936.

Davies, Margaret Llewellyn, ed. *Maternity: Letters from Working-women Collected by The Women's Co-operative Guild*. London: G. Bell and Sons, 1915. Introd. Linda Gordon. NY: Norton, 1978.

Dickens, Charles. *Martin Chuzzlewit*. 1843–44. Ed. P. N. Furbank. Harmondsworth: Penguin, 1986.

Duffin, Lorna. "The Conspicuous Consumptive: Woman as Invalid." Sara DeLamont and Lorna Duffin, eds., *The Nineteenth-Century Woman: Her Cultural and Physical Worlds*. London: Croom Helm; NY: Barnes and Noble, 1978. 26–56.

Erdrich, Louise. *The Blue Jay's Dance: A Birth Year*. NY: HarperCollins, 1995.

Forster, John. *The Life of Charles Dickens*. 3 vols. Philadelphia: Lippincott, 1874.

Haraway, Donna. "Investment Strategies for the Evolving Portfolio of Primate Females." In *Body/Politics: Women and the Discourses of Science*. Ed. Mary Jacobus, Evelyn Fox Keller, and Sally Shuttleworth. NY: Routledge, 1990. 139–62.

Hibbert, Christopher. *Queen Victoria in her Letters and Journals*. New York: Viking, 1984.

Lee, Holme [Harriet Parr]. *Sylvan Holt's Daughter*. 1858. New York: Harper, 1859.

Lewis, Judith Schneid. *In the Family Way: Childbearing in the British Aristocracy, 1760–1860*. New Brunswick, NJ: Rutgers UP, 1986.

Mason, Michael. *The Making of Victorian Sexuality*. Oxford: Oxford UP, 1994.

Matus, Jill L. *Unstable Bodies: Victorian Representations of Sexuality and Maternity*. Manchester: Manchester UP, 1995.

Moore, George. *Esther Waters*. 1894. NY: Liveright, 1932.

Perkin, Joan. *Victorian Women*. NY: New York UP, 1993.

Perry, Ruth. "Colonizing the Breast: Sexuality and Maternity in Eighteenth-Century England." In *Forbidden History: The State, Society, and the Regulation of Sexuality in Modern Europe*. Ed. John C. Fout. Chicago: U. of Chicago P, 1992. 107–37.

Poovey, Mary. *Uneven Developments: The Ideological Work of Gender in Mid-Victorian England*. Chicago: U of Chicago P, 1988.

Reade, Charles. *White Lies*. 1857. In *A Simpleton; White Lies*. Boston: Dana Estes and Co., n.d.

Ross, Ellen. *Love and Toil: Motherhood in Outcast London, 1870–1918*. Oxford: Oxford UP, 1993.

Shuttleworth, Sally. "Demonic Mothers: Ideologies of Bourgeois Motherhood in the Mid-Victorian Era." In *Rewriting the Victorians: Theory, History and the Politics of Gender*. NY: Routledge, 1992. 31–51.

Wohl, Anthony S. *Endangered Lives: Public Health in Victorian Britain*. Cambridge: Harvard UP, 1983.

Recent Dickens Studies: 1998

Harland S. Nelson

This essay surveys 40 items having to do with Dickens. It does not include studies in languages other than English, dissertations, novel reprints, video cassettes, or study guides. Various modes of criticism are represented: traditional explication of the text, psychoanalytic criticism, reader response, Marxist, postcolonial: the gamut. Bakhtin, Benjamin, Derrida, Foucault, Lacan—these and other current critical authorities occur regularly, sometimes usefully, sometimes touch-and-go. The essays in the collection on Bleak House *date from 1971 to 1993, those in the collection on* A Tale of Two Cities *from 1970 to 1992. Standing out in the year's production: volume 10 of the Pilgrim* Letters; *Paul Davis's* Charles Dickens from A to Z; *Deborah Vlock's concept of the imaginary text; and Suzanne Keen's of the narrative annex.*

This review covers reference works, editions of Dickens, monographs, collections of essays, and journal articles. Also a film. It includes only a few paperback editions of the course text sort, and no dissertations. And only work in English (after a morning's work on Anny Sadrin's review of *The Old Curiosity Shop* and Annie Ramel's " 'Brooks of Sheffield,' ou la Question de la Coupure dans *David Copperfield*" demonstrated the state of my French). The various data bases Luther College librarians (to whom I owe a large debt of gratitude) led me to listed scores of reprints of Dickens's novels, video cassettes, and study guides; I left them alone, drawing moral support from Philip Collins (in his chapter on Dickens in *Victorian Fiction: A Second Guide to Research* [1978]), who recognized "the high degree of fallibility inevitable in a chapter such as this on an author so much discussed, unless it

Dickens Studies Annual, Volume 29, Copyright © 2000 by AMS Press, Inc. All rights reserved.

is written by a person (who, I hope, does not exist) whose sole mission in life is reading current writings about Dickens'' (104n).

To specify. I cover five reference works, two editions of Dickens's work, three paperbacks, eight monographs (five the "Dickens and" variety), five works of biographical interest, four collections (two of them reprinting articles [twenty in all] devoted to specific novels), two volumes of this journal, the year's run of *The Dickensian* and *Dickens Quarterly,* and thirty articles found in other journals or on the Internet; and two novels. In all, 140 items.

How to characterize these studies. They include a fair amount of psychoanalytic criticism and work tracing theological and Biblical themes, as well as studies of influences and affinities. Joel Brattin does his usual painstaking work on Dickens's manuscripts, and Jerome Meckier his on *All The Year Round.* Hye-Joon Yoon's book is larger-caliber Marxism, and Marxist concepts inform a fair number of articles. Postcolonialism turns up occasionally, more or less traditional explication of the text often. Bakhtin, Benjamin, Derrida, Foucault, Lacan—these and others appear regularly, sometimes usefully, sometimes as bases to be touched.

Musings. The collections of essays on *Bleak House* and *A Tale of Two Cities* raise the question whether they should be seen as gatherings for convenient current use or as monuments to recently flourishing modes of criticism. There should be a prize for a title like Timothy Peltason's "Esther's Will," and a moratorium on the colon.

Final thoughts. The standouts for me include, of course, volume 10 of the Pilgrim *Letters;* Paul Davis's *Charles Dickens A to Z;* and Deborah Vlock's concept of the imaginary text and Suzanne Keen's of the narrative annex in their monographs. By way of overall summary, I return to Philip Collins, who judged one of the books he reviewed to be "often most valuable in perception analysis of verbal detail, independent of the larger case being argued" (72).

Reference Works

Guides to Dickens on my own shelves include Gilbert A. Pierce's pioneering *Dickens Dictionary* (1872; also the date of my Houghton Mifflin eleventh "edition," probably meaning "impression"), nearly falling apart from use in the thirty-five years since I picked it up in a New York bookshop; a 1989 reprint of the second edition (1928) of *The Dickens Dictionary* by Alex Philip and Laurence Gadd, originally published by Philip in 1908; and *The Dickens Index* (1988), a project originated by Nicolas Bentley and completed after his death by Michael Slater and Nina Burgis. Turning to Preus Library at Luther College, I find (besides *The Dickens Index*) *The Charles Dickens*

Encyclopedia (1973), compiled by Michael and Mollie Hardwick; and the awe-inspiring three-volume *Everyone in Dickens* (1995), by George Newlin, augmented in 1996 by his *Everything in Dickens*. All are useful: Pierce and the Hardwicks include extensive quotations; Pierce and Bentley/Slater/Burgis include chapter references in their entries on characters: Bentley/Slater/ Burgis and the Hardwicks include a time chart of Dickens and events of the period. Newlin justifies his title.

This year three more guides were published. The least conventional is Norrie Epstein's *The Friendly Dickens,* subtitled *a good-natured guide to the art and adventures of the man who invented Scrooge.* The format and style are decidedly not academic. The text is organized as a series of brief essays, the style chatty. The narrative frame is biographical: works come in for attention accordingly. Interspersed are interviews with writers and Dickens scholars. It may be unjust to call the book superficial—Epstein has a lot of the right stuff, as might be expected of someone who dedicates her book to "the memory of my teacher, George H. Ford"—but it is fair to call it fleeting. And who is the intended reader? Not a high school student, I think, although readers of that age will not be turned off. The title may be the best clue: Epstein would appear to be after the occasional reader who has heard of Scrooge (without necessarily having read the book Paul Davis calls a culture text—a story so widely known as to have become part of the age's ambience), while probably inclined to dismiss ancient writers as pompous and distant: i.e., not friendly.

Donald Hawes's *Who's Who in Dickens,* however, is pretty clearly for students from secondary school age on up; David Parker's foreword claims "specialist scholars" will also find it useful for brushing up on details. (One hopes they will use with discretion Parker's suggestion that entries can serve "school students and undergraduates with writing assignments" as "spring-boards for essays.") Hawes has selected forty illustrations by eleven illustra- tors of Dickens, and (according to Parker) covers more of Dickens's fiction than did John Greaves's 1972 work of the same title, as well as his *Uncom- mercial Traveller,* plays, and collaborative works. Entries identify chapters in which characters appear as well as works. They are concise but often include quotations; there are of course no plot summaries, but Hawes provides considerable narrative context in describing characters.

His introduction is brief and traditional (that is, not viewing the characters through the lens of any particular critical theory), focusing on the plenitude and variety of Dickens's cast of thousands (calculated by Newlin as "a total of 3,592 name usages, and nearly that many named characters"). Hawes includes "about 1,650 personages (and a few animals and birds)." Heading the dictionary proper is a list of all characters grouped work by work. A selected bibliography is mainly British. All in all, *Who's Who in Dickens* is modest in scale by comparison to *The Dickens Index*, which includes entries on individual works, editions in Dickens's lifetime, his professional acquaintances, obsolete words and phrases, quotations, places, and more. But a useful book.

Paul Davis's *Charles Dickens A to Z* is a much more ambitious work, subtitled with assurance *The Essential Reference to His Life and Work. The Dickens Index* may outdo it in a count of items, but not in depth of information. Davis produces brief entries for short stories, journalistic essays, sketches, poems, and plays. But for each novel he gives a part-by-part synopsis ("since [the parts] were so important in defining the structure of the work as Dickens imagined it"); an informal and judicious commentary on action and theme; a summary of critical opinion of the work; and an account of theatrical and cinematic treatments ("Adaptations"). (The commentaries, collected and published separately, would constitute a fine overview of Dickens.) Characters are discussed individually, though members of a family (the Dombeys, for example) will be treated in a single entry; chapter appearances are identified. Matters important in the period are dealt with ("Corn Laws"), as are places ("The Albany"), topics important in the novels ("Divorce"), literary matters ("Allegory"), and more. Dickens's friends and acquaintances come in for attention, as do others who had any connection with him; and Davis includes a concise biographical sketch of Dickens. Finally (for my purposes in this essay, though much more could be detailed), Davis has provided entries on a goodly number of Dickens scholars and critics, both contemporary from the past.

A work as comprehensive as this one is bound to misfire here and there. I ran across a startling error (Podsnap assigned to *Little Dorrit*), and Dickens's first meeting with John Forster gets advanced a few years. But it would be silly to dwell on such blemishes. *Charles Dickens A to Z* is a splendid reference work—what one would expect from the author of *The Life and Times of Ebenezer Scrooge.*

"Finally, unless an entry includes a notation indicating otherwise, all items have actually been seen"—this guarantee from Don Richard Cox's preface (xi) to his *Charles Dickens's "The Mystery of Edwin Drood": An Annotated Bibliography* resonates with me from my experience with a single year of Dickens Studies. The more than 1,900 items are organized into three parts: texts, studies, and biography and bibliography. Among the studies, literary criticism fills two long chapters, the first covering 1871–1939, the second 1940–1997 (a division roughly corresponding to the shift in Dickens studies followed from Edmund Wilson's "Dickens: The Two Scrooges" (xi). Entries are consecutively numbered in a single series throughout, and cross-referenced, since many items are parts of ongoing discussions and disputes (xi). Within each chapter items are alphabetized by authors (except in chapter 4,

"Editions from 1870 to the Present"; 1870 editions are listed in order of appearance, the rest according to year of publication).

His bibliography is not complete, Cox says: "There have simply been too many essays, too many opinions, too much commentary (from Dickensians both wise and not-so-wise). . ."(ix). But he believes that he has annotated "virtually all" of it: this bibliography "lists and annotates at least 90% of the *Drood* commentary that has ever been published, perhaps as much as 95%. . . ." To the possible charge that he has not sifted out the "trivial, insignificant, or just plain silly," he concedes that the wheat is mingled with "a great deal of chaff also." His defense is twofold: that *Drood* material is full of chaff—debates go on and on, over trivial matters as well as important ones; and secondly, that including and annotating it all will help scholars avoid wasting their time tracking down junk (x). (Some indication of the problem: *The Dickensian* declared a moratorium on *Drood* publications three times from 1908 to 1928 [xxii, xxv, xxvii].)

Topical and alphabetical organization have obvious merits, but there is a major drawback: for instance, item 738 is about a 1905 piece by William Archer attacking a solution to the mystery proposed by Cuming Walters, and the next four items are 1924–1925 articles by Felix Aylmer about a wholly different topic. Cox's introduction cancels any objections on this ground; it is a prose narrative of the *Drood* phenomenon itemized in the bibliography. Cox shows the shifting foci of criticism: the early commentary, continuations of the story, professed solutions to the mystery (if there is a mystery—one of the subjects of dispute), and movie versions. He organizes his account by twenty-year periods (except the first, 1870–1899), and helpfully identifies relevant items in the course of the narrative. The "golden age" was 1905–1914, generating a fourth of the annotated items. Interest had risen high enough in 1914 to support "trials" of John Jasper in London and Philadelphia; George Bernard Shaw was foreman at the former, and declared for the jury a verdict of manslaughter (because there was no body), while the Philadelphia trial ended in a hung jury that voted 11:1 for acquittal (xxiv). Solving the mystery is the concern of most commentary (calling it "literary criticism" is "possibly misleading" [xv]). Cox makes this story interesting, and one should be on the watch for some deadpan humor, especially when he mentions any of the continuations channeled by mediums (xviii, xix, xxvii).

Dickens on Disk (925 text files on thirty-four disks, each file a chapter of a book) includes the fifteen novels, *The Uncommercial Traveller,* and *A Christmas Carol; Sketches by Boz* is in preparation. Three computer programs for working with this edition are included. In his review, Eric Johnson's claim is that certain kinds of research are greatly facilitated by this edition, although the source texts are not always reliable (printed volumes not in copyright).

Editions and Letters

Volume 10 of the Pilgrim *Letters* (covering 1862–1864) appeared this year, including forty-nine discovered since volume 9 appeared in 1997:918 in all (including extracts and mentions), 435 published for the first time, thirty-five for the first time complete; 864 are transcribed from the originals or photographs of the originals. There is the usual awesome annotation, a virtual record of the whirl of Dicken's life in these three years. There are new strains, two of them relating to health: for the first time a book contract contains a clause dealing with the consequences of the author's death while the novel is in progress. And Dickens's subeditor Wills begins to have health problems the summer of 1864, creating more work for Dickens.

Considerable editing goes on by mail from France, facilitated by rapid railroad service between Paris and London: for instance, writing from Paris Sunday 1 February 1863, Dickens tells Wills that his man John will be back in London Thursday night, and he wants a letter from Wills about the next number of *All The Year Round* "before John leaves me, [so that I may] answer it per John aforesaid" (207). Writing again Wednesday, he acknowledges receiving Wills's letter about the number that morning (210). The reason for so much long-distance editing was probably Dickens's visits to Ellen Ternan; there are nine occasions by my count of trips of a week or more, beginning in August 1862 and continuing through November 1864, unheralded except for one brief trip in March 1863, when Dickens writes of visiting a friend who is ill. (The editors cite Clair Tomalin's strong case in *The Invisible Woman* for believing Ellen lived in France at this time, and for the evidence that the illness was "just possibly a pregnancy" [xii].)

Public readings go on now, including three in Paris in winter 1863; Dickens exults to Wills about his reception. Curiously, speaking of his reading from *David Copperfield,* it is as if he was an observer of his own performance: "I really listened in ecstasy" (211).

In volume 9 the editors noted that Kathleen Tillotson had been unable to complete her work for that volume. She is listed as a consultant on the title page of volume 10, and the editors thank her for her contribution. Professor Tillotson's distinguished work for the Pilgrim *Letters* and the Clarendon editions of the novels goes back to the beginnings of both projects in the 1960s.

Oddly, there is no mention of her in the Pilgrim *Letters* entry of the bibliography for volume 3 of "The Dent Uniform Edition of Dickens' Journalism." *"Gone Astray" and Other Papers from "Household Words" 1851–1859,* edited by Michael Slater. According to his preface, this volume prints in chronological order "the great majority" of the single-authored articles and essays'' Dickens wrote between July 1851 and January 1859, and includes all but one of his choices for *Reprinted Pieces* in the Library Edition (1858). Items Dickens did not collect first appeared in 1908 in B. W. Matz's National Edition as *Miscellaneous Papers,* enlarged and retitled *Collected Papers* in 1937 in Walter Dexter's Nonesuch Edition. The 1908 collection was reprinted in 1983, and a selection, *Charles Dickens: Selected Journalism,* edited by David Pascoe, in 1997. Slater provides a chronology of Dickens's life and times, and his headnotes to the essays give background biographical and historical information and identify literary allusions. Illustrations relevant to Dickens's essays are drawn form such sources as *Punch* and *The Illustrated London News.*

Dickens's marriage broke up in 1858; Slater includes his 12 June denunciaton of the rumors about ''some domestic troubles of mine, of long standing [as] arising out of wickedness, or out of folly, or out of inconceivable wild chance, or out of all three . . .'' (489–90). Appendices print ''An Appeal,'' addressed to women of the streets about the avenue of escape from prostitution afforded by Urania Cottage; Dickens's descriptive headlines for the *Reprinted Papers* in this collection; a complete list of his contributions to *Household Words* from 12 July 1851 through 1 January 1859 (including collaborative pieces as found in Harry Stone's *Uncollected Writings of Charles Dickens: ''Household Words'' 1850–1859* [2 vols., 1969]). Finally, the ''Index and Glossary'' covers Dickens's texts and Slater's editorial material (including modern scholars and critics referred to).

No new Clarendon editions of Dickens's novels were published in 1998 to my knowledge, but two Penguin Classics and an Everyman Dickens were.[1] Kate Flint edited the Penguin Classic *Pictures from Italy* (1846), adding as an appendix ''The Italian Prisoner,'' and an *Uncommercial Traveller* essay from *All The Year Round* (13 October 1860), and providing twenty-four pages of notes (for 180 pages of text). She uses the one-volume first edition text by Bradbury and Evans, with corrections from the Charles Dickens Edition of 1868. Flint's introduction is very good, whether or not she owes her mastery to her familiarity with Bakhtin on Rabelais or Benjamin on Baudelaire; she points out how Dickens's consciousness of political realities in the 1840s (oppression of the people, including violent physical forms, is uppermost to him) ''permeates *Pictures from Italy*'' (xxv) in his selection of topics, and in frequent direct allusions (xxvi). He observed the ''inter-layering of past and present'' (xxvii) in the material and spiritual culture, and the book shows a continuing dialogue between ''picturesqueness and poverty, past and present, and between conflicting impulses in Dickens's own response to Italy'' (xxviii). Dickens was indignant about Italian injustices past and present, but he also seemed to fear ''that recurrent patterns of violence are inherently latent in the country and in its people.''

The new Penguin Classics *Little Dorrit* is edited and introduced by Stephen Wall; Helen Small provided the notes (greatly augmenting those in John Holloway's 1967 Penguin English Library edition) and appendices B (the number plans), C (a Marshalsea map and essay), and D (a map of London). Appendix A is by Holloway, "The Denouement of *Little Dorrit*," taken over from his earlier edition (and still not quite correct). Appendices B, C, and D are of course new; the blank page following the map of London could well have been used for the 1967 editor's list of *Little Dorrit* localities. The novel text is that of the Bradbury and Evans first edition in one volume (1857). Holloway's edition used the 1868 Charles Dickens Edition text, and Dickens's 1857 preface and table of contents. Holloway also used Dickens's running titles composed for the Charles Dickens Edition; Wall does not.)

Wall takes a different tack in his introduction than Holloway, who deals briefly with specific relevances of the story before turning to the theme, and then to details of fictive craft. Wall starts with Dickens's own prison experiences and interests; proceeds to his characters' varieties of prison experience, the satiric treatment of the Merdles et al., and then to Dickens's criticisms of bureaucracy, with special attention to the dispute with James Fitzjames Stephen; and then returns to the prison theme. Wall focuses more closely than Holloway did on story detail and circumstances surrounding publication; Holloway is stronger on theme and philosophy. Teachers will be well served by the markedly superior new edition, but they would be prudent to save their old Penguin English Library edition and mine Holloway for additional insights.

The other new paperback Dickens is *The Pickwick Papers* edited by Malcolm Andrews in the Everyman Dickens series. Andrews's introduction is fresh and interesting, focusing on the changing "generic identity [of *Pickwick Papers*] as it evolved" (xxvii) and on Dickens's shifting stance as a writer (starting as "editor" and ending as "author"). A separate essay, "Dickens and His Critics," begins with Dickens's contemporary reception, including substantial quotation. Andrews continues his survey up to the recent past, noting the "gradual turning of critical attention to the middle and later novels" (830) after the work of George Orwell (1940) and Edmund Wilson (1941); oddly he neglects to mention Humphry House's *The Dickens World* (1941). Among recent and contemporary critics he makes special mention of John Butt and Kathleen Tillotson, William Axton, Stephen Marcus, W. H. Auden, Northrop Frye, Garrett Stewart, Kathryn Chittick, and James Kinsley; in his introduction he also credits J. Hillis Miller and Paul Schlicke.

Andrews includes a chronology of Dickens's life and times (life on the left-hand page, times on the right), Dickens's preface to the first one-volume edition (1837) and the 1867 preface to the Charles Dickens Edition (noting that the Cheap Edition [1847] and Library Edition [1858] prefaces are "substantially the same" as the 1867 one except that Dickens added two paragraphs there about the Seymour controversy); all the illustrations; thirty-two pages of notes; a glossary of items concerning transport, clothing, food, and drink; appendices (the mock-heroic Athenaeum advertisement most likely by Dickens himself, his addresses to readers after numbers 10 and 15, and selected re-etched plates by Browne); suggestions for further reading; and a chapter-by-chapter summary of the action. All in all, an edition well-suited to meet the Penguin classic edited by Robert Patten, which has held the field since its introduction in 1972 (as a Penguin English Library edition, reprinted without change in the Penguin Classics format in 1986).

Trey Philpotts, reviewing with high praise Ruth Glancy's Everyman *Christmas Stories* for *DSA* 27, expressed some disappointment in the Everyman Dickens series overall, citing poor reproduction of illustrations and inner margins "uncomfortably close to the binding" in the thicker volumes, and finding that "the odd-sized books themselves are clumsy to hold," while granting that the introductions are "generally good" and annotations "reasonably thorough." I don't know what other Everyman editions he had in mind, but this one, compared to the Penguin Classic edition, comes off very well. Both editors wrote good introductions; critical apparatus differs—Andrews provides those chronologies, Patten does not; Patten gives a list of characters, Andrews a glossary—but formats are nearly identical as to page and print and text body size. Patten indicates monthly part number beginnings in the text and includes useful maps of Pickwick's London and of the Pickwickian tours. Andrews, of course, provides a more up-to-date select bibliography and that essay on Dickens and his critics. Teachers will be well served by either edition (unless they expect to require further reading, in which case the Everyman has an edge).

Monographs

Some of these are about Dickens, others about some aesthetic, social, or political topic, Dickens being brought in to illustrate. Monica Cohen's *Professional Domesticity in the Victorian Novel: Women, Work, and Home* belongs to the latter group. She devotes two chapters to Dickens: "*Great Expectations* and vocational domesticity" (ch. 3) and "*Little Dorrit* in a home: institutionalism and form" (ch. 4). She sees her book as complementing the work of Mary Poovey and Nancy Armstrong, who showed "how the separate sphere doctrine of Victorian England used emotion and psychology to displace politics and to effectively elide class conflict from the collective consciousness. In this light, the domestic ideology represented by cultural products like novels can be seen as middle-class political interest masquerading as psychology'' (8). Wemmick's castle is a satire on the idea of home as a separate domain and refuge; Amy Dorritt is made to serve the communitarian ideal at the expense of character realism, and social virtues are allied with the prison. Cohen finds the collectivist spirit intrinsic to the ideal of domesticity in mid-century Victorian novels edged out the "psychoanalytic dimensions of humanist novel-craft'' (2); this is "the ironic, if not tragic, tale that *Little Dorrit*'s domesticity unfolds'' (124).

For rather more than the Marxist undercarriage evident in Cohen's book, consider Hye-Joon Yoon's *Physiognomy of Capital in Charles Dickens: An Essay in Dialectical Criticism.* Yoon's book began in his graduate study in English at SUNY-Buffalo and was revised, he says, in the light of professional activities in Seoul, including his experience in two English departments, at Dankook University and Hankuk University of Foreign Studies (xiv). A generating image for him was an "unrecorded but not altogether implausible encounter in the streets of London between two men of letters, Charles Dickens and Karl Marx'' (xi)—an imaginative leap somewhat short of Peter Ackroyd's, but of that order. Yoon dismisses the "genealogy of twentieth-century academic discourse on Dickens [and] its business of managing 'cultural capital' '' (26–27), giving no more than a nod to contemporary critical icons (his index lists three references each to Derrida and Foucault, one to Lacan).

As his title suggests, "physiognomy'' is a crucial term of Yoon's analysis: "the concrete 'material' appearance of the subject as seen from the others alien viewpoint'' (166). For Yoon's purpose, the physiognomy Dickens attempted to sketch was "the concretely visible manifestation of capital on the variegated surface of the capitalist metropolis'' (20). His attempts (that is, his "production,'' his novels) operated at three levels, presenting (1) novelistic confrontations with capital in (2) the "materiality'' of a version of the physical city, by means of (3) the avenues of publication available to him (27). "Dickens, for us, is . . . an active focus of mutations, shifts, and contradictions that a dialectical confrontation with capital brings about . . . [The name] denotes a space of antagonism, an field of multiple confrontations with capital . . .'' (27). This is Dickens's own physiognomy as text, formulated in Yoon's argument; more traditionally, the term might denote his entrepeneurial busyness, Dickens as Rouncewell in *Bleak House* (177–78)—or Dickens as grasped by a series of "antinomic pairs; entrepeneur/uncommercial traveler, flâneur/solitary brooder-wanderer,'' and so on (192–93).

Having anatomized London himself in part one ("Dialectics in the Capital City'') and Dickens in part two ("Dickens in the Relations of Production''), Yoon turns in part three ("Physiognomy of Capital in Three Novels'') to *Dombey and Son, Little Dorritt,* and *Our Mutual Friend.* As my description thus far indicates, this is a densely conceptual study, and I can do no more than register a couple of Yoon's insights from his ideological point of view, and mine from mine.

In *Little Dorrit* Merdle as capitalist is no longer idiosyncratic, Yoon says, as were Ralph Nickleby, Scrooge, and Dombey; he is the "extreme climactic point" (223). The Marshalsea embodies the "physiognomy of capital behind its shabby courts and dingy walls," while the inventor-engineer Doyce shows Dickens's ambivalence about the Victorian bourgeoisie (234; presumably Yoon means Doyce's narrow concern with technology). Arthur Clennam's "soul-searching misgivings" about the source of his family's wealth "register a sharp break within Dickens's novels from dominent bourgeois ideology" (231). This "space" is where the plots of *Little Dorrit, Great Expectations,* and *Our Mutual Friend* unfold.

In the chapter on *Dombey and Son* Yoon sees Dombey as an emblem of the firm, or capital itself. This tendency to allegorize is not wrong of him, but that Dombey equals capital is only a deduction from the materialist paradigm that underlies Yoon's concept of physiognomy. ("Physiognomic perspective at once rejects essentialism and anti-essentialism, since it redeems mere appearance from its meaninglessness and the projection of invisible essence from its lack of substance" [20].) Very little novelistic substance supports such an equation. Dickens does in fact make Dombey stand for an abstraction; pride in the theological sense, virtual deification of self; and the story's details flesh that out. So one's base of values determines how one sees things. In a way this confirms the poststructural view that the text is all, indeterminate, open to multiple readings. On that premise, which is to be preferred, Yoon's materialist assumptions, which disallow essentialist and anti-essentialist views, or a transcendentalist position, which does not entirely or absolutely cancel materialist insights?

This is an interesting book; viewing Dickens as a producer in a particular sector of nineteenth-century capitalism (and an observer as well) turns up unexpected insights. Generally Yoon sees Dickens, himself a capitalist, recording the excesses of capitalism, and opposing them; his opposition, however, is traditional and Christian, not proto-Marxist. One has to get past the opening chapter, which is stiff with Marxist teminology and authority; and the "Conclusion: Dickens and History" returns to that in lesser degree, quoting Ernst Bloch, Raymond Williams, Theodor Adorno, Engel, Georg Lukács, Pierre Macherey, Louis Althusser, Frederick Jameson, and Étienne Balibar. Naturally the text is prodigiously footnoted. The cover blurb is a pretty good thumbnail characterization: "A materialist approach to the fictions of Charles Dickens, based on a reading-in of the historical background [and] creative application of Walter Benjamin's methodology. . . . Reconfigures the canonical novels within the framework of 19th century London, and the capital/cash nexus of Charles Dickens's fictive network." Yoon's purpose, according to John Dings in his foreword, is "to understand Dickens as both the historian of capital and capital's utopian antagonist," as both chronicler of the vast economic and social changes going on around him, and as "the 'subjective' Dickens driven to set things right . . ." (vii).

Brenda Ayres's *Dissenting Women in Dickens' Novels: The Subversion of Domestic Ideology* is an argument for another, less conscious contradiction. What Ayres says about *Our Mutual Friend* may stand as her thesis about the whole of Dickens: "Even as Dickens' text overtly promotes an ideology of womanhood [the "domestic ideology" of the subtitle], however, at the same time it modifies and subverts that ideology" (2). Ayres cites Sarah Ellis's *The Women of England* (1843) regularly as a convenient embodiment of "angel-in-the-house" ideals: woman as wife and mother, rearer of children, manager of the household, keeper of the family moral high ground, provider and guardian of a retreat for her husband home from the strife and tumult of the public commercial and political world, maritally (and before that, in her parental home, filially) loving and subservient. Ayres finds this pattern embedded in all fifteen of Dickens's novels, giving most attention to *Oliver Twist, Barnaby Rudge, David Copperfield,* and *Bleak House.* And of course she finds Dickens undercutting the pattern everywhere as well: in *Bleak House,* for instance, by giving Esther a part of the narrative, Dickens "inadvertently but severely undercuts the benevolence and the absolute value of the domestic ideology that the Dickensian text has attempted to construct and advocate," providing her "the space to articulate struggle and pain when women were supposed to aspire and moderate their behavior toward an angel-in-the-house ideal naturally and joyfully" (153). Ayres's argument is replete with such illustrative detail, and supported by impressive marshaling of relevant criticism and scholarship. Still, I have some reservations, not about Ayres's general point, but about her execution of it. Not to obliterate my endorsement by a lengthy overlay of doubts, I will keep this short.

Ayres's handling of story detail is accurate as a rule, but not always. Factual error: it is a bit startling to be told that Miss Havisham is only "nearly" killed when her gown catches fire (89), and that Edith Dombey (like Lady Dedlock in *Bleak House* and Nancy in *Oliver Twist*) dies violently (55). Misreading: she considers Dickens's satiric treatment of Mercy Chuzzlewit's arch girlishness to be his subtle eroticism "for a Victorian audience" (68), apparently missing his tone. Elsewhere, she argues that David's dwelling on Dora's physicality, in contrast to his description of Agnes "only as having a 'heavenly face,' " makes Dora a "flesh and blood" character while denying Agnes "physicality and essence" (22). But David's point is surely to show that his infatuation was based on superficial sensual attraction. Such misreadings weaken the force of the point being made. Elsewhere Ayres's conscientious assimilation of her argument to current critical modalities gets her in trouble. One may be grateful for this occasionally, as when she writes (of the gender roles endorsed in *The Women of England*), "This ideological function of gender was for the furthering of the British empire" (4)—stripped of critical jargon, the idea stands bare to scrutiny. But Ayres's recurrent resort to a certain critical locution which personifies the text—'"The text tries to master her" (81), "the text retaliates" (88), " 'Agnes' name has additional potential that the text denies her" (116)—is annoying because it implies an existence for the character independent of the text.

Which brings me to my final reservation. Is a text deconstructing a value system when showing its downside(s)? especially if humor is involved. It is hard to distinguish what Ayres calls "dissent" from ordinary received interpretations in current critical idioms. This can of course be a useful thing to do: showing the longevity of a "text." Sometimes, though—and I don't mean to imply that Ayres is a case in point, because I read Dickens pretty much as she does—sometimes more is involved than reinscription, sometimes a whole alternative reading is being proposed. Occam's razor should be kept well stropped.

The next two monographs are both concerned with the special importance of literary form to meaning. Robert Higbie's focus in *Dickens and Imagination* is on religious belief. Actually his scope is wider than that: he approaches "works of literature as attempts to imagine some desired object but also as efforts to deal with the difficulties created by such attempts. . . " (1). Naming critics who have influenced him one way or another, he closes in on his central topic by way of singling out Garrett Stewart's *Dickens and the Trials of the Imagination* to distinguish his own focus from Stewart's: not on "the imagination of Dickens's characters [but on] the way Dickens relates imagination to the search for spiritual belief" (3).

Higbie's approach is historical as well as conceptual, sketching Romantic concepts of imagination inherited and revised by Victorians, and in the course of that introducing the terms and concepts in his argument: besides imagination, idealism, realism, belief, and desire. He devotes a chapter to the Romantic theory of imagination and another to the imaginative basis of religious belief—important for him to establish if he means to show Dickens in quest of religious belief in his fiction. Belief, he says, attempts to reconcile reason, which is aware of reality (in the marketplace sense of the term), and imgination, which at the bidding of desire generates illusory images: "we can define [belief] as reason's acceptance of the mental image, seeing it as real" (12). The concept is close to what Newman calls "assent" and William James " 'a sentiment of reality' [attached] to an unseen object" (13). There is more to Higbie's analysis, but I must move on to its relevance to Dickens's fiction. Higbie thinks "what happens in literature is closely related to this process. . . . [L]iterature aspires to create a similar kind of belief, asking us in a less serious way to accept its images as real" (15).

Higbie sees the accommodation of the ideal to the real by the play of imagination as Dickens's career-long preoccupation: "From *Dombey* on, Dickens makes the conversion of imagination into belief a central organizing principle" (75). He is most successful, Higbie thinks, in *Little Dorrit,* where he persuasively envisions the power of the ideal to penetrate in hospital reality (144). But in his last two complete novels Dickens was unable to maintain that persuasiveness; "the sense of reality" so resists "the wish for belief" that "imagining the ideal is the best one can hope for" (158).

Higbie's final chapter is about "the way Dickens's imagination actually finds expression . . . [in] the constant imaginative play in his novels" (159). His explications of the action here—including Dickens's various plays on the parent-child relationship, which he notes frequently in earlier chapters—are illuminating. The main difficulty I find in Higbie's book is the rush of abstractions entailed in his method. Schooled to expect abstractions at the top of a ladder of concrete detail, I find the abstract heights Higbie expects me to scale at a leap rather much. A related problem is the regular allegorizing of story; Dickens's stories are treated (without attention to such grounding in life experience as the parent-child business has) as sublimations of his personal yearning for assured religious belief. Not that Dickens was indifferent to that dimension of life; I have argued otherwise myself, and Steven Marcus, Angus Wilson, Jane Vogel, and Janet Larson, to name no others, have effectively dispelled that notion. In general agreement with Higbie's outlook on Dickens, I am reluctant to go against Edwin Eigner's pre-publication recommendation: "A work which all 19th century scholars will find useful and which Dickens scholars will find indispensable." My impression is that *Dickens and Imagination* tries to map a very large terrain at rather many miles to the inch, but I hope Eigner is right.

Brian Nelson's *The Basis of Morality and Its Relation to Dramatic Form in a Study of "David Copperfield,"* as his title suggests, has to do more directly with literary structure than Higbie's study does, and the focus of his study is moral rather than religious. But just as Higbie thinks the literary process is closely related to the process by which religious belief is created, Nelson is convinced "that moral philosophy and literature are to a significant degree embedded in each other" (xii). Nelson's study has two parts (again, as is title suggests), in the first of which, "A Theory Concerning the Nature of Morality," he argues that the proper base of a moral attitude is "the concern of a moral being about its own worth" (45, 47, et passim: his tag phrase). He discusses Hume and Freud as examples of empirical theorists, Kant as a theorist who worked from abstract principle; all are dismissed as flawed because inevitably dependent on the moral attitudes of the theorist. In Part II, "A Theory Concerning the Nature of Dramatic Form, Demonstrated in Relation to *David Copperfield,*" Nelson argues that the best way to discern

such a moral attitude is by close analysis of the moral complexities of the
action in the dramatic form (in Joyce's sense) of the novel, rather than by
discursive thought, because the novel shows a character "in the actual circumstances of his or her psychological development" (xii).

Nelson proceeds to analysis of *David Copperfield*. His analysis is close
and discriminating, of a sort that takes literature as a criticism of life, not
just text. (Nelson would probably agree with William Myers, who in a study
I will come to later asserts that "character analysis of the most unfashionable
kind remains a central task of the critic. . . .") After using John Carey (*The
Violent Effigy*) and Q. D. Leavis (*Dickens the Novelist*) to demonstrate what
he is *not* doing, he hardly ever refers directly to critics again. He doesn't
retell the story; he proceeds from chapter to chapter focusing on the moral
implications for David of successive situations (attending as well to accumulation of experience), demonstrating what he points out in his abstract, "that
[while] our ordinary understanding of a person's character is unavoidably
partial" (xii), in a novel we know the character more completely, as we can't
know real people—what the author tells us, or provides us the data to infer
from, *is* all there is to know.

Nelson's position is similar to Martha Nussbaum's in another article I
touch on later; she holds there to be human conditions that only literary
treatment—not abstract theoretical discussion, but embodiment in fiction—can do justice to, providing "guides to what is mysterious and messy
and dark in our experience." Nelson does a good job it seems to me—subject
only to his own caveat in his abstract: "that dramatic form can achieve a
true representation where discursive thought on its own must fail" (xii).
Inevitably, in such a work at this discourse is the medium; the saving grace
must be the fineness of the analysis.

What Nelson is at the mercy of is the reader's familiarity with *David
Copperfield*. That reader's consciousness, in Dickens's day, was constituted
differently from ours, according to Deborah Vlock's *Dickens, Novel Reading,
and the Victorian Popular Theatre*. Her subject is "the construction of a
Victorian reading subject, a reader of Dickens and others, primarily constituted in the dialogic spaces between theatre and novel" (159). This is a
"public" constituting (not D. A. Miller's idea of novel reading as a private
affair), reacting to certain "contextual signs of the theatre" and "freezing
them . . . into the status of mythical or universal ideas." This "imaginary
text" is a basic concept in the book, something like the "culture text" Paul
Davis says the story of Scrooge has become (*The Lives and Times of Ebenezer
Scrooge*), as Vlock points out (6). She develops the concept in her chapter
"Dickens and the "imaginary text," proposing with impressive detail that
for Victorian readers theatrical conventions and renditions—a "theatre of
assumptions" (11)—shaped their reception of Dickens's novels, as indeed

they strongly influenced Dickens's invention (she points out striking evidence in Browne's illustrations of influence by the stylized poses in Henry Siddon's *Practical Illustrations of Rhetorical Gesture and Action* [1882]). Thus, she concludes, "Theatrical signs were received as genuine and normative" (26), so that "even those Dickensian characters who seem most exaggerated to us were routinely accepted as true to life" (32).

Impressive and persuasive as this demonstration of reader response criticism is, thoroughly grounded in research into Victorian rhetorical and theatrical practice, it is less impressive and persuasive as part of the case Vlock tries to make that "bourgeois industrial ideology depended on linguistic controls . . ." (102). She proposes Dickens's public readings as an example, suggesting a motive on his part to "harness" the power of his texts to prevent their inciting "acts of social disruption." The evidence she offers: Dickens's notes and cues in his prompt copies, "serving the purpose of containing the text and directing its oral delivery . . . suggest[ing] a kind of struggle, or negotiation, between Dickens and his text. One can almost sense danger beneath those crosses and bars, as if a story unmarked and undirected could erupt into the unexpected . . . surging out of control" (61–62). This is a feverishly imaginative extrapolation from Dickens's careful preparation for public readings. Presumably Vlock thinks he was acting out of hegemonic anxiety, the same motive he had, Vlock suggests, for his "ruthless treatment" in *Our Mutual Friend* of the seller of street ballads, Silas Wegg, in his "profound anxiety over Wegg's possible social influence" (125).

Seen through Vlock's ideological lens, Victorian eminences like Dickens experience "anxiety" regularly, manipulating those "linguistic controls" to maintain the dominant socio-politico-economic orthodoxy. To stay with Dickens, he "suppresses" the stories of "redundant" women like Flora Finching and Mrs. Nickleby by giving them "patter" speech that instantly places them for Victorian readers (164). (Vlock's chapter on theatrical patter—"a language which means meaninglessness, and therefore means something desperately significant" [94]—is extremely interesting.) He is even "downright hostile" to Mrs. Gamp (97), assigning her patter speech which goes beyond good-natured comedy (Vlock thinks: being constituted as a reader by another imaginary text than the Victorians').

But this is a good book after all; these irritations have not overriden my impression after the first couple of chapters that it is deeply researched, knowledgeable about current academic idols but not bowed in worship, imaginatively insightful. When those insights are harnessed to Marxist clichés or enlisted in gender wars, the ideology is usually detachable. Vlock's concept of the "imaginary text" is illuminating; so is her discussion of patter, though the ideological application does not persuade me. (I suppose Vlock might reasonably attribute my annoyance to anxiety.)

Suzanne Keen detects mid-Victorian anxiety, too, in her *Victorian Renovations of the Novel: Narrative Annexes and the Boundaries of Representation;* not so much the anxiety of the dominant social and political elites, however, but anxiety showing up in contemporary novel criticism, "caused by unconventional subjects of representation, and by challenges to normative novelistic techniques" (17). Literary or aesthetic anxiety, then, not socio-politico-economic (in the main, that is: note an exception below). These two causes are often found together in the "narrative annex"—"annex" in the architectural sense. An annex, according to Keen, is not the same as authorial comment, which steps out of the fictive world. It is a "bounded, temporary alternative miniature" world, entry to which is through "a boundary line or border region," accomplishing a shift of place and genre which permits a larger "space" than the regular world of the novel, allowing "unexpected characters, impermissible subjects, and plot-altering events to appear . . ." (1–2). All four of these features—change of genre and setting, a boundary crossing, and consequentially for the plot of the novel—must be present for Keen to call the section an annex (3). The Eden episode of *Martin Chuzzlewit* is an example (5–6). Annexes contain material challenging to mid-Victorian critics, operating according to Keen by an evolving body of "rules" governing concepts of the novel genre, "social and cultural assumptions of probability and permissibility" (180). The annexes, however, enabled Victorian writers to "send their characters across borders into representational realms that deepen and complicate the terrain of nineteenth-century fiction" (183) without mortal offense to critics, though troubling them to greater or less degree.

Keen gives a chapter each to Trollope and Charlotte Brontë, one to Kingsley and Hardy (in which she links narrative annexes to "class anxiety," but without the ideological coloration I noticed in Vlock's book), and one of Disraeli's *Coningsby,* Dickens's *Hard Times,* and Well's *Tono-Bungay:* all "condition-of-England" novels, she argues, rejecting the assumption that this subgenre died with the Chartist movement (146). As to the device of the annex, she closes with a chapter entitled "Victorian annexes and modern form," where she writes that "the realm of contrasting place and genre, entered by crossing a boundary between worlds, retains its power as an imaginative construction" (188). In fact she finds the strategy of the Victorian annex came from "the tool-box of technique inherited from earlier narrative artists" (2–3), embodied in "the houses within Spenser's Faerie Land, the woods of Shakespeare, and the ubiquitous islands of Renaissance fiction" (182).

Obviously this is a book about the Victorian novel, not centrally about Dickens. Keen does refer (besides to *Martin Chuzzlewit*) to *Pickwick Papers, Oliver Twist, Bleak House,* and *Little Dorrit,* and she takes up *Hard Times* in some detail. *Martin Chuzzlewit* seems to me to provide a better example of the narrative annex, but she needs *Hard Times* for her condition-of-England section.

Keen's book is an admirable piece of work. It had its beginnings in her dissertation, she says (vii); the signs are there in her copious and far-ranging bibliography, and such features of her text as her discovery that Trollope did a narrative annex once (in his forty-seven novels, which she must have read all of!), and her exhaustive survey of fictional worlds and their theorists in her opening chapter: the sort of thing one does to satisfy one's advisor that the ground has been thoroughly mapped. Some of this might have been omitted, I think, without damage to her apartment. But if it helped her to her final achievement, it would be niggling to object strongly. *Victorian Renovations* is the best of the monographs I have read for this review.

I come finally to Carolyn Dever's *Death and the Mother from Dickens to Freud: Victorian Fiction and the Anxiety of Origins*. (Anxiety here, too.) Psychoanalysis, Dever believes, "provides a useful lens" (3) for studying "the significance of maternal loss in the construction of subjectivity, domesticity, and desire, and the ideological implications of this representational practice" in mid-Victorian fiction (1). But she thinks "the analyst of Victorian fiction has as much to teach us about psychoanalysis as psychoanalysis teaches about the Victorian novel . . ." (3). Her first chapter shows "the passage from anxiety to stability, from loss to mastery, occur[ring] by appropriating maternal loss" in selected pre-Victorian novels; her second is about the "staging [of] that loss as the child's first and most significant rite of passage" (34) in Freud, Melanie Klein, and D. W. Winnicott. In the remaining two-thirds of her book she analyzes *Bleak House,* Wilkie Collins's *Woman in White,* George Eliot's *Daniel Deronda, The Autobiography of Charles Darwin,* and Virginia Woolf's *To the Lighthouse* (her "Victorian novel," as Dever calls it).

As this table of contents suggests, psychoanalysis is more in the foreground than fiction is, not only in the first two chapters, but also in *Bleak House* (and I judge in the other chapters, on the basis of my dipping and skimming). In fact, far into the chapters on *Bleak House* Dever reveals where her main investment is, when she says *Bleak House* is "an allegory of the psychoanalytic process" (97).The search for the missing mother "constitutes the detective plot"; but the outcome is not persuasive because "the world of the text is so inundated with narrative, with the prolilferation of the Symbolic. . . ." Sad, indeed, for a novel to be full of narrative, and of symbolism. The judgment shows the warping effect of Dever's twin commitments: there is much more to *Bleak House* than the mother-daughter story. Narrative gets adjusted to enhance the psychoanalytic theory: Nemo's packet of love letters pass from him "to Guppy to Mr. Tulkinghorn, then to Bucket, to Sir Leicester and Mr.

Jarndyce, and finally to Esther'' (95). But Guppy never sees the letters, and they simply disappear from the story after they get to Bucket. Nor would the packet include ''the handwriting of [Esther's] two parents,'' as Dever says, but only her mother's. These narrative additions enforce the completion of Esther's identity, of course—I kept thinking of the little boy's book report, ''This is a good book about fish; it told me more about fish than I want to know.'' It's more about psychoanalysis than about fiction—*Bleak House* is a proof text for the doctrine. (I expect the other novels are, too.) Very heavy going, for me anyway.

Collections

Seven collections of essays have come my way for attention in this review: volumes 26 and 27 of *Dickens Studies Annual;* two collections on individual novels, *Bleak House* (edited by Jeremy Tambling) and *A Tale of Two Cities* (Michael Cotsell); *Homes and Homelessness in the Victorian Imagination* (Murray Baumgarten and H. M. Daleski); *Imperial Objects: Essays on Victorian Emigration and the Unauthorized Imperial Experience* (Rita S. Kranidis); and *Readings on Charles Dickens* (Clarice Swisher). The *DSA* essays, being on a wide variety of topics, will be found in appropriate topical categories; four of the Baumgarten/Daleski collection make up the group under the head ''Homes and Homelessness'' (the rest distributed into other sections); and I review the Cotsell and Tambling collections in the groups devoted to *Bleak House* and *A Tale of Two Cities*.

That leaves Kranidis and Swisher to deal with here. Swisher first. *Readings on Charles Dickens* appears in the ''Literary Companion to British Authors'' series published by Greenhaven Press ''designed for young adults'' to provide ''an engaging and comprehensive introduction to literary analysis and criticism'' (Foreword,11). It sounds like just the thing for the Dickens part of an undergraduate British novel course. In time, the collection ranges from Louis Cazamian's ''Dickens's Philosophy of Christmas'' (1905) to Nicola Bradbury's ''Multiple Narratives in *Great Expectations*'' (1990) and includes Chesterton and Shaw as well as British and American critics from the 1940s through the 1970s. (Several important critics are missing: John Butt and Kathleen Tillotson, Philip Collins, K. J. Fielding, George Ford.) The traditionalist cast of the collection further appears in its organization: a group on ''Major Themes,'' another on ''Entertaining Stories for Serial Publication,'' a third on Dickens's Semiautobiographical novels,'' and a fourth on ''Novels of Reform, History, and Morality.'' The selection is shaky, though; there are no essays centering on *Dombey and Son, Bleak House, Little Dorritt,* or *Our Mutual Friend,* the last three certainly suitable for attention as novels of reform. The organization is uncertain, too: two of the essays on *Great Expectations* in the fourth group would fit better in the group on serial publication, and three of the four essays in the second group are not on serial publication at all (two of them belong in the first group, really).

Misgivings grow as one scans the essays; they are oddly compact, running 4 to 10 pages (including a synoptic headnote), most of them 8 or 9 pages. Back to the Foreword: which says essays were "chosen for their accessibility to a young adult audience and are expertly edited in consideration of both the reading and comprehension level of this audience" (11). "Expertly edited": read "abridged," with the result, for example, that A. O. J. Cockshut's essay on prison experiences leaves out *Little Dorrit*. Who are these "young adults?" The implied definition in the Foreword ("accessibility," "suitability") becomes clearer in the description of the biographical sketch as "in-depth" and the chronology as "detailed." Neither claim is true. The biographical sketch makes no mention of Ellen Ternan; Swisher says only that "Dickens had a fight with Bradbury and Evans" (29) that led to his changing publishers. Swisher's account of the marital breakup is grossly simplified and sanitized, and minimizes Dickens's initiative in the matter. No Gen-Xers, these "young adults"—perhaps nobody at all among today's youth.

One could ignore the Foreword; the critics represented are worth rereading, and the collection could be enjoyable and valuable as a reminder of an era in Dickens criticism now past. But the "expertly edited" versions of these essays are distressing; the abridgments strip out important parts and distort the emphases of their authors. It is unfortunate if the series guidelines compel this butchery; in any event, my inclination is to warn off, not recommend.

In her introduction to *Imperial Objects: Essays on Victorian Women's Emigration and the Unauthorized Imperial Experience*, Rita S. Kranidis argues for the current relevance of the topic: "[C]olonial emigration and emigrant women's relation to the Victorian imperial project surface as significant analogues to our present preoccupation with cultural boundaries" (1). ("Unauthorized" in the subtitle puzzles me—does it mean "not deliberately planned?") The Victorian debate over emigration was about whether emigration was a solution to England's socio-economic problems. Gender complicated it: what should the role of women be? which question resolved itself into, "What are women for?" and after that, "What women?"

Two of the essays ring Dickens into the debate, although the first, Shannon Russell's "Recycling the Poor and Fallen: Emigration Politics and the Narrative Resolutions of *Mary Barton* and *David Copperfield*," is misleadingly titled: the article refers only occasionally to details from the novels, and then only to illustrate in passing points made by argument and factual published material from the period. The issues as Russell frames them are the problems faced by women emigrants, and the political implications and consequences of their emigration. Emigration "as a narrative solution in *David Copperfield*" shows that Dickens believed the colonies were for people unfit, morally or economically, for England (58); and as to women in particular he cooperated lustily in figuring female emigrants as marriage objects—all of them in *David Copperfield* get proposals (47).

The assumption that marriage was the only suitable occupation is central to Carmen Faymonville's " 'Waste Not, Want Not': Even Redundant Women Have Their Uses." It underlies, she says, the opinion supposedly confirmed by the 1851 census that there was a "dramatic oversupply of women" (66)—hence the category "redundant." Dickens, Elizabeth Gaskell, and Eliza Meteyard "believed that the so-called 'fallen women,' working-class women, paupers, and even impoverished middle-class gentlewomen, might profit from emigration assistance [to] escape marginalization"—that is, spinsterhood—in Britain (64–65). Faymonville sees Dickens as "defining women's subjectivity through biology and determinism" (75), and sketches his vigorous activity in connection with Urania Cottage (with its financial underwriter, the heiress Angela Burdett Coutts), a project for rehabilitating prostitutes and holding out to them the hope of emigration and marriage. Emily and Martha in *David Copperfield* come in for discussion; Martha the repentant prostitute finds a husband in Australia, but for Emily emigration is a way to hide, not "empowering" (76). Faymonville seems to have missed the reason for that in the moral economy of the novel: Emily owes a debt to her saintly uncle Daniel Peggotty that can only be paid by resumption of her place in his household.

Biographical

Kate Field's *Pen Photographs of Charles Dickens's Readings: Taken from Life* (the enlarged edition of 1871) has been reprinted with an introduction and appendices by Carolyn J. Moss. Field, a young American freelance journalist, attended twenty-five Dickens's 1867–68 public readings in Boston and New York. Though always an appreciative fan, she was not uncritical, spotting interpolations not in the novel texts, regretting the omission of favorite scenes, and noting some readings when Dickens's performance fell short of her expectations. (She noted his health problems late in the tour). She attended to style and technique, speculating that his "rising inflection" at the ends of sentences was an expedient "to overcome the defects of an imperfect voice" (65), and she tried by typographical means (a musical scale in print) to suggest how Dickens's humor derived from pitch and inflections (65–67).

Fred Kaplan's fine *Dickens: A Biography* published in 1988 is now in paperback from Johns Hopkins with a new preface in which he identifies and comments on the Dickensian warts that contemporary biographers have found especially interesting—his self-image as the survivor of an abused childhood, his relations with women, and his double life—as well as on the nature of our interest in these matters (12). He identifies "the two major biographical studies of the women in [Dickens's] life" as Michael Slater's *Dickens and Women* (1983) and Claire Tomalin's "pursuit of Ellen Ternan *in The Invisible Woman*" (1990). Still, he points out, our interest in "any of the women in Dickens's life resides primarily in what our attention to them can teach us about Dickens" (13). He thinks we are unlikely ever to know much more about Dickens's private life: "Dickens was good, perhaps brilliant, at covering his tracks" (14). As usual, Kaplan is centered and concise; anyone already owning his *Dickens* should find a way to get at this preface.

Catherine Peters's *Charles Dickens* in the Pocket Biography Series is a good hour-and-a-half read for a general adult audience. (An unabridged audio edition runs 135 minutes.) Peters doesn't condescend to the reader or patronize her subject. She is in control of her material, condensing and selecting admirably to give a clear and just sketch of Dickens's life. (I noticed only one factual error, his daughter Mary's birthdate, wrongly given in one place as 1816.) She limits herself to describing subjects and themes of his novels, abjuring criticism; chapter titles provide the contour of his life and career. Unlike Swisher, she doesn't write Ellen Ternan out of Dickens's final years. But she points out, "[H]e was forty-five, she was eighteen, the age of his daughter Kate" (79); and having given an objective assessment of the understandable elements in Dickens's attraction to Ellen, she writes, "Less than two years after first meeting Ellen Ternan, Dickens had ended his marriage, destroyed his magazine, fallen out with some of his closest friends, and seriously compromised his position in English society" (83–84). Unsparing, but just, I think, and not disproportionate in context. Peters reports Claire Tomalin's cautious conjectures about children by Ellen (if any, they died in infancy). Journalists will probably "smoke" Tomalin; if they do, Malcolm Andrews will doubtless give them the same acid treatment he gave (in a *Dickensian* editorial) the January 8 *Sunday Times* writer who precipitated a footnote in volume 9 of the Pilgrim *Letters* (conjecturing that a letter to Dickens's physician referred to a venereal infection) into "historical fact in the newspaper article" and went on to buttress the "fact" with speculation that Dickens got it from a French prostitute on one of his jaunts with Wilkie Collins. (John Sutherland handled the matter responsibly in *TLS* [6 February].)

David Paker's esssay "Dickens at Home" says a lot about Dickens in describing what he did with his homes: "He sought in homes the stimulation to be had from story" (65); so his interiors were designed with a sense of theatre (68), and his furniture showed "a demand for narrative significance"

(72). He always remodelled; he saw a house in a Romantic light, as requiring "adaptation to the needs of the occupiers . . . affirming their identities" (66). He bought Gads Hill Place (home ownership was uncommon), located on the hill where Shakespeare's Falstaff held rendezvous with his "lads"; for Dickens, Gads Hill Place thus rooted him in "the larger story of English comic literature" (74).

Information about Dickens's reading is more conventionally relative to his work. Leon Litvack's "What Books Did Dickens Buy and Read?" reports the "Evidence from the Book Accounts with his Publishers" (his subtitle). Earlier studies by T. W. Hill (1949), Harry Stone (1955), and Philip Collins (1964) worked over an 1844 inventory of books at 1 Devonshire Terrace and the catalog of the Gads Hill library prepared for the 1878 sale. Litvack categorizes the books Dickens bought from 1845 on, as recorded in these accounts. He prints the account pages (including a facsimile of Bradbury and Evans account #1) and annotates the titles appearing in the accounts. Litvack rightly considers this article to be a data base for future studies.

Sources, Influences, Affinities

How better to begin this group than with something on classical literature? Pauline Fletcher's "Bacchus in Kersey: Dickens and the Classics" traces the classics in Dickens from his early parodic use of classical matter (as in Jingles's ejaculatory talk—it is he who denominates Pickwick as a Bacchus in a suit of kersey), through more mordant satiric force in *Martin Chuzzlewit* (6–7) and *Dombey and Son* (8), and into *Bleak House,* which displays "a new rhetorical element [:] . . . the use of an extended classical reference as an ironic commentary on the action, or to foreshadow future developments" (12)—that figure of Allegory on Tulkinghorn's ceiling. The circus performers who put up at the Pegasus' Arms in *Hard Times,* and Jenny the doll's dressmaker in *Our Mutual Friend,* show the late Dickens using classics more organically: Latinate graminiferous quadrupeds of the Utilitarian classroom are set over against the Greek winged horse of imagination, and Jenny, Fletcher argues, with her advice on the rooftop to "come up and be dead," is the guide Mercury—but her advice is Christian, not pagan (15–16). The Dickens who early used classical material with bouncy irreverence by the end of his life was using it, in Jenny, "in the service of [his] moral, and essentially humanistic, vision"; such figures as Jenny help define "an alternative world of imaginative license, subtle subversions, compassion, and extraordinary inclusiveness" (17). References to Bakhtin et al. often constitute mainly the critic's claim to be au courant. In Fletcher's illuminating text-centered article, her quotation from Bakhtin provides some of that light.

Before passing on to matters of influence, I should note Ray Dubberke's convincing proposal ("Dickens's Favorite Detective") that "Dickens's favorite detective W—," who conducted Dickens and his American friend James T. Fields on London underworld tours in 1869, was Adolph Frederick Williamson, then head of the Detective Department at Scotland Yard, and not Charles Frederick Field (as Philip Collins suggests in *Dickens: Interviews and Recollections),* Dickens's underworld guide in the *Household Words* years, who had long since retired.

Dickens's church bells rang in the works of Edgar Allan Poe and Virginia Woolf, according to Burton R. Pollin and Gary Hollington. Pollin's article "Dickens's Chimes and Its Pathway into Poe's 'Bells' " argues that the four-stanza structure of Poe's final version (considering as well the numerous similarities in words and phrasings) was modelled on the four quarters (chapters) of Dickens's 1844 Christmas book *The Chimes,* which Poe probably read in the pirated *New-York Evening Mirror* printing of 28 January 1845. Hollington ("Woolf's *Mrs. Dalloway")* thinks that the central image of "the bells that ring emphatically at crucial junctures and resonate metaphorically throughout" *Mrs. Dalloway* possibly originates in David Copperfield's reflections stirred by the cathedral bells of Canterbury, which he hears on his return from abroad (144); David's noting that the reverberations " 'lost themselves in air, as circles do in water' may have provided a model for . . . a leitmotif in *Mrs. Dalloway:* 'the leaden circles dissolved in the air' " (145).

Simon David Trezise finds "numerous links, some superficial and some profound, between the life and work of Dickens and Baring-Gould" (123), and thinks Baring-Gould "has been neglected as a link in the chain of literary and political thinking from Dickens to Shaw" (132). A parson and landowner in Devon, Sabine Baring-Gould had a "Dickensian attitude to life . . . combining comic and moral vision" (126). Dickensian themes are modulated in Baring-Gould's numerous novels; Trezise discusses one of them, *Court Royal: A Story of Cross Currents* (1886), as a representative example (128–32), finding parallels with *Bleak House* (and foreshadows of Shaw). Trezise's article draws parallels rather easily, but is interesting as an overview of a man prominent in his time and place, and as an instance of Dickens's wide influence.

In "Dickens's *Oliver Twist* and Mendele's *The Book of Beggars"* Gershon Shaked never quite claims that the latter was influenced by the former, but clearly he thinks it was, on the basis of publication dates and similarities of structure and content. He begins by sketching *Oliver Twist* in psychological and mythic terms; Oliver is "the victim of Victorian sexual and social repression" (297), and his story is an instance of "the descent of the newborn" into "daemonic hell [the workhouse] and non-identity," ascending "through the metropolitan inferno of greed, sadism and lust" with the aid of "a good surrogate father'' (297–98). The plot of *The Book of Beggars,* Shaked says, is comparable but much more complicated (298). Judging from his summary, I agree to the latter, but the comparability escapes me.

Philip Rogers is not making a case for direct influence; there is no evidence that Evgenii Zamiatin (or Yevgeni? Rogers gives both spellings) read *Hard Times.* Rogers thinks it most likely that he did; however, his main point is that Zamiatin stands in the line of descent from nineteenth century dystopian disclosure. The ''similarities of motif and symbol,'' he says, indicate the continuity, the differences the ''adaptations of the evolving genre to the historic contexts of mid-Victorian British and Russian modernist fiction'' (394). He aims also ''to extend and refine the reading of *Hard Times* as dystopian fiction'' and to ''focus on Dickens [sic] and Zamiatin's self-referential preoccupation with imagination and the arts to show that the metafictionality of both works may be read as defenses of the novel and novel writing in worlds dominated by empirical science and philosophy'' (394). He does just about that, devoting more space to *Hard Times* than to *We,* which is consistent with his expressed purpose. Not having read *We,* I cannot judge Rogers's summary of that work, but I take exception to some opinions of *Hard Times:* that it belongs to the ''heart-centered genre'' of the love story (love in *Hard Times* is more about agape than eros), and that ''*Hard Times* laments (as did Thomas Carlyle, to whom it is dedicated) the lack of a Hero, a reformed Gradgrind to unify and inspire the nation'' (399). Dickens does not in *Hard Times* go beyond excoriating the blue-book systematizers running Parliament. Rogers thinks both novels show control being maintained by proscription of imagination; subtextually, both Dickens and Zamiatin are defending fiction ''as more real in its apprehension of human experience than bluebook facts . . .'' (405). There is a convincing solidity to Rogers's argument, and he supplies exhaustive documentation of supporting critical work (though I think he rather overdoes the use of footnotes to elaborate on textual statements and/or carry on sidebars).

Being only slightly more familiar with Salman Rushdie's work than Zamiatin's, I will not attempt to do much more than report what Martine Hennard Dutheil intends to show in ''Rushdie's Affiliation with Dickens'': that ''Dickens's fatherly—or indeed fathering—presence is felt at crucial moments in [Rushdie's] *Midnight's Children, Shame,* and *The Satanic Verses.* More precisely, Dickens's paternity is both acknowledged and ironized, in an ambivalent mode characteristic of most postcolonial writing'' (210). *The Satanic Verses* contains ''straightforward references to *Our Mutual Friend* in the crucial scene of the party . . .'' (211), while in *Midnight's Children* and *Shame* Dickens's presence is ''held in suspense,'' constituted by allusions to *David Copperfield.* Rushdie's main debt to *David Copperfield* in *Midnight's Children* is ''the motif of the child of uncertain origin who needs to replace a traumatic past with his own inventions'' (213). This jars slightly—we know David's origins—but just before this Dutheil cites with approval Edward Said's belief that ''mainstream Victorian fiction [enacts] the power relation between the metropolitan center and its overseas territories,'' and says Rushdie, like Said, uses moments ''when the colonial relationship is played out in Dickens's text and alters their significance by repeating and displacing them from a postcolonial perspective.'' So that must be what she thinks is going on here with respect to *David Copperfield*. (Said's example however is the relation between Pip and Magwitch in *Great Expectations*.) I don't see the parallel here; but Dutheil's essay is interesting and hangs together pretty well. (Her use of footnotes reminds me of Rogers.)

Texts, Language, Narrative Devices

Two items on Dickens turned up in *Proverbium* this year. Pilar Orero's ''Spanish Wellerisms'' discusses the absence in Spanish translations of *Pickwick Papers* of those Weller witticisms; they miss the ''as the . . . said'' part. The rhetorical figure does exist in 1627 and 1941 collections of Spanish proverbs, she says, so a proper translation of *Pickwick Papers* ought to be possible. Wolfgang Mieder ('' 'Conventional Phrases Are a Sort of Fireworks': Charles Dickens's Proverbial Langauge'') says that a ''Wellerism'' is a proverb joined to humorous comment; the name of the figure obviously comes from Dickens's use of it (189). Dickens used proverbs often, sometimes by allusion, sometimes in playful elaboration; he used folk proverbs more often than Biblical ones (187–88). Proverbs not only add ''metaphorical color to [Dickens's] prose''; they form ''intrinsic parts of the entire meaning and message of the novels'' (195). Mieder took his title from chapter 41 of *David Copperfield*, and he quotes the rest of the sentence: ''easily let off, and liable to take a great variety of shapes and colours not at all suggested by their original forms.''

Joel Brattin published two articles this year on Dickens's texts, on *David Copperfield* and *Our Mutual Friend*. In '' 'Let Me Pause Once More': Dickens' Manuscript Revisions in the Retrospective Chapters of *David Copperfield*'' he illustrates how Dickens maintains the double perspective of narrator and character (76), finding (as narrator) his younger self ''amusing, but not quite ridiculous,'' opening the reader's way to the same view (78). Dickens develops important themes—''memory, affection, time, reflection, and love''—in these chapters that focus on ''milestones'' in David's emotional developmental and in his relationship with Agnes (89). '' 'I will not have my words misconstrued': The Text of *Our Mutual Friend*'' is a technical job, explaining what he has done as editor of the Everyman Paperbacks

Classic edition. Series policy is to use as copy text the Charles Dickens Edition of 1867–68, the last one Dickens could have revised. Could have: Brattin confirms the recent skepticism of editors about that, asserting that "every single one of the 2,203 textual corrections, alterations, and mistakes" could have been made by anybody (172). So he finds it hard to believe Dickens did any of them. The light that the Charles Dickens Edition sheds on Dickens's creative process, then, is "at best a diffuse and weak" light. For the record, Brattin includes a table of variants, organized in categories, between the 1868 Charles Dickens Edition of *Our Mutual Friend* and the 1864–65 first edition.

Toru Sasaki's "Dickens in Confusion? Discrepancies in the Denouement of *Martin Chuzzlewit*" may be said to be for the record also: confusions and contradictions in chapters 49–52. Without following the trail closely, I am content to agree that the slips escape notice because of "Dickens's ability to sweep the reader along with his powerful narrative . . ." (24)—and, I would add, his cascade of events. Barbara Hill Hudson's "Sociolinguistic Analysis of Dialogues and First-Person Narratives in Fiction" turns out to be less forbidding than the title; she uses *Great Expectations* and a Dorothy Parker story, "The Standard of Living," as texts for exercises in detecting social class dialect discrimination. This is one of many publications for school use; I quailed at the prospect of covering them all.

However, I did read an unassuming and interesting analysis of the way Dickens's characters deal with each other's "face" that would be very useful in class: Deniz Tarba Ceylan's "Intimidation and Embarrassment in Conversations of Dickens's Novels." Threats to "face"—status, or standing, or reputation—occur often when Dickens's characters face off; a "face threat" may be unintentional, deliberate, or incidental. Ceylan illustrates with episodes from *Pickwick Papers, The Old Curiosity Shop, David Copperfield,* and *Little Dorrit.* She might have used also the interchange between Podsnap and the French gentleman in *Our Mutual Friend*—a stellar example of both intimidation and embarrassment, deliberate of course: intimidation is Podsnap's mode of discourse. The device is discoverable in any Dickens novel, and illustrates how Dickens's character interchanges are humanly credible.

Finally, another useful article for a teacher is Yael Halevi-Wise's "Little Dorrit's Story: A Window into the Novel," an unpretentious and perceptive explication of the significance of the story Amy Dorrit tells Maggie, to the reader clearly enough a fairy-tale version of her own romantic predicament. The poor little spinning woman of the story is Amy, and telling the story "helps Amy rearrange her feelings and behavior towards Clennam . . ." (184). Maggie interrupts often, to get Amy to tailor the story to her preferences, but Dickens uses the interruptions "to clarify the most obvious connections between the tale and the teller's current life" (187). Mainly, however, "allegorizing" Amy's case generates the reader's sympathy for her better than telling us how she feels, or just showing her sad in her Marshalsea garret (190).

Modes of Criticism

Martha Nussbaum and Richard Posner debated the legitimacy of ethical criticism. Nussbaum's "Exactly and Responsibly: A Defense of Ethical Criticism" takes issue with Posner's "Against Ethical Criticism," which appeared in 1997; and Posner's "Against Ethical Criticism: Part Two" is a response to Nussbaum. Nussbaum notes that Posner invoked with approval Oscar Wilde's famous credo: that literature is not "moral or immoral," only "well or badly written" (342). In his earlier piece Posner had mentioned Nussbaum's *Love's Knowledge* (1990) and *Poetic Justice* (1996) as belonging to "the counter tradition in literary criticism [which] originates with Plato" that privileges "ethical or political content and effects of works of literature" (2, 1997). Nussbaum had used *Hard Times* in *Poetic Justice,* and she defends her evaluation of Dickens's work on grounds that "ethical and political values are not 'extraneous,' but absolutely central, to his works" (360). She claims Posner is against reading literature for ethical instruction, that to him aesthetic pleasure is the only legitimate use. In his rejoinder Posner picks up on Nussbaum's analysis of Henry James's *The Ambassadors* in *Love's Knowledge,* leaving Dickens alone except for some mentions in passing, and a dismissive footnote.

As is often the case in such scuffles, the disputants talk past each other to some extent. Posner is not striking an outrageously amoral attitude in his first article, but taking a thoroughly traditional and respectable position about aesthetic values. Nussbaum is not contemptuous of aesthetic values; she assumes them; she is arguing (invoking Henry James's preface to *The Golden Bowl*) "that James is correct in thinking . . . that responsible criticism of literary works can legitimately invoke ethical categories" (344). Posner's tone in his rejoinder strikes me as dismissive, but Nussbaum may have evoked that by her own passionate style (which may in turn have been set on by the energy and magisterial tone of Posner's first essay). But the exchange is instructive and thought-provoking. It seems to me that these two are in substantial agreement about the effects of literature. Nussbaum (like Brian Nelson in his monograph) holds there to be human conditions that only literary treatment—not abstract theoretical discourse but embodiment in fiction—can provide: "guides to what is mysterious and messy and dark in our experience" (348). Surely that resonates with Posner here: "[In reading literature] we are expanding our emotional as well as our intellectual horizons. . . . Imaginative literature can engender in its readers emotional responses to experiences that they have not had" (19, 1997).

William Myers's *The Presence of Persons: Essays on Literature, Science and Philosophy in the Nineteenth Century* is a collection "based mainly on unpublished conference papers and teaching materials amassed over a very long time." (He says this in his Acknowledgments, where he also says he is "grateful to a now defunct university culture" which encouraged him in this kind of scholarship. Presumably he speaks of his own University of Leicester; how much more widely his remark applies is worth thinking about.) His essays on *Oliver Twist* and *Little Dorrit* come up later in this review, but his introduction belongs here. Myers is another defender of imaginative literature as a way of knowing; "language [is] not the exclusive determinant of understanding" (3), and readers of literature "can share an awareness of intentions which can never be expressed" (17) because what Newman called our "illative sense" enables us to speak "figuratively but with certitude about the complex system of human experience which logically lies beyond language, but which casts faithful shadows on its use." It reaches "back beyond the 'always already' which is [J. Hillis Miller's et al.] starting point and their limit" (10); Miller thinks literally analysis must stop with analysis of language, which Myers thinks sets "intolerable limits," and wrong if Newman is right. This is why Myers believes in "character analysis of the most unfashionable kind" (12). (One sees why Myers credits Newman with anticipating "deconstructionist notions of narrative as a makeshift version of a fuller, absent truth, forever, as far as its expression goes, deferred" [7].)

Peter Hunt's "Chesterton and Wilson on Dickens: An Instructive Comparison" is a modest foray into the history of Dickens criticism. Hunt defends Chesterton (shunted from the main line by Wilson and his followers) by showing they agree on a lot. He attributes their differences to their basic takes on Dickens: Wilson saw Dickens as "a Dostoevskian figure" and took "a very dark view of Dickens's work and character" (18), while Chesterton's idea of Dickens was that "whatever his restlessness and periods of depression, [he] was, to the last, a man of fundamentally joyful vision" (13). For instance, Chesterton gives us full attention to the unhappy episodes in Dickens's life—the blacking-factory, the marriage wreck—as Wilson does, but shows "a greater readiness to diagnose weakness without judging"; Wilson "builds on the trauma" and "tends to turn human frailty into almost the inevitable price of genius . . ." (14). Hunt provides a number of telling parallels and contrasts in their analyses of Dickens's novels, and points out that Chesterton was not ignorant of the Dickensian symbolism that Wilson has been credited with discovering. Hunt takes a parting shot at J. Hillis Miller for elevating Wilson at the expense of earlier critics, noting (as a reason?) that "Miller's Dickens is heavily reliant on Freudian assumptions and subjectivist views of what creative writing is," whereas Chesterton's comes from "penetrating insight into Dickens's own experience and personality [and] the evidence of the novels" (19): not necessarily a logically disjunct discrimination. But about Chesterton, Hunt says things worth saying.

Grahame Smith (''Dickens and Critical Theory'') thinks that what he calls ''open'' critical theory (which he associates with Derrida) is more productive (''listening'') than ''closed'' (''constraining''), or Foucaultian theory. Open theory consorts better, he says (following J. Hillis Miller here), with the comic linguistic exuberance characteristic of the Dickens *oeuvre* as a whole, which has features ''particuarly amenable to the fluidities of post-structuralist criticism.'' He thinks three of Bakhtin's emphases are especially rewarding, applied to Dickens: his belief in the necessary social relevance of a literary text, his privileging of the dialogic or polyphonic novel (as opposed to the monologic text), and his concept of the carnivalesque. (The first two of these put Smith in the same part of the critical forest as Martha Nussbaum and Brian Nelson.)

Jeremy Tambling's psychoanalytic essay ''Carlyle in Prison: Reading *Latter-Day Pamphlets*'' includes a kind of postscript on chapter 61 of *David Copperfield,* ''I am shown two interesting Penitents,'' where David experiences ''great relief'' when Uriah Heep is returned to his cell: ''the ugly, the disgusting, the under-class, the phallic—Heep is all of these things—has [sic]been excluded again'' (325). Tambling argues that David's anxiety ''to establish his subjectivity and his point of view,'' his ''desire for control,'' is behind this relief (326). In fact the episode, Tambling says, is revealing in another way: Heep and Littimer coming out of their cells are ''uncannily like the appearance of the unconscious,'' and ''the anxiety constructing [the text] is that of the power of the unconscious—that it cannot be repressed'' (328–29). The threat to an ''anxious masculinity'' cannot be left behind. (But the text drives them back to their cells, and to transportation: is that to be taken as mere wish fulfillment, or as evidence of a power to control?)

Mark M. Hennelly, Jr. has had a big year (two and a half years, really) in print: an article in volume 26 of this journal on Dickens and Hardy, a two-part article on *David Copperfield, Bleak House,* and *Great Expectations* in the fall and winter numbers of *Dickens Quarterly,* and a five-part article on *Oliver Twist* (so far as Dickens is concerned) in the *Journal of Evolutionary Psychology* running in consecutive numbers from March 1997 through March 1999. ''Courtly Wild Men and Carnivalesque Pig Women in Dickens and Hardy'' develops concepts of courtly and carnivalesque play (which Hennelly says are not, contra Bakhtin, opposing but ''different tides of the same archetypal play current'' [8]) to illuminate things in *Pickwick Papers, David Copperfield, Barnaby Rudge, The Old Curiosity Shop,* and particularly the Wild Man tradition as found in *Nicholas Nickleby* (that amorous neighbor in ch. 41). Hardy's play motifs are most like Dickens's of any nineteenth-century novelists (20), and the two of them do more than any others with ''carnivalesque popular festive motifs'' (26), though in widely contrasting ways.

From here on I am in another country without a visa. The best I can do about ''The 'Mysterious Portal': Liminal Play in *David Copperfield, Bleak*

House, and *Great Expectations"* is to begin by quoting Hennelly's intention: "to outline the pertinent points of [Victor] Turner's liminal theory, point out some general and rather basic applications to *David Copperfield, Bleak House,* and *Great Expectations* [in part one], and conclude [in part two] with a more detailed application of D. W. Winnicott's related play theory to the initiation trials of Mr. Dick and Esther Summerson" (158). "Liminal play," if I understand this, is what happens in an episode which amounts to a threshold, the doorway into a critical turn in the action, "a crucial rite of initiation" (155). Winnicott, like Dickens, is concerned with the search for the self and the importance of play to this search (195). His theory of the "good-enough mother, [who] teaches her children to trust the real world by playing with them" (196), is pertinent because of the importance of mothers in these novels (195–96).—I abandon further effort to render Hennelly; the article is far too detailed to do justice to. Bakhtin and Lacan, Freud, Turner, and Winnicott are braided into the fabric. Adumbrations of and allusions to them swaddle specific references to the novels, which may be strenuously adjusted to fit psychoanalytic theory: since David and Emily played as children on the beach, David finds Steerforth's body there among "heaps of such toys"—a phrase occurring earlier, in reference not to what David and Emily found on the beach but to the "men, spars, casks, planks, bulwarks" washed overboard from the wreck—toys to the storm waves. Hennelly has a wrong take on Esther, too: that she has to "die to her old agape-bound self and be reborn to passionate fulfillment with her courtier Woodcourt" (204). Rather, remaining true to her "agape-bound self" (she is the most tried of Dickens's patient Griseldas) is what earns her her Woodcourt.

" 'Deep Play' and 'Women's Ridicules' in *Oliver Twist"* is the most ambitious of Hennelly's three articles; in fact it amounts to a brief monograph published serially. To stick the two 1998 segments was to be lost in medias res. So in part I, I learned that the phrase "deep play" was uttered by Fagin, suspecting Nancy of some hidden purpose; and that it also denotes an anthropological theory of play in which the stakes are so high as to render the play irrational; but Dickens's readers would probably have known the phrase from its occurrence in Bentham's *Theory of Legislation* (original French edition 1802); and that "women's ridicules" is Noah Claypole's malapropism for "reticules" (102). (We have much to do with women's containers [also signified by the O in Oliver] in this article.) Part I also introduces the "play codes [which] reflexively circulate around and matriculate from" the opening chapter, where *Oliver Twist* "seminally situates its very high, very surface, and very deep play stakes, structures and antistructures . . ." (104–05). These codes (with "their modern advocates") are the romance (Frye), the carnivalesque (Bakhtin), liminal (Turner), psychoanalytic (Lacan), and deconstructive (Derrida) (105). The interplay of these codes creates "[what Barthes calls] a twisted 'braid' of multiple 'understandings' [which] 'enables the discourse to engage in a game of equivocations . . . originally' saturated with sexualities . . . virtually a kind of *foreplay,* which the reader can either enjoy or interrupt'' (105).

In parts II-IV, "before finally tracing textual play through the opening of *Oliver Twist*'' (II, 144), Hennelly prolegomanically lays out the codes—romance and carnivalesque in II, liminal and psychoanalytic in III, and deconstructive in IV—to help the reader by "minimiz[ing] theoretical interference during the eventual (modified) 'step-by-step commentary [Barthes's phrase]' on the opening [of *Oliver Twist*] (II, 144). Hennelly is certainly right to deploy his material this way; the theoretical discourses, erudite and intricate, would utterly decompose the 'step-by-step commentary' if inserted parenthetically at relevant points.

Part V, then, is where Hennelly promises at the end of IV to "finally interrogate" the opening of *Oliver Twist* (172). And so he does, discovering Barthes's sexualities in the game of equivocations that the text seems reduced to. What of "the possibility of a solution to this polysemy" that he encouraged us to look forward to? Alas: at the end the reader is left "liminally hanging, if not twisting from the five braided play codes (among many, many others), with nothing left to do but speculate on and/or participate in the overlapping games of literature and life" (V, 98). Really, I trusted my guide through thorny thickets of erudition to lead me to more of a clearing than this. I discounted "Hills" for "Hillis" (in "J. Hills Miller") and "Humphrey" (Humphry House), besides mangled words in the text, as faulty proofreading by somebody. But "Elaine Showister"?—and everywhere the goddess of the underworld "Prosperine"?—is there some inattention to detail here? And what about Hennelly's assertion that Dickens's 1858 preface for the Library Edition of *Oliver Twist* "provocatively opens the curtain on play motifs . . . by introducing criminal 'merry-makings in the snuggest of all caverns' '' (V, 93), when Dickens's sentence begins "Here are no canterings on moonlit healths, no merry-makings . . .''? I suppose Hennelly's frequent word play (e.g., "brothel or betrothal," II, 147; "demanding if not demented mentors," III, 119; "models or medlies [sic] of meddling carnivalesque impulses," II, 148; "re-presentation of a peter-pan, if not pederastic, paradise (lost)," III, 124) is offered in the spirit of play, but the style calls attention to itself. The last example illustrates too the pervasive use of parentheses and dashes, as in "(per)version" (II, 145), "(tor)mentors" (III, 119), "p(l)ay-load" (V, 93), "dis-eased" (III, 125), "a-mazing" (IV, 170), and "(p)re-presents": ". . . the initial letter *O* in *Oliver* . . . calligraphically (p)re-presents the opening of the text . . ." (V, 93). These shifts provide a suspended quality to Hennelly's meaning: not "tentative," but keeping a strategic retreat open from the position taken by suggesting an alternative or supplemental read-ing—what one might call indeterminacy as a critical strategy. Or perhaps as I suggested earlier, just playfulness; puns occur often, too. P(f)unny stuff.

Finally, consider that "the underground play of underprivileged feminine *différance(s)* further eludes, differs, and ambivalently disarms or even rearms the other codes (including Barthes's and the present essay's code of 'codes') by ludicly, crossly, and ludicrously—*ludicrossly* [a portmanteau word Hen-nelly coins for later use]—'crackling' about and against 'women's ridicules' and reticules, thus creating *catechresis*" (I, 106). This is a fair example of Hennelly's prose. One must decide whether a journey through forty pages of it (plus seven pages of notes, and eight of works cited) is worth being left "liminally hanging."

Requiring—and rewarding—close attention, Paul A. Kran's "Signification and Rhetoric in *Bleak House*" analyzes the novel's structure according to categories of Hayden White in *Metahistory* (1973) in combination with an idea of Lacan's in "Seminar on 'The Purloined Letter' '': that behavior is determined by "displacement of the signifier" rather than by more traditional notions of psychology (148). Kran claims this methodology avoids "pitfalls of both the traditional humanist critique and the radical anti-humanist formalist critique as well" (1947). He works through Esther's handkerchief, Lady Dedlock's letters, smallpox, and the suit in Chancery to show that "it is through the circulation of these signifiers, rather than through the active agency of any of the characters, that the complex plot(s) of the novel unfold, and their passing between and among characters creates the system of per-sonal and social interconnections the text makes explicit ["What connexion can there be, between . . ."]it wishes to establish" (148). Kran's engaging modesty as a critic inspires confidence: to some critics' claim that the dual narrative in *Bleak House* "undermines itself and the intentions of its author," he says, "The text amply demonstrates that we can attribute to Dickens an ironic self-consciousness at least as acute as that of our most subtle critics"; and about his own comment on a particular matter he posts this wry dis-claimer: "I have a painfully ironic awareness as I say so that—given my own ideological predispositions and professional training—this is exactly what I *would* say" (164).

Biblical and Theological Themes

Six studies demonstrate how deeply Biblical story and Christian theology were embedded in Dickens's imagination. Five of them deal with one novel only; Baruch Hochman's "Bulrush and Harvest Home" ranges over five from *Oliver Twist* to *Great Expectations*, paying most attention to *David*

Copperfield and *Little Dorrit.* The bulrush is in *Oliver Twist,* from Monk's warning to Bumble during their meeting at the abandoned factory to beware the trapdoor opening to the river below, "or your life's not worth a bulrush" (ch. 38). This improbable link to the story of Moses introduces the "powerful threat of extinction ... [the] equally powerful promise of redemption ... [and] the constellation of redeeming women" (53) which figure in Dickens's many treatments of "the orphan condition" which is Hochman's subject, along with "the radical homelessness it entails" as well as Dickens's amplification and illumination of that experience by biblical motifs (51). He finds allusion to the Egyptian bondage in *Bleak House,* the Cain-Abel story in *Oliver Twist* and *Little Dorrit,* and of course King David in *David Copperfield,* where "some curious implications of Dickens's naming of David, Uriah, and Agnes" imply that "Agnes is rightfully Uriah's, and that Dickens, at some level, knows it" (59). This is certainly an example of Hochman's view that "the positives of the Dickens texts" have undersides, "striking negations and subversions" (60). So, he says, while Amy Dorrit's "healing presence" makes a home possible, it "may, finally, be imagined to partake, in a limited way, of the desolation of the world Miss Wade inhabits ..." (62); and there was "no safe haven among the bulrushes ... [nor] a meaningful possibility of harvest, or of home: only the ordeal of achieving such consciousness of loss and of falsifications as the Pips of the late Dickens's imaginative world can achieve" (63). Hochman's findings are interesting though not all persuasive; in *David Copperfield* the implication of the names does not fit the feel of the story, and the world of Amy and Arthur is walled off from Miss Wade's by love. Hochman seems to me to be operating from a determinedly dark outlook on Dickens. (I don't know where "harvest" comes from in the novels, incidentally.)

Jon Surgal's "The Parable of the Spoons and Ladles: Sibling and Crypto-Sibling Typology in *Martin Chuzzlewit*" carries out neither the comic implication of "spoons and ladies" nor the sociological freight of the subtitle. Surgal works out something more interesting: a theological analysis of why young Martin comes to a good end and his cousin Jonas does not. He uses the parallels that he finds with the parable of the prodigal son, the story of Cain and Abel, and most significantly, God's "transformation of Jacob into Israel, designated heir to the family estate ["The land which I gave Abram and Isaac, to thee will I give it ..." (Genesis 35:12)]. This transformation parallels the change in Martin "into a worthy legatee of his grandfather's name and possessions" (64). Both selections are offers of grace: "prevenient grace, the opportunity to earn sanctifying grace by 'coming out strong' from a purgative trial by suffering" (64). Jonas, however, gets no such offer, and he is "among those Dickens characters ... who do evil ... because it is their nature" (65). In the end, Surgal says, Dickens follows St. Paul, who "tells us that 'the purpose of God according to election' is determined 'not of works, but of him that calleth' (Romans 9:11)'' (66). Surgal speculates that this "arbitrariness of salvation in the novel" (66) reflects Dickens's own experience in the blacking factory. Placed there by family power and later rescued by the same power, he learned that "fate was unfair . . . [and] capricious as well. . . . Martin and Jonas recapitulate the helplessness of Dickens' abandonment to the mercy of that arbitrary and indecipherable Will which supercedes all other wills" (67).

Robert Polhemus ("The Favorite Child: *David Copperfield* and the Scriptual Issue of Child-Wives") argues that Dickens "parallels, re-interprets, and revises for the Victorian age the generative story of the Biblical David, who in Scripture issues from child-wives" (4). He points out that Lot and his daughters—"child-wives with a vengeance" (10)—belong to the lineage of David, and finds many echoes of "the Lot chapter and its Scriptural consequences" (12) in Dickens's novel. There are many child-wives in Dickens—Polhemus lists them (5)—and the child-wife is the marital expression of Dickensian model man-woman relations: "an affectionate, very close parent-child or sibling relationship" (6), not a Freudian sexual one. "In the word 'child-wife,' . . . the 'child' drains the 'wife' of its mature sexual connotation and infantilizes the marital relationship''; but the threat of sexuality is not entirely banished, for " 'wife' casts a sexual potential and a threat about the life of a child" (8). Still, Polhemus says, the term "has cultural significance beyond the personal," suggestive of "desires for secure family structure, . . . peace and harmony" between generations, and so on (5). Polhemus's packed prose style sometimes extends to sentences Faulknerian in length if not obscurity (I quote there from one), but generally he is perspicuous enough, and his article is a rich read.

Anthony Julius's "Dickens the Law-Breaker" frames his analysis of *Bleak House* as a test whether "Nabokov's antimony" is unassailable. An antimony is "an ostensible paradox" resolvable only by the revision "of some tacit and trusted pattern of reasoning" (45), literary analysis in the present case; and the antimony in *Bleak House* is the perceived tension between aesthetic form and reformist sentiment. Nabokov says the antimony is inescapable, "we must choose form over content, style over satire" (46). Julus says no, the two are related, and to see this in *Bleak House* one must "take seriously the novel's attack on the law. . . ." Julius draws on St. Paul often in doing that, to make the point that "law and love [are] in contest in the novel" (50), and that the action shows Dickens to be a literary antinomialist whose hostility to the law is "insurrectionary destructiveness . . . 'lawbreaking' of the most fundamental kind," an attack on law as such (55). This law breaking, in *Bleak House*, belongs to both form and content, and thus the Nabokovian antimony is reconciled. Is that clear? Julius does it better, and his recourse to St. Paul is much more important than this adumbration indicates.

Volume 27 of this journal includes two articles discerning theological dimensions in *A Tale of Two Cities:* David Rosen's *"A Tale of Two Cities:* Theology of Revolution" and Kenneth Sroka's "A Tale of Two Gospels: Dickens and John." Both pay attention to Biblical parallels, Sroka rather more concerned with particular details, and Rosen with theological patterns. Sroka makes a lot of tiger and lamb images, finding them at times "ambivalent . . . suggesting the mixed and paradoxical realities they ultimately symbolize" (154); he also spots the reference to Jesus Christ in Jerry Cruncher's initials (but misses the near-profane comic play on the Resurrection). Much of his article lays out permutations and combinations of parallels and doubles. Rosen thinks that Dickens saw the French Revolution as following "the pattern of pagan fertility rites" (172); France under the aristocracy is infertile, and the deaths of aristocrats are sacrificial (174). But the revolution ends in barbarism of its own, and it is the Christian pattern of redemptive sacrifice that Dickens affirms (182–83). The tale of two cities is really about Augustine's "two cities of man and God" as well as London and Paris, and "Biblical typology is fully operative"; the French incur guilt "of all sorts of blasphemy" by invoking the pagan counter-myth (184). Rosen cites Alexander Welsh about Augustine's two cities (*The City of Dickens,* 1968); according to Davis's *Charles Dickens A to Z,* Joseph Gold calls up the same comparison in *Charles Dickens: Radical Moralist* (1972). Sroka finds more of parallel than embodiment: "John's theology and Dickens's poetic prose are complementary guides for the human spirit, one with its eye on an other-worldly heaven, the other looking more to earth" (166). There is a certain wavering in his overview, though; *A Tale of Two Cities* might be "another Victorian 'gospel' " like Carlyle's work substituting for "conventional religious faith" (145). On the whole, Rosen's article is more provocative and engaging.

Dickens and the City

Chapter 4 of Julian Wolfrey's *Writing London: The Trace of the Urban Text from Blake to Dickens* is "Dickensian architextures or, the city and the ineffable." The word "architexture" puns on "text," of course (*Writing London,* remember); Wolfreys invents it to suggest the desire ("always present in Dickens") to shake the solidity of the monumental"(148). To Wolfreys, Dickens's London is a radical state of flux: "not a location or base [but] a multiplicity of events, chance occurrences, and fields of opportunities" (7). (This outlook comes from Derrida, of whom there is more in Wolfreys's bibliography than even Dickens.) So Wolfreys quotes *Bleak House*'s opening description of London ("Michaelmas term lately over," etc.; "implacable November weather," etc.; "mud," "smoke," "fog," etc.) right up to the naming of Temple Bar, where November weather, fog, and muddy streets are at their rawest, densest and muddiest (154–55). He claims that this "London" infects Chancery (158), rather than symbolizing Chancery's effect on England. But stopping at Temple Bar, Wolfreys suppresses the information in the next sentence that the Lord High Chancellor presides over the High Court of Chancery "hard by Temple Bar, in Lincoln's Inn Hall, *at the very heart of the fog . . .*" (my italics.) Context and Dickensian symbolic technique confute Wolfreys. Dickens is not "writing London," even here; he is writing Chancery, and providing a London appropriate to his subject and theme. That "London" changes from novel to novel is not because of its ineffability, but because Dickens's subjects and themes change. Wolfreys's Derridean lens, like Dever's Freudian one, distorts.

Grahame Smith's "Dickens and the City of Light" connects the importance of the visual in Dickens, his interest in life as lived in city streets, and his consciousness of the value of light, in proposing "a reading of the genesis of cinema in relation to Dickens" (1). Smith comes at this convolutedly (and superfluously) via Baudelaire and Benjamin, and more materially via Michael Hollington's 1981 article "Dickens the Flâneur," which deals with Dickens's well-known need of city streets for inspiration. Not streets, really, but people. It is the city as spectacle in motion (5)—whether London, the city of darkness as it became to Dickens, or Paris, the city of light to him, as seen through the window of his apartment on the Champs Elyseés in 1855–56—that Smith thinks of in connecting Dickens to the emergence of film. That, and Dickens's perception that ordinary people want—need—"*something in motion*" in their amusements; a mere picture gallery "is too still after their lives of machinery" (7), as he wrote to Macready in a letter Smith thinks "reveals Dickens' awareness of some of the pressures, and opportunities, leading towards the advent of cinema . . ." (7).

Cinema

A stretch, that, perhaps. But Smith's right to our attention is certified by his excellent review of the March 1998 BBC *Our Mutual Friend* (broadcast in the U.S. by PBS in January 1999). He rates this production very highly; his fears set on by technical deficiencies of the opening scene were "unconfirmed by almost all that followed" (145). He thinks the liberties taken with Dickens's text—omission of Podsnap and Fledgeby, for instance—make this a "version," not the "adaptation" that the credits announce it to be. He commends the "daring substitution of visual and aural alternatives" occasioned by "the loss of densely textured narrative prose," and singles out one such—"the voyeuristic spying of the characters upon one another"—as "a visual motif of real power" embodying the spirit of the novel. Generally complimentary of the cast, he singles out David Bradley (Rogue Riderhood) and Kenneth Cranham (Silas Wegg) as especially effective.

As to this production of *Our Mutual Friend,* I would second everything Smith says is good about it, dissenting only about the opening: the docks did not strike me as "a wretched mock-up," nor did I notice the "painted back-cloth of decaying warehouses" (145). I regret the loss of Podsnap, though the viewer unfamiliar with Dickens's text will not miss him. (The script neatly substitutes Bella for the absent Miss Podsnap as the object of the Lammles' mercenary attention.) The music is occasionally obtrusive, and dialog (especially between Eugene Wrayburn and Lizzie Hexam) is too often muttered. (Perhaps it strikes Brit ears differently.) Even if this is a "version," not an "adaptation," too much is sacrificed in the casting of the Wilfers—Mr. Wilfer is too burly, and Mrs. Wilfer not dominant enough—and John Harmon needs more force of character than Steven Mackintosh conveys, to justify the violence with which he breaks out at Silas Wegg at the end. Perhaps that it a matter of direction, as may be also the over-the-top moments of Bradley Headstone and Mr. Veneering. But David Bradley is superb as Rogue Riderhood, as Smith says; and so are Peter Vaughan and Pam Ferris as the Boffins.

The story line is clear (barring a few puzzling moments—editing cuts, perhaps), and as Smith says, the absence of Dickens's narrative voice is not a problem in this production (a noticeable defect in most films of Dickens novels). All in all, Smith is entirely justified in calling this a "triumphant version" of *Our Mutual Friend.*

In the same number of *The Dickensian* (Summer 1998), Malcolm Andrews defends in his editorial the principle of adapting Dickens in modern film/radio/TV productions, offering as examples this *Our Mutual Friend* and the new American version of *Great Expectations,* transplanted to twentieth-century Florida and New York City. After all, Dickens himself adapted his works for his public readings. Andrews says the new *Great Expectations* turned out to be a bad movie, opting for "garish sensuality and *Grand Guignol*"; it would better have "us[ed] the original text to illuminate changing social values [or] differences between the two cultures" (84). Andrews is confident, however, that "[Dickens] will survive his adapters."

Elham Afnan begins "Imaginative Transformations: *Great Expectations* and *Sunset Boulevard*" by discriminating among three kinds of film adaptations of novels: "translation . . . from the literary to the cinematic medium"; a version "like a critical essay which stresses what the critic sees as the main theme of the original"; and an "imaginative transformation" (5), a phrase borrowed from Neil Sinyard's *Filming Literature: The Art of Screen Adaptation. Sunset Boulevard,* he says, has that third relation to *Great Expectations,* and Afnan's essay seems to be a fleshing-out of his view. The clue to the relationship is supplied early, when the hero, Joe Gillis, describes his impression of the aging movie star Norma Desmond's home as having "an unhappy look . . . like that . . . Miss Havisham and her rotting wedding dress and her torn veil . . ." (5). Citations of numerous parallels follow, not always clearly distinguished from those pointed out by Sinyard (6). Afnan involves David Lean's *Great Expectations* ("a good example of film as an essay on the original" [5]) in her analysis from time to time. Afnan's theme is interesting as developed, plausible in spite of some misinterpretations (Estella does not "[break] Pip's heart" [11] to avoid being jilted by him). But at the end, *Sunset Boulevard,* which began in Afnan's essay as an "imaginative transformation," has become "a critical essay on Dickens's novel" (12). What gives?

Homes and Homelessness

The four essays in this group are in Murray Baumbarten and H. M. Daleski's *Homes and Homelessness in the Victorian Imagination* (I treat five others under other heads); two are about Dickens, two refer to Dickens as illustrative on broader topics. Efraim Sicher's "Bleak Homes and Symbolic Houses: At-homeness and Homelessness in Dickens," although his conscientious credit to other critics can look like a parade of learning ("Without repeating Dominick LaCapra's critique of D. A. Miller's analysis . . ." [142]), sets *Bleak House* "on the foundations of an alternate political and ethical agenda" (34). It is definitely not a parallel to Deadly London, as David Storer says in an article I discuss later. "Delightfully irregular," Bleak House provides "imaginative space" not to be found in "the tyrannical regularity of architectural and legal boundaries in Coketown [and] negates the idea of property as acquisition [and represents] the ideal of home" (37). There is much more, about *Oliver Twist* and *Great Expectations* as well as *Bleak House,* and about Dickens's own at-homeness. Sicher's article is densely rich and will repay (perhaps require) rereading.

Patrick McCarthy's opening paragraph to "Making for Home: David Copperfield and His Fellow Travelers" is really an abstract of his article, making the point that *David Copperfield* (unlike other novels of development) "draws its protagonist toward its particular idea—middle-class domestic achieved happiness" (21). Other protagonists either reject that hope, reaching for some other fulfillment "that they do not attain within the novel, [or] glimpse the domestic satisfactions of others" but do not reach them, or reject them (22). McCarthy spells out how all the action in *David Copperfield* centers on the domestic economy; the thematic focus is at "the expense of novelistic rendering of close-grained, realistic characterization" (26–27). Agnes does not come alive, but she "carries a symbolic burden" (30). Knowing that domestic happiness must end—"that at the heart of all this warmth and hominess lies a radical instability" (31)—Dickens uses Agnes to "thrust through the present moment into an indeterminate future." Her "pointing upward"—the closing words of *David Copperfield*—is Dickens's "startling assertion of energy's response to atrophy, of home seeking transmutation into non-worldly hope" (31).

John O. Jordan explores what the Ruskinian image of home as the retreat from the rush and tensions and injustices "outside" ignores (as do the manual writers for Victorian householders): the "potentially disruptive qualities that the presence of servants risks introducing into the middle-class home" (80; "Domestic Servants and the Victorian Home"). To provide perspectives from above and below stairs Jordan uses Isabella Beeton's *Book of Household Management* (1861, often reprinted and revised) and *The Diaries of Hannah Cullwick, Victorian Maidservant.* In Dickens, servants may "blend in harmoniously" as in *Pickwick Papers* and *The Old Curiosity Shop* (85), and are regularly "the old family retainer" type, as Orwell noted (84). But sometimes they express class hostility: in *Little Dorritt* Tattycoram, and Miss Wade, once a governess (86), and perhaps in *Dombey and Son,* in Polly Toodles (85). Jordan ends by considering Thackeray's essay "Our Chalk-Mark on the Door," which he says "deconstruct[s] the idea of Home . . . [collapsing] the distinction . . . between the safe, orderly domestic world and the world of 'terror, doubt, and division' that hovers just outside its doorstep" (88–89).

The story of the sexually exploited housemaid is familiar, but Murray Roston's "Disrupted Homes: The Fallen Woman in Victorian Art and Literature" focuses on two "of the most familiar images in Victorian thought" (96): besides the Fallen Woman of his title, the Angel in the House, "as Coventry Patmore termed her" (97). Rosen thinks that the cluster of Fallen Women appearing in art and literature around 1850 is not a reflection of burgeoning prostitution, a "strictly sociological" phenomenon (95), but the "obverse" of the Angel image: allegorical representation of the incompatibility of "Christian ideals of selflessness, compassion, and love," represented by the Angel (keeper of the family morals), with the "ruthless pursuit of worldly profit . . . so intrinsic to the material prosperity of the age . . ." (109). Roston traces this opposition in *David Copperfield*, and in *Hard Times,* where he sees drawing consciousness of the contradictions in Victorian domestic ideology (100–01). He also cites Thackeray, Gaskell, and Eliot, and among painters, Rossetti, Egg, Watts, and Hunt; his analysis of the Biblical inscription on the frame of *The Awakening Conscience* shows that Hunt meant the picture to be an allegory of "society's failure to fulfill its duties and, like the cat beneath the table playing with a helpless bird, cruelly ill-treating those within its power" (106). (According to William Palmer's *Dickens Quarterly* review [March 1991], Roston's *Victorian Contexts. Literature and the Visual Arts* [1997] is rich in such "cultural readings of the visual works of artists" [53].)

Politics and Society

Some of these studies, as is evident, could fit just as well as in other categories; they are here because they seem to me to be more about Dickens's views than about formal considerations. Three of them are about Dickens and middle-class Victorian attitudes toward the lower classes. Patrick Brantlinger's introduction to *The Reading Lesson: The Threat of Mass Literacy in Nineteenth-Century British Fiction*, "The Case of the Poisonous Book," tells how "novels and novel-reading were viewed, especially by novelists themselves, as both causes and symptoms of the rotting of minds and the decay of culture and society" (24). Perhaps that is why characters in Dickens's novels did not uniformly display the benefits that he claimed for education in speeches and articles. Illiteracy is less dangerous than the abuse of literacy: witness Joe and Pip in *Great Expectations*, and Boffin as contrasted to Wegg and Headstone in *Our Mutual Friend* (5). It is unfortunate that Brantlinger, in support of his point that serial publication made for "dialogic" relations between the novelist and his readers, repeats the canard—disproven by Robert Patten relative to *The Old Curiosity Shop* nearly thirty years ago—that Dickens's novels unfolded in accordance with fan mail and sales figures (13). (I summarize Patten's case and the evidence as to other novels in my *Charles Dickens*, 74–76).

Robert Tracy's title ("Queens' Parlours, Queens' Bedrooms, and Queens' Gardens: Raping the Locks") highlights one aspect of middle-class fears "of the mob taking over as it had done in France during the Revolution" (323), the fancied threat to the chastity of wives, daughters, and sisters in the event of working-class rebellion. Dickens's *A Tale of Two Cities* responds to this anxiety by "shrink[ing] history to personalize it" (337), making the French Revolution a sort of family affair. Tracy works out in convincing detail that "the Darnay/Evrémonde family, Charles, Lucie, and little Lucie, are a fictional version of the French royal family, domesticated and sentimentalized" (337). Thus he "connect[s] political revolution with danger to the home" (340–41)—though the Darnays are reassuringly spared the fate of the Bourbons. (The title refers to the mob's invasion of the palace of Versailles on 6 October 1789, sensationally developed in Burke's *Reflections on the Revolution in France*.).

Scott Dransfield sees the mob in *Barnaby Rudge* as "fixed in a middle-class perception of working-class pathologies" (83) which Dickens seems to equate with Chartism, or at least makes to imply aspects of Chartism ("Reading the Gordon Riots in 1841:Social Violence and Moral Management in *Barnaby Rudge*"). Dickens's "horror of the mob" (a phrase Dransfield borrows from Humphry House) appears in his "construction of the mob as a pathological entity," and Gabriel Varden exemplifies the "disciplined subject who has internalized the means of his own moral control . . ." (86), the hoped-for outcome of "active and interventionist moral management of the social body" (84). This societal "pathological entity" is symbolized at the individual level by "Barnaby's moral oblivion and Hugh's sociopathic impulses" (86); Protestant religious zeal has nothing to do with the matter. ("Moral Management" was a new idea for treatment of the insane, a development away from the eighteenth century's reliance on physical restraint, the object being to develop "self command" in the insane person [72].)

Stephen Hake's "Becoming Poor to Make Many Rich: The Resolution of Class Conflict in Dickens" could have gone into the group devoted to theological and Biblical themes, since Hake grounds his argument on a handful of Biblical texts which he says shows that "Christianity always works from the bottom up" (107). The "Christian concept of salvation through a forgiving and self-sacrificing love" (107) appears in those working-class people who "suffer for and save the rich and sophisticated, or those who aspire to be rich and sophisticated" (108). Hake demonstrates his thesis in *David Copperfield, Great Expectations,* and *Our Mutual Friend,* and points out how the idea develops in Dickens's career (Steerforth is redeemed as Wrayburn [114]). There is something to this idea, although Hake simplifies class structure in his demonstration, and his argument often carves narrative detail in the shape required by his thesis.

Rodney Stenning Edgecombe thinks that the statesman George Canning's lampoon in heroic couplets of what he saw as "feckless moral relativism" in "the Tories' left-leaning critics . . . might well underpin a similar passage in *Little Dorrit*" (484–85) where Dickens characterizes Henry Gowan, whose "moral flattening" enraged Dickens the way Jacobin relativism did Canning ("*Little Dorrit* and Canning's 'New Morality' "). Edgecombe argues that the character Rigaud stands in for Napoleon III as Gowan does for Thackeray, and that they embody Dickens's perception that what he saw as Thackeray's cynicism parallels British merchants' financial interest in Napoleon's empire (that is, Gowan's admiration for Rigaud's style, regardless of his moral depravity, is like British merchants' winking at Second Empire reaction). Edgecombe credits Edmund Wilson (as quoted in Edgar Johnson, *Charles Dickens: His Tragedy and Triumph,* II: 886) with perceiving the Rigaud-Napoleon III connection; Wilson, however, makes the house of Clennam stand in for the British merchants. Edgecombe needlessly goes beyond proof of a Canning/ Dickens link in saying Dickens "blurred the allusion by paraphrasing the source'' (486); his argument for similar moral outrage does not require that there be direct influence.

William Myers's essay "The Radicalism of *Little Dorrit*" in his *Presence of Persons* (I discuss his introduction in the section on modes of criticism) depicts Dickens writing of his own world, an inhabitant himself of the middle-class world of which the values are the object of the most penetrating (though not the most biting) satire: Mr. Meagles's deference to "Blood," for example. It is a world of unremitting and unresolved tensions, "not externally observed, but internally enacted" (129); Miss Wade's "History" is not assimilable, "intrud[ing] as something gratuitous and ugly, which cannot be ignored . . . challeng[ing] the security of all the Meagles-type households in which it is being read . . ." (115). The revolutionary thrust is embodied in the entrapment of characters like Fanny Dorrit and Pancks by system (social, economic), and the novel "makes a comprehensive statement of political despair" (127), of "the complete incompatibility between a humanity which lays claim not to traditional but to full human status, and nineteenth-century Western Europe" (129). The world of *Little Dorrit* as Myers sees it, then, is pretty much the world Anthony Julius sees in *Bleak House.*

Sambudha Sen's "*Bleak House* and *Little Dorrit*: The Radical Heritage" is persuasive on the survival and transformation of radical rhetoric from the era of writers like Paine, Cobbett, and Hone in "continued (if displaced) development in novels like *Bleak House* and *Little Dorrit*" (945). "Dis-placed": radical periodical, journalism, reified in novel form, addressed an audience attuned to entertainment, not politics (949), in "a discursive space capable of generating a discussion or an argument from the point of view of the excluded [a recurrent phrase]" about topical problems and state institu-tions (950). Sen explains how Dickens's novels deploy "the language of radicalism [within what Bakhtin calls] a stylistic aura" belonging to the genre (951), ridiculing the rhetoric of the elite by parody and caricature (951–56) and translating the visual satire of graphic art into verbal form (956–63). Dickens offended "*Westminster Review* ideas of the novel as a work of art" (945); he was criticized as beyond his depth as a socio-political critic. (Sen is up on current critical authority [Bakhtin, Bourdieu, Kristeva, Arac] and uses them intelligently.)

It seems to me, however, that Bakhtin and Co. get in David Storer's way ("Grotesque Storytelling: Dickens's Articulation of the 'Crisis of the Know-able Community' in *Bleak House* and *Little Dorrit*"); the quoted phrase is Raymond Williams's term for what was happening in nineteenth-century England. Storer's "story" is that *Bleak House* and *Little Dorrit* "are essen-tially similar articulations" of that crisis but resolve it differently. In *Bleak House* Dickens funks his vision of things with "a paradoxical retreat into a bourgeois utopian remove [Esther and Allan's new Bleak House in York-shire]"; in *Little Dorrit* "Arthur Clennam and Little Dorrit's going down into the roaring streets" indicates the survival of human values to provide "a solution to the grim social order he [envisions]" (40). Storer's narrative is complicated by his projects to show the slum Tom-All-Alone's as "the focus of the bourgeois gaze" according to Kristeva's idea of "the abject" (29); cast Inspector Bucket and Pancks as Bakhtinian grotesques (Pancks also as carnivalesque); and identify both of them as Benjaminian "storytellers" to this community in crisis (39). Seeing the action through these critical lenses displaces Bucket and Pancks to the centers of Dickens's designs; and the new Bleak House is no "bourgeois utopian remove," but Dickens's vision of hoped-for harmony between human society and its home in the natural world: "a thriving place, pleasantly situated; streams and streets, town and country, mill and moor" (*Bleak House*, ch. 60).

In "Imaginary Capital: The Shape of the Victorian Economy and the Shaping of Dickens's Career" Tatiana M. Holway discerns "a critique of the practical and ethical contradictions of capitalism" that runs from the satire in *Nicholas Nickleby* on "the fictional, fraudulent language of speculation" (28) embodied in the United Metropolitan Improved Hot Muffin [etc.] Company to the Merdle fraud in *Little Dorrit,* which also levitates in language. Holway adumbrates the evolution of a paper economy and credit (disguised debt), drawing a parallel between Dickens's career development as a serial novelist and the development of the general economy; and she offers a detailed explanation how *Little Dorrit* corresponds mimetically to Victorian culture and the credit system. Holway's occasional practice of appropriating a quotation from Dickens for her own purpose without regard to context is disconcerting, but not particularly consequential. The rush of concluding explicatory sensations, however, contributes to a somewhat Delphic cast to her case.

Whatever his stance toward Victorian capitalism, Dickens supported "the politics of imperialism" (172), according to Laura Peters in "Perilous Adventures: Dickens and Popular Orphan Adventure Narratives." The evidence is in his contribution to the genre, "The Perils of Certain English Prisoners, and Their Treasure in Women, Children, Silver and Jewels," written during English calls for vengeance after the 1857 Cawnpore mutiny. "Popular orphan adventure narratives . . . justify imperialism as a patriotic impulse in order to mask the nature of its capitalist ideology" (173). 'Perils" is narrated by Gill, a male orphan who to escape "the oppressed existence of the marginalised" (177) in England has joined the Royal Marines and survives a mutiny in South America. Dickens thus combines "the orphan narrative of internal colonization (in the face of domesticity and the family narrative) with the imperial or orphan adventure narratives (where the orphan unwittingly acts as colonial agent) . . ." (175).

Like Peters's essay in postcolonial criticism, Leona Toker's "Veblen, Dickens, and Martin Chuzzlewit's America" could have fit into my organizational grid elsewhere, since she deals with certain affinities of Dickens and Veblen. That is, Dickens's satiric targets in the United States and in England are recognizable as Veblenian categories, although the nuances are different in the two national settings. The predatory behavior characteristic in Veblen's view of modern acquisitive culture in Dickens's America consists in bullying and bluffing; in his England "the bluffing . . . takes precisely the form of the Veblenian conspicuous consumption"—Tigg's magnificent porter and imposing office, "meant to suggest that his company commands huge capital" (149). Similarly, good manners: to Veblen, a sociological phenomenon having to do with class status, for Dickens an ethical one, a matter of considerateness for others. Good manners may mask predatory intent in the Chuzzlewit England; "the absence of upper-class polish" (151) young Martin finds in America suggests singleminded pursuit of business or political success.

Anthony Trollope's jibe at "Mr. Popular Sentiment" in *The Warden* "aligned [Dickens] with ninetenth-century cultural constructions of *femininity,*" Mary Lenard believes (" 'Mr. Popular Sentiment': Dickens and the Gender Politics of Sentimentalism and Social Reform Literature," 52); Fitzjames Stephen ticketed him as "a feminine, irritable, and noisy mind" in 1857 (61). Lenard shows how good male characters in *Oliver Twist* are endorsed for "feminine" behavior; however, Dickens showed little sympathy for female social reformers in *Bleak House* (58). Still, she argues that "many of Dickens's central themes and literary techniques . . . mark [him] as a part of a feminized, sentimental discourse of social reform" (60), and contends that "the disjunction between Dickens's own gender and the 'gender' of his fiction" shaped his work and its critical reception through the years (51).

The Christmas Books

The baby in James Reed's title—"Dickens, Christmas, and the Baby in the Egg-Box"—was one Dickens saw in a slum home in Edinburgh; Reed sees it as a symbol of the "darker region" at one pole of the Dickensian Christmas (165), the other pole being the uplifting spirit of his Christmas books. Negotiating that polar distance, Dickens moves from counting on benevolence as a sufficient motive to reform our baser nature to a perception of the intransigence of that based part which requires something more; in method, 'from the abstractions of *A Christmas Carol* [the children Ignorance and Want) . . . to a more robust presentation of the brutalizing effect of ignorance and want on an individual child [in *The Haunted Man*] . . .'' (171). Scrooge is "a brilliantly conceived pantomine villain''; by 1848 and Redlaw (the haunted man), Dickens "is looking more profoundly and more sombrely into the nature of the haunted mind" (167).

Speaking of poles, volume 27 of this journal includes a pair of articles a small world apart in tone: H. M. Daleski's "Seasonal Offerings: Some Recurrent Features of the Christmas Books" and Robert Tracy's " 'A Whimsical Kind of Masque': The Christmas Books and Victorian Spectacle." Daleski's recurrent features are basically structural: the opposition between home and life and street life, the "imagination of disaster—and its recuperation" (102), and the ghost machinery. Tracy, too, deals with the structure of the Christmas books, linking them to the Victorian theater's preoccupation with spectacle, and to the tradition of the masque (the quotation in his title is from Dickens' preface to the one-volume 1852 edition), as well as to the conventions of the Christmas pantomime, which descended "in adulterated form" (121) from the masque. Daleski and Tracy strike a couple of notes in common—how Dickens's ghosts are his machinery for achieving dramatic transformation (whether of character or place) in the short order necessitated by the brevity of the tale (Daleski 107, Tracy 116); how characters and events anticipate those in Dickens's full-length novels (Daleski 109–10, Tracy 126–27).

But Daleski cocks a quizzical eyebrow at Dickens's plots, "the deliberate titillation of the reader" (102), making especial game of *The Chimes,* where Trotty's tribulations turn out to have been only a dream, and *The Cricket on the Hearth,* in which the narrator, he points out, "is not only unreliable; he deliberately prevaricates" (105). As to the plausibility of Scrooge's conversion, he thinks the point is moot: "Scrooge's transformation . . . is Dickens's donnée and the supernatural its means" (107). Tracy might not disagree about any of this, since his concerns are more wide-ranging. But he also provides thoughtful analysis of the Spirits, "in effect projections of the author . . . presenting a series of vignettes . . . which will work upon Scrooge, arousing his pity and so his potential for charity, or showing the pleasures of social revelry to arouse his suppressed instinct for engaging himself with other people—Dickens's basic social and moral aims as a writer" (124). Daleski would probably not disagree with *that,* but suggests that Marley is Scrooge's double, and his ghost a projection of Scrooge's fears (108). Daleski is irreverent but just; Tracy coins the *mot juste*: " 'Dead: to begin with' like Marley, Scrooge is alive to end with" (125).

The Weeklies

Much of Elizabeth Dale Samet's "When Constabulary Duty's To Be Done': Dickens and the Metropolitan Police" is about *Household Words*'s generally admiring coverage of the relatively new metropolitan police force, especially the detective police, who the public thought likely to be "spy police'' because they ''seemed to undermine the theoretical concepts of high-visibility preventive policing'' (133). *Household Words* defined police as conscience, not surveillance (136), and contrasted English police to continental law officers (135; ineffective criminal police, omnipresent political police). But Dickens's fictional Inspector Bucket, Samet says, does not measure up to the *Household Words* image of the real thing; his ''expert power of surveillance and detection'' are insufficient to prevent the death of Lady Dedlock (140). Samet's conclusion that his failure shows Dickens's lack of confidence in the value of policing in unwarranted; Bucket's failure belongs to the moral necessities of Lady Dedlock's story, not to Dickens's exemplification of police operations.

Jerome Meckier's '' 'Dashing In Now': *Great Expectations* and Charles Lever's *A Day's Ride*'' is a thoroughgoing account of Dickens's strategy for offsetting the depressing effect of Lever's serial on *All The Year Round*'s circulation. Besides coming up with *Great Expectations*, he moved *Ride* to the back pages (231–33) and conducted in his own novel ''parodic revaluation'' of *Ride*'s ''unrealistic world view'' (227). Meckier's detailed analysis of the seventeenth number of *Great Expectations* shows how that worked; he appropriated and sobered Lever's comic theme of ''snobbery's perils and pitfalls'' (235). Meckier thinks Dickens was admonishing Thackeray, too; his case for that, though, depends rather much on assertions that ''Dickens believed,'' ''Dickens belatedly realized,'' and the like. An appendix gives a chapter-by-chapter summary of *A Day's Ride*.

Studies of Individual Works

OLIVER TWIST ''How Oliver Twist Learned to Read, and What He Read,'' the second chapter of Patrick Brantlinger's *The Reading Lesson,* is about the relations between poverty and education, poverty and crime, and most of all crime and education. *Oliver Twist* figures only as a springboard, illustrating the contradiction between Dickens's conviction that ignorance bred crime, and his fiction, where criminals are literate and reading corrupts: Fagin puts Oliver to reading a crime manual to set him on the right path (72). (That Oliver can read is plausible, Brantlinger says, in light of an 1838 survey of workhouse children [69].)

Dickens's ''Sikes and Nancy'' reading trips up Joseph Litvak (in ''Bad Scene: *Oliver Twist* and the Pathology of Entertainment'') as it did Brantlinger, but his mistake is more glaring. Brantlinger merely gave new currency to the long-lived error about ''a dozen to twenty ladies taken out stiff and rigid'' that Philip Collins disproved in 1971 (*Charles Dickens: The Public Readings* [1975], 470). Litvak gives the clear impression that the intensity of

Dickens's identification with "the villainous Jew" was what accounted for the damage performance did to Dickens's health (41), leaving entirely out of account the climax, the murder itself. But then, his article is all about Dickens's Fagin, "whom the book charges most heavily, most saliently, most allegorically, with the function of representing repulsiveness . . ." (36), physical and moral, with overtones of cannibalism and intimations of pederasty: "Oliver's surname, of course, may hint that he already has tendencies that way—just as his aptly termed Christian name, in so far as it has liver in it, already tastes like rich Jewish offal" (43). Awful, indeed. I offer this sentence as an example of Litvak's style of analysis. (Litvak's evidence for Fagin's pederastic intent, incidentally, is a perverse reading of the last sentence in chapter 18.)

Dickens held conventional Victorian views about Jews, and given his teeming imagination, the macabre and the grotesquery that Litvak detects can certainly not be dismissed out of hand. Perhaps the creative furor informing Litvak's own efforts led to that mistake about "Sikes and Nancy." Anyway, his exuberant style of analysis is hard for stodgier minds to keep track of.

William Myers thinks that both psychological critics and social critics (in the present context, Litvak and Brantlinger may serve as examples) miss "the moral positives with which [Dickens] proposes to counter the evils he describes so graphically" ("Celibate Men and Angelic Women in *Oliver Twist*," in Myers's *The Presence of Persons,* 100). All those celibate middle-aged men with their various imperfections (Brownlow, Dr. Losberne, Bumble, even Sikes and Fagin) "contribute to the novel's discreet but sustained preoccupation" with the human condition (104). Rose, on the other hand, is angelic, a "deeply improper" presence in this mode of fiction; she is there not as a model for imitation or " 'solution' to the problem of human deformation, but rather as a light by which the darkness is able to disclose itself." The final retirement to the country is similarly "improper and as necessary . . . [,] a logical consequence of the historically shaped, concretely realised and penetratingly understood feeling of helplessness symbolized in the celibate Mr. Brownlow and the angelic Rose." This ending "suggests how seriously the young Dickens tried to specify and enlarge the tragic complexity at the heart of his comic gift" (108). Myers's view of Rose has implications for critics to consider before dismissing the saintly young women in Dickens's later novels as simply unrealistic.

BLEAK HOUSE Besides the several articles on *Bleak House* and some other novel(s) this year, I found two which I treat elsewhere, Anthony Julius's in the section "Biblical and Theological Themes" and Paul Kran's under "Modes of Criticism." Here I discuss two new essays and a collection of essays first published from 1971 to 1993. I take up the current ones individually first, and then the collection.

Stanley Tick's "In the Case of *Bleak House*: A Brief Brief in Defense of Mr. Tulkinghorn" makes the point succinctly that Tulkinghorn's motives are neither "impenetrable or obscure" (210); what he tells Lady Dedlock in their climactic interview, that his sole object is "to save the [Dedlock] family credit" (212), accounts for what he does. A reader's confusion, Tick thinks, arises from Dickens's "growing ambivalence about the conflict of old vs. new, of tradition vs. modernity" (213). Tulkinghorn is part of that Dickens's original conception, but he develops worthy traits. The greatness of *Bleak House* lies in Dickens's success in "dramatizing his doubts into significant questions" (215). Tick is on to something, but "old" and "old-fashioned" are not synonymous in Dickens. (Chancery is never called "old-*fashioned*.") A Dickens novel begins in a condition of disharmony, usually originating in events antedating the opening, and moves toward (in the novels from *Bleak House* on, more likely only "envisions") a harmony not new but "old-fashioned"—fashioned like the *original*. Little Paul Dombey is old-fashioned; so is Agnes's home; so is the furniture in Bleak House, "old-fashioned rather than old" (ch. 6).

Timothy J. Caren's concern in "The Civilizing Mission at Home: Empire, Gender, and National Reform in *Bleak House*" is "to show how Esther's theory of reform ['concentric gradualism,' a phrase borrowed from Bruce Robbins's essay (in the collection I review next)] represents, like the satire on Mrs. Jellyby which it complements, a rhetorical intersection of anxieties related to the location of philanthropic duties in the context of empire [,] and the division of those duties into gendered spheres of influence." Both the imperium and the middle-class woman should begin at home; thus her activity will "sustain the imperial economy of reform" (122). Dickens was ambivalent about imperialism, Carens thinks, citing the scene where the narrator suggests the sun might better" sometimes set upon the British dominions, than that it should ever rise upon so vile a wonder as [Tom-All-Alone's]' " (131; *BH* ch. 46). Thus, "concentric gradualism." Carens sees Dickens's placing of the new Bleak House in Yorkshire as despairing of the possibility of reform at home: it is "less an outpost of progress than a tactical retreat to an ideal place in which the social forces which necessitate the civilizing mission 'at home' can be easily controlled" (140). I take Carens's "tactical retreat to an ideal place" in Yorkshire to be about the same as David Storer's "paradoxical retreat into a bourgeois utopian remove" in the article I reviewed in the section on politics and society, and my objection to Storer's reading which I explained there applies here as well.

I turn now to *Bleak House,* the New Casebook edited by Jeremy Tambling. It carries out competently the series project "to bring together in an illuminating way those critics who best illustrate the ways in which contemporary criticism has established new methods of analysing texts and who have reinvigorated the important debate about how we 'read' literature" (xi). The collection is chronologically organized, beginning with J. Hillis Miller's 1971 introduction to the Penguin English Library edition, which Tambling says "influences nearly every other [essay] in this collection" (9), and ending with an essay published in 1993. The date and place of original publication appears at the end of each essay. (See my "Works Cited" for the complete list. "Chronologically" is not quite accurate; Virginia Blain's 1985 article ought not to precede but follow D. A. Miller's dated 1988 and Dominick LaCapra's response to Miller dated 1984; a puzzle resolved by the fact that Miller's essay, a chapter of *The Novel and the Police,* first appeared in 1983). Two pieces are not complete essays but edited portions of texts.

Tambling does an excellent job of providing the information the series editors John Peck and Martin Coyle recognize readers may need to cope with "unfamiliar critical language . . . but without simplifying the essays or the issues they raise" (xi). His Introduction sketches what contemporary theory is about, naming as the main figures Derrida, Foucault, and Lacan, and identifying the concerns of the essayists. He also identifies two lines of earlier criticism grounded in the work of British critics: the historical approach of John Butt, Philip Collins, Humphry House, and Kathleen Tillotson, and the moral approach of F. R. Leavis and his followers. (He says—wrongly, I think—that both "lines" made Dickens out to be more the entertainer than the serious novelist). It is noteworthy, Tambling says, that his collection "actually reprints nothing from Britain," being mostly American; and he speculates that Dickens may best be interpreted "from outside—where Dickens is not part of the national ideology . . ." (2–3). He identifies and discusses four "key concepts or methodologies that underpin the essays reprinted—realism, deconstruction, psychoanalysis, feminism" (3). He wants finally, he says, "to ask where this criticism gets us . . . [and] to suggest . . . that there are still other new ways for thinking about Dickens's text" (3–4). He adds Bakhtin and Benjamin to the mix in suggesting those ways, and drops in a considerable number of other names as well.

In addition to his Introduction, Tambling provides a bracketed editorial note to each essay (following the essay and preceding the essayist's notes), in which he characterizes the essay as to critical genre and theme, and points out connections he perceives to other essays. So Tambling's Introduciton and these headnotes, taken together, constitute his own contribution to the profile of this new criticism. His Introduction is a valuable contribution (about the editorial notes, more later), more lucid than his *Dickens, Violence and the Modern State* (1995), which received mixed reviews (including one by an essayist in this collection). The answer to his question "where this criticism gets us," diffused through his discussions of the essayists, is not of a nature to adumbrate here. He may be forgiven for missing in the profusion of narrative detail in *Bleak House* that Esther does find out who her father was (from Mr. Jarndyce, in ch. 64). But his wondering why Esther "conceal[s] throughout the narrative that she is a happily married woman with two children" (7) raises the question whether his critical commitments involve discussing the long tradition of conventions of narration.

Tambling's editorial notes to each essay give local habitations and names to those commitments. J. Hillis Miller's approach "rests on Derrida" (52), and while my (lamentably scant) acquaintance with Derrida disqualifies me for jousting with Tambling on the point, I don't see much of Derrida in Miller's essay, only ("only"!) a sensitive close reading of the text which, for Miller's prominence and the notorious opening sentence (*"Bleak House* is a document about the interpretation of documents"*) might not have gotten the particular fame it has. (As to that sentence, it is the rhetoric that commands, not the fact asserted; *Bleak House* is only one of many novels that turn on the interpretation of documents.)

Timothy Peltason's "Esther's Will" is another essay built on careful attention to the text, persuasively developing Esther's (mostly) submerged desire for full female personhood (firmly discrediting the lesbian longings imputed to her by some). Tambling's note aims to bring Peltason to heel, reasserting a pervasive sexual theme in the novel (224–25). His notes to the essays of Audrey Jaffe and Bruce Robbins are similar in that they cast a net of theory over the texts, drawing them firmly within the bounds of the New Casebooks series. Jaffe's is a psychological analysis, *"David Copperfield* and *Bleak House:* On Dividing the Responsibility of Knowing," about the evasion of connection in *Bleak House* between knowledge and responsibility, in the divided responsibility implied by the two narratives (165, 176). Tambling injects ideology: on Jaffe's view about Esther's self-construction, he says, "This fits with the dream of omniscience, another name for which is the power of ideology . . . [recalling] what Althusser says about ideology [etc.]. . . " (179). Bruce Robbins ("Telescopic Philanthropy: Professionalism and Responsibility in *Bleak House*") is a Foucaultian and Althusserian (147, 149); Tambling gives him a Marxist slant and coherence that is not evident in the essay (159–60).

Robbins seems to have the large purpose of defending professionalism focused on "particular local situations of conflict, danger and rapid change" (159), using *Bleak House* as a case study in contradiction: Dickens disapproved of both telescopic philanthropy—a global outlook—and an impersonal style of professionalism in personal relations (think Mrs. Jellyby and Mrs. Pardiggle). Unfortunately he is given to sweeping unsupported assertions ("most readers," "by now a critical commonplace," "as generations of readers have observed") and the global generality (Comte, Spencer, and Durkheim are said to link Foucault and Dickens [154]). His argument is also blemished by misreadings of Dickens's text: he misconstrues "disinterested" in Dickens's preface (144), mistakes the point of the humor (145), argues a Dickens point by dissecting his metaphor (142).

But inaccuracy about the novel text is not uncommon among this set of critics. Christine Van Boheemen-Saaf interprets the danger of disease spreading from Tom-All-Alone's as "the subversive threat of the levelling of hierarchical distinctions" (58; would that be the anagogical level of allegory?); thinks Esther did not acknowledge her mother until finding her dead at the burial ground (59), and totally misstates the resolution of Esther's romantic life (59). Virginia Blain says Lady Dedlock fled Chesney Wold "to legitimize Esther [by taking] upon herself society's hostility towards the illegitimate" (77); but the text is clear that she flees because she thinks all is known, and she is overwhelmed—there is no mention of Esther (ch. 55). Nor is there any causal relation between Inspector Bucket's relentless pursuit and Lady Dedlock's death, as Blair asserts (81); she had that burial ground in mind from the start (ch. 59). Audrey Jaffe repeatedly disregards context to fit quotations into her interpretive statements, "to use the novel's own words" (171), implying a significance that, if pressed, she could deny. But she also attributes to Vholes Esther's words about Vholes's motive to "divide the responsibility of knowing" about Richard's difficulties (165). Esther is also said to be " 'full of business' [busyness] . . . because about herself she is 'content to know no more' " (172); the latter phrase is two dozen pages and three episodes on from the former, in the next chapter, and the former is in context mere narrative statement of her activity as Mr. Jarndyce's household manager. These are not serious warpings of the text, but a use of quotation that diminishes my trust. I suspect theory of interposing a veil between the critic and the text in these representative instances. Foregrounding of theory probably also accounts for the relatively distant presence of Dickens's text in these essays generally (with the notable exceptions of Hillis Miller's, Peltason's, and Blain's).

D. A. Miller is properly absolved by Dominick LaCapra on this score ("Ideology and Critique in Dickens's *Bleak House*"), but he does argue that in Miller's representation of "certain 'objects' in the novel (bureaucracy, police, family; Esther, Bucket, etc.)" (131) he ignores the effect of dual narration on their representation. Miller argues that the disorder of Chancery, resisting closure, calls forth desire that is satisfied by the detective story form: hence, the transformation of *Bleak House* halfway through, and the installation of the police, "desirable as a sort of institutional 'alternative' to Chancery, . . . providing, from within a total system of power, *a representation of the containment of power*" ("Discipline in Different Voices: Bureaucracy, Police, Family, and *Bleak House*," 99; Miller's italics). Miller's article is the major essay of the collection next to Hillis Miller's, and I may be saying more about my own powers than his when I confess that I find him nearly unreadable. LaCapra characterizes his style as "sinuous complexity" (129); a good start. Rhetorically, there seems to be a compulsion to say it *all,* extrude all the implications of a sliver of theory; and prolixity—a sentence to the effect that a novel about dreariness has to avoid being dreary itself (106) is embedded in a paragraph saying, difficultly and ponderously, no more than that. Miller glances repeatedly at the length of *Bleak House*; everything he says is patly appropriate to his own argument.

Katherine Cummings leaves me bewildered; Tambling's notes help me out here. Her "Rereading *Bleak House*: The Chronicle of a 'Little Body' and Its Perverse Defence," he says, is "a short, heavily cut extract" from her *Telling Tales: The Hysteric's Seduction in Fiction and Theory,* "a feminist reading of *Bleak House*, part of a longer playful argument about 'seduction' (and about who seduces who [sic]) . . ." (200). I leave it at that, commending the essay to the reader who wants more. Kevin McLaughlin's "Losing One's Place: Displacement and Domesticity in *Bleak House*" bewilders me, too, in a different way; he takes me through "the 'self-estranged subject' of Hegel's *Phenomenology of the Spirit*" to show how Dickens's novel "departs from Hegel's model," and how "analysis of subjectivity in *Bleak House* suggests the ongoing relevance of this speculative tradition for the study of social and institutional questions in nineteenth-century novels" (229).

The sidebar endnote is considerably in evidence among these critics: what amount to mini-essays on related topics. D. A. Miller does a lot of this; so do Cummings, Peltason, and most extensively of all, Tambling himself. And this reader needs more help than explication of the "unfamiliar critical language" noted by the series editors (if by that phrase they mean terminology). He would rewrite their statement "Because much of this criticism is difficult and often employs an unfamiliar critical terminology" by dropping "and" and moving "because" to its place. This criticism is not all as sinuously complex, global, and prolix as D. A. Miller's, but more of it is more like his style than like Hillis Miller's or Peltason's.

I do believe that Tambling's New Casebook on *Bleak House* displays the spectrum of the "new" criticism from the last twenty years or so. But like Tambling (though obviously in a different mood) I want to ask where this criticism gets us.

HARD TIMES Beatriz Vegh says Rafael Barraclas's illustrations are a kind of "paratext," in narratological nomenclature a form of "transtextualilty," that which "denotes what sets a text in a manifest or secret relation to another text . . ." ("*Hard Times* Gone Modernist: The 1921 Rafael Barradas Illustrations for *Tiempos Díficiles*," 3). The placement of the full-page color illustrations (all reproduced in *Dickens Quarterly* black and white) is deliberately out of sync with the text, creating a counterpoint with it (19). The contrapuntal effect is repeated in the "Clownism" style which deliberately suppresses individuality in the human figures, providing what Barthes was to call in *S/Z* characters free from " 'civility,' impersonal, achronological, drawn with symbolic, encompassing and projective outlines' " (17). A flower motif running through the series refers to Sissy (11); reproduction in *Dickens Quarterly* cannot do justice to the effect.

Anthony Giffone's "The Sleary Circus" is part of a collection entitled *Fools and Jesters in Literature, Art, and History.* The Editor, Vicki K. Janik, distinguishes four categories of fool (2–4); Giffone does not place Dickens's circus people accordingly, but quotes Paul Schlicke approvingly, who says they "exist more as idealized alternatives to pernicious attitudes than as actual representatives of the Victorian business of entertainment" (398). "Despite its roots in realistic observation," Giffone concludes, "the Sleary Circus remains more symbol than reality." The format for articles is brisk and brief: sections on background, description and analysis, critical reception (missing from Giffone's), and select bibliography. The pieces are all short, ranging from superficial through slight to summary (Giffone).

Malcolm Pittock believes late nineteenth- and early twentieth-century critical opinion of Dickens's shortcomings has been unjustly buried ("Taking Dickens to Task: *Hard Times* Once More"), taking the Leavises' turnaround in *Dickens the Novelist* as representative of the critical tide (107). Intending "to reinstate a way of looking at Dickens which has been lost sight of" (109), he dissects the plot, the characters, and the theme, finding defects everywhere. Rereading his essay, I thought again of Collins: many assertions command assent, but they depend on an unspoken premise, that Dickens offends against realism. Pittock does not see the moral fable which *Hard Times* deploys across a story that echoed contemporary events and beliefs: he does not (or will not) see that Dickens's description of Gradgrind's house, for example, signifies the Gradgrind philosophy, not disapproval of "gas and ventilation, draining and water-service, all of the primest quality" (114–15). His peroration suggests that disapproval of Dickens's personal behavior—his stand late in life on the Governor Eyre affair (125–26), and his "deplorable treatment of his wife" (127)—may be the real engine of his attack.

Valerie Wainwright's "On Goods, Virtues, and *Hard Times*" contests the idea that Dickens had no "coherent and consistent viewpoint" on "moral/ political issues in the novel" (169). On the contrary, he constructs "a neat typology of moral character" featuring especially "the capacities for accurate perception and emotive attachment or commitment. . . . [To these] a good will is foundational . . ." (177). Wainwright suggests Dickens was influenced by the Unitarian minister Edward Tagart, who disputed the Augustinian idea of a fundamentally corrupt will, and who also denied the Mills' view that the will is the servant of desire, therefore finally of self-interest (176–78). Bitzer finely illustrates the absence of such good will, and "the very center of the classic theory of individualism" (179). But the good characters are not perfectly free (Harthouse, who has no will, is); Sissy and Rachel are moral beings because their freedom consists in their (will) power to govern their impulses (181). They are assertive, not passive, displaying "adherence to the Christian virtues of love, faith, and hope. . . . [S]pontaneous and self-disciplined, they are both free and yet obedient" (181–82).

LITTLE DORRIT These four essays center on Miss Wade's importance in the novel and address one way or another her sexuality. (Several other studies that I surveyed besides these deal with *Little Dorrit:* Halevi-Wise in the section "Texts, Language, Narrative Devices," and in the section "Politics and Society," Edgecombe, Myers, Sen, and Storer.) The question whether she is a lesbian has been and continues to be debated. Annamarie Jagose, is an important article, argues that Miss Wade bodies forth a "subsequent order of female homosexuality" which critics commit anachronism to call lesbianism ("Remembering Miss Wade: *Little Dorrit* and the Historicizing of Female Perversity," 424–25). Not that she is anything but lesbian; but Dickens establishes what she is—perverse, in our sense of the word—"without ever having to struggle after that name which is not yet hers," by wreathing her in suspicion, "figuring her as diseased, pathological, illegitimate, angry, immodest, indecent . . ." (428)—a very effective way of saying by not saying. Jagose also has much to say about Victorian specifications of femininity and how they "shore up the hegemonic interests of masculinity, class, industrial capitalism, nation, and empire" (425). (I hesitate to traffic in labels, preferring to leave quotations to speak for themselves.)

Janet Retseck believes Miss Wade "neither enters nor leaves the novel as a lesbian"; she comes on stage "a threat of political rebellion" and is later reshaped "into a paranoid, delusional woman" ("Sexing Miss Wade," 217). (Retseck helpfully lists the lesbianites in a note.) Miss Wade puts a check on Mr. Meagles at their first meeting, which Retseck sees as emphasizing her potential for anger and defiance, coded to recall the French Revolution (218–19); her sexuality is not emphasized here (221). Miss Wade is tinder to the "smouldering discontent" of Tattycoram, who "rises up in anger at the slightest provocation, as Dickens feared the subjects of the British crown might do in the absence of reform" (221). The remodeling of Miss Wade is completed in her "History." Retseck speculates that the lesbian theory has been attractive because it seems to accommodate the early and late images of Miss Wade (224). She acknowledges Jagose's article, in print too late for her to respond to.

In "On History, Case History, and Deviance: Miss Wade's Symptoms and Their Interpretation," Anna Wilson takes on Miss Wade's "History of a Self-Tormentor" in the context of "contemporary discourses on governesses and on madness" (188), and finds that the structure of *Little Dorrit* does not support the "History" as an "authentic narrative of social injustice" (193). But Mr. Meagles sees political threat in Miss Wade's mentorship of Tatty-coram: the danger of a group or class entity emerging (195–96). As for the question of lesbianism, Wilson suggests that lesbian identity is the "major metaphor" of the "History," not its ultimate truth (197). Wilson's is an interesting reading, hovering among several interpretations of Miss Wade: "a symptomatic reading—of Miss Wade *as* symptom [she says]—within a larger cultural context" (189). This is more satisfying, I think, than Retseck's "para-noid delusional" Miss Wade—why would Dickens skewer a paranoid delu-sional woman? Jagose's analysis, though, seems to me most persuasive (not because of but in spite of the turgid style).

Barbara Black quotes the same paragraph about Miss Wade that Retseck does, but for Black, in "A Sisterhood of Rage and Beauty: Dickens' Rosa Dartle, Miss Wade, and Madame Defarge," the passage "suggests the narra-tor's erotic surge" (94). These beautiful women who seethe with rage are quite unlike the good Dickens women with their power to "resurrect and repair" the world-stained men in their lives (91). But even Esther "shares with Miss Wade a peculiarly female rage" (92). Black thinks these women embodied Dickens's male unease, "the psychic traces of a male authorial imagination" (93) conscious of some threat in femininity (96). So they "re-peatedly disrupt the narrative" (97), assaulting "privilege in its numerous manifestations" (101). They are intricately entangled with "Dickens's own imaginative and psychic states," but they require to be erased if the "good Dickens heroines" are to triumph (103). Black manages to touch these many bases (imperialism, male gaze, erasure, semiotics), and in such a wide-ranging essay it is often touch-and-go ("Rosa's scar is a grotesque erogenous zone . . . an image for the female genitalia . . ." [95]; "*A Tale of Two Cities* depicts the growing pains and growing concerns of a developing British empire—alle-gorically coded in Carton's and Darnay's struggles" [100]). I found Black suggestive on authorial anxieties informing the text, detected by examination through up-to-date critical lenses.

A TALE OF TWO CITIES (Articles by Rosen and Sroka are discussed in "Biblical and Theological Studies.")

George Newlin's *Understanding "A Tale of Two Cities": A Student Case-book to Issues, Sources, and Historical Documents* devotes only the first brief chapter to the novel itself, cast in brief summary discussions of literary mat-ters. The rest of the book consists of chapters on pre-revolutionary France, the events of the Revolution, Carlyle's *French Revolution,* Dickens and Car-lyle, the mob in London and Paris (and the Terror), letters and memoirs of prisoners of the Terror, the nature of political revolutions in Britain, France, the United States, and Russia; the Rights of Man; capital punishment (the guillotine and before); solitary confinement; and human dissection and "res-urrection men." For each chapter there are study questions and (except for the first) a brief bibliography (the items also appearing in the general bibliography for the whole volume), and a glossary. Newlin includes copious selections from Carlyle, Arthur Young's *Travels in France,* contemporary letters and memoirs, Thomas Paine, Anthony Trollope's *La Vendée,* and Dickens's *Barnaby Rudge* and *American Notes.* There are hardly any quotations from *A Tale of Two Cities,* but frequent references to it, and events in the novel are placed in the chronology of the Revolution in chapter 3 (set off in italics).

But is this really a student casebook? Yes and no. Yes: there is the usual apparatus of study questions and suggestions for further reading. No: some of the topical foci are out of the range of student vision, and the language is not the carefully leveled (read "condescending") sort; it's adult. The book is not academic in the narrow sense. It's solidly informative in broad strokes, a good read for anybody with an interest in the French revolution, whether interested in Dickens's take on it or not; but readers of Dickens will find their understanding of *A Tale of Two Cities* broadened, in some ways challenged. I don't think it would be very useful, except to superior students, for writing a research paper on *A Tale of Two Cities* and the French Revolution. The study questions do often relate the topic to *A Tale of Two Cities,* it's true, but on the whole this collection would serve history students better. All in all, the sort of meaty book to be expected from the author of *Everybody and Everything in Dickens.*

Michael Cotsell's collection *Critical Essays on Charles Dickens: "A Tale of Two Cities"* is one of the series "Critical Essays on British Literature" (Zack Brown, general editor) originated by G. K. Hall & Co., and published in 1998 as "an imprint of Simon Schuster Macmillan." Cotsell includes, by way of background, passages from Carlyle's *French Revolution,* a chapter of Dickens's *American Notes* (the effects of solitary confinement on prisoners), two of Walter Bagehot's "Letters on the French *Coup d'Etat* of 1851" (on the French national character), two excerpts from the Marxist George Lukács's *The Historical Novel* (the crisis of bourgeois realism), and an account of the fall of the Bastille from George Rudé's *Paris and London in the Eighteenth Century.* The critical essays are printed in chronological order (like those in Tambling's collection), beginning with a 1970 psychoanalytic essay by Leonard Manheim and ending with a feminist study by Lisa Robson published in 1992. Three essays that Harold Bloom included in his 1987 collection in the Chelsea House "Modern Critical Interpretations" series reappear here, by Albert Hutter (1978), John Kucich (1980), and J. M. Rignall (1984).

In his Introduction Costell shows a strong predilection for a psychoanalytic approach to interpretation. He finds sources for many novelistic details in Dickens's life, including his childhood stint in the blacking factory ("Here, clearly, is one source of Manette's shoemending" [3]). He is probably right to see Carton's dying with the little French seamstress as somehow reflecting Dickens's liaison with Ellen Ternan, though surely wrong to call that liaison Dickens's "French idyll"—not so early as 1859. Costell also raises the question of Dickens's obsession with mob violence, and he applies the concept of splitting (Freudian, he says, but developed by Melanie Klein) at some length, finding it in evidence in the famous opening paragraph, in the titular settings of course, in the doubled hero Carton/Darnay, and elsewhere.

The essays by Manheim, Hutter, and Frank follow this psychoanalytic line. Leonard Manheim ("A Tale of Two Characters: A Study in Multiple Projection") and Lawrence Frank ("Dickens' A Tale of Two Cities: The Poetics of Impasse") have in common, over against Albert Hutter ("Nation and Generation in A Tale of Two Cities"), a view of the novel as personal and psychological. Manheim works from a model of the novel as psychological construct; he looks for the decayed virgin, the mother figure, and father figures. Hutter says the Tale correlates family and nation, using "the language of psychological conflict and psychological identification to portray social upheaval and the restoration of social order" (89). He sees the characters as "moved by something larger than their own desires" (94). Frank thinks not; the real subject, he says, is not national and political, but "a family drama . . . the conflict between generations . . . recurring and inescapable . . . the son's complex, perhaps doomed, struggle to free himself from the father's tyranny" (113). Hutter sees that conflict, Dickens's "familial and political revolutions," embodied in various splittings: Carton/Darnay, Carton/Stryker, Madame Defarge/Lucie (100ff.). Frank sees Darnay's renunciation of his French patrimony as an evasion of responsibility (115); Carton, who "embodies the unacknowledged failure of Charles Evrémonde, called Darnay" (129), dies to restore Darnay to life (130). Hutter's analysis is largely structured by the concept of splitting (and elaborated by extensive use of the endnote sidebar—about half as much text in those mini-essays as in the article itself). Frank's article is more persuasive to me; Manheim's is alloyed by a tone of amusement at the 45–year-old Dickens's persistent adolescence.

A second emphasis of Cotsell's in the collection is political (particularly Marxist). The title of Michael Goldberg's "Carlyle, Dickens, and the Revolution of 1848" correctly indicates he is more concerned with Carlyle than with Dickens, and 1848 than 1789. Goldberg notes that the failure of the 1848 revolutions "broke Dickens' faith in the adequacy of reform and alerted him to . . . the constant possibility of the fire next time" (155). Cotsell says this "shows how different Dickens's response to revolution in France could be" (13), a somewhat obscure conclusion.

Nicholas Rance's "Charles Dickens: A Tale of Two Cities (1859)" (ch. 3 of his The Historical Novel and Popular Politics in Nineteenth-Century England [1975]) shows how the French Revolution was on English minds in the 1850s, either as "vital prehistory" and a warning, or a historical anomaly; *A Tale of Two Cities,* Rance says, "wavers between the two positions and gradually settles for the more comfortable" (76)—the latter. At the beginning of the novel, France and England are much alike, "ripe for violent change"; but writing the violence of revolution induced Dickens to settle for "any society that is non-revolutionary" (84). Finally, "Carton prophesies a secure and happy England" quite unbelievable in light of the opening (87). The action yearns toward an escape from history, and "the theme of resurrection pervades the novel" (88).

A Tale of Two Cities takes a wide view of history and the historical process, but that view is not a vision of progress, according to J. M. Rignall ("Dickens and the Catastrophic Continuum of History in *A Tale of Two Cities*"). The historical process is the catastrophe of the title, "the single catastrophe, piling wreckage on wreckage" that Walter Benjamin sees (197). Dickens is unable to see any escape, although some passages of the narrative look like authorial interruption implying a desire for another end than the grim one implied by historical determinism: the opening paragraph of chapter 3 on the secrecy of the individual heart (159); the Darnays' escape from Paris (160). Carton's Christlike act is the final such "moment of resistance to the grimly terminal linearity . . ." (158). Rignall too finds Carton's vision of an idyllic future incredible, "not so much a vision of redeeming historical development . . . a vision of the end of time" (165).

Cates Baldridge contends ("Alternatives to Bourgeois Individualism in *A Tale of Two Cities*") that "Dickens's deep dissatisfaction with the social relations fostered by his own acquisitive and aggressively individualist society" is to be seen in a subversive subtext to the narrator's middle-class horror at the collectivist Revolutionary ideology . . ." (168). He finds that opening paragraph of chapter 3 to belong to this subtext, and unlike Rignall, hears "a broadly thematic resonance to the passage . . . crucial to the book's attitudes concerning bourgeois individualism and its supposedly detested alternatives" (171). That resonance however is displaced "toward the comic and toward the private" (174); the former is illustrated by Jarvis Lorry, the latter by Carton. Baldridge concludes that Carton's death "and his subsequent life after death" refute collectivist ideology by endorsing the individual's influence on history (184). I have to leave Baldridge at that; his argument is too involved to be adumbrated.

John Kucich agrees that Carton's suicide is the only possible resolution of the *Tale,* but his is a different resolution than Baldridge's. He argues that "The Purity of Violence: *A Tale of Two Cities*" that Dickens works in melodrama here, "toward an escape from the realm of the analytical, the ethical, and the useable altogether, [endorsing] desires for irrational extremity that [are satisfied] finally in Carton's chaste suicide" (134). The validation is in terms of Hegel's Master-Slave dialectic; the Master will give up life "for a greater, intangible good," the Slave opts for survival (139). Self-violence is "pure" when not designed for profit; the revolutionary mob violence turns "impure" when it becomes self-gratifying revenge (141). Carton's "suicide" is selfless, violence "redeemed through the preservation of Darnay and his family" (144). Hegel aside, Kucich's analysis would make better sense to Victorian readers than Rignall's or Baldridge's because of the "unstated relationship between Sydney Carton's death and the reader's awareness of that significance" (145) grounded in the Christian view of life.

Tom Lloyd's "Language, Love, and Identity: *A Tale of Two Cities*" does not mention Hegel, but Carlyle, Schlegel, Schiller, Goethe, Tennyson, and Dante get to take bows in the course of Lloyd's demonstration that the *Tale* "affirms the value of the word" (187). "Revivification of language" (196)—what Carton experiences on recalling Jesus' words—is empowering, but not, in Lloyd's view, definitively so, apparently: "[Carton's] prophecy, like so much else in the novel reveals an insecurity on Dickens's part about our capacity to 'name' and thus control the future, an even more precarious act than defining our identities against the onrush of contemporary events" (200). Since the substance of the prophecy is anything but uncertain, Lloyd must mean Dickens felt it inappropriate to put in the narrator's mouth. (Alternatively, I would suggest, giving it to Carton was to provide narratival validation to his self-sacrifice.)

In the final essay in Cotsell's collection Lisa Robson undertakes to examine the "female role in Dickens's representation of the Revolution," a subject she says current criticism, "focussing on a patriarchal world of politics and historical development in which men dominate the scene," has ignored ("The 'Angels' in Dickens's House: Representation of Women in *A Tale of Two Cities*," 204). She argues in convincing detail that Dickens gives Lucie Manette, Miss Pross, and Madame Defarge room to act "in unconventional situations and positions . . . exploring new spaces for women to inhabit" (205). But in the end he "recontains" them: "This circumscription of a potentially progressive depiction of women by a chauvinistic need for their repression and confinement underscores Dickens's gender bias" (220). This final sentence of Robson's cast, in the rhetoric of militantly ideological feminist criticism, is inconsistent in tone and focus with the body of her essay, where she analyzes the action and the relations of these three female characters objectively and sensitively.

The essays in this collection speak to each other, sometimes by explicit cross-reference, and more generally by the contrast in modes of criticism. One subset explores the text for its revelations about Dickens's psyche, another for what it says about Dickens's understanding of the French Revolution; both sets raise the fundamental question of what imaginative literature is and is for. Personally I find the latter more interesting, without denying that what the former set may discover can be important for the latter (For example, there is surely an avatar of Dickens's personal romantic predicament embodied in the inaccessibility of Lucie to Carton, making self-sacrifice the noble solution.) Some of the critics belonging to the second subset to see a secular Dickens retreating to the defense of reaction; Kucich sees farther into the text, I think, accounting for Dickens's "escape" from reality as his commitment to melodrama, and his affirmation of the Christian idea of selflessness.

One last item in this section: Bjørn Tysdahl's "Europe Is Not the Other: *A Tale of Two Cities*," the first part of which sensibly points out similarities of the English and the French settings implied in his title. Thereafter he undertakes to support that idea by a not very convincing analysis of Dickens's imagery, particularly imagery of "the fluid, the boundless and the all-embracing," which he of course finds in both England and France, and which also calls up for him "Old Testament echoes that underline the evil ways of the mob" (115), and turns out to have temporal as well as spatial application, which brings him to echoes and journeys (116–17). Tysdahl also invokes Romantic poetry and *Dombey and Son* in the space of half a page, and remarkably asserts that Carton's last Biblical thought "stresses *human* connections" (118). The imperative for Dickens studies, he concludes, "must be 'Never generalize!' " (119)

THE UNCOMMERCIAL TRAVELLER In a two-part essay in *Dickens Quarterly*, "The Nineteenth-Century Commercial Traveler and Dickens's 'Uncommercial' Philosophy," John M. L. Drew sets Dickens's traveling salesman for the Human Interest Brothers in the historical context established by contemporary commercial practice and discusses ten of the "Uncommercial Traveller" papers published in *All The Year Round*. Drew is particularly concerned with the tonal and attitudinal variety evident in this uncommercial traveler (hereafter UT); there is a "strong satirical cross-current" (90). But UT is even-handed; "mature acceptance of commercial imperatives" underlies whimsy and satire, and UT does not write off people or systems "on a 'wholesale' or general basis until he has dealt with them on a 'retail' or first-hand basis" (93), contrasting, for example, "the far-seeing [economic] schemes of Thisman and Thatman" with what he learns "by turn[ing] down a narrow street to look into a house or two" (97). By this "uncommercial" dialectic, Drew concludes, Dickens conducted a "particularly convincing critique of the essence of 1860s socio-political thought which equated the dictates of political economy with the commands of moral law as the grounds for human action" (104). This is a solid piece of work. Drew co-edits the Dent Uniform Edition of Dickens's journalism, for which he is annotating *The Uncommercial Traveller*.

GREAT EXPECTATIONS Goldie Morgantaler's thoughtful "Meditating on the Low: A Darwinian Reading of *Great Expectations*" argues that, on the evidence of *Great Expectations,* after Darwin Dickens was no longer a "hereditary determinist" (708) as to character formation: that Estella and Pip both illustrate the force of circumstances. Morgantaler sees Darwinian thought in "the idea of the primitive or low and its relation to 'civilized' society; the idea of adaptation . . . " and finally, the conception of time [as linear rather than] a reanimation of the past" (712). The last of these is why Pip cannot return to the (primitive) village world; the first underlies the universal criminality of Pip's world, especially the interconnection of the upper-class gentleman and underclass criminality (713). Morgantaler's examples can be read otherwise; that interconnection is evident well before Darwin, explicitly in oft-quoted passages from *Dombey and Son* and *Bleak House.* The shaft of light emphasizing the absolute equality of judge and prisoners before the bar (ch. 56) is, according to Morgantaler, "a reassertion of the Darwinian belief in the interdependence of all living things" (714); but it is at least as likely, in the narrative context and given Dickens's religious outlook, an expression of basic Christian theology.

Another worthwhile essay, Kathleen Sell's "The Narrator's Shame: Masculine Identity in *Great Expectations,*" is a very complicated mesh of theses about class, hetero- and homosocial relations, guilt, shame, the basis of male identity, and the fundamental importance of the feminine to that identity, distilled out of Pip's narrative. (Sell's [uneasy?] consciousness of the complexity appears in the frequency of "clear" and "clearly" in her argument—nearly subliminal suasion.) Pip's narrative "sets in motion a dynamic of shame that has class, sexual, and gendered aspects . . ." (203), and his failure to fully achieve masculine identity—based in Victorian times on heterosexual competition and heterosexual love—is due to the failure of women (especially of course Estella) to fulfill the Victorian ideal of selfless femininity (that angel in the house again). Pip's shame (the main engine of the novel) is first social (the character Pip) and later moral (the narrator Pip's recognition of his attitude toward Joe growing out of his class ambition). A complex scaffold of ideas from feminist criticism and cutlural studies supports all this.

The main force of Timothy A. Spurgin's fine " 'It's Me Wot Has Done It!': Letters, Reviews, and *Great Expectations*" is to show "that although [GE] is a product of bitter self-knowledge, it is also an opportunity for unapologetic self-assertion" (200). Thus Magwitch's "exhilarating declaration of authorship" that Spurgin quotes in his title he takes to express Dickens's pride in his professional accomplishment in this novel: he was dishing the critics who condescended to him as a "feminine" writer of soft sentiment as well as a caterer to coarse audience taste (191–93). He was also acting decisively to counter the threat to circulation posed by the failure of Charles Lever's *A Day's Ride,* as his letters to Lever show (194–97; see my review of Jerome Meckier's " 'Dashing In Now' . . . " about that correspondence, in the section above on Dickens's weeklies). Spurgin glances at a larger thesis: that letters especially, and reviews, need to be considered in a wider light than they often are (200).

Jerome Meckier's "*Great Expectations:* Symmetry in (Com)motion" confirms that Dickens had a right to the pride in his craft that Spurgin says he was expressing there. Awe is in order, both at Meckier's analysis of the novel's structure and at Dickens the architect. With two charts, Meckier diagrams the relations of weekly parts, monthly parts, and chapters, to show the symmetry of Dickens's deployment. He argues that Dickens's placement of critical chapters and events shows he had monthly-part publication in mind as he wrote the weekly installments for *All the Year Round.* The three parts are almost exactly equal in length, whether measured by chapters or pages. (Meckier's whole article is a stream of symmetries, balances, and counters in the action, and so on, that he detects. Persuasive as his article is, the implication that *all* this was consciously contrived is almost too much to swallow. . . . Almost.)

OUR MUTUAL FRIEND Lisa Surridge published an article in 1997 on Dickens's ambivalence about the feminine in *Dombey and Son.* This year she sees *Our Mutual Friend* as looking at first like well-known sensation novels serialized between 1859 and 1863, but it soon "frustrate[s] many of the generic expectations that this sets up" (269) and centers instead on "two of the central anxieties of the sensation genre: the instability of the middle-class home, and the moral unreliability of the woman at its center" (" 'John Rokesmith's Secret': Sensation, Detection, and the Policing of the Feminine in *Our Mutual Friend,*" (270). The woman is Bella Wilfer, morally unreliable because in her wilfulness she refuses to subside into the angel in the house. Surridge observes all the spying that goes in the course of containing Bella (she provides a catalog [276]), and this external policing must become internal à la Foucault (277). Surridge makes a good case for the thesis she has been developing via the transformation of Bella Wilfer, summing it up admirably in her final paragraph, which I can only adumbrate here: *Our Mutual Friend* "presents itself as a sensation novel . . . only to [violate] the teleological nature of the classic mystery plot, [returning] obsessively to sensation fiction's central anxieties—the beleaguered home and the criminal angel in the house" (279).

Not Much About Dickens

Winding down, but preferring not to close on a blue note, I have a short list of tangentially Dickensian items to notice here. Robert Googins's "Reflections on Delinquency, Dickens, and Twain" is part of a collection by scholars from different disciplines and perspectives, on "selected aspects of criminal and violent behavior among young people" (vii). Googins is professor of law at the University of Connecticut and teaches a course on Dickens and the law; his article, about the development of the law's treatment of juveniles, has about a page on Dickens crediting him with interest and compassion and concluding that present legal practice does not provide the "forgiving firmness . . . in the pleas of Dickens" (10). Nick Gillespie's title "Darwin and Dickens" is a metaphor; his article is about the emergence of a movement in literary criticism that takes account of evolution as a factor in literary creation (Morgantaler's article comes to mind). The critics he discusses are generally on the nature side of the nature/nurture argument; they oppose poststructural orthodoxy, he says, in which even "nature" is an ideological construct—evolutionary critics affirm "the idea that there is something approaching objective, knowable reality" (39). Very interesting. Murray Baumgarten's "Staging the Ruins: David Roberts's Paintings . . ." is really about Roberts, especially his paintings of scenes in the Holy Land. The connection to Dickens is that they were friends; the point of the article as to Dickens is that his London is a wilderness overwhelming the London homeless as crumbling Holy Land ruins in Roberts's paintings overwhelm the homeless inhabitants there. Linda H. Peterson's "Mother-Daughter Productions: Mary Howitt and Anna Mary Howitt . . ." concerns Dickens only in that he published material from Anna Mary's letters from Munich, as edited by her mother Anna, in *Household Words*. Joseph Clayton Clark (1857–1937) was an illustrator, according to Robert R. Wark ("The Curious Case of . . ."), best known for his pen-and-water-color drawings of Dickens characters: "among the last and most prolific" of Dickens illustrators in the tradition of Cruikshank. The Huntington Library has the largest collection of his work, 840 illustrations in all.

Riffing on Dickens

Two novels published in 1998 take their points of departure from Dickens's life and career. The title character of Peter Carey's *Jack Maggs* (British edition, 1997, U.S. 1998), a transported convict, returns from Australia in 1837 to see his "son," Henry Phipps; afflicted with tic douloureux, he is ministered to by an amateur mesmerist and upstart writer, Tobias Oates, who scents material for a novel here. (Oates is having an affair with his wife's sister, who lives with the young couple.) The premise of Ross Gilfillan's *The Snake-Oil Dickens Man* is that during the western leg of his 1842 trip to the United States Dickens fathered a son on a frontier landlord's daughter. The action of the novel is set during Dickens's 1867–68 reading tour of the United

States; his son, Billy Talbot, is sent by his foster father Elijah Putnam to make himself known to Dickens, who Putnam expects will make it worth their while to keep mum. On the way Billy meets a con man who has been giving readings, passing himself off as Dickens, and thereafter Billy is ''Dickens's'' tour manager Dolby.

I will go no further into the action of either novel. Both use suggestive names: Carey's Maggs and Phipps echo Magwitch and Pip, but Tobias Oates calls to mind Titus Oates, giving a hoaxer tint to the shadow Dickens. Gilfillan's Elijah Putnam is very near *Martin Chuzzlewit's* Elijah Pogram, and Dora, Emily, and Katherine (Kate) occur as women's names. Carey conflates Dickens's life and *Great Expectations*, with copious additions; the point of view is usually situated in Maggs or Oates. The story begins in medias res with Maggs's return to London, and the element of mystery is occasionally enhanced by proleptic introduction of narrative material. Gilfillan's fictive matrix is Dickens's life; the narrator is the aged Billy Talbot, looking back from the early twentieth century and establishing in a prologue that his memoir is a quest for self-understanding. In his epilogue he sums himself up as a successful fraud, one like many another respected person in the United States, ''where the con man is king of the heap'' (280). Gilfillan's plotting nods to Dickens in frequent coincidences and characters popping up repeatedly; the adventures of the fraudulent Dickens/Dolby, however, recall those of Huckleberry Finn's unwanted companions, the duke and the king. (Gilfillan acknowledges in an authorial afterword the difficulty of ''setting a novel in another time and in another country'' [281].) Carey's plotting does not strike me as particularly Dickensian; his is a modern novel in this respect, as it is in themes. There is no ostentatious Victorianizing of setting (or language, for that matter); Carey writes as a Victorian to Victorians, simply matter-of-fact about the details of everyday Londodn life in 1837.

Both novels are good reads. Both of them will stand alone for a reader unacquainted with Dickens, Carey better than Gilfillan. The Dickens angle gives each of them considerable extra interest for anybody reading this review; Gilfillan relies on that in more obvious ways than Carey, whose story is more complexly Dickensian.

Dickens as a Criticism of Life

Joyce Zonana uses Frank Edwin Elwell's statue *Dickens and Little Nell* in West Philadelphia's Clark Park to frame her essay about how *The Old Curiosity Shop* seized her at the age of ten; how she had identified her own fears of her grandmother (''a personage as grotesque to me then as any of the curiosities in Nell's life'' [579]) with Nell's fears, climaxing in the episode of her

grandfather's nocturnal theft of her purse—a symbolic rape (584). Rereading
that passage as an adult, she understood that her grandmother's nightly preparations for bed in the cramped room they shared in her parents' apartment—a
nightly disassembly of her person, as it were—so "fascinated and horrified"
her (580) as to make Nell's victimization by her grandfather "an image of
my own life—a girl violated by a grandparent" (584). She realizes why she
had "experienced the book as a refuge" (584), a shelter "of printed words,
words that took seriously my own circumstances, that gave shape to my own
fantasies and fears" (589). Now, as an adult, she has brought Nell "into
consciousness" and sees her as the embodiment of her childish self-image
of injured innocence. "Giving up identification with her involves giving up
a schematized vision of good and evil . . . I come to see my grandmother not
as a witch but as a broken woman, my parents as themselves bewildered
children trying to balance their loyalties and responsibilities" (589). Zonana's
personal story is skilfully drawn out of her analysis of Nell's. Her view that
Quilp "is a dramatic displacement, . . . a safe focus for Nell's and the reader's
anxieties" (586), and that the real villain is Nell's grandfather, is not an
ingenious academic argument grounded on a new angle of vision or a new
critical theory; it draws support from her own life.

NOTES

1. I should mention a number of other paperback reprints: *Oliver Twist* and *The
   Old Curiosity Shop* (Oxford World's Classics, edited by Kathleen Tillotson and
   Elizabeth Brennan respectively); *The Old Curiosity Shop, Bleak House,* and *A
   Tale of Two Cities* (from Andrew Lang's Gadshill Edition); and five editions of
   Great Expectations, one of them the Penguin Classic newly edited in 1996 (re-
   viewed by Trey Philpotts in *DSA* 27), and another, the only one of these paper-
   backs that I have seen, the Signet Classic edition with a new introduction by
   Stanley Weintraub. In it he notices anachronisms in the story (he attributes them
   to the pressure of the weekly schedule) and identifies allusions. There were also
   several audio cassettes, which I have not attempted to track down. The American
   Printing House for the Blind issued a Braille edition of *Great Expectations*.

WORKS CITED

If an article was published in one of the Dickens journals or in a volume of essays, it is cross-referenced to the journal or volume entry, thus:

Andrews, Malcolm, "Editorial," *D* 94:1.

Titles of Dickens journals and edited collections are abbreviated in cross-references: *The Dickensian (D); Dickens Quarterly (DQ); Dickens Studies Annual (DSA);* Jeremy Tambling (ed.), *"Bleak House"*: *Contemporary Critical Essays* (Tambling); Michael A. Cotsell (ed.), *Critical Essays on Charles Dickens's "A Tale of Two Cities"* (Cotsell); Murray Baumgarten and H. M. Daleski (eds.), *Homes and Homelessness in the Victorian Imagination* (Baumgarten/Daleski).

Afnan, Elham. "Imaginative Transformations: *Great Expectations* and *Sunset Boulevard.*" See *D* 94:1.

Andrews, Malcolm. "Editorial." *D* 94:1.

—— "Editorial." *D* 94:2.

Ayres, Brenda. *Dissenting Women in Dickens' Novels: The Subversion of Domestic Ideology.* Contributions in Women's Studies No. 168. Westport, Connecticut: Greenwood Press, 1998.

Baldridge, Cates. "Alternatives to Bourgeois Individualism in *A Tale of Two Cities.*" Cotsell.

Baumgarten, Murray. "Staging the Ruins: David Roberts's Paintings of the Holy Land and Charles Dickens London Theatre of Homelessness." See next entry.

Baumgarten, Murray and H. M. Daleski, eds. *Homes and Homelessness in the Victorian Imagination.* AMS Studies in Nineteenth-Century Literature and Culture No. 2. New York: AMS Press, 1998.

Baumgarten, Murray. "Staging the Ruins: David Roberts's Paintings of the Holy Land and Charles Dickens' London Theatre of Homelessness." 127–66.
Hochman, Baruch. "Bulrush and Harvest Home." 51–64.
Jordan, John O. "Domestic Servants and the Victorian Home." 79–90.
McCarthy, Patrick. "Making for Home: David Copperfield and His Fellow Travelers." 21–32.
Parker, David. "Dickens at Home." 65–75.
Polhemus, Robert M. "The Favorite Child: *David Copperfield* and the Scriptual Issue of Child-Wives." 3–20.
Roston, Murray. "Disrupted Homes: The Fallen Woman in Victorian Art and Literature." 91–110.
Shaked, Gershon. "Dickens's *Oliver Twist* and Mendele's *The Book of Beggars.*" 297–305.

Sicher, Efraim. "Bleak Homes and Symbolic Houses: At-homeness and Home-lessness in Dickens." 33–49

Tracy, Robert. "Queens' Parlours, Queens' Bedrooms, and Queens' Gardens: Raping the Locks." 323–45.

Black, Barbara. "A Sisterhood of Rage and Beauty: Dickens' Rosa Dartle, Miss Wade, and Madame Defarge." *DSA* 26.

Blain, Virginia. "Double Vision and the Double Standard in *Bleak House:* A Feminist Perspective." Tambling.

Brantlinger, Patrick. *The Reading Lesson: The Threat of Mass Literacy in Nineteenth-Century British Fiction.* Bloomington and Indianapolis: Indiana UP, 1998.
"Introduction: The Case of the Poisonous Book." 1:24
"How Oliver Twist Learned to Read, and What He Read." Ch. 4, 69–92.

Brattin, Joel J. " 'I Will Not Have My Words Misconstrued': The Text of *Our Mutual Friend.*" *DQ* 15:3.

———— " 'Let Me Pause Once More': Dickens' Manuscript Revisions in the Retrospective Chapters of *David Copperfield.*" *DSA* 26.

Carens, Timothy L. "The Civilizing Mission at Home: Empire, Gender, and National Reform in *Bleak House.*" *DSA* 26.

Carey, Peter. *Jack Maggs.* New York: Alfred A. Knopf, 1998. (Published 1997 in Great Britain.)

Ceylan, Deniz, Tarba. "Intimidation and Embarrassment in Conversations of Dickens's Novels." British Council Sixth British Novelists Seminar, "Charles Dickens and His Work." Ankara, Turkey: Middle East Technical University, March 1998. http: //www.stg.brown.edu/projects/hyperte . . . ow/victorian/dickens/turkey/tur-lit16.html.

Childers, Joseph W. "Recent Dickens Studies: 1995." *DSA* 26.

Cohen, Monica F. *Professional Domesticity in the Victorian Novel: Women, Work, and Home.* Cambridge Studies in Nineteenth-Century Literature and Culture 14. Cambridge: Cambridge UP, 1998.

Cotsell, Michael A., ed. *Critical Essays on Charles Dickens's "A Tale of Two Cities."* Critical Essays on British Literature Series, Zack Bowen, general editor. New York: G. K. Hall & Co., an Imprint of Simon & Schuster Macmillan, 1998.

Baldridge, Cates. "Alternatives to Bourgeois Individualilsm in *A Tale of Two Cities.*" 168–86. (1990).
Cotsell, Michael. "Introduction." 1–15.
Frank, Lawrence. "Dickens' *A Tale of Two Cities:* The Poetics of Impasse." 111–32. (1979)
Goldberg, Michael. "Carlyle, Dickens, and the Revolution of 1848. 148–56. (1983)

Hutter, Albert. "Nation and Generation in *A Tale of Two Cities.*" 89–110 (1978)

Kucich, John. "The Purity of Violence: *A Tale of Two Cities.*" 133–47 (1980)

Lloyd, Tom. "Language, Love, and Identity: *A Tale of Two Cities.*" 187–203. (1992)

Manheim, Leonard. "A Tale of Two Characters: A Study in Multiple Projection." 61–73. (1970)

Rance, Nicholas. "Charles Dickens: *A Tale of Two Cities* (1859)." 74–88 (1975)

Rignall, J. M. "Dickens and the Catastrophic Continuum of History in *A Tale of Two Cities.*" 157–67. (1984)

Robson, Lisa. "The 'Angels' in Dickens's House: Representation of Women in *A Tale of Two Cities.*" 204–21. (1992)

Cox, Don Richard. *Charles Dickens's "The Mystery of Edwin Drood": An Annotated Bibliography.* AMS Studies in the Nineteenth Century No. 17. New York: AMS Pres, Inc., 1998.

Cummings, Katherine. "Re-reading *Bleak House:* The Chronicle of a 'Little Body' and Its Perverse Defence." Tambling.

Daleski, H. M. "Seasonal Offerings: Some Recurrent Features of the *Christmas Books." DSA* 27.

Davis, Paul. *Charles Dickens A to Z: The Essential Reference to His Life and Work.* New York: Facts on File, Inc., 1998.

Dever, Carolyn. *Death and the Mother from Dickens to Freud: Victorian Fiction and the Anxiety of Origins.* Cambridge Studies in Nineteenth-Century Literature and Culture 17. Cambridge: Cambridge UP, 1998.

Dickens, Charles. *"Gone Astray" and Other Papers from "Household Words" 1851–59.* Ed. Michael Slater. The Dent Uniform Edition of Dickens' Journalism. vol. 3. Columbus: Ohio State UP, 1999. (Introduction, preliminary material, headnotes, and index © J. M. Dent 1998).

—— *Great Expectations.* Ed. Stanley Weintraub. Signet Classic. New York: New Amsterdam Library, 1998.

—— *The Letters of Charles Dickens.* The British Academy Pilgrim Edition. Vol. 10:1862–1864. Ed. Graham Storey. Oxford: Clarendon, 1998.

—— *Little Dorrit.* Introduction by Stephen Wall. New notes and appendices by Helen Small. Penguin Classics. Harmondsworth: Penguin, 1998.

—— *The Pickwick Papers.* Ed. Malcolm Andrews. The Everyman Dickens, Michael Slater, series editor. London: J. M. Dent and Rutland, Vermont: Charles E. Tuttle, 1998.

—— *Pictures from Italy.* Introduction and notes by Kate Flint. Penguin Classics. Harmondsworth: Penguin, 1998.

The Dickensian 94:1 (Spring 1998).

Afnan, Elham. "Imaginative Transformation: *Great Expectations* and Sunset Boulevard." 5:12.

Andrews, Malcolm. "Editorial." 3–4.

Dubberke, Ray. "Dickens's Favourite Detective." 45–49.

Hunt, Peter. "Chesterton and Wilson on Dickens: An Instructive Comparison." 13–20.

Long, William F. "Rejecting the Golden Dustman: An Uncollected Letter." 42–44.

Sasaki, Toru. "Dickens in Confusion? Discrepancies in the Denouement of *Martin Chuzzlewit*." 21–24.

Storer, David. "Grotesque Storytelling: Dickens's Articulation of the 'Crisis of the Knowable Community' in *Bleak House* and *Little Dorrit*." 25–41.

The Dickensian 94:2 (Summer 1998).

Andrews, Malcolm. "Editorial." 83–84.

Litvack, Leon. "What Books did Dickens Buy and Read? Evidence from the Book Accounts with His Publishers." 85–129.

Smith, Grahame. "Television Review" (BBC2's *Our Mutual Friend*). 145–46.

The Dickensian 94:3 (Winter 1998).

Halevi-Wise, Yael. "Little Dorrit's Story: a Window into the Novel." 184–94.

Peters, Laura. "Perilous Adventures: Dickens and Popular Orphan Adventure Narratives." 172–83.

Reed, James. "Dickens, Christmas and the Baby in the Egg-Box." 165–71.

Dickens Quarterly 15:1 (March 1998).

Drew, John M. L. "The Nineteenth-Century Commerical Traveler and Dickens's 'Uncommercial' Philosophy: (Part One)." 50–61.

Meckier, Jerome. "*Great Expectations:* Symmetry in (Com)motion." 28–49.

Vegh, Beatriz. "*Hard Times* Gone Modernist: The 1921 Rafael Barradas Illustrations for *Tiempos Difíciles*." 3–27.

Dickens Quarterly 15:2 (June 1998).

Drew, John M. L. "The Nineteenth-Century Commercial Traveler and Dickens's 'Uncommercial' Philosophy: (Part Two)." 83–110.

Trezise, Simon David. "Dickensian Influences on the Life and Work of Sabine Baring-Gould." 123–32.

Tysdahl, Bjørn. "Europe Is Not the Other: *A Tale of Two Cities*." 111–22.

Dickens Quarterly 15:3 (September 1998).

Brattin, Joel J. " 'I will Not Have My Words Misconstrued': The Text of *Our Mutual Friend*." 167–76.

Hennelly, Mark M. Jr. "The 'Mysterious Portal': Liminal Play in *David Copperfield, Bleak House,* and *Great Expectations*: (Part One). 155–66.

Toker, Leona. "Veblen, Dickens, and Martin Chuzzlewit's America." 147–54.

Dickens Quarterly 15:4 (December 1998).

Hennelly, Mark M. Jr. "The 'Mysterious Portal': Liminal Play in *David Copperfield, Bleak House,* and *Great Expectations*: (Part Two)." 195–209.
Retseck, Janet. "Sexing Miss Wade." 217–25.
Tick, Stanley. "In the Case of *Bleak House:* A Brief Brief in Defense of Mr. Tulkinghorn." 210–16.

Dickens Studies Annual: Essays on Victorian Fiction. Ed. Stanley Friedman, Edward Guiliano, and Michael Timko. Vol. 26. New York: AMS Press, 1998.

Black, Barbara. "A Sisterhood of Rage and Beauty: Dickens' Rosa Dartle, Miss Wade, and Madame Defarge." 91–106.
Brattin, Joel J. " 'Let Me Pause Once More': Dickens' Manuscript Revisions in the Retrospective Chapters of *David Copperfield*." 73–90.
Carens, Timothy L. "The Civilizing Mission at Home: Empire, Gender, and National Reform in *Bleak House*." 121–45.
Childers, Joseph W. "Recent Dickens Studies: 1995." 335–53.
Hake, Stephen. "Becoming Poor to Make Many Rich: The Resolution of Class Coflict in Dickens." 107–19.
Hennelly, Mark M. Jr. "Courtly Wild Men and Carnivalesque Pig Women in Dickens and Hardy." 1–32.
Kran, Paul A. "Signification and Rhetoric in *Bleak House*." 147–67.
Litvak, Joseph. "Bad Scene: *Oliver Twist* and the Pathology of Entertainment." 33–49.
Meckier, Jerome. " 'Dashing in Now': *Great Expectations* and Charles Lever's *A Day's Ride*." 227–64.
Sell, Kathleen. "The Narrator's Shame: Masculine Identity in *Great Expectations*." 203–26.
Surgal, Jon. "The Parable of the Spoons and Ladles: Sibling and Crypto-Sibling Typology in *Martin Chuzzlewit*." 51–71.
Surridge, Lisa. " 'John Rokesmith's Secret': Sensation, Detection, and the Policing of the Feminine in *Our Mutual Friend*." 265–84.
Tambling, Jeremy. "Carlyle in Prison: Reading *Latter-Day Pamphlets*." 311–33.
Wainwright, Valerie L. "On Goods, Virtues, and *Hard Times*." 169–86.
Wilson, Anna. "On History, Case History, and Deviance: Miss Wade's Symptoms and Their Interpretation." 187–201.

Dickens Studies Annual: Essays on Victorian Fiction. Ed. Stanley Friedman, Edward Guiliano, and Michael Timko. Vol. 27. New York: AMS Press, 1998.

Daleski, H. M. "Seasonal Offerings: Some Recurrent Features of the *Christmas Books*." 97–111.
Dransfield, Scott. "Reading the Gordon Riots in 1841:Social Violence and Moral Management in *Barnaby Rudge*." 69–95.
Dutheil, Martine Hennard. "Rushdie's Affiliation with Dickens." 209–26.

Fletcher, Pauline. "Bacchus in Kersey: Dickens and the Classics." 1–22.

Holway, Tatiana M. "Imaginary Capital: The Shape of the Victorian Economy and the Shaping of Dickens's Career." 23–43.

Lenard, Mary. " 'Mr. Popular Sentiment': Dickens and the Gender Politics of Sentimentalism and Social Reform Literature." 45–68.

Philpotts, Trey. "Recent Dickens Studies: 1996." 307–63.

Rosen, David. "*A Tale of Two Cities:* Theology of Revolution." 171–85.

Samet, Elizabeth Dale. " 'When Constabulary Duty's To Be Done': Dickens and the Metropolitan Police." 131–43.

Spurgin, Timothy. " 'It's Me Wot Has Done It!': Letters, Reviews, and *Great Expectations.*" 187–208.

Sroka, Kenneth M. "A Tale of Two Gospels: Dickens and John." 145–69.

Tracy, Robert. " 'A Whimsical Kind of Masque': The Christmas Books and Victorian Spectacle." 113–30.

Dransfield, Scott. "Reading the Gordon Riots in 1841; Social Violence and Moral Management in *Barnaby Rudge.*" *DSA* 27.

Drew, John M. L. "The Nineteenth-Century Commercial Traveler and Dickens's 'Uncommercial Philosophy.' " *DQ* 15:1 and 2.

Dubberke, Ray. "Dickens's Favorite Detective." *D* 94:1.

Dutheil, Martine Hennard. "Rushdie's Affiliation with Dickens." *DSA* 27.

Edgecombe, Rodney Stenning. "*Little Dorrit* and Canning's 'New Morality.' " *Modern Philology* 95:4 (May 1998): 484–89.

Epstein, Norrie. *The Friendly Dickens: being a good-natured guide to the art and adventures of the man who invented Scrooge.* A Winokur-Boates Book. New York: Viking Penguin, 1998.

Faymonville, Carmen. " 'Waste Not, Want Not': Even Redundant Women Have Their Uses." In Kranidis, Rita S., ed. *Imperial Objects* . . . (below). 64–84.

Field, Kate. *Pen Photographs of Charles Dickens's Readings: Taken from Life.* Introduction by Carolyn J. Moss. Troy, New York: Whitston, 1998.

Fletcher, Pauline. "Bacchus in Kersey: Dickens and the Classics." *DSA* 27.

Frank, Lawrence. "Dickens' *A Tale of Two Cities:* The Poetics of Impasse." Cotsell.

Giffone, Anthony. "The Sleary Circus: (England: in Charles Dickens's *Hard Times:* 1854)." *Fools and Jesters in Literature, Art, and History: A Bio-Bibliographical Sourcebook.* Ed. Vicki K. Janik. Westport, Connecticut: Greenwood Press, 1998, 395–99.

Gilfillan, Ross. *The Snake-Oil Dickens Man.* London: Fourth Estate Limited, 1998.

Gillespie, Nick. "Darwin and Dickens." *Reason* 30–6 (November 1998): 38–47.

Goldberg, Michael. "Carlyle, Dickens, and the Revolution of 1848." Cotsell.

Googins, Robert. "Reflections on Delinquency, Dickens and Twain." *Delinquent Violent Youth: Theory and Interventions.* Ed. Thomas P. Gullotta, Gerald R. Adams, and Raymond Montemayor. Advances in Adolescent Development Series, vol. 9. Thousand Oaks, California: SAGE Publications, 1998. 1–11.

Hake, Stephen. "Becoming Poor to Make Many Rich: The Resolution of Class Conflict in Dickens." *DSA* 26.

Halevi-Wise, Yael. "Little Dorrit's Story: A Window into the Novel." *D* 94–3.

Harrington, Gary. "Woolf's *Mrs. Dalloway.*" *Explicator* 56:3 (Spring 1998): 144–46.

Hawes, Donald. *Who's Who in Dickens.* Foreword by David Parker. Who's Who Series. London: Routledge, 1998.

Hennelly, Mark M. Jr. "Courtly Wild Men and Carnivalesque Pig Women in Dickens and Hardy." *DSA* 26.

——— " 'Deep Play' and 'Women's Ridicules' in *Oliver Twist.*" *Journal of Evolutionary Psychology* 18:1–2 (March 1997): 102–11 (Part I); 18:3–4 (August 1997): 143–55 (Part II); 19:1–2 (March 1998): 116–31 (Part III); 19:3–4 (August 1998): 165–74 (Part IV); 20:1–2 (March 1999): 92–102 (Part V).

——— "The 'Mysterious Portal': Liminal Play in *David Copperfield, Bleak House,* and *Great Expectations.*" *DQ* 15:3 and 4.

Higbie, Robert. *Dickens and Imagination.* Gainesville, Florida: UP of Florida, 1998.

Hochman, Baruch. "Bulrush and Harvest Home." Baumgarten/Daleski.

Holway, Tatiana M. "Imaginary Capital: The Shape of the Victorian Economy and the Shaping of Dickens's Career." *DSA* 27.

Hudson, Barbara Hill. "Sociolinguistic Analysis of Dialogues and First-Person Narratives in Fiction." *Language: Readings in Language and Culture.* Eds. Virginia P. Clark, Paul A. Eschholz, and Alfred F. Rosa. New York: St. Martin's, 1998. 740–48.

Hunt, Peter. "Chesterton and Wilson on Dickens: An Instructive Comparison." *D* 94:1.

Hutter, Albert. "Nation and Generation in *A Tale of Two Cities.*" Cotsell.

Jaffe, Audrey. "*David Copperfield* and *Bleak House*: On Dividing the Responsibility of Knowing." Tambling.

Jagose, Annamarie. "Remembering Miss Wade: *Little Dorrit* and the Historicizing of Female Perversity." *GLQ: A Journal of Gay and Lesbian Studies* 4 (1998): 423–51.

Johnson, Eric. "Dickens on Disk." *Computers and Humanities* 31 (1997–98): 257–60.

Jordan, John O. "Domestic Servants and the Victorian Home." Baumgarten/Daleski.

Julius, Anthony. "Dickens the Lawbreaker." *Critical Quarterly* 40:3 (Autumn 1998): 43–66.

Kaplan, Fred. *Dickens: A Biography.* Johns Hopkins Paperback. Baltimore: Johns Hopkins UP, 1998. (Originally published in 1988.)

Keen, Suzanne. *Victorian Renovations of the Novel: Narrative Annexes and the Boundaries of Representation.* Cambridge Studies in Nineteenth-Century Literature and Culture 15. Cambridge: Cambridge UP, 1998.

Kran, Paul A. "Signification and Rhetoric in *Bleak House.*" *DSA* 26.

Kranidis, Rita S., ed. *Imperial Objects: Essays on Victorian Women's Emigration and the Unauthorized Imperial Experience.* New York: Twayne Publishers, An Imprint of Simon & Schuster Macmillan, 1998. "Introduction: New Subject, Familiar Grounds." 1–18.

Kucich, John. "The Purity of Violence: *A Tale of Two Cities.*" Cotsell.

LaCapra, Dominick. "Ideology and Critique in Dickens's *Bleak House.*" Tambling.

Lenard, Mary. " 'Mr. Popular Sentiment': Dickens and the Gender Politics of Sentimentalism and Social Reform Literature." *DSA* 27.

Litvack, Leon. "What Books did Dickens Buy and Read? Evidence from the Book Accounts with His Publishers." *D* 94:2.

Litvak, Joseph. "Bad Scene: *Oliver Twist* and the Pathology of Entertainment." *DSA* 26.

Lloyd, Tom. "Language, Love, and Identity: *A Tale of Two Cities.*" Cotsell.

Long, William F. "Rejecting the Golden Dustman: An Uncollected Letter." See *D* 94:1.

Manheim, Leonard. "A Tale of Two Characters: A Study in Multiple Projection." Cotsell.

McCarthy, Patrick. "Making for Home: David Copperfield and His Fellow Travelers." Baumgarten/Daleski.

McLaughlin, Kevin. "Losing One's Place: Displacement and Domesticity in Dickens's *Bleak House.*" Tambling.

Meckier, Jerome. " 'Dashing In Now': *Great Expectations* and Charles Lever's *A Day's Ride.*" *DSA* 26.

————.*"Great Expectations:* Symmetry in (Com)motion." *DQ* 15:1.

Mieder, Wolfgang. " 'Conventional Phrases Are a Sort of Fireworks': Charles Dickens's Proverbial Language." *Proverbium* 15 (1998): 179–99.

Miller, D. A. "Discipline in Different Voices: Bureaucracy, Policy, Family, and *Bleak House."* Tambling.

Miller, J. Hillis. "Interpretation in *Bleak House."* Tambling.

Morgantaler, Goldie. "Meditating on the Low: A Darwinian Reading of *Great Expectations." Studies in English Literature 1500–1900* 38:4 (Autumn 1998): 707–21.

Myers, William. *The Presence of Persons: Essays on Literature, Science and Philosophy in the Nineteenth Century.* The Nineteenth Century Series. Vincent Newey and Joanne Shattock, general editors. Aldershot, Hants and Brookfield, Vermont: Ashgate, 1998.

"Introduction: Nothing New." 1–17.
"Celibate Men and Angelic Women in *Oliver Twist."* 99–108.
"The Radicalism of *Little Dorrit."* 109–29.

Nelson, Brian R. *The Basis of Morality and Its Relation to Dramatic Form in a Study of "David Copperfield."* Studies in Comparative Literature, vol. 3. Lewiston, New York: Edwin Mellen, 1998.

Newlin, George. *Understanding "A Tale of Two Cities": A Student Casebook to Issues, Sources, and Historical Documents.* "Literature in Context" Series. Westport, Connecticut: Greenwood, 1998.

Nussbaum, Martha C. "Exactly and Responsibly: A Defense of Ethical Criticism." *Philosophy and Literature* 22:2 (1998): 343–65.

Orero, Pilar. "Spanish Wellerisms." *Proverbium* 15 (1998): 235–42.

Parker, David. "Dickens at Home." Baumgarten/Daleski.

Peltason, Timothy. "Esther's Will." Tambling.

Peters, Catherine. *Charles Dickens.* Pocket Biographies Series. C. S. Nicholls, series editor. Thrupp, Stroud, Gloucestershire: Sutton, 1998.

Peters, Laura. "Perilous Adventures: Dickens and Popular Orphan Adventure Narratives." *D* 94:3.

Peterson, Linda H. "Mother-Daughter Productions: Mary Howitt and Anna Mary Howitt in *Howitt's Journal, Household Words,* and *Other Mid-Victorian Publications." Vitorian Periodicals Review* 31:1 (Spring 1998): 31–54.

Philpotts, Trey. "Recent Dickens Studies: 1996." *DSA* 27.

Pittock, Malcolm. "Taking Dickens to Task: *Hard Times* Once More." *Cambridge Quarterly* 27:2 (1998): 107–28.

Polhemus, Robert M. "The Favorite Child: *David Copperfield* and the Scriptural Issues of Child-Wives." Baumgarten/Daleski.

Pollin, Burton R. "Dickens's *Chimes* and Its Pathway into Poe's 'Bells.' " *Mississippi Quarterly* 51:2 (Spring 1998): 217–31.

Posner, Richard A. "Against Ethical Criticism." *Philosophy and Literature* 21:1 (1997): 1–27.

———."Against Ethical Criticism." *Philosophy and Literature* 22:2 (1998): 394–412.

Rance, Nicholas. "*Charles Dickens: 'A Tale of Two Cities'* (1859)." Ch. 3 of *The Historical Novel and Popular Politics in Nineteenth-Century England.* Barnes & Noble Critical Studies. New York: Barnes & Noble Books, 1975. Cotsell.

Reed, James. "Dickens, Christmas, and The Baby in the Egg-Box." *D* 94:3.

Retseck, Janet. "Sexing Miss Wade." *DQ* 15:4.

Rignall, J. M. "Dickens and the Catastrophic Continuum of History in *A Tale of Two Cities.*" Cotsell.

Robbins, Bruce. "Telescopic Philanthropy: Professionalism and Responsibility in *Bleak House.*" Tambling.

Robson, Lisa. "The 'Angels' in Dickens's House: Representations of Women in *A Tale of Two Cities.*" Cotsell.

Rogers, Philip. "Dystopian Intertexts: Dickens' *Hard Times* and Zamiatin's *We.*" *Comparative Literature Studies* 35 (1998): 393–411.

Rosen, David. "*A Tale of Two Cities:* Theology of Revolution." *DSA* 27.

Roston, Murray. "Disrupted Homes: The Fallen Woman in Victorian Art and Literature." Baumgarten/Daleski.

Russell, Shannon. "Recycling the Poor and Fallen: Emigration Politics and the Narrative Resolutions of *Mary Barton* and *David Copperfield.*" In Rita S. Kranidis, ed., *Imperial Objects* . . . (above). 43–63.

Samet, Elizabeth Dale. "When Constabulary Duty's To Be Done: Dickens and the Metropolitan Police." *DSA* 27.

Sasaki, Toru. "Dickens in Confusion? Discrepancies in the Denouement of *Martin Chuzzlewit.*" *D* 94:1.

Sell, Kathleen. "The Narrator's Shame: Masculine Identity in *Great Expectations.*" *DSA* 26.

Sen, Sambudha. "*Bleak House* and *Little Dorrit:* The Radical Heritage." *ELH* 65:4 (Winter, 1998): 945–70.

Shaked, Gershon. "Dickens's *Oliver Twist* and Mendele's *The Book of Beggars.*" Baumgarten/Daleski.

Sicher, Efraim. "Bleak Homes and Symbolic Houses: At-homeness and Homelessness in Dickens." Baumgarten/Daleski.

Smith, Grahame. "Dickens and Critical Theory." British Council Sixth British Novelists Seminar, "Charles Dickens and His Work." Ankara, Turkey: Middle East Technical University, March 1998. http: //www.britcoun.org.tr/elt/lit/turlit09.htm

———."Dickens and the City of Light." See above for venue. Now in print in *DQ* 16:3 (September 1999): 178–90.

———."Television Review" (BBC2's *Our Mutual Friend*). *D* 94:2.

Spurgin, Timothy A. " 'It's Me Wot Has Done It!': Letters, Reviews, and *Great Expectations.*" *DSA* 27.

Sroka, Kenneth M. "A Tale of Two Gospels: Dickens and John." *DSA* 27.

Storer, David. "Grotesque Storytelling: Dickens's Articulation of the 'Crisis of the Knowable Community' in *Bleak House* and *Little Dorrit.*" *D* 94:1.

Surgal, John. "The Parable of the Spoons and Ladles: Sibling and Crypto-Sibling Typology in *Martin Chuzzlewit.*" *DSA* 26.

Surridge, Lisa. " 'John Rokesmith's Secret': Sensation, Detection, and the Policing of the Feminine in *Our Mutual Friend.*" *DSA* 26.

Swisher, Clarice, ed. *Readings on Charles Dickens.* Literary Companion to British Authors Series. San Diego: Greenhaven Press, 1998.

Tambling, Jeremy, ed. *Bleak House.* New Casebooks. New York: St. Martin's, 1998.

Blain, Virginia. "Double Vision and the Double Standard in *Bleak House:* A Feminist Perspective." 65–86. (1985)
Cummings, Katherine. "Re-reading *Bleak House:* The Chronicle of a 'Little Body' and its Perverse Defence." 183–204. (1991)
Jaffe, Audrey. "*David Copperfield* and *Bleak House*: On Dividing the Responsibility of Knowing." 163–82. (1991)
LaCapra, Dominick. "Ideology and Critique in Dickens's *Bleak House.*" 128–38. (1984)
McLaughlin, Kevin. "Losing One's Place: Displacement and Domesticity in Dickens's *Bleak House.*" 228–45. (1993)
Miller, D. A. "Discipline in Different Voices: Bureaucracy, Police, Family and *Bleak House.*" 87–127. (1983)
Miller, J. Hillis. "Interpretation in *Bleak House.*" 29–53. (1971)

Peltason, Timothy. "Esther's Will." 205–27. (1991)

Robbins, Bruce. "Telescopic Philanthropy: Professionalism and Responsibility in *Bleak House*." 139–62. (1990)

Tambling, Jeremy. "Introduction." 1–28.

Van Boheemen-Saaf, Christine. " 'The Universe Makes an Indifferent Parent': *Bleak House* and the Victorian Family Resonance." 54–64. (1983)

———."Carlyle in Prison: Reading *Latter-Day Pamphlets*." *DSA* 26.

Tick, Stanley. "In the Case of *Bleak House:* A Brief Brief in Defense of Mr. Tulkinghorn." *DQ* 15:4

Toker, Leona. "Veblen, Dickens, and Martin Chuzzlewit's America." *DQ* 15:3.

Tracy, Robert. "Queens' Parlours, Queens' Bedrooms, and Queens' Gardens: Raping the Locks." Baumgarten/Daleski.

———." 'A Whimsical Kind of Masque': The Christmas Books and Victorian Spectacle." *DSA* 27.

Trezise, Simon David. "Dickensian Influences on the Life and Work of Sabine Baring-Gould." *DQ* 15:2.

Tysdahl, Bjørn. "Europe Is Not the Other: *A Tale of Two Cities*." *DQ* 15:2.

Van Boheemen-Saaf, Christine. " 'The Universe Makes an Indifferent Parent': *Bleak House* and the Victorian Family Romance." Tambling.

Vegh, Beatriz. "*Hard Times* gone Modernist: The 1921 Rafael Barradas Illustrations for *Tiempos Difíciles*." *DQ* 15–1.

Vlock, Deborah. *Dickens, Novel Reading, and the Victorian Popular Theatre*. Cambridge Studies in Nineteenth-Century Literature and Culture 19. Cambridge: Cambridge UP, 1998.

Wainwright, Valerie L. "On Goods, Virtues, and *Hard Times*." *DSA* 26.

Wark, Robert R. "The Curious Case of Joseph Clayton Clark." *Huntington Library Quarterly* 59:4 (1998): 551–55.

Wilson, Anna. "On History, Case History, and Deviance: Miss Wade's Symptoms and Their Interpretation." *DSA* 26.

Wolfreys, Julian. *Writing London: The Trace of the Urban Text from Blake to Dickens*. London and New York: Macmillan and St. Martin's, 1998. Ch. 4, "Dickensian Architexture or, the city and the ineffable," 141–78. (An expansion of a chapter in *Victorian Identities* ed. Ruth Robbins and Julian Wolfreys [London: Macmillan, 1996].)

Yoon, Hye-Joon. *Physiognomy of Capital in Charles Dickens: An Essay in Dialectical Criticism*. Bethesda, Maryland: International Scholars, 1998.

Zonana, Joyce. "Nell and I." *Hudson Review* 50:4 (Winter 1998): 573–90.

Recent Studies in Thomas Hardy's Fiction 1987–99

David Garlock

This survey assesses the current state of critical scholarship dealing with Hardy's novels, offering synopses and commentary on the profusion of book-length studies that have surfaced during the period 1987–99. The variety of critical postures discernible among recent Hardy studies is suggested by the diversity of classificatory divisions presented in the essay, including feminist readings, multivalent analyses of individual novels, collections of essays, "poststructuralist" readings, biographical studies, and "critically eclectic" readings that often eschew tidy categorization. This overview focuses on the full gamut of often-contradictory interpretative strategies proffered by leading Hardy scholars of our time. In addition, this essay underscores the impact of the relatively recent appearance of previously unpublished personal correspondence and related Hardyan arcana upon Hardy scholars, especially those concerned with biographical and historical contextualization of the novels. In this review attention is also focused upon recent publications offering guided excursions through and around the contemporary labyrinth of theory-based criticism. Overall, this collection of capsule-sized reviews aspires to provide an informed awareness of the breadth and robust vitality of the thriving "Hardy industry."

The period encompassed by this survey frames the centenary of Thomas Hardy's abandonment of novel-writing in 1897, capping one hundred years of Hardy studies and attesting to the novelist's persistent popularity with both literary scholars and the reading public. In response to the sheer volume of recent critical assessments, I have resorted to some "desperate remedies," in particular, restricting the scope of this review to book-length criticism. In the course of preparing this survey, I found myself adopting as a kind of mantra the oft-quoted line from Ecclesiastes, " . . . of making many books there is no end" (12:12). Hardy would have been amused.

Commentary on the first-rate scholarship that brought Hardy studies to a new plateau during the mid-1980s can be found in Dale Kramer's comprehensive survey of the period 1980–86 (*DSA* 17 [1988], 249–84). I have omitted evaluation of the final volume of *Collected Letters* (Richard Little Purdy and Michael Millgate [eds.], Oxford: Clarendon, 1978–88), although it technically falls within the parameters of this essay, because the bulk of that massive project has been amply discussed by Kramer. The now completed multi-volume collection of Hardy's letters appears recurrently as marginalia in much of the criticism discussed below, indicative of the contribution that compendious undertaking has made to current scholarship.

In this essay, I have elected to group my appraisals in a manner that I hope will convey some sense of the diverse vitality of critical postures discernible among recent Hardy studies. While categories inevitably overlap, much significant criticism of the last decade or so seems to cluster around some familiar rubrics: namely, (1) feminist and/or gender-conscious readings, (2) exposition and textual analyses of individual novels, (3) collections of essays (with or without an organizing "theme"), (4) works with an explicit allegiance to one or more critical stances broadly classifiable as "poststructuralist," and (5) biographical studies. A sixth category I have elected to label (6) "critically eclectic" includes works that, while frequently offering a nod of recognition to current theory, seem to chart their own course.

1.

Among recent feminist readings, one of the freshest is Rosemarie Morgan's *Women and Sexuality in the Novels of Thomas Hardy* (London: Routledge, 1988), in which she argues against the frequently proffered assumption that the greater part of Hardy's female characters are passive objects of sexual desire. Morgan advances the premise that many of Hardy's women actually embody an aggressive sexuality. While focusing primarily on Hardy's most popular heroines—Elfride Swancourt, Bathsheba Everdene, Eustacia Vye, Tess Durbeyfield and Sue Bridehead—Morgan suggests that the role of aggressive female eroticism in Hardy may have been underestimated by earlier critics. Morgan positions Hardy among forward-thinking, evolving proto-feminist writers who defied the expectations of their time and created memorable heroines capable of transcending the conventional Victorian madonna/whore dichotomy. "On the contrary, his heroines' best faculties are presented in the context of their less-than-perfect natures in a less-than-perfect world not yet ready to take them at face value" (xiv).

Setting forth a recurrent Hardyan plot paradigm, in her discussion of *A Pair of Blue Eyes*, Morgan underscores the significance of role reversal in the relationships between Elfride Swancourt and her lovers. Passages from the text are cited to advance the argument that Elfride, though trapped in a society that encourages female passivity, is forced by the passivity of her suitors to become sexually aggressive. "She is not only sexually instigative, then, where the male is less so, she also sets the pace" (8). In Morgan's view, the unconventionality of Hardy's heroines, interpreted as flawed characterizations in his own time, is still underappreciated. In a similar mode, she views Hardy's Bathsheba Everdene as a woman whose inherent sexuality transcends societal constraints and prejudices. Describing her early encounters with Sergeant Troy, Morgan states: "On the threshold of sexual maturity, her impulse is to explore and experiment freely" (34). According to Morgan's revisionist take on some of Hardy's best-known heroines, Eustacia Vye's smoldering eroticism is the factor that causes us to identify her so closely with the smoldering fires on Egdon Heath in *Return of the Native*. The pagan, elemental forces of nature—represented by the Heath's raw, unfettered landscape—are represented synecdochially in Eustacia's unfulfilled passions. Accordingly, frustrated sexual vitality plays a major role in the character development and destinies of both Tess Durbeyfield and Sue Bridehead. Morgan's Tess rises above victimization: "Hardy retains, then, for Tess, with her emotional generosity, sexual vitality and moral strength, the capacity to rise above her fall and, ultimately, to redeem the man who, bearing the values and sexual prejudices and double-standards of the society, fails to rise above them in the hour of need" (109). Sue Bridehead's frustrated sexuality is treated similarly: " . . . in denying her a sexual reality, in nullifying her needs and desires, Jude unwittingly enforces her subjugation" (154). Some Hardy readers may feel that Morgan is engaging in a kind of retrospective wishful thinking, projecting contemporary feminist views onto Hardy's work. But whatever take one has on Hardy's position regarding "the woman question," Morgan defends her viewpoint with intelligence and conviction.

While somewhat less overtly feminist in approach, H. M. Daleski, in *Thomas Hardy and Paradoxes of Love* (Columbia, Missouri: U of Missouri P, 1997), shares with feminist critics a suspicion of readings that assume essentialist-based gender typologies in Hardy, as if the novelist's work required only contextualization within the received wisdom of his age, particularly in the area of traditional gender dichotomization. Instead of placing Hardy's fictive Wessex within the context of Victorian sexist propriety and prudery, Daleski offers bracingly fresh insights into the dynamics of the multiple love triangles (and quadrangles) around which many of Hardy's plots are built. Recognizing Hardy's casting and re-configuring one persistent plot paradigm, discernible throughout his fiction, Daleski selects seven novels (the most widely-read and critically acclaimed of the fourteen Hardy published) and explores the significance of romantic versus conjugal love in each—the tension between idealized romantic loves and the flesh-and-blood realities of conjugal unions comprising one of the "paradoxes" to which Daleski's title alludes. Like Rosemarie Morgan, Daleski detects among many of Hardy's female characters an erotic assertiveness running against the grain of reader expectations. Positing his own catalogue of gender typologies detectable among Hardy's creations, Daleski delineates the characteristics of the novelist's "diffident man," a character "type" surfacing in several of the novels, whose traits and predilections are frequently juxtaposed against a more traditional "manly hero," an unmistakably virile, albeit irresponsible, rake. This is another one of the paradoxes under consideration. Yet another paradox is Hardy's ambivalence toward the embodiments of male sexuality he exploits: "... Hardy is preoccupied with two opposed conceptions of male sexuality, fascinated and repelled by his rake figures and wary and skeptical of his sexually diffident heroes" (3). According to Daleski, Hardy's female characters, while certainly as bound by circumstance as the men who pursue them, are, nevertheless, granted wide-ranging freedoms in their choices among sexual partners: "His female characters are repeatedly and sympathetically portrayed as at the center of his fictional worlds, and they are always granted the freedom of choice, refuting the view of them as victims and of the novelist as a crass determinist weighting the scales against them" (3).

Daleski explores the issue of complicated sexuality and unacknowledged passion in his analysis of Michael Henchard's character in *The Mayor of Casterbridge*. He compares Henchard's self-imposed asceticism and celibacy with that of Bathsheba Everdene, ignoring traditional gender-specific typologies when referring to the "Diana complex" that drives them both. Daleski goes farther than most critics, positing unacknowledged homosexuality as a significant motivator behind some of Henchard's nearly inexplicable actions in the novel. He views the wrestling scene between Henchard and the younger Farfrae as a possible model for D. H. Lawrence's nude wrestling match between Birkin and Gerald in *Women in Love*. "It is true that the homoerotic dimension of the male relationship in the earlier novel is much more muted, but when we read back from Lawrence to Hardy, the relationship of Henchard to Farfrae is placed in a context that brings out its undertones" (124). Whether or not one accepts this interpretation of the early attraction and subsequent anguish Henchard feels toward another man, this reading effectively disrupts facile gender stereotyping of an extremely complex personality. Daleski's

investigation of recurrent gender-transcendent consciousness perceivable in
some of Hardy's major characters opens the door to further re-consideration
of the complexities of human sexuality throughout Hardy's work. According
to Daleski, the paradoxes of love encompass the full range of human passion,
from the forbidden to the conventional. It is hardly inconsistent with what
we know of Hardy's life and work to characterize his treatment of love's
paradoxes in a manner that spills across the restrictive boundaries of Victorian propriety.

Gender-based criticism informs and enlivens the analyses of several of
Hardy's major male characters in Annette Federico's *Masculine Identity in
Hardy and Gissing* (Cranbury: Associated UP, 1991). Federico has chosen
George Gissing and Thomas Hardy as exemplars of their age's response to
gender role awareness in the late nineteenth century—"my first criterion in
choosing these authors is their status as popular late-century English novelists
who work in the realist tradition" (14). Within the context of fluctuating sex-
role expectations, realistic novelists of this period were engaged in re-defining
"how notions of masculine identity were beginning to evolve from the solid,
monolithic patriarchal role of the mid-1800s to more malleable, less confident
styles of manhood" (16), according to Federico, whose focus on the reassessment of masculine identities parallels Daleski's probing of traditional
masculine stereotypes. Another parallel between Daleski's approach and Federico's is the latter's identification of specific character types, representative
of particular masculine identities. Federico presents us with four distinct models: (1) the virile man, or seducer (2) the chaste man, or the saint, (3) the
idealist, or romantic personality and, finally, (4) the realist. The realist functions in the novels discussed as the practical counterpart to the New Woman
of the Victorian Age. Federico presents both Hardy and Gissing as novelists
who were engaged in the creation of male characters (as well as female
characters) struggling against society-imposed norms of behavior and self-
actualization. In a discussion of Jude Fawley's character in her chapter entitled "The Other Victim," Federico explores the pressures of sex-role expectations imposed by society; men have traditionally accepted the patriarchal
straightjacket as their birthright, but find it as burdensome as the compliant
role assigned to the "weaker sex." The overall effect is debilitating and
constrictive, producing sexual and personality dysfunction. "If women's personalities appear fragmented because they are vulnerable to contradictory
emotions, men's identities are tense to the breaking point because of the
urgent personal need to remain self-protectively whole" (110). In her concluding chapter, Federico singles out Jude as Hardy's only male character
who may possibly transcend the patriarchal tradition, with its uncritical acceptance of masculine superiority over women. But, for most of Hardy's male
characters, in Federico's view, the individual man must adapt his inner being
to fit the mask imposed by a society reluctant to relinquish an antique mold.

In *Thomas Hardy, Femininity and Dissent* (London: Macmillan, 1999), Jane Thomas focuses on Hardy's so-called "minor novels," a body of fiction that is currently attracting unprecedented critical attention. Thomas maintains that Hardy's focus on female identity in these novels foregrounds "the historically specific determinants of identity itself and, more importantly, its unstable and temporary nature" (9). Close readings of the "marginalised" novels are offered, emphasizing "how they examine women's struggle to make language express a transformed sense of self and a new interpretation of experience" (51). Focusing throughout on "the tendentiousness of language" (67), Thomas argues that Hardy's female characters are engaged in a kind of dialectic opposition to the social milieux in which they find themselves and to the very narrators whose "male gaze" defines them.

2.

Among books devoted to a single novel, Rosemarie Morgan's *Cancelled Words, Rediscovering Thomas Hardy* (London: Routledge, 1992) stands apart, relying almost exclusively on comparative textual analyses of archival documents to support her exegetical commentary on Hardy's *Far from the Madding Crowd*. Based on close examination of the holograph manuscript housed at the Beinecke Rare Book and Manuscript Library at Yale University, surviving fragments of early drafts held in the Dorset County Museum, facsimiles of the serialized novel as issued in twelve numbers (from January to December, 1874) of Leslie Stephen's *Cornhill Magazine* and the first edition published by Smith, Elder & Company, Morgan escorts the reader's embarkation on an illuminating excursion through the creative processes that helped shaped current editions of Hardy's first major popular and critical success. Having been privileged to handle and explore the holograph manuscript at Yale a number of years ago, I can readily identify with Morgan's succumbing to the mystery and lure of the manuscript's interpolative marginalia, much of it hastily scrawled in Hardy's own hand. Of equal interest are the many Grundyan expurgations and "improvements" pencilled in by Leslie Stephen. Morgan's book is greatly enhanced by thirty-one facsimile pages of the holograph manuscript, which amply illustrate the process by which the serialized version of Hardy's novel evolved. In the introductory chapter, describing her critical approach to her task, Morgan raises "the vexed question of intentionality" (11), but then dismisses it as irrelevant to the kind of critical interpretation she is undertaking: "If there is a way of exploring the creative mind at work without second-guessing first Hardy's and then Stephen's developing interests and concerns, I have not discovered it" (11).

Morgan offers us the benefit of her exhaustive research, in which she has compared a variety of extant documents that hold particular value in terms of assessing Hardy's artistic mindset and the kinds of restrictive parameters imposed by Victorian prudery. She has also examined some of Hardy's correspondence relevant to *Far from the Madding Crowd* in the published *Letters* (see above). Overall, Morgan's painstaking comparative analyses yield illuminating insights into the nature of Victorian prudery and the concerns of editors like Leslie Stephen, whose readership possessed a sense of propriety almost incomprehensible within the context of our own contemporary tell-all/how-all culture.

Harold Bloom's *Thomas Hardy's The Mayor of Casterbridge* (New York: Chelsea, 1988) is a collection of essays dealing with a single novel. Part of the Modern Critical Interpretations Series, the six essays included (in addition to Bloom's introductory critical overview) are culled from a wide range of critical viewpoints spanning a time period from 1971 to 1986. It is interesting to note that Elaine Showalter's "The Unmanning of the Mayor of Casterbridge," taken from Dale Kramer's 1979 edition of *Critical Approaches to the Fiction of Thomas Hardy* (Macmillan), resurfaces in Bloom's collection as well as in Margaret Higonnet's *The Sense of Sex* (reviewed below), attesting to the essay's resonance with feminist reassessments of Hardy's work. In Showalter's words: "To the feminist critic, Hardy presents an irresistible paradox" (53). Hardy's paradoxes— particularly his paradoxical take on gender, sex, and sex-role reversal—continue to invite diverse modes of explication. Harold Bloom's introductory essay presents Michael Henchard as a traditional tragic hero: "[H]ardy specifically sets out to show that Henchard's character is his fate" (7). This is followed by Bert G. Hornback's essay, which deals with the metaphoric aspect of atmosphere and milieu in *The Mayor of Casterbridge*—"a close and minute awareness of physical objects" (13). For Hornback, the narrator's expansion of Henchard's character and the tragic dimensions of his misalliances and mistakes are brought into focus by Hardy's contextualizing the mayor's personal history within the framework of "the unchanging and timeless fate of man" (14). Ian Gregor's essay deals with Henchard's character in terms of the separation between his public and private worlds. George Levine takes up the issue of Hardyan realism, delineating ways in which the facade of realistic narrative masks a deeper level of romantic individualism, in which the individual character imposes his/her own structure upon surface realities. Hence, realism becomes a kind of artfully crafted discipline, "a discipline to be learned in the containment of the monstrous and the self-divided energies that make of mankind such an anomaly in a hostile universe" (93). Bruce Johnson, like Levine, views Henchard as Hardy's highest achievement in terms of creating a truly tragic figure, a position he defends in his essay "True Correspondence." The final essay that Bloom has included is J. B. Bullen's "Visual Appearance and Psychological Reality in *The Mayor of Casterbridge*." Bullen applies the clothes philosophy of Carlyle's *Sartor Resartus* to Michael Henchard's world of exterior objects and material surfaces: "Sometimes it is the substantial projection of man's spirit; at other times it is ephemeral and phantasmagoric" (117). Bullen's Carlylian exploration of the interplay of appearances and reality in the world of Casterbridge provides a fitting conclusion to Harold Bloom's collection of essays, all of which open up issues worthy of further consideration and study.

Roger Ebbatson's *The Mayor of Casterbridge* (London: Penguin Books, 1994) follows the same format as most of the books reviewed in this section. The first part provides a history of the novel's composition and publication, followed by an overview of the work's critical reception. Ebbatson provides his own explication of the novel in Part Two, offering snippets of historical background that facilitate interpretation of significant events in the novel. In describing Michael Henchard's almost incomprehensible cruelty toward his wife after leaving the furmity-woman's tent, Ebbatson offers this contextualization of the act: "The fairground possesses a long literary pedigree as a site of folly and recklessness" (57). Ebbatson also places the novel within the context of Hardy's appropriation of what he considered to be the Darwinism view of society and the world. The wheat market symbolizes "the vagaries of chance" (68), and synecdochially suggests the role circumstances play in determining individual destinies. Ebbatson's observations bring into significant focus the tensions between the individual and the community, reflecting the tensions the buried past imposes upon the shifting realities of the present in the novel. An emphasis on Hardy's valuation of enduring community life comprises a major theme throughout this interpretive guide through the novel's intricacies of plot and characterization.

Among books dealing with a single novel, Dale Kramer's assiduously researched and carefully documented *Thomas Hardy, Tess of the d'Urbervilles*, part of the Landmarks of World Literature Series published by Cambridge University Press (1991), provides an excellent reader's guide to one of Hardy's most enduringly popular novels. This slim volume (109 pages) is packed with useful background data that any reader of Hardy's *Tess* should find illuminating and insightful. A major strength of this study is Kramer's thoroughgoing exploration of mid-century rural England's social and cultural milieu, a way of life with which Hardy was intimately familiar and whose prejudices and preconceptions shape so much of Tess Durbeyfield's destiny. Exploring the literary milieu of the age in a chapter devoted to "Some Literary Influences," Kramer recreates for the reader the literary marketplace of Hardy's time: "Novels were selected for publication in mass-circulation magazines on the criterion that they could be read in rural parsonages to young daughters—a standard which several of Hardy's novels did not meet, according to letters from the parson fathers which have survived in publishers' archives'' (25). Kramer goes on to explore parallels between Hardy's treatment of the sexual double standard and the treatment of the same subject in the then popular sub-genre known as the Seduction Novel, especially Elizabeth Gaskell's *Ruth*. Kramer effectively synthesizes and applies his own encyclopedic comprehension of the Victorian zeitgeist when he describes ''a direct line of descent and influence'' upon Hardy that includes Wordsworth, Carlyle, Ruskin, Newman, Arnold, and, finally, Pater. Much is made of the Paterian elements in Hardy's fiction, particularly after a meeting between the two writers in 1886: ''In Walter Pater, Hardy found not only a kindred spirit, but a literary and scientific theorist'' (31). From Pater Hardy derived the impulse toward a kind of literary impressionism, whose light and ethereal evocations suited the narrative portraiture of Tess and her world.

Another book dealing with the same subject is Peter J. Casagrande's *Tess of the d'Urbervilles, Unorthodox Beauty* (New York: Twayne, 1992). In his second chapter dealing with ''The Importance of the Work,'' Casagrande discusses ways in which Hardy took the conventional story of a ruined maid, an antique plot with roots going back to Samuel Richardson's *Clarissa*, and flouted the expectations of critics and the general public. After presenting a brief history of Hardy's novel—its early reception and its significance in the Hardy canon—Casagrande offers a reading of the novel itself. He develops the theme of Hardy's elevation of the ungainly to the level of transcendent beauty and grace, ''Hardy's unorthodox notion that in art, as in life, beauty can dwell with ugliness'' (44). Casagrande develops a theory of the importance of ''beaugliness,'' a neologism he introduces early in his explication of the novel, and one he explores as he describes the evolution of Tess's character, with all of the ambiguities and ambivalent emotions to which she is subjected. For Casagrande, Hardy's *Tess* celebrates an embracing of the world's ugliness through a transcendent sensibility that perceives worth and beauty in the unpleasantness one encounters in the grimy everyday realities. According to this reading of the novel, Angel is ''our intellectual and emotional contemporary'' (110) and his separatist distancing of himself from distasteful realities provides an illuminating contrast to Tess's tragic acceptance.   Another excellent treatise dealing with a single novel is Gary Adelman's *Jude the Obscure, a Paradise of Despair* (New York: Twayne, 1992). Like Kramer, Adelman provides a wealth of historical context and furnishes the reader with a valuable synthesis of critical appraisals, including an informative synopsis of early critical reception of the novel and its effect on the novelist. Approximately two-thirds of the text is taken up with Adelman's own reading of *Jude*, comprising a scholarly composite enriched with numerous references to earlier criticism (from D.H. Lawrence to Terry Eagleton), which he cleverly interlaces with his own. This book may serve as a particularly valuable resource to the classroom instructor seeking to present a balanced approach to conflicting viewpoints concerning the major characters or to disparate takes on Hardy's narrative stance. Adelman considers Hardyan experiments with narratological technique in the novel one of the writer's stellar accomplishments: "Should the author express indignation, farce, or black comedy? . . . Hardy responded to these problems with an ambiguous narrative point of view that is the chief marvel of the novel" (30). Adelman's organization of his analytical commentary is sequential, following the progress of the novel from "Part First" onward, a device that makes his detailing of narrative shifts easy to follow. Describing Jude Fawley's early encounters with Arabella Donn, he offers concrete examples of narrative instability underscoring the novel's permutable narrative focus: "The point of view that constantly shifts from sympathy to mockery, and the occasional switches from close to distant perspective mean that the ethical, social, and philosophical inferences are always changing" (39). A major strength of Adelman's exegetical treatment of *Jude* is the way he contextualizes the novel's narrative tensions, relating these ambivalences to the perceived conflicts between faith and science that plagued Hardy's generation. In his concluding chapter, Adelman draws an interesting parallel between the lives and anxieties of Darwin and Hardy, concerns he sees mirrored in the struggles and frustrations endured by the major protagonists in Hardy's last novel: "Jude and Sue act out the anxiety-ridden dilemmas of late Victorians who face an insentient universe they fear, and cling to a Christian world order that is collapsing" (102). While Adelman effectively contextualizes Hardy's creation of Jude and Sue within the framework of Victorian social and cultural realities, he also charts *Jude*'s significance as an artistic landmark, pinpointing the novel's high profile on the map of that genre's evolving history.

3.

Among collections loosely bound together by a common theme, Margaret Higonnet's collection of essays *The Sense of Sex, Feminist Perspectives on Hardy* (Urbana: U of Illinois P, 1993) provides a thoughtfully-chosen selection of recent criticism with a feminist focus. Inherently revisionist, these critiques range from textual analyses that purport to uncover Hardy's late-Victorian, male-privileging sexism to analytical readings that position Hardy at the vanguard of progressive feminist ideology. An admirably comprehensive survey of the diversity offered, issues of gender and sexuality are dealt with from a wide variety of approaches; Higonnet's inclusion of contradictory perspectives enlivens the collection, making for an invigorating reassessment of gender-awareness in Hardy. In her introductory chapter, Higonnet offers as the collection's unifying premise the notion that Hardy's fiction readily accommodates gender-based analysis: "Hardy tested and subverted constraining gender definitions to an unusual extent" (3). The first three essays in the collection (by Margaret Higonnet, Elizabeth Langland, and Linda Shires) deal with narrative structure and gender, as these relate to the conflict between a given character's inner voice and the narrative voice that seems to encode the norms of society. For example, in "Becoming a Man in *Jude the Obscure*," Langland relates Hardy's genius to his capturing the essence of this conflict: "Part of the novel's brilliance derives from Hardy's ability to represent Jude's battle with the class and gender self-constructions his culture offers him" (32). The ten essays which follow in the collection represent the current gamut of feminist approaches to Hardy. One of the most startlingly provocative and inevitably controversial essays in the collection is James R. Kincaid's "Girl-watching, Child-beating and Other Exercises for Readers of *Jude the Obscure*." Kincaid implicates readers of Hardy's *Jude* as voyeuristically sadistic participants in the torture of the novel's "victims," an extreme point of view the ramifications with which many readers may take issue. The thirteen essays included in this collection represent widely divergent viewpoints, many of which will engender lively debate within the ranks of feminist critics as well as among general readers. At times contentious, challenging, unsettling, nettlesome—Higonnet's collection of essays will elicit its share of descriptive adjectives, but few will find it "dull."

Critical Essays on Thomas Hardy: The Novels edited by Dale Kramer (Boston: G. K. Hall, 1990) provides a wide-ranging sampling of critical postures in a collection of sixteen essays that admirably support Kramer's characterization of Hardy's "continuing and indeed increasing relevance for students of interpretation and of culture" (16). Kramer's introductory essay places the essays which follow within the historical context of Hardy criticism, tracing the development of critical approaches from the late nineteenth century to the present. Following this initiatory survey, the book is divided into two sections, the first dealing with overviews of Hardy's complete novelistic oeuvre, and the second dealing with various novels treated individually. The first essay in the first section, "Hardy and Marxism," by John Goode, is published for the first time in this collection, as is the first essay in the second section, "Emma Hardy's Helping Hand," by Alan Manford, and the final essay in the collection, "Hardy's Comic Tragedy: Jude the Obscure," by Ronald P. Draper. The balance of the essays offered are reprinted chapters from books or journal articles, offering a representative sampling of critical postures and topics, with publication dates ranging from 1960 to 1987.

A recent collection of essays published under the title *Celebrating Thomas Hardy, Insights and Appreciations* (London: Macmillan, 1996), edited by Charles P. C. Pettit, presents eleven lectures given at the July 1994 International Thomas Hardy Conference held in Dorchester, England. These lectures fall into two categories: analyses dealing directly with Hardy's work itself and treatment of Hardy's impact on later writers. Pettit has succeeded admirably in "rounding up the usual suspects" among leading Hardy critics, providing a diverse and stimulating cross-section of contemporary approaches to the novels and poetry. Although all eleven selected lectures by scholars from many parts of the world (specifically, Canada, England, the United States, and Germany) represent some of the most lucid voices in contemporary Hardy criticism, I found Rosemarie Morgan's discussion of Hardy and Toni Morrison notably fresh and original. She cites numerous examples from both writers to illustrate ways in which language articulates and reinforces societal norms and constructs: "[T]he public world of standard speech is indivisible from the public world of standard patriarchal values" (137). Morgan explores ways in which Hardy and Morrison foreground the sexism and classism embedded in the very language they employ, and the ways in which they subvert these formulations. Morgan cites *A Laodicean*'s conclusion as a particularly telling example: "In fact the closure of this novel performs in all ways Hardyan and subversive. There is ambiguity, indeterminacy and more" (156). Gillian Beer's contribution to this collection, "Hardy and Decadence," delineates ways in which Hardy's work seeks congruence with the science of his age, while, at the same time, railing against a despairing shudder in the face of entropy and dissolution. Like many recent critics, Beer suggests that some of the "minor novels" may be less minor than previously assumed. In particular, her reading of *The Well-Beloved* elevates Hardy's last novel published in book form to the status of a concluding, valedictory comic statement regarding artistic endeavor, life and passion: "In *The Well-Beloved* sex is a form of hope, of revival and lightness" (99). Beer's call to "lighten up" may be indicative of a new trend among Hardy critics.

4.

Of special interest to anyone intrigued by application of current critical theory to the works of Thomas Hardy is Marjorie Garson's *Hardy's Fables of Integrity, Woman, Body, Text* (Oxford: Clarendon, 1991), an intellectual roller-coaster ride, complete with de rigueur bumps, jolts, and dips missing from analyses maintaining a safer distance from the poststructuralist "cutting edge." Garson offers critical readings of seven Hardy novels, selecting the works ordinarily classified as "major"—the most popular as well as the most critically acclaimed. Her readings are explicitly Lacanian, which Garson acknowledges in the introduction. Not surprisingly, the focus on text and mythical subtext extends to the classification of the novelist himself as a text: "Indeed I treat Hardy himself less as a real person than as a text" (4). Somatic anxiety, defined as "fear of corporeal dissolution" (1), is a pervasive theme detectable in the novels discussed, according to Garson's reading. Concerns about "the constitution of the self and about its inevitable dissolution" (1) certainly haunt much of Hardy's work, and it is not difficult to relate this "somatic anxiety" to many of the biographical details gleaned from Hardy's autobiographical *Life* and other biographies. (The author's well-documented dread of being physically touched comes to mind as an example of "somatic anxiety"—a fact peculiarly amenable to poststructuralist psycho-analytic reading.) As an example of the way Garson applies psychoanalytic theories of Jacques Lacan to Hardy's novels, I offer a capsule summary of her analysis of *Under the Greenwood Tree*. This reading focuses on the novel's portraiture of "the integrity and dissolution of bodies" (13). The bodies in question are not just the physical bodies of major characters, but comprise, in a much wider sense, corporate bodies consisting of several individual bodies. A primary example is the Mellstock Choir, which is a "body" of singers. The dissolution of this body is, unquestionably, a major subject of the narrative. According to Garson, "[t]here is considerable emphasis on isolated bodily parts; the human body, especially the male body, seems potentially fragmented or disconnected, ready to come apart" (13). A close reading of descriptions of the choir reveals ways in which consciousness of one's individual human body, along with the anxieties that attend its inevitable vulnerability, get projected onto the corporate body of singers. Garson explains: "There is the suggestion of figurative dismemberment as well as emasculation: in losing its 'Dick' . . . the choir might as well lose its *head*" (13). (What *would* Mrs. Grundy say?!) In her analysis of a later novel, *The Return of the Native*, Garson explores the "somatic imagery" (65) embodied in Hardy's enigmatic, primordial evocation of the Heath, which emerges in the novel as a dominant and domineering personality. "The gender of the heath-creature is undecidable" (65). The relationship of major characters to this mythic androgynous entity seems to be intimately associated with their destiny—their perseverance or extinction. The deeply layered, somatically androgynous and mysterious nature of the ancient heath supports a reading geared toward the novel's deeper mythic substrata. While some of Garson's projected images of male and female bodily characteristics onto inanimate nature may seem strained, her readings are often provocative and arresting. She acknowledges the limitations of this kind of theorizing in her concluding chapter: "Not all of Hardy's fiction is equally amenable to the kind of analysis I have attempted" (179). A reading which integrates psychic/mythic land-scapes with physical components of the fe/male human body, human socie-ties, and physical milieux may seem an ill-cobbled, visionary chimera to some. However, the audacious verve with which Garson makes her case has the capacity to represent and re-present a familiar literary landscape through an unfamiliar interpretive lens.

Hardy and the Erotic by T. R. Wright (London: Macmillan, 1989) also sets out to test some contemporary critical theories of literature by applying them to Hardy's novels. His opening chapter, dealing with "Wessexuality," introduces the notion that "[Hardy's] world, it might be argued, is at least half-comprised of libido" (1). Emphasizing the frequently voyeuristic character of narrative description in Hardy, Wright suggests that Hardy's work is particularly susceptible to Lacanian analysis: "What seems particularly appropriate to Hardy in Lacanian theory is the emphasis placed upon the visual . . . the lure of the gaze" (16). Like Marjorie Garson, Wright treats Hardy's accounts of his own life as a kind of fiction, a fiction he explores in the book's second chapter. Throughout this analysis of the erotic and the illusory nature of the objects of erotic desire, Wright traces the development of Hardy's fictive imagination, and, consistent with a recurrent trend among recent critics, focuses particularly on some of the so-called "minor novels." Wright's reading displays explicit allegiance to current critical theory in a number of passages: "A whole critical doctrine opposed to the fixation of meaning, the premature foreclosure of the text, celebrates the analogy between the reading and the sexual act" (13). (Teachers of required undergraduate literature courses may find mentioning the alleged link between the sexual act and the comparatively sedate process of reading a method of enlivening class discussion!) The focus of Wright's monograph throughout is "recognition of the indissoluble link between art and desire" (19), an association he traces through an exploration of underlying eroticism driving plot structure and character motivation from the earliest novels through a final chapter dealing with Hardy's *The Well-Beloved*, a valedictory recognition of the link between the erotic imagination and the creative impulse.

Peter Widdowson's *On Thomas Hardy: Late Essays and Earlier* (London: Macmillan, 1998) offers an overview of the critic's own induction into the arcana of contemporary critical theory. "Suffice to say here, that both Hardy and Hardy studies have been changed out of all recognition in the course of the theorization of criticism, and so too has the nature of the mystification in which he nevertheless continues to envelop me" (9). In the collection's introduction, Widdowson describes how his earlier tradition-bound exegetical treatment of Hardy (begun around the time of his first teaching assignment in Sweden in 1968) has evolved, and "is today transmogrified into a Deconstructionist *avant la lettre* . . . " (9). The seven essays he has included encompass a much shorter time span (1983–1997). The focus on indeterminacy which characterizes the work of so many critical theorists of the last two or three decades pervades Widdowson's readings of *The Hand of Ethelberta, A Laodicean, Tess,* and *Jude,* the four novels he has elected to dissect in this book. Each of Widdowson's essays is grounded in the assumption that all readings are provisional, inevitably signifying and illuminating some historical/social context. According to Widdowson, the so-called "minor novels" lend themselves particularly well to this kind of reading. Hence, Hardy's *Hand of Ethelberta* can be read as a truer account of the life of the son of Jemima Hand (the significance of the name in the title has been noted before) than the official biography written by Hardy and attributed to Florence Emily Hardy. Widdowson's fourth essay offers a fresh reading of a work tradition- ally considered inferior, Hardy's *A Laodicean*. Widdowson views Hardy's novel dealing with social, religious and cultural backsliding as "at once a sophisticated, self-conscious mockery of the misrepresentations implicit in a realism which purports to 'tell things as they really are,' and a further satire on the artifice/iality of a class system in volatile transition" (7). In a similar mode, Widdowson reads *Tess*, a novel often praised for its tragic realism, as a critique of the realist tradition—a novel in which "representation becomes *mis*representation" (123). This misrepresenting process is presumed to domi- nate the narrative perspective throughout the novel, and it is through these mispresentations that "the dominant ideology and culture sentence us all to lives of false being" (123). Widdowson's concluding chapter on *Jude* classi- fies Hardy's late novel as satire; he interprets Arabella's role as crucial to an understanding of the novel's primary focus. Deconstructionist patois aside, Widdowson's radical reassessments of Hardy's work and his world are often bracingly fresh and provocative.

An earlier monograph, *Hardy in History, a Study in Literary Sociology* (London: Routledge, 1989) provides an interesting introduction to the evolu- tion of Widdowson's critical posture. The relationship between social norms and literature is explored in depth by Widdowson, as he attempts to articulate a sociology of literature. Early in this study, he explores ways in which the Hardy canon itself reflects social values among critics and the reading public. For example, Widdowson challenges the notion that *Tess* is superior to *The Hand of Ethelberta*, a daring position which he defends admirably. He main- tains that Hardy's "failures of realist decorum" (218) are not failures at all, but merely reflect critical tastes that have prevailed for decades and which are employed to shape the Hardyan canon. "It seems to me quite absurd to purport to be discussing a writer's 'work,' if one deletes from it substantial amounts of its constituent discourse" (218). For Widdowson, the allegedly unrealistic elements in Hardy's portrayal of Ethelberta Chickerel are neces- sary components in his "demystification of class and gender relations" (218). His arguments for reassessment of Hardy's canon will strike many readers as cogent and compelling.

5.

Anyone interested in following the stages of development through which Hardy's work passed as he advanced from his insecure beginnings toward the summit of his literary career will be enthralled by Simon Gatrell's *Hardy the Creator, a Textual Biography* (Oxford: Clarendon, 1988). This book provides a detailed account of the interactive dynamic between a writer who tended to chafe against the boundaries imposed by popular taste and the incursive editorial bowdlerizations negotiated by Grundy-sensitive publishers. In his preface, Gatrell defends the value of understanding this process: "No reading is so rich as that which proceeds from a full awareness of the work's development" (viii). One comes away from this study sensitized to the fluidity of creative process, gained from Gatrell's exhaustive combing through an avalanche of archival minutiae. The fortuitous result is a kind of "insider's view" of the evolution of particular novels, and of Hardy's entire oeuvre. Gatrell traces in great detail the metamorphic process that shaped individual works, in some cases outlining the full history of a novel from initial serialization in a popular (and usually constrictively prudish) magazine through further tampering and/or polishing required for rendering a narrative suitable for a three-volume edition hungrily anticipated by the immensely lucrative lending libraries of Hardy's day. Gatrell's calling his book a biography is singularly appropriate, since his account of the development of a text or collection of texts does, indeed, constitute a "life." Like any other biographer, Gatrell presents a history, not of an individual man called Thomas Hardy, but of a palpable body of work conceived and nurtured, from birth to maturity, by Hardy and his editors. The gradual evolution of Hardy's Wessex in the writer's mind is a specific focus in chapter seven, which deals with the first collected edition of Hardy's novels published from 1895 to 1897. This chapter, like the rest of Gatrell's study, will prove invaluable to scholars specializing in textual studies or the history of publishing from the late nineteenth century onward. Gatrell's meticulously detailed chronicling of the creative process through which Hardy's fictive world developed will also be of considerable worth to fiction writers and/or anyone intrigued by the inner workings of a truly creative mind and the challenges of accommodation to the outer world's demands, limitations and expectations.

Like Simon Gatrell, James Gibson focuses primarily on Hardy's literary career in *Thomas Hardy, a Literary Life* (London: Macmillan, 1996), part of the Literary Lives series produced under the general editorship of Richard Dutton. Gibson's literary biography differs from Gatrell's in that the emphasis centers around the writer's personal development as it relates to his artistic development. In his preface, Gibson acknowledges that Michael Millgate's *Thomas Hardy: A Biography* (New York: Random, 1982) remains the definitive biography. Approximately one-third the length of Millgate's all-inclusive chronicle, Gibson's pared down summary of Hardy's literary life "cuts to the chase" for those primarily interested in Hardy's development as a writer; Gibson devotes very little space to family background and influences other than literary. The second chapter, "Phase the Second: The Novelist (1870–97)" deals extensively with literary influences. Gibson places Hardy's first published novel, *Desperate Remedies*, within the context of the popular "whodunnit?" tradition. He touches upon all of the primary mentors who helped shape Hardy's growth as a fiction writer, always emphasizing Hardy's evolution as a skilled and capable novelist, managing to craft his fiction in a manner consistent with the public's taste, while, at the same time, breaking new ground as a creative artist. Gibson's last chapter, "Phase the Third: The Poet (1898–1928)," summarizes Hardy's abandonment of novel-writing and his successful attempt to establish a reputation as a poet, albeit late in life. In Gibson's words: "Hardy was determined to go out, as he had begun, still challenging complacency and expressing his own realistic, honest view of life" (194).

Some recent biographical studies focus on one particular aspect of Hardy's literary career. His lifelong fascination with the theater is the subject of Keith Wilson's *Thomas Hardy on Stage* (London: Macmillan, 1995), a carefully researched monograph filled with interesting minutiae related to late-Victorian theatrical conventions and production values, as well as revealing anecdotal accounts of Hardy's diffident attitude toward theatrical performances of his own work. During the period when Hardy was publishing his novels (1871–1897), he often displayed considerable disdain toward the idea of having his work adapted for the stage, and Wilson explores some of the reasons for this disaffection toward the commercial theater of the late Victorian period. As with so many of his disclaimers and disinclinations, Hardy's own behavior in this regard was inconsistent with his written correspondence and public statements. Hardy was an avid playgoer, especially during his annual sojourns to London when "the season" was in full swing. Wilson presents in chronological order, the stages of development through which Hardy passed as his attitude toward commercial theatrical performance of his work softened in later years. Wilson devotes two chapters to Hardy's relationship with The Hardy Players of Dorchester, providing insights into the kinds of concerns Hardy had with issues such as casting, insertion of additional dialogue into his work, and gratuitous tampering with the novels' original plot structures or eccentricities associated with characters. Apparently, Hardy had a particular concern with tampering that caricatured his "rustics." Wilson's last chapter deals with the role of Tess as realized on the stage in both Dorchester and London. By 1924 Hardy was in his eighties and an international celebrity. The history surrounding his selection of the actress Gertrude Bugler to play the role of Tess, and his involvement in adaptation of the novel provides a kind of behind-the-scenes snapshot of the process of bringing a popular novel to the English stage in the 1920s. In particular, I found Wilson's account of Hardy's concern with the distinction between amateur and professional production of interest. Overall, this volume offers a close-up portrait of a major novelist's adaptation to the theater, chronicling an important aspect of Hardy's life and career.

While not biographical in any strict sense of the term, Edward Neill's *Trial by Ordeal, Thomas Hardy and the Critics* (Columbia, South Carolina: Camden House, 1999) does describe the manner in which Hardy criticism has taken on a ''life'' of its own. His critical assessment of Hardy's critics—often acerbic but always entertaining and provocative—provides an informative and quite comprehensive survey of a vast body of work which Neill warns ''might be called 'fast food' produced by critical processings'' (xi). Neill's grasp of current Hardy criticism, ranging from the cautiously conservative to the most radical outer limits of poststructuralist arcana, is dazzlingly encyclopedic. He contextualizes current theories about Hardy's significance within the historical framework of critical assessments, both positive and negative, that prevailed during Hardy's lifetime and when Hardy's stature was further enhanced by homage paid by literary progeny such as D. H. Lawrence and his generation. Neill's ''trial'' of the Hardyan tribunal provides an excellent overview of the current state of Hardy criticism, and of how the ''Hardy industry'' grew and prospered. One may not always agree with Neill's assessments, which in some cases seem hastily dismissive, but his roster of major critical voices is compendious and impressive.

While many Hardy scholars still consider Michael Millgate's monumentally comprehensive *Thomas Hardy, a Biography* definitive and unsurpassed, no review of recent Hardy studies would be complete without mention of the more recent full-length biography (886 pages), *Thomas Hardy* by Martin Seymour-Smith (London: Bloomsbury, 1994). Seymour-Smith acknowledges Millgate's equally compendious tome throughout this work, particularly when he takes issue with Millgate's rendering of some significant event. The instances of an alternate reading of some detail in Hardy's personal or professional life are too numerous to document in this review. Suffice it to say that, given Hardy's secretive nature and the strictures of Victorian prudery, contradictory speculations about the possibility that Emma Gifford believed herself pregnant prior to Hardy's proposal of marriage or that Hardy may have been impotent during some period in his life remain unresolvable. Seymour-Smith's biography is written in a pleasing, readable style, following the progress of Hardy's personal life and his development as a literary artist. Events are presented in chronological order, and this recording of Hardy's life, like the Millgate biography, provides a useful introduction to the man, his heritage, and the world he created.

6.

Taking his title from Pope's *Essay on Man*, Simon Gatrell has assembled in *Thomas Hardy and the Proper Study of Mankind* (Charlottesville: UP of

Virginia, 1993) a collection of his essays which cluster around a familiar Hardyan theme—the relation between the natural environment and human beings whose lives foreground Hardy's incursive landscapes. In contrast with Garson's treatment of Hardy the novelist as "a text," Gatrell adopts the more traditional posture, assuming that historical and canonic contextualization is both realizable and worth the attempt. Linking Hardy with Alexander Pope may seem far-fetched at first blush, but the book's introductory preface qualifies the comparison: "In his examination of humankind Pope considers how individuals stand in relation to divine power, to Nature, and to each other . . ." (2). Gatrell makes the point that Hardy takes up the same issues in his novels, but "any answers to such fundamental questions that are derivable from Hardy's fiction are often provisional and contradictory" (2). A recurrent theme that runs through this assessment of mankind's "proper study" according to Hardy is the significance of community life, a disappearing phenomenon threatened by urbanization. The dissolution of the Mellstock Choir is an example of loss through usurpation of community rituals that sustain essential bonds vital to a harmonious, functional society. In his second chapter, "Hardy's Dances," Gatrell relates Hardy's personal history to the author's fascination with dance, and provides examples from the novels of the role dance plays in the rural societies which Hardy portrays so vividly. The role of dance as metaphor in several major works is viewed as an indicator of the individual's significance within that society: "We have been considering dance as an epitome of aspects of society, and there is no doubt that Hardy was aware of the potential of dance as social indicator, even as social criticism" (34). Exploring the decline of the traditional rural community is central to any consideration of Hardy's work, according to Gatrell. His chapter devoted to analysis of *Jude*, "Sex, Marriage and the Decline of Traditional Community in *Jude the Obscure*" articulates the would-be scholar's tragedy as his failed search for "a community to sustain the individual through lovingkindness" (171). In his last chapter, Gatrell summarizes Hardy's *The Dynasts* along with other works in terms of frustrated yearning for a kind of global community, perhaps realizable in some far-off future epoch only vaguely perceived by Hardy the meliorist.

Thomas Hardy in Our Time by Robert Langbaum (London: Macmillan, 1995) combines genre classification with insightful psychoanalytic readings of Hardy's fictions, delineating the novelist's effect on the evolution of the novel in the twentieth century. In his exploration of the latter phenomenon, Langbaum highlights the psychological complexity of Hardy's major characters to support his argument relating Hardy's persistent popularity to the novelist's insights into the workings of the unconscious. Citing the influence Hardy had on D. H. Lawrence, Langbaum maintains that "Hardy is important in the history of the English novel because he is the first to elaborate the sphere of unconscious motivation'' (15). The relationship between the natural world and human perception of the natural world in Hardy's novels is a central theme elucidated by Langbaum in his chapter entitled "Versions of Pastoral." The distinction between poetry and prose is blurred: "*The Return of the Native* is Hardy's greatest nature poem" (64). Langbaum views Hardy's pastoralism as a subversion of the pastoral tradition and a post-Darwinian critique of idealism. He points out that in an anti-pastoral world, heroes such as Giles Winterborne, Clym Yeobright and Angel Clare all fail the women who love them. A final chapter, "The Minimisation of Sexuality," concludes with an insightful reading of *The Well-Beloved*, a novel that has been traditionally slighted by critics and one that, in my opinion, is only now beginning to achieve the recognition it merits in the Hardy canon. Like so many of Hardy's male characters, the anti-hero/artist in Hardy's last published novel " is spoiled by the excessive imagination and inadequate sexuality which make him unable to attend sufficiently to the individual woman before him" (152). According to Langbaum, Hardy's persistent popularity in our own time owes much to his prescient modernity—his rejection of essentialist-based definitions of gender, social and sexual propriety, as well as the proper domains of science and faith. No advocate of crass, despiritualized materialism, Hardy remains for Langbaum, like Jocelyn Pierston, a time-chidden, but undefeated proponent of "a proper balance between the ideal and the real" (155).

Two recent studies exploring Hardy's tortured relationship with the complex issue of lapsed religious faith are *Thomas Hardy and His God: a Liturgy of Unbelief* by Deborah L. Collins (London: Macmillan, 1990) and Jan Jedrzejewski's *Thomas Hardy and the Church* (London: Macmillan, 1996). Collins offers a dialogic reading of both Hardy's oeuvre and his career, emphasizing what she perceives to be a Bakhtinian polyphony, pervading not only the novels, poetry, short stories and *The Dynasts*, but also Hardy's surviving notebooks and letters, all of which she quotes extensively. Collins traces the history of Hardy's intellectual development from the biblical literalism and faithful church attendance of his early youth through his belief-shattering grapplings with the century's two great threats to traditional doctrines of Scriptural inerrancy: the Darwinian challenge to a naive reading of Genesis and the skeptical textual parsings of the age's "higher critics." According to Collins, shifting dialogic perspectives discernible throughout Hardy's work center around the disaffected churchman's tenacious adherence to the underlying principles of Christian morality: "Hardy had no quarrel with a more practical brand of Christianity in which the teachings of Christ are accepted as excellent moral instruction, but neither had he patience with creeds which offered false hopes of eternal life in exchange for obedience" (158). The book's concluding chapter presents evidence from Hardy's later life that indicate a tentative resolution of the conflicts underlying Hardy's

Laodicean angst, suggesting that his doctrine of the Immanent Will may be viewed as a melding of the evolutionary meliorist mindset with an emergent secularized faith in the future of humankind. This, however, has little to do with traditional hope of individual salvation or visions of the soul's immortality.

Jedrzejewski's monograph focuses on Hardy's lifelong lover's quarrel with the trappings and traditions specific to the Church of England, as Hardy experienced the power and allure of that imposing institution. The first chapter outlines Hardy's religious biography, describing his parents' High Church affiliation and his father's playing of sacred music at Stinsford Church. Hardy's cutting free from the moorings of traditional orthodoxy is described as a gradual process. Jedrzejewski documents this drift through a careful cataloging of Hardy's autodidactic readings of "the classics of mid-nineteenth-century English thought" (29), classics which tended toward agnosticism and the contextualization of Christianity within a burgeoning pluralistic consciousness. Following the biographical chapter, Jedrzejewski explores Hardy's treatment of church-related motifs in his work. He devotes a chapter to each of the following familiar subjects: church architecture, liturgical spectacle, and the character of the clergy. Like Collins, Jedrzejewski adopts a viewpoint that attempts to accommodate the complexity of Hardy's emotionally charged attraction/revulsion toward the accoutrements of religious worship. This viewpoint rejects the glib assumption that Hardy's agnosticism was uncomplicated and without reservation. This study offers many examples of how church architecture looms large in some of Hardy's novels, while functioning as a melancholy backdrop in others. The chapter entitled "Religion as Spectacle" further explores Hardy's deeply ingrained responsiveness to the beauty and texture of religious observance, while repudiating the narrowness of orthodox creeds. Similarly, the chapter dealing with Hardy's assessment of the English clergy demonstrates his veneration of the humanistic values they sometimes represent, while satirizing their less appealing characteristics. In his concluding chapter, Jedrzejewski summarizes Hardy's relationship with the church in terms of a kind of evolutionary process, consisting of early-life orthodoxy followed by an increasing attitude of bitterness that seems to deepen as one proceeds through the novels, an attitude whose harshness appears to wane, however, in some of Hardy's later poetry. Jedrzejewski's study provides compelling evidence that Hardy the skeptic never quite severed his emotional ties to his church's external trappings, however irrelevant those archaic relics might appear within the context of modern life.

Peter J. Casagrande's *Hardy's Influence on the Modern Novel* (London: Macmillan, 1987) assesses the impact of Hardy's novels on novelists of succeeding generations. That D. H. Lawrence was profoundly affected by his reading of Hardy's work is well documented in his well-known *Study of*

Hardy first published in 1914. Casagrande describes Lawrence's awareness of significant parallels between the depiction of a close mother-son relationship in *Sons and Lovers* and the relationship between Clym Yeobright and Mrs. Yeobright in *Return of the Native*. He also explores the similarities and differences between the complicated male/female relationships in *Jude* and *Tess* and those we encounter in Lawrence's *Women in Love*. Hardy's influence on a wide range of twentieth-century writers is explored extensively throughout the book. He makes much of the fact that in France Marcel Proust and Alain-Fournier were great admirers of Hardy's work. According to Casagrande, the French attitude towards Hardy was less critical than the British: "[T]hey sympathized with, even embraced, Hardy's heterodoxy, both religious and emotional" (149). Among American writers, traces of Hardyan influence can be found among some of the greatest early twentieth-century literary figures, from Theodore Dreiser to Sherwood Anderson, Ellen Glasgow, and William Faulkner. Even those who derided Hardy's much-maligned "pessimism" admired his realism and sharply-drawn portraiture of individual characters in his novels. The parallels between Faulkner's Yoknapatawpha County and Hardy's Wessex have been noted by many critics, and Faulkner himself readily acknowledged his debt to the earlier novelist. Casagrande concludes his study by drawing an analogy between the relationship of Hardy to his literary successors and a nurturing parent whose offspring prove capable of exceeding the guiding example they will ultimately out-distance.

While I have generally omitted references to books that include Hardy within the context of a broader subject, I wish to call special attention to Alison Byerly's illuminating *Realism, Representation and the Arts in Nineteenth-Century Literature* (Cambridge: Cambridge UP, 1997). Hardy's affinity for the "sister arts," most notably music, painting, architecture, and the theater, is well documented and has been treated elsewhere in scrupulous detail. Byerly's study is unique among these critiques in that she deals explicitly with Hardy's deliberate allusions to related art forms, concluding with some interesting insights into Hardyan resonance with the Aestheticism that coincided with the production of his more mature work of the 1880s and 1890s. Byerly interweaves biographical anecdotes regarding Hardy's abiding interest in specific works of art with analyses of his allusive incorporation of these creations into his work. Traditionally, critics have admired Hardy's pictorial style, but have shuddered at his strained and often-pedantic references to specific productions: "The critics who praise Hardy's pictorialism, however, are not impressed by his allusions to actual paintings" (151). His sensitivity to light and shadow in some of his most compelling descriptive passages are explored in detail by Byerly, who informs us that J.M.W. Turner was the painter whom Hardy most admired—a fact not difficult to relate to his "impressionistic" style of writing. Hardy's association with the theater, which increased with his growing popularity after publication of *Far from the Madding Crowd*, is another aspect of his personal history which Byerly relates to his work as a novelist. She offers interesting readings of some key passages in Hardy in which an event charged with theatricality signals the relationship of a major character to the social environment of the novel. Eustacia Vye's participation in the mummers' play in *Return of the Native* and the horrendous skimmity ride in *The Mayor of Casterbridge* , for example, represent false social values, "an artificial standard of value that is contrasted with the gold standard embodied in the arts of painting, music, and architecture . . ." (165). In contrast with theater, music is for Hardy a "truer" art form, closely associated with daily functions and deep-rooted rituals, expressive of natural rhythms associated with everyday activities. Byerly cites the tranquility of the Mellstock Choir's music, in contrast with the incursions of more modern forms of church music in *Under the Greenwood Tree*, as an example of Hardy's assessment of music's role within the societies he portrays. There is good and bad art, and that which approximates nature is the superior form, within the context of Hardy's world. Likewise, in the field of architecture, it is the functional forms that Hardy prizes, while the excessively ornamented and effete clumsily linked to the modern (like the Stancy Castle of *A Laodicean* hastily equipped with a jerry-built telegraphic connection) suggests dysfunction and conflicting aesthetic values.

Once again invoking Ecclesiastes (in a reference Hardy would have immediately recognized), "Let us hear the conclusion of the whole matter" (12:13). My conclusion is that the "Hardy industry" remains hardy (to borrow one of his favorite puns)! Any attempt to survey its scope must, perforce, be selective and, to some degree, idiosyncratic. Perhaps extensive reading of poststructuralist critics informs my conclusion that the selections reveal as much about the selector as the selected. Arbitrary elisions and inadvertent omissions notwithstanding, I hope the range and diversity covered in this survey suggest that any door facilitating access to the richly textured world of Hardy's creative imagination constitutes a legitimate port of entry—one from which the individual reader may then wander at will from trodden paths.

INDEX

Ackroyd, Peter, 198, 202
Adelman, Gary, *Jude the Obscure*, 43–74
Afnan, Elham, 424–25
Aiken, Conrad, 306
Alain-Fournier, 486
Alter, Robert, 355
Andrews, Malcolm, "Dickens, Washington Irving, and English National Identity," 1–16; ed., *The Pickwick Papers*, 394
Armstrong, Karen, *In the Beginning*, 362
Armstrong, Nancy, 347 n.1
Arnold, Matthew, *Culture and Anarchy*, 210
Austen, Jane
    Persuasion, 370, 371
    Pride and Prejudice, 299 n.13
    Sense and Sensibility, 370, 371
Australia, 32–33
Ayres, Brenda, *Dissenting Women in Dickens's Novels: The Subversion of Domestic Ideology*, 398–99

Bakhtin, Mikhail, 294, 378–79, 380

Baldridge, Cates, 445
Barraclas, Rafael, 439–40
Barthes, Roland, 417–18
Baumgarten, Murray, 450
Bedient, Calvin, 305–06, 307, 309, 313, 314, 315, 317
Beer, Gillian, *Darwin's Plots*, 352, 358, 476
Benjamin, Walter, 397, 397, 445
Berger, John, *Ways of Seeing*, 272, 291
Besant, Annie, 373–74
Bible, 419–22
Binfield, Clyde, 223
Black, Barbara, 442
Bloom, Harold, ed., *Thomas Hardy's "The Mayor of Casterbridge,"* 471–72
Boheemen-Saaf, Christine Von, 438
Branca, Patricia, 378, 379
Brantlinger, Patrick, 427
    The Reading Lesson, 433
Brattin, Joel, "'Let me pause once more': Dickens's Manuscript Revisions in

the Retrospective Chapters of *David Copperfield*," 412; "'I will not have my words misconstrued': The Text of *Our Mutual Friend*," 412–13

British Museum, 7–8

Brontë, Charlotte, 323–24
  Jane Eyre, 323–24, 326–35
  Villette, 323–24, 326–35

Brontë, Emily, *Wuthering Heights*, 168–69

Brooks, Cleanth, 313, 315–16, 317

Browne, Hablot K., 369, 402

Bull, John, 8–9, 10

Bull, Thomas, Dr., *Hints to Mothers*, 374

Bullen, J. B., 471–72

Bunyan, John, *Pilgrim's Progress*, 212–13

Buxton, Thomas Fowell (Niger expedition, 1841), 210–11

Byerly, Alison, *Realism, Representation and the Arts in Nineteenth-Century Literature*, 486–87

Byron, George Gordon Byron, 6th baron, *Childe Harold's Pilgrimage*, 5

Canning, George, 428–29

Caren, Timothy J., 435

Carey, Peter, *Jack Maggs*, 450

Carlyle, Thomas
  French Revolution, The, 166, 188, 443
  Latter-Day Pamphlets, 204, 237
  Nigger Question, The, 204
  Sartor Resartus, 471–72

Casagrande, Peter J.
  Tess of the d'Urbervilles, 473
  Hardy's Influence on the Modern Novel, 485–86

Charles Dickens Encyclopedia, comp. Michael and Mollie Hardwick, 388–89

Chalmers, Thomas (evangelist), 239–41, 258–59

Chartist uprisings, 198

Chavasse, Dr. Pye Henry, *Ladies' Family Physician*, 374–75

Chesterfield, Philip Dormer Stanhope, 4th earl of, *Letters to His Son*, 10

Chesterton, George, 21

Chesterton, G. K., 415

Chodorow, Nancy, 272

Clark, Joseph Clayton (illustrator), 450

Cohen, Monica, *Professional Domesticity and the Victorian Novel*, 395

Coldbath Fields (prison), 21

Coleridge, Samuel Taylor, 279, 280, 281

Colligan, Collette, "Raising the House Tops: Sexual Surveillance in Charles Dickens's *Dombey and Son*," 99–144

Collins, Deborah L., *Thomas Hardy and His God*, 484–85

Collins, Philip, 19, 387–88
  Dickens and Crime, 18, 226 n.9, 317
  Critical Commentary on Dickens's "Bleak House," 198

Collins, Wilkie, *The Woman in White*, 282

Cornhill Magazine, 470

Cotsell, Michael, 443–44, 446

Cox, Don Richard, *Charles Dickens's "The Mystery of Edwin Drood": An Annotated Bibliography*, 390–91

Crawford, Robert, 310

Crimean War (1853–56), 196

Crystal, Palace, 196, 225 n.1

Cummings, Katherine, 439

Darwin, Charles, 270, 284, 289, 361, 450
  Descent of Man, 358
  Origin of Species, 270–71, 282–83, 352, 355, 357–58, 448

Davis, Paul, *Charles Dickens A to Z*, 388, 390

Defoe, Daniel, *Robinson Crusoe*, 259–60

Derrida, Jacques, 274, 277, 274, 278–79, 298 n.8, 437

Dever, Carolyn, *Death and the Mother from Dickens to Freud: Victorian Fiction and the Anxiety of Origins*, 404–05

Dickens [Burnett], Fanny, 212

Dickens, Catherine, 4, 378

Dickens, Charles, in America, 3–4; on British institutional disorder and corruption (*Bleak House*), 195–99, 200–201, 224–25; (*Little Dorrit*), 236–42; childhood, Victorian theories of, 83–94; Christmas, the invention of, 4–5; CD on the Church of England, 214–21; CD on debt, 18, 38 n.26, 246; CD on debtors' prisons and penal reform (Fleet, Marshalsea), 17–36, 255–57, 259–61; CD on evangelical vengeance, sin, and redemption, 242–56; growth, novel of (*bildungsroman*), 163–90; hereditary determinism, 86–89; human body, CD's frankness about, 145–58; Irving, Washington, CD's friendship with, 1–16; Jews, CD's attitudes toward, 206, 434; Malthusian economist, CD as , 238–39; Metropolitan Police, 226 n.9, 432–33; Poor Laws and debt, CD on, 18, 41, 46; pregnancy, CD's satire on prudish Victorian attitudes about, 367–80; CD on prostitution and illegitimate offspring, 67–77; religious Dissent and Victorian status quo, CD on, 195–225; sexuality of Paul Dombey, 101–02, 113–18; CD on speculation as disease, 235–36, "uncivilized" colonials, CD's views on, 226–27 n.9; Warren's Blacking factory, 19, 22, 23, 24, 46, 263 n.15; *Waste Land, Our Mutual Friend* as source of Eliot's, 303–19

  Works written or edited by:
  All the Year Round, 271, 392, 393

American Notes, 19, 24, 35, 36, 443

Barnaby Rudge, 35, 427–28

Bleak House, 6–7, 36, 146, 147, 150, 153, 154–55, 157–58, 163–90, 195–225, 236, 243, 294, 398, 404–05, 419, 421, 425, 429–30, 434

Chimes, The, 410, 432

Christmas Carol, A, 4, 153, 243, 431–32

Christmas Stories, 431–32

Cricket on the Hearth, The, 432

Collected Papers (1937), 37 n.9

David Copperfield, 23, 148, 150, 167, 177, 196, 243, 392, 400–401, 407, 412, 421, 425–26

Dombey and Son, 99–144, 147, 149, 150, 397, 400

Great Expectations, 66, 177, 282, 283, 447–49

Hard Times, 69, 181, 403–04, 439–41

Haunted Man, The, 431

Household Words, 208, 392, 432–33

Letters, 37 n.11, 55, 392

Little Dorrit, 19, 35, 36, 38 n.26, 55, 149, 185,-86, 196, 233–61, 292, 294, 295, 395, 397, 400, 413, 429–30, 441–42

Martin Chuzzlewit, 90, 243, 292, 367–85, 403, 413, 420, 430–31

Master Humphrey's Clock, 8

Mystery of Edwin Drood, The, 18

Nicholas Nickleby, 4, 45, 53, 430 "Nurse's Stories," 148

Old Curiosity Shop, The, 2, 4, 31, 86–87, 150, 156, 243

Oliver Twist, 4, 20, 35, 41–56,
  61–81, 83–98, 418, 420,
  433–34,
Our Mutual Friend, 9, 147,
  148–49, 154, 191 n.14,
  269, 270, 282–96, 303–19,
  402, 413, 423, 449
Pickwick Papers, The, 1, 3, 4,
  10, 14, 17–39, 53, 149,
  196, 197–243, 204, 206,
  394
Pictures from Italy, 393
Sketches by Boz, 7–8, 42
  "Some Recollections of
  Mortality," 67
Sunday under Three Heads,
  202, 205–06, 209, 214
Tale of Two Cities, A, 19, 24,
  35, 36, 86, 198, 422, 427,
  442–47
  Uncommercial Traveller, The,
  148, 226 n.3, 393, 447
Dickens Dictionary, The, (Alex Philip
  and Lawrence Gadd), 388
Dickens Index, The (Bentley, Slater and
  Burgis), 388, 390
Dickens on Disk, 391
Dickensian, The, 424
Dransfield, Scott, 427–28
Draper, Ronald P., 475
Dresner, Samuel, 353
Drew, John M. L., 447
Dubberke, Ray, "Dickens's Favorite
  Detective," 410
Dunn, Richard J., 217

Easson, Angus, 18, 34–35
Ebbatson, Roger, ed., *The Mayor of
  Casterbridge*, 472
Eliot, George
  Daniel Deronda, 323–24,
    335–49
  Middlemarch, 323–24,
    335–49, 368
  Adam Bede, 371–72

Eliot, T. S., 303
  Waste Land, The, 303–19
Edgecomb, Rodney Stenning, 428–29
Epstein, Norrie, *The Friendly Dickens*,
  389
Ermarth, Elizabeth Deeds, 325
Evans, David Morier, 236–37
Everyone in Dickens (Newlin), 389
Everything in Dickens (Newlin), 389
Ewen, Stuart, 290

Fahnestock, Jeanne, 325
Farkas, Carol-Ann, "Beauty is as Beauty
  Does: Action and Appearance in
  Brontë and Eliot," 323–49
Faymanville, Carmen, 407
Federico, Annette, "Dickens and
  Disgust," 145–62
  *Masculine Identity in Hardy
    and Gissing*, 469
Field, Kate, *Pen Photographs of Charles
  Dickens's Readings: Taken from
  Life*, 407
Fielding, Henry, *Tom Jones*, 368, 370
Fisher King (Grail), 315–16
Fleet prison, 18–20, 25–31, 32
Fletcher, Pauline, "Bacchus in Kersey:
  Dickens and the Classics," 409
Ford, George, 197
Forster, John, 23, 24, 214
Foucault, Michel, 18, 33, 270, 279–80,
  282, 290,
  History of Sexuality, 279
Frank, Lawrence, 309–10, 444
Freud, Sigmund, 245, 270, 273–74
Fromm, Erich, 247

Gallup, Donald, 304
Garlock, David, "Recent Studies in
  Thomas Hardy's Fiction
  1987–99," 465–87
Garson, Marjorie, *Hardy's Fables of
  Integrity, Woman, Body, Text*,
  476–77

Gatrell, Simon, *Hardy the Creator, a Textual Biography*, 480; *Thomas Hardy and the Proper Study of Mankind*, 482–83
Genesis, 351–55, 357, 361–63
Gibbon, Edward, *Decline and Fall of the Roman Empire*, 310, 311
Gibson, James, *Thomas Hardy, a Literary Life*, 480–81
Giffone, Anthony, 440
Gilfillan, Ross, *The Snake-Oil Dickens Man, 450–51*
Gillespie, Nick, "Darwin and Dickens," 450
Gindele, Karen C., "Desire and Deconstruction: Reclaiming Centers," 269–301
Gissing, George, *The Odd Women*, 361
Godwin, William, *Caleb Williams*, 20
Goethe, Johann Wolfgang von, 264 n.21
Goldberg, Michael, 444
Goode, John, 475
Googins, Robert, 449–50
Gordon, Lyndall, 305, 315, 316
Grass, Sean C., "Pickwick, the Past, and the Prison," 17–39
Great Exhibition (1851), 196
Greg, W. R., 356
Gregor, Ian, 471
Grosz, Elizabeth, *Volatile Bodies*, 296 n.1
Gurney, Michael, 235–36

Hake, Stephen 428
Hale, Keith, "Doing the Police in Different Voices: The Search for Identity in Dust Heaps and Waste Lands," 303–22
Halevi-Wise, Yael, "Little Dorrit's Story: A Window into the Novel," 413
Hardy, Thomas, 351–63, 416, 465–87; Hardy and the arts, 486–87; H's influence on writers, 475–76, 485–86; H. and lapsed religious faith, 484–85; H. and sexuality, 466–70, 472–73, 474–75, 477–78; H. and the theater, 481–82, 486–87

Collected Letters, 466, 471
Desperate Remedies, 481
Dynasts, The, 483, 484
Far from the Madding Crowd,
Hand of Ethelberta, 478, 479
Jude the Obscure, 357–58, 473–75, 478, 483
Mayor of Casterbridge, The, 471, 472, 487
Pair of Blue Eyes, A, 467
Return of the Native, 467, 484, 486, 487
Tess of the d'Urbervilles, 351–65, 472–73, 478, 479, 481
Under the Greenwood Tree, 477, 487
Well-Beloved, The, 478, 484
Haroway, Donna, 377–78
Harvey, C. J. D., 311, 316–17
Hawes, Donald, *Who's Who in Dickens*, 389–90
Hayles, Katherine, *The Cosmic Web: Scientific Field Models and Literary Strategies in the Twentieth Century*, 282
Hazlitt, William, 205
Hegel, G. W. F., 446
Henderson, Andrea, 251, 262 n.3
Hennelly, Mark M., Jr., 416–19
Higbie, Robert, *Dickens and Imagination*, 399–400
Higgonet, Margaret, *The Sense of Sex*, 471, 474–75
Hill, James, Authority and the *Bildungsroman*: The Double Negative of *Bleak House*," 163–94
Hilton, Boyd, 239, 244
Hochman, Baruch, "Bulrush and Harvest Home," 419–20
Hogarth, George (CD's father-in-law), 7
Hogarth, William, 325
Homes and Homelessness in the Victorian Imagination, ed. Murray Baumgarten and H. M. Daleski, 425–31

Holway, Tatiana M., 430
Hood, Theodore, 11
Hornback, Bert G., 471
Horney, Karen, 274
House, Humphry, 195, 197, 214, 224
Hume, David, *Enquiry concerning Human Understanding*, 298 n.7
Hunt, Peter, *Chesterton and Wilson on Dickens*, 415
Hutter, Albert, 444

Irigaray, Luce, 274
Irving, Edward (millenarian preacher), 213
Irving, Washington, 1–16; tourism and travels to England, 5
　　Alhambra, The, 2
　　Bracebridge Hall, 2, 4, 10–14
　　Sketchbook of Geoffrey Crayon, 1, 2, 4, 5, 6
　　Tales of a Traveler, 2

Jackson, Thomas A., *Charles Dickens: The Progress of a Radical* (1937), 198
Jaffe, Audrey, 18, 166, 437
James, Henry, 414
　　Ambassadors, The, 414
　　Golden Bowl, The, 414
Jameson, Frederic, *The Political Unconscious: Narrative as a Socially Symbolic Act*, 168
Jarrett, David, 255
Jedrzejewski, Jan, *Thomas Hardy and the Church*, 484–85
John, Saint
　　Gospel, 213, 314
Johnson, Bruce, 471
Johnson, Edgar, *Charles Dickens: His Tragedy and Triumph*, 21, 22, 206, 297 n.2, 304
Jordan, John O., 426
Julius, Anthony, "Dickens the Law-Breaker," 421
Jung, Carl, 290

Kaplan, Fred
　　Dickens: A Biography, 1998, 202, 263 n.15, 407–08
　　Dickens and Mesmerism: The Hidden Springs of Fiction, 287–88
Keen, Suzanne, 388, 403–04
Kelly, Thomas, and Brian Kelly, 304–05
Kiely, Robert, 290, 318
Kincaid, James R., 475
Korg, Jacob, 222
Kramer, Dale, 466
　　Thomas Hardy, Tess of the d'Urbervilles, 472–73, 475
Kran, Paul A., 419
Kranidis, Rita S., *Imperial Objects: Essays on Victorian Women's Emigration and the Unauthorized Imperial Experience*, 406–07
Kristeva, Julia, 251, 277, 305,
　　Powers of Horror, 252–53, 260
Kucich, John, 273, 445–46

Lacan, Jacques, 270, 274–75, 277, 278, 291, 477
LaCapra, Dominick, 438–39
Langbaum, Robert, *Thomas Hardy in Our Time*, 483–84
Lawrence, D. H., 468, 483, 485–86
Lecky, W. E. H., *Religious Tendencies of the Age*, 199
Lee, Holme (Harriet Parr), *Sylvan Holt's Daughter*, 372
Lefkovitz, Lori Hope, 324–25
Lenard, Mary, 431
Lever, Charles, *A Day's Ride*, 433
Levine, George, 471
　　Darwin and the Novelists, 298 n.10
Lewis, Judith Schneid, 369
Lewis, Peter, 305
Little Britain (London), 8–9, 11
Litvack, Leon, "What Books Did Dickens Buy and Read," 409
Litvak, Joseph, 433–34

Lloyd, Tom, 446
Lytton, Edward George Earl Bulwer-
    Lytton, 1ˢᵗ baron
    Eugene Aram, 20
    Paul Clifford, 20

Macaulay, Thomas Babington, 225 n.1
McCarthy, Patrick, 425–26
McCulloch, J. R., 234, 241, 247
Malone, Cynthia Northcutt, "Near
    Confinement: Pregnant Women in
    the Nineteenth-Century British
    Novel," 367–85
Malthus, Thomas, 238–39, 240
Manford, Alan, 475
Manheim, Leonard, 444
Marcus, Steven, 25
Mark, Saint, 213, 219
Marshalsea prison, 20, 22, 23, 24, 31, 32,
    33, 235, 244, 257, 397
Marx, Karl, 265 n.28, 396
Matthew, Saint, 216, 219, 315
Matus, Jill, *Unstable Bodies*, 371–72
Meckier, Jerome, 433, 449
Mesmer, Franz Anton, 287–88
Metz, Nancy Aycock, 294
Mieder, Wolfgang, 412
Milbank Penitentiary, 21
Mill, John Stuart, *Subjection of Women*,
    297 n.4
Millbank, Alison, 245
Miller, D. A., 438–39
Miller, J. Hillis, 201, 222, 415, 438
Miller, John Hawkins, 374
Millgate, Michael, *Thomas Hardy: A
    Biography*, 480, 482, and Richard
    Little Purdy, eds. *Collected Letters*
    (Hardy), 466
Moore, George, *Esther Waters*, 382 n.1
Moretti, Franco, 169–70
Morgan, Rosemarie
    *Women and Sexuality in the
        Novels of Thomas Hardy*,
        466–67, 468, 476
    *Cancelled Words:
        Rediscovering Thomas
        Hardy*, 470

Morgentaler, Goldie, "The Long and the
    Short of Oliver and Alice: The
    Changing Size of the Victorian
    Child," 83–98; 447–48
Myers, William, *The Presence of
    Persons: Essays on Literature,
    Science, and Philosophy in the
    Nineteenth Century*, 429, 434

Neill, Edward, *Trial by Ordeal, Thomas
    Hardy and the Critics*, 482
Nelson, Harland S., "Recent Dickens
    Studies: 1998," 387–464
Newgate prison, 21
Newlin, George, 442–43
Newsome, Robert, 305
Nunokawa, Jeff, 265 n.28
Nussbaum, Martha, 401, 414

Orwell, George, 224
O'Toole, Fintan, 204
Owen, Alex, 244

Parker, David, "*Oliver Twist* and the
    Fugitive Family," 41–60; "Dickens
    at Home," 408–09
Parsons, Gerald, 204
Pater, Walter, 279, 280, 281–82, 295, 473
Patterson, Annabel, 314–15, 316
Peacham, Henry, *The Compleat
    Gentleman*, 10
Peltason, Timothy, 437
Perkin, Joan, 369
Perry, Ruth, 376
Peters, Catherine, *Charles Dickens*, 408
Peters, Laura, 430
Peterson, Linda H., 450
Pettit, Charles P. C., 475–76
Philpotts, Trey, 395
Pittock, Malcolm, 440
Polhemus, Robert, 421
Poor Law (1821), 22, 23, 24; (1834), 21
Poovey, Mary, 292, 297 n.3
Pope, Norris, 243
Porter, Roy, 237–38

Posner, Richard, 414
Pound, Ezra, 310
Proust, Marcel, 486

Quiller-Couch, Arthur, 199–200, 225 n.2

Rance, Nicholas, 444–45
Retseck, Janet, 441, 442
Robbins, Bruce, 437–38
Rushdie, Salman, 411–12
Reade, Charles, *White Lies*, 372–73
Reform Bill (1832), 13, 21, 196
Richardson, Samuel, *Clarissa*, 473
Robson, Catherine, "Down Ditches, on Doorsteps, in Rivers: *Oliver Twist's* Journey to Respectability." 61–82
Robson, John, 307
Robson, Lisa, 446
Rogers, Philip, 411
Roston, Murray, 426–27
Ruskin, John, 426
        Unto This Last, 237

Sadler's Ten-hour Bill, 21
Sadrin, Anny, 30
St. Bartholomew's Fair, 8
Samet, Elizabeth Dale, 432–33
Sasaki, Toru, "Dickens in Confusion," 413
Schacht, Paul, 330
Scoggin, Daniel P. "Speculative Plagues and the Ghosts of *Little Dorrit*," 233–68
Scott, Sir Walter, *Waverley*, 11
Sedgwick, Eve Kosofsky, 296
Seduction novel, 473
Sekora, John, *Luxury: The Concept in Western Thought*, 256; 262n.8
Seldes, Gilbert, 315, 316
Sell, Kathleen, 448
Sen, Sambudha, 429
Sepoy Rebellion (1857–58), 226 n.9
Seymour-Smith, Martin, 352
        Thomas Hardy, 353, 482
Shaked, Gershwin, 410–11

Shapiro, James, *Shakespeare and the Jews*, 200
Shaw, George Bernard, 198
Shelley, Percy Bysshe, 279, 280
Showalter, Elaine, 471
Shuttleworth, Sally, 376–77
Sicher, Efraim, 425
Slater, Michael, 392–93
Smith, Grahame, 416; "Dickens and the City of Light," 423
Smith, Adam, 238–39, 240
Smollett, Tobias, 256
        Peregrine Pickle, 368–69
Spurgeon, Charles Haddon (baptist preacher), 210
Spurgin, Timothy A., 448–49
Sternlieb, Lisa, "'Three Leahs to Get One Rachel': Redundant Women in *Tess of the d'Urbervilles*," 351–65
Stewart, Garrett, 35
Storer, David, 429–30
Surgal, Jon, 420–21
Surridge, Lisa, 449
Sutherland, John, 360
Swisher, Clarice, *Readings on Charles Dickens*, 405–06

Tambling, Jeremy, 416, 435–39
Ternan, Ellen, 392, 408, 444
Thackeray, William Makepeace, *Vanity Fair*, 256
Thomas, Jane, *Thomas Hardy, Femininity and Dissent*, 470
Tick, Stanley, 435
Tillotson, Kathleen, 199
Tokev, Leona, 430–31
Tracy, Robert, 427, 432
Trezise, Simon David, 410
Trilling, Lionel, *A Gathering of Fugitives*, 304
Turner, J. M. W., 486
Tysdahl, Bjørn, 447

Urania College, 393, 407

Veblen, Thorstein, 430–31
Vegh, Beatriz, 439–40

Vlock, Deborah, 388, 390
    *Dickens, Novel Reading and
    the Popular Theatre*,
    401–02

Wainwright, Valerie, 440–41
Walder, Dennis, *Dickens and Religion*,
    200, 243
Walpole, Horace
    Castle of Otranto, The, 235,
    245–46, 254
    Mysteries of Udolpho, The, 246
Walton, Isaak, *The Compleat Angler*,
    314–15
Ward, David A., "Distorted Religion:
    Dickens, Dissent, and *Bleak
    House*," 195–232
Watts, Isaac (Nonconformist), 219
Weir, Allison, 277
Widdowson, Peter
    *Hardy in History, a Study in
    Literary Sociology*, 479

*On Thomas Hardy: Late Essays
    and Earlier*, 478–79
Wilson, Anna, 441–42
Wilson, Edmund, 428
Wilson, Keith, *Thomas Hardy on Stage*,
    481–82
Winnecott, D. W., 272, 299 n.15, 417
Wolff, Robert Lee, 199
Wolfren, Julian, *Writing London: The
    Trace of the Urban Text from Blake
    to Dickens*, 422–23
Wollstonecraft, Mary, *Vindication of the
    Rights of Women*, 297 n.4
Woodruff, Douglas, 200
Woolf, Virginia, *Mrs. Dalloway*, 410
Wright, T. R., *Hardy and the Erotic*, 478

Yitzhak, Levi, 354
Young, G. M., *Portrait of an Age*, 234
Yoon, Hye-Joon, *Physiognomy of Capital
    in Charles Dickens: An Essay in
    Diolectical Criticism*, 396–98

Zonana, Joyce, 451–52